Benner's Translation of the Torah

~~~~~~~~~~~~~~~~~~~~~~~~~~~~~~~~~~~~

Jeff A. Benner
~~~~~~~~~~~~~~~~~~~~~~~~~~~~~~~~~~~~

Cover design by Jeff A. Benner

"Benner's Translation of the Torah," by Jeff A. Benner. ISBN 978-1-951985-55-4.

Published 2020 by Virtualbookworm.com Publishing. P.O. Box 9949, College Station, TX 77842, US.

Manufactured in the United States of America.

Contents

About this Translation

The Mechanical Translation

The translation in this book is the *Revised Mechanical Translation*, which is derived from Mr. Benner's *The Torah: A Mechanical Translation* (available at mechanical-translation.org). In the *The Torah: A Mechanical Translation* (MT) each Hebrew word is translated faithfully according to its original linguistic and cultural perspective. Mr. Benner's vision of this translation included a translation that;

1. eliminates personal and religious bias on the part of the translator,
2. translates each Hebrew word, prefix and suffix, exactly the same way, every time it occurs in the text,
3. can be read and understood by the average person who does not have any prior knowledge of the Hebrew language,
4. includes a dictionary of each word used in the translation as well as a concordance, and
5. can be used as a tool by those who are learning to read Biblical Hebrew.

The mechanical translation will always translate each Hebrew word, prefix and suffix the same way every time it appears and no two Hebrew words are translated with the same English word.

To demonstrate, below is Genesis 1:1 from *The Torah: A Mechanical Translation*.

> **1:1** in~ SUMMIT (בְּרֵאשִׁית *bê'rey'shit*) *he~ did~* SHAPE(V) (בָּרָא *ba'ra*) Elohiym (אֱלֹהִים *e'lo'him*) AT (אֵת *eyt*) the~ SKY~ s2 (הַשָּׁמַיִם *ha'sha'ma'yim*) and~ AT (וְאֵת *wê'eyt*) the~LAND (הָאָרֶץ *ha'a'rets*) **RMT:** In the summit Elohiym shaped the skies and the land,

The first word is בְּרֵאשִׁית (pronounced *bê'rey'shit*), which is the Hebrew word רֵאשִׁית (rey'shit), which is always translated as "summit" in this translation, unlike other translations that will translate it in different ways. For instance, the King James

Translation translates this word as; beginning, first, firstfruits, chief and principle thing.

This word is prefixed with the ב (the Hebrew letter *beyt*), which means "in" and is always translated as "in" in the Mechanical Translation.

Each verse in the translation includes the *Revised Mechanical Translation*, which rearranges the words so that it will follow English syntax. For instance, Hebrew syntax places the subject of the verb (*Elohiym*) after the verb (shaped *Elohiym*). However, in English syntax the subject comes before the verb (*Elohiym* shaped). In addition, some words will be changed for clarity. For example, in Hebrew, one says "in a mountain," but we would say "on a mountain" and this translation will reflect such changes. This *Revised Mechanical Translation* is the translation found in this book.

The Revised Mechanical Translation

You will notice, as you read this translation, it does not "flow" as easily as the translations you are used to. The reason for this is that this translation is designed to allow the reader to see the Hebrew behind the English by using the English language. So while this translation may not read easily, you are getting a glimpse of the Hebrew language behind the translation.

Names

This translation transliterates all names straight from the Hebrew, rather than using the conventional names found in other translation. For instance, the name Moses, which is in reality derived from the Greek form of this name, will appear as *Mosheh* in this translation.

Alternate Translations

Where the MT of a given Hebrew word will make no sense in English, it will be necessary to change the translation of that Hebrew word. As an example, the Hebrew word בית (*bayit*) is always translated as "house" in the MT and RMT, but in the phrase מבית ומחוץ (from the house and from the outside) the translation "house" does not make any sense in English. Therefore, the word "house" is changed to "inside" (another meaning of the Hebrew word בית) in the RMT.

Compound Phrases

Certain combinations of Hebrew words have a specific meaning. For example, the Hebrew phrase על כן (*al keyn*) would literally be translated as "upon so" but means "therefore." This phrase is then translated in the RMT as "therefore." Another example is the word כאשר (*k'asher*), which literally means "like which," but is translated as "just as" in the RMT. (These "compound phrases" are also indicated in the dictionary that accompanies *The Torah: A Mechanical Translation*)

Verb Forms

Different verb forms can change the meaning of a verb. For instance, the Hebrew verb אמן (*aman*) means "secure," but when this verb is written in the 'hiphil' form (identified as *make*~SECURE(V) in the MT), it literally means "to cause to be secure" and means "support." Therefore, this verb will be written as "support" in the RMT.

Plural Forms

The Hebrew word אף (*aph*) means "nose," but when it is written in the plural form, אפים (*aphiym*), it means "nostrils." Therefore, this plural form will appear in the RMT as "nostrils."

Intensifying Infinitive Absolute

The Hebrew language uses the unique style of doubling the use of a verb to show intensity. As an example, the phrase ראה ראיתי (*ra'oh ra'iy'tiy*) includes the Hebrew verb ראה (*R.A.H*), meaning "see," twice and is translated in the RMT as "I surely saw."

Past Perfect Verbs

In Hebrew Syntax, the subject of the verb follows the verb. For instance, we would say in English, "Mosheh walked," but in Hebrew it would be, "walked Mosheh." However, there are times when the subject of the verb precedes the verb. In this case, the structure is identifying the verb as a past perfect. As an example, the Hebrew phrase היה משה (*hayah mosheh*) would be translated in the RMT as

"Mosheh existed," but when this phrase is written as משה היה (*mosheh hayah*), it is translated as "Mosheh had existed."

Added Words

It is frequently required to add words in the RMT that do not exist within the Hebrew text in order to have the translation make sense in English. A common example in the Hebrew text is the phrase בני ישראל (*b'ney yisra'el*), which is translated in the MT as "SON~s Yisra'el," but appears in the RMT as "the sons of Yisra'el," where the words "the" and "of" have been added to the text.

Pronouns

The MT may have the pronoun "~you" but may be translated as "your" (showing possession) in the RMT. This translation will also retain the pronoun genders from the Hebrew. For instance, in Numbers 31:54 the King James Version has the phrase "and brought <u>it</u> into the tabernacle" where the word "it" is referring to the word "gold." In the RMT this phrase is translated as "and they brought <u>him</u> to the appointed tent" where the word "him" is a translation of the Hebrew masculine pronoun, which is referring to the word "gold," which is a masculine noun in Hebrew.

The word "it" will appear in the RMT for clarity, where no pronoun exists in the Hebrew. For instance, in Leviticus 9:12 is the phrase, "and he sprinkled <u>him</u> upon the altar all around." The "him" is the translation of the third person, masculine, singular pronoun that is present in the Hebrew. However, in Leviticus 8:30 is the phrase, "and he spattered <u>it</u> upon Aharon." In this case, there is no pronoun in the Hebrew, so the word "it" was added for clarity.

Plural nouns

Most plural forms of nouns are simply the singular form of the noun with the letter "s" suffixed to the noun. Examples from the MT are the plural HAND~s and HOUSE~s, which simply appear as "hands" and "houses" in the RMT. However, the plural words MAN~s and FOOT~s will be translated in the RMT as "men" and "feet."

Verbs

The Hebrew verb אמר (*amar*) is translated as "*he~did*~SAY(V)" in the MT, where the word "he" identifies the gender (masculine) and number (singular) of the subject of the verb and the word "did" identifies the tense (perfect, similar to the English past tense) of the verb. This word is translated as "he said" in the RMT. When the prefix "and~" is attached to a verb, the tense of the verb is reversed. So, the verb ואמר (*wa'omar*) would be translated in the MT as "and~*he*~*did*~SAY(V)," but as "and he will say" in the RMT. Below are a few examples of how a verb and its subject would be translated in the MT and the RMT.

About the Glossary and Dictionary

Because of the nature of this translation, where each Hebrew word is always translated the same, it is possible to identify the Hebrew word behind each English word. In the back of this book is a list of English words used in this translation, along with the *Strong's Dictionary* number associated with Hebrew word behind the English.

However, there is a precaution. It was previously mentioned that no two Hebrew words are translated with the same English word. While this is true for the mechanical translation, it is not always the case in the *Revised Mechanical Translation*. In the mechanical translation, the Hebrew verb אבד (*A.B.D*, Strong's #6) is always translated as "PERISH." But when this verb is written in the hiphil (causative) form, it is translated as "make~PERISH" in the mechanical translation, but as "destroy" in the *Revised Mechanical Translation*. This can cause some confusion as the Hebrew verb שמד (*Sh.M.D*, Strong's #8045) is always translated as "DESTROY" in the mechanical translation.

Also included in the back of this book is a dictionary of all the names in the Torah, along with their meaning and *Strong's Dictionary* number.

History of the Torah

Oral Tradition

It is widely believed that the *Torah* was written by Moses. While this is the traditional origins of the Judeo-Christian religions, there is no record in the *Torah* of its author. Whether the *Torah* was written by Moses or another author, how did he know about the events of creation, the flood, and the history of the Hebrew people? Two possibilities exist to explain this knowledge. One possibility is that God had revealed the facts to him through divine inspiration. The other possibility is that the stories and events were handed down from generation to generation and the author would have been very familiar with these traditional stories and could have simply written them down.

In the Hebrew language, the Hebrew word דבר (*davar*) is used for a "thing," something of substance:

> KJV Exodus 22:9 *For all manner of trespass, whether it be for ox, for ass, for sheep, for raiment, or for any manner of lost thing...*

> KJV Leviticus 5:2 *Or if a soul touch any unclean thing...*

> KJV Leviticus 23:37 *These are the feasts of the LORD, which ye shall proclaim to be holy convocations, to offer an offering made by fire unto the LORD, a burnt offering, and a meat offering, a sacrifice, and drink offerings, every thing upon his day:*

> KJV Numbers 18:7 *Therefore thou and thy sons with thee shall keep your priest's office for every thing of the altar...*

This same Hebrew word is also used for an action or an important event:

> Genesis 18:14 *Is any thing too hard for the LORD?...*

> KJV Exodus 12:24 *And ye shall observe this* <u>*thing*</u> *(referring to the Passover) for an ordinance to thee and to thy sons for ever.*

> KJV Numbers 32:20 *And Moses said unto them, If ye will do this* <u>*thing*</u>*, if ye will go armed before the LORD to war,*

> KJV Deuteronomy 23:9 *When the host goeth forth against thine enemies, then keep thee from every wicked* <u>*thing*</u>.

From this we can conclude that actions were perceived as things of substance, much in the same way as physical objects. The word דבר is also used for "words" as seen in the following passages:

> KJV Genesis 15:1 *After these things the word of the LORD came unto Abram in a vision...*

> KJV Genesis 44:2 *...And he did according to the word that Joseph had spoken.*

> KJV Exodus 14:12 *Is not this the word that we did tell thee in Egypt...*

> KJV Numbers 11:23 *...thou shalt see now whether my word shall come to pass unto thee or not.*

In our Western culture, the written word carries much more weight than the oral word and all official documents, contracts and agreements are written to record specific events. While it may seem strange or even impossible, in our culture, the opposite was true in the ancient Hebrew cultures: the oral word carried more weight than the written word, as the oral word was considered something of substance. This concept is clearly demonstrated in Genesis chapter 27. Isaac is about to give his blessing to his eldest son, Esau, before he dies. Esau's younger brother, Jacob, deceives his father by impersonating Esau, and Isaac gives his blessing to Jacob. When Esau comes to his father to receive his blessing, Isaac tells him, "Your brother came with treachery and has taken away your blessing." Esau then begs his father for the blessing, but Isaac states that he had already given it Jacob and he will be blessed because of it. The "words" of Isaac were given to Jacob and he could not take them back, no more than if he had tried to take back a stone that he had thrown into the sea.

The ancients placed much weight on the oral traditions which were handed down from generation to generation. The stories and traditions were spoken from father to son and memorized with complete accuracy. The written document could be lost or destroyed but the story lived forever in the mind and could never be lost or destroyed. It would have been these stories that Moses would have heard since childhood and long ago put to memory.

The Original Manuscripts

The original manuscripts of the Hebrew Bible, which would have been written on animal skins or papyrus, have long since deteriorated, and what remains today are copies from these original autographs.

In the digital age, electronic copies are perfect representations of the original. However, in ancient times, making a copy of a manuscript was much more tedious and not as precise, and this allowed for human intervention or error.

Oldest Known Copies of Biblical Texts

The manuscripts discovered in the Dead Sea Caves include all of the Canonical Books of the Hebrew Bible with the exception of the book of Esther. Additionally, non-Canonical Books such as Enoch, Jubilees, Tobit and Sirach, as well as Psalms that are not part of the 150 Psalms in the Canonical Bible were found among the scrolls. Less-familiar Sectarian Books such as the Community Rule, the War Scroll, the Damascus Document and commentaries on books of the Bible complete the findings in the caves.

There are several different theories on the origin of these texts.

The predominating theory is that the scrolls were the work of a Jewish sect called the Essenes who, it is believed, resided in nearby Qumran and hid the scrolls in the caves to protect them from the advancing Roman army.

Other theories about the writers' identities include Early Messianics (often called Christians) or Zadokite Priests.

A newer theory posits that the scrolls were from various libraries and synagogues, in Jerusalem, located about 15 miles from the caves.

The Masoretic Texts

The Masorites were a group of Jewish scribes and scholars from the 6th to 10th centuries that compiled the entire Tenakh (Old Testament) into one Codex (book). The Masorites added the nikkud (vowel pointings) to the text in an attempt to standardize pronunciation, added paragraphs and verse divisions, and added cantillation marks to the text.

The two oldest Masoretic texts are the *Aleppo Codex* and the *Leningrad Codex*. Both of these codices are virtually identical, with only a slight variation in the paragraphs, verse numbers and spellings of words.

Ancient Translations

As the Jewish people began to spread out beyond Israel, they adopted the language of their new neighbors. This necessitated the need for translations of the Bible in their new languages in order for them to continue reading the Bible. While there have been many translations of the Hebrew Bible into many different languages, the three most widely used in ancient times were the Latin, Aramaic and Greek.

Benner's Translation of the Torah

The Book of Genesis

Chapter 1

1 In the summit *Elohiym* shaped the skies and the land, **2** and the land had
existed in confusion and was unfilled, and darkness was upon the face of the
deep water and the wind of *Elohiym* was fluttering upon the face of the
waters, **3** and *Elohiym* said, light will exist, and light existed, **4** and *Elohiym*
saw the light, given that it was functional, and *Elohiym* made a separation
between the light and the darkness, **5** and *Elohiym* called out to the light,
day, and to the darkness he called out, night, and evening existed and
morning existed, a day unit, **6** and *Elohiym* said, a sheet will exist in the
midst of the waters, and he existed, making a separation between waters to
waters, **7** and *Elohiym* made the sheet, and he made a separation between
the waters which are below for a sheet and the waters which are above for a
sheet, and he existed so[1], **8** and *Elohiym* called out to the sheet, skies, and
evening existed and morning existed, a second day, **9** and *Elohiym* said, the
waters will be bound up below the skies to one area, and dry ground
appeared, and he existed so, **10** and *Elohiym* called out to the dry ground,
land, and to the collection of the waters he called out, seas, and *Elohiym*
saw that it was functional, **11** and *Elohiym* said, the land will make grass
sprout, herbs producing seeds, trees of produce making produce to his kind
which his seed is in him upon the land, and he existed so, **12** and the land
brought out grass, herbs sowing seeds to his kind, and trees making produce
which has his seed in him to his kind, and *Elohiym* saw that it was functional,
13 and evening existed and morning existed, a third day,[2] **14** and *Elohiym*
said, the luminaries will exist in the sheet of the skies to make a separation
between the day and the night and they exist for signs and for appointed
times and for days and years, **15** and they exist for luminaries in the sheet of
the skies to make light upon the land, and he existed so, **16** and *Elohiym*
made two of the great luminaries, the great luminary for the regulation of
the day, and the small luminary for the regulation of the night, and the
stars[3], **17** and *Elohiym* placed them in the sheet of the skies to make light

---

[1] The phrase "he existed so" means "it is firmly established." (also in verses 9, 11,15, 24 and 30)

[2] Days one through three are the "separating" of the skies and land. On the first day the light is separated from the darkness. On the second day the water is separated from the skies. On the third day, the water is separated from the land.

[3] The phrase "and the stars" is grammatically and contextually out of place and appears to have been added to the text. In addition, this phrase does not appear in some of the Dead Sea Scrolls of Genesis.

upon the land, **18** and to regulate in the day and in the night, and to make a
separation between the light and the darkness, and *Elohiym* saw that it was
functional, **19** and evening existed and morning existed, a fourth day, **20** and
Elohiym said, the waters will swarm with swarmers of living souls and flyers
will fly upon the land, upon the face of the sheet of the skies, **21** and *Elohiym*
shaped the great crocodile[4] and all the living souls, the treaders which
swarm the waters to their kind, and all the flyers of the wing to his kind, and
Elohiym saw that it was functional, **22** and *Elohiym* exalted them saying,
reproduce and increase and fill the waters in the seas, and the flyers
increased in the land, **23** and evening existed and morning existed, a fifth
day, **24** and *Elohiym* said, the land will bring out living souls to her kind,
beasts and treaders and living ones[5] of the land to her kind, and he existed
so, **25** and *Elohiym* made living ones of the land to her kind and the beast to
her kind and all of the treaders of the ground to his kind, and *Elohiym* saw
that it was functional, **26** and *Elohiym* said, we will make a human in our
image, like our likeness, and he will rule in the fish of the sea and in the
flyers of the skies, and in the beast, and in all the land, and in all the treaders
treading upon the land, **27** and *Elohiym* shaped the human in his image, in
the image of *Elohiym* he shaped him, male and female he shaped them,
28 and *Elohiym* exalted them, and *Elohiym* said to them, reproduce and
increase and fill the land and subdue her, and rule in the fish of the sea and
in the flyers of the skies, and in all the living ones treading upon the land,
29 and *Elohiym* said, look, I gave to you all of the herbs sowing seed which
are upon the face of all the land, and all of the trees which are in him the
produce of a tree sowing seed, he will exist for food for you, **30** and to all the
living ones of the land, and to all the flyers of the skies, and to all the
treaders upon the land which is in him a living soul, all the green herbs for
food, and he existed so, **31** and *Elohiym* saw all which he made, and look, it
is very functional, and evening existed and morning existed, a sixth day,[6]

---

[4] This Hebrew word is translated in various ways, including; whale, sea-monster, dragon, serpent, asp and jackal (see Exodus 7:9, Deuteronomy 32:33, Nehemiah 2:13, Job 7:12). According to these texts, this is a very large creature that lives on the land and in the water, which is characteristic of the crocodile.

[5] The Hebrew literally reads "his living ones," but may be written incorrectly.

[6] Days four through six are the "filling" of the skies and land and are paralleled with the first three days (see the footnote at Genesis 1:13). On the fourth day the light is filled with the sun and the night with the moon. On the fifth day the water is filled with fish and the skies with birds. On the sixth day the land is filled with animals and man.

Chapter 2

1 and the skies and the land and all of their armies were finished, **2** and *Elohiym* finished in the seventh day his business which he did, and he ceased in the seventh day from all his business which he did, **3** and *Elohiym* exalted the seventh day and he set him apart, given that in him he ceased from all of his business which *Elohiym* shaped to make. **4** These are the birthings of the skies and the land in their being shaped in the day ***YHWH*** the *Elohiym* made land and skies, **5** and all the shrubs of the field before existing in the land, and all the herbs of the field before springing up, given that ***YHWH*** the *Elohiym* did not make it precipitate upon the land and it was without a human to serve the ground, **6** and a mist will go up from the land and he made all the face of the ground drink, **7** and ***YHWH*** the *Elohiym* molded the human of dirt from the ground and he exhaled in his nostrils a breath of life and the human existed for a living soul, **8** and ***YHWH*** the *Elohiym* planted a garden in *Eden* from the east and placed there the human which he molded, **9** and ***YHWH*** the *Elohiym* made all the trees spring up from the ground to be a craving for appearance and functional for nourishment, and the tree[7] of life in the midst of the garden, and the tree of discernment of function and dysfunction, **10** and a river was going out from *Eden* to make the garden drink, and from there he will be divided apart existing to four heads. **11** The title of the one is *Pishon*, he is the one going around all the land of the *Hhawilah* where there is the gold, **12** and the gold of that land is functional, there is the amber and the stone of onyx, **13** and the title of the second river is *Giyhhon*, he is the one going around all the land of *Kush*, **14** and the title of the third river is *Hhideqel*, he is the one walking eastward of *Ashur*, and the fourth river, he is *Perat*, **15** and ***YHWH*** the *Elohiym* took the human and he deposited him in the garden of *Eden* to serve her and to safeguard her, **16** and ***YHWH*** the *Elohiym* directed upon the human saying from all the trees of the garden you will surely eat, **17** but from the tree of discernment of function and dysfunction you will not eat from him, given that in the day you eat from him you will surely die, **18** and ***YHWH*** the *Elohiym* said, it is not functional for the human to exist by himself, I will make for him a helper[8] as his opposite, **19** and ***YHWH*** the *Elohiym* molded from the ground all the living ones of the field, and all the flyers of the skies, and he brought to the human to see what he will call out to him and all the living souls, which the human will call out to him, that is his title, **20** and the human called out the titles to all the beasts and to the flyers of the skies, and to all the living ones

---

[7] The singular word "tree" may imply a "tree" or "trees." the context of this and following verses do not specify if there is one tree or a forest of trees. Compare this with 2:16.

[8] The helper will have the character traits that are complimentary to his own.

of the field, but for the human he did not find a helper as his opposite[9], **21** and ***YHWH*** the *Elohiym* made a trance fall upon the human and he slept, and he took a unit from his ribs and he shut the flesh under her, **22** and ***YHWH*** the *Elohiym* built the rib which he took from the human for a woman, and he brought her to the human, **23** and the human said, this time it is bone from my bones and flesh from my flesh, for this, he will be called out woman[10], given that from man this was taken. **24** Therefore a man will leave his father and his mother, and he will adhere with his woman, and they will exist as one flesh, **25** and the two of them, the human and his woman, existed nude, and they were not ashamed of themselves,

---

Chapter 3

1 and the serpent had existed as a subtle one more than all the living ones of the field which ***YHWH*** the *Elohiym* made, and he said to the woman, did *Elohiym* really say you will not eat from all the trees of the garden, **2** and the woman said to the serpent, from the produce of the trees of the garden we eat, **3** but from the produce of the tree which is in the midst of the garden *Elohiym* said, you will not eat from him, and you will not touch him, otherwise you must die, **4** and the serpent said to the woman, you shall certainly not die, **5** given that *Elohiym* knows that in the day you eat from him, then your eyes will be opened up and you will exist like *Elohiym*, knowing function and dysfunction, **6** and the woman saw that the function of the tree is for nourishment and that he is a yearning to the eyes, and the tree is a craving for making calculations, and she took from his produce and she ate, and she gave also to her man with her, and he ate, **7** and the eyes of the two of them were opened up and they knew that they were naked, and they sewed together leaves of the fig, and they made for themselves loin wraps, **8** and they heard the voice[11] of ***YHWH*** the *Elohiym* walking himself in the garden for the wind of the day, and the human and his woman withdrew themselves from the face of ***YHWH*** the *Elohiym* into the midst of the trees of the garden, **9** and ***YHWH*** the *Elohiym* called out to the human and he said to him, where are you, **10** and he said, I heard your voice in the garden and I feared, given that I am naked, and I withdrew, **11** and he said, who told you that you are naked, are you eating from the tree which I directed you to not eat from, **12** and the human said, the woman which you placed by me, she gave to me from the tree and I ate, **13** and ***YHWH*** the *Elohiym* said to the

---

[9] See verse 18.

[10] The Hebrew phrase יִקָּרֵא אִשָּׁה literally translates as "he will be called out woman." Either the "he" is an error and should be "she," or the text originally read יִקְרָא שְׁמָהּ אִשָּׁה, which would then be translated as "he called out her title woman."

[11] This Hebrew word can also mean "sound" (see also verse 10).

woman, what is this you did, and the woman said, the serpent had deceived me and I ate, **14** and ***YHWH*** the *Elohiym* said to the serpent, given that you did this, spat upon[12] are you from all the beasts and from all the living ones of the field, upon your belly you will walk, and dirt you will eat all the days of your life, **15** and I set down hostility between you and the woman, and between your seed and her seed, he will fall upon you a head[13], and you will fall upon him a heel[14]. **16** To the woman he said, I will make a great increase of your hardship and your pregnancy, in distressing pain you will bring forth sons[15], and to your man is your following, and he will regulate in you, **17** and to the human he said, given that you listened[16] to the voice of your woman and you ate from the tree which I directed you saying, you will not eat from him, spat upon[17] is the ground on account of you, in your hardship you will eat of her all the days of your life, **18** and she will make brambles and thistles spring up for you, and you will eat the herbs of the field. **19** With the sweat of your nostrils you will eat bread, until you turn back to the ground, given that from her you were taken, given that you are dirt and to dirt you will turn back, **20** and the human called out the title of his woman *Hhawah*, given that she existed as the mother of all the living, **21** and ***YHWH*** the *Elohiym* made for the human and his woman tunics of skin and he clothed them, **22** and ***YHWH*** the *Elohiym* said, though the human had existed like one of us[18], knowing function and dysfunction, and now otherwise, he will send his hand and he will take also from the tree of life, and he will eat and he will live to a distant time, **23** and ***YHWH*** the *Elohiym* sent him from the garden of *Eden* to serve the ground which from there he was taken, **24** and he cast out the human, and the keruvs and the blazing one dwelt from the east to the garden of *Eden*, the sword overturning herself to safeguard the road of the tree of life,

---

[12] "Spat upon" is an idiom for "cursed."

[13] The Hebrew word ראש (a head) could also be translated as "first."

[14] The Hebrew word עָקֵב (a heel) could also be translated as "last."

[15] Hebrew masculine plural nouns may refer to only males or a group of males and females. Therefore, the word "sons" may also be translated as "children."

[16] The Hebrew verb שמע (sh'ma) means "to hear" or "listen," but also to respond.

[17] "Spat upon" is an idiom for "cursed."

[18] The Hebrew phrase כְּאַחַד מִמֶּנּוּ can be translated as "like one of us" (referring to the *Elohiym*, a plural word) or "like one of him" (referring to the serpent). Compare with the words of the serpent in verse 5.

Chapter 4

1 and the human had known *Hhawah* his woman and she conceived and she
brought forth *Qayin*, and she said, I purchased a man with ***YHWH***[19], **2** and
she brought forth again his brother *Hevel*, and *Hevel* existed as a feeder of
the flocks, and *Qayin* existed as a server of the ground, **3** and it came to pass
at the conclusion[20] of days, *Qayin* brought from the produce of the ground,
a deposit to ***YHWH***, **4** and *Hevel* had brought also, he from the firstborn
females of his flocks and from their fat, and ***YHWH*** looked with respect to
Hevel and to his deposit, **5** and to *Qayin* and to his deposit he did not look
with respect, and *Qayin* flared up[21] and his face fell[22], **6** and ***YHWH*** said to
Qayin, why were you flared up, and why is your face fallen. **7** If you do well,
will there not be a lifting up, but if you do not do well, there will be an
opening of failure stretching out, and to you is his[23] following and you will
regulate in him, **8** and *Qayin* said to *Hevel* his brother[24], let us go out into the
field, and it came to pass in their existing in the field, and *Qayin* rose to
Hevel his brother and he killed him, **9** and ***YHWH*** said to *Qayin*, where is
Hevel your brother, and he said, I do not know, am I the guardian of my
brother, **10** and he said, what did you do, the voice of the bloodshed of your
brother is crying out to me from the ground, **11** and now, you are spat
upon[25] from the ground which parted her mouth to take the bloodshed of
your brother from your hand, **12** given that you will serve the ground, she
will not again give her strength to you, you will exist in the land staggering

---

[19] If the Hebrew word אֵת (et) is being used as a preposition (with), then the translation provided is correct. However, if it is being used as the marker of the definite object, then the translation should be "I purchased the man ***YHWH***."

[20] This Hebrew word is usually followed by a number of years or days to identify the end of that time frame, such as in Genesis 8:6 where it states "at the conclusion of the forty days." In this verse, it appears that the period of time is missing.

[21] "Flared up" is an idiom for "anger."

[22] "Face fell" is an idiom for sadness."

[23] It is often assumed the pronoun "him" is referring to the "failure." However, the word "failure" is a feminine noun. One interpretation is that the pronoun "him" is referring to his brother. Compare the phrase "to you is his following and you will regulate in him" with the same phrasing in Genesis 3:16 where it is referring to the man and his woman.

[24] The conversation between *Qayin* and *Hevel* is missing from the text. In the Greek *Septuagint* this is followed by "let us go out into the field." The *Septuagint* may have been translated from a Hebrew text with the conversation intact or the translators may have supplied the phrase to clarify the text.

[25] "Spat upon" is an idiom for "cursed."

and nodding[26], **13** and *Qayin* said to ***YHWH***, great is my twistedness, it is
more than I can lift up. **14** Though you cast me out today from upon the face
of the ground, and I will be hidden from your face, but I will exist in the land
staggering and nodding, and it will come to pass, all the ones finding me will
kill me, **15** and ***YHWH*** said to him, because of this, all the ones killing *Qayin*
will be avenged sevenfold, and ***YHWH*** placed for *Qayin* a sign for all the
ones finding him to not attack him, **16** and *Qayin* went out from before the
face of ***YHWH***, and he settled in the land of *Nod*, eastward of *Eden*, **17** and
Qayin knew his woman and she conceived and she brought forth *Hhanokh*,
and he existed as a builder of a city[27], and called out the title of the city
Hhanokh, like the title of his son, **18** and *Irad* was brought forth to *Hhanokh*,
and *Irad* had brought forth *Mehhuya'el* and *Mehhuya'el* had brought forth
Metusha'el and *Metusha'el* had brought forth *Lamekh*, **19** and *Lamekh* took
for himself two women, the title of the one is *Adah* and the title of the
second is *Tsilah*, **20** and *Adah* brought forth *Yaval*, he existed as the father[28]
of tent and livestock settlers[29], **21** and the title of his brother is *Yuval*, he
existed as the father of all the ones seizing hold[30] of the harp and reed-pipe,
22 and *Tsilah* also had brought forth *Tuval-Qayin*, a sharpener[31] of all the
craftsmen of copper and iron, and the sister of *Tuval-Qayin* is *Na'amah*,
23 and *Lamekh* said to his women, *Adah* and *Tsilah*, hear my voice, women
of *Lamekh*, pay attention to my speech, given that I killed a man for my
wound and a boy for my striped bruise, **24** given that *Qayin* will be avenged
sevenfold, then *Lamekh* seventy and seven, **25** and the human knew yet
again his woman and she brought forth a son, and she called out his title
Shet, given that *Elohiym* set down for me another seed in place of *Hevel*,
given that *Qayin* killed him, **26** and to *Shet* also, he brought forth a son, and
he called out his title[32] *Enosh*, at that time he began to call out in the title of
YHWH.

---

26 "Staggering and nodding" mean to wander aimlessly.

27 The phrase וַיְהִי בֹּנֶה עִיר may be translated as "he existed as a builder of a city" or "he existed, building a city."

28 A father can be the father of a son, an ancestor, or the creator of a trade or profession.

29 "Tent and livestock settlers" are nomads.

30 "Seizing hold," in this context, means "players," who grab hold of an instrument.

31 Or "instructor," in the sense of sharpening the skills of students.

32 The phrase "call out his title" may also be translated as "meet with the character."

Chapter 5

1 This is the scroll of the birthings of the human in the day *Elohiym* shaped
the human, in the likeness of *Elohiym* he made him. **2** Male and female he
shaped them, and he exalted them, and he called out their title human in
the day he shaped them, **3** and the human lived thirty and a hundred
years[33], and he caused to bring forth in his likeness, like his image, and he
called out his title *Shet*, **4** and the days of the human, after his causing to
bring forth, were eight hundred years, and he caused to bring forth sons and
daughters, **5** and all the days of the human, which he lived, were nine
hundred and thirty years, and he died, **6** and *Shet* lived five and a hundred
years[34], and he caused to bring forth *Enosh*, **7** and *Shet* lived, after his
causing to bring forth *Enosh*, seven and eight hundred years, and he caused
to bring forth sons and daughters, **8** and all the days of *Shet* were twelve and
nine hundred years, and he died, **9** and *Enosh* lived ninety years[35], and he
caused to bring forth *Qeynan*, **10** and *Enosh* lived, after causing to bring
forth *Qeynan*, fifteen and eight hundred years, and he caused to bring forth
sons and daughters, **11** and all the days of *Enosh* were five and nine hundred
years, and he died, **12** and *Qeynan* lived seventy years[36], and he caused to
bring forth *Mahalalel*, **13** and *Qeynan* lived, after his causing to bring forth
Mahalalel, forty and eight hundred years, and he caused to bring forth sons
and daughters, **14** and all the days of *Qeynan* were ten and nine hundred
years, and he died, **15** and *Mahalalel* lived five and sixty years[37], and he
caused to bring forth *Yared*, **16** and *Mahalalel* lived, after his causing to
bring forth *Yared*, thirty and eight hundred years, and he caused to bring
forth sons and daughters, **17** and all the days of *Mahalalel* were five and
ninety and eight hundred years, and he died, **18** and *Yared* lived two and
sixty and a hundred years, and he caused to bring forth *Hhanokh*, **19** and
Yared lived, after his causing to bring forth *Hhanokh*, eight hundred years,
and he caused to bring forth sons and daughters, **20** and all the days of
Yared were two and sixty and nine hundred years, and he died, **21** and
Hhanokh lived five and sixty years[38], and he caused to bring forth
Metushelahh, **22** and *Hhanokh* walked himself with the *Elohiym*, after his
causing to bring forth *Metushelahh*, three hundred years, and he caused to
bring forth sons and daughters, **23** and all the days of *Hhanokh* were five and
sixty and three hundred years, **24** and *Hhanokh* walked himself with the
Elohiym and he was not, given that *Elohiym* took him, **25** and *Metushelahh*
lived seven and eighty and a hundred years, and he caused to bring forth

---

[33] The *Septuagint* has 230 years.

[34] The *Septuagint* has 205 years.

[35] The *Septuagint* has 190 years.

[36] The *Septuagint* has 170 years.

[37] The *Septuagint* has 165 years.

[38] The *Septuagint* has 165 years.

Lamekh, **26** and *Metushelahh* lived, after his causing to bring forth *Lamekh*, two and eighty and seven hundred years, and he caused to bring forth sons and daughters, **27** and all the days of *Metushelahh* were nine and sixty and nine hundred years, and he died, **28** and *Lamekh* lived two and eighty and a hundred years, and he caused to bring forth a son, **29** and he called out his title *No'ahh* saying, this one will comfort us from our work, and from the hardship of our hands, from the ground which ***YHWH*** spat upon[39], **30** and *Lamekh* lived, after his causing to bring forth *No'ahh*, five and ninety and five hundred years, and he caused to bring forth sons and daughters, **31** and all the days of *Lamekh* were seven and seventy and seven hundred years, and he died, **32** and *No'ahh* was a son[40] of five hundred years, and *No'ahh* caused to bring forth *Shem*, *Hham* and *Yaphet*,

---

Chapter 6

1 and it came to pass that the human began to increase in number upon the face of the ground, and daughters were brought forth for them, **2** and the sons of the *Elohiym* saw the daughters of the human, that they were functional, and took for them women from all which they chose, **3** and ***YHWH*** said, my wind will not moderate[41] in the human for a distant time, whereas he is flesh and his days will exist a hundred and twenty years. **4** The *Nephilim* existed in the land in those days and also afterward, when the sons of the *Elohiym* came to the daughters of the human, and they brought forth for them, they are the courageous ones which are from a distant[42] time, men of the title[43], **5** and ***YHWH*** saw that the dysfunctions of the human in the land was abundant, and all the thoughts of inventions of his heart was only dysfunctional every day, **6** and ***YHWH*** regretted that he made the human in the land, and he was distressed within his heart, **7** and ***YHWH*** said, I will wipe away the human which I shaped from upon the face of the ground, from the human as well as the beast as well as the treader and as well as the flyer of the skies, given that I regretted that I made them, **8** and *No'ahh* found beauty in the eyes of[44] ***YHWH***. **9** These are the birthings of *No'ahh*, *No'ahh* was a steadfast one and mature man in his generations, *No'ahh* walked himself with the *Elohiym*, **10** and *No'ahh* caused to bring forth three sons, *Shem*, *Hham* and *Yaphet*, **11** and the land was damaged to

---

39 "Spat upon" is an idiom for a "curse."

40 "Son" is an idiom for years "old."

41 The Hebrew word דון means to moderate, judge or rule over.

42 The word מֵעוֹלָם can mean "from a distant time" (meaning ancient), but can also mean "from a distant place."

43 "Men of the title" may be interpreted as "men of character."

44 "Found beauty in the eyes of" is an idiom meaning "was accepted by."

the face[45] of the *Elohiym* and the land was filled with violence[46], **12** and *Elohiym* saw the land and look, she was damaged, given that all the flesh destroyed his road[47] upon the land, **13** and *Elohiym* said to *No'ahh*, a conclusion of all the flesh has come to my face[48], given that the land of violence was filled from their face[49], and look at me, I am destroying them with the land. **14** Make for yourself a vessel of gopher wood, you will make nests for the vessel, and you will cover her from the inside and the outside with the covering, **15** and this is how you will make her, three hundred *ammah*s is the length of the vessel, fifty *ammah*s is her width, and thirty *ammah*s is her height. **16** You will make a glistening[50] for the vessel, and to an *ammah* you will finish her above[51], and you will place an opening of the vessel in her side, you will make her with lower parts, second ones and third ones, **17** and look at me, I am bringing the flood of waters upon the land to damage all the flesh, which has in him the wind of life, below the skies, all which are in the land will expire, **18** and I will make my covenant rise with you and you will come to the vessel, you and your sons and your woman and the women of your sons with you, **19** and from all of the living ones, from all the flesh, two from all you will bring to the vessel to live with you, male and female will exist. **20** From the flyer to his kind, and from the beast to her kind, from all of the treaders of the ground to his kind, two from all will come to you to live, **21** and you, take for you from all the nourishment which will be eaten, and you will gather for you, and he will exist for you and for them for food, **22** and *No'ahh* did everything *Elohiym* directed him, so he did,

---

Chapter 7

1 and ***YHWH*** said to *No'ahh*, come, you and all of your house to the vessel, given that I saw you are a steadfast one to my face[52] in this generation.

---

45 "To the face" means "in front" or "before."

46 The grammar of the Hebrew text can be translated as "the land of violence was filled." the Hebrew appears to be missing the word אֵת or the prefix ב (both can be translated as "with") before the word violence. Compare this with Genesis 6:13.

47 The "road" of man is his customs, manner or actions.

48 "To my face" is an idiom meaning "before me."

49 "From their face" means "with their presence."

50 The meaning of this Hebrew word in this context is uncertain. It is usually translated as "window," but the window of the vessel, mentioned in Genesis 8:6, is a different Hebrew word.

51 The meaning of the phrase "to an *ammah* you will finish her above" is uncertain.

52 "To my face" is an idiom meaning "in front of me."

2 From all of the clean beasts you will take for you seven, seven men and his
women[53], and from the beasts which are not clean, two men and his
women. **3** Also from the flyers of the skies seven, seven males and females
to keep alive the seed upon the face of all the land, **4** given that within seven
more days, I will make a precipitating upon the land, forty days and forty
nights, and I will wipe away all the substance, which I made, from upon the
face of the ground, **5** and *No'ahh* did everything which ***YHWH*** directed him,
6 and *No'ahh* was a son[54] of six hundred years, and the flood had existed as
waters upon the land, **7** and *No'ahh* and his sons and his woman and the
women of his sons with him came to the vessel from the face of the waters
of the flood. **8** From the clean beasts, and from the beasts which are not
clean, and from the flyers, and all which are treading upon the ground.
9 Two by two they came to *No'ahh* to the vessel, male and female just as
Elohiym directed *No'ahh*, **10** and it came to pass within the seven days, and
the waters of the flood existed upon the land. **11** In the year of the six
hundredth year to the life of *No'ahh*, in the second new moon, in the
seventeenth day to the new moon, in this day all the springs of the deep
water were cleaved open abundantly, and the chimneys of the skies had
been opened, **12** and the rain showers existed upon the land, forty days and
forty nights. **13** In the bone of this day[55], *No'ahh*, and *Shem* and *Hham* and
Yaphet, the sons of *No'ahh*, and the woman of *No'ahh*, and the three
women of his sons with them, came to the vessel. **14** They and all the living
ones to her kind, and all the beasts to her kind and all the treaders treading
upon the land to his kind, and all the flyers to his kind, all the birds of all the
wings, **15** and they came to *No'ahh*, to the vessel, two by two from all the
flesh which in him is the wind of life, **16** and the ones coming of the males
and females from all the flesh, came just as *Elohiym* directed him, and
YHWH shut it on his behalf, **17** and the flood existed forty days upon the
land, and the waters increased and lifted up the vessel, and she rose up
from upon the land, **18** and the waters overcame and increased much upon
the land, and the vessel walked upon the face of the waters, **19** and the
waters had overcome very much upon the land and they covered over all
the high hills which are under all the skies. **20** The waters overcame fifteen
ammahs above her, and they covered over the hills, **21** and all the flesh
treading upon the land expired, with the flyer and with the beasts and with
the living ones and with all the swarmers swarming upon the land and all
the humans. **22** All which have the breath of the wind of life in his nostrils,
from all which are in the wasteland had died, **23** and he wiped away all the

---

[53] In context, the "men and his women" are the" males and their mates" from the pure beasts.

[54] "Son" is an idiom for years "old."

[55] "Bone of this day" is an idiom of uncertain meaning, but may mean "this very same day" or the "middle of this day."

substance which was upon the face of the ground, from the human, as well
as the beast, as well as the treader and as well as the flyer of the skies, and
they were wiped away from the land, and only *No'ahh* remained and who
were with him in the vessel, **24** and the waters overcame upon the land fifty
and a hundred days,

Chapter 8

1 and *Elohiym* remembered *No'ahh* and all the living ones and all the beasts
which were with him in the vessel, and *Elohiym* made a wind cross over
upon the land and the waters subsided, **2** and the springs of the deep water
and the chimneys of the skies were shut, and the rain showers from the
skies were restricted, **3** and the waters turned back from upon the land,
walking and turning back, and the waters diminished at the extremity of fifty
and a hundred days, **4** and the vessel rested in the seventh new moon, in the
seventeenth day to the new moon, upon the hills of *Ararat*, **5** and the waters
had existed, walking and diminishing until the tenth new moon, in the tenth
one, in one[56] to the new moon, the heads of the hills appeared, **6** and it
came to pass at the conclusion of the forty days, and *No'ahh* opened the
window of the vessel which he made, **7** and he sent the raven and he went
out, going out and turning back, until the drying out of the waters from
upon the land, **8** and he sent the dove from him to see, were the waters
belittled from upon the face of the ground, **9** and the dove did not find an
oasis for the palm of her foot, and she turned back to him to the vessel,
given that the waters were upon the face of the land, and he sent his hand
and he took her, and he brought her to him to the vessel, **10** and he
twisted[57] yet again another seven days, and he again sent the dove from the
vessel, **11** and the dove came to him at the appointed time of the evening,
and look, a leaf of the olive, a prey in her mouth, and *No'ahh* knew that the
waters were belittled from upon the land, **12** and he twisted yet again
another seven days, and he sent the dove and she did not continue turning
back to him, **13** and it came to pass in one and six hundred years, in the
first[58], in the one[59] to the new moon, the waters dried up from upon the
land, and *No'ahh* removed the roof covering of the vessel and he saw, and
look, the face of the ground dried up, **14** and in the second new moon, in the
twenty and seventh day to the new moon, the land was dried out, **15** and
Elohiym spoke to *No'ahh* saying, **16** go out from the vessel, you and your
woman and your sons and the women of your sons with you. **17** All the living
ones which are with you, from all the flesh, with the flyers and with the

---

[56] Probably meaning "in the first day."

[57] In the sense of "anxiously awaiting." (also in verse 12)

[58] It appears that the Hebrew word for "new moon" is missing from the text.

[59] Probably meaning "in the first day."

beast and with all the treaders treading upon the land, bring out with you,
and they swarmed in the land, and they reproduced and they increased
upon the land, **18** and *No'ahh* went out, and his sons and his woman and the
women of his sons with him. **19** All the living ones, all the treaders and all
the flyers, all the treaders upon the land, according to their clan, they went
out from the vessel, **20** and *No'ahh* built an altar to ***YHWH***, and he took from
all the clean beasts and from all the clean flyers, and he brought up
ascension offerings in the altar, **21** and ***YHWH*** smelled the sweet aroma, and
YHWH said to his heart, I will not continue to belittle the ground on account
of the human, given that the thoughts of the heart of the human are
dysfunctional from his young age, and I will not continue to attack all the
living ones which I made. **22** Yet again are all the days of the land, seed and
harvest and cold and hot and summer and winter and day and night, they
will not cease,

Chapter 9

1 and *Elohiym* exalted *No'ahh* and his sons, and said to them, reproduce and
increase and fill the land, **2** and a fearing of you and a trembling in fear of
you will exist upon all the living ones of the land, and upon all the flyers of
the skies, in all which tread upon the ground, and in all the fish of the sea, in
your hand they were given. **3** All the treaders which are living will exist for
you for food, like all the green herbs I gave to you. **4** Surely, flesh is in his
soul, you will not eat his blood, **5** and surely, for your soul I will seek your
blood, from the hand of all the living I will seek him, and from the hand of
the human, from the hand of the man of his brother, I will seek the soul of
the human. **6** One pouring out the blood of the human by the human, his
blood will be poured out, given that in the image of *Elohiym* he made the
human, **7** and you, reproduce and increase, swarm in the land and increase
in her, **8** and *Elohiym* said to *No'ahh* and to his sons with him, saying, **9** and I,
look at me, am making my covenant rise with you and your seed after you,
10 and with all the souls of the living ones which are with you, with the flyer,
with the beast, and with all the living ones of the land with you, from all the
ones going out of the vessel, to all the living ones of the land, **11** and I made
my covenant rise with you, and all the flesh will not be cut again from the
waters of the flood, the flood will not exist again to damage the land, **12** and
Elohiym said, this is the sign of the covenant which I am giving between me
and you and all the living souls which are with you, for generations of a
distant time. **13** I placed my bow in the cloud, and she will exist for a sign of
the covenant between me and the land, **14** and it will come to pass, with my
conjuring a cloud over the land, and the bow[60] will appear in the cloud,
15 and I will remember my covenant which is between me and you and all

---

[60] This is assumed to be a "rainbow."

the living souls, with all the flesh, and the waters for a flood will not again
exist to damage all the flesh, **16** and the bow will exist in the cloud, and I will
see her to remember the covenant of a distant time, that is between
Elohiym and all living souls with all the flesh which is upon the land, **17** and
Elohiym said to *No'ahh*, this is the sign of the covenant which I made rise
between me and all the flesh which is upon the land, **18** and the sons of
No'ahh going out from the vessel were *Shem* and *Hham* and *Yaphet*, and
Hham, he is the father of *Kena'an*. **19** These three are the sons of *No'ahh*,
and from these all the land scattered[61], **20** and *No'ahh* began as a man of
the ground, and he planted a vineyard, **21** and he gulped from the wine and
he became drunk, and he uncovered himself in the midst of her tent[62],
22 and *Hham*, the father of *Kena'an*, saw the nakedness of his father[63], and
he told his two brothers in the outside, **23** and *Shem* and *Yaphet* took the
apparel and they placed it upon the shoulder of the two of them, and they
walked backward, and they covered over the nakedness of their father, and
their faces were backward and they did not see the nakedness of their
father, **24** and *No'ahh* awoke from his wine and he knew what his small son
did to him, **25** and he said, spat upon is *Kena'an*, he will exist as a servant of
servants to his brothers, **26** and he said, ***YHWH*** the *Elohiym* of *Shem* is
exalted, and *Kena'an* will exist as a servant to them. **27** *Elohiym* will make
Yaphet spread wide, and he will dwell in the tents of *Shem*, and *Kena'an* will
exist as a servant to them, **28** and *No'ahh* lived after the flood three hundred
and fifty years, **29** and all the days of *No'ahh* existed nine hundred and fifty
years and he died,

---

[61] In context, the word "scattered" means that the land was divided into sections (see Genesis 10:5).

[62] All modern translations have "his tent," but the Hebrew spelling of this Hebrew word should be translated as "her tent." the Hebrew spelling may be in error, but in the modern Bedouin culture, which is very similar to the ancient Hebrew culture, the family tent is owned by the wife. Therefore, it is possible that the Hebrew text may use the word "her tent" in reference to this cultural context.

[63] The phrase "nakedness of the father" is an idiom for "sexual relations with the wife of the father" as seen in Leviticus 18:8. Also, the phrase "uncover the nakedness" is another idiom for "sexual relations." the common interpretation of this verse is that *Hham* saw his father naked; however this is not a wrongful act. The idiomatic phrasing of this verse means that *Hham* had sexual relations with his mother. This type of relationship is forbidden and is the reason why *Kena'an*, the product of this union, is cursed in verse Genesis 9:25.

Chapter 10

1 and these are the birthings of the sons of *No'ahh*, *Shem*, *Hham* and
Yaphet, and sons were brought forth to them after the flood. **2** The sons of
Yaphet were *Gomer* and *Magog* and *Madai* and *Yawan* and *Tuval* and
Meshek and *Tiras*, **3** and the sons of *Gomer* were *Ashkanaz* and *Riphat* and
Togarmah, **4** and the sons of *Yawan* were *Elishah* and *Tarshish* and the ones
of *Kit* and the ones of *Dodan*. **5** From these the islands[64] of the nations were
divided apart in their lands, each to his tongue[65], to their clans in their
nations, **6** and the sons of *Hham* were *Kush* and *Mits'rayim* and *Put* and
Kena'an, **7** and the sons of *Kush* were *Seva* and *Hhawilah* and *Savtah* and
Ramah and *Savtekha*, and the sons of *Ramah* were *Sheva* and *Dedan*, **8** and
Kush had brought forth *Nimrod*, he began to exist as a courageous one in
the land. **9** He existed as a courageous hunter to the face of[66] ***YHWH***,
therefore it will be said, like *Nimrod*, a courageous hunter to the face of
YHWH, **10** and the summit of his kingdom existed as *Bavel* and *Erekh* and
Akad and *Kalneh*, in the land of *Shinar*. **11** From that land, *Ashur* went out[67]
and he built *Ninweh* and *Rehhovot-Ghir* and *Kalahh*, **12** and *Resen* between
Ninweh and *Kalahh*, she is the great city, **13** and *Mits'rayim* had brought
forth the ones of *Lud* and the ones of *Anam* and the ones of *Lehav* and the
ones of *Naphtuhh*, **14** and the ones of *Patros* and the ones of *Kasluhh*, which
the ones of *Peleshet* went out from there, and the ones of *Kaphtor*, **15** and
Kena'an had brought forth *Tsidon* his firstborn and *Hhet*, **16** and the one of
Yevus and the one of *Emor* and the one of *Girgash*, **17** and the one of *Hhiw*
and the one of *Araq* and the one of *Sin*, **18** and the one of *Arwad* and the
one of *Tsemar* and the one of *Hhamat* and after the clans of the one of
Kena'an were scattered abroad, **19** and the border of the one of *Kena'an*
existed from *Tsidon* as you come unto *Gerar* as far as *Ghaza*, as you come
unto *Sedom* and *Ghamorah* and *Admah* and *Tseviim*, as far as *Lesha*.
20 These are the sons of *Hham*, to their clans, to their tongues[68], in their
lands, in their nations, **21** and for *Shem* sons were also brought forth, he is
the father of all the sons of *Ever*[69], the brother of *Yaphet* the great. **22** The

---

[64] This Hebrew word can also mean "country."

[65] The word tongue can mean "language."

[66] The phrase "to the face of" is an idiom meaning "in front of."

[67] The construction of the sentence identifies *Ashur* (as a person) as the subject of the verb "GO.OUT" and would be translated as "*Ashur* went out." If however, the original meaning of the phrase was "he went out to *Ashur*," (where the "he" is *Nimrod* and *Ashur* is a place, see Genesis 2:14) the word "to" should have preceded the word *Ashur*.

[68] The word tongue can mean "language."

[69] That is, the Hebrews, which in the Hebrew language is עברים (ivrim) meaning "ones of *Ever*."

sons of *Shem* were *Elam* and *Ashur* and *Arpakhshad* and *Lud* and *Aram*[70], **23** and the sons of *Aram* were *Uts* and *Hhul* and *Getar* and *Mash*, **24** and *Arpakhshad* had brought forth *Shelahh*, and *Shelahh* had brought forth *Ever*,[71] **25** and to *Ever* were brought forth two sons, the title of the one was *Peleg*, given that in his days the land was split, and the title of his brother was *Yaqtan*, **26** and *Yaqtan* had brought forth *Almodad* and *Sheleph* and *Hhatsarmawet* and *Yerahh*, **27** and *Hadoram* and *Uzal* and *Diqlah*, **28** and Oval and *Aviyma'el* and *Sheva*, **29** and *Ophir* and *Hhawilah* and *Yovav*, all these are the sons of *Yaqtan*, **30** and their settling existed from *Mesha* as you come unto *Sephar*, the hill of the east. **31** These are the sons of *Shem*, to their clans, to their tongue[72], in their lands, to their nations. **32** These are the clans of the sons of *No'ahh*, to their birthings, in their nations, and from these the nations were divided apart in the land after the flood,

Chapter 11

1 and all of the land existed as one lip and a unit of words, **2** and it came to pass in their journey from the east, then they found a level valley in the land of *Shinar*, and they settled there, **3** and they said each to his companion, come, we will make bricks and we will cremate them, and the bricks existed to them for stone, and the slime existed for them for mortar, **4** and they said, come, we will build for us a city and a tower, and his head will be in the skies, and we will make for us a title, otherwise we will scatter abroad upon the face of all the land, **5** and ***YHWH*** went down to see the city and the tower which the sons of the human built, **6** and ***YHWH*** said, though the people are a unit and to all of them is one lip, and this is what they will begin to do, and now not a thing will be fenced in[73] from them, all which they will plot to do. **7** Come, we will go down and we will mix their lip[74] there, that each will not hear[75] the lip of his companion, **8** and ***YHWH*** scattered them abroad from there upon the face of all the land, and they terminated to build the city. **9** Therefore he called out her title *Bavel*, given that there ***YHWH*** mixed the lip of all the land, and from there ***YHWH*** scatter them abroad upon the face of all the land. **10** These are the birthings of *Shem*, *Shem* was a son[76] of a hundred years, and he caused to bring forth

---

[70] The *Septuagint* also has; "and *Qeynan*."

[71] The *Septuagint* and Dead Sea Scrolls read; "and *Arpakhshad* had brought forth Keynan, and *Qeynan* brought forth *Shelahh*, and *Shelahh* had brought forth *Ever*."

[72] This Hebrew word can also mean "language." (also in verses 11:1, 6 and 9)

[73] "Fenced in" in this context means limited or restricted.

[74] This Hebrew word can also mean "language."

[75] Possibly meaning "understand."

[76] "Son" is an idiom for years "old."

Arpakhshad two years after the flood, **11** and *Shem* lived five hundred years after his causing to bring forth *Arpakhshad,* and he caused to bring forth sons and daughters, **12** and *Arpakhshad* had lived five and thirty years[77] and he caused to bring forth *Shelahh*[78], **13** and *Arpakhshad* lived three and four hundred years after his causing to bring forth *Shelahh,* and he caused to bring forth sons and daughters,[79] **14** and *Shelahh* lived thirty years[80] and he caused to bring forth *Ever,* **15** and *Shelahh* lived three and four hundred years after his causing to bring forth *Ever,* and he caused to bring forth sons and daughters, **16** and *Ever* lived four and thirty years, and he caused to bring forth *Peleg,* **17** and *Ever* lived thirty and four hundred years after his causing to bring forth *Peleg,* and he caused to bring forth sons and daughters, **18** and *Peleg* lived thirty years and he caused to bring forth *Re'u,* **19** and *Peleg* lived nine and two hundred years after his causing to bring forth *Re'u,* and he caused to bring forth sons and daughters, **20** and *Re'u* lived two and thirty years and he caused to bring forth *Serug,* **21** and *Re'u* lived seven and two hundred years after his causing to bring forth *Serug,* and he caused to bring forth sons and daughters, **22** and *Serug* lived thirty years and he caused to bring forth *Nahhor,* **23** and *Serug* lived two hundred years after his causing to bring forth *Nahhor,* and he caused to bring forth sons and daughters, **24** and *Nahhor* lived nine and twenty years and he caused to bring forth *Terahh,* **25** and *Nahhor* lived nineteen and a hundred years after his causing to bring forth *Terahh,* and he caused to bring forth sons and daughters, **26** and *Terahh* lived seventy years and he caused to bring forth *Avram, Nahhor* and *Haran,* **27** and these are the birthings of *Terahh, Terahh* had caused to bring forth *Avram, Nahhor* and *Haran,* and *Haran* had caused to bring forth *Lot,* **28** and *Haran* died upon the face of[81] *Terahh* his father, in the land of his kindred in *Ur* of the ones of *Kesed,* **29** and *Avram* and *Nahhor* took women for themselves, the title of the woman of *Avram* was *Sarai,* and the title of the woman of *Nahhor* was *Milkah,* the daughter of *Haran,* the father of *Milkah,* and the father of *Yiskah,* **30** and *Sarai* existed sterile, there was not a child to her, **31** and *Terahh* took *Avram* his son, and *Lot,* the son of *Haran,* the son of his son, and *Sarai,* his daughter-in-law, the woman of *Avram* his son, and they went

---

[77] The *Septuagint* has "a hundred and thirty-five years."

[78] The *Septuagint* has *Qeynan* instead of *Shelahh.*

[79] The *Septuagint* for this verse reads; "And *Arpakhshad* lived after he had begotten *Qeynan,* four hundred years, and brought forth sons and daughters, and died. And *Qeynan* lived a hundred and thirty years and brought forth *Shelahh*; and *Qeynan* lived after he had brought forth *Shelahh,* three hundred and thirty years, and brought forth sons and daughters, and died."

[80] The *Septuagint* has "a hundred and thirty years."

[81] "Upon the face of" is an idiom meaning "in the presence of."

out with them from *Ur* of the ones of *Kesed,* to walk unto the land of *Kena'an,* and they came as far as *Hharan,* and they settled there, **32** and the days of *Terahh* existed five and two hundred years, and *Terahh* died in *Hharan,*

Chapter 12

1 and ***YHWH*** said to *Avram,* walk yourself from your land and from your kindred and from the house of your father to the land which I will show you, **2** and I will make you a great nation and I will exalt you and I will magnify your title and exist as a present, **3** and I will exalt ones exalting you and ones belittling you I will spit upon and all of the clans of the ground will be exalted with you, **4** and *Avram* walked just as ***YHWH*** spoke to him and *Lot* walked with him and *Avram* was a son of seventy-five years in his going out from *Hharan,* **5** and *Avram* took *Sarai* his woman and *Lot* the son of his brother and all their goods which they accumulated and the souls which they did in *Hharan* and they went out to walk unto the land of *Kena'an* and they came unto the land of *Kena'an,* **6** and *Avram* crossed over in the land, as far as the area of *Shekhem,* as far as the great tree of *Moreh* and the one of *Kena'an* was at that time in the land, **7** and ***YHWH*** appeared to *Avram* and said, to your seed I will give this land, and he built there an altar to ***YHWH*** the one appearing to him, **8** and he advanced from there unto the hill, from the east to *Beyt-El* and he stretched her tent[82], *Beyt-El* was from the sea[83] and *Ay* was from the east and he built there an altar to ***YHWH*** and he called out in the title of ***YHWH***[84], **9** and *Avram* journeyed, walking and journeying unto the south, **10** and a hunger existed in the land and *Avram* went down unto *Mits'rayim* to immigrate there, given that the hunger was heavy in the land, **11** and it came to pass just as he came near to come unto *Mits'rayim* and he said to *Sarai* his woman, please look, I know that you are a woman of beautiful appearance, **12** and it will come to pass that the ones of *Mits'rayim* will see you and they will say this is his woman and they will kill me and they will keep you alive. **13** Please say you are my sister so that it will go well for

---

[82] All modern translations have "his tent" but the Hebrew spelling of this word should be translated as "her tent." the Hebrew spelling may be in error, but in the modern Bedouin culture, which is very similar to the Ancient Hebrew culture, the family tent is owned by the wife. Therefore, it is possible that the Hebrew text may use the word "her tent" in reference to this cultural context. The phrase "he called out in the title" may also be translated as "he met with the title."

[83] This Hebrew word can also mean "west," as the Mediterranean "sea" is "west" of Israel.

[84] The phrase "and he called out in the title of ***YHWH***" can also be translated as "and he met with the character of ***YHWH***."

me with your crossing over, and my soul will live on account of you, **14** and it came to pass as *Avram* came unto *Mits'rayim* and the ones of *Mits'rayim* saw the woman, given that she was very beautiful, **15** and the nobles of *Paroh* saw her and they endorsed her to *Paroh* and took the woman to[85] the house of *Paroh*, **16** and to *Avram* it was made well on account of her, and flocks existed for him and cattle and donkeys and servants and maids and she-donkeys and camels, **17** and ***YHWH*** touched *Paroh* and his house with great plagues because of the word[86] of *Sarai*, the woman of *Avram*, **18** and *Paroh* called out to *Avram* and he said, what is this you did to me, why did you not tell to me that she is your woman. **19** Why did you say she is my sister, and I took her for me for a woman and now look, take your woman and walk, **20** and *Paroh* directed men concerning him and they sent him and his woman and all which belong to him,

---

Chapter 13

1 and *Avram* went up from *Mits'rayim*, he and his woman and all which belong to him, and *Lot* who was with him, unto the south, **2** and *Avram* was much heavy[87] in livestock, in silver and in gold, **3** and he walked on his journey from the south and as far as *Beyt-El*, as far as the area where her tent[88] existed the first time, between *Beyt-El* and the *Ay*. **4** To the area of the altar which he made there first, and there *Avram* called out in the title of ***YHWH***[89], **5** and also belonging to *Lot*, the one walking with *Avram*, existed flocks and cattle and tents, **6** and the land did not lift them up[90] to settle together, given that their goods existed abundantly and they were not able to settle together, **7** and a dispute existed between the feeders of the livestock of *Avram* and the feeders of the livestock of *Lot*, and the ones of *Kena'an* and the ones of *Perez* were at that time settling in the land, **8** and *Avram* said to *Lot*, please, do not let contention exist between me and you, and between my feeders and your feeders, given that we are men of brothers. **9** Is not all of the land to your face, please, be divided apart from

---

[85] The word "to" appears to be missing before the word "house" in the Hebrew, otherwise this phrase should be translated as "and took the woman of the house of *Paroh*."

[86] This Hebrew word can also mean "matter."

[87] Meaning "wealthy."

[88] The *ketiv*, meaning "her tent," may be correct. In the modern Bedouin culture, which is very similar to the Ancient Hebrew culture, the family tent is owned by the wife. Therefore, it is possible that the Hebrew text may use the word "her tent" in reference to this cultural context.

[89] The phrase "he called out in the title of ***YHWH***" can also be translated as "he met with the character of ***YHWH***."

[90] The phrase "lift up" can mean "support."

upon me, if the left hand, I will go right and if the right hand, I will go left,
10 and *Lot* lifted up his eyes and he saw all of the roundness of the *Yarden*, given that all of her was drinking[91], before ***YHWH*** damaged *Sedom* and *Ghamorah*, it was like the garden of ***YHWH***, like the land of *Mits'rayim* as you come to *Tso'ar*,
11 and *Lot* chose for him all of the roundness of the *Yarden*, and *Lot* journeyed from the east and they divided apart, each from upon his brother.
12 *Avram* had settled in the land of *Kena'an*, and *Lot* had settled in the cities of the roundness, and he pitched the tent as far as *Sedom*,
13 and the men of *Sedom* were dysfunctional and of many failures to ***YHWH***,
14 and ***YHWH*** had said to *Avram* after *Lot* was divided apart from him, please, lift up your eyes and see the area from where you are, unto the north and unto the south and unto the east and unto the sea,
15 given that all the land which you are seeing for yourself, I will give her and to your seed unto a distant time,
16 and I will place your seed like the dirt of the land, which if a man will be able to reckon the dirt of the land, also your seed will be reckoned.
17 Rise and walk yourself in the land, to her length and to her width, given that I will give her to you,
18 and *Avram* pitched the tent and he came and he settled in the great trees of *Mamre*, which is in *Hhevron*, and he built there an altar to ***YHWH***,

---

Chapter 14

1 and it came to pass in the days of *Amraphel* king of *Shinar*, *Aryokh* king of *Elasar*, *Kedarla'omer* king of *Elam* and *Tidal* king of *Goyim*.
2 They did battle with *Bera* king of *Sedom*, and with *Birsha* king of *Ghamorah*, *Shinav* king of *Admah*, and *Shemever* king of *Tseviim*, and the king of *Bela*, she is *Tso'ar*.
3 All of these coupled[92] to the valley of the *Sidim*, he is the sea of salt.
4 Twelve years they served *Kedarla'omer* and the thirteenth year they rebelled,
5 and in the fourteenth year *Kedarla'omer* came, and the kings which were with him, and they attack the ones of *Rapha* in *Ashterot-Qar'nayim*, and the ones of *Zuz* in *Ham*, and the ones of *Eym* in *Shaweh-Qiryatayim*,
6 and the one of *Hhor* in their mount of *Se'iyr*, as far as *Eyl-Paran* which is upon the wilderness,
7 and they turned back and they came to *Eyn-Mishpat*, she is *Qadesh*, and they attack all of the fields of the ones of *Amaleq* and also the ones of *Emor*, the ones settling in *Hhats'tson-Tamar*,
8 and the king of *Sedom* went out, and the king of *Ghamorah*, and the king of *Admah*, and the king of *Tseviim*, and the king of *Bela*, she is *Tso'ar*, and they arranged with them a battle in the valley of *Sidim*.
9 With *Kedarla'omer* the king of *Elam*, and *Tidal* the king of *Goyim*, and *Amraphel* the king of *Shinar*, and *Aryokh* the king of *Elasar*, four kings with the five,
10 and the valley of *Sidim* was wells of wells of slime, and the king of *Sedom* and

---

[91] Meaning "well watered."

[92] Meaning "came together."

Ghamorah fled, and they fell there and the remaining ones fled unto the hill, **11** and they took all the goods of *Sedom* and *Ghamorah*, and all their foodstuff, and they walked, **12** and they took *Lot*, the son of the brother of *Avram*, and his goods, and they walked and he settled in *Sedom*, **13** and the one that escaped came and he told to *Avram*, the one of *Ever* and dwelling in the great trees of *Mamre*, the one of *Emor*, the brother of *Eshkol* and the brother of *Aner*, they were the masters of the covenant of *Avram*, **14** and *Avram* heard that his brother was captured, and he emptied his three hundred and eighteen experienced ones born of his house, and he pursued as far as *Dan*, **15** and he was distributed upon them at night, he and his servants had hit them, and he pursued them as far as *Hhovah* which is from the left hand to *Dameseq*, **16** and he returned all the goods and also *Lot* his brother, and his goods he returned, and also the women and the people, **17** and the king of *Sedom* went out to meet him after his turning back from attacking *Kedarla'omer* and the kings who were with him, at the valley of *Shaweh*, he is the valley of the king, **18** and *Malkiy-Tsedeq*, king of *Shalem*, had brought out bread and wine, and he was the administrator to the mighty one of *Elyon*, **19** and he exalted him and he said, exalted is *Avram* to the mighty one of *Elyon*, the purchaser of skies and land, **20** and exalted is the mighty one of *Elyon* who delivered up your narrowness[93] in your hand, and he gave to him a tenth part from all, **21** and the king of *Sedom* said to *Avram*, give to me the soul, and take the goods for yourself, **22** and *Avram* said to the king of *Sedom*, I rose up my hand to ***YHWH***, the mighty one of *Elyon*, purchaser of skies and land. **23** If I do not[94] take from a thread or even the lace of a sandal or from anything which belongs to you, then you cannot say, I made *Avram* rich. **24** Apart from only what the young men ate, and the distribution of the men which walked with me, *Aner*, *Eshkol* and *Mamre*, they will take their distribution.

Chapter 15

1 After these words, the word of ***YHWH*** existed for *Avram* in the vision saying, do not fear *Avram*, I am a shield for you, your wages will increase greatly, **2** and *Avram* said, *Adonai* of ***YHWH***, what will you give to me as I am walking barren and the son of acquisition of my house is *Eli'ezer* of *Dameseq*[95], **3** and *Avram* said, though you did not give me seed, look, a son

[93] The word "narrowness" may mean "difficult."

[94] The word "NOT," at the beginning of *Abram*'s statement, according to the context, appears to be missing from the text.

[95] The Hebrew text has these names written as "*Dameseq Eli'ezer*" which requires the translation "*Dameseq* of *Eli'ezer*" or as a compound name – "*Dameseq- Eli'ezer*." If the standard translation of "*Eli'ezer* of Damascus" is correct, then the names must be reversed to "*Eli'ezer Dameseq*."

of my house is possessing me, **4** and look, the word of ***YHWH*** was for him
saying, this one will not possess you, instead he which will go out from your
abdomens, he will possess you, **5** and he brought him out unto the outside
and he said, please, stare unto the skies and count the stars, if you are able
to count them, and he said to him, in this way your seed will exist, **6** and he
supported in ***YHWH*** and he thought it was steadfastness for him, **7** and he
said to him, I am ***YHWH*** who brought you out from *Ur* of the ones of *Kesed*,
to give to you this land to possess her, **8** and he said, *Adonai* of ***YHWH*** how
will I know that I will inherit her, **9** and he said to him, take for me a heifer
being a threefold[96], and a she-goat being a threefold, and a buck being a
threefold and a turtledove and a young pigeon, **10** and he took for himself
all these, and he cut them in two in the midst[97], and he gave each cut piece
of him to meet his companion, and the bird he had not cut in two, **11** and
the bird of prey went down upon the corpses, and *Avram* made a gust at
them, **12** and it came to pass, the sun came, and a trance had fallen upon
Avram, and look, a terror of a great darkness was falling upon him, **13** and
he said to *Avram*, you will surely know that your seed will exist as an
immigrant in a land not belonging to them, and they will serve them and
they will afflict them four hundred years, **14** and also, the nation which they
will serve, I am moderating, and afterward they will go out with great goods,
15 and you will come to your fathers in completeness, you will be buried
with a functional gray-head, **16** and the fourth generation will turn back to
this point, given that the twistedness of the ones of *Emor* are not complete
at this point, **17** and it came to pass, the sun came and it was twilight, and
look, an oven of smoke and a torch of fire that crossed over between these
divided parts. **18** In that day ***YHWH*** cut with *Avram* a covenant saying, to
your seed I gave this land, from the river of *Mits'rayim* as far as the great
river, the river *Perat*. **19** The ones of *Qayin*, and the ones of *Qenaz*, and the
ones of *Qadmon*, **20** and the ones of *Hhet*, and the ones of *Perez*, and the
ones of *Rapha*, **21** and the ones of *Emor*, and the ones of *Kena'an*, and the
ones of *Girgash*, and the ones of *Yevus*,

Chapter 16

1 and *Sarai*, the woman of *Avram*, did not bring forth for him, and belonging
to her was a maid of *Mits'rayim*, and her title was *Hagar*, **2** and *Sarai* said to
Avram, please look, ***YHWH*** stopped me from bringing forth, please come to
my maid, possibly I will build from her, and *Avram* heard the voice of *Sarai*,
3 and after ten years of the settling of *Avram* in the land of *Kena'an*, *Sarai*,
the woman of *Avram*, took *Hagar*, the one of *Mits'rayim*, her maid, and she

---

[96] The word threefold probably means "three years old."

[97] The Samaritan Pentateuch has the word בתור (*batur*) which means "with the turtledove."

gave her to *Avram*, her man, for him for a woman, **4** and he came to *Hagar* and she conceived, and she saw that she conceived, and her female owner was belittled in her eyes, **5** and *Sarai* said to *Avram*, my violence is upon you, I gave my maid in your bosom, and she saw that she conceived, and I am belittled in her eyes, ***YHWH*** will decide between me and you, **6** and *Avram* said to *Sarai*, look, your maid is in your hand, do to her what is functional in your eyes, and *Sarai* afflicted her, and she fled from her face, **7** and the messenger of ***YHWH*** found her upon the eye[98] of the waters in the wilderness, upon the eye in the road of *Shur*, **8** and he said, *Hagar*, the maid of *Sarai*, from where did you come and wherever are you walking, and she said, I am fleeing away from the face of *Sarai* my female owner, **9** and the messenger of ***YHWH*** said to her, turn back to your female owner and afflict yourself under her hands, **10** and the messenger of ***YHWH*** said to her, I will surely make your seed an increase, and he will not be counted from an abundance, **11** and the messenger of ***YHWH*** said to her, look, you are pregnant and you will bring forth a son, and you will call out his title *Yishma'el*, given that ***YHWH*** will hear your affliction, **12** and he will exist as a wild ass of a human, his hand will be in all and the hand of all will be in him, and he will dwell upon the faces of[99] all his brothers, **13** and she called out the title of ***YHWH***, the one speaking to her, you are *El-Ra'iy*, given that she said, will I also see at this point after seeing me. **14** Therefore he called out to the well *Be'er-Lahhiy-Ro'iy*, look, it is between *Qadesh* and *Bered*, **15** and *Hagar* brought forth for *Avram* a son, and *Avram* called out the title of his son which *Hagar* brought forth *Yishma'el*, **16** and *Avram* was a son[100] of eighty six years in the giving birth of *Hagar* to *Yishma'el* for *Avram*,

---

Chapter 17

1 and *Avram* existed as a son[101] of ninety nine years, and ***YHWH*** appeared to *Avram* and he said to him, I am the mighty one of *Shaddai*, walk yourself to my face and exist whole, **2** and I will give my covenant between me and you, and I will make you increase with a great many, **3** and *Avram* fell upon his face, and *Elohiym* spoke with him saying, **4** look, I am here, my covenant is with you, and you will exist as a father of a multitude of nations, **5** and your title *Avram* will not again be called out, but your title will exist as *Avraham*, given that I gave you as a father of a multitude of nations, **6** and I will make you reproduce with a great many, and I will give you for nations, and from you kings will go out, **7** and I will make my covenant rise between me and you, and your seed after you to their generations for a covenant of a distant

---

98 Meaning a "fountain."

99 "Upon the faces of" means "in the presence of."

100 "Son" is an idiom for years "old."

101 "Son" is an idiom for years "old."

time, to exist for you for *Elohiym*, and for your seed after you, **8** and I will
give to you and to your seed after you the land of your immigration, all the
land of *Kena'an* for holdings of a distant time, and I will exist for them for
Elohiym, **9** and *Elohiym* said to *Avraham*, and you, you will safeguard my
covenant, you and your seed after you to their generations. **10** This is my
covenant, which you will safeguard, between me and you and your seed
after you, all of your males will be snipped, **11** and you will cut off the flesh
of your foreskin, and he will exist as the sign of the covenant between me
and you, **12** and the son[102] of eight days will be snipped for you, all of the
males to your generations born of the house or acquired by silver, from all
of the sons of a foreigner which is not from your seed. **13** Be snipped, one
born of your house or acquired of your silver will be snipped, and my
covenant will exist in your flesh for a covenant of a distant time, **14** and an
uncircumcised male whose flesh of his foreskin is not being snipped, then
that soul will be cut from her people, he broke my covenant, **15** and *Elohiym*
said to *Avraham*, of *Sarai* your woman, her title will not be call out as *Sarai*,
given that *Sarah* is her title, **16** and I will exalt her, and also I gave[103] to you a
son from her, and I will exalt her, and she will exist for nations, kings of
peoples will exist from her, **17** and *Avraham* fell upon his face and he
laughed and he said in his heart, will he be brought forth to one who is a
son[104] of a hundred years, and if *Sarah* is the daughter[105] of ninety years will
she bring forth, **18** and *Avraham* said to the *Elohiym*, would that *Yishma'el*
live to your face[106], **19** and *Elohiym* said, nevertheless, *Sarah* your woman is
bringing forth for you a son, and you will call out his title *Yits'hhaq*, and I will
make my covenant rise with him for a covenant of a distant time to his seed
after him, **20** and to *Yishma'el*, I heard you, look, I exalted him and I will
make him reproduce, and I will make him increase with a great many, he will
cause to bring forth twelve captains and I will give him for a great nation,
21 and I will make my covenant rise with *Yits'hhaq*, which *Sarah* will bring
forth for you at this appointed time in another year, **22** and he finished
speaking with him, and *Elohiym* went up from upon *Avraham*, **23** and
Avraham took *Yishma'el* his son and all of the ones born of his house and all
of the ones acquired of his silver, all the males with the men of the house of
Avraham, and he snipped the flesh of their foreskin in the bone of this
day[107] just as *Elohiym* spoke with him, **24** and *Avraham* was a son[108] of

---

[102] "Son" is an idiom for years "old."

[103] The perfect tense of the verb requires it to be translated as "I gave," but the context indicates that the verb tense should have been in the imperfect, which would then be translated as "I will give."

[104] "Son" is an idiom for years "old."

[105] "Daughter" is an idiom for years "old."

[106] "To your face" is an idiom for "in front of you."

[107] "Bone of this day" is an idiom of uncertain meaning, but may mean "this very same day" or the "middle of this day."

ninety nine years in his being snipped of the flesh of his foreskin, **25** and *Yishma'el* his son was a son[109] of thirteen years in his being snipped of the flesh of his foreskin. **26** In the bone of this day[110] *Avraham* was snipped, and *Yishma'el* his son, **27** and all of the men of his house, ones born of the house or acquired of silver from the son of a foreigner, were snipped with him,

---

Chapter 18

1 and ***YHWH*** appeared to him in the great trees of *Mamre*, and he was settling in the opening of the tent as the day was hot, **2** and he lifted up his eyes and he saw and look, three men were standing upon him, and he saw, and he ran from the opening of the tent to meet them, he bent himself down unto the land, **3** and he said, *Adonai*[111], please, if I find beauty in your eyes, please do not cross over from upon your servant. **4** Please, a small amount of waters will be taken and bathe your feet and lean under the tree, **5** and I will take a fragment of bread and hold up[112] your heart, afterward you will cross over since you crossed over upon your servant, and they said, you will do so just as you spoke, **6** and *Avraham* much hurried unto the tent to *Sarah* and he said, hurry, knead three *se'ah*s of grain flour and make baked breads, **7** and *Avraham* ran to the cattle and he took a son of the cattle, tender and functional, and he gave it to the young man, and he hurried to make him, **8** and he took cheese and fat and a son of the cattle, which he made, and he gave it to their face, and he was standing upon them under the tree and they ate, **9** and they said to him, where is *Sarah* your woman, and he said, look, in the tent, **10** and he said, I will surely turn back to you at the appointed time of life[113], and look, a son for *Sarah* your woman, and *Sarah* was hearing in the opening of the tent and he was behind him, **11** and *Avraham* and *Sarah* were bearded ones, coming in the days[114], the path like the women terminated to exist[115] for *Sarah*, **12** and

---

108 "Son" is an idiom for years "old."

109 "Son" is an idiom for years "old."

110 "Bone of this day" is an idiom of uncertain meaning, but may mean "this very same day" or the "middle of this day."

111 The name "*Adonai*" may be translated as a name, "*Adonai*," or as the possessive plural noun meaning "my lords." Context supports both translations as there are three men before *Avraham* allowing for the "my lords" translation, but the three uses of the pronoun "you" in the singular implies that he is speaking to one individual supporting the use of the word as a name.

112 Meaning to "refresh."

113 Possibly an idiom for the season of "spring."

114 "Coming in the days" means "advanced in age."

Sarah laughed inside herself saying, after I am worn out[116], pleasure exists for me and my lord who is old, **13** and ***YHWH*** said to *Avraham*, why is this, *Sarah* laughed saying, will I really bring forth when I am old. **14** Is a word[117] too difficult for ***YHWH***, at the appointed time I will turn back to you, at the appointed time of life[118], and to *Sarah* will be a son, **15** and *Sarah* lied, saying, I did not laugh, given that she feared, and he said, no, given that you did laugh, **16** and the men rose from there and they looked down upon the face of *Sedom*, and *Avraham* was walking with them to send them off, **17** and ***YHWH*** had said, shall I cover over[119] from *Avraham* what I am doing, **18** and *Avraham* will surely exist as a great and numerous nation, and all the nations of the land will be exalted with him, **19** given that I knew him, so that he will direct his sons, and his house after him, and they will safeguard the road of ***YHWH*** to do steadfastness and decisions, so that ***YHWH*** will bring upon *Avraham* what he spoke upon him, **20** and ***YHWH*** said, given that the yell of *Sedom* and *Ghamorah* had increased in number and, given that their failure had become very heavy. **21** I will go down to her please, and I will see whether her yell that is coming to me is a completion, and if not, I will know, **22** and the men turned from there and they walked unto *Sedom*, and yet again *Avraham* was standing to the face[120] of ***YHWH***, **23** and *Avraham* drew near and he said, moreover, will you consume the steadfast one with the lost. **24** Possibly there are fifty steadfast ones in the midst of the city, moreover will you consume and not lift up[121] to that area on account of the fifty steadfast ones which are inside her. **25** Far be it to you from doing in this manner to kill the correct with the lost and the correct will be like the lost, far be it to you, will the judge of all of the land not do judgment, **26** and ***YHWH*** said, if I will find in *Sedom* fifty correct ones in the midst of the city I will lift up to all of the place on account of them, **27** and *Avraham* answered and he said, please look, I take upon to speak to *Adonai* and I am dirt and dust. **28** Possibly the fifty correct ones diminish by five, will you destroy all of the city with the five, and he said, I will not cause damage if I will find there forty-five, **29** and he continued to speak to him and he said, possibly forty will be found there, and he said, I will not do on account of the forty, **30** and he said to *Adonai*, please do not flare up and I will speak, possibly thirty will be found there, and he said, I will not do if I will find there thirty, **31** and he said, please look, I will take upon to speak to *Adonai*, possibly twenty will be found there, and he said, I will not cause damage on

---

[115] The phrase "the path like the women terminated to exist" means "the time of childbearing has ended."

[116] In reference to being beyond childbearing age (see verse 11).

[117] This Hebrew word can also mean "thing."

[118] Possibly an idiom for the season of "spring."

[119] Meaning "hide."

[120] "To the face" is an idiom for "in front."

[121] Meaning "spare."

account of the twenty, **32** and he said to *Adonai*, please do no flare up and I will speak, surely this time, possibly ten will be found there, and he said I will not cause damage on account of the ten, **33** and ***YHWH*** walked just as he finished to speak to *Avraham* and *Avraham* turned back to his place,

---

Chapter 19

1 and two of the messengers came unto *Sedom* in the evening and *Lot* was settling in the gate of *Sedom* and *Lot* saw and he rose to meet them and he bent himself down, nostrils unto the land, **2** and he said, please look my lords, please turn aside to the house of your servant and stay the night and wash your feet and you will depart early and you will walk to your road and they said, no, given that in the street we will stay the night, **3** and he pressed very hard with them and they turned aside to him and they came to his house and he made for them a feast and he baked unleavened bread and they ate. **4** Before they laid down, and the men of the city, the men of *Sedom*, from the young men and also the bearded ones, all of the people from the far end, went around upon the house, **5** and they called out to *Lot* and they said to him, where are the men which came to you tonight, bring them out to us and we will know them, **6** and *Lot* went out to them, unto the opening and he shut the door after him, **7** and he said, please no my brothers, you will be made dysfunctional. **8** Please look, I have two daughters which do not know a man, please, I will bring them out to you and do to them as is functional in your eyes only to these men you will not do a thing because they came in the shadow of my rafter, **9** and they said, draw near to a distance, and they said, the one had come to immigrate and he will judge a judgment, now we will cause you to be dysfunctional rather than them and they pressed very hard with the man, with *Lot*, and they drew near to burst the door, **10** and the men sent their hand and they made *Lot* come to them unto the house and they shut the door. **11** They attack the men which were at the opening of the house with the blindness from the small and also the great and they were weary for finding the opening, **12** and the men said to *Lot* yet again, who also belongs to you here, in-laws and your sons and your daughters and all of the ones which belong to you in the city, go out from the place, **13** given that we will destroy this place, given that their cry will magnify at the face of ***YHWH*** and ***YHWH*** sent us to damage her, **14** and *Lot* went out and he spoke to his in-laws, ones taking his daughters, and he said rise, go out from this place, given that ***YHWH*** will destroy the city and he was like one greatly laughing in the eyes of his in-laws, **15** and as the dawn had come up, then the messengers compelled *Lot* saying, rise, take your woman and your two daughters, the ones being found, otherwise you will be consumed in the twistedness of the city, **16** and he lingered himself and the men seized his hand and the hand of his woman and the hand of his two daughters, ***YHWH*** had pity upon him and they

brought him out and they left him outside the city, **17** and it came to pass as
they brought them out unto the outside and he said, slip away upon your
soul, you will not stare behind you and you will not stand in all of the
roundness, slip away unto the hill, otherwise you will be consumed, **18** and
Lot said to them, please no my lords. **19** Please look, your servant found
beauty in your eyes and you magnified your kindness which you did by me,
making my soul live and I will not be able to slip away unto the hill otherwise
dysfunction will adhere to me and I will die. **20** Please look, this city is near,
to flee unto there and she is few, please, I will slip away unto there, is she
not few, and my soul will live, **21** and he said to him, look, I lifted up your
face also to this word for I will not overturn the city which you spoke.
22 Hurry, slip away unto there, given that I will not be able to do a word
until you come unto there, therefore he called out the title of the city *Tso'ar*.
23 The sun went out upon the land and *Lot* came unto *Tso'ar*, **24** and ***YHWH***
caused to precipitate upon *Sedom* and upon *Ghamorah* brimstone and fire
from ***YHWH*** from the skies, **25** and he overturned these cities and all of the
roundness and all of the settlers of the cities and the spring up things of the
ground, **26** and his woman stared from behind him and she existed as a post
of salt, **27** and *Avraham* departed early in the morning to the place where he
stood there with the face of ***YHWH***, **28** and he looked down upon the face of
Sedom and *Ghamorah* and upon all of the face of the land of the roundness
and he saw and look, a smoldering of the land went up like a smoldering
furnace, **29** and it came to pass *Elohiym* greatly damaged the cities of the
roundness and *Elohiym* remembered *Avraham* and he sent *Lot* from the
midst of the overturning, in overturning the cities which *Lot* settled in,
30 and *Lot* and his two daughters with him, went up from *Tso'ar* and settled
in the hill, given that he feared to settle in *Tso'ar* and he and his two
daughters settled in the cave, **31** and the firstborn woman said to the little
one, our father is old and not a man in the land to come upon us like the
road of all of the land. **32** Walk, we will make our father drink wine and we
will lie down with him and we will live from our father a seed, **33** and they
made their father drink wine in that night and the firstborn woman came
and she laid down with her father and he did not know in her lying down
and in her rising, **34** and it came to pass the next day and the firstborn
woman said to the little one, though I laid down last night with my father we
will make him drink wine also tonight and come and lay down with him and
we will live from our father a seed, **35** and they made their father drink wine
also in that night and the little one rose and she laid down with him and he
did not know in her lying down and in her rising, **36** and the two daughters
of *Lot* conceived from their father, **37** and the firstborn woman brought
forth a son and she called out his title *Mo'av*, he is the father of the *Mo'av*
until today, **38** and the little one, she also brought forth a son and she called
out his title *Ben-Amiy*, he is the father of the sons of *Amon* until today,

Chapter 20

1 and *Avraham* lifted up from there unto the land of the south, and he settled between *Qadesh* and *Shur* and he immigrated in *Gerar*, **2** and *Avraham* said to *Sarah* his woman, she is my sister and *Aviymelekh* the king of *Gerar* sent and he took *Sarah*,[122] **3** and *Elohiym* came to *Aviymelekh* in the dream in the night and he said to him, look at you, dying because of the woman whom you took and she is the married of a master, **4** and *Aviymelekh* had not come near to her and he said, *Adonai* will you kill also a correct nation. **5** Did he not say to me she is my sister and she also said he is my brother, in the maturity of my heart and in the innocence of my palms I did this, **6** and the *Elohiym* said to him in the dream, also I, I knew that in the maturity of your heart, you did this, and I also kept you back from his failure to me[123], therefore I did not give you to touch her, **7** and now, make the woman of the man return, given that he is an announcer and he will plead on your behalf and live and if you do not make a returning, know that you will surely die and all which belongs to you, **8** and *Aviymelekh* departed early in the morning and he called out to all of his servants and he spoke all of these words in their ears and the men greatly feared, **9** and *Aviymelekh* called out to *Avraham* and said to him what did you do to us and how did I fail to you, given that you brought upon me and upon my kingdom place a great failure, works which were not done, you did by me, **10** and *Aviymelekh* said to *Avraham*, what did you see, given that you did this word, **11** and *Avraham* said, given that I said, fearfulness of *Elohiym* is not at all in this place and they will kill me because of the word[124] of my woman, **12** and indeed she is my sister, daughter of my father, surely not the daughter of my mother and she exists to me for a woman, **13** and it came to pass just as *Elohiym* caused me to wander from the house of my father and I said to her, this is your kindness which you will do by me to all of the places which we will come unto, say for me he is my brother, **14** and *Aviymelekh* took flocks and cattle and servants and maids and he gave to *Avraham* and turned *Sarah* his woman back to him, **15** and *Aviymelekh* said, look, my land is to your face, functional in your eyes, settle, **16** and to *Sarah* he said, look, I gave a thousand silver to your brother, look, he is to you a raiment of the

---

[122] The Hebrew of this verse appears to be missing some text. It appears this verse should read something like "and *Avraham* said to *Sarah* his woman [possible text missing, "say you are my brother"] [possible text missing, "and he said to *Aviymelek* the king of *Gerar*"] she is my sister and *Aviymelekh* the king of *Gerar* sent [possible text missing, "his servant"] and he took *Sarah* (See 20:5)

[123] Most translations have something like "and it was I who kept you from sinning against me" implying the sin of *Aviymelekh*. The Hebrew however implies it is the sin (fault) of *Avraham*.

[124] This Hebrew word can also mean "matter."

eyes to all who are with you and with all, and being rebuked, **17** and
Avraham pleaded to the *Elohiym* and *Elohiym* healed *Aviymelekh* and his
woman and his bondwomen and they brought forth, **18** given that ***YHWH***
stopped up on behalf of all the bowels to the house of *Aviymelekh* because
of the word[125] of *Sarah* the woman of *Avraham*,

Chapter 21

1 and ***YHWH*** had visited *Sarah* just as he said, and ***YHWH*** did to *Sarah* just as
he spoke, **2** and *Sarah* conceived and she brought forth for *Avraham* a son to
his extreme old age to the appointed time which *Elohiym* spoke to him,
3 and *Avraham* called out the title of his son, being brought forth for him
which *Sarah* brought forth for him, *Yits'hhaq*, **4** and *Avraham* snipped
Yits'hhaq his son, a son of eight days just as *Elohiym* directed him, **5** and
Avraham was a son of a hundred years with *Yits'hhaq* his son, being brought
forth for him, **6** and *Sarah* said, *Elohiym* did laughter to me, all the ones
hearing will laugh for me, **7** and she said, who talked to *Avraham*, *Sarah*
made sons suckle, given that I brought forth a son to his extreme old age,
8 and the boy will magnify and he will be yielded and *Avraham* will do a
great feast in the day *Yits'hhaq* is being yielded, **9** and *Sarah* saw the son of
Hagar, the one of *Mits'rayim* which brought forth for *Avraham*, much
mocking, **10** and she said to *Avraham*, cast out this bondwoman and her son,
given that the son of this bondwoman will not inherit with my son *Yits'hhaq*,
11 and the word was very dysfunctional in the eyes of *Avraham* on account
of his son, **12** and *Elohiym* said to *Avraham*, it is not dysfunctional in your
eyes upon the young man and upon your bondwoman, all which *Sarah* says
to you, hear in her voice, given that in *Yits'hhaq*, seed will be called out to
you, **13** and also I will set in place the son of the bondwoman for a nation,
given that he is your seed, **14** and *Avraham* departed early in the morning
and he took bread and a skin bag of waters and he gave to *Hagar* placing
upon her shoulder and the boy and he sent her and she walked and she
wandered in the wilderness of *B'er-Sheva*, **15** and they finished the waters
from the skin bag and she threw out the boy under one of the shrubs,
16 and she walked and she settled herself opposite afar, like the hurling of a
bow, given that she said I will not see in the death of the boy and she settled
opposite and she lifted up her voice and she wept. **17** *Elohiym* heard the
voice of the young man and the messenger of *Elohiym* called out to *Hagar*
from the skies and he said to her, what is to you *Hagar*, you will not fear,
given that *Elohiym* heard the voice of the young man whereas he is there.
18 Rise, lift up the young man and make your hand seize with him, given that
I will set him in place for a great nation, **19** and *Elohiym* opened up her eyes
and she saw a well of waters and she walked and she filled the skin bag of

---

[125] This Hebrew word can also mean "matter."

waters and she made the young man drink, **20** and *Elohiym* existed with the
young man and he magnified and he settled in the wilderness and he existed
increasing of a bow, **21** and he settled in the wilderness of *Paran* and his
mother took for him a woman from the land of *Mits'rayim*, **22** and it came to
pass in that appointed time *Aviymelekh* and *Pikhol*, the noble of his army,
said to *Avraham* saying, *Elohiym* is with you in all which you are doing,
23 and now, swear to me in *Elohiym* thus far, if[126] you will deal falsely to me
and to my heir and to my posterity, like the kindness which I did with you,
you will do by me and with the land which you immigrated in, **24** and
Avraham said, I will be sworn, **25** and *Avraham* rebuked *Aviymelekh*
concerning the well of waters which the servants of *Aviymelekh* plucked
away, **26** and *Aviymelekh* said, I do not know who did this thing and also you
did not tell me and also I did not hear except today, **27** and *Avraham* took
flocks and cattle and he gave to *Aviymelekh* and the two of them cut a
covenant, **28** and *Avraham* made seven ewe lambs of the flock stand erect
by themselves, **29** and *Aviymelekh* said to *Avraham*, what is this, these seven
ewe lambs, which you made stand erect by themselves, **30** and he said,
given that you will take the seven ewe lambs from my hand on account of
that she will exist for me for a witness, given that I dug out this well.
31 Therefore he called out to that place *B'er-Sheva*, given that there the two
of them were sworn, **32** and they cut a covenant in *B'er-Sheva* and
Aviymelekh rose and *Pikhol* the noble of his army and they turned back to
the land of the ones of *Peleshet*, **33** and he planted a tamarisk in *B'er-Sheva*
and he met there with the title of ***YHWH***, a mighty one of a distant time,
34 and *Avraham* immigrated in the land of the ones of *Peleshet* an abundant
days,

Chapter 22

1 and it came to pass after these words and the *Elohiym* greatly tested
Avraham and he said to him, *Avraham*, and he said here am I, **2** and he said,
please take your son, your solitary one which you love, *Yits'hhaq* and you
will walk to the land of *Moriyah* and make him go up there for an ascension
offering upon one of the hills which I will say to you, **3** and *Avraham*
departed early in the morning and he saddled his donkey and took two of
his young men with him and with *Yits'hhaq* his son and he cleaved the wood
of the ascension offering and he rose and he walked to the place which the
Elohiym said to him. **4** In the third day *Avraham* lifted up his eyes and saw
the place from a distance, **5** and *Avraham* said to his young men, you will

---

[126] The Hebrew word אם (*iym*), meaning "if," may be written in error for the word לא (*lo*), meaning "not." In which case, this would be translated as, "you will not deal falsely to me," which agrees with the translation in the *Septuagint*.

settle here with the donkey and I and the young man will walk as far as this way and we will bend ourselves down and we will turn back to you, **6** and *Avraham* took wood of the ascension offering and set in place upon *Yits'hhaq* his son and he took in his hand the fire and the knife and the two of them walked together, **7** and *Yits'hhaq* said to *Avraham* his father and he said, my father, and he said, here am I my son, and he said, look, the fire and the trees and where is the ram for the ascension offering, **8** and *Avraham* said, *Elohiym* will see to him the ram for an ascension offering my son and the two of them walked together, **9** and they came to the place which the *Elohiym* said to him and *Avraham* built there the altar and arranged the trees and he bound *Yits'hhaq* his son and he set him in place upon the altar, on top of the wood, **10** and *Avraham* sent his hand and he took the knife to slay his son, **11** and the messenger of ***YHWH*** called out to him from the skies and he said, *Avraham*, *Avraham*, and he said, here am I, **12** and he said, you will not send your hand to the young man and you will not do to him anything, given that now I know that you are fearful of *Elohiym* and you did not keep back your solitary son from me, **13** and *Avraham* lifted up his eyes and he saw and look, a buck was behind and he was held in a net[127] with his horns and *Avraham* walked and he took the buck and he made him go up for an ascension offering in place of his son, **14** and *Avraham* called out the title of that place ***YHWH-Yireh*** which today will be said, in a hill ***YHWH*** appeared, **15** and the messenger of ***YHWH*** called out to *Avraham* a second time from the skies, **16** and he said, in me I was sworn an utterance of ***YHWH*** seeing that you did this thing and you did not keep back your solitary son, **17** given that I will greatly exalt and I will greatly make an increase of your seed like the stars of the skies and like the sand which is upon the lip of the sea and your seed will inherit the gate of his hostile ones, **18** and all nations of the land will exalt themselves with your seed, as a consequence of that, you listened to my voice, **19** and *Avraham* turned back to his young men and they rose and they walked together to *B'er-Sheva* and *Avraham* settled in *B'er-Sheva*, **20** and it came to pass after these words and he told to *Avraham* saying, look, *Milkah* also brought forth sons for *Nahhor* your brother. **21** *Uts* his firstborn and *Buz* his brother and *Qemu'el* the father of *Aram*, **22** and *Kesed* and *Hhazo* and *Pildash* and *Yidlap* and *Betu'el*, **23** and *Betu'el* brought forth *Rivqah*, these eight *Milkah* brought forth for *Nahhor* the brother of *Avraham*, **24** and his concubine and her title was *Re'umah* and she also brought *Tevahh* and *Gahham* and *Tahhash* and *Ma'akhah*,

---

Chapter 23

1 and the life of *Sarah* existed a hundred and twenty and seven years, the years of the life of *Sarah*, **2** and *Sarah* died in *Qiryat-Arba*, she is *Hhevron* in

[127] Probably meaning a "thicket."

the land of *Kena'an* and *Avraham* came to lament for *Sarah* and to weep for her, **3** and *Avraham* rose from upon the face of his dead and he spoke to the sons of *Hhet* saying, **4** I am an immigrant and settler with you, give to me a holdings of a grave with you and I will bury my dead from before my face, **5** and the sons of *Hhet* answered *Avraham* saying to him. **6** Hear us my lord you are a captain of *Elohiym* in the midst of us, with the chosen of our graves bury your dead, not a man from us will restrict his grave from you from burying your dead, **7** and *Avraham* rose and bent himself down to the people of the land, to the sons of *Hhet*, **8** and he spoke to them saying, if it is your soul to bury my dead from before my face, hear me and reach for me with *Ephron* the son of *Tsohhar*, **9** and he will give to me the cave *Makhpelah* which belongs to him which is in the far end of his field, with full silver he will give to me in your midst for holdings of a grave, **10** and *Ephron* was settling in the midst of the sons of *Hhet* and *Ephron*, the one of *Hhet*, answered in the ears of the sons of *Hhet* to all coming to the gate of his city saying, **11** no my lord hear me, the field I give to you and the cave which is in him I give her to you to the eyes of the sons of my people I give her to you, bury your dead, **12** and *Avraham* bent himself down to the face of the people of the land, **13** and he spoke to *Ephron* in the ears of the people of the land saying, surely, if you would hear me, I give the silver of the field, take from me and I will bury my dead unto there, **14** and *Ephron* answered *Avraham* saying to him. **15** My lord, hear me, what is a land of four hundred *sheqel*s of silver between me and you, bury your dead, **16** and *Avraham* heard *Ephron* and *Avraham* weighed to *Ephron* the silver which he spoke in the ears of the sons of *Hhet*, four hundred *sheqel*s of silver, a crossing over for the trading, **17** and the field of *Ephron* rose, which is in *Makhpelah* which is to the face of *Mamre*, the field and the cave which is in him and all the trees which are in the field which are in all his borders around. **18** To *Avraham* to acquire to the eyes of the sons of *Hhet* with all coming at the gate of his city, **19** and afterward, *Avraham* buried *Sarah* his woman to the cave of the field of *Makhpelah* upon the face of *Mamre*, she is *Hhevron*, in the land of *Kena'an*, **20** and the field rose, and the cave which is in him, belonging to *Avraham* for holdings of a grave from the sons of *Hhet*,

---

Chapter 24

1 and *Avraham* was old, he came in the days and ***YHWH*** had exalted *Avraham* in all, **2** and *Avraham* said to his servant, the bearded one of his house the one regulating in all which belonged to him, please set your hand in place under my midsection, **3** and I will make you swear with ***YHWH*** the *Elohiym* of the skies and the *Elohiym* of the land that you will not take a woman for my son from the daughters of the ones of *Kena'an* which I am settling inside, **4** given that to my land and to my kindred you will walk and you will take a woman for my son *Yits'hhaq*, **5** and the servant said to him,

possibly the woman will not consent to walk after me to this land, will I
return your son to the land which you went out from, **6** and *Avraham* said to
him, you be safeguarded, otherwise you will turn my son back unto there.
7 ***YHWH*** the *Elohiym* of the skies who took me from the house of my father
and from the land of my kindred and who spoke to me and who was sworn
to me saying, I will give to your seed this land, he will send his messenger to
your face and you will take a woman for my son from there, **8** and if the
woman will not consent to walk after you, then you will be acquitted from
my swearing of this, only you will not turn back my son unto there, **9** and the
servant sat his hand in place under the midsection of *Avraham* his lord and
he was sworn to him upon this word, **10** and the servant took ten camels
from the camels of his lord and he walked and all the functional ones of his
lord were in his hand and he rose and he walked to *Aram-Nahara'im*, to the
city of *Nahhor*, **11** and he made the camels kneel outside the city to the well
of the waters to the appointed time of the evening, to the appointed time
the waters drawers go out, **12** and he said, ***YHWH*** the *Elohiym* of my lord
Avraham, please make a meeting before today and do kindness with my lord
Avraham. **13** Look, I am standing erect upon the eye of the waters and the
daughters of the men of the city are going out to draw waters, **14** and it will
come to pass the young woman which I will say to her, please make your jar
stretch and I will gulp and she will say, gulp and I will also make your camels
drink, you rebuked her to your servant *Yits'hhaq* and in her I will know that
you did kindness with my lord, **15** and it came to pass before he finished
speaking and look, *Rivqah* was going out, who was brought forth to *Betu'el*,
the son of *Milkah*, the woman of *Nahhor*, the brother of *Avraham* and her
jar was upon her shoulder, **16** and the young woman was very functional of
appearance, a virgin and a man had not known her and she went down unto
the eye and she filled her jar and she got up, **17** and the servant ran to meet
her and he said, please make me guzzle a small amount of waters from your
jar, **18** and she said, gulp my lord and she much hurried and she made her
jar go down upon her hand and she made him drink, **19** and she finished
making him drink and she said, I will also draw waters for your camels until
they finish gulping, **20** and she much hurried and she uncovered her jar to
the watering trough and she ran yet again to the well to draw waters and
she drew waters for all his camels, **21** and the man was crashing himself to
her, keeping silent, to know, did ***YHWH*** make his road prosper or not, **22** and
it came to pass just as the camels finished gulping and the man took a ring of
gold of a *beqa* weight and two bracelets upon her hands, ten weights of
gold, **23** and he said whose daughter are you, please tell me, is there a house
of your father, a place for us to stay the night, **24** and she said to him, I am
the daughter of *Betu'el* the son of *Milkah* who was brought forth to *Nahhor*,
25 and she said to him, also straw, also abundant provender with us, also a
place to stay the night, **26** and the man bowed the head and he bent himself
down to ***YHWH***, **27** and he said, exalted is ***YHWH*** the *Elohiym* of my lord
Avraham who did not leave his kindness and his truth from my lord, I am in

the road of the house of the brothers of my lord, ***YHWH*** guided me, **28** and
the young woman ran and she told to the house of her mother these words,
29 and to *Rivqah* was a brother and his title was *Lavan* and *Lavan* ran unto
the man outside, to the eye, **30** and it came to pass at seeing the ring and
the bracelets upon the hands of his sister and at the hearing of the words of
Rivqah his sister saying, in this way the man spoke to me and he came to the
man and look, standing upon the camels, upon the eye, **31** and he said,
come, exalted is ***YHWH***, why will you stand in the outside and I turned the
house and the place for the camels, **32** and the man came unto the house
and he opened the camels and he gave straw and provender to the camels
and waters to wash his feet and the feet of the men who were with him,
33 and he put to his face to eat and he said, I will not eat until I speak my
words, and he said, speak, **34** and he said, I am a servant of *Avraham*, **35** and
YHWH had exalted my lord and he magnified and he gave to him flocks and
cattle and silver and gold and servants and maids and camels and donkeys,
36 and *Sarah*, the woman of my lord, brought forth a son for my lord after
her old age and he gave to him all which belongs to him, **37** and my lord
made me swear saying, you will not take a woman for my son from the
daughters of the one of *Kena'an* where I am settling in his land, **38** but to the
house of my father you will walk and to my family and you will take a
woman for my son, **39** and I said to my lord, possibly the woman will not
walk after me, **40** and he said to me, I walked myself to the face of ***YHWH***,
he will send his messenger to you and he will make your road prosper and
you will take a woman for my son from my family and from the house of my
father. **41** At that time you will be innocent from my oath, given that you will
come to my family and if they will not give to you and you will exist
acquitted from my oath, **42** and I came today to the eye and I said, ***YHWH***
the *Elohiym* of my lord *Avraham*, if you are there please make my road
which I am walking upon prosper. **43** Look, I am standing erect upon the eye
of the waters and it came to pass the young maiden was going out to draw
waters and I said to her please make drink a small amount of waters from
your jar, **44** and she said to me, you also gulp and also for your camels, I will
draw waters, she is the woman which ***YHWH*** rebuked for the son of my lord.
45 Before I finished speaking to my heart and behold *Rivqah* was going out
and her jar was upon her shoulder and she went down unto the eye and she
drew waters and I said to her, please make me drink, **46** and she hurried and
she made her jar go down from upon her and she said, gulp and also your
camels I will make drink and I gulped and also the camels she made drink,
47 and I inquired of her and I said whose daughter are you and she said the
daughter of *Betu'el*, the son of *Nahhor* who *Milkah* brought forth to him and
I set in place the ring upon her nose and the bracelets upon her hands,
48 and I bowed the head and I bent myself down to ***YHWH*** and I exalted
YHWH the *Elohiym* of my lord *Avraham* which he guided me in the road of
truth to take a daughter of the brother of my lord for his son, **49** and now if

you will do kindness and truth to my lord tell to me and if not tell to me and
I will turn upon the right hand or upon the left hand, **50** and *Lavan* answered
and *Betu'el*, and they said, the word went out from ***YHWH***, we will not be
able to speak to you dysfunction or function. **51** Look, *Rivqah* is to your face,
take and walk and she will exist as a woman for the son of your lord just as
YHWH spoke, **52** and it came to pass just as the servant of *Avraham* heard
their words and bent himself down unto the land to ***YHWH***, **53** and the
servant brought out utensils of silver and utensils of gold and garments and
he gave to *Rivqah* and he gave ornaments to her brother and to her mother,
54 and they ate and they gulped, he and the men which were with him and
they stayed the night and they rose in the morning and he said, send me to
my lord, **55** and her brother said, and her mother, the young woman will
settle days or the tenth one, afterward, walk, **56** and he said to them, you
will not delay me and ***YHWH*** has made my road prosper, send me and I will
walk to my lord, **57** and they said we will call out to the young woman and
inquire at her mouth, **58** and they called out to *Rivqah* and they said to her,
will you walk with this man and she said, I will walk, **59** and they sent *Rivqah*
their sister and her nurse and the servant of *Avraham* and his men, **60** and
they exalted *Rivqah* and they said to her, you are our sister, exist for a
myriad thousands and your seed will inherit the gate of the ones hating him,
61 and *Rivqah* rose and her young women and they rode upon the camels
and they walked after the man and the servant took *Rivqah* and he walked,
62 and *Yits'hhaq* had come from coming of *Be'er-Lahhiy-Ro'iy* and he is
settling in the land of the south, **63** and *Yits'hhaq* went out to meditate in
the field at the turning of the evening and he lifted up his eyes and he saw,
and look, camels were coming, **64** and *Rivqah* lifted up her eyes and she saw
Yits'hhaq and she fell from upon the camel, **65** and she said to the servant,
who is this man, the one walking in the field to meet us and the servant said,
he is my lord and she took the veil and concealed herself, **66** and the servant
recounted to *Yits'hhaq* all the words which he did, **67** and *Yits'hhaq* brought
her unto the tent of *Sarah* his mother and he took *Rivqah* and she existed to
him for a woman and loved her and *Yits'hhaq* was comforted after his
mother,

Chapter 25

1 and *Avraham* again took a woman and her title was *Qeturah*, **2** and she
brought forth to him *Zimran* and *Yaq'shan* and *Medan* and *Mid'yan* and
Yish'baq and *Shu'ahh*, **3** and *Yaq'shan* had brought forth *Sheva* and *Dedan*
and the sons of *Dedan* existed, the ones of *Ashur* and the ones of *Letush* and
the ones of *Le'um*, **4** and the sons of *Mid'yan* are *Eyphah* and *Epher* and
Hhanokh and *Avida* and *Elda'ah*, all these are the sons of *Qeturah*, **5** and
Avraham gave all which belonged to him to *Yits'hhaq*, **6** and to the sons of
the concubines which were to *Avraham*, *Avraham* gave contributions and he

sent them from upon *Yits'hhaq* his son, while he was alive unto the east, to
the land of the east, **7** and these were the days of the years of the life of
Avraham which was a life of a hundred and seventy five years, **8** and
Avraham expired and he died with a gray-head, functional beard and plenty
and he was gathered to his people, **9** and *Yits'hhaq* and *Yishma'el* his sons
buried him at the cave of *Makhpelah*, at the field of *Ephron*, the son of
Tsohhar of the ones of *Hhet* which is upon the face of *Mamre*. **10** The field
which *Avraham* purchased from the sons of *Hhet*, unto there *Avraham* was
buried and *Sarah* his woman, **11** and it came to pass after the death of
Avraham and *Elohiym* exalted *Yits'hhaq* his son and *Yits'hhaq* settled by
Be'er-Lahhiy-Ro'iy, **12** and these are the birthings of *Yishma'el* the son of
Avraham who *Hagar*, the one of the *Mits'rayim*, the maid of *Sarah*, brought
forth to *Avraham*, **13** and these are the titles of the sons of *Yishma'el* in their
titles to their birthings, the firstborn of *Yishma'el* was *Nevayot* and *Qedar*
and *Adbe'el* and *Mivsam*, **14** and *Mishma* and *Dumah* and *Masa*. **15** *Hhadad*
and *Teyma*, *Yetur*, *Naphish* and *Qedmah*. **16** These are the sons of *Yishma'el*
and these are their titles in their courtyards and in their rows of tents,
twelve captains to their tribes, **17** and these are the years of the life of
Yishma'el, a hundred and thirty seven years and he expired and he died and
he was gathered to his people, **18** and they dwelt from *Hhawilah* as far as
Shur which is upon the face of *Mits'rayim* as you come unto *Ashur*, upon the
face of all his brothers he fell, **19** and these are the birthings of *Yits'hhaq*,
the son of *Avraham*, *Avraham* had caused to bring forth *Yits'hhaq*, **20** and
Yits'hhaq was a son of forty years in his taking of *Rivqah*, the daughter of
Betu'el the one of *Aram*, from *Padan-Aram*, the sister of *Lavan*, the one of
Aram, to him for a woman, **21** and *Yits'hhaq* interceded to ***YHWH*** in front of
his woman, given that she was sterile and ***YHWH*** was interceded to him and
Rivqah, his woman, conceived, **22** and the sons crushed themselves inside
her and she said, if it is so, why am I this and she walked to seek ***YHWH***,
23 and ***YHWH*** said to her, two nations are in your womb and two
communities from your abdomens will be divided apart and the community
from the community will be strong and abundant, he will serve the little
one, **24** and her days were filled to bring forth and look, twins are in her
womb, **25** and the first went out ruddy, all of him was like a robe of hair and
they called out his title *Esaw*, **26** and afterward, his brother went out and his
hand was holding in the heel of *Esaw* and he called out his title *Ya'aqov* and
Yits'hhaq was a son of sixty years in bringing them forth, **27** and the young
men magnified and *Esaw* was a man knowing game and a man of the field
and *Ya'aqov* was a man of maturity a settler of tents, **28** and *Yits'hhaq* loved
Esaw, given that game was in his mouth and *Rivqah* was loving *Ya'aqov*,
29 and *Ya'aqov* seethed a stew and *Esaw* came from the field and he was
tired, **30** and *Esaw* said to *Ya'aqov* please provide food to me from the red
thing, given that I am tired, therefore he called out his title *Edom*, **31** and
Ya'aqov said, as of today, sell your birthright to me, **32** and *Esaw* said, look, I

am walking to die and what is this birthright to me, **33** and *Ya'aqov* said be
sworn to me as of today and he was sworn to him and he sold his birthright
to *Ya'aqov*, **34** and *Ya'aqov* had given to *Esaw* bread and stew of lintels and
he ate and he gulped and he rose and he walked and *Esaw* disdained the
birthright,

Chapter 26

1 and hunger existed in the land apart from the first hunger which existed in
the days of *Avraham* and *Yits'hhaq* walked to *Aviymelekh* king of the ones of
Peleshet unto *Gerar*, **2** and ***YHWH*** appeared to him and he said, you will not
go down unto *Mits'rayim*, dwell in the land which I will say to you.
3 Immigrate in this land and I will exist with you and I will exalt you, given
that to you and to your seed I will give all these lands and I will make rise the
swearing which I was sworn to *Avraham* your father, **4** and I will make your
seed increase like the stars of the skies and I will give to your seed all these
lands and all the nations of the land will exalt themselves with your seed.
5 As a consequence of that, *Avraham* listened to my voice and he guarded
my charge, my directives, my customs and my teachings, **6** and *Yits'hhaq*
settled in *Gerar*, **7** and the men inquired to his woman and he said, she is my
sister, given that he feared saying, my woman, otherwise the men of the
place will kill me because of *Rivqah*, given that she is functional in
appearance, **8** and it came to pass that the days were prolonged to him
there and *Aviymelekh* the king of the ones of *Peleshet* looked down round
about the window and he saw and look, *Yits'hhaq* was laughing with *Rivqah*
his woman, **9** and *Aviymelekh* called out to *Yits'hhaq* and he said, surely
look, she is your woman and why did you say, she is my sister and *Yits'hhaq*
said to him, if I said otherwise, I will die because of her, **10** and *Aviymelekh*
said what is this you did to us, one of the people might have lain down with
your woman and you will make guilt come upon us, **11** and *Aviymelekh*
directed all the people saying, the touching with this man and with his
woman, he will surely be put to death, **12** and *Yits'hhaq* sowed in that land
and he found in that year a hundred *sha'ar*s and ***YHWH*** exalted him, **13** and
the man magnified and he walked a walking and magnified until he much
magnified, **14** and livestock of flocks and livestock of cattle and an abundant
household existed to him and the ones of *Peleshet* were envious of him,
15 and all the wells which the servants of his father dug out in the days of
Avraham his father, the ones of *Peleshet* shut them up and they filled them
with dirt, **16** and *Aviymelekh* said to *Yits'hhaq*, walk from us, given that you
are much more abundant from us, **17** and *Yits'hhaq* walked from there and
he camped in the wadi of *Gerar* and settled there, **18** and *Yits'hhaq* turned
back and dug out the wells of waters which they dug out in the days of
Avraham his father and the ones of *Peleshet* shut them up after the death of
Avraham and he called out to them titles like the titles which his father

called out to them, **19** and the servants of *Yits'hhaq* dug out in the wadi and they found there a well of waters of life, **20** and the feeders of *Gerar* disputed with the feeders of *Yits'hhaq* saying, the waters is to us, and he called out there the well *Eseq*, given that they quarreled with him, **21** and they dug out another well and they also disputed upon her and he called out her title *Sitnah*, **22** and he made an advance from there and he dug out another well and they did not dispute upon her and he called out her title *Rehhovot* and he said, given that now ***YHWH*** made a widening for us and we will reproduce in the land, **23** and he went up from there to *B'er-Sheva*, **24** and ***YHWH*** appeared to him in that night and he said, I am the *Elohiym* of *Avraham* your father, you will not fear, given that I am with you, I will exalt you and I will make an increase to your seed on account of *Avraham* my servant, **25** and he built an altar there and called out in the title[128] of ***YHWH*** and he will stretch his tent there and the servants of *Yits'hhaq* dug a well there, **26** and *Aviymelekh* had walked to him from *Gerar* and *Ahhuzat* his partner and *Pikhol* the noble of his army, **27** and *Yits'hhaq* said to them, why did you come to me and you hated me and you sent me from you, **28** and they said, we surely see that ***YHWH*** existed with you and we said, please, an oath will exist between us and you and we will cut a covenant with you. **29** If you will not[129] do dysfunction with us just as we did not touch and just as we did with you only function and we sent you in completeness, you are now exalted of ***YHWH***, **30** and he made for them a feast and they ate and they gulped, **31** and they departed early in the morning and each were sworn to his brother and *Yits'hhaq* sent them and they walked from him in completeness, **32** and it came to pass in that day and the servants of *Yits'hhaq* came and they told to him concerning the well which they dug out and they said to him we found waters, **33** and he called her *Shivah*, therefore the title of the city is *B'er-Sheva* until this day, **34** and *Esaw* existed a son of forty years and he took a woman, *Yehudit*, the daughter of *Be'eri*, the one of *Hhet* and *Basmat* the daughter of *Eylon*, the one of *Hhet*, **35** and they existed a grief of wind to *Yits'hhaq* and to *Rivqah*,

---

[128] The phrase "he called out in the title" may also be translated as "he met with the title."

[129] The Hebrew literally reads, "if you will do dysfunction with us just as we did not touch," is problematic. The phrase "just as," implies the phrase before it is similar in meaning to the phrase after it. If the phrase after the "just as" is positive then the phrase before must also be positive, but the phrase is negative. The probable solution is that the word "Not" is missing in the original phrase "you will do."

Chapter 27

1 and it came to pass that *Yits'hhaq* was old and his eyes dimmed from
seeing and he called out *Esaw* his great son and he said to him, my son, and
he said to him, here am I, **2** and he said, please look, I am old, I do not know
the day of my death, **3** and now please lift up your utensil, your quiver and
your bow and go out to the field and hunt for me provisions, **4** and do for
me delicacies just as I love and bring to me and I will eat in order that my
soul will exalt you before I die, **5** and *Rivqah* was hearing in the speaking of
Yits'hhaq to *Esaw* his son and *Esaw* walked to the field to hunt game to
bring, **6** and *Rivqah* had said to *Ya'aqov* her son saying, look, I heard your
father speaking to *Esaw* your brother saying, **7** bring to me game and make
for me delicacies and I will eat and I will exalt you before ***YHWH***, before my
death, **8** and now my son, hear in my voice which I am directing you.
9 Please walk to the flocks and take for me from there two functional male
kids of the she-goats and I will make them, delicacies for your father just as
he loves, **10** and you will bring to your father and he will eat so that he will
exalt you before his death, **11** and *Ya'aqov* said to *Rivqah* his mother, though
Esaw my brother is a hairy man and I am a slick man. **12** Possibly my father
will feel me and I will exist in his eyes as imitating and I will bring upon me
an annoyance and not a present, **13** and his mother said to him, your
annoyance is upon me my son, surely, hear in my voice and walk, take for
me, **14** and he walked and he took and he brought to his mother and his
mother made delicacies just as his father loved, **15** and *Rivqah* took
garments of *Esaw* her great son which were with her in the house and she
clothed *Ya'aqov* her small son, **16** and with the skins of the male kids of the
she-goats she clothed his hands and the smooth of the back of his neck,
17 and she gave delicacies and bread which she made in the hand of *Ya'aqov*
her son, **18** and he came to his father and he said, my father, and he said,
here am I, who are you my son, **19** and *Ya'aqov* said to his father, I am *Esaw*
your firstborn I did just as you spoke to me, please rise, settle and eat from
my game in order that your soul will exalt me, **20** and *Yits'hhaq* said to his
son, what is this you quickly hurried to find my son, and he said, given that
YHWH your *Elohiym* caused to meet before me, **21** and *Yits'hhaq* said to
Ya'aqov, please draw near and I will grope my son, is this you my son *Esaw*
or not, **22** and *Ya'aqov* drew near to *Yits'hhaq* his father and he groped him
and he said, the voice is the voice of *Ya'aqov* and the hands are the hands of
Esaw, **23** and he did not recognize him, given that his hands existed like the
hands of *Esaw* his brother was hairy, and he exalted him, **24** and he said, this
is you my son *Esaw*, and he said, I am, **25** and he said, draw near to me and I
will eat from the game of my son so that my soul will exalt you, and he drew
near to him and he ate and he brought wine to him and he gulped, **26** and
Yits'hhaq his father said to him, please draw near and kiss me my son,
27 and he drew near and he kissed him and he smelled the aroma of his
garments and he exalted him and he said, see the aroma of my son is like

the aroma of the field which ***YHWH*** presented him many gifts, **28** and the *Elohiym* gave to you from the dew of the skies[130] and from the oil of the land and the abundance of cereal and fresh wine. **29** Peoples will serve you and the communities will bend down to you, be an owner to your brothers and the sons of your mother will bend down to you, one spitting upon you is spat upon, one exalting you is exalted, **30** and it came to pass just as *Yits'hhaq* finished exalting *Ya'aqov* and he was surely going out, *Ya'aqov* went out from the face of *Yits'hhaq* his father and *Esaw* his brother came from his game, **31** and he also made delicacies and brought to his father and he said to his father, my father will rise and he will eat from the game of his son on account of this your soul will exalt me, **32** and *Yits'hhaq* his father said to him, who are you, and he said, I am your son, your firstborn *Esaw*, **33** and *Yits'hhaq* trembled a great trembling and many more and he said who then is he of the hunt of the game and he brought to me and I ate from all before you came and I exalted him, also, the one exalted will exist. **34** As *Esaw* heard the words of his father and he cried out a great and bitter cry and many more and he said to his father, exalt me, also me my father, **35** and he said, your brother came in deceit and he took your present, **36** and he said, is it that he called out his title *Ya'aqov* and he restrained me these two times, he took my birthright and look, now he took my present, and he said, did you not set aside for me a present, **37** and *Yits'hhaq* answered and he said to *Esaw*, though I set him in place as owner to you and all his brothers I gave to him for servants and with cereal and fresh wine I supported him, and to you then, what will I do my son, **38** and *Esaw* said to his father, is there to you one present my father, exalt me, also me my father and *Esaw* lifted up his voice and he wept, **39** and *Yits'hhaq* his father answered and he said to him, look, from the oils of the land a settling will exist and from the dew of the skies from above, **40** and upon your sword you will live and you will serve your brother and it will come to pass, you will roam and you will tear away his yoke from upon the back of your neck, **41** and *Esaw* held a grudge at *Ya'aqov* because of the present which his father exalted and *Esaw* said in his heart, the days of mourning of my father will come near and I will kill *Ya'aqov* my brother, **42** and he told to *Rivqah* the words of *Esaw* her great son and she sent and she called out to *Ya'aqov* her small son and she said to him, look, *Esaw* your brother is comforting himself for you to kill you, **43** and now my son, hear in my voice and rise, flee away for you to *Lavan* my brother unto *Hharan*, **44** and you will settle with him a unit of days until the fury of your brother turns back. **45** Until the nose of your brother turns back from you and he forgets what you did to him and I will send and I will take you from there, why should I be childless

---

[130] This phrase Hebrew text for the phrase "and the *Elohiym* gave to you from the dew of the skies" could also be translated as "and he gave to you the *Elohiym* from the dew of the skies."

of the two of you of one day, **46** and *Rivqah* said to *Yits'hhaq*, I will loathe in my life from the faces of the daughters of *Hhet*, if *Ya'aqov* is taking a woman from the daughters of *Hhet* such as these from the daughters of the land what is to me a life,

---

Chapter 28

1 and *Yits'hhaq* called out to *Ya'aqov* and he exalted him and he directed him and he said to him, you will not take a woman from the daughters of *Kena'an*. **2** Rise, walk unto *Padan-Aram*, unto the house of *Betu'el* the father of your mother and take for you from there a woman, from the daughters of *Lavan*, the brother of your mother, **3** and the mighty one of *Shaddai* will exalt you and he will make you reproduce and he will make you increase and you will exist for an assembled flock of peoples, **4** and he gave to you the present of *Avraham* for you and for your seed with you for you to inherit the land of your immigrations, which *Elohiym* gave to *Avraham*, **5** and *Yits'hhaq* sent *Ya'aqov* and he walked unto *Padan-Aram* to *Lavan* the son of *Betu'el* the one of *Aram* the brother of *Rivqah* the mother of *Ya'aqov* and *Esaw*, **6** and *Esaw* saw that *Yits'hhaq* exalted *Ya'aqov* and he sent him unto *Padan-Aram* to take for him from there a woman, in exalting him and he directed upon him saying, you will not take a woman from the daughters of *Kena'an*, **7** and *Ya'aqov* heard his father and his mother and he walked unto *Padan-Aram*, **8** and *Esaw* saw that the daughters of *Kena'an* were dysfunctional in the eyes of *Yits'hhaq* his father, **9** and *Esaw* walked to *Yishma'el* and he took *Mahhalat* the daughter of *Yishma'el* the son of *Avraham*, the sister of *Nevayot*, for him for a woman in addition to his women, **10** and *Ya'aqov* went out from *B'er-Sheva* and he walked unto *Hharan*, **11** and he reached the place and he stayed the night there, given that the sun came and he took from the stones of the place and he set his headrest in place and he laid down in that place, **12** and he dreamed and look, a ladder is standing erect unto the land and his head was touching unto the skies and look, messengers of *Elohiym* were going up and going down him, **13** and look, ***YHWH*** is standing erect upon him and he said, I am ***YHWH*** the *Elohiym* of *Avraham* your father and the *Elohiym* of *Yits'hhaq*, the land which you are lying down upon I will give her to you and to your seed, **14** and your seed will exist like the dirt of the land and you will break out unto the sea and unto the east and unto the north and unto the south and all the families of the ground will be exalted with you and with your seed, **15** and look, I am with you and will guard you in all where you will walk and I will return you to this ground, given that I will not leave you until I do which I spoke to you, **16** and *Ya'aqov* awoke from his snooze and he said, surely ***YHWH*** is in this place and I did not know, **17** and he feared and he said, what is being feared of this place this is nothing except the house of *Elohiym* and this is the gate of the skies, **18** and *Ya'aqov* departed early in the morning and he took the stone which he set in place as his headrest, and he set her in place as a monument and poured down oil upon her head, **19** and he called out the title of that place *Beyt-El* but *Luz* was the title of the city at first, **20** and *Ya'aqov* vowed a vow saying, if ***YHWH*** the *Elohiym* is by me and he will guard me in this road which I am walking and he will give to me bread to eat and garments to clothe, **21** and I will turn back in completeness to the house of my father then ***YHWH*** will exist for me for *Elohiym*, **22** and this stone which I set in place as a monument will exist as the house of *Elohiym* and all which you will give to me I will surely give a tenth of him to you,

---

Chapter 29

1 and *Ya'aqov* lifted up his feet and he walked unto the land of the sons the east, **2** and he saw and look, a well in the field and look, there were three droves of flocks stretching out upon her, given that from that well the droves will drink and the stone upon the mouth of the well was great, **3** and all the droves gathered unto there and they rolled the stone from upon the mouth of the well and the flocks drank and they returned the stone back upon the mouth of the well to her place, **4** and *Ya'aqov* said to them, my brothers, from where are you and they said, we are from *Hharan*, **5** and he said to them, do you know *Lavan* the son of *Nahhor* and they said we know, **6** and he said to them, is completeness to him and they said completeness and look, *Rahhel* his daughter was coming with the flocks, **7** and he said, while it is yet a great day it is not the appointed time for the gathering of the livestock, make the flocks drink, walk and feed, **8** and they said, we will not be able until all the droves be gathered and they will roll the stone from upon the mouth of the well and they will make the flocks drink. **9** While he was speaking with them then *Rahhel* was coming with the flocks which belonged to her father, given that she was feeding, **10** and it came to pass just as *Ya'aqov* saw *Rahhel* the daughter of *Lavan* the brother of his mother and the flocks of *Lavan* the brother of his mother and *Ya'aqov* drew near and he rolled the stone from upon the mouth of the well and he made the flocks of *Lavan*, the brother of his mother, drink, **11** and *Ya'aqov* kissed *Rahhel* and he lifted up his voice and he wept, **12** and *Ya'aqov* told *Rahhel* that he was the brother of her father and that he was the son of *Rivqah* and she ran and she told her father, **13** and it came to pass as *Lavan* heard the report of *Ya'aqov* the son of his sister and he ran to meet him and he embraced him and he kissed him and he brought him to his house and he recounted to *Lavan* all these words, **14** and *Lavan* said to him surely you are my bone and my flesh and he settled with him a new moon of days, **15** and *Lavan* said to *Ya'aqov*, given that you are my brother, will you serve me freely, tell me what is your payment, **16** and to *Lavan* were two daughters, the title of the magnificent one was *Le'ah* and the title of the small one was *Rahhel*, **17** and the eyes of *Le'ah* were tender and *Rahhel* had existed

beautiful of form and beautiful of appearance, **18** and *Ya'aqov* loved *Rahhel*
and he said, I will serve you seven years in *Rahhel* your small daughter,
19 and *Lavan* said, it is functional that I give her to you rather than give her
to another man, settle by me, **20** and *Ya'aqov* served in *Rahhel* seven years
and they existed in his eyes like a few days with the affection to her, **21** and
Ya'aqov said to *Lavan*, bring my woman, given that my days are filled and I
will come to her, **22** and *Lavan* gathered all the men of the place and he
made a feast, **23** and it came to pass in the evening and he took *Le'ah* his
daughter and he brought her to him and he came to her, **24** and *Lavan* gave
her *Zilpah*, his maid, to *Le'ah*, his daughter, for a maid, **25** and it came to
pass in the morning and look, she is *Le'ah*, and he said to *Lavan* what is this
you did to me, did I not serve in *Rahhel* with you and why did you betray me,
26 and *Lavan* said, he will not be done so in our place, to give the little one
before the firstborn woman. **27** Fulfill this week and we will also give to you
this one with the service which you will serve by me yet again another seven
years, **28** and *Ya'aqov* did so and he fulfilled this week and he gave to him
Rahhel, his daughter, for him for a woman, **29** and *Lavan* gave *Rahhel*, his
daughter, *Bilhah* his maid to her for a maid, **30** and he also came to *Rahhel*
and he also loved *Rahhel* rather than *Le'ah* and he served with him yet again
another seven years, **31** and ***YHWH*** saw that *Le'ah* was hated and he opened
her bowels and *Rahhel* was sterile, **32** and *Le'ah* conceived and she brought
forth a son and she called out his title *Re'uven*, given that she said, given
that ***YHWH*** saw in my affliction, given that now my man will love me, **33** and
she conceived yet again and she brought forth a son and she said, given that
YHWH heard, given that I am hated and he also gave to me this and she
called out his title *Shimon*, **34** and she conceived yet again and she brought
forth a son and she said, now this time my man will be joined to me, given
that I brought forth to him three sons, therefore she called out his title *Lewi*,
35 and she conceived yet again and she brought forth a son and she said,
this time I will thank ***YHWH***, therefore, she called out his title *Yehudah* and
she stood from bringing forth,

Chapter 30

1 and *Rahhel* saw that she did not bring forth for *Ya'aqov* and *Rahhel* was
envious with her sister and she said to *Ya'aqov*, bring me sons and if not I
am dead, **2** and the nose of *Ya'aqov* flared up with *Rahhel* and he said, am I
in the place of *Elohiym* who withheld from you the produce of the womb,
3 and she said, look, my bondwoman *Bilhah*, come to her and she will bring
forth upon my knee and I will also be built from her, **4** and she gave to him
Bilhah her maid for a woman and *Ya'aqov* came to her, **5** and *Bilhah*
conceived and she brought forth for *Ya'aqov* a son, **6** and *Rahhel* said,
Elohiym will moderate me and he also heard in your voice and he gave to
me a son, therefore, she called out his title *Dan*, **7** and she conceived yet

again and *Bilhah*, the maid of *Rahhel*, brought forth a second son for *Ya'aqov*, **8** and *Rahhel* said, with wrestlings of *Elohiym* I was entwined with my sister, also I was able and she called out his title *Naphtali*, **9** and *Le'ah* saw that she stood from bringing forth and she took *Zilpah* her maid and she gave her to *Ya'aqov* for a woman, **10** and *Zilpah* the maid of *Le'ah* brought forth for *Ya'aqov* a son, **11** and *Le'ah* said, fortune came, and she called out his title *Gad*, **12** and *Zilpah*, the maid of *Le'ah*, brought forth a second son for *Ya'aqov*, **13** and *Le'ah* said, I am in happiness, given that the daughters are very happy for me and she called out his title *Asher*, **14** and *Re'uven* walked in the days of the wheat harvest and he found mandrakes in the field and he brought them to *Le'ah* his mother and *Rahhel* said to *Le'ah*, please give me from the mandrakes of your son, **15** and she said to her, is it a small thing for you to take my man and also to take the mandrakes of my son and *Rahhel* said, because of this he will lay down with you tonight under the mandrakes of your son, **16** and *Ya'aqov* came from the field in the evening and *Le'ah* went out to meet him and she said, you will come to me, given that I surely hired you with the mandrakes of my son and he laid down with her in that night, **17** and *Elohiym* heard *Le'ah* and she conceived and she brought forth for *Ya'aqov* a fifth son, **18** and *Le'ah* said, *Elohiym* gave my wage because I gave my maid to my man and she called out his title *Yis'sas'khar*, **19** and *Le'ah* conceived yet again and she brought forth a sixth son for *Ya'aqov*, **20** and *Le'ah* said, *Elohiym* endowed me a functional dowry, will my man reside with me this time, given that I brought forth for him six sons and she called out his title *Zevulun*, **21** and afterward she brought forth a daughter and she called out her title *Dinah*, **22** and *Elohiym* remembered *Rahhel* and *Elohiym* listened to her and he opened her bowels, **23** and she conceived and she brought forth a son and she said, *Elohiym* gathered my disgrace, **24** and she called out his title *Yoseph*, saying, ***YHWH*** will add to me another son, **25** and it came to pass, just as *Rahhel* brought forth *Yoseph*, *Ya'aqov* said to *Lavan*, send me and I will walk to my place and to my land. **26** Give my women and my boys, which I served with you in them and I will walk, given that you knew my service which I served you, **27** and *Lavan* said to him, please, if I found beauty in your eyes, I will divine and ***YHWH*** exalted me on account of you, **28** and he said, pierce through your wage upon me and I will give, **29** and he said to him, you know that I served you, that your livestock existed with me, **30** given that the small amount which existed to you before me and he will break out for an abundance and ***YHWH*** will exalt you to my foot and now, how long will I make also for my house, **31** and he said, what will I give to you, and *Ya'aqov* said, you will not give to me anything if you will do to me this word, I will turn back, I will feed your flock, I will guard. **32** I will cross over in all your flocks today, removing from there all the speckled and spotted rams and all of the black rams with the sheep and the spotted and speckled with the she-goats and he will exist as my wage, **33** and my correctness will answer in me in a later day, given that you will come because of my wage before you, all which are without the speckled and the spotted in the she-goats and the black in the sheep, he is stolen with me, **34** and *Lavan* said, though that would exist like your word, **35** and he removed in that day the stripped and spotted he-goats and all the speckled and spotted she-goats, all which was white in him and all the black in the sheep and he gave in the hand of his sons, **36** and he sat in place a road of three days between him and *Ya'aqov* and *Ya'aqov* was feeding the flocks of *Lavan*, the ones being reserved, **37** and *Ya'aqov* took to him a rod of a moist poplar and of hazel and of chestnut and he peeled white strips in them, exposing the white which was upon the rods, **38** and he set the rods which he peeled in troughs, in the watering troughs of waters where the flocks come to gulp, to the front of the flocks, and they will heat in their coming to gulp, **39** and the flocks will heat to the rods and the flocks brought forth striped ones, speckled ones and spotted ones, **40** and *Ya'aqov* divided apart the sheep and he gave the faces of the flocks to the striped and all the black in the flocks of *Lavan* and he set down to him droves by himself and he did not set them down upon the flocks of *Lavan*, **41** and it came to pass in all the heating of the robust flocks and *Ya'aqov* set in place the rods to the eyes of the flocks in the troughs, for her heating in the rods, **42** and with the ones of the flocks made enveloped, he will not set in place, and the enveloped ones existed to *Lavan* and the robust ones to *Ya'aqov*, **43** and the man broke out very greatly and he existed to him abundant flocks and maids and servants and camels and donkeys,

---

Chapter 31

1 and he heard the words of the sons of *Lavan* saying, *Ya'aqov* took all which belongs to our father and from which belongs to our father he will do all this honor, **2** and *Ya'aqov* saw the face of *Lavan* and look, it was not with him previously, **3** and ***YHWH*** said to *Ya'aqov*, turn back to the land of your father and to your kindred and I will exist with you, **4** and *Ya'aqov* sent and he called out to *Rahhel* and to *Le'ah*, to the field of his flock, **5** and he said to them, I am seeing the face of your father, given that it was not to me as previously and the *Elohiym* of my father existed by me, **6** and you know that in all my strength I served your father, **7** and your father has dealt deceitfully in me and he changed my payment ten times and *Elohiym* did not give him to be made dysfunctional by me. **8** If in this way he will say, the speckled ones will exist as your wage, then all of the flocks will bring forth speckled ones and if in this way he will say, striped ones will exist as your wage, then all of the flocks will bring forth striped ones, **9** and *Elohiym* delivered the livestock of your father and he gave to me, **10** and it came to pass, in the appointed time of the heat of the flocks and I lifted up my eyes and I saw in the dream and look, the male goats going up upon the flocks were striped ones, speckled ones and spotted ones, **11** and the messenger of the *Elohiym*

said to me in the dream, *Ya'aqov*, and I said, here am I, **12** and he said,
please lift up your eyes and see all the male goats going up upon the flocks
were striped ones, speckled ones and spotted ones, given that I saw all
which *Lavan* is doing to you. **13** I am the mighty one of *Beyt-El*, where you
smeared there a monument, where there you made a vow to me, now rise,
go out from this land and turn back to the land of your kindred, **14** and
Rahhel answered, and *Le'ah*, and they said to him, is there also for us a
distribution and inheritance in the house of our father. **15** Were we not
thought of as foreigners to him, given that he sold us and he also greatly ate
our silver, **16** given that all the riches, which *Elohiym* delivered from our
father, to us is he and to our sons and now, all which *Elohiym* said to you,
do, **17** and *Ya'aqov* rose and he lifted up his sons and his women upon the
camels, **18** and he drove all his livestock and all his goods which he
accumulated, the livestock of his possession, which he accumulated in
Padan-Aram, to come to *Yits'hhaq* his father, unto the land of *Kena'an*,
19 and *Lavan* had walked to shear his flocks and *Rahhel* stole the family idols
which belonged to her father, **20** and *Ya'aqov* stole the heart of *Lavan*, the
one of *Aram*, because it was not told to him that he was fleeing away,
21 and he fled away and all which belonged to him and he rose and he
crossed over the river and he set his face in place toward the hill of *Gil'ad*,
22 and he told to *Lavan* in the third day that *Ya'aqov* fled away, **23** and he
took his brothers with him and he pursued after him a road of seven of the
days and he adhered to him in the hill of *Gil'ad*, **24** and *Elohiym* came to
Lavan, the one of *Aram*, in a dream of the night and he said to him, be
guarded to yourself, otherwise you will speak with *Ya'aqov* out of function
as well as dysfunction, **25** and *Lavan* overtook *Ya'aqov* and *Ya'aqov* had
thrust his tent in the hill and *Lavan* had thrust his brothers in the hill of
Gil'ad, **26** and *Lavan* said to *Ya'aqov*, what did you do and you stole my
heart and you drove my daughters like captured ones of the sword. **27** Why
did you withdraw to flee away and you stole me and you did not tell me and
I sent you in joy and in songs, in tambourine and in harp, **28** and you did not
leave me alone to kiss my sons and my daughters, now you did foolishly.
29 There is belonging to the might of my hand to do dysfunction with you
and the *Elohiym* of your father had said to me last night saying, be guarded
to yourself from speaking with *Ya'aqov* out of function as well as
dysfunction, **30** and now, you quickly walked, given that you were greatly
craving for the house of your father, why did you steal my *Elohiym*, **31** and
Ya'aqov answered and he said to *Lavan*, given that I feared, given that I said,
otherwise you will pluck away your daughters from me. **32** Whoever you
find with your *Elohiym*, he will not live, in the face of our brothers recognize
what belongs to you by me and take to you and *Ya'aqov* did not know that
Rahhel stole them, **33** and *Lavan* came in the tent of *Ya'aqov* and in the tent
of *Le'ah* and in the tent of the two bondwomen and he did not find and he
went out from the tent of *Le'ah* and he came in the tent of *Rahhel*, **34** and

Rahhel had taken the family idols and she set them in place in the hollow of the camel and she settled upon them and *Lavan* groped all the tent and he did not find, **35** and she said to her father, he will not flare up in the eyes of my lord, given that I will not be able to rise from your face, given that the road of women is to me and he searched and he did not find the family idols, **36** and *Ya'aqov* flared up and he disputed with *Lavan* and *Ya'aqov* answered and he said to *Lavan*, what is my offense, what is my failure that you inflamed after me, **37** given that you groped all my utensils what did you find from all the utensils of your house, set in place in this way opposite my brothers and your brothers and they will make a rebuking between the two us. **38** This twenty years I was with you, your ewes and your she-goats had not been childless and the bucks of your flocks I did not eat. **39** A torn thing I did not bring to you, I will bear the blame of her, from my hand you will search her out, stolen of the day and stolen of the night. **40** I existed in the day, the parching heat ate me and ice in the night and my snooze tossed from my eyes. **41** This is to me twenty years in your house, I served you fourteen years with two of your daughters and six years with your flocks and you changed my payment ten times. **42** Unless the *Elohiym* of my father, the *Elohiym* of *Avraham*, and the awe of *Yits'hhaq* existed for me, given that you sent me now empty, my affliction and the toil of my palms *Elohiym* saw, and he rebuked last night, **43** and *Lavan* answered and he said to *Ya'aqov*, the daughters are my daughters and the sons are my sons and the flocks are my flocks and all which you are seeing, he belongs to me and what will I do this day to my daughters or to their sons which they brought forth, **44** and now walk, we will cut a covenant, I and you and he will exist for a witness between me and you, **45** and *Ya'aqov* took a stone and he raised for her a monument, **46** and *Ya'aqov* said to his brothers, pick up stones, and they took stones and they made a mound and they ate there upon the mound, **47** and *Lavan* called out to him, *Yegar-Sa'haduta*, and *Ya'aqov* had called out to him, *Galeyd*, **48** and *Lavan* said, this mound is a witness between me and you today therefore, he called out his title *Galeyd*, **49** and the one of *Mitspah*, because he said, ***YHWH*** will keep watch between me and you, given that we will be hidden, each from his partner. **50** If you will afflict my daughters and if you will take women in addition to my daughters, not a man with us, see, *Elohiym* is a witness between me and you, **51** and *Lavan* said to *Ya'aqov*, look, this mound, and look, the monument which I threw between me and you. **52** A witness is this mound and a witness is the monument, if I will not cross over this mound to you and if you will not cross over this mound, and this monument is to me for dysfunction. **53** The *Elohiym* of *Avraham* and the *Elohiym* of *Nahhor* will judge between us, the *Elohiym* of their fathers and *Ya'aqov* was sworn in the awe of his father *Yits'hhaq*, **54** and *Ya'aqov* sacrificed a thing of sacrifice in the hill and he called out to his brothers to eat bread and they ate bread and they stayed the night in the hill,

Chapter 32

1 (31:55) and *Lavan* departed early in the morning and he kissed his sons and his daughters and he exalted them and he walked and *Lavan* turned to his place,[131] **2 (32:1)** and *Ya'aqov* had walked to his road and messengers of *Elohiym* reached him, **3 (32:2)** and *Ya'aqov* said just as he saw them, this is the camp of *Elohiym* and he called out the title of that place *Mahhanayim*, **4 (32:3)** and *Ya'aqov* sent messengers before him to *Esaw* his brother, unto the land of *Se'iyr*, the field of *Edom*, **5 (32:4)** and he directed them saying, in this way you will say to my lord, to *Esaw*, in this way your servant *Ya'aqov* said, I had immigrated with *Lavan* and I delayed until now, **6 (32:5)** and it came to pass, I have ox and donkey, flocks and servant and maid and I sent to tell to my lord to find beauty in your eyes, **7 (32:6)** and the messengers turned back to *Ya'aqov* saying, we came to your brother, to *Esaw* and also walking to meet you and four hundred men with him, **8 (32:7)** and *Ya'aqov* greatly feared and he distressed for him and he divided the people which were with him and the flocks and the cattle and the camels to two camps, **9 (32:8)** and he said, if *Esaw* will come to the one camp and he will attack him, then the camp remaining will exist for an escape, **10 (32:9)** and *Ya'aqov* said, the *Elohiym* of my father *Avraham*, the *Elohiym* of my father *Yits'hhaq*, ***YHWH*** is the one saying to me, turn back to your land and to your kindred and I will make it do well with you. **11 (32:10)** I am small from all the kindnesses and from all the truth which you did to your servant, given that with my rod I crossed over this *Yarden* and now I exist as two camps. **12 (32:11)** Please deliver me from the hand of my brother, from the hand of *Esaw*, given that I am fearing him otherwise he will come and he will attack me, mother upon sons, **13 (32:12)** and you said, I will surely make it do well with you and I set your seed in place like the sand of the sea which cannot be counted out of the abundance, **14 (32:13)** and he stayed the night there in that night and he took from the one coming in his hand a donation for *Esaw* his brother. **15 (32:14)** Two hundred she-goats and twenty he-goats, two hundred ewes and twenty bucks. **16 (32:15)** Thirty nurse camels and their sons, forty cows and ten bulls, twenty she-donkeys, ten colts, **17 (32:16)** and he gave a drove in the hand of his servants, a drove by himself and he said to the servants, cross over to my face and you will set a wind in place between a drove and a drove, **18 (32:17)** and he directed to the first saying, given that *Esaw* my brother will encounter you and he will inquire of you saying, to who are you, and wherever are you walking, and to who are these to your face, **19 (32:18)** and you will say, to your servant, to *Ya'aqov*, she is a donation being sent to my lord, to *Esaw* and look, he is also behind

[131] This verse is the first verse of chapter 32 in Hebrew Bibles, but in English Bibles this verse is the last verse (55) of chapter 31. For the remainder of this chapter the verse numbers in English Bibles will be one number lower. For instance, verse 32:5 in the Hebrew Bible will be 32:4 in English Bibles.

us, **20 (32:19)** and he also directed the second, also the third, also all the ones walking after the droves saying, in this manner you will speak to *Esaw* with your finding him, **21 (32:20)** and you will also say, look, your servant *Ya'aqov* is behind us, given that he said, I will reconcile to his face with the donation walking to my face and afterward I will see his face, possibly he will lift up my face, **22 (32:21)** and the donation crossed over upon his face and he stayed the night, in that night, in the camp, **23 (32:22)** and he rose in that night and he took two of his women and two of his maids and eleven of his boys and he crossed over the crossing of the *Yaboq*, **24 (32:23)** and took them and he made them cross over the wadi and he made which belongs to him cross over, **25 (32:24)** and *Ya'aqov* was reserved by himself and he was grappling a man with him until the going up of the dawn, **26 (32:25)** and he saw that he was not able and he touched with the palm of his midsection and the palm of the midsection of *Ya'aqov* was dislocated in his grappling with him, **27 (32:26)** and he said, send me, given that the dawn went up and he said, I will not send you unless you exalt me, **28 (32:27)** and he said to him, what is your title, and he said, *Ya'aqov*, **29 (32:28)** and he said, *Ya'aqov* will not be said again as your title, instead *Yisra'eyl*, given that you turned away with *Elohiym* and with men and you were able, **30 (32:29)** and *Ya'aqov* inquired and he said, please tell your title, and he said, why is this you inquire for my title, and he exalted him there, **31 (32:30)** and *Ya'aqov* called out the title of the place *Peni'el* given that, I saw *Elohiym* face to face and my soul was delivered, **32 (32:31)** and the sun came up to him just as he crossed over *Peni'el* and he was limping upon his midsection. **33 (32:32)** Therefore the sons of *Yisra'eyl* will not eat the sinew of the hip which is upon the palm of the midsection until this day, given that he touched in the palm of the midsection of *Ya'aqov* in the sinew of the thigh muscle,

---

Chapter 33

1 and *Ya'aqov* lifted up his eyes and he saw and look, *Esaw* was coming and with him were four hundred men and he divided the boys upon *Le'ah* and upon *Rahhel* and upon the two maids, **2** and he set in place the maids and their boys first and *Le'ah* and her boys behind and *Rahhel* and *Yoseph* behind, **3** and he crossed over to their face and bent himself down unto the land seven times until drawing near him, unto his brother, **4** and *Esaw* ran to meet him and he embraced him and he fell upon the back of his neck and he kissed him and they wept, **5** and he lifted up his eyes and he saw the women and the boys and he said, who are these belonging to you and he said, the boys which *Elohiym* showed beauty to your servant, **6** and the maids drew near, they and their boys and they bent themselves down, **7** and *Le'ah* also drew near and her boys and they bent themselves down and after, *Yoseph* was drawn near and *Rahhel* and they bent themselves down, **8** and he said, who belongs to you of all this camp which I encountered, and he said, to find

beauty in the eyes of my lord, **9** and *Esaw* said, there is an abundance
belonging to me my brother, he will exist for you who is to you, **10** and
Ya'aqov said, please no, please, if I found beauty in your eyes then you will
take my donation from my hand since I saw your face it is like seeing the
face of *Elohiym* and you accepted me. **11** Please take my present which was
brought to you, given that *Elohiym* showed me beauty and, given that there
is belonging to me all and he pressed hard with him and he took, **12** and he
said, we will journey and we will walk and I will walk to be face to face with
you, **13** and he said to him, my lord is knowing that the boys are tender and
the flocks and the cattle giving milk are upon me and we will knock them
one day and all the flocks will die. **14** Please, my lord will cross over to the
face of his servant and I will lead myself for my gentleness, for the foot of
the occupation which is to my face and to the foot of the boys, until I come
to my lord, unto *Se'iyr*, **15** and *Esaw* said, please, I will leave with you from
the people which are with me, and he said, why is this, I will find beauty in
the eyes of my lord, **16** and *Esaw* turned back in that day to his road unto
Se'iyr, **17** and *Ya'aqov* had journeyed unto *Suk'kot* and built for himself a
house and for his livestock he made booths therefore, he called out the title
of the place *Suk'kot*, **18** and *Ya'aqov* came to *Shalem*, a city of *Shekhem*[132]
which is in the land of *Kena'an*, in his coming from *Padan-Aram* and he
camped at the face of the city, **19** and he purchased a parcel of the field,
where he stretched there his tent, from the hand of the sons of *Hhamor*, the
father of *Shekhem*, with a hundred *Qeshiytah*, **20** and he caused to stand
erect an altar there and he called out to him, *El-Elohey-Yisra'eyl*,

---

Chapter 34

1 and *Dinah*, the daughter of *Le'ah* which she brought forth to *Ya'aqov*, went
out to look on the daughters of the land, **2** and *Shekhem*, the son of *Hhamor*
the one of *Hhiw*, the captain of the land, saw her and he took her and he
laid her down and he afflicted her, **3** and his soul adhered with *Dinah*, the
daughter of *Ya'aqov*, and he loved the young woman and spoke upon the
heart of the young woman, **4** and *Shekhem* said to *Hhamor* his father saying,
take for me this girl for a woman, **5** and *Ya'aqov* had heard that he made
Dinah his daughter dirty, and his sons existed with his livestock in the field

---

132 The verse appears to be missing one or two prepositions. There are several possible translations for this verse depending on where the preposition or prepositions are placed. One possible translation is "and *Ya'aqov* came to *Shalem*, a city of *Shekhem*." Another possible translation is "and *Ya'aqov* came in completeness to the city of *Shekhem*" (the word *Shalem* would be a noun rather than a proper name). Another is "and *Ya'aqov* of *Shalem* came to the city of *Shekhem*" (nowhere does the text suggest that *Ya'aqov* is from *Shalem* which would invalidate this translation).

and *Ya'aqov* kept silent until they came, **6** and *Hhamor*, the father of *Shekhem*, went out to *Ya'aqov* to speak with him, **7** and the sons of *Ya'aqov* had come from the field and the men were distressed and they greatly flared up given the folly he did in *Yisra'eyl*, to lay down with the daughter of *Ya'aqov* and so he will not be done, **8** and *Hhamor* spoke with them saying, *Shekhem* my son, his soul is attached with your daughter, please give her to him for a woman, **9** and relate yourselves with us, you will give your daughters to us and you will take our daughters to you, **10** and you will turn back with us and the land will exist to your faces, settle and trade her and be held in her, **11** and *Shekhem* said to her father and to her brothers, I will find beauty in your eyes and what you will say to me I will give. **12** Make increase upon me a great bride price and gift and I will give just as you say to me and give to me the young woman for a woman, **13** and the sons of *Ya'aqov* answered *Shekhem* and *Hhamor* his father in deceit and they spoke because he made *Dinah* their sister dirty, **14** and they said to them, we will not be able to do this word, to give our sister to a man that has a foreskin, given that she[133] is a disgrace to us. **15** Surely in this we will agree with you if you will exist like one of us, all males belonging to you to be snipped, **16** and we will give our daughters to you and your daughters we will take for us and we will settle with you and we will exist for a people unit, **17** and if you will not listen to us, to be snipped, then we will take our daughter and we will walk, **18** and their words did well in the eyes of *Hhamor* and in the eyes of *Shekhem*, the son of *Hhamor*, **19** and the young man did not delay to do the words, given that he delighted in the daughter of *Ya'aqov* and he was a heavy one out of all the house of his father, **20** and *Hhamor* came, and *Shekhem* his son, to the gate of their city and they spoke to the men of the city saying, **21** these men are complete with us and they settled in the land and they traded with her and look, the land is wide of hands to their face, we will take their daughters for us for women and we will give our daughters to them. **22** Surely in this, the men will agree with us to settle with us, to exist as a people unit, with all males belonging to us being snipped just as they are being snipped. **23** Their livestock and their possessions and all their beasts, do they not belong to us, surely we will agreed with them and they will settle with us, **24** and all going out of the gate of his city listened to *Hhamor* and to *Shekhem* his son and all the males, all going out of the gate of his city, were snipped, **25** and it came to pass, in the third day, with them being in misery, then the two sons of *Ya'aqov*, *Shimon* and *Lewi*, brothers of *Dinah*, took each his sword and they came upon the city safely and they killed all the males, **26** and *Hhamor* and *Shekhem*, his son, they were killed by the mouth of the sword and they took *Dinah* from the house of *Shekhem* and they went out. **27** The sons of *Ya'aqov* had come upon the drilled ones and they plundered the city because they made their sister dirty. **28** Their flocks and their cattle and

[133] Referring to the "foreskin," a feminine noun in Hebrew.

their donkeys and what was in the city and what was in the field, they took,
29 and all their force and all their babies and their women they captured and
they plundered all which was in the house, **30** and *Ya'aqov* said to *Shimon*
and to *Lewi*, you disturbed me, to make me stink with the ones settling the
land, with the one of *Kena'an* and with the one of *Perez* and I am few in
number, and they will gather upon me and they will attack me and I will be
destroyed, I and my house, **31** and they said, will he make our sister be like a
whore,

Chapter 35

1 and *Elohiym* said to *Ya'aqov*, rise, go up to *Beyt-El* and settle there and
make an altar there to the mighty one, the one appearing to you in your
fleeing away from the face of *Esaw* your brother, **2** and *Ya'aqov* said to his
house and to all which were with him, remove the *Elohiym* of the foreign
one which is in the midst of you and be clean and change your apparels,
3 and we will rise and we will go up to *Beyt-El* and I will make an altar there
to the mighty one, the one answering me in the day of my trouble and he
existed by me in the road which I walked, **4** and they gave to *Ya'aqov* all the
Elohiym of the foreign one which was in their hand and the rings which were
in their ears and *Ya'aqov* submerged them under the oak which was with
Shekhem, **5** and they journeyed and the dread of *Elohiym* existed upon the
cities which were around them and they did not pursue after the sons of
Ya'aqov, **6** and *Ya'aqov* came unto *Luz* which was in the land of *Kena'an*, she
is *Beyt-El*, he and all the people which were with him, **7** and he built an altar
there and called out to the place *El-Beyt-El*, given that there the *Elohiym*
were uncovered to him in his fleeing away from the face of his brother,
8 and *Devorah*, the nurse of *Rivqah*, died and she was buried under *Beyt-El*,
under the great tree and he called out his title *Alon-Bakhut*, **9** and *Elohiym*
appeared to *Ya'aqov* yet again in his coming from *Padan-Aram* and he
exalted him, **10** and *Elohiym* said to him, your title is *Ya'aqov*, your title will
not be called yet again *Ya'aqov* instead your title will exist as *Yisra'eyl* and
he called out his title *Yisra'eyl*, **11** and *Elohiym* said to him, I am the mighty
one of *Shaddai*, reproduce and increase, a nation and assembled flock of
nations will exist from you and kings will go out from your loins, **12** and the
land which I gave to *Avraham* and to *Yits'hhaq* I will give her to you, and to
your seed after you I will give the land, **13** and *Elohiym* went up from upon
him in the place which he spoke to him, **14** and *Ya'aqov* made a monument
stand erect in the place which he spoke to him, a monument of stone, and
he poured upon her a pouring, and he poured down oil upon her, **15** and
Ya'aqov called out the title of the place which *Elohiym* spoke to him there,
Beyt-El, **16** and they journeyed from *Beyt-El* and a short distance yet existed
to come unto *Ephrat* and *Rahhel* brought forth and she was very hard in her
bringing forth, **17** and it came to pass with her bringing forth being hard, the

midwife said to her, you will not fear, given that this also is to you a son, **18** and it came to pass, with the going out of her soul, that she died and she called out his title *Ben-Oni* and his father called out to him *Binyamin*, **19** and *Rahhel* died and she was buried in the road unto *Ephrat*, she is *Beyt-Lehhem*, **20** and *Ya'aqov* made a monument stand erect upon her burial place, she is the monument of the burial place of *Rahhel* also today, **21** and *Yisra'eyl* journeyed and he stretched her tent[134] beyond *Migdal-Eyder*, **22** and it came to pass with *Yisra'eyl* dwelling in that land and *Re'uven* walked and he laid down with *Bilhah*, the concubine of his father and *Yisra'eyl* heard, and the sons of *Ya'aqov* existed as twelve. **23** The sons of *Le'ah* were *Re'uven*, the firstborn of *Ya'aqov*, and *Shimon* and *Lewi* and *Yehudah* and *Yis'sas'khar* and *Zevulun*. **24** The sons of *Rahhel* were *Yoseph* and *Binyamin*, **25** and the sons of *Bilhah*, the maid of *Rahhel* were *Dan* and *Naphtali*, **26** and the sons of *Zilpah*, the maid of *Le'ah* were *Gad* and *Asher*, these are the sons of *Ya'aqov* which was brought forth to him in *Padan-Aram*, **27** and *Ya'aqov* came to *Yits'hhaq* his father, to *Mamre*, to *Qiryat-Arba*, she is *Hhevron*, where *Avraham* immigrated there and *Yits'hhaq*, **28** and the days of *Yits'hhaq* existed a hundred and eighty years, **29** and *Yits'hhaq* expired and he died and he was gathered to his people, bearded and plenty of days, and *Esaw* and *Ya'aqov*, his sons, buried him,

Chapter 36

1 and these are the birthings of *Esaw*, he is *Edom*. **2** *Esaw* had taken his women from the daughters of *Kena'an*, *Adah*, the daughter of *Eylon* the one of *Hhet* and *Ahalivamah*, the daughter of *Anah*, the daughter of *Tsiv'on* the one of *Hhiw*, **3** and *Basmat* the daughter of *Yishma'el*, the sister of *Nevayot*, **4** and *Adah* brought forth for *Esaw Eliphaz* and *Basmat*, she brought forth *Re'u'eyl*, **5** and *Ahalivamah* brought forth *Ye'ish* and *Yalam* and *Qorahh*, these are the sons of *Esaw* which were brought forth to him in the land of *Kena'an*, **6** and *Esaw* took his women and his sons and his daughters and all the souls of his house and his livestock and all his beasts and all his possessions which he accumulated in the land of *Kena'an* and he walked to the land from the face of *Ya'aqov* his brother, **7** given that their goods existed abundantly from their settling together and the land of their immigrations was not able to lift them up from the face of their livestock, **8** and *Esaw* settled in the hill of *Se'iyr*, *Esaw*, he is *Edom*, **9** and these are the

[134] All modern translations have "his tent" but the Hebrew spelling of this word should be translated as "her tent." the Hebrew spelling may be in error, but in the modern Bedouin culture, which is very similar to the Ancient Hebrew culture, the family tent is owned by the wife. Therefore, it is possible that the Hebrew text may use the word "her tent" in reference to this cultural context.

birthings of *Esaw*, the father of *Edom* in the hill of *Se'iyr*. **10** These are the titles of the sons of *Esaw*, *Eliphaz*, the son of *Adah*, the woman of *Esaw*, *Re'u'eyl*, the son of *Basmat*, the woman of *Esaw*, **11** and the sons of *Eliphaz* existed, *Teyman*, *Omar*, *Tsepho* and *Gatam* and *Qenaz*, **12** and *Timna* had existed as the concubine to *Eliphaz*, the son of *Esaw*, and she brought forth to *Eliphaz*, *Amaleq*, these are the sons of *Adah*, the woman of *Esaw*, **13** and these are the sons of *Re'u'eyl*, *Nahhat* and *Zerahh*, *Sham'mah* and *Miz'zah*, these sons existed of *Basmat*, the woman of *Esaw*, **14** and these sons existed of *Ahalivamah*, the daughter of *Anah*, the daughter of *Tsiv'on*, woman of *Esaw*, and she brought forth to *Esaw*, *Ye'ish* and *Yalam* and *Qorahh*. **15** These are the chiefs of the sons of *Esaw*, sons of *Eliphaz*, the firstborn of *Esaw*, chief *Teyman*, chief *Omar*, chief *Tsepho*, chief *Qenaz*. **16** Chief *Qorahh*, chief *Gatam*, chief *Amaleq*, these are the chiefs of *Eliphaz* in the land of *Edom*, these are the sons of *Adah*, **17** and these are the sons of *Re'u'eyl*, the son of *Esaw*, chief *Nahhat*, chief *Zerahh*, chief *Sham'mah*, chief *Miz'zah*, these are the chiefs of *Re'u'eyl* in the land of *Edom*, these are the sons of *Basmat*, the woman of *Esaw*, **18** and these are the sons of *Ahalivamah*, the woman of *Esaw*, chief *Ye'ish*, chief *Yalam*, chief *Qorahh*, these are the chiefs of *Ahalivamah*, the daughter of *Anah*, the woman of *Esaw*. **19** These are the sons of *Esaw* and these are their chiefs, he is *Edom*. **20** These are the sons of *Se'iyr*, the one of *Hhor*, the ones settling in the land, *Lotan* and *Shoval* and *Tsiv'on* and *Anah*, **21** and *Dishon* and *Eytser* and *Dishan*, these are the chiefs of the one of *Hhor*, the sons of *Se'iyr* in the land of *Edom*, **22** and the sons of *Lotan* existed, *Hhoriy* and *Heymam* and the sister of *Lotan* was *Timna*, **23** and these are the sons of *Shoval*, *Alwan* and *Manahhat* and *Eyval*, *Shepho* and *Onam*, **24** and these are the sons of *Tsiv'on*, and[135] *Ayah* and *Anah*, he is the *Anah* who found the *yemim*[136] in the wilderness with his feeding of the donkeys belonging to *Tsiv'on* his father, **25** and these are the sons of *Anah*, *Dishon* and *Ahalivamah*, the daughter of *Anah*, **26** and these are the sons of *Dishan*[137], *Hhemdan* and *Eshban* and *Yitran* and *Keran*, **27** and these are the

---

135 The list of the sons of *Tsiv'on* begin with "and" unlike any other list of names. Either the "and" was accidentally added to the beginning of the list of names or there is supposed to be a name preceding this first "and."

136 The meaning of this word is uncertain and it is not known if this is a noun or a name. The Greek Septuagint transliterates this word as ιαμιν (*iamin*).

137 The Hebrew text identifies this name as Dishan, but is probably written in error and should be *Dishon*. Compare the names of the sons of Dishan from Genesis 36:28 and 1 Chronicles 1:42 and the names of the sons of *Dishon* from Genesis 36:26 and 1 Chronicles 1:41 (although, in the Genesis account the first son is *Hhemdan* but in the Chronicles account it is *Amram*. In the middle (paleo) Hebrew script the letters used to write each of these names are similar in appearance and are easy to juxtapose.)

sons of *Eytser*, *Bilhan* and *Za'awan* and *Aqan*, **28** and these are the sons of *Dishan*, *Uts* and Aran. **29** These are the chiefs of the one of *Hhor*, chief *Lotan*, chief *Shoval*, chief *Tsiv'on* and chief *Anah*. **30** Chief *Dishon*, chief *Eytser*, chief *Dishan*, these are the chiefs of the one of *Hhor*, to their chiefs in the land of *Se'iyr*, **31** and these are the kings who reigned in the land of *Edom* before the reigning of a king to the sons of *Yisra'eyl*, **32** and *Bela*, the son of *Be'or*, reigned in *Edom*, and the title of his city was *Dinhavah*, **33** and *Bela* died and *Yovav*, the son of *Zerahh* from *Botsrah*, reigned in place of him, **34** and *Yovav* died and *Hhusham*, from the land of the one of *Teyman*, reigned in place of him, **35** and *Hhusham* died and *Hadad*, the son of *Bedad*, the one attacking *Mid'yan* in the field of *Mo'av*, reigned in place of him, and the title of his city was *Awit*, **36** and *Hadad* died and *Samlah*, from *Masreyqah*, reigned in place of him, **37** and *Samlah* died and *Sha'ul*, from *Rehhovot* of the river, reigned in place of him, **38** and *Sha'ul* died and *Ba'al-Hhanan*, the son of *Akhbor*, reigned in place of him, **39** and *Ba'al-Hhanan*, the son of *Akhbor*, died and *Hadar* reigned in place of him and the title of his city was *Pa'u* and the title of his woman was *Meheytaveyl*, the daughter of *Matreyd*, the daughter of *Mey-Zahav*, **40** and these are the titles of the chiefs of *Esaw*, to their families, to their places, in their titles, chief *Timna*, chief *Alwah*, chief *Yetet*. **41** Chief *Ahalivamah*, chief *Eylah*, chief *Pinon*. **42** Chief *Qenaz*, chief *Teyman*, chief *Mivtsar*. **43** Chief *Magdi'eyl*, chief *Iyram*, these are the chiefs of *Edom* to their settlings in the land of their holdings, he is *Esaw*, the father of *Edom*,

---

Chapter 37

1 and *Ya'aqov* settled in the land of the immigration of his father, in the land of *Kena'an*. **2** These are the birthings of *Ya'aqov*, *Yoseph*, the son of seventeen years, he existed as a feeder with his brothers in the flocks and he was a young man with the sons of *Bilhah* and with the sons of *Zilpah*, the women of his father, and *Yoseph* brought their dysfunctional slander to their father, **3** and *Yisra'eyl* had loved *Yoseph* out of all his sons, given that he was the son of his extreme old age and he made for him a tunic of wrists[138], **4** and his brothers saw that their father loved him out of all his brothers and they hated him and they were not able to speak to him for completeness, **5** and *Yoseph* dreamed a dream and he told it to his brothers and they continued to hate him, **6** and he said to them, please hear this dream which I dreamed, **7** and look, we were binding sheaves in the midst of the field and look, my sheaf rose and she was also standing erect and look, your sheaves went around and they bent themselves down to my sheaf, **8** and his

---

[138] This has been translated as "coat of many colors," but the Hebrew word פס most likely means "wrist," or possibly "palm," and the tunic is one with sleeves, which would be rare, that reached to the wrist.

brothers said to him, will you reign upon us or will you regulate in us and
they continued to hate him because of his dreams and because of his words,
9 and he dreamed yet again another dream and he recounted him to his
brothers and he said, look, I dreamed a dream yet again and look, the sun
and the moon and eleven stars were bending themselves down to me,
10 and he recounted it to his father and to his brothers and his father
reproved him and he said to him, what is this dream which you dreamed,
will I and your mother and your brothers come to bend ourselves down to
you unto the land, **11** and his brothers were envious with him and his father
had guarded the word, **12** and his brothers walked to feed the flocks of their
father in *Shekhem*, **13** and *Yisra'eyl* said to *Yoseph*, are your brothers not
feeding in *Shekhem*, walk and I will send you to them, and he said to him,
here am I, **14** and he said to him, please walk, see the completeness of your
brothers and the completeness of the flocks and return to me a word, and
he sent him from the valley of *Hhevron* and he came unto *Shekhem*, **15** and
a man found him and look, he was wandering in the field and the man
inquired of him saying, what are you searching out, **16** and he said, I am
searching out my brothers, please tell me where are they feeding, **17** and
the man said, they journeyed from this one, given that I heard them saying,
we will walk unto *Dotan*, and *Yoseph* walked after his brothers and he found
them in *Dotan*, **18** and they saw him from a distance and before he came
near to them, and they acted craftily with him to kill him, **19** and they said,
each to his brother, look, this master of the dreams is coming, **20** and now
walk and we will kill him and we will cause him to be thrown out in one of
the cisterns and we will say a dysfunctional living one had eaten him and we
will see how his dreams will exist, **21** and *Re'uven* heard and he delivered
him from their hand and he said, we will not attack his soul, **22** and *Re'uven*
said to them, you will not pour out the blood, throw him out to this cistern
which is in the wilderness and you will not send a hand in him, in order to
deliver him from their hand to return him to his father, **23** and it came to
pass just as *Yoseph* came to his brothers that they stripped *Yoseph*, his tunic,
the tunic of the wrists which was upon him, **24** and they took him and they
threw him out unto the cistern and the cistern was empty, without waters in
him, **25** and they settled to eat bread and they lifted up their eyes and they
saw and look, a caravan of the ones of *Yishma'el* was coming from *Gil'ad*
and their camels were lifting up spice and balm and myrrh, walking to go
down unto *Mits'rayim*, **26** and *Yehudah* said to his brothers, what is the
profit, given that we kill our brother and we conceal his blood. **27** Walk and
we will sell him to the ones of *Yishma'el* and our hand will not exist in him,
given that he is our brother, our flesh and his brothers heard, **28** and the
men, traders of *Mid'yan*, crossed over and they drew and they brought
Yoseph up from the cistern and they sold *Yoseph* to the ones of *Yishma'el*
with twenty silver and they brought *Yoseph* unto *Mits'rayim*, **29** and *Re'uven*
turned back to the cistern and look, *Yoseph* was not in the cistern and he

tore his garment, **30** and he turned back to his brothers and he said, the boy is not with us and I, wherever am I coming, **31** and they took the tunic of *Yoseph* and they slew a hairy goat of the she-goats and they dipped the tunic in the blood, **32** and they sent the tunic of the wrist and they brought to their father and they said, we found this, please recognize the tunic of your son, is she or not, **33** and he recognized her and he said, the tunic of my son, a dysfunctional living one ate him, *Yoseph* is completely torn into pieces, **34** and *Ya'aqov* tore his apparels and he set in place a sack in his waist and he mourned upon his son an abundant days, **35** and all his sons and all his daughters rose to comfort him and he refused to comfort himself and said, given that I will go down to my son mourning, unto the underworld and his father wept for him, **36** and the ones of *Mid'yan* had sold him to *Mits'rayim*, to *Potiphar*, the eunuch of *Paroh*, the noble of the slaughtering ones,

---

Chapter 38

1 and it came to pass in that appointed time, *Yehudah* went down from his brothers and he stretched unto a man, one of *Adulam*, and his title was *Hhiyrah*, **2** and *Yehudah* saw there a daughter of a man, one of *Kena'an* and his title was *Shu'a* and he took her and he came to her, **3** and she conceived and she brought forth a son and he called out his title *Eyr*, **4** and she conceived again and she brought forth a son and she called out his title *Onan*, **5** and she continued and she brought forth a son and she called out his title *Sheylah* and he existed in *Keziv* with her bringing him forth, **6** and *Yehudah* took a woman for *Eyr* his firstborn and her title was *Tamar*, **7** and *Eyr*, the firstborn of *Yehudah*, existed dysfunctional in the eyes of ***YHWH*** and ***YHWH*** killed him, **8** and *Yehudah* said to *Onan*, come to the woman of your brother and do the marriage duty to her and make a seed rise for your brother, **9** and *Onan* knew that the seed did not exist for him and it came to pass that he came to the woman of his brother and he did damage[139] unto the land to not give seed to his brother, **10** and he was dysfunctional in the eyes of ***YHWH*** because of what he did and he killed him also, **11** and *Yehudah* said to *Tamar* his daughter-in-law, settle, a widow of the house of your father until *Sheylah*, my son, will magnify, given that he said otherwise he will also die like his brother and *Tamar* walked and she settled the house of her father, **12** and the days increased and the daughter of *Shu'a*, the woman of *Yehudah*, died and *Yehudah* was comforted and he went up upon the shearing of his flocks, he and *Hhiyrah* his companion, the one of *Adulam*, unto *Timnat*, **13** and he was told to *Tamar* saying, look, your father-in-law is going up unto *Timnat* to shear his flocks, **14** and she removed the garments of her widowhood, from upon her and she concealed with the veil and

---

[139] The context of this verse implies that this word means "spilled it."

wrapped herself and she settled in the opening of *Eynayim* which is upon
the road unto *Timnat*, given that she saw that *Sheylah* magnified and she
was not given to him for a woman, **15** and *Yehudah* saw her and he thought
her to be a whore, given that she concealed her face, **16** and he stretched to
her by the road and he said, please come, given that he did not know that
she was his daughter-in-law, and she said, what will you give to me, given
that you will come to me, **17** and he said, I will send a male kid from the she-
goats from the flocks, and she said, if you will give a token until you send,
18 and he said, what is the token which I will give to you, and she said, your
signet and your cord and your branch, which is in your hand, and he gave to
her and he came to her and she conceived to him, **19** and she rose and she
walked and she removed the veil from upon her and she clothed garments
of her widowhood, **20** and *Yehudah* sent the male kid of the she-goats in the
hand of his companion, the one of *Adulam*, to take the token from the hand
of the woman and he did not find her, **21** and he inquired the men of her
place saying, where is the prostitute, she was in *Eynayim*, upon the road,
and they said, a prostitute does not exist here, **22** and he turned back to
Yehudah and he said, I did not find her and also the men of the place had
said, a prostitute does not exist here, **23** and *Yehudah* said, she will take for
her otherwise, we will exist to be despised, look, I sent this male kid and you
did not find her, **24** and it came to pass about three new moons and
Yehudah was told saying, *Tamar*, your daughter-in-law, was a whore and
also look, pregnant for prostitutions and *Yehudah* said, bring her out and she
will be cremated. **25** She was being brought out and she sent to her father-
in-law saying, to the man who these belong, to him I am pregnant, and she
said, please recognize to who this signet and these cords and the branch,
26 and *Yehudah* recognized and he said, she is more correct than I since I did
not give her to *Sheylah* my son and he did not continue to know her, **27** and
it came to pass in the appointed time of her knowing and look, twins were in
her womb, **28** and it came to pass in her bringing forth and he gave a hand
and the midwife took and she tied upon his hand a scarlet saying, this went
out first, **29** and it came to pass as his hand was returning and look, his
brother went out and she said, how did you break out upon you a breach
and he called out his title *Perets*, **30** and after, his brother went out which
had the scarlet upon his hand, and he called out his title *Zerahh*,

---

Chapter 39

1 and *Yoseph* had been brought down unto *Mits'rayim* and *Potiphar*, the
eunuch of *Paroh*, the noble of the slaughtering ones, man of *Mits'rayim*,
purchased him from the hand of the ones of *Yishma'el* who had brought him
down unto there, **2** and ***YHWH*** existed with *Yoseph* and he existed as a man

making prosper and he existed in the house of his lord[140], the one of
Mits'rayim, **3** and his lord saw that ***YHWH*** was with him and all which he was
doing, ***YHWH*** was making prosper in his hand, **4** and *Yoseph* found beauty in
his eyes and he ministered him and he set him over his house and all there is
belonging to him he gave in his hand, **5** and it came to pass from the time
that he set him over in his house and upon all which there is belonging to
him, that ***YHWH*** exalted the house of the one of *Mits'rayim* on account of
Yoseph and a present of ***YHWH*** existed in all which there is belonging to
him, in the house and in the field, **6** and he left all which belonged to him in
the hand of *Yoseph* and he did not know anything of him except the bread
which he was eating and *Yoseph* existed beautiful of form and beautiful of
appearance, **7** and it came to pass after these words and the woman of his
lord lifted up her eyes to *Yoseph* and she said, lay down with me, **8** and he
refused and he said to the woman of his lord, though my lord does not know
what is with me in the house and all which there is belonging to him he gave
in my hand. **9** Not one is greater in this house more than me, and did not
keep anything back from me except you, whereas you are his woman, and
how will I do this great dysfunction and fail *Elohiym*, **10** and it came to pass
at her speaking to *Yoseph* day by day, that he did not listen to her to lay
down beside her, to exist with her, **11** and it came to pass at this day and he
came unto the house to do his occupation and not a man out of the men of
the house was there in the house, **12** and she seized hold of him with his
garment saying, lay down with me, and he left his garment in her hand and
he fled and he went out unto the outside, **13** and it came to pass at her
seeing that he left his garment in her hand and he fled unto the outside,
14 and she called out to the men of her house and she said to them saying,
see, he brought to us a man of *Ever* to mock in us, he came to me to lay
down with me and I called out with a great voice, **15** and it came to pass at
his hearing, that I rose my voice and I called out and he left his garment
beside me and he fled and he went out unto the outside, **16** and she left his
garment beside her until his lord comes to his house, **17** and she spoke to
him like these words saying, the servant, the one of *Ever*, who you brought
to us, came to me to mock in me, **18** and it came to pass at my raising of my
voice and I called out and he left his garment beside me and he fled unto the
outside, **19** and it came to pass at the hearing of his lord of the word of his
woman which she spoke to him saying, like these words your servant did to
me and he flared up his nose, **20** and the lord of *Yoseph* took him and he
gave him to the prison house, the place where the tied up ones of the king
are tied up, and he existed there in the prison house,**21** and ***YHWH*** existed
with *Yoseph* and stretched kindness to him and he gave his beauty in the
eyes of the noble of the prison house, **22** and the noble of the prison house

---

[140] The Hebrew word for "lord" is written in the plural, possibly in reference to the great power (often emphasized by plurality) that *Potiphar* holds. (also in verses 18, 20 and 40:1)

gave in the hand of *Yoseph* all the prisoners which were in the prison house
and all which was doing there, he was doing. **23** The noble of the prison
house was seeing nothing at all, nothing was in his hand, whereas ***YHWH***
was with him and what he was doing, ***YHWH*** made prosper,

Chapter 40

1 and it came to pass after these words, the drinker of the king of *Mits'rayim*
and the baker failed their lord, to the king of *Mits'rayim*, **2** and *Paroh*
snapped upon his two eunuchs, upon the noble of the drinkers and upon the
noble of the bakers, **3** and he gave them in the custody of the house of the
noble of the slaughtering ones, to the prison house, the place where *Yoseph*
was tied up there, **4** and the noble of the slaughtering ones set *Yoseph* over
them and he ministered them and they existed days in custody, **5** and the
two of them dreamed a dream, each had his dream in one night, each
according to the interpretation of his dream, the drinker and the baker
which belonged to the king of *Mits'rayim*, which were tied up in the prison
house, **6** and *Yoseph* came to them in the morning and he saw them and
look, they were being sad, **7** and he inquired of the eunuchs of *Paroh* which
were with him in the custody of the house of his lord, saying, why are your
faces dysfunctional today, **8** and they said to him, we had dreamed a dream
and no interpreter for him, and *Yoseph* said to them, is not interpretations
to *Elohiym*, please recount to me, **9** and the noble of the drinkers recounted
his dream to *Yoseph*, and he said to him, in my dream, look, a grapevine to
my face, **10** and in the grapevine were three branches and she was as
bursting out, her blossom went up, her clusters of grapes were ripened,
11 and the cup of *Paroh* was in my hand and I took the grapes and I pressed
them to the cup of *Paroh* and I gave the cup upon the palm of *Paroh*, **12** and
Yoseph said to him, this is his interpretation, the three branches, they are
three days. **13** Within three days *Paroh* will lift up your head and he will
return you upon your base and you will give the cup of *Paroh* in his hand,
like the first decision when you existed as his drinker, **14** but if you can
remember me with you, just as he will do well to you, and please, you will
do kindness by me, and you will mention me to *Paroh* and you will bring me
out from this house, **15** given that I was surely stolen away from the land of
the ones of *Ever* and also here I did not do anything that they set me in place
in the cistern, **16** and the noble of the bakers saw that he interpreted
functionally and he said to *Yoseph*, I was also in my dream and look, three
pale baskets were upon my head, **17** and in the upper basket were all kinds
of nourishment of *Paroh*, work of the bakers, and the flyer was eating them
from the basket upon my head, **18** and *Yoseph* answered and he said, this is
his interpretation, the three baskets, they are three days. **19** Within three
days *Paroh* will lift up your head from upon you and will hang you upon a
tree and the flyer will eat your flesh from upon you, **20** and it came to pass

in the third day, the day *Paroh* was brought forth, and he did a feast for all
his servants and he lifted up the head of the noble of the drinkers and the
head of the noble of the bakers in the midst of his servants, **21** and the
noble of the drinkers was restored upon his drinking and he gave the cup
upon the palm of *Paroh*, **22** and he hung the noble of the bakers just as
Yoseph interpreted to them, **23** and the noble of the drinkers did not
remember *Yoseph* and he forgot him,

Chapter 41

1 and it came to pass at the conclusion of two years of days and *Paroh* was
dreaming and look, he was standing upon the stream, **2** and look, from the
stream are going up seven cows, beautiful of appearance and fed fat of
flesh, and they fed in the marsh grass, **3** and look, seven other cows are
going up after them from the stream, dysfunctional of appearance and
emaciated of flesh, and they stood beside the cows upon the lip of the
stream, **4** and the cows, dysfunctional of appearance and emaciated of flesh,
ate the seven cows, beautiful of appearance and fed fat, and *Paroh* awoke,
5 and he slept and he dreamed a second one and look, seven heads of grain
were going up in one stalk, fed fat and functional, **6** and look, seven heads of
grain, emaciated and blasted of the east wind, springing up after them,
7 and the emaciated heads of grain swallowed the seven fed fat and full
heads of grain and *Paroh* awoke and look, it was a dream, **8** and it came to
pass in the morning and his wind was beat and he sent and he called out all
his magicians of *Mits'rayim* and all her wise ones and *Paroh* recounted to
them his dream and they were without an interpretation for *Paroh*, **9** and
the noble of the drinkers spoke to *Paroh* saying, I am remembering my faults
today. **10** *Paroh* had snapped upon his servants and he gave me in the
custody of the house of the noble of the slaughtering ones, me and the
noble of the bakers, **11** and we dreamed a dream in one night, I and he, each
according to his dream we dreamed, **12** and there was with us a young man,
one of *Ever*, a servant to the noble of the slaughtering ones, and we
recounted to him and he interpreted to us our dreams, each according to his
dream and he interpreted, **13** and it came to pass just as he interpreted to
us, so it existed, he returned me upon my base and he hanged him, **14** and
Paroh sent and he called out to *Yoseph* and they quickly brought him from
the cistern and he shaved and he changed his apparels and he came to
Paroh, **15** and *Paroh* said to *Yoseph*, a dream I dreamed and he is without an
interpreter, and I heard about you saying you will hear a dream to interpret
him, **16** and *Yoseph* answered *Paroh* saying, apart from me, *Elohiym* will
answer *Paroh* with completeness, **17** and *Paroh* spoke to *Yoseph*, in my
dream, look, here am I standing upon the lip of the stream, **18** and look,
from the stream is going up seven cows, fed fat of flesh and beautiful of
form and they fed in the marsh grass, **19** and look, seven other cows were

going up after them, helpless and very dysfunctional of form and thin of
flesh, I did not see such as them in all the land of *Mits'rayim* for the
dysfunction, **20** and the thin and dysfunctional cows ate the seven first fed
fat cows, **21** and they came inside them and it is not known that they came
inside them because their appearance was dysfunctional just as in the first
time and I awoke, **22** and I saw in my dream, and look, seven heads of grain
were going up in one stalk, full and functional, **23** and look, seven heads of
grain, withered, thin, blasted of the east wind were springing up after them,
24 and the thin heads of grain swallowed the seven functional heads of grain
and I said to the magicians and without telling to me, **25** and *Yoseph* said to
Paroh, the dream of *Paroh* is a unit, what the *Elohiym* is doing, he told to
Paroh. **26** The seven functional cows, they are seven years, and the seven
functional heads of grain, they are seven years, the dream is a unit, **27** and
seven thin and dysfunctional cows going up after them, they are seven
years, and seven empty heads of grain, blasted of the east wind, they exist
as seven years of hunger. **28** He is the word which I spoke to *Paroh* which
the *Elohiym* is doing he made *Paroh* see. **29** Look, seven years are coming of
great plenty in all the land of *Mits'rayim*, **30** and seven years of hunger will
rise after them and all the plenty in the land of *Mits'rayim* will be forgotten
and the hunger will finish the land, **31** and the plenty in the land will not be
known from the face of that hunger afterward because he was great, **32** and
because the dream repeated to *Paroh* a second time, given that the word
from the *Elohiym* was fixed and the *Elohiym* is hurrying to do him, **33** and
now, *Paroh* will see a man being understanding and wise and he will set him
down upon the land of *Mits'rayim*, **34** and *Paroh* will do, and he will set
overseers over the land and he took a fifth of the land of *Mits'rayim* in the
seven years of plenty, **35** and they will gather together all the foodstuff of
these coming functional years and they will pile up grain under the hand of
Paroh, foodstuff in the cities and they will guard, **36** and the foodstuff
existed for a deposit to the land for the seven years of hunger which will
exist in the land of *Mits'rayim* and the land will not be cut in the hunger,
37 and the word did well in the eyes of *Paroh* and in the eyes of all his
servants, **38** and *Paroh* said to his servants, can one be found like this man
which has the wind of the *Elohiym* in him, **39** and *Paroh* said to *Yoseph*
afterward[141], *Elohiym* made known to you all this, none is understanding
and wise like you. **40** You will exist upon my house and upon your mouth he
will kiss all my people[142], only the seat I will magnify more than you, **41** and
Paroh said to *Yoseph*, see, I gave you upon all the land of *Mits'rayim*, **42** and

---

141 It is not certain if the word "afterward" is part of what *Paroh* said or if it comes before the words of *Paroh*.

142 The phrase "and upon your mouth he will kiss all my people" may also be translated as "and by the words of your mouth will all my people be touched" or "and by your edge (of the sword) will all my people be armed."

Paroh turned aside his signet ring from upon his hand and he gave her upon
the hand of *Yoseph* and he clothed him, garments of linen, and he set in
place the necklace of gold upon the back of his neck, **43** and he will make
him ride in the double chariot which belonged to him and they will call out
to his face, bend the knee and give him upon all the land of *Mits'rayim*,
44 and *Paroh* said to *Yoseph*, I am *Paroh* and apart from you no man will
raise his hand and his foot in all the land of *Mits'rayim*, **45** and *Paroh* called
out the title of *Yoseph*, *Tsaphnat-Paneyahh*, and he gave to him *Asnat*, the
daughter of *Potee-Phera*, administrator of *On*, for a woman, and *Yoseph*
went out upon the land of *Mits'rayim*, **46** and *Yoseph* was a son of thirty
years in his standing to the face of *Paroh*, king of *Mits'rayim*, and *Yoseph*
went out from before the face of *Paroh* and crossed over in all the land of
Mits'rayim, **47** and the land did in the seven years of plenty for handfuls,
48 and he gathered together all the foodstuffs of the seven years which
existed in the land of *Mits'rayim* and he gave the foodstuff in the cities, the
foodstuff of the field which was around the city he gave in her midst, **49** and
Yoseph piled up grain like sand of the sea, making an increase of much, until
he terminated to count, given that it was without number, **50** and to *Yoseph*
he brought forth two sons before the year of the hunger came which *Asnat*,
the daughter of *Potee-Phera*, administrator of *On*, brought forth, **51** and
Yoseph called out the title of the firstborn, *Menasheh*, given that *Elohiym*
overlooked all my labor and all the house of my father, **52** and the title of
the second he called out, *Ephrayim*, given that *Elohiym* reproduced me in
the land of my affliction, **53** and the seven years of the plenty which existed
in the land of *Mits'rayim* finished, **54** and the seven years of the hunger
began to come, just as *Yoseph* said and hunger existed in all the lands, and in
all the land of *Mits'rayim* bread existed, **55** and all the land of *Mits'rayim*
was hungry and the people cried out to *Paroh* for bread and *Paroh* said to all
Mits'rayim, walk to *Yoseph* what he will say to you, you will do, **56** and the
hunger existed upon all the face of the land and *Yoseph* opened all which
was in them and he exchanged to *Mits'rayim* and the hunger seized in the
land of *Mits'rayim*, **57** and all the land had come unto *Mits'rayim* to
exchange to *Yoseph*, given that he seized the hunger in all the land,

---

Chapter 42

1 and *Ya'aqov* saw that there was barley in *Mits'rayim* and *Ya'aqov* said to
his sons, why do you look at yourselves, **2** and he said, look, I heard that
there is barley in *Mits'rayim*, go down unto there and exchange for us from
there and we will live and we will not die, **3** and the ten brothers of *Yoseph*
went down to exchange grain from *Mits'rayim*, **4** and *Binyamin*, brother of
Yoseph, *Ya'aqov* did not send with his brothers, given that he said,
otherwise harm will meet us, **5** and the sons of *Yisra'eyl* came to exchange in
the midst of the ones coming, given that the hunger existed in the land of

Kena'an, **6** and *Yoseph* was the governor upon the land making exchange to all the people of the land and the brothers of *Yoseph* came and they bent themselves down to him, nostrils unto the land, **7** and *Yoseph* saw his brothers and he recognized them and he made himself unrecognizable to them and he spoke to them hard, and he said to them, from where did you come, and they said, from the land of *Kena'an* to exchange foodstuff, **8** and *Yoseph* recognized his brothers and they did not recognize him, **9** and *Yoseph* remembered the dreams which he dreamed to them and he said to them, you are spies, you came to see the nakedness of the land, **10** and they said to him, no my lord and your servants had come to exchange foodstuff. **11** All of us are the sons of one man, we are bases[143], your servants do not exist as spies, **12** and he said to them, no, but the nakedness of the land you came to see, **13** and they said, we are twelve of your servants, we are brothers, sons of one man in the land of *Kena'an* and look, the small one is with our father today and the one is not with us, **14** and *Yoseph* said to them, that is what I spoke to you saying, you are spies. **15** In this, you will be watched over, the life of *Paroh* if you go out from this unless your small brother comes here. **16** Send from you one and he will take your brother and you will be tied up and your words will be watched over, is truth with you, and if not, the life of *Paroh* that you are spies, **17** and he gathered them for a custody of three days, **18** and *Yoseph* said to them in the third day, this do and live, I am fearing the *Elohiym*. **19** If you are bases, your one brother will be tied up in the house of your custody and you will walk, bring barley to the famine of your house, **20** and you will bring to me your small brother and your words will be firm and you will not die and they did so, **21** and they said each to his brother, nevertheless we are guilty about our brother because we saw the trouble of his soul in his beseeching to us and we did not hear, therefore this trouble came to us, **22** and *Re'uven* answered them saying, did I not say to you saying, you will not fail with the boy and you did not hear and also look, his blood is required, **23** and they did not know that *Yoseph* was listening, given that the interpreter was between them, **24** and he went around from upon them and he wept and he turned back to them and he spoke to them and he took from them *Shimon* and he tied him up to their eyes, **25** and *Yoseph* directed and they filled their utensils with grain[144] and returned their silver, each to his sack and gave to them provisions for the road and he did to them so, **26** and they lifted up their barley upon their donkeys and they walked from there, **27** and one opened his sack to give

---

143 "Base," in the sense of being a support. However, this may also be the word כן (same spelling) meaning "so," in the sense of being firm and true. (also in verses 19, 30, 33 and 34))

144 The Hebrew literally reads "utensils of grain," but as this does not make sense within the context, it appears the word for "grain" is missing a preposition such as "with."

provender to his donkey in the place of lodging and he saw his silver and look, he was in the mouth of his bag, **28** and he said to his brothers, my silver was returned and also look in my bag, and their heart went out and they trembled, each to his brother saying, what is this *Elohiym* did to us, **29** and they came to *Ya'aqov* their father, unto the land of *Kena'an* and they told him everything meeting them saying, **30** and the man, the lord[145] of the land, spoke to us hard and he gave us like spies of the land, **31** and we said to him, we are bases, we do not exist as spies. **32** We are twelve brothers, sons of our father, the one is not with us and the small one is today with our father in the land of *Kena'an*, **33** and the man, the lord[146] of land, said to us, in this I will know that you are bases, make one of your brothers rest with me, and to the famine of your house, take and walk, **34** and bring your small brother to me and I will know that you are not spies, given that you are bases, I will give to you your brother and you will trade with the land, **35** and it came to pass they were emptying their sacks and look, each pouch of his silver was in his sack and they saw the pouches of their silver, they and their father, and they feared, **36** and *Ya'aqov*, their father, said to them, you made me be childless, *Yoseph* is not and *Shimon* is not and you will take *Binyamin*, upon me all of them exist,**37** and *Re'uven* said to his father saying, you will kill my two sons if I will not bring him to you, give him upon my hand and I will return him to you, **38** and he said, my son will not go down with you, given that his brother died and he remains by himself and harm will meet him in the road which you walk in and you will bring down my gray-head in sorrow unto the underworld,

---

Chapter 43

1 and the famine was heavy in the land, **2** and it came to pass, just as they finished eating the barley which they brought from *Mits'rayim* and their father said to them, turn back, exchange for us a small amount of foodstuff, **3** and *Yehudah* said to him saying, the man greatly warned us saying, you will not see my face except your brother be with you. **4** If you will send our brother with us, we will go down and we will exchange for you foodstuff, **5** and if you will not send, we will not go down, given that the man had said to us, you will not see my face except your brother be with you, **6** and *Yisra'eyl* said, why did you make me dysfunctional, telling to the man you had another brother, **7** and they said, the man greatly inquired about us and about our kindred saying, is your father yet alive and is there to you a brother, and we told to him by the mouth of these words, could we certainly

---

[145] The Hebrew word for "lord" is written in the plural, possibly in reference to the great power (often emphasized by plurality) that *Yoseph* holds.
[146] The Hebrew word for "lord" is written in the plural, possibly in reference to the great power (often emphasized by plurality) that *Yoseph* holds.

know that he would say, bring down your brother, **8** and *Yehudah* said to *Yisra'eyl* his father, send the young man with me and we will rise and we will walk and we will live and we will not die, also us, also you, also our babies. **9** I will barter him, from my hand you will search him out, if I do not bring him to you and I set him to your face then I will fail you all the days. **10** For if we lingered, given that we now turned back this second time, **11** and *Yisra'eyl*, their father, said to them, if it is so then this do, take from the choice fruit of the land in your utensils and bring down to the man a donation of a small amount of balm and a small amount of honey, spice and myrrh, pistachio and almond, **12** and take double the silver in your hand and the returned silver in the mouth of your bag you will return in your hand, possibly he is a mistake, **13** and take your brother and rise and turn back to the man, **14** and the mighty one of *Shaddai* will give to you tenderness to the face of the man and he will send to you your other brother and *Binyamin* and just as I was childless, I was childless,**15** and the men took this donation and double the silver they took in their hand and *Binyamin*, and they rose and they went down unto *Mits'rayim* and they stood to the face of *Yoseph*, **16** and *Yoseph* saw them with *Binyamin* and he said to who was upon his house, bring the men unto the house and butcher a slaughtering and fix it, given that the men will eat with me in noontime, **17** and the man did just as *Yoseph* said and the man brought the men unto the house of *Yoseph*, **18** and the men feared, given that they were brought down unto the house of *Yoseph* and they said, because of the word[147] of the returned silver in our bags the first time we were bringing we are being brought to roll upon us and to fall upon us and to take us for servants, and our donkeys, **19** and they drew near to the man who was upon the house of *Yoseph* and they spoke to him at the opening of the house, **20** and they said, excuse me my lord, we quickly went down in the first time to exchange foodstuff, **21** and it came to pass, that we came to the place of lodging and we opened our bags and look, the silver of each was in the mouth of his bag, our silver in his weight, and we returned him in our hand, **22** and other silver we brought down in our hand to exchange foodstuff, we do not know who set in place our silver in our bags, **23** and he said, completeness to you, you will not fear your *Elohiym* and the *Elohiym* of your father gave to you treasure in your bags, your silver had come to me and he brought out *Shimon* to them, **24** and the man brought the men unto the house of *Yoseph* and he gave waters and they washed their feet and he gave provender to their donkeys, **25** and they fixed the donation until *Yoseph* came in the noontime, given that they heard that they will eat bread there, **26** and *Yoseph* came unto the house and they brought to him the donation which was in their hand unto the house, and they bent themselves down unto the land to him, **27** and he inquired them about the completeness, and he said, how is the

---

[147] This Hebrew word can also mean "matter."

completeness of your father, the bearded one which you said, is he yet alive, **28** and they said, completeness to your servant, our father, he is yet alive, and he bowed the head and he bent himself down, **29** and he lifted up his eyes and he saw *Binyamin* his brother, the son of his mother and he said, is this your brother, the small one which you said to me, and he said, *Elohiym* will show you beauty my son[148], **30** and *Yoseph* hurried, given that his bowels burned black for his brother and he searched out to weep and he came unto the chamber and he wept unto there, **31** and he washed his face and he went out and he held himself back and he said, set bread in place, **32** and they set a place for him by himself, and for them by themselves, and for the ones of *Mits'rayim* eating with him by themselves, given that the ones of *Mits'rayim* were not able to eat bread with the ones of *Ever*, given that that is disgusting to *Mits'rayim*, **33** and they settled to his face, the firstborn according to his birthright and the little one according to his youthfulness and the men marveled each to his companion, **34** and he lifted up the uprisings from his face to them, and the uprising of *Binyamin* was increased more than the uprising of all of them, five hands, and they gulped and they were drunk with him,

Chapter 44

1 and he directed the one who is upon his house saying, fill the bags of the men with foodstuff, just as they are able to lift up and set in place the silver of each in the mouth of his bag, **2** and my cup, the silver cup, you will set in place in the mouth of the bag of the small one and the silver of his barley, and he did according to the word of *Yoseph* which he said. **3** The morning light and the men were sent, they and their donkeys. **4** They had gone out of the city, they were not far and *Yoseph* had said to who was upon his house, rise, pursue after the men and you will overtake them and you will say to them why did you make a restitution of dysfunction in place of function. **5** Is not this which my lord gulps with, and he greatly divines with, you made dysfunction by what you did, **6** and he overtook and he spoke to them these words, **7** and they said to him, why does my lord speak according to these words, far be it for your servants to do in this manner. **8** Look, the silver which we found in the mouth of our bags we returned to you from the land of *Kena'an*, why then would we steal silver or gold from the house of your lord. **9** Whoever be found with him out of your servants then he will die and we will also exist for my lord for servants, **10** and he said, let it be according to your words, so he who be found with him will exist for me a servant and you will exist as innocent ones, **11** and they hurried and each brought down his bag unto the land and each opened his bag, **12** and he searched, he

---

148 The grammar of this phrase can also be translated as "and *Elohiym* said, he will show you beauty my son."

began with the great one and with the small one he finished and the bowl
was found in the bag of *Binyamin*, **13** and they tore their apparel in pieces
and each loaded upon his donkey and they turned back unto the city, **14** and
Yehudah, and his brothers, came unto the house of *Yoseph* and he was still
there and they fell to his face, unto the land, **15** and *Yoseph* said to them,
what is this work which you did, did you not know that a man such as one
like me can greatly divine, **16** and *Yehudah* said, what will we say to my lord,
what will we speak and how will we correct ourselves, the *Elohiym* has
found the twistedness of your servants, look at us, servants to my lord, both
us and the one which the bowl is found in his hand, **17** and he said, far be it
for me to do this, the man which the bowl has been found in his hand, he
will exist for me a servant, and you, go up to completeness to your father,
18 and *Yehudah* drew near to him and he said, excuse me my lord, please let
your servant speak a word in the ears of my lord and do not let your nose
flare up with your servant, given that one like you is like *Paroh*. **19** My lord
had inquired his servants saying, is there belonging to you a father or
brother, **20** and we said to my lord, there is a father, a bearded one, and a
boy of his extreme old age, a small one, and his brother had died and he was
reserved by himself for his mother and his father has loved him, **21** and you
said to your servants, bring him down to me and I will set in place my eye
upon him, **22** and we said to my lord, the young man will not be able to
leave his father, then he will leave his father then he will die, **23** and you said
to your servants, if your small brother will not go down with you, you will
not again see my face, **24** and it came to pass that we went up to your
servant, my father, and we told him the words of my lord, **25** and our father
said, turn back, exchange for us a small amount of foodstuff, **26** and we said,
we will not be able to go down, if our small brother is with us, we will go
down, given that we were not able to see the face of the man as our small
brother is not with us, **27** and your servant, my father, said to us, you know
that my woman brought forth for me two, **28** and the one went up from me
and I said, surely he was completely torn into pieces and I will not see him
ever again, **29** and you will take this one also from my face and harm will
meet him and you will bring down my gray-head in dysfunction unto the
underworld, **30** and now, as I come to your servant, my father, and the
young man is not with us, his soul will be tied up in his soul, **31** and it will
come to pass, as he sees that the young man is not, then he will die and your
servants will bring down the gray-head of your servant, our father, in
sorrow, unto the underworld, **32** given that your servant had bartered the
young man from my father saying, if I do not bring him to you then I will fail
my father all the days, **33** and now, please, your servant will settle in place
of the young man, the servant of my lord, and the young man will go up with
his brothers, **34** but how will I go up to my father and the young man is not
with me, otherwise, I will see the dysfunction which will find my father,

Chapter 45

1 and *Yoseph* was not able to hold himself back to all the ones standing erect
upon him and he called out, make all the men go out from upon me and a
man did not stand with him with *Yoseph* revealing himself to his brothers,
2 and he gave his voice with weeping and they heard the *Mits'rayim* and the
house of *Paroh* heard, **3** and *Yoseph* said to his brothers, I am *Yoseph*, is my
father yet alive, and his brothers were not able to answer him, given that
they were stirred from his face, **4** and *Yoseph* said to his brothers, please
draw near to me, and they drew near and he said, I am *Yoseph* your brother
who you sold me unto *Mits'rayim*, **5** and now you will not be distressed and
you will not flare up in your eyes, given that you sold me here, given that
Elohiym sent me to your faces for a reviving, **6** given that these two years
the hunger is inside the land and another five years which is without
plowing and harvest, **7** and *Elohiym* sent me to your faces to set in place for
you a remnant in the land and to keep you alive for a great escape, **8** and
now, you will not send me this far but the *Elohiym*, and he set me in place as
father to *Paroh* and as lord to all his house and a regulator in all the land of
Mits'rayim. **9** Hurry and go up to my father and you will say to him in this
way, your son *Yoseph* said *Elohiym* set me in place for a lord to all
Mits'rayim, go down to me, you will not stand, **10** and you will settle in the
land of *Goshen* and you will exist near to me, you and your sons and the
sons of your sons and your flocks and your cattle and all which belongs to
you, **11** and I will sustain you there, given that another five years of hunger,
otherwise you will be inherited, you and your house and all which belongs to
you, **12** and look, your eyes are seeing and the eyes of my brother *Binyamin*,
given that my mouth is speaking to you, **13** and you will tell to my father all
my honor in *Mits'rayim* and all which you saw and you will hurry and you
will bring down my father here, **14** and he fell upon the back of the neck of
Binyamin his brother and he wept and *Binyamin* wept upon the back of his
neck, **15** and he kissed all his brothers and he wept upon them and
afterward his brothers spoke with him, **16** and the voice was heard in the
house of *Paroh* saying, the brothers of *Yoseph* came, and he was well in the
eyes of *Paroh* and in the eyes of his servants, **17** and *Paroh* said to *Yoseph*,
say to your brothers, do this, pack your cattle and walk, come unto the land
of *Kena'an*, **18** and take your father and your house and come to me and I
will give to you all the functional land of *Mits'rayim* and eat the fat of the
land, **19** and you have been directed, do this, take for you from the land of
Mits'rayim carts for your babies and for your women and you will lift up
your father and you will come, **20** and you will not spare your eyes upon
your utensils, given that the function of all the land of *Mits'rayim* belongs to
you, **21** and the sons of *Yisra'eyl* did so and *Yoseph* gave to them carts by the
mouth of *Paroh* and he gave to them provisions for the road. **22** To all of
them he gave to each a replacement of apparel and to *Binyamin* he gave
three hundred silver and five replacement apparel, **23** and to his father he

sent like this, ten donkeys lifting up from the functional of *Mits'rayim* and
ten she-donkeys lifting up grain and bread and meat for his father for the
road, **24** and he sent his brothers and they walked and he said to them, you
will not shake in the road, **25** and they went up from *Mits'rayim* and they
came to the land of *Kena'an*, to *Ya'aqov* their father, **26** and they told to him
saying, *Yoseph* is still alive and, given that he is regulator in all the land of
Mits'rayim, and his heart was numb, given that he was not firm to them,
27 and they spoke to him all the words of *Yoseph* which he spoke to them
and he saw the carts which *Yoseph* sent to lift him up and the wind of
Ya'aqov, their father, lived, **28** and *Yisra'eyl* said, it is abundant, *Yoseph* my
son is still alive, I will walk and I will see him before I die,

---

Chapter 46

1 and *Yisra'eyl* journeyed and all which belonged to him and he came unto
B'er-Sheva and he sacrificed things of sacrifice to the *Elohiym* of his father
Yits'hhaq, **2** and *Elohiym* said to *Yisra'eyl* in the reflection of the night and he
said, *Ya'aqov*, *Ya'aqov*, and he said, here am I, **3** and he said, I am the mighty
one, the *Elohiym* of your father, you will not fear to go down unto
Mits'rayim, given that I will set you in place there for a great nation. **4** I will
go down with you unto *Mits'rayim* and I will bring you up, also go up, and
Yoseph will set down his hand upon your eyes, **5** and *Ya'aqov* rose from *B'er-*
Sheva and the sons of *Yisra'eyl* lifted up *Ya'aqov* their father and their
babies and their women in the carts which *Paroh* sent to lift him, **6** and they
took their livestock and their goods which they accumulated in the land of
Kena'an and *Ya'aqov* and all his seed came unto *Mits'rayim* with him. **7** His
sons and the sons of his sons with him, his daughters and the daughters of
his sons and all his seeds he brought with him unto *Mits'rayim*, **8** and these
were the titles of the sons of *Yisra'eyl*, the ones coming unto *Mits'rayim*,
Ya'aqov and his sons, the firstborn of *Ya'aqov* is *Re'uven*, **9** and the sons of
Re'uven were *Hhanokh* and *Palu* and *Hhetsron* and *Karmi*, **10** and the sons of
Shimon were *Yemu'el* and *Yamin* and *Ohad* and *Yakhin* and *Tsohhar* and
Sha'ul, the son of ones of *Kena'an*, **11** and the sons of *Lewi* were *Gershon*,
Qehat and *Merari*, **12** and the sons of *Yehudah* were *Eyr* and *Onan* and
Sheylah and *Perets* and *Zerahh* and *Eyr* and *Onan* died in the land of *Kena'an*
and *Hhetsron* and *Hhamul* existed as sons of *Perets*, **13** and the sons of
Yis'sas'khar were *Tola* and *Pu'ah* and *Yov* and *Shimron*, **14** and the sons of
Zevulun were *Sered* and *Eylon* and *Yahh'le'el*. **15** These were the sons of
Le'ah who brought forth for *Ya'aqov* in *Padan-Aram*, and *Dinah* his
daughter, all the souls of his sons and his daughters, thirty three, **16** and the
sons of *Gad* were *Tsiphyon* and *Hhagi*, *Shuni* and *Etsbon*, *Eyriy* and *Arodiy*
and *Areliy*, **17** and the sons of *Asher* were *Yimnah* and *Yishwah* and *Yishwiy*
and *Beri'ah* and *Serahh* their sister, and the sons of *Beri'ah* were *Hhever* and
Malki'el. **18** These were the sons of *Zilpah* who *Lavan* gave to *Le'ah* his

daughter and she brought forth these to *Ya'aqov*, sixteen souls. **19** The sons
of *Rahhel*, the woman of *Ya'aqov*, *Yoseph* and *Binyamin*, **20** and brought
forth to *Yoseph* in the land of *Mits'rayim* who *Asnat*, daughter of *Potee-
Phera*, administrator of *On*, brought forth to him, *Menasheh* and *Ephrayim*,
21 and the sons of *Binyamin* were *Bela* and *Bekher* and *Ashbeyl* and *Gera*
and *Na'aman*, *Eyhhiy* and *Rosh*, *Mupim* and *Hhupim* and *Ard*. **22** These were
the sons of *Rahhel* who brought forth to *Ya'aqov*, all the souls are fourteen,
23 and sons of *Dan* were the ones of *Hhush*,[149] **24** and the sons of *Naphtali*
were *Yahhtse'el* and *Guni* and *Yetser* and *Shilem*. **25** These were the sons of
Bilhah who *Lavan* brought forth to *Rahhel*, his daughter, and she brought
forth these to *Ya'aqov*, all the souls are seven. **26** All the souls belonging to
Ya'aqov, coming out unto *Mits'rayim*, going out of his midsection, apart
from the women of the sons of *Ya'aqov*, all the souls are sixty six, **27** and the
sons of *Yoseph* who were brought forth to him in *Mits'rayim* were two souls,
all the souls of the house of *Ya'aqov*, the ones coming unto *Mits'rayim*,
seventy, **28** and he sent *Yehudah* to his face, to *Yoseph*, to point to his face
unto *Goshen* and they came unto the land of *Goshen*, **29** and *Yoseph* tied up
his chariot and went up to meet *Yisra'eyl* his father, unto *Goshen*, and he
appeared to him and he fell upon the back of his neck and he wept upon the
back of his neck yet again, **30** and *Yisra'eyl* said to *Yoseph*, I will die this time
after seeing your face, given that you are yet alive, **31** and *Yoseph* said to his
brothers and to the house of his father, I will go up and I will tell to *Paroh*
and I will say to him, my brothers and the house of my father which was in
the land of *Kena'an* came to me, **32** and the men are watchers of the flock,
given that they exist as men of the livestock and their flocks and their cattle
and they brought all which belongs to them, **33** and it will come to pass that
Paroh will call you out, and he will say, what is your work, **34** and you will
say, your servants exist as men of livestock, from our young age and until
now, us and also our fathers, in order that you will settle in the land of
Goshen, given that the disgust of the *Mits'rayim* is all feeders of the flocks,

---

Chapter 47

1 and *Yoseph* came and he told to *Paroh*, and he said, my father and my
brothers and their flocks and their cattle and all which belonged to them
came from the land of *Kena'an* and look at them in the land of *Goshen*,
2 and from the far end of his brothers he took five men and he presented

---

[149] It is uncertain if the text here identifies one descendant of *Dan* named *Hhushim* (a plural name due to the "*im*" suffix) or if it refers to the descendants of *Hhush* (plural in number). Because the verse begins with "and the sons" (plural), it would appear that it refers to the descendants of *Hhush*, but the total number of children born to *Bilhah* are seven (see vs. 25) and *Hhushim* would be only one of these.

them to the face of *Paroh*, **3** and *Paroh* said to his brothers, what is your
work, and they said to *Paroh*, your servants are feeders of the flocks, us and
also our fathers, **4** and they said to *Paroh*, to immigrate in the land have we
come, given that no pastures for the flocks which belong to your servants,
given that the hunger is heavy in the land of *Kena'an* and now, please, your
servants will settle in the land of *Goshen*, **5** and *Paroh* said to *Yoseph* saying,
your father and your brothers came to you. **6** The land of *Mits'rayim* is to
your face, she is in the best of the land, your father and your brothers will
surely settle in the land of *Goshen* and if you know and there is in them men
of force then you will set them in place as nobles of livestock upon which
belong to me, **7** and *Yoseph* brought *Ya'aqov* his father and he stood him to
the face of *Paroh* and *Ya'aqov* exalted *Paroh*, **8** and *Paroh* said to *Ya'aqov*,
how many are the days of the years of your life, **9** and *Ya'aqov* said to *Paroh*,
the days of the years of my immigration are a hundred and thirty years, a
small and dysfunctional amount have the days of the years of my life existed
and they did not reach the days of the years of the life of my father in the
days of their immigrations, **10** and *Ya'aqov* exalted *Paroh* and he went out
from before the face of *Paroh*, **11** and *Yoseph* settled his father and his
brothers and he gave to them holdings in the land of *Mits'rayim*, in the best
of the land, in the land of *Ra'meses* just as *Paroh* directed, **12** and *Yoseph*
sustained his father and his brothers and all the house of his father, bread to
the mouth of the babies, **13** and bread was not in all the land, given that the
hunger was very heavy and the land of *Mits'rayim* was faint and the land of
Kena'an from the face of the hunger, **14** and *Yoseph* picked up all the silver
being found in the land of *Mits'rayim* and in the land of *Kena'an*, with the
barley which they were exchanging, and *Yoseph* brought the silver unto the
house of *Paroh*, **15** and the silver was whole from the land of *Mits'rayim* and
from the land of *Kena'an* and all *Mits'rayim* came to *Yoseph* saying, bring for
us bread, why should we die opposite you, given that the silver came to an
end, **16** and *Yoseph* said, provide your livestock and I will give to you with
your livestock if the silver came to an end, **17** and they brought their
livestock to *Yoseph* and *Yoseph* gave to them bread with the horses and with
the livestock of the field and with the donkeys and he led them with the
bread with all their livestock in that year, **18** and that year was whole and
they came to him in the second year and they said to him, we will not keep
secret from my lord that the silver has been whole and the livestock of the
beast belong to my lord, we will not remain to the face of my lord except
our body and our ground. **19** Why should we die to your eyes, us and also
our ground, purchase us and our ground with bread and we will exist, we
and our ground will be servants for *Paroh* and give seed and we will live and
we will not die and the ground will not be desolate, **20** and *Yoseph*
purchased all the ground of *Mits'rayim* for *Paroh*, given that *Mits'rayim* sold
each his field, given that the hunger seized upon them and the land existed
for *Paroh*, **21** and he made the people cross over to cities from the far end of

the border of *Mits'rayim* and until his far end. **22** Only the ground of the
administrators he did not purchase, given that the custom for the
administrators is from *Paroh*, and they ate their custom[150] that *Paroh* gave
to them, therefore they did not sell their ground, **23** and *Yoseph* said to the
people, though I purchased you today and your ground for *Paroh*, lo, to you
is seed and you will sow the ground, **24** and it will come to pass in the
production and you will give a fifth to *Paroh*, and four of the hands will exist
for you for seed of the field and for you to eat, and to who is in your house
and for your babies to eat, **25** and they said, you made us live, we will find
beauty in the eyes of my lord and we will exist as servants for *Paroh*, **26** and
Yoseph set her in place for a custom until this day concerning the ground of
Mits'rayim for *Paroh* for the fifth part, only the ground of the administrators
is for themselves and did not exist for *Paroh*, **27** and *Yisra'eyl* settled in the
land of *Mits'rayim* in the land of *Goshen*, and they were held in her and they
reproduced and they increased greatly, **28** and *Ya'aqov* existed in the land of
Mits'rayim seventeen years and the days of *Ya'aqov*, the years of his life,
existed a hundred and forty seven years, **29** and the days of *Yisra'eyl* came
near to die and he called out to his son, to *Yoseph*, and he said to him,
please, if I found beauty in your eyes, please set in place your hand under
my midsection and you will do by me kindness and truth, please, you will
not bury me in *Mits'rayim*, **30** and I will lay down with my fathers and you
will lift me up from *Mits'rayim* and you will bury me in their burial place and
he said, I will do like your word, **31** and he said, be sworn to me and he was
sworn to him and *Yisra'eyl* bent himself down upon the head of the bed,

---

Chapter 48

1 and it came to pass, after these words, and he said to *Yoseph*, look, your
father is sick and he took his two sons with him, *Menasheh* and *Ephrayim*,
2 and he told *Ya'aqov* and he said, look, your son *Yoseph* had come to you
and *Yisra'eyl* strengthened himself and he settled upon the bed, **3** and
Ya'aqov said to *Yoseph*, the mighty one of *Shaddai* appeared to me in *Luz*, in
the land of *Kena'an* and he exalted me, **4** and he said to me, here am I,
making you reproduce and I will make you increase and I will give you for an
assembled flock of peoples and I will give this land to your seed after you, a
holdings for a distant time, **5** and now, your two sons are being brought
forth to you in the land of *Mits'rayim* before I came to you unto *Mits'rayim*,
they belong to me, *Ephrayim* and *Menasheh*, like *Re'uven* and *Shimon*, they
will belong to me, **6** and your kindred which you caused to bring forth after
them belong to you, they will exist in addition to the title of their brothers,
they will be called out in their inheritance, **7** and I, I came from *Padan*,

---

[150] The Hebrew word translated as "custom," which is *hhoq* (see vs. 26), may have been miswritten for the word *hheleq* meaning a "portion" (see 31:14).

Rahhel died upon me in the land of *Kena'an*, in the road while a short land[151] coming unto *Ephrat* and I buried her there in the road of *Ephrat*, she is *Beyt-Lehhem*, **8** and *Yisra'eyl* saw the sons of *Yoseph* and he said, who are these, **9** and *Yoseph* said to his father, they are my sons which *Elohiym* gave to me here, and he said, please take them to me and I will exalt them, **10** and the eyes of *Yisra'eyl* were heavy from age and he was not able to see and he drew them near to him and he kissed them and he embraced them, **11** and *Yisra'eyl* said to *Yoseph*, not seeing your face and I pleaded and look, *Elohiym* caused me to also see your seed, **12** and *Yoseph* brought them out from by his knees and he bent himself down, his nose unto the land, **13** and *Yoseph* took the two of them, *Ephrayim* in his right hand to the left hand of *Yisra'eyl* and *Menasheh* in the left hand to the right hand of *Yisra'eyl* and he caused to draw near to him, **14** and *Yisra'eyl* sent his right hand and he set it down upon the head of *Ephrayim* and he was the little one and his left hand upon the head of *Menasheh*, he calculated his hands, given that *Menasheh* was the firstborn, **15** and he exalted *Yoseph* and he said, the face of *Elohiym* which my fathers, *Avraham* and *Yits'hhaq*, walked to, the *Elohiym* was the one feeding my whole life to this day. **16** The messenger redeeming me from all dysfunction will exalt the young men and my title was called out in them, and the title of my fathers, *Avraham* and *Yits'hhaq*, and they will amplify as an abundance inside the land, **17** and *Yoseph* saw that his father set down the hand of his right hand upon the head of *Ephrayim* and he was dysfunctional in his eyes and he upheld the hand of his father to remove her from upon the head of *Ephrayim*, upon the head of *Menasheh*, **18** and *Yoseph* said to his father, not so my father, given that this is the firstborn, set in place your right hand upon his head, **19** and his father refused and he said, I know my son, I know, he will also exist for a people and he will also magnify but, his small brother will magnify more than him and his seed will exist as a filling of the nations, **20** and he exalted them in that day saying, in you *Yisra'eyl* will exalt saying, *Elohiym* will set you in place like *Ephrayim* and like *Menasheh* and will set in place *Ephrayim* to the face of *Menasheh*, **21** and *Yisra'eyl* said to *Yoseph*, look, I am dying and *Elohiym* will exist with you and he will remove you to the land of your fathers, **22** and I gave to you one shoulder in addition to your brothers which I took from the hand of the one of *Emor*, with my sword and with my bow,

Chapter 49

1 and *Ya'aqov* called out to his sons and he said, be gathered and I will tell to you what will meet you in the end of days. **2** Be gathered together and hear, sons of *Ya'aqov*, and listen to *Yisra'eyl* your father. **3** *Re'uven*, you are my firstborn, my strength and the summit of my vigor, the remainder of

[151] The phrase "short land" means a "short distance."

elevation and the remainder of the strong. **4** Reckless like waters, you will not be reserved, given that you went up to the lying place of your father, at that time you defiled, my couch had gone up. **5** *Shimon* and *Lewi* are brothers, utensils of violence are their caves. **6** In their council you will not come, my soul is in their assembled flock, my honor will not unite, given that in their nose they killed a man and by their will they plucked up an ox. **7** Spat upon is their nose, given that their wrath was strong, given that she was hard, I will distribute them in *Ya'aqov* and I will scatter them abroad in *Yisra'eyl*. **8** *Yehudah*, your brothers will thank you, your hand is in the neck of the hostile ones, the sons of your father will bend themselves down to you. **9** A whelp of a lion is *Yehudah*, from the prey, my son, you went up, he stooped, he stretched out like a lion, like a lioness, who will make him rise. **10** The staff will not turn aside from *Yehudah* and the inscribing from between his feet until tranquility comes and to him is the obedience of the peoples. **11** Tying me up to the grapevine of his colt, and to the choice vine, my son, his she-donkey, he treaded upon in the wine his clothing and in the blood of the grapes of his coat. **12** Dull red are the eyes from wine, and white the teeth from fat. **13** *Zevulun*, to the shore of the waters he will dwell and he is for the shore of ships, his hollow is upon *Tsidon*. **14** *Yis'sas'khar* is a donkey of cartilage, stretching out between the saddlebags, **15** and he saw the place of rest, given that it was functional and the land, given that she is sweet and he will stretch his shoulder to carry and he will exist for the task work of the server. **16** *Dan* will moderate his people like one of the staffs of *Yisra'eyl*. **17** *Dan* will exist as a serpent upon the road, an adder upon the path, the one biting the heels of a horse and his rider will fall back. **18** ***YHWH***, I was bound up for your relief. **19** *Gad* is a band, he will invade us and he will invade the heel. **20** From *Asher* is oil of his bread and he will give tasty food of the king. **21** *Naphtali* is a doe sent, the giver of bright statements. **22** A son being fruitful is *Yoseph*, a son being fruitful upon the eye, daughters had marched upon the ox, **23** and the masters of the arrows were bitter of him and they increased in number and they held a grudge of him, **24** and his bow settled in consistency and they refined the arms of his hands, from the hands of the valiant of *Ya'aqov*, from there are the feeders, the stone of *Yisra'eyl*. **25** From the mighty one of your father, he will help you, and with *Shaddai* he will exalt you, presents of the skies from upon the presents of the deep water stretching out underneath, presents of the breasts and bowels. **26** Presents of your father will overcome upon the presents of my conceivers until the yearning of the knolls of a distant time, they will exist for a head of *Yoseph* and to the top of the head, dedicated of his brothers. **27** *Binyamin* is a wolf, he will tear into pieces, in the morning he will eat again and to the evening he will distribute the spoil. **28** All these staffs of *Yisra'eyl* are twelve, and this is what their father spoke to them, and he exalted them, each according to his present he exalted them, **29** and he directed them and he said to them, I am being gathered to my people, bury me to my fathers, to the cave which is in the field of *Ephron* the one of *Hhet*.

30 In the cave which is in the field of *Makhpelah* which is upon the face of
Mamre in the land of *Kena'an* which *Avraham* purchased with the field from
Ephron the one of *Hhet* for a holdings of a grave. **31** Unto there they buried
Avraham and *Sarah* his woman, unto there they buried *Yits'hhaq* and *Rivqah*
his woman and unto there I buried *Le'ah*. **32** The livestock of the field and
the cave which is in him from the sons of *Hhet*, **33** and *Ya'aqov* finished
directing his sons and he gathered his feet to the bed and he expired and he
was gathered to his people,

Chapter 50

1 and *Yoseph* fell upon the face of his father and he wept upon him and he
kissed him, **2** and *Yoseph* directed his servants, the healers, to ripen his
father and the healers ripened *Yisra'eyl*, **3** and the forty days were filled for
him, for so will the days of the ripening be filled, and *Mits'rayim* wept for
him for seventy days, **4** and the days of the time of his weeping crossed over
and *Yoseph* spoke to the house of *Paroh* saying, please, if I found beauty in
your eyes, please speak in the ears of *Paroh* saying, **5** my father made me
swear saying, look, I am dying in my grave which I dug for me in the land of
Kena'an, unto there you will bury me, and now, please, I will go up and I will
bury my father and I will turn back, **6** and *Paroh* said, go up and bury your
father just as he made you swear, **7** and *Yoseph* went up to bury his father
and all the servants of *Paroh* went up with him, the bearded ones of his
house and all the bearded ones of the land of *Mits'rayim*, **8** and all the house
of *Yoseph* and his brothers and the house of his father, only their babies and
their flocks and their cattle were left in the land of *Goshen*, **9** and the rider
also went up with him, also the horsemen, and the camps existed very
heavy, **10** and they came unto *Goren-Ha'atad* which is on the other side of
the *Yarden*, and they lamented there a great and very heavy lamenting and
he did a mourning to his father seven days, **11** and the settlers of the land of
the one of *Kena'an* saw the mourning in *Goren-Ha'atad* and they said, this is
a heavy mourning for *Mits'rayim*, therefore he called out her title *Aveyl-
Mitsrayim* which is on the other side of the *Yarden*, **12** and his sons did to
him so, just as he directed them, **13** and his sons lifted him up unto the land
of *Kena'an* and they buried him in the cave of the field of the *Makhpelah*,
the field for holdings of a grave which *Avraham* purchased, from *Ephron*, the
one of *Hhet*, upon the face of *Mamre*, **14** and *Yoseph* turned back from unto
Mits'rayim, he and his brothers and all the ones going up with him to bury
his father after he buried his father, **15** and the brothers of *Yoseph* saw that
their father died and they said, will *Yoseph* hold a grudge to us and return to
us all the dysfunction which we yielded to him, **16** and directed *Yoseph*
saying, your father had directed before his death saying, **17** in this way you
will say to *Yoseph*, please lift up the offense of your brothers and their
failure, given that they yielded you dysfunction, and now please, lift the

offense of your servants of the *Elohiym* of your father, and *Yoseph* wept in
their speaking to him, **18** and his brothers also walked and they fell to his
face and they said, look, we belong to you for servants, **19** and *Yoseph* said
to them, you will not fear, given that I am in the place of *Elohiym*, **20** and
you had thought dysfunction upon me, *Elohiym* had thought her for
function, on account of it being done like this day, to make the people live
abundantly, **21** and now, you will not fear, I will sustain you and your babies,
and he comforted them and he spoke upon their heart, **22** and *Yoseph*
settled in *Mits'rayim*, he and the house of his father and *Yoseph* lived a
hundred and ten years, **23** and *Yoseph* saw the sons of the third generation
belonging to *Ephrayim*, also the sons of *Makhir*, the son of *Menasheh*, they
were brought forth upon the knees of *Yoseph*, **24** and *Yoseph* said to his
brothers, I am dying and *Elohiym* will surely visit you, and he will bring you
up from this land to the land which he was sworn to *Avraham*, to *Yits'hhaq*
and to *Ya'aqov*, **25** and *Yoseph* caused the sons of *Yisra'eyl* to swear saying,
Elohiym will surely visit you and you will bring up my bones from this, **26** and
Yoseph died, a son of a hundred and ten years, and they ripened him and he
was set in place in the box in *Mits'rayim*,

The Book of Exodus

Chapter 1

1 and[152] these are the titles of the sons of *Yisra'eyl*, the ones coming unto
Mits'rayim with *Ya'aqov*, each and his house had come. **2** *Re'uven*, *Shimon*,
Lewi, and *Yehudah*. **3** *Yis'sas'khar*, *Zevulun*, and *Binyamin*. **4** *Dan*, and
Naphtali, *Gad* and *Asher*, **5** and it came to pass, all the souls going out of the
midsection of *Ya'aqov* were seventy[153] souls and *Yoseph* had existed in
Mits'rayim, **6** and *Yoseph* died and all his brothers and all that generation,
7 and the sons of *Yisra'eyl* had reproduced and they swarmed and they
increased and they were abundant with a great many, and the land was
filled with them, **8** and a new king rose upon *Mits'rayim* who did not know
Yoseph, **9** and he said to his people, look, the people of the sons of *Yisra'eyl*
are abundant and numerous, more than us. **10** Come, we will act skillfully
toward him, otherwise he will increase, and it will come to pass that a battle
will meet us, also in addition, our haters will wage war with us, and he will
go up from the land, **11** and they placed nobles of the task works upon him
so that he was afflicted in their burdens, and he built storehouse cities for
Paroh great house at *Pitom* and at *Ra'meses*, **12** and just as they will afflict
him, so he will increase, and so, he will break out, and they loathed the face
of the sons of *Yisra'eyl*, **13** and *Mits'rayim* made the sons of *Yisra'eyl* serve
by the whip, **14** and their lives were very bitter with the hard service, with
mortar and with bricks and with all the service in the field, all their service
which they served in them with the whip, **15** and the king of *Mits'rayim* said
to the midwives of *Ever*, of whom the title of the one is *Shiphrah* and the
title of the second is *Pu'ah*, **16** and he said with the ones of *Ever* acting as a
midwife, if you see upon the stone stool that he is a son, then you will kill
him, and if she is a daughter, then she will live, **17** and the midwives feared
the *Elohiym* and they did not do just as the king of *Mits'rayim* spoke to
them, and they kept alive the boys, **18** and the king of *Mits'rayim* called out
to the midwives and he said to them, why did you do this matter and kept
alive the boys, **19** and the midwives said to *Paroh*, because the women of
Mits'rayim are not like the ones of *Ever*, because they are lively before the
midwife comes to them, and they bring forth, **20** and *Elohiym* made it go
well for the midwives and the people increased and they became greatly
abundant, **21** and it came to pass that the midwives feared the *Elohiym* and
he made houses for them, **22** and *Paroh* directed all his people saying, you

---

152 The first verse of the book of Exodus begins with "and," indicating that this is a continuation of the final verse of Genesis.

153 The *Septuagint* and the Dead Sea Scrolls have 75.

will throw all the birthed sons out unto the stream and you must keep alive all the daughters,

Chapter 2

1 and a man from the house of *Lewi* walked and he took a daughter of *Lewi*, **2** and the woman conceived and she brought forth a son and she saw that he was functional and she concealed him for three moons, **3** and she was not able to continue to make him concealed and she took for him a vessel of bulrush and she pasted it with the slime and with the pitch and she placed the boy in her and she placed it in the reeds upon the lip of the stream, **4** and his sister stationed herself at a distance to know what will be done to him, **5** and the daughter of *Paroh* went down to bathe upon the stream, and her young women were walking upon the hand[154] of the stream, and she saw the vessel in the midst of the reeds and she sent her bondwoman, and she took her, **6** and she opened it and she saw the boy, and look, a young man was weeping and she showed pity upon him, and she said, this is from the boys of the ones of *Ever*, **7** and his sister said to the daughter of *Paroh*, should I walk and should I call out for you a woman, a nurse from the ones of *Ever*, and should she nurse the boy for you, **8** and the daughter of *Paroh* said to her, walk, and the young maiden walked and she called out to the mother of the boy, **9** and the daughter of *Paroh* said to her, take this boy and nurse him for me and I will give your wage, and the woman took the boy and she nursed him, **10** and the boy magnified, and she brought him to the daughter of *Paroh*, and he existed to her for a son, and she called out his title *Mosheh*, and she said, given that from the waters I plucked him out, **11** and it came to pass in those days that *Mosheh* magnified, and he went out to his brothers and he saw them with their burdens, and he saw a man of *Mits'rayim* attacking a man of *Ever*, one from his brothers, **12** and he turned this way and that way, and he saw that there was no man, and he attack the one of *Mits'rayim* and he submerged him in the sand, **13** and he went out in the second day, and look, two men of *Ever* were struggling, and he said to the lost one, why would you attack your companion, **14** and he said, who placed you as a noble man and decider[155] over us, are you saying you will kill me just as you killed the one of *Mits'rayim*, and *Mosheh* feared, and he said, surely the matter is known, **15** and *Paroh* heard of this matter, and he searched out to kill *Mosheh*, and *Mosheh* fled away from the face of *Paroh*, and he settled in the land of *Mid'yan* and he settled upon the well, **16** and to the administrator of *Mid'yan* were seven daughters, and they came and they drew up and they filled the troughs to make the flocks of

---

[154] The word "hand" may be in error and may have originally been "lip," meaning "edge."
[155] That is, a "judge," as one who decides.

their father drink, **17** and the feeders[156] came and they cast them out, and
Mosheh rose and he rescued them and he made their flocks drink, **18** and
they came to *Re'u'eyl* their father, and he said, why did you hurry to come
today, **19** and they said, a man of *Mits'rayim* had delivered us from the hand
of the feeders, and also, he surely drew it up for us and he made the flocks
drink, **20** and he said to his daughters, and where is he, for what reason did
you leave the man, call out to him and he will eat bread, **21** and *Mosheh*
agreed to settle with the man, and he gave *Tsiporah*, his daughter, to
Mosheh, **22** and she brought forth a son, and he called out his title *Gershom*,
given that he said, I existed as an immigrant in a foreign land, **23** and it came
to pass in those abundance of days, and the king of *Mits'rayim* died, and the
sons of *Yisra'eyl* sighed from the service and they yelled out, and their
outcry went up to the *Elohiym* from the service, **24** and *Elohiym* heard their
groaning, and *Elohiym* remembered his covenant with *Avraham* with
Yits'hhaq and with *Ya'aqov*, **25** and *Elohiym* saw the sons of *Yisra'eyl* and
Elohiym knew,

Chapter 3

1 and *Mosheh* had been feeding the flocks of *Yitro*, his in-law, the
administrator of *Mid'yan*, and he drove the flocks behind the wilderness and
he came to the hill of the *Elohiym*, unto *Hhorev*, **2** and the messenger of
YHWH appeared to him in a glimmering of fire from the midst of the thorn
bush, and he saw, and look, the thorn bush was burning with the fire and
the thorn bush was not eaten, **3** and *Mosheh* said, please, let me turn aside
and I will see this great appearance, why the thorn bush will not burn, **4** and
YHWH saw that he turned aside to see, and *Elohiym* called out to him from
the midst of the thorn bush, and he said, *Mosheh*, *Mosheh*, and he said,
here I am, **5** and he said, do not come near to this point, cast off your
sandals from upon your feet, given that the area which you are standing
upon is the ground of a special place, **6** and he said, I am *Elohiym* of your
father, *Elohiym* of *Avraham*, *Elohiym* of *Yits'hhaq* and *Elohiym* of *Ya'aqov*,
and *Mosheh* hid his face, given that he feared from staring toward the
Elohiym, **7** and ***YHWH*** said, I surely saw the affliction of my people who are
in *Mits'rayim*, and I heard their cry from the faces of his pushers, given that I
know his miseries, **8** and I will go down to deliver him from the hand of
Mits'rayim, and to make him go up from that land to a functional and wide
land, to a land issuing fat[157] and honey[158], to the area of the one of *Kena'an*
and the one of *Hhet* and the one of *Emor* and the one of *Perez* and the one

---

[156] That is, "shepherds." (also in verse 19)
[157] This Hebrew word can also mean "milk."
[158] The Hebrew word דבש means a "sticky mass" and can also mean "dates" from the palm tree.

of *Hhiw* and the one of *Yevus*, **9** and now look, the cry of the sons of *Yisra'eyl* had come to me, and also, I saw the squeezing because *Mits'rayim* is squeezing them, **10** and now walk, and I will send you to *Paroh*, and make my people, the sons of *Yisra'eyl*, go out from *Mits'rayim*, **11** and *Mosheh* said to the *Elohiym*, who am I that I should walk to *Paroh* and that I will make the sons of *Yisra'eyl*, go out from *Mits'rayim*, **12** and he said, given that I will exist with you, and this is the sign for you that I had sent you, in your making the people go out from *Mits'rayim*, you must serve the *Elohiym* upon this hill, **13** and *Mosheh* said to the *Elohiym*, look, I am coming to the sons of *Yisra'eyl* and I will say to them, *Elohiym* of your fathers had sent me to you, and they will say to me, what is his title, what will I say to them, **14** and *Elohiym* said to *Mosheh*, I will exist which I will exist, and he said, in this way you will say to the sons of *Yisra'eyl*, *Ehyeh* had sent me to you, **15** and *Elohiym* said yet again to *Mosheh*, in this way you will say to the sons of *Yisra'eyl*, ***YHWH*** the *Elohiym* of your fathers, *Elohiym* of *Avraham*, *Elohiym* of *Yits'hhaq* and *Elohiym* of *Ya'aqov* had sent me to you, this is my title for a distant time and this is my memorial for a generation and a generation[159]. **16** Walk, and you will gather the bearded ones of *Yisra'eyl*, and you will say to them, ***YHWH*** the *Elohiym* of your fathers had appeared to me, *Elohiym* of *Avraham*, *Yits'hhaq* and *Ya'aqov*, saying, I surely registered you and what was done to you in *Mits'rayim*, **17** and I said, I will make you go up from the affliction of *Mits'rayim*, to the land of the one of *Kena'an* and the one of *Hhet* and the one of *Emor* and the one of *Perez* and the one of *Hhiw* and the one of *Yevus*, to a land issuing fat[160] and honey[161], **18** and they listened to your voice, and you will come, you and the bearded ones of *Yisra'eyl*, to the king of *Mits'rayim* and you will say to him, ***YHWH*** the *Elohiym* of the ones of *Ever* had met with us, and now, please, we will walk the road for three days in the wilderness and we will sacrifice to ***YHWH*** our *Elohiym*, **19** and I had known that the king of *Mits'rayim* will not allow you to walk without a forceful hand, **20** and I will send my hand and I will attack *Mits'rayim* with all my performances which I will do inside him, and afterward he will send you, **21** and I will place the beauty[162] of this people in the eyes[163] of *Mits'rayim*, and it will come to pass, when you must walk, you will not walk empty, **22** and a woman will inquire from her dweller, and from the immigrant of her house, utensils of silver, and utensils of gold, and apparels, and you will place them upon your sons and upon your daughters, and you will deliver *Mits'rayim*,

---

[159] "For a generation and a generation" is an idiom meaning "throughout the generations," or "for all time."

[160] This Hebrew word can also mean "milk."

[161] The Hebrew word דבש means a "sticky mass" and can also mean "dates" from the palm tree.

[162] "Place the beauty" means to "make accepted."

[163] "In the eyes of" is an idiom meaning "in the sight of."

Chapter 4

1 and *Mosheh* answered and he said, but they will not support me, and they
will not hear my voice, given that they will say, ***YHWH*** did not appear to you,
2 and ***YHWH*** said to him, what is this in your hand, and he said, a branch,
3 and he said, throw him out unto the land, and he threw him out unto the
land, and he existed as a serpent, and *Mosheh* fled from his face, **4** and
YHWH said to *Mosheh*, send your hand and take hold by his tail, and he sent
his hand and he seized him, and he existed as a branch in his palm. **5** So that
they will support, given that ***YHWH*** the *Elohiym* of their fathers appeared to
you, *Elohiym* of *Avraham*, *Elohiym* of *Yits'hhaq* and *Elohiym* of *Ya'aqov*,
6 and ***YHWH*** said to him yet again, please bring your hand in your bosom,
and he brought his hand in his bosom, and he made her go out, and look, his
hand was being infected like the snow, **7** and he said, make your hand turn
back to your bosom, and he made his hand turn back to his bosom, and he
made her go out from his bosom, and look, she turned back like his flesh,
8 and it will come to pass, if they will not support you, and they will not
listen to the voice[164] of the first sign and they will not support the voice of
the last sign, **9** and it will come to pass, if they will not support both of these
two signs, and they will not listen to your voice, then you will take from the
waters of the stream and you will pour it out to the dry ground, and the
waters, which you took from the stream, will exist, and they will exist as
blood in the dry land, **10** and *Mosheh* said to ***YHWH***, excuse me *Adonai*, I am
not a man of words, since previously, since that time you spoke to your
servant, given that I have a heavy mouth and heavy tongue, **11** and ***YHWH***
said to him, who placed the mouth of the human, or who placed the mute
or the silent or the seeing or the blind, is it not I, ***YHWH***, **12** and now walk,
and I will exist with your mouth, and I will teach you what you will speak,
13 and he said, excuse me *Adonai*, please send, by the hand you will send[165],
14 and ***YHWH*** flared up the nose with *Mosheh* and he said, is not *Aharon*
your brother, the one of *Lewi*, I know that he will surely speak well, also
look, he is going out to meet you and he will see you and he will rejoice in
his heart, **15** and you will speak to him, and you will place the words in his
mouth, and I will exist with your mouth and with his mouth, and I will teach
you what you must do, **16** and he will speak for you to the people, and it will
come to pass, he will exist for you as a mouth, and you, you will exist for him
as *Elohiym*, **17** and this branch, you will take in your hand, which is what you
will do the signs with, **18** and *Mosheh* walked and he turned back to *Yeter*[166],

---

[164] In context, the phrase "listen to the voice" means "heed the message."

[165] The Hebrew text appears to be missing text. The *Septuagint*, which may preserve the original wording, reads, "please send another by the hand that you can send."

[166] *Mosheh*'s father-in-law is called יתרו (*yitro*) later in this verse and in every other occurrence of his name. But here he is identified as יתר (*yeter*).

his in-law, and he said to him, please, I will walk and I will turn back to my
brothers who are in *Mits'rayim*, and I will see, are they still living, and *Yitro*
said to *Mosheh*, walk to completeness, **19** and ***YHWH*** said to *Mosheh* in
Mid'yan, walk, turn back unto *Mits'rayim*, given that all the men died, the
ones searching out your soul, **20** and *Mosheh* took his woman and his sons,
and he made them ride upon the donkey, and he turned back unto the land
of *Mits'rayim*, and *Mosheh* took the branch of the *Elohiym* in his hand,
21 and ***YHWH*** said to *Mosheh*, in your walking to turn back unto *Mits'rayim*,
see all the wonders which I placed in your hand, and you will do them to the
face of *Paroh*, and I will strengthen his heart and he will not send the
people, **22** and you will say to *Paroh* in this way, ***YHWH*** said, my firstborn
son is *Yisra'eyl*, **23** and I say to you, send my son and he will serve me, and
you refused to send him, look, I am killing your firstborn son, **24** and it came
to pass, in the road, in the place of lodging, and ***YHWH*** encountered him[167]
and he searched out to kill him, **25** and *Tsiporah* took a sharp stone and she
cut the foreskin of her son, and she touched it to his feet, and she said, given
that you are an in-law of bloodshed to me, **26** and he sunk down from him,
at that time she said, an in-law of bloodshed for the circumcisions, **27** and
YHWH said to *Aharon*, walk unto the wilderness to meet *Mosheh*, and he
walked and he encountered him in the hill of the *Elohiym*, and he kissed
him, **28** and *Mosheh* told *Aharon* all the words of ***YHWH*** which he sent him
and all the signs which he directed him, **29** and *Mosheh* walked, and *Aharon*,
and they gathered all the bearded ones of the sons of *Yisra'eyl*, **30** and
Aharon spoke all the words which ***YHWH*** spoke to *Mosheh*, and he did the
signs to the eyes of the people, **31** and the people supported, and they
heard that ***YHWH*** registered the sons of *Yisra'eyl*, and, given that he saw
their affliction, and they bowed the head and they bent themselves down,

---

Chapter 5

1 and afterward, *Mosheh* and *Aharon* came, and they said to *Paroh*, in this
way, ***YHWH*** the *Elohiym* of *Yisra'eyl* said, send my people and they will hold
a feast to me in the wilderness, **2** and *Paroh* said, who is ***YHWH*** that I should
listen to his voice to send *Yisra'eyl*, I do not know ***YHWH***, and also, I will not
send *Yisra'eyl*, **3** and they said, *Elohiym* of the ones of *Ever* has met with us,
please, we will walk the road for three days in the wilderness, and we will
sacrifice to ***YHWH*** our *Elohiym*, otherwise, he will reach us with the
epidemic or with the sword, **4** and the king of *Mits'rayim* said to them, why
will you, *Mosheh* and *Aharon*, loose the people from his work, walk to your
burdens, **5** and *Paroh* said, though the people of the land are now abundant,
will you make them cease from their burdens, **6** and in that day, *Paroh*
directed the pushers over the people and his officers, saying, **7** you must not

---

[167] The "him" may be *Mosheh*, but may also be his son (see 4:25).

again give straw to the people to make bricks like the bricks previously, they will walk and they, they will collect straw for themselves, **8** and the sum of the bricks which they were doing previously, you will place upon them, you will not take away from him, given that they are lazy, therefore they are crying out saying, we will walk, we will sacrifice to our *Elohiym*. **9** The service will be heavy upon the men and they will do with her, and they will not do words of falseness, **10** and the pushers of the people, and his officers, went out and they said to the people saying, in this way *Paroh* said, I am not giving straw to you. **11** You, walk, take straw for yourself from which you will find, given that not a thing will be taken away from your service, **12** and the people scattered abroad in all the land of *Mits'rayim* to collect stubble for straw, **13** and the pushers were compelling, saying, finish your work, it is a word of the day in his day[168], just as with the existence of the straw, **14** and the officers of the sons of *Yisra'eyl*, which the pushers of *Paroh* placed upon them, were attacked, saying, why did you not finish your custom to make bricks, both yesterday and today like previously, **15** and the officers of the sons of *Yisra'eyl* came and they cried out to *Paroh* saying, why will you do this to your servants in this way. **16** No straw is being given to your servants, and they are saying to us, make bricks, and look, your servants are being attacked, and it is a failure of your people, **17** and he said, you are very lazy, therefore you are saying, we will walk, we will sacrifice to ***YHWH***, **18** and now, walk, serve, and straw will not be given to you, and you will give the measured amount of bricks, **19** and the officers of the sons of *Yisra'eyl* saw them in dysfunction, saying, you will not take away from your bricks, it is a word of the day in his day, **20** and they reached *Mosheh* and *Aharon* standing to meet them in their going out from *Paroh*, **21** and they said to them, ***YHWH*** will look upon you, and he will decide, because you made our aroma stink in the eyes of *Paroh* and in the eyes of his servants, to give a sword in their hand to kill us, **22** and *Mosheh* turned back to ***YHWH*** and he said, *Adonai*, why did you make it dysfunctional for this people, what is the reason you sent me, **23** and from that time, I came to *Paroh* to speak in your title, he made it dysfunctional to this people and you never delivered your people,

Chapter 6

1 and ***YHWH*** said to *Mosheh*, now you will see what I will do to *Paroh*, given that with a forceful hand he will send them, and with a forceful hand he will cast them out from his land, **2** and *Elohiym* spoke to *Mosheh* and he said to him, I am ***YHWH***, **3** and I appeared to *Avraham*, to *Yits'hhaq*, and to *Ya'aqov* with the mighty one of *Shaddai*, and my title is ***YHWH***, I was not known to

168 "Word of the day in his day" is an idiom meaning a "daily matter." (also in verse 19)

them,[169] **4** and also, I made my covenant rise with them, to give to them the
land of *Kena'an*, the land of their immigration which they immigrated in,
5 and also, I had heard the groaning of the sons of *Yisra'eyl*, because
Mits'rayim was making them serve, and I remembered my covenant.
6 Because of this, say to the sons of *Yisra'eyl*, I am ***YHWH***, and I will make
you go out from under the burdens of *Mits'rayim*, and I will deliver you from
their service, and I will redeem you with an extended arm, and with great
judgments, **7** and I will take you for me for a people, and I will exist for you
for *Elohiym*, and you will know that I am ***YHWH*** your *Elohiym*, the one
making you go out from under the burdens of *Mits'rayim*, **8** and I will bring
you to the land which I lifted up with my hand to give to *Avraham*, to
Yits'hhaq, and to *Ya'aqov*, and I gave her to you for a possession, I am
YHWH, **9** and *Mosheh* spoke to the sons of *Yisra'eyl*, and they did not listen
to *Mosheh* from the shortness of wind[170] and from the hard service, **10** and
YHWH spoke to *Mosheh* saying, **11** come, speak to *Paroh*, king of *Mits'rayim*,
and he will send the sons of *Yisra'eyl* from his land, **12** and *Mosheh* spoke to
the face of ***YHWH*** saying, since the sons of *Yisra'eyl* had not listened to me,
then how will *Paroh* hear me and I am of uncircumcised lips, **13** and ***YHWH***
spoke to *Mosheh* and to *Aharon*, and he directed them to the sons of
Yisra'eyl and to *Paroh*, king of *Mits'rayim*, to make the sons of *Yisra'eyl* go
out from the land of *Mits'rayim*. **14** These are the heads of the house of
their fathers, the sons of *Re'uven*, firstborn of *Yisra'eyl*, *Hhanokh* and *Palu*,
Hhetsron and *Karmi*, these are the families of *Re'uven*, **15** and the sons of
Shimon, *Yemu'el* and *Yamin* and *Ohad* and *Yakhin* and *Tsohhar* and *Sha'ul*, a
son of the ones of *Kena'an*, these are the families of *Shimon*, **16** and these
are the titles of the sons of *Lewi*, to their birthings, *Gershon* and *Qehat* and
Merari, and the years of the life of *Lewi* is seven and thirty and a hundred
years. **17** The sons of *Gershon*, *Liyvniy* and *Shiymiy*, to their families, **18** and
the sons of *Qehat*, *Amram* and Yits'har and *Hhevron* and *Uziy'eyl*, and the
years of the life of *Qehat* is three and thirty and a hundred years, **19** and the
sons of *Merari*, *Mahh'liy* and *Mushiy*, these are the families of the *Lewi* to
their birthings, **20** and *Amram* took *Yokheved*, his aunt, for him for a woman,
and she brought forth for him, *Aharon* and *Mosheh*, and the years of the life
of *Amram* is seven and thirty and a hundred years, **21** and the sons of
Yits'har, *Qorahh* and *Nepheg* and *Zikh'riy*, **22** and the sons of *Uziy'eyl*,
Miysha'eyl and *El'tsaphan* and *Sitriy*, **23** and *Aharon* took *Eliysheva*,
daughter of *Amiynadav*, sister of *Nahhshon*, for him for a woman, and she
brought forth for him *Nadav* and *Aviyhu*, *Elazar* and *Iytamar*, **24** and the
sons of *Qorahh*, *Asiyr* and *Elqanah* and *Aviyasaph*, these are the families of
the one of *Qorahh*, **25** and *Elazar*, son of *Aharon*, had taken for him from the

---

[169] Compare this verse with Genesis 17:1, but also see Genesis 15:7 and 28:13.

[170] The phrase "shortness of wind," being paralleled with "hard service," means "shortness of breath."

daughters of *Putiy'eyl*, for him for a woman, and she brought forth for him *Piynhhas*, these are the heads of the fathers of the ones of *Lewi* to their families. **26** This is what ***YHWH*** said to *Aharon* and *Mosheh*, make the sons of *Yisra'eyl* go out from the land of *Mits'rayim* upon their armies. **27** They, the ones speaking to *Paroh*, king of *Mits'rayim*, are to make the sons of *Yisra'eyl* go out from *Mits'rayim*, this is *Mosheh* and *Aharon*, **28** and it came to pass, in the day ***YHWH*** spoke to *Mosheh* in the land of *Mits'rayim*, **29** and ***YHWH*** spoke to *Mosheh* saying, I am ***YHWH***, speak to *Paroh*, king of *Mits'rayim*, all which I am speaking to you, **30** and *Mosheh* said to the face of ***YHWH***, since I am of uncircumcised lips, then how will *Paroh* listen to me,

Chapter 7

1 and ***YHWH*** said to *Mosheh*, see, I made you *Elohiym* for *Paroh*, and *Aharon*, your brother, he exists as your announcer. **2** You, you will speak all which I will direct you, and *Aharon*, your brother, will speak to *Paroh* and he will send the sons of *Yisra'eyl* from his land, **3** and I will make the heart of *Paroh* be hard, and I will make my signs and my wonders increase in the land of *Mits'rayim*, **4** and *Paroh* will not listen to you, and I will give my hand in *Mits'rayim*, and I will make my armies, my people, the sons of *Yisra'eyl*, go out from the land of *Mits'rayim* with great judgments, **5** and *Mits'rayim* will know that I am ***YHWH*** with my extending of my hand upon *Mits'rayim*, and I will make the sons of *Yisra'eyl* go out from the midst of them, **6** and *Mosheh* did, and *Aharon*, just as ***YHWH*** directed them, so they did, **7** and *Mosheh* was a son[171] of eighty years and *Aharon* was a son of three and eighty years in their speaking to *Paroh*, **8** and ***YHWH*** said to *Mosheh* and to *Aharon* saying, **9** given that *Paroh* will speak to you saying, give for you a wonder, and you will say to *Aharon*, take your branch and throw it out to the face of *Paroh*, he will exist as a crocodile[172], **10** and *Mosheh* came, and *Aharon*, to *Paroh*, and they did so, just as ***YHWH*** directed, and *Aharon* threw out his branch to the face of *Paroh* and to the face of his servants, and he existed as a crocodile[173], **11** and *Paroh* also called out to the skilled ones and to the

[171] "Son" is an idiom for the age of a person.

[172] This Hebrew word is translated in various ways, including; whale, sea-monster, dragon, serpent, asp and jackal (see Exodus 7:9, Deuteronomy 32:33, Nehemiah 2:13, Job 7:12). According to these texts, this is a very large creature that lives on the land and in the water, which is characteristic of the crocodile.

[173] This Hebrew word is translated in various ways, including; whale, sea-monster, dragon, serpent, asp and jackal (see Exodus 7:9, Deuteronomy 32:33, Nehemiah 2:13, Job 7:12). According to these texts this is a very large creature and lives on the land and in the water, which are characteristics of the crocodile.

sorcerers, and they, the magicians of *Mits'rayim,* also did so with their blazings[174], **12** and each threw out his branch and they existed as crocodiles[175], and the branch of *Aharon* swallowed their branches, **13** and he seized the heart of *Paroh*[176] and he did not listen to them, just as ***YHWH*** spoke, **14** and ***YHWH*** said to *Mosheh,* heavy is the heart of *Paroh,* he refuses to send the people. **15** Walk to *Paroh* in the morning, look, he is going out unto the waters, and you will be standing up to meet him upon the lip of the stream, and the branch, which was overturned to a serpent, you will take in your hand, **16** and you will say to him, ***YHWH*** the *Elohiym* of the ones of *Ever* sent me to you saying, send my people and they will serve me in the wilderness, and look, you still did not hear. **17** In this way, ***YHWH*** said, in this you will know that I am ***YHWH***, look, I am attacking, with the branch which is in my hand, upon the waters which are in the stream, and they will be overturned to blood, **18** and the fish, which are in the stream, will die and the stream will stink, and *Mits'rayim* will be too weary to gulp waters from the stream, **19** and ***YHWH*** said to *Mosheh,* say to *Aharon,* take your branch and extend your hand upon the waters of *Mits'rayim,* upon their rivers, upon their streams, and upon their pools and upon all the collections of their waters, and they will exist as blood, and blood will exist in all the land of *Mits'rayim* and in the wood and in the stones[177], **20** and *Mosheh* and *Aharon* did just as ***YHWH*** directed, and he rose with the branch, and he attacked the waters, which were in the stream, to the eyes of *Paroh* and to the eyes of his servants, and all the waters which were in the stream were overturned to blood, **21** and the fish which were in the stream died and the stream stank, and *Mits'rayim* was not able to gulp waters from the stream, and the blood existed in all the land of *Mits'rayim,* **22** and the magicians of *Mits'rayim* did so with their secrets, and he seized the heart of *Paroh*[178] and he did not listen to them just as ***YHWH*** spoke, **23** and *Paroh* turned and he came to his house and he also did not set his heart down by this, **24** and all

---

[174] The word "blazing" is the same word used for the sword of the *Keruv* (cherub in most other translations) in Genesis 3:24, but the meaning of its use in this verse is obscure.

[175] This Hebrew word is translated in various ways, including; whale, sea-monster, dragon, serpent, asp and jackal (see Exodus 7:9, Deuteronomy 32:33, Nehemiah 2:13, Job 7:12). According to these texts this is a very large creature and lives on the land and in the water, which are characteristics of the crocodile.

[176] The phrase וַיֶּחֱזַק לֵב פַּרְעֹה may be translated as "and he seized the heart of *Paroh*" or "and the heart seized *Paroh*," but compare with Exodus 4:21 and 9:12.

[177] Probably referring to containers made of wood and stone.

[178] The phrase וַיֶּחֱזַק לֵב פַּרְעֹה may be translated as "and he seized the heart of *Paroh*" or "and the heart seized *Paroh*." Compare this phrase with Exodus 4:21 and 9:12.

of *Mits'rayim* dug out all around the stream of waters to gulp, given that
they were not able to gulp from the waters of the stream, **25** and seven days
were filled after ***YHWH*** attacked the stream, **26 (8:1)** and ***YHWH*** said to
Mosheh, come to *Paroh* and you will say to him in this way, ***YHWH*** said,
send my people and they will serve me,[179] **27 (8:2)** and if you are refusing to
send them, look, I am smiting all your borders with the frogs, **28 (8:3)** and
the stream will swarm with frogs, and they will go up, and they will come in
your house, and in the chamber of your lying place, and upon your bed, and
in the house of your servants, and in your people, and in your ovens, and in
your kneading bowls, **29 (8:4)** and in you, and in your people, and in all your
servants the frogs will go up,

Chapter 8

1 (8:5) and ***YHWH*** said to *Mosheh*, say to *Aharon*, extend your hand, with
your branch, upon the rivers, upon the streams and upon the pools, and
make the frogs upon the land of *Mits'rayim* go up, **2 (8:6)** and *Aharon*
extended his hand upon the waters of *Mits'rayim*, and the frogs went up
and covered over the land of *Mits'rayim*, **3 (8:7)** and the magicians did so
with their secrets, and frogs went up upon the land of *Mits'rayim*, **4**
(8:8) and *Paroh* called out to *Mosheh* and to *Aharon* and he said, intercede
to ***YHWH*** and he will make the frogs turn aside from me and from my
people, and I will send the people and they will sacrifice to ***YHWH***, **5**
(8:9) and *Mosheh* said to *Paroh*, decorate yourself upon me for how long I
will intercede for you and for your servants and for your people, to make the
frogs cut from you and from your houses, only in the streams will they
remain,[180] **6 (8:10)** and he said, tomorrow, and he said, it will be like your
word so that you will know that there is none like ***YHWH*** our *Elohiym*, **7**
(8:11) and the frogs will turn aside from you and from your houses and from
your servants and from your people, only in the stream will they remain, **8**
(8:12) and *Mosheh* went out, and *Aharon*, away from *Paroh*, and *Mosheh*
cried out to ***YHWH*** because of the word[181] of the frogs which he placed for
Paroh, **9 (8:13)** and ***YHWH*** did just like the word of *Mosheh*, and the frogs
died, from the houses, from the courtyards, and from the fields, **10**
(8:14) and they piled them up as much slime, and the land stank, **11**
(8:15) and *Paroh* saw that the respite existed, and his heart was made
heavy, and he did not listen to them just as ***YHWH*** spoke, **12 (8:16)** and
YHWH said to *Mosheh*, say to *Aharon*, extend your branch and attack the

---

[179] This verse is the first verse of chapter 8 in Christian Bibles. For the remainder of chapter 7 and all of chapter 8, the verse numbers in Christian Bibles will be four numbers higher than Hebrew and Bibles.

[180] The meaning of the phrase "decorate yourself upon me" is uncertain.

[181] This Hebrew word can also mean "matter."

dirt of the land and he will exist as gnats in all the land of *Mits'rayim*, **13 (8:17)** and they did so, and *Aharon* extended his hand, with his branch, and he attacked the dirt of the land and the gnats existed on the human and on the beast, all the dirt of the land had existed as gnats in all the land of *Mits'rayim*, **14 (8:18)** and the magicians did so with their secrets, to make the gnats go out, and they were not able, and the gnats existed on the human and on the beast, **15 (8:19)** and the magicians said to *Paroh*, this is the finger of *Elohiym*, and he seized the heart of *Paroh*[182] and he did not listen to them, just as ***YHWH*** spoke, **16 (8:20)** and ***YHWH*** said to *Mosheh*, depart early in the morning and stand yourself up to the face of *Paroh*, look, he is going out unto the waters, and you will say to him in this way, ***YHWH*** said, send my people and they will serve me. **17 (8:21)** Instead you are not sending my people, look at me, I am sending the horde on you and on your servants and on your people and in your houses, and the houses of *Mits'rayim* will be filled with the horde, and also the ground which they are upon, **18 (8:22)** and I will make the land of *Goshen*, which my people are standing upon, be distinct in this day, by not letting the horde exist there, so that you will know that I am ***YHWH*** inside the land, **19 (8:23)** and I will place a ransom between my people and your people, tomorrow this sign will exist, **20 (8:24)** and ***YHWH*** did so, and the horde came heavy unto the house of *Paroh* and the house of his servants and in all the land of *Mits'rayim*, the land was damaged from the face of the horde, **21 (8:25)** and *Paroh* called out to *Mosheh* and to *Aharon*, and he said, walk, sacrifice to your *Elohiym* in the land, **22 (8:26)** and *Mosheh* said, it is not being prepared to do so, given that we will sacrifice to ***YHWH*** our *Elohiym* it is a disgusting thing to *Mits'rayim*, since we sacrifice a disgusting thing to *Mits'rayim* to their eyes, then will they not stone us. **23 (8:27)** We will walk the road for three days in the wilderness, and we will sacrifice to ***YHWH*** our *Elohiym*, just as he said to us, **24 (8:28)** and *Paroh* said, I will send you and you will sacrifice to ***YHWH*** your *Elohiym* in the wilderness, only you will not walk very far, intercede on my behalf, **25 (8:29)** and *Mosheh* said, look, I am going out away from you, and I will intercede to ***YHWH***, and he will turn aside the horde from *Paroh*, from his servants, and from his people tomorrow, only do not let *Paroh* again deal deceitfully, by not sending the people to sacrifice to ***YHWH***, **26 (8:30)** and *Mosheh* went out away from *Paroh* and he interceded to ***YHWH***, **27 (8:31)** and ***YHWH*** did just like the word of *Mosheh*, and he made the horde turn aside from *Paroh*, from his servants, and from his people, not one was remaining, **28 (8:32)** and *Paroh* made his heart heavy, also in this footstep[183], and he did not send the people,

---

[182] The phrase וַיֶּחֱזַק לֵב פַּרְעֹה may be translated as "and he seized the heart of *Paroh*" or "and the heart seized *Paroh*." Compare this phrase with Exodus 4:21 and 9:12.

[183] The phrase "also in this footstep" means "also at this time."

Chapter 9

1 and ***YHWH*** said to *Mosheh*, come to *Paroh* and you will speak to him in this way, ***YHWH*** the *Elohiym* of the ones of *Ever* said, send my people and they will serve me. **2** Instead you are refusing to send them, and you continue seizing them. **3** Look, the hand of ***YHWH*** is existing in your livestock, which are in the field, in the horses, in the donkeys, in the camels, in the cattle, and in the flocks, it is a very heavy epidemic, **4** and ***YHWH*** will make a distinction between the livestock of *Yisra'eyl* and the livestock of *Mits'rayim*, and not a thing will die from among the sons of *Yisra'eyl*, **5** and ***YHWH*** placed an appointed time saying, tomorrow ***YHWH*** will do this matter in the land, **6** and ***YHWH*** did this matter the next day, and all the livestock of *Mits'rayim* died, and from the livestock of the sons of *Yisra'eyl* not one died, **7** and *Paroh* sent, and look, not a single one died from the livestock of *Yisra'eyl*, and the heart of *Paroh* was heavy, and he did not send the people, **8** and ***YHWH*** said to *Mosheh* and to *Aharon*, take for you the soot of the furnace, filling your cupped hands, and *Mosheh* will sprinkle him unto the skies to the eyes of[184] *Paroh*, **9** and he will exist as dust upon all the land of *Mits'rayim*, and he will exist upon the human and upon the beast as boils, bursting out pustules in all the land of *Mits'rayim*, **10** and they took the soot of the furnace and they stood to the face of *Paroh*, and *Mosheh* sprinkled him unto the skies and boils existed, pustules bursting out on the human and on the beast, **11** and the magicians were not able to stand to the face of *Mosheh* because of the face of the boils, given that the boils existed on the magicians and on all *Mits'rayim*, **12** and ***YHWH*** strengthened the heart of *Paroh* and he did not listen to them, just as ***YHWH*** spoke to *Mosheh*, **13** and ***YHWH*** said to *Mosheh*, depart early in the morning and stand yourself up to the face of *Paroh* and you will say to him in this way, ***YHWH*** the *Elohiym* of the ones of *Ever* said, send my people and they will serve me, **14** given that in this footstep[185], I am sending all my pestilences to your heart and in your servants and in your people, in order that you will know that there is not one like me in all the land, **15** given that now I sent my hand, and I attack you and your people with the epidemic, and you will be kept secret from the land, **16** but, on account of this, I made you stand, with the intention to show you my strength, and so that there will be a recounting of my title in all the land. **17** Yet again, you are building yourself up with my people, by not sending them. **18** Look at me, about this time tomorrow, will be a precipitating of very heavy hailstones, which had not existed like this in *Mits'rayim*, before the day she was founded and until now, **19** and now, send, seek refuge with your livestock and with all which belongs to you in the field, all the humans and the beasts which will be found in the field, and those not gathered unto the house, then the

[184] "To the eyes of" is an idiom meaning "in the sight of."
[185] The phrase "in this footstep" means "at this time."

hailstones will go down upon them and they will die. **20** The one fearing the
word of ***YHWH*** from the servants of *Paroh*, he will make his servants and his
livestock flee to the houses, **21** and who does not set his heart in place to
the word of ***YHWH***, then he will leave his servants and his livestock in the
field, **22** and ***YHWH*** said to *Mosheh*, extend your hand upon the skies and
hailstones will exist in all the land of *Mits'rayim*, upon the human and upon
the beast and upon all the herbs of the field in the land of *Mits'rayim*,
23 and *Mosheh* extended his branch upon the skies, and ***YHWH*** had given
thunder and hailstones, and fire walked unto the land, and ***YHWH*** made it
precipitate hailstones upon the land of *Mits'rayim*, **24** and hailstones
existed, and fire was taking itself in the midst of the very heavy hailstones,
which had not existed like this in all the land of *Mits'rayim*, from the time
she existed as a nation, **25** and the hailstones attacked in all the land of
Mits'rayim, all which were in the field, from the human and even the beast,
and all the herbs of the field, the hailstones attacked, and all the trees of the
field he shattered. **26** Only in the land of *Goshen*, which there is the sons of
Yisra'eyl, the hailstones did not exist, **27** and *Paroh* sent and he called out to
Mosheh and *Aharon*, and he said to them, I failed this time, ***YHWH*** is the
correct one and I and my people are the lost ones. **28** Intercede to ***YHWH***,
there is enough thunder of *Elohiym* and hailstones, and I will send you, and
you must not again stand here, **29** and *Mosheh* said to him, in my going out
of the city, I will spread out my palms to ***YHWH***, the thunder must
terminate, and the hailstones will not exist again, so that you will know that
the land belongs to ***YHWH***, **30** and you, and your servants, I know that you
do not yet fear the face of ***YHWH*** the *Elohiym*, **31** and the flax and the barley
were hit, given that the barley was green and the flax was budding, **32** and
the wheat and the spelt were not beaten, given that they were late, **33** and
Mosheh went out of the city, away from *Paroh*, and he spread out his palms
to ***YHWH*** and the thunder terminated, and the hailstones and precipitation
did not drop down unto the land, **34** and *Paroh* saw that the precipitation
and the hailstones and the thunder terminated, and he again failed and his
heart was made heavy, he and his servants, **35** and he seized the heart of
Paroh[186], and he did not send the sons of *Yisra'eyl* just as ***YHWH*** spoke by
the hand of *Mosheh*,

Chapter 10

1 and ***YHWH*** said to *Mosheh*, come to *Paroh*, given that I made his heart
heavy, and the heart of his servants, so that I can set down these, my signs,
inside him, **2** and so that you will recount in the ears of your son and the son

---

[186] The phrase וַיֶּחֱזַק לֵב פַּרְעֹה may be translated as "and he seized the heart of *Paroh*" or "and the heart seized *Paroh*." Compare this phrase with Exodus 4:21 and 9:12.

of your son, that I abused *Mits'rayim* with my signs which I placed in them, then you will know that I am ***YHWH***, **3** and *Mosheh*, and *Aharon*, came to *Paroh* and they said to him, in this way ***YHWH*** the *Elohiym* of the ones of *Ever* said, for how long will you refuse to afflict yourself at my face, send my people and they will serve me. **4** Instead you are refusing to send my people, look at me, tomorrow I am bringing locust in your borders, **5** and he will cover over the eye of the land, and he[187] will not be able to see the land, and he will eat the remainder of the ones escaping, the ones remaining to you from the hailstones, and he will eat all the springing up trees that belong to you from the field, **6** and they will fill your houses and the houses of all your servants and the houses of all *Mits'rayim*, which your fathers, and the fathers of your fathers, did not see, from the day you existed upon the ground until this day, and he turned and he went out away from *Paroh*, **7** and the servants of *Paroh* said to him, for how long will this exist to us as a snare, send the men and they will serve ***YHWH*** their *Elohiym*, do you not yet know that *Mits'rayim* is perished, **8** and *Mosheh* was turned back, and *Aharon*, to *Paroh*, and he said to them, walk, serve ***YHWH*** your *Elohiym*, who and who are the ones walking, **9** and *Mosheh* said, with our young men and with our bearded ones we will walk, with our sons and with our daughters, with our flocks and with our cattle we will walk, given that a feast of ***YHWH*** is for us, **10** and he said to them, ***YHWH*** will exist so with you, just as I will send you and your babies, see that dysfunction is before your faces. **11** Not so, please walk the warriors and serve ***YHWH***, given that you are searching this out, and he cast them out from the face of *Paroh*, **12** and ***YHWH*** said to *Mosheh*, extend your hand upon the land of *Mits'rayim* with the locust, and he will go up upon the land of *Mits'rayim*, and he will eat all the herbs of the land, all which the hailstones left, **13** and *Mosheh* extended his branch upon the land of *Mits'rayim*, and ***YHWH*** had driven a wind of the east wind in the land all that day and all the night, the morning had existed and the wind of the east wind had lifted up the locust, **14** and the locust went up upon all the land of *Mits'rayim*, and he rested in all the borders of *Mits'rayim*, very heavy to his face, locust like this did not exist so, and after he will not exist so, **15** and he covered over the eye of all the land, and the land was darkened, and he ate all the herbs of the land and all the produce of the trees which the hailstones left behind, and not any of the green in the trees was left behind or in the herbs of the field, in all the land of *Mits'rayim*, **16** and *Paroh* hurried to call out to *Mosheh* and to *Aharon* and he said, I failed ***YHWH*** your *Elohiym* and to you, **17** and now, please lift up my failure, only this time, and intercede to ***YHWH*** your *Elohiym*, and he will turn aside this death from upon me only, **18** and he went out away from *Paroh* and he interceded to ***YHWH***, **19** and ***YHWH*** overturned a very forceful

---

[187] Grammatically the "he" is referring to the locust, but contextually it is referring to the people.

wind of the sea[188], and he lifted up the locust, and he thrust him unto the sea of reeds[189], not one locust was remaining in all the borders of *Mits'rayim*, **20** and ***YHWH*** strengthened the heart of *Paroh*, and he did not send the sons of *Yisra'eyl*, **21** and ***YHWH*** said to *Mosheh*, extend your hand upon the skies and darkness will exist upon the land of *Mits'rayim*, and the darkness will make one grope, **22** and *Mosheh* extended his hand upon the skies, and a darkness of thick gloominess existed in all the land of *Mits'rayim* for three days. **23** Each could not see his brother, and each could not rise from underneath him for three days, and to all the sons of *Yisra'eyl* light existed in their settling place, **24** and *Paroh* called out to *Mosheh* and he said, walk, serve ***YHWH***, only your flocks and your cattle will be left in place, also your babies will walk with you, **25** and *Mosheh* said, also you, you will place in our hand the sacrifices and ascension offering, and we will do them for ***YHWH*** our *Elohiym*, **26** and also our livestock will walk with us, a split hoof will not remain, given that from him we will take to serve ***YHWH*** our *Elohiym*, and we will not know what we will serve ***YHWH*** until we come unto there, **27** and ***YHWH*** strengthened the heart of *Paroh* and he did not consent to send them, **28** and *Paroh* said to him, walk from upon me, safeguard yourselves, do not again see my face, given that in the day you see my face, you will die, **29** and *Mosheh* said, so you spoke, I will not ever again see your face,

Chapter 11

1 and ***YHWH*** said to *Mosheh*, I will bring one more plague upon *Paroh* and upon *Mits'rayim*, afterward he will send you from this place, as he is completely sending you, he will surely cast you out from this place. **2** Please speak in the ears of the people and each will inquire, from his companion and each from her friend, utensils of silver and utensils of gold, **3** and ***YHWH*** placed the beauty[190] of the people in the eyes of *Mits'rayim*, also the man *Mosheh* was very great in the land of *Mits'rayim* in the eyes of the servants of *Paroh* and in the eyes of the people, **4** and *Mosheh* said, in this way ***YHWH*** said, about the center of the night[191], I am going out in the midst of *Mits'rayim*, **5** and all the firstborn in the land of *Mits'rayim* will die, from the firstborn of *Paroh*, the one settling upon his seat, unto the firstborn of the maid which is behind the millstones, and all the firstborn beasts, **6** and a great cry will exist in all the land of *Mits'rayim*, which had not existed like this and will not again exist like this, **7** and to all of the sons of *Yisra'eyl*, the

---

[188] Meaning "west."

[189] "Sea of reeds," or "*Yam Suph*," is usually mistranslated as "red sea."

[190] "Place the beauty" means to "make accepted."

[191] "Center of the night" is midnight.

dog will not cut his tongue sharply[192], from the man and even the beast, so that you must know that ***YHWH*** will make a distinction between *Mits'rayim* and *Yisra'eyl*, **8** and all these, your servants, will go down to me and they will bend themselves down to me saying, go out, you and all the people which are with your feet[193], and afterward I will go out, and he went out away from *Paroh* with the flaming nose[194], **9** and ***YHWH*** said to *Mosheh*, *Paroh* will not listen to you so that my wonders will increase in the land of *Mits'rayim*, **10** and *Mosheh* and *Aharon* did all these wonders to the face of *Paroh*, and ***YHWH*** strengthened the heart of *Paroh* and he did not send the sons of *Yisra'eyl* from his land,

---

Chapter 12

1 and ***YHWH*** said to *Mosheh* and to *Aharon* in the land of *Mits'rayim*. **2** This new moon is for you the head of the new moons, he is the first for you for the new moons of the year. **3** Speak to all the company of *Yisra'eyl* saying, in the tenth one[195] to this new moon, each will take for themselves a ram to the house of the fathers, a ram to the house, **4** and if the house will be less than what is needed from a ram, then he and his dweller, the one near to his house, will take one that is with the worth of the souls of each[196], according to the mouth of his eating, you will estimate upon the ram. **5** A ram will exist for you, it will be whole, a male, a son[197] of a year, you will take it from the sheep and from the she-goats, **6** and he will exist for you for a charge until the fourteenth day to this new moon, and all the assembly of the company of *Yisra'eyl* will slay him between the evenings[198], **7** and they will take from the blood, and they will place it upon the two doorposts and upon the lintel upon the houses which they will eat him in, **8** and they will eat the flesh in this night, a roast of fire, and unleavened bread, upon bitter herbs they will eat him. **9** You will not eat from him raw or boiled by being boiled in the waters, instead, a roast of fire, his head, also his legs and also his insides, **10** and you will not leave him behind until morning, and what is

---

192 "The dog will not cut his tongue sharply" is probably an idiom, but of unknown origin or meaning.
193 "With your feet" is an idiom meaning "following after you."
194 "Flaming nose" is an idiom for "fierce anger."
195 Meaning "the tenth day."
196 "In the worth of the souls of man" means "one that is sufficient for all those eating it."
197 "Son" is an idiom for years "old."
198 As the word for "evening" is written in the double plural. This is literally translated as "between the 'two' evenings," but is of uncertain meaning. It may be the time between sunset and dark or between sunrise (as the word ערב literally means the "mixing" of light) and sunset.

being left behind of him until morning, you will cremate in the fire, **11** and just like this you will eat him, your waists girded up, your sandals on your feet, and your rod in your hand, and you will eat him in haste, he is the *Pesahh* for ***YHWH***, **12** and I will cross over in the land of *Mits'rayim* in this night, and I will attack all the firstborn in the land of *Mits'rayim*, from the human and even the beast, and in all the *Elohiym* of *Mits'rayim* I will do judgments, I am ***YHWH***, **13** and the blood will exist for you for a sign upon the houses which you are in, and I will see the blood and I will hop over you and the striking to destruction will not exist in you in my attacking in the land of *Mits'rayim*, **14** and this day will exist to you for a remembrance, and you will hold a feast with him, a feast to ***YHWH*** for your generations, you will hold a feast, it is a ritual of a distant time. **15** You will eat unleavened bread for seven days, in the first day you will surely make leaven cease from your houses, given that anyone eating leavened bread from the first day until the seventh day, that soul will be cut from *Yisra'eyl*, **16** and in the first day a meeting of a special time, and in the seventh day a meeting of a special time will exist for you, no business will be done in them, only what will be eaten by any soul, that alone will be done to you, **17** and you will safeguard the unleavened bread, given that in the bone of this day[199] I will make your armies go out from the land of *Mits'rayim*, and you will safeguard this day for your generations, it is a ritual of a distant time. **18** In the first month, in the fourteenth day to the new moon[200] in the evening, you will eat unleavened bread until the day of the one and twenty to the new moon in the evening. **19** For seven days leaven will not be found in your houses, given that anyone eating leaven, that soul will be cut from the company of *Yisra'eyl*, with the immigrant and with the native of the land. **20** You will not eat any leaven in any of your settlings, you will eat unleavened bread, **21** and *Mosheh* called out to all the bearded ones of *Yisra'eyl* and he said to them, draw and take for yourself one from the flocks for your families and slay the *Pesahh*, **22** and you will take a bunch of hyssop, and you will dip it in the blood which is in the basin, and you will smite it on the lintel and on the two doorposts, from the blood which is in the basin, you will not go out, each from the opening of his house until morning, **23** and ***YHWH*** will cross over to smite *Mits'rayim*, and he will see the blood upon[201] the lintel and upon the two doorposts, and ***YHWH*** will hop upon the opening, and he will not allow the damager to come to your houses to smite, **24** and you will safeguard this word for a custom for you, and for your generations until[202] a distant time, **25** and it will come to pass, you will come to the land, which ***YHWH*** will give to you just as he spoke, and you will safeguard this service,

---

[199] "Bone of this day" is an idiom of uncertain meaning, but may mean "this very same day" or the "middle of this day."

[200] This Hebrew word may mean "after the new moon."

[201] The word "upon" may also be translated as "over."

[202] Or "unto."

26 and it will come to pass that your sons will say to you, what is this service
to you, **27** and you will say, he is a sacrifice of *Pesahh* for ***YHWH***, who
hopped over the houses of the sons of *Yisra'eyl* in *Mits'rayim*, in his smiting
of *Mits'rayim*, and he delivered our houses, and the people bowed the head
and they bent themselves down[203], **28** and the sons of *Yisra'eyl* will walk and
they did just as ***YHWH*** directed *Mosheh* and *Aharon*, so they did, **29** and it
came to pass in the middle of the night, and ***YHWH*** had attacked all the
firstborn in the land of *Mits'rayim*, from the firstborn of *Paroh*, the one
settling upon his seat, unto the firstborn of the captives, which are in the
house of the cistern[204], and all the firstborn of the beasts, **30** and *Paroh* rose
that night and all his servants and all *Mits'rayim*, and a great cry existed in
Mits'rayim, given that there was not a house which was without a dying
one, **31** and he called out to *Mosheh* and to *Aharon* in the night and he said,
rise, go out from the midst of my people, both you, and the sons of *Yisra'eyl*
and walk, serve ***YHWH*** as you spoke. **32** Also your flocks and your cattle,
take them just as you spoke, and walk, and you will exalt me also, **33** and
Mits'rayim seized upon the people to hurry to send them from the land,
given that they said, all of us are dying, **34** and the people lifted up his dough
before he was soured, their kneading bowls were pressed in with their
apparel upon their shoulder, **35** and the sons of *Yisra'eyl* had done like the
word of *Mosheh*, and they inquired from *Mits'rayim* utensils of silver and
utensils of gold and apparel, **36** and ***YHWH*** had placed the beauty[205] of the
people in the eyes of *Mits'rayim*, and they granted it to them and they
delivered *Mits'rayim*, **37** and the sons of *Yisra'eyl* journeyed from *Ra'meses*
unto *Suk'kot*, about six hundred thousand warriors on foot, aside from the
babies, **38** and also an abundant mixture had gone up with them, and flocks
and cattle, the livestock was very heavy[206], **39** and they will bake the dough
which they made go out from *Mits'rayim*, these are baked breads of
unleavened bread, given that he was not soured, given that they were cast
out from *Mits'rayim*, and they were not able to linger, and also, they did not
do provisions for themselves, **40** and the settling of the sons of *Yisra'eyl*,
who settled in *Mits'rayim*[207], was thirty and four hundred years, **41** and it
came to pass, at the conclusion of the thirty and four hundred years, and it
came to pass in the bone of this day[208], all the armies of ***YHWH*** went out
from the land of *Mits'rayim*. **42** This is a night of safeguardings to ***YHWH***, to

---

[203] "Bending oneself down" means to prostrate oneself down to the ground in respect to another.

[204] The "house of the cistern" is probably a prison.

[205] "Place the beauty" means to "make accepted."

[206] "Heavy" means abundant.

[207] The *Septuagint* and the Samaritan Pentateuch state that Israel was in *Mits'rayim* (Egypt) "and Canaan" for 430 years.

[208] "Bone of this day" is an idiom of uncertain meaning, but may mean "this very same day" or the "middle of this day."

make them go out from the land of *Mits'rayim*, that this night is to ***YHWH***, safeguardings to all the sons of *Yisra'eyl*, to their generations, **43** and ***YHWH*** said to *Mosheh* and *Aharon*, this is the ritual of the *Pesahh*, not one son of a foreigner will eat him, **44** and you will snip every man servant acquired by silver, at that time he will eat him. **45** A settler or a hireling will not eat him. **46** He will be eaten in one house, you will not make anything from the flesh go out from the house unto the outside, and you will not crack a bone of him. **47** All the company of *Yisra'eyl* will do him, **48** and if an immigrant will immigrate with you, and he will do the *Pesahh* to ***YHWH***, all the males will be circumcised to him, and at that time, he will come near to do him, and he will exist like a native of the land, and all the uncircumcised will not eat him. **49** One teaching will exist to the native and to the immigrant, the immigrant in the midst of you, **50** and all the sons of *Yisra'eyl* did just as ***YHWH*** directed *Mosheh* and *Aharon*, so they did, **51** and it came to pass, in the bone of this day[209], ***YHWH*** made the sons of *Yisra'eyl* go out from the land of *Mits'rayim*, with their armies,

Chapter 13

1 and ***YHWH*** spoke to *Mosheh* saying, **2** set apart for me all the firstborn bursting of all the bowels[210] in the sons of *Yisra'eyl*, in the human and in the beast, he belongs to me, **3** and *Mosheh* said to the people, remember this day, which is when you went out from *Mits'rayim*, from the house of servants, given that with a grasp of the hand ***YHWH*** made you go out from this, and leavened bread will not be eaten. **4** Today you are going out in the new moon of the green grain, **5** and it will come to pass that ***YHWH*** will bring you to the land of the one of *Kena'an* and the one of *Hhet* and the one of *Emor* and the one of *Hhiw* and the one of *Yevus*, which was sworn to your fathers to give to you, a land issuing fat[211] and honey[212], and you will serve this service in this new moon. **6** Seven of the days you will eat unleavened bread, and in the seventh day is the feast to ***YHWH***. **7** Unleavened bread will be eaten seven of the days, and leavened bread will not appear to you, and leaven will not appear to you in all your borders, **8** and you will tell to your son in that day saying, on account of this ***YHWH*** did to me in my going out from *Mits'rayim*, **9** and he will exist for you for a sign upon your hand, and for a remembrance between your eyes, so that the teaching of ***YHWH*** will exist in your mouth, given that with a forceful hand ***YHWH*** made you go out

---

[209] "Bone of this day" is an idiom of uncertain meaning, but may mean "this very same day" or the "middle of this day."

[210] "Bursting of all the bowels" is an idiom for "births."

[211] This Hebrew word can also mean "milk."

[212] The Hebrew word דבש means a "sticky mass" and can also mean "dates" from the palm tree.

from *Mits'rayim*, **10** and you will safeguard this ritual according to her appointed time, from days unto days[213], **11** and it will come to pass, that ***YHWH*** will bring you to the land of the one of *Kena'an*, just as he swore to you and to your fathers, and he will give her to you, **12** and you will make all the burstings of the bowels[214] cross over to ***YHWH***, and all the burstings of the births of the beasts will exist for you, the males belong to ***YHWH***, **13** and you will ransom all the bursting of the donkeys with a ram, and if you will not ransom it, then you will behead[215] him, and all the firstborn of the humans *among* your sons, you will ransom, **14** and it will come to pass tomorrow[216], that your son will inquire of you saying, what is this, and you will say to him, with the grasp of the hand, ***YHWH*** made us go out from *Mits'rayim*, from the house of servants, **15** and it came to pass, that *Paroh* made it hard to send us, and ***YHWH*** killed all the firstborn in the land of *Mits'rayim*, from the firstborn human and even the firstborn beast, therefore I am sacrificing to ***YHWH*** all the bursting of the bowels[217], the males, and all the firstborn of my sons I will ransom, **16** and he will exist for a sign upon your hand, and for markers between your eyes, given that with the grasp of the hand, ***YHWH*** made us go out from *Mits'rayim*, **17** and it came to pass, with *Paroh* sending the people, and *Elohiym* did not guide them on the road to the land of the ones of *Peleshet* when he was near, given that *Elohiym* said, otherwise, the people will regret it in their seeing the battle, and they will turn back unto *Mits'rayim*, **18** and *Elohiym* made the people go around the road of the wilderness of the sea of reeds[218], and armed for battle, the sons of *Yisra'eyl* went up from the land of *Mits'rayim*, **19** and *Mosheh* took the bones of *Yoseph* with him, given that he surely made the sons of *Yisra'eyl* swear, saying, *Elohiym* will surely register with you, and you will make my bones go up from this place with you, **20** and they journeyed from *Suk'kot*, and they camped in *Eytam*, in the extremity of the wilderness, **21** and ***YHWH*** was walking before them, by daytime in a pillar of cloud to guide them in the road, and by night in a pillar of fire to make light for them to walk, daytime and night. **22** He will not make the pillar of the cloud of the daytime and the pillar of the fire of the night move away from to the face of the people,

---

213 "From days unto days" is a Hebrew idiom meaning "continually."

214 "Bursting of the bowels" is an idiom meaning "births."

215 This Hebrew verb can also mean "break the neck."

216 "Tomorrow" can mean "later," a time in the future.

217 "Bursting of the bowels" is an idiom meaning "births."

218 "Sea of reeds," or "*Yam Suph*," is usually mistranslated as "red sea."

Chapter 14

1 and ***YHWH*** spoke to *Mosheh* saying, **2** speak to the sons of *Yisra'eyl* and they will turn back and they will camp in front of *Piy-Hahhiyrot*, between *Migdol* and the sea, to the face of *Ba'al-Tsephon*, in front of him you will camp, upon the sea, **3** and *Paroh* will say to the sons of *Yisra'eyl*, they are being entangled in the land, the wilderness shut in upon them, **4** and I will strengthen the heart of *Paroh*, and he will pursue after them, and I will be heavy in *Paroh*, and in all his forces, and *Mits'rayim* will know that I am ***YHWH***, and they will do so, **5** and it was told to the king of *Mits'rayim* that the people fled away, and the heart of *Paroh*, and his servants, were overturned to the people, and they said, what is this we did, given that we sent *Yisra'eyl* from serving us, **6** and he tied up[219] his vehicle, and he took his people with him, **7** and he took six hundred chosen vehicles, and all the vehicles of *Mits'rayim*, and the lieutenants over all of them, **8** and ***YHWH*** strengthened the heart of *Paroh*, the king of *Mits'rayim*, and he pursued after the sons of *Yisra'eyl*, and the sons of *Yisra'eyl* were going out with the hand raising[220], **9** and *Mits'rayim* pursued after them, and all the horses of the vehicles of *Paroh*, and his horsemen, and his forces overtook them camping upon the sea, upon *Piy-Hahhiyrot*, to the face of *Ba'al-Tsephon*, **10** and *Paroh* had come near, and the sons of *Yisra'eyl* lifted up their eyes and saw *Mits'rayim* journeying after them, and they feared greatly, and the sons of *Yisra'eyl* cried out to ***YHWH***, **11** and they said to *Mosheh*, is it from a lack of graves in *Mits'rayim* that you took us to die in the wilderness, what is this you did to us, to make us go out from *Mits'rayim*. **12** Is not this the word which we spoke to you in *Mits'rayim* saying, terminate from us and we will serve *Mits'rayim*, given that it is functional for us to serve *Mits'rayim* rather than us dying in the wilderness, **13** and *Mosheh* said to the people, do not fear, station yourself and see the relief of ***YHWH***, which he will do for you today, even though you saw *Mits'rayim* today, you will not again see them, even unto a distant time. **14** ***YHWH*** will wage war for you, and you must keep silent, **15** and ***YHWH*** said to *Mosheh*, what will you cry out to me[221], speak to the sons of *Yisra'eyl* and they will journey, **16** and you, raise your branch and extend your hand upon the sea and cleave him, and the sons of *Yisra'eyl* will come[222] in the midst of the sea on the dry ground, **17** and I, look at me, strengthening the heart of *Mits'rayim*, and they will come after them, and I will be heavy[223] with *Paroh*, and with all his forces, with his vehicles, and with his horsemen, **18** and *Mits'rayim* will know that I am

[219] Meaning "harnessed."

[220] "The hand raising" is an idiom meaning "boldly."

[221] This phrase may also be translated as "What? Will you cry out to me?"

[222] Or "go."

[223] "Being heavy" means that ***YHWH*** will bring his power on *Mits'rayim* to show his might.

YHWH with my being heavy[224] with *Paroh*, with his vehicles, and with his horsemen, **19** and the messenger of the *Elohiym*, the one walking to the face of the camp of *Yisra'eyl*, journeyed, and he walked behind them, and the pillar of the cloud journeyed from their face, and he stood behind them, **20** and he came between the camp of *Mits'rayim* and the camp of *Yisra'eyl*, and the cloud existed, and the darkness, and he made the night light, and this one did not come near that one all the night, **21** and *Mosheh* extended his hand upon the sea, and ***YHWH*** made the sea walk with a strong east wind all the night, and he placed[225] the sea for a wasteland, and the waters were cleaved, **22** and the sons of *Yisra'eyl* came in the midst of the sea in the dry ground, and the waters were a rampart for them, at their right hand and at their left hand, **23** and *Mits'rayim* pursued, and all the horses of *Paroh*, his chariots and his vehicle, came after them to the midst of the sea, **24** and it came to pass in the night watch of the morning, and ***YHWH*** looked down to the camp of *Mits'rayim*, in the pillar of fire and the cloud, and he confused the camp of *Mits'rayim*, **25** and he made the wheels of his chariots turn aside, and he drove him with heaviness[226], and *Mits'rayim* said, I will flee from the face of *Yisra'eyl*, given that ***YHWH*** will wage war for them *among Mits'rayim*, **26** and ***YHWH*** said to *Mosheh*, extend your hand upon the sea and the waters will turn back upon *Mits'rayim*, upon his vehicles, and upon his horsemen, **27** and *Mosheh* extended his hand upon the sea and the sea turned back to his consistency by the turning of the morning, and *Mits'rayim* was fleeing to meet him, and ***YHWH*** shook off *Mits'rayim* in the midst of the sea, **28** and the waters turned back and they covered over the vehicles, and the horsemen, and all the forces of *Paroh*, the ones coming after them in the sea, not a single one was remaining with them, **29** and the sons of *Yisra'eyl* had walked on the dry ground in the midst of the sea, and the waters were a rampart for them, at their right hand and at their left hand, **30** and ***YHWH*** rescued *Yisra'eyl* from the hand of *Mits'rayim* in that day, and *Yisra'eyl* saw *Mits'rayim* dying upon the lip[227] of the sea, **31** and *Yisra'eyl* saw the great hand[228], which ***YHWH*** did in *Mits'rayim*, and the people feared ***YHWH***, and they supported ***YHWH*** and *Mosheh*, his servant.

---

[224] "Being heavy" means that ***YHWH*** will bring his power on *Mits'rayim* to show his might.
[225] This verb, שים, appears to be out of context and may be an error. A possible correction may be the verb עשה meaning "to make."
[226] "With heaviness" probably means to "turn with difficulty,"
[227] Meaning "edge."
[228] A "great hand" is a "powerful action."

Chapter 15

1 At that time, *Mosheh,,* and the sons of *Yisra'eyl*, will sing this song to ***YHWH***, and they said saying, I will sing to ***YHWH***, given that he surely rose up, the horse and his rider, he threw down in the sea. **2** My boldness and music is ***Yah***, and he will exist to me for a relief, this is my mighty one, and I will make him abide, *Elohiym* of my father, and I will raise him. **3** ***YHWH*** is a man of battle, ***YHWH*** is his title. **4** He threw the chariots of *Paroh* and his forces in the sea, and his chosen lieutenants had sunk in the sea of reeds[229]. **5** The deep water will cover them over, they will go down in the depths like a stone. **6** Your right hand ***YHWH***, is being eminent with strength, your right hand ***YHWH***, she will dash to pieces the attacker, **7** and with the abundance of your majesty, you will demolish the rising one, you will send your burning wrath, he will eat them like the stubble, **8** and with the wind of your nose, the waters were piled, they were stood up like a flowing heap, the deep water curdled in the heart of the sea. **9** The attacker said, I will pursue, I will overtake, I will distribute the spoil, my soul will be filled[230] with them, I will make my sword drawn out, my hand will dispossess them. **10** You blew with your wind, the sea covered them over, they were overshadowed[231] like lead in the eminent waters. **11** Who is like you *among* the mighty ones, ***YHWH***, who is like you, being eminent in specialness, being feared of adorations, doing performances. **12** You extended your right hand and the land swallowed them. **13** You guided the people with your kindness, wherein you redeemed, you lead with your boldness to the abode of your special place. **14** The people heard, they trembled, agony had taken hold of the settlers of *Peleshet*. **15** At that time, the chiefs of *Edom* were stirred, the bucks[232] of *Mo'av*, a shaking in fear will take hold of them, all the settlers of *Kena'an* were dissolved. **16** Terror will fall upon them, and awe, with your great arm they will be silent like a stone, until your people ***YHWH***, will cross over, until the people wherein you purchased, cross over. **17** You will bring them, and you will plant them in the hill of your inheritance, a pedestal for your settling, ***YHWH***, you made a sanctuary, *Adonai*, your hands prepared it. **18** ***YHWH*** will reign to a distant time and beyond, **19** given that the horse of *Paroh*, with his vehicle and with his horsemen, came in the sea, and ***YHWH*** made the waters of the sea turn back upon them, and the sons of *Yisra'eyl* had walked on the dry ground in the midst of the sea, **20** and *Mir'yam*, the announcer, the sister of *Aharon*, took the tambourine in her hand, and all the women went out after her, with tambourines and with dances, **21** and *Mir'yam* answered them, sing to ***YHWH***, given that he surely rose up, the

---

[229] "Sea of reeds," or "*Yam Suph*," is usually mistranslated as "red sea."

[230] "Be filled" probably means "outraged," in the sense of being filled with anger.

[231] Meaning "they dropped to the dark depths."

[232] Meaning "mighty men."

horse and his rider, he threw down in the sea, **22** and *Mosheh* journeyed
Yisra'eyl from the sea of reeds[233], and they went out to the wilderness of
Shur, and they walked three days in the wilderness, and they did not find
waters, **23** and they came unto *Marah*, and they were not able to gulp
waters from *Marah*, given that they were bitter, therefore he called out her
title *Marah*, **24** and the people were murmuring upon *Mosheh* saying, what
will we gulp, **25** and he cried out to ***YHWH***, and ***YHWH*** pointed to him a tree,
and he threw it out to the waters and the waters tasted sweet, there he
placed[234] for him a custom and a decision, and there he tested him, **26** and
he said, if you surely listen to the voice of ***YHWH*** your *Elohiym*, and you will
do the straight thing in his eyes, and you will pay attention to his directives,
and you will safeguard all his customs, all the sickness which I placed in
Mits'rayim, I will not place upon you, given that I am ***YHWH***, your healer,
27 and they came unto *Eyliym*, and there were twelve eyes[235] of waters, and
seventy date palms, and they camped there upon the waters,

Chapter 16

1 and all the company of the sons of *Yisra'eyl* journeyed from *Eyliym* and
they came to the wilderness of *Sin*, which is between *Eyliym* and *Sinai*, on
the fifteenth day to the second new moon of their going out from the land
of *Mits'rayim*, **2** and all the company of the sons of *Yisra'eyl* were
murmuring upon *Mosheh* and upon *Aharon* in the wilderness, **3** and the sons
of *Yisra'eyl* said, who will allow us to die by the hand of ***YHWH*** in the land of
Mits'rayim, with our settling upon the pot of flesh with us eating bread to
satisfaction, given that you made us go out to this wilderness to kill this
assembly with hunger, **4** and ***YHWH*** said to *Mosheh*, look at me making it
precipitate bread for you from the skies, and the people will go out and they
will pick it up, it is a word[236] of the day in his day[237], so that I will test him,
will he walk in my teaching or not, **5** and it will come to pass, in the sixth day,
and they will prepare what they will bring, and double will exist in addition
to what they will pick up daily, **6** and *Mosheh*, and *Aharon* said to all the
sons of *Yisra'eyl*, evening[238], and you will know that ***YHWH*** had made you go

---

[233] "Sea of reeds," or "*Yam Suph*," is usually mistranslated as "red sea."
[234] Meaning "established" or "appointed."
[235] That is, a spring.
[236] This Hebrew word can also mean "matter."
[237] "A word of the day in his day" is an idiom meaning a "daily matter."
[238] The passage does not make sense contextually and appears to be written incorrectly. A possible solution is that the passage originally read, "and in the evening you will eat flesh" (compare with verse 8 and 12).

out from the land of *Mits'rayim*, **7** and morning[239], and you will see the
armament of ***YHWH***, in his hearing of your murmurings upon ***YHWH***, and
what are we that you will murmur upon us, **8** and *Mosheh* said, with ***YHWH***
giving you flesh to eat in the evening, and bread in the morning to be
satisfied, with ***YHWH*** hearing your murmurings which you are murmuring
upon him, and what are we, your murmurings are not upon us, given that
they are upon ***YHWH***, **9** and *Mosheh* said to *Aharon*, say to all the company
of the sons of *Yisra'eyl*, come near to the face of ***YHWH***, given that he heard
your murmurings, **10** and it came to pass as *Aharon* spoke to all the
company of the sons of *Yisra'eyl*, and they turned to the wilderness, and
look, the armament of ***YHWH*** appeared in the cloud, **11** and ***YHWH*** spoke to
Mosheh saying, **12** I heard the murmurings of the sons of *Yisra'eyl*, speak to
them saying, between the evenings[240] you will eat flesh and in the morning
you will be satisfied with bread, and you will know that I am ***YHWH*** your
Elohiym, **13** and it came to pass in the evening, and the quail went up and
she covered over the camp, and in the morning the lying down of the dew
existed all around the camp, **14** and the lying down of the dew went up, and
look, upon the face of the wilderness was a scrawny flake, scrawny like the
hoarfrost upon the land, **15** and the sons of *Yisra'eyl* saw, and they said each
to his brother, what is he[241], given that they did not know what he was, and
Mosheh said to them, he is the bread which ***YHWH*** gave to you for food.
16 This is the word which ***YHWH*** directed, pick him up, each according to the
mouth of his eating[242], an omer to the skull[243], a number of your souls, you
will take for each that is in his tent, **17** and the sons of *Yisra'eyl* did so, and
they picked it up, the one taking an increase and the other taking less,
18 and they measured with the omer, and the one making an increase was
not made to exceed, and the one taking less was not diminished, each

---

239 The passage does not make sense contextually and appears to be written incorrectly. A possible solution is that the passage originally read, "and in the morning you will eat bread" (compare with verse 8 and 12).

240 As the word for "evening" is written in the double plural. This is literally translated as "between the 'two' evenings," but is of uncertain meaning. It may be the time between sunset and dark or between sunrise (as the word ערב literally means the "mixing" of light) and sunset.

241 The phrase מָן הוּא (*mahn hu*) means, "*Mahn* is he" or "he is *Mahn*" (where *Mahn* is the bread-like substance). However, if the text originally read, מָה הוּא (*mah hu*), then this would be translated as "What is he," which explains the next phrase which states, "given that they did not know what he was," where "what he was" is מָה הוּא in Hebrew.

242 "To the mouth of his eating" means that each person was to gather only what was needed for their meals.

243 "Skull" is a euphemism for a "person."

picked up according to the mouth of his eating[244], **19** and *Mosheh* said to them, a man will not leave him behind until morning, **20** and they did not listen to *Mosheh* and the men left him behind until morning, and kermes[245] raised and he stank and *Mosheh* snapped upon them, **21** and they picked him up morning by morning, each according to the mouth of his eating[246], and the sun will be warm and he will be melted away, **22** and it came to pass in the sixth day, they picked up double the bread, two of the omers for a unit, and all the captains of the company came, and they told this to *Mosheh*, **23** and he said to them, that is what ***YHWH*** said, tomorrow is a rest period, a ceasing, a special time for ***YHWH***, bake what you will bake, boil what you will boil, and leave for yourself all the exceeding for a charge until the morning, **24** and they left him until the morning, just as *Mosheh* directed, and he did not stink and maggots did not exist in him, **25** and *Mosheh* said, eat him today, given that today is a ceasing for ***YHWH***, today you will not find him in the field. **26** Six days you will pick him up, and in the seventh day is a ceasing, he will not exist in him, **27** and it came to pass in the seventh day, they went out from the people to pick it up and they did not find it, **28** and ***YHWH*** said to *Mosheh*, how long will you refuse to safeguard my directives and my teachings. **29** See, given that ***YHWH*** had given to you the ceasing, therefore he is giving to you in the sixth day the bread of two days, each will settle underneath[247], each will not go out from his area in the seventh day, **30** and the people will cease in the seventh day, **31** and the house of *Yisra'eyl* called out his title *Mahn*, and he was like the seed of a coriander, it was white, and his flavor was like a wafer in honey, **32** and *Mosheh* said, this is the word which ***YHWH*** directed, make a filling of the omer from him for a charge for your generations so that they will see the bread which I made you eat in the wilderness with my making you go out from the land of *Mits'rayim*, **33** and *Mosheh* said to *Aharon*, take one woven basket and place unto there the filling of the omer of the *Mahn*, and make him rest to the face of ***YHWH*** for a charge for your generations. **34** Just as ***YHWH*** directed to *Mosheh*, and *Aharon* left him to the face of the evidence for a charge, **35** and the sons of *Yisra'eyl* had eaten the *Mahn* forty years until they came to the land being settled, they had eaten the *Mahn* until they came to the extremity of the land of *Kena'an*, **36** and the omer is a tenth of the *eyphah*,[248]

---

[244] "To the mouth of his eating" means that each person gathered what was needed for their meals.

[245] *Kermes*, a species of worms, were found on the mahn (compare with verse 24).

[246] "Like the mouth of his eating" means that each person gathered what was needed for their meals.

[247] Probably meaning "underneath his tent."

[248] This verse is a parenthetical statement.

Chapter 17

1 and all the company of the sons of *Yisra'eyl* journeyed from the wilderness of *Sin*, according to their breaking camps by the mouth of ***YHWH***, and they camped in *Rephiydiym*, and the people were without waters to gulp, **2** and the people disputed with *Mosheh* and they said, give us waters and we will gulp, and *Mosheh* said to them, why must you dispute with me, why must you test ***YHWH***, **3** and the people thirsted there for waters, and the people murmured upon *Mosheh*, and he[249] said, for what reason did you make us go up from *Mits'rayim*, to kill me and my sons, and my acquirings with the thirst, **4** and *Mosheh* cried out to ***YHWH*** saying, what will I do for this people, in a moment they will stone me, **5** and ***YHWH*** said to *Mosheh*, cross over to the face of the people and take with you from the bearded ones of *Yisra'eyl*, and your branch, which you attacked the stream with, take it in your hand and you will walk. **6** Here, I am standing to your face, there upon the boulder in *Hhorev*, and you will attack the boulder and waters will go out from him, and the people will gulp, and *Mosheh* did so to the eyes of the bearded ones of *Yisra'eyl*, **7** and he called out the title of the area, *Mas'sah* and *Meriyvah*, because of the dispute of the sons of *Yisra'eyl*, and because of their testing ***YHWH*** saying, is ***YHWH*** inside us or not, **8** and *Amaleq* came and he waged war with *Yisra'eyl* in *Rephiydiym*, **9** and *Mosheh* said to *Yehoshu'a*, choose for us men and go out, wage war with the *Amaleq*, tomorrow I will be standing up upon the head of the knoll, and the branch of the *Elohiym* will be in my hand, **10** and *Yehoshu'a* did just as *Mosheh* said to him, to wage war with the *Amaleq*, and *Mosheh*, *Aharon* and *Hhur*, had gone up to the head of the knoll, **11** and it came to pass, just as *Mosheh* made his hand rise, then *Yisra'eyl* will overcome, and just as he made his hand rest, then *Amaleq* will overcome, **12** and the hands of *Mosheh* were heavy, and they took a stone and they placed it underneath him, and he settled upon her, and *Aharon* and *Hhur* upheld his hands, from this one and from that one[250], and his hands were secure until the coming[251] of the sun, **13** and *Yehoshu'a* weakened *Amaleq* and his people by the mouth of the sword, **14** and ***YHWH*** said to *Mosheh*, write this remembrance in the scroll and place it in the ears[252] of *Yehoshu'a*, given that I will surely wipe away the memorial of *Amaleq* from under the skies, **15** and *Mosheh* built an altar and he called out his title ***YHWH-Nisiy***, **16** and he said, given that a hand is upon

---

[249] This is the "people," a masculine singular word in Hebrew.

[250] The phrase "from this unit and from this unit" means "one on this side and one on the other side."

[251] The Hebrew verb may mean "come" or "go" and probably refers to the "going down" of the sun.

[252] "Place it in the ears" is an idiom meaning to "speak."

the stool[253] of ***Yah***, the battle is for ***YHWH*** with the ones of *Amaleq*, from a
generation and a generation[254],

Chapter 18

1 and *Yitro*, administrator of *Mid'yan*, in-law of *Mosheh*, heard all which
Elohiym did for *Mosheh* and for *Yisra'eyl* his people, given that ***YHWH*** made
Yisra'eyl go out from *Mits'rayim*, **2** and *Yitro*, in-law of *Mosheh*, took
Tsiporah, woman of *Mosheh*, after sending her off, **3** and with her two sons,
which the title of the one is *Gershom*, given that he said, I existed as an
immigrant in a foreign land, **4** and the title of the other one is *Eli'ezer*, given
that *Elohiym* of my father is in my help, he will deliver me from the sword of
Paroh, **5** and *Yitro*, in-law of *Mosheh*, and his sons and his woman, came to
Mosheh, to the wilderness, where he was camping, there was the hill of the
Elohiym, **6** and he said to *Mosheh*, I am your in-law *Yitro*, coming to you, and
your woman and her two sons with her, **7** and *Mosheh* went out to meet his
in-law, and he bent himself down and he kissed him, and each inquired to
his companion according to the completeness, and they came unto the tent,
8 and *Mosheh* recounted to his in-law all which ***YHWH*** did to *Paroh* and to
Mits'rayim on account of *Yisra'eyl*, all the trouble which found them in the
road, and ***YHWH*** delivered them, **9** and *Yitro* was amazed over all the
functional things which ***YHWH*** did for *Yisra'eyl*, when he delivered them
from the hand of *Mits'rayim*, **10** and *Yitro* said, exalted is ***YHWH*** who
delivered you from the hand of *Mits'rayim*, and from the hand of *Paroh* who
delivered the people from under the hand of *Mits'rayim*. **11** Now I know that
YHWH is great, more than all the *Elohiym*, because of the matter which they
simmered[255] upon them, **12** and *Yitro*, in-law of *Mosheh*, took an ascension
offering and sacrifices to *Elohiym*, and *Aharon* came, and all the bearded
ones of *Yisra'eyl*, to eat bread with the in-law of *Mosheh* to the face of the
Elohiym, **13** and it came to pass on the morrow, and *Mosheh* settled to
decide[256] the people, and the people stood by *Mosheh* from the morning
until the evening, **14** and the in-law of *Mosheh* saw all which he was doing
for the people, and he said, what is this matter which you are doing for the
people, why are you settling by yourself, and all the people are standing by
you from morning until evening, **15** and *Mosheh* said to his in-law, because
the people will come to me to seek *Elohiym*, **16** given that a matter will exist
for them, it is coming to me and I will decide between each and his

---

[253] The phrase "a hand is upon the stool (or throne)" is of uncertain meaning.

[254] "From a generation and a generation" is an idiom meaning "throughout the generations," or "for all time."

[255] Probably referring to the hard labor forced on the people.

[256] Or, to judge.

companion, and I will make known the customs of the *Elohiym* and his teachings, **17** and the in-law of *Mosheh* said to him, the matter which you are doing is not functional. **18** You will surely fade, both you and this people who are with you, given that the matter is heavier than you, you will not be able to do him by yourself. **19** Now, hear my voice, I will give you advice, and *Elohiym*[257] will exist with you, you will exist for the people, in place of *Elohiym*, and you will bring the matters to the *Elohiym*, **20** and you will warn them of the customs and the teachings, and you will make them know the road they will walk in and the work which they must do, **21** and you, you will perceive out of all the people, men of force, fearful of *Elohiym*, men of truth, hating profit, and you will place upon them nobles of thousands, nobles of hundreds, nobles of fifties[258] and nobles of tens, **22** and they will decide for the people at all times, and it will come to pass, of all the great matters they will bring to you, and of all the small matters they will decide themselves, it will be made little upon you, and they will lift you up. **23** If you will do this matter, and *Elohiym* will direct you, then you will be able to stand, and also, this people will come upon his[259] area in completeness, **24** and *Mosheh* heard the voice of his in-law and he did all which he said, **25** and *Mosheh* chose men of force from all of *Yisra'eyl*, and he gave them heads upon the people, nobles of thousands, nobles of hundreds, nobles of fifties[260] and nobles of tens, **26** and they will decide for the people at all times, they must bring the hard matters to *Mosheh*, and they will decide all the small matters themselves, **27** and *Mosheh* sent his in-law, and he walked himself, to his land.

Chapter 19

1 In the third new moon to the going out of the sons of *Yisra'eyl* from the land of *Mits'rayim*, in this day they came to the wilderness of *Sinai*, **2** and they journeyed from *Rephiydiym*, and they came to the wilderness of *Sinai*, and they camped in the wilderness, and *Yisra'eyl* camped there, opposite the hill, **3** and *Mosheh* had gone up to the *Elohiym* and ***YHWH*** called out to him from the hill saying, in this way you will say to the house of *Ya'aqov*, and you will tell to the sons of *Yisra'eyl*. **4** You saw what I did to *Mits'rayim*, and I will lift you up upon the wings of the eagle[261], and I will bring you to me,

---

[257] The three uses of the Hebrew word *Elohiym* in this verse may refer to the judges.
[258] The Hebrew word חֲמִשִּׁים, the plural form of חֲמֵשׁ, means fifty. However, the context of the word חֲמִשִּׁים in this verse means fifties.
[259] The "his" is "the people," a masculine singular word in Hebrew.
[260] The Hebrew word חֲמִשִּׁים, the plural form of חֲמֵשׁ, means fifty. However, the context of the word חֲמִשִּׁים in this verse means fifties.
[261] An unknown bird, but probably a hawk or eagle.

5 and now, if you will carefully hear my voice, and you will safeguard my covenant, then you will exist for me as a jewel more than all the peoples, given that all the lands belong to me, **6** and you will exist for me as a kingdom of administrators and a unique nation, these are the words which you will speak to the sons of *Yisra'eyl*, **7** and *Mosheh* came and he called out to the bearded ones of the people, and he placed all these words, which ***YHWH*** directed him, to their faces, **8** and all the people answered together, and they said, all which ***YHWH*** spoke, we will do, and *Mosheh* returned the words of the people to ***YHWH***, **9** and ***YHWH*** said to *Mosheh*, look, I am coming to you in the thick of the cloud, in order that the people will hear me speaking with you, and also, they will support you for a distant time, and *Mosheh* told the words of the people to ***YHWH***, **10** and ***YHWH*** said to *Mosheh*, walk to the people and you will set them apart today and tomorrow, and they will wash their apparel, **11** and they will be ready for the third day, given that in the third day ***YHWH*** will go down to the eyes of all the people upon the hill of *Sinai*, **12** and you will make bounds all around the people saying, safeguard yourselves, go up in the hill[262], and touch his extremity, all the ones touching the hill will surely be killed. **13** The hand will not touch him, given that he will surely be stoned or he will surely be thrown, if it is a beast, if it is a man, he will not live, with the drawing of the jubilee horn, they, they will go up in the hill, **14** and *Mosheh* went down from the hill to the people, and he set apart the people, and they washed their apparel, **15** and he said to the people, be ready for three days, do not draw near to a woman, **16** and it came to pass in the third day, in the existing of the morning, and it came to pass, thunder and flashes and a heavy cloud were upon the hill, and the voice of the ram horn was very forceful, and all the people, which were in the camp, trembled, **17** and *Mosheh* made the people go out from the camp to meet the *Elohiym*, and they were made to stand up in the lower part of the hill, **18** and all of the hill of *Sinai* had smoked from all his face[263], because ***YHWH*** went down upon him in the fire, and his smoke went up like the smoke of the furnace, and all the hill trembled greatly, **19** and the voice of the ram horn was walking[264] and was very forceful, *Mosheh* will speak and the *Elohiym* will answer him with the voice, **20** and ***YHWH*** went down upon the hill of *Sinai*, to the head of the hill, and ***YHWH*** called out to *Mosheh* to the head of the hill, and *Mosheh* went up, **21** and ***YHWH*** said to *Mosheh*, go down, warn the people, otherwise, they will cast down[265] to ***YHWH*** to see, and many will fall from him, **22** and also the administrators, drawing near to ***YHWH***, they will be

---

262 The passage as it is written is a contradiction. It appears the word לא (not) is missing and should read "do not go up in the hill."

263 "From all his face" means the entire surface.

264 Meaning "sounding."

265 "Cast down" probably means to "throw down" the boundary that was to be made (see 19:12).

made set apart, otherwise, ***YHWH*** will break out in them, **23** and *Mosheh* said to ***YHWH***, the people will not be able to go up to the hill of *Sinai*, given that you, you warned us saying, make bounds at the hill, and you will set him apart, **24** and ***YHWH*** said to him, walk, go down, and you will go up, you and *Aharon* with you, and the administrators, and do not let the people cast down[266] to go up to ***YHWH***, otherwise he will break out with them, **25** and *Mosheh* went down to the people and he said to them,[267]

Chapter 20

1 and *Elohiym* spoke all these words saying, **2** I am ***YHWH*** your *Elohiym*, who made you go out from the land of *Mits'rayim*, from the house of servants. **3** Another *Elohiym* will not exist for you in my face[268]. **4** You will not make for you a sculpture and any resemblance which is in the skies above, and which is in the land below, and which is in the waters below the land. **5** You will not bend yourself down to them, and you will not be made to serve them, given that I am ***YHWH*** your *Elohiym*, the mighty one of zealousness, registering the twistedness of the fathers upon the sons, upon the third generation, and upon the fourth generation, to the ones hating me, **6** and doing kindness to the thousands, to the ones loving me, and to the ones safeguarding my directives. **7** You will not lift up the title of ***YHWH*** your *Elohiym* for the falseness, given that ***YHWH*** will not acquit one who will lift up his title for the falseness. **8** Remember the day of ceasing, to set him apart. **9** Six days you will serve, and you will do all your business, **10** and the seventh day is a ceasing to ***YHWH*** your *Elohiym*, you will not do any business, you and your son and your daughter, your servant and your bondwoman, and your beast, and your immigrant which is in your gates, **11** given that six days ***YHWH*** made the skies and the land, the sea and all which is in them, and he rested in the seventh day, therefore ***YHWH*** exalted the day of the ceasing, and he set him apart. **12** Honor your father and your mother so that your days will be made long upon the ground which ***YHWH*** your *Elohiym* is giving to you. **13** You will not murder. **14** You will not commit adultery. **15** You will not steal. **16** You will not afflict your companion with a witness of falseness. **17** You will not crave the house of your companion, you will not crave the woman of your companion, and his servant, and his bondwoman, and his ox, and his donkey, and all which belongs to your companion, **18** and all the people were seeing the thunder and the torches and the voice of the ram horn and the hill of smoke, and the people saw, and staggered, and they stood from a distance, **19** and they said to *Mosheh*, you will speak with us

---

[266] "Cast down" probably means to "throw down" the boundary that was to be made (see 19:12).

[267] What *Mosheh* said to the people appears to be missing.

[268] The word "face" can mean "presence."

and we will hear, and do not let *Elohiym* speak with us, otherwise we will die, **20** and *Mosheh* said to the people, do not fear, given that *Elohiym* came with the intention to test you, and with the intention that his fearfulness will exist upon your faces so you will not fail, **21** and the people stood at a distance, and *Mosheh* had been drawn near to the thick darkness which there, is the *Elohiym*, **22** and ***YHWH*** said to *Mosheh*, in this way you will say to the sons of *Yisra'eyl*, you saw that I spoke with you from the skies. **23** You must not make me a *Elohiym* of silver and a *Elohiym* of gold, you will not make them for yourselves. **24** You will make an altar of ground for me, and you will sacrifice upon him your ascension offerings and your offerings of restitution, your flocks and your cattle, in all the area where I will make my title remembered, I will come to you and I will exalt you, **25** and if you will make an altar of stones, you will not build them of hewn stone, given that you waved your sword[269] upon her, and you made her defiled, **26** and you will not go up with steps upon my altar, because you will not uncover your nakedness upon him,

---

Chapter 21

1 and these are the decisions which you will place to their faces. **2** If you will purchase a servant of *Ever*, he will serve six years, and in the seventh he will go out freely to freedom. **3** If he comes by himself, he will go out by himself, if he is the master of a woman, then his woman will go out with him. **4** If his lord will give him a woman, and she will bring forth for him sons or daughters, the woman and her boys[270] will exist for her lord, and he, he will go out by himself, **5** but if the servant will say, I love my lord, my woman and my sons, I will not go out free, **6** then his lord will make him draw near to the *Elohiym*[271], and he will make him draw near to the door, or to the doorpost, and his lord will bore through his ear with the awl and he will serve him to a distant time, **7** and if a man will sell his daughter as a bondwoman, she will not go out like the going out of the servants. **8** If she is dysfunctional in the eyes of her lord, which he did not appoint[272], then he will ransom her, he will not regulate[273] to sell her in his treacherous act with her, **9** and if he will

---

269 The "sword" is probably a sharp instrument used for shaping stone.
270 The masculine plural suffix (ים) may be used for a group of males or males and females. In the context of this verse, the word "boys" refers to the children, the sons and daughter.
271 The word *Elohiym* may refer to the judges.
272 If לא (*lo*), the *ketiv* meaning "not," is correct, this would be translated as "which he did not appoint." If לו (*lo*), the *qere* meaning "to him," is correct, then it would be translated as "who appointed her to himself."
273 That is to "rule" or "decide."

appoint her to his son, he will do to her just like the decision[274] of the daughters. **10** If he will take another, he will not take away her remains, her raiment and her habitation, **11** and if he will not do these three to her, then she will go out freely without silver. **12** The one attacking a man, and dies, he will be killed, **13** and when he did not lay in wait, and the *Elohiym*[275] delivers him to his hand, then I will place an area for you where he will flee unto, **14** and if a man simmers[276] upon his companion to kill him with subtlety, you will take him from my altar to die, **15** and the one attacking his father or his mother, will surely be killed, **16** and anyone stealing a man and sells him or is found in his hand[277], he will surely be killed, **17** and anyone belittling his father or his mother, he will surely be killed, **18** and if men must dispute, and a man will attack his companion with a stone, or with a fist, and he does not die, then he will fall to the lying place. **19** If he will rise, and he walks himself to the outside upon his stave, then the one attacking him will be acquitted, only his ceasing he will give him[278] and he will be completely healed[279], **20** and if a man attacks his servant or his bondwoman with the staff, and he dies by his hand, he will surely be avenged. **21** However, if he will stand for a day or two days, he will not be avenged, given that he is his silver, **22** and if men struggle, and they smite a pregnant woman, and her boys[280] go out, but harm did not exist, he will surely be fined just as the master of the woman will set down upon him, and he will give the judgments, **23** but if harm does exist, then you will give a soul in place of a soul. **24** An eye in place of an eye, a tooth in place of a tooth, a hand in place of a hand, a foot in place of a foot. **25** A singeing in place of a singeing, a bruise in place of a bruise, a striped bruise in place of a striped bruise, **26** but if a man will attack the eye of his servant, or the eye of his bondwoman, and he damages her, he will send him to freedom in place of his eye, **27** and if the tooth of his servant, or the tooth of his bondwoman, is made to fall out, he will send him to freedom in place of his tooth, **28** and if an ox will gore a man, or a woman, and he dies, the ox will surely be stoned, and his flesh will not be eaten, and the master of the ox is innocent, **29** but if that ox was a gorer previously, and his master was warned, and he does not safeguard him, and he kills a man or a woman, the ox will be stoned, and also his master will be killed. **30** If a covering is set down upon him, and he will give

---

[274] Or "manner."

[275] The word *Elohiym* may refer to the judges.

[276] Possibly meaning a premeditated action.

[277] Meaning "in his possession."

[278] The phrase "only his ceasing he will give him" is probably an idiom for compensating the injured person for his time lost.

[279] The injured is physically as well as financially healed.

[280] The masculine plural suffix (ים) may be used for a group of males or males and females. In the context of this verse, the word "boys" refers to the children, the sons and daughters.

the ransom price of his soul, just like all that was set down upon him. **31** Or
he gores a son, or he gores a daughter, likewise, this decision, will be done
to him. **32** If the ox gores a servant, or a bondwoman, he will give to his lords
a silver of three *sheqel*s, and the ox will be stoned, **33** and if a man opens a
cistern, or if a man digs a cistern, and he does not cover him over, and an ox
or a donkey falls into it. **34** The master of the cistern will make restitution,
he will return silver to his master, and the dead one will exist for himself,
35 and if the ox of a man smites the ox of his companion, and he dies, then
they will sell the living ox, and they will divide his silver, then they must also
divide the dead one. **36** Or if it was known that that ox was a gorer
previously, and he does not safeguard him, his master will make full
restitution, an ox in place of the ox, and the dead one will exist for himself.
37 (22:1) If a man steals an ox or a ram, and he butchers him, or he sells him,
he will make restitution with five cattle in place of the ox, and four flocks in
place of the ram.[281]

Chapter 22

1 (22:2) If the thief is found in the act of searching, and he is attacked, and
he dies, the bloodshed does not belong to him. **2 (22:3)** If the sun comes up
upon him, the bloodshed belongs to him, he will make full restitution, if
nothing belongs to him, then he will be sold with his theft. **3 (22:4)** If the
theft is surely found in his hand, from the ox, even the donkey, even a ram,
he will make restitution with double the life. **4 (22:5)** If a man causes a field
or vineyard to burn[282], or he sends his cattle, and they ignite another field,
he will make restitution with his best field and his best vineyard. **5 (22:6)** If a
fire will go out[283], and she finds brambles, and stacks, or grain stalks, or a
field is eaten[284], the one making the burning will make full restitution. **6**
(22:7) If a man gives silver or utensils to his companion for safeguarding, and
he was stolen from the house of the man, if the thief is found, he will make
restitution of two times. **7 (22:8)** If the thief is not found, then the master of
the house will be brought near to the *Elohiym*[285], to see if he did not send

---

[281] This verse is the first verse of chapter22 in Christian Bibles. In all of chapter 22, the verse numbers in Christian Bibles will be one number higher.
[282] The word "burn" is probably meaning "grazing" and not a "burning" of fire. The "he" is referring to the "cattle," a masculine singular noun in Hebrew.
[283] To "go out" in the sense of "spreading out," not in the sense of being extinguished.
[284] This Hebrew word means "to eat," but also "to devour" or "destroy."
[285] The word *Elohiym* may refer to the judges. The text appears to be missing text at this point and may have originally included "to see," or "to determine."

his hand into the business of his companion. **8 (22:9)** Over all manners of offense, over an ox, over a donkey, over a ram, over an outer garment, over all lost things, of which it is said, that one is this, the manner of the two of them will come unto the *Elohiym*[286], the one which *Elohiym* must convict, he will make full restitution of two times to his companion. **9 (22:10)** If a man will give to his companion a donkey, or an ox, or a ram or any beast for safeguarding, and he dies, or he is cracked, or he is captured, without being seen. **10 (22:11)** A swearing of ***YHWH*** will exist between the two of them, if he did not send his hand into the business of his companion, then his master[287] will take[288] it, and he will not make restitution, **11 (22:12)** but if he was surely stolen away from him, he will make restitution to his master[289]. **12 (22:13)** If he was surely torn into pieces, he will bring him as a witness, he will not make restitution of the torn thing, **13 (22:14)** and if a man will inquire[290] away from his companion, and he is cracked, or he dies, and his master is not with him, he will make full restitution. **14 (22:15)** If his master is with him, he will not make restitution, if he is a hireling, he, he came with his wage, **15 (22:16)** and if a man will persuade a virgin who has not been betrothed, and he lays down with her, he will quickly hurry her to be a woman for himself. **16 (22:17)** If her father completely refuses to give her to him, he will weigh out silver just like the bride price of the virgin. **17 (22:18)** You will not keep alive a sorceress. **18 (22:19)** All lying down with a beast will surely be killed. **19 (22:20)** Anyone sacrificing to the *Elohiym*, except to ***YHWH*** himself, will be assigned, **20 (22:21)** and you will not suppress an immigrant, and you will not squeeze him, given that you existed as immigrants in the land of *Mits'rayim*. **21 (22:22)** You must not afflict any widow or orphan. **22 (22:23)** If you greatly afflict him instead, he will greatly cry out to me, I will surely hear his cry, **23 (22:24)** and my nose will flare up[291], and I will kill you with the sword, and your women will exist as widows, and your sons as orphans. **24 (22:25)** If you loan silver to my people, the ones afflicted within you, you will not exist to him as a deceiver[292], you must not place a usury upon him. **25 (22:26)** If you insist to take the outer garment of your companion as a pledge, you will return him to him by the coming[293] of the sun, **26 (22:27)** given that she is his only raiment, she is his

---

[286] The word *Elohiym* may refer to the judges. However, unlike the other uses of this Hebrew word in this section, the verb associated with *Elohiym* is singular (he).

[287] "His master" is the owner of the beast.

[288] Meaning "accept."

[289] "His master" is the owner of the beast.

[290] Or "borrow."

[291] "My nose will flare up" is an idiom meaning "I will be fiercely angry."

[292] This Hebrew word can also mean a "lender."

[293] The Hebrew verb may mean "come" or "go" and contextually must be referring to the "going down" of the sun.

apparel for his skin, how will he lay down, and it will come to pass that he will cry out to me and I will hear him, given that I am gracious. **27 (22:28)** You will not belittle *Elohiym*[294], and you will not spit upon the captains *among* your people. **28 (22:29)** You will not delay your ripe fruit and your juice, you will give to me your firstborn sons. **29 (22:30)** Thus you will do to your ox, to your flocks, he will exist with his mother for seven days, in the eighth day you will give him to me, **30 (22:31)** and you must exist as men of specialness for me, and you will not eat torn flesh in the field, you must throw it to the dog.

Chapter 23

1 You will not lift up a report of falseness, you will not set your hand down with the lost to be a witness of violence. **2** You will not follow the abundant[295] to dysfunction, and you will not answer upon a dispute, extending after the abundant by turning away from it, **3** and you will not swell the helpless in his dispute. **4** If you reach the ox of your attacker, or his donkey, and it is wandering, you will surely return him to him. **5** If you see the donkey of your hater stretching out under his load[296], you will terminate from leaving it to him, you will surely leave it with him.[297] **6** You will not turn away from a decision of your needy in his dispute. **7** You will be far from a false word, and you will not kill the innocent or the correct, given that I will not correct the lost, **8** and you will not take a bribe, given that the bribe will blind the seeing ones, and he will twist correct words backwards, **9** and you will not squeeze an immigrant, and you know the soul of the immigrant, given that you existed as immigrants in the land of *Mits'rayim*, **10** and you will sow your land six years, and you will gather her production, **11** and in the seventh you will release her, and you will leave her alone, and the needy ones of your people will eat, and the living ones of the field will eat their remainder[298], so you will do to your vineyard, and to your olive grove. **12** Six days you will do your work, and in the seventh day you will cease, so that your ox and your donkey will rest, and the son of your bondwoman and the immigrant will breathe deeply[299], **13** and in all which I said to you, you will

[294] Context suggests this may be the judges.
[295] That is, a "crowd," as a great multitude, the majority.
[296] "Stretching out under his load" means "lying down from the heavy load."
[297] The second part of this passage is ambiguous. One possible interpretation is, "you will not leave the donkey to struggle with its load, but will help it with its load." Another interpretation is, "you will not release the load from the donkey and leave it behind, but will help it up to carry its load."
[298] The "remainder" is what the needy ones leave behind.
[299] "Breathe deeply" means "to take a break" or "to refresh ones' self."

be safeguarded, and you will not remember the title of other *Elohiym*, he will not be heard by your mouth. **14** You will hold a feast three times for me in the year. **15** You will safeguard the feast of unleavened bread, for seven days you will eat unleavened bread, just as I directed you, it is for an appointed time in the month of the green grain, given that in him you went out from *Mits'rayim*, and they will not appear to my face empty, **16** and the feast of the harvest, the first-fruits of your works, which you will sow in the field, and the feast of the gathering in the going out of the year[300], with your gathering of your works from the field. **17** Three times in the year, your men will appear to the face of the lord ***YHWH***. **18** You will not sacrifice the blood of my sacrifice upon leavened bread, and the fat of my feast will not stay the night until morning. **19** You will bring the summit of the first-fruits[301] of your ground to the house of ***YHWH*** your *Elohiym*, you will not boil a male kid in the fat[302] of his mother. **20** Look, I am sending a messenger to your face to safeguard you in the road, and to bring you to the area which I prepared. **21** Be safeguarded from his face, and hear his voice, you will not provoke him, given that he will not lift up[303] your offense, given that my title is inside him. **22** Instead you will surely hear his voice, and you will do all which I will speak, then I will attack your attackers, and I will smack your oppressors, **23** given that, my messenger will walk to your face, and he will bring you to the one of *Emor* and the one of *Hhet* and the one of *Perez* and the one of *Kena'an*, the one of *Hhiw* and the one of *Yevus*, and I will hide him[304]. **24** You will not bend yourself down to their *Elohiym*, and you will not be made to serve them, and you will not do like their works, given that you will surely cast them down, and you will surely shatter their monuments, **25** and you will serve ***YHWH*** your *Elohiym*, and he will exalt your bread and your waters, and I will remove sickness from inside you. **26** You will not miscarry or be sterile in your land, I will fulfill the number of your days. **27** I will send my terror to your face, and I will confuse all the people which you come to, and I will give the neck of all your attackers to you[305], **28** and I will send the hornet to your face, and she will cast out the one of *Hhiw*, the one of *Kena'an* and the one of *Hhet*, from before your face[306]. **29** I will not cast him out from your face in one year, otherwise, the land will be desolate and the

---

[300] "In the going out of the year" means "at the end of the year."

[301] "The summit of the first-fruits" may mean the "first" or the "best" of the harvest.

[302] Or "milk."

[303] Meaning to "remove" or "forgive."

[304] In context, probably meaning to remove these people from the land.

[305] "Give the neck of all your attackers to you" is an idiom meaning "all your enemies will be defeated." In the Ancient Near East, the victorious king would place his foot on the neck of his enemy as a sign of victory over the defeated.

[306] "From before your face" is an idiom meaning "from your presence."

living ones of the field[307] will increase in number upon you. **30** I will cast him
out little by little from your face[308], until you reproduce and you inherit the
land, **31** and I will set down your border from the sea of reeds[309] and unto
the sea of the ones of *Peleshet*, and from the wilderness unto the river,
given that I will give the settlers of the land in your hand, and you will cast
them out from your face[310]. **32** You will not cut a covenant with them or with
their *Elohiym*. **33** They will not settle in your land, otherwise, they will make
you fail me, given that you will serve their *Elohiym*, given that he will exist
for you for a snare,

Chapter 24

1 and to *Mosheh* he said, go up to ***YHWH***, you and *Aharon*, *Nadav* and
Aviyhu, and seventy from the bearded ones of *Yisra'eyl*, and you will bend
yourself down at a distance, **2** and *Mosheh* alone will be drawn near to
YHWH, and they will not draw near, and the people will not go up with him,
3 and *Mosheh* came and he recounted to the people all the words of ***YHWH***
and all the decisions, and all the people of one voice answered, and they
said, all the words which ***YHWH*** spoke, we will do, **4** and *Mosheh* wrote all
the words of ***YHWH***, and he departed early in the morning, and he built an
altar under[311] the hill, and twelve monuments for the twelve staffs[312] of
Yisra'eyl, **5** and he sent the young men of the sons of *Yisra'eyl*, and they
made ascension offerings go up, and they sacrificed sacrifices, offerings of
restitutions of bulls to ***YHWH***, **6** and *Mosheh* took half of the blood and he
placed it in the goblets, and half of the blood he sprinkled upon the altar,
7 and he took the scroll of the covenant and he called[313] it out in the ears of
the people, and they said, all which ***YHWH*** spoke, we will do and we will
hear, **8** and *Mosheh* took the blood and he sprinkled it upon the people, and
he said, look, the blood of the covenant, which ***YHWH*** cut with you
concerning all these words, **9** and *Mosheh* went up, and *Aharon*, *Nadav* and
Aviyhu, and seventy from the bearded ones of *Yisra'eyl*, **10** and they saw
Elohiym of *Yisra'eyl*, and under his feet was like a work of brick[314] of the lapis

---

307 "The living ones of the field" is an idiom meaning "wild animals."

308 "From your face" is an idiom meaning "from your presence."

309 "Sea of reeds," or "*Yam Suph*," is usually mistranslated as "red sea."

310 "From your face" is an idiom meaning "from your presence."

311 Meaning "the base."

312 Also meaning "tribes," as each tribe was represented by a staff or standard.

313 Or "read."

314 This Hebrew word may also mean a "poplar tree" or the "moon."

lazuli, and like a bone of the skies for cleanliness[315], **11** and to the leaders of the sons of *Yisra'eyl* he did not send his hand, and they perceived the *Elohiym*, and they ate and they gulped, **12** and ***YHWH*** said to *Mosheh*, go up to me unto the hill and exist there, and I will give to you slabs of the stone, and the teaching and the directive which I wrote to teach them, **13** and *Mosheh* rose, and *Yehoshu'a* his minister, and *Mosheh* went up to the hill of the *Elohiym*, **14** and to the bearded ones he said, settle for us here, until we turn back to you, and look, *Aharon* and *Hhur* are with you, whoever is a master of words[316] will draw near to them, **15** and *Mosheh* went up to the hill, and the cloud covered over the hill, **16** and the armament of ***YHWH*** dwelled upon the hill of *Sinai*, and the cloud covered over him for six days, and he called out to *Mosheh* in the seventh day from the midst of the cloud, **17** and the appearance of the armament of ***YHWH*** was like a fire eating in the head of the hill[317] to the eyes of the sons of *Yisra'eyl*, **18** and *Mosheh* came in the midst of the cloud, and he went up to the hill, and *Mosheh* existed in the hill for forty days and forty nights,

---

Chapter 25

1 and ***YHWH*** spoke to *Mosheh* saying, **2** speak to the sons of *Yisra'eyl* and they will take for me an offering from every man whose heart will offer willingly, you will take my offering, **3** and this is the offering which you will take from them, gold and silver and copper, **4** and blue and purple and kermes of scarlet and linen and she-goats, **5** and skins of bucks being red, and the skins of the deer, and wood of acacia. **6** Oil for the luminary, sweet spices for the oil of ointment and for the incense of aromatic spices. **7** Stones of the onyx and stones of the installations for the ephod and for the breastplate, **8** and they will make for me a sanctuary, and I will dwell in their midst. **9** Like everything that I showed you, the pattern of the dwelling and the pattern of all his utensils, and so you will make, **10** and they will make a box of wood of acacia, two *ammah*s and a half is his length, and an *ammah* and a half is his width, and an *ammah* and a half is his height, **11** and you will overlay him with clean gold, from the inside and the outside you will overlay him, and you will make upon him a molding of gold all around, **12** and you will pour down[318] for him four rings of gold, and you will place upon it his

---

[315] The meaning of the phrase "like a bone of the skies for cleanliness" is uncertain.

[316] The phrase "master of words" apparently means "one with a dispute."

[317] The phrase "like a fire eating in the head of the hill" means "like a fire devouring everything on top of the hill."

[318] In this context, to "pour down" means to "cast" an object from a molten metal.

four footsteps[319], and two rings upon his one rib, and two rings upon his
second rib, **13** and you will make strands of wood of acacia, and you will
overlay them with gold, **14** and you will bring the strands in the rings upon
the ribs of the box to lift up the box with them. **15** The strands will exist in
the rings of the box, they will not turn aside from him, **16** and you will place
into the box, the evidence which I will give to you, **17** and you will make a lid
of clean gold, two *ammahs* and a half is her length, and an *ammah* and a
half is her width, **18** and you will make two keruvs of gold of beaten work,
you will make them at the two extremities of the lid, **19** and make one *keruv*
at this extremity, and one *keruv* at that extremity, from the lid you will make
the keruvs upon two of his extremities, **20** and the keruvs will be spreading
out the wings above, fencing around with their wings upon the lid, and their
faces each to his brother, the faces of the keruvs will exist toward the lid,
21 and you will place the lid upon the top of the box, and by the box you will
place the evidence which I will give to you, **22** and I will meet with you there,
and from upon the lid, from between the two keruvs, which are upon the
box of the evidence, I will speak with you of all which I will direct you for the
sons of *Yisra'eyl*, **23** and you will make a table of wood of acacia, two
ammahs is his length, and an *ammah* is his width, and an *ammah* and a half
is his height, **24** and you will overlay him with clean gold, and you will make
for him a molding of gold all around, **25** and you will make for him a rim of a
hand span all around, and you will make a molding of gold for his rim all
around, **26** and you will make for him four rings of gold, and you will place
the rings upon the four edges which belong to his four feet. **27** The rings will
exist alongside the rim for houses[320] for the strands to lift up the table,
28 and you will make the strands of wood of acacia, and you will overlay
them with gold, and the table will be lifted up with them, **29** and you will
make his platters, and his palms[321] and his jugs and his sacrificial bowls,
which will be for pouring, with clean gold you will make them, **30** and you
will place upon the table the bread of the face, to my face continually,
31 and you will make a lampstand of clean gold, the midsection of the
lampstand will be made of beaten work, and her stalk, her bowls, her knobs
and her buds will exist from her[322], **32** and six stalks are going out from her
sides, three stalks of the lampstand out of her one side, and three stalks of
the lampstand out of her second side. **33** Three bowls, being almond shaped
in the stalk of the one with a knob and a bud, and three bowls, being
almond shaped in the stalk of the other with a knob and a bud, so it is for
the six stalks going out from the lampstand, **34** and in the lampstand are

---

319 Or "feet."

320 Or "housings."

321 The Hebrew word for the "palms" can also mean "palm" shaped and here refers to "spoons" or "shovels."

322 "From her" means that each of these parts is beaten (molded) out of the one piece. (also in verse 32)

four bowls being almond shaped with her knobs and her buds, **35** and a knob under two of the stalks from her[323], and a knob under two of the stalks out of her, and a knob under two of the stalks out of her, for the six stalks going out from the lampstand. **36** Their knobs and their stalks from her[324], all of her will exist as one beaten work of clean gold, **37** and you will make her seven lamps, and he will make her lamps go up[325], and he will make light upon the other side of her face, **38** and her tongs and her fire pans with clean gold. **39** A *kikar* of clean gold he will make her with all these utensils, **40** and see and do them with their pattern which you were being shown in the hill,

Chapter 26

1 and you will make the dwelling, ten curtains of twisted linen and blue and purple and kermes of scarlet, you will make them with keruvs of a work of thinking[326]. **2** The length of the one curtain is eight and twenty by the *ammah*, and the width is four by the *ammah*, the one curtain measurement is one for all the curtains. **3** Five of the curtains will exist, coupling each to her sister, and five curtains coupling each to her sister, **4** and you will make loops of blue upon the lip of the one curtain from the extremity in the coupling, and so you will make in the lip of the outer curtain in the joint of the second. **5** You will make fifty loops in the one curtain, and you will make fifty loops in the extremity of the curtain which is in the joint of the second receiving the loops of each to her sister, **6** and you will make fifty hooks of gold, and you will couple the curtains each to her sister in the hooks, and the dwelling will exist as a unit, **7** and you will make the curtains of she-goats[327] for the tent upon the dwelling, eleven curtains you will make. **8** The length of the one curtain is thirty by the *ammah*, and the width is four by the *ammah*, the one curtain measurement is one for the eleven curtains, **9** and you will couple five of the curtains alone and six of the curtains alone, and you will double over the sixth curtain to the forefront face of the tent, **10** and you will make fifty loops upon the lip of the one outer curtain with the coupling, and fifty loops upon the lip of the curtain of the second coupling, **11** and you will make fifty copper hooks, and you will bring the hooks in the loops, and you will couple the tent, and he will exist as a unit,

323 "From her" means that each of these parts is beaten (molded) out of the one piece.

324 "From her" means that each of these parts is beaten (molded) out of the one piece.

325 "Make her lamps go up" means to light the wicks.

326 This may be a work of thinking, in the sense of an intricate design, a work of a thinker, in the sense of a designer.

327 The curtains were made of "goats" hair.

12 and the overhang of the exceeding part in the curtains of the tent, half of
the curtain, the exceeding part, you will overhang upon the backs of the
dwelling, **13** and the *ammah* from this side, and the *ammah* from that side,
in the exceeding part in the length of the curtains of the tent, will be
overhung upon the sides of the dwelling, from this side and from that side to
cover him over, **14** and you will make a roof covering for the tent, skins of
bucks being red, and a roof covering of skins of deer on top, **15** and you will
make the boards for the dwelling of wood of acacia standing up. **16** Ten
ammahs is the length of the board, and an *ammah* and half the *ammah* is
the width of the one board. **17** Two hands[328] for the one board for being
joined together, each to her sister, so you will make for all the boards of the
dwelling, **18** and you will make the boards for the dwelling, twenty boards
for the edge unto the south, unto the southward, **19** and you will make forty
footings of silver under twenty of the boards, two footings under the one
board for his two hands, and two footings under the other board for his two
hands, **20** and for the second rib of the dwelling, to the north edge, is twenty
boards, **21** and their forty footings of silver, two footings under the one
board, and two footings under the other board, **22** and for the flanks[329] of
the dwelling, unto the sea[330], you will make six boards, **23** and you will make
two boards for the corner posts of the dwelling in the flanks, **24** and they will
exist being double beneath, and together they will exist whole upon his
head for the one ring, so he will exist for the two of them, for two of the
buttresses they will exist, **25** and eight boards will exist, and their footings of
silver are sixteen footings, two footings under the one board and two
footings under the other board, **26** and you will make wood bars of wood of
acacia, five for the boards of the one rib of the dwelling, **27** and five wood
bars for the boards of the second rib of the dwelling, and five wood bars for
the boards of the rib for the flanks of the dwelling unto the sea[331], **28** and
the middlemost wood bar in the midst of the boards will reach from the
extremity to the extremity, **29** and you will overlay the boards with gold, and
their rings you will make with gold, houses[332] for the wood bars, and you will
overlay the wood bars with gold, **30** and you will make the dwelling rise, like
his decision[333], which you were shown in the hill, **31** and you will make a tent
curtain of blue and purple and kermes of scarlet and twisted linen, a work of
a thinking[334], he will make her with keruvs, **32** and you will place her upon

---

328 These "hands" are probably notched tenons which are cut into the board to join the boards together. (also in verse 19)

329 That is, "sides."

330 Meaning "west."

331 Meaning "seaward" or "westward."

332 Or "housings."

333 Meaning "according to the manner."

334 This may be a work of thinking, in the sense of an intricate design, a work of a thinker, in the sense of a designer.

the four pillars of acacia, being overlaid with gold, their pegs of gold, upon the four footings of silver, **33** and you will place the tent curtain under the hooks, and you will bring unto there, inside the tent curtain, the box of the evidence, and the tent curtain will make a separation for you, between the special place and the special of specials[335], **34** and you will place the lid upon the box of the evidence in the special of specials, **35** and you will place the table outside the tent curtain, and the lampstand in front of the table upon the rib of the dwelling unto the south, and the table you will place upon the rib of the north, **36** and you will make a screen for an opening of the tent of blue and purple and kermes of scarlet and twisted linen, a work of embroidering[336], **37** and you will make for the screen five pillars of acacia, and you will overlay them with gold, their pegs of gold, and you will pour down[337] for them five footings of copper,

---

Chapter 27

1 and you will make the altar of wood of acacia, five *ammahs* is the length and five *ammahs* is the width, the altar will exist squared, and three *ammahs* is his height, **2** and you will make his horns upon the four of his corners, from him his horns will exist, and you will overlay him with copper, **3** and you will make his pots for removing fat residue, and his shovels, and his sprinkling basins, and his forks, and his fire pans, you will make all his utensils with copper, **4** and you will make for him a grate work of netting with copper, and you will make upon the netting four rings of copper upon his four extremities, **5** and you will place her under the outer rim of the altar beneath, and the netting will exist in the middle of the altar, **6** and you will make strands for the altar, strands of wood of acacia, and you will overlay them with copper, **7** and his strands will be brought in the rings, and the strands will exist upon the acacia ribs of the altar in lifting him up. **8** With hollowed out slabs you will make him, just as shown you in the hill, so they will do, **9** and you will make a courtyard of the dwelling to the edge, unto the south of the south, slings for the courtyard of twisted linen, a hundred by the *ammah* is the length for the one edge, **10** and his twenty pillars, and their twenty footings are of copper, the pegs of the pillars and their binders are of silver, **11** and so, for the edge of the north in the length, the slings are a hundred in length, and his twenty pillars and their twenty footings of copper, the pegs of the pillars and their binders of silver, **12** and the width of

---

[335] The phrase "special of specials" means a "very special thing, one or place." (also in verse 34)

[336] This may refer to a work of embroidery or the work of an embroiderer.

[337] In this context, to "pour down" means to "cast" an object from a molten metal.

the courtyard for the edge of the sea[338] are the slings of fifty *ammahs*, their ten pillars and their ten footings, **13** and the width of the courtyard for unto the edge of the east, unto the sunrise, is fifty *ammah*s, **14** and fifteen *ammahs* are the slings for the shoulder piece, their three pillars and their three footings, **15** and for the second shoulder piece are fifteen slings, their three pillars and their three footings, **16** and for the gate of the courtyard is a screen of twenty *ammah*s of blue and purple and kermes of scarlet and twisted linen, a work of embroidering[339], their four pillars and their four footings. **17** All the pillars of the courtyard all around it, being attached with silver, their pegs of silver and their footings of copper. **18** The length of the courtyard is a hundred by the *ammah*, and the width is fifty by the *ammah*s, and the height is five *ammah*s, with twisted linen and their footings of copper. **19** To all the utensils of the dwelling, in all his service, and all his tent pegs, and all the tent pegs of the courtyard are copper, **20** and you, you will direct the sons of *Yisra'eyl*, and they will take to you the refined and crushed oil of the olive for the luminary, to make the lamp go up[340] continually. **21** In the appointed tent, outside the tent curtain, which is upon the evidence, *Aharon*, and his sons, will arrange him, from the evening until the morning to the face of ***YHWH***, a ritual of a distant time for their generations, from the sons of *Yisra'eyl*,

Chapter 28

1 and you, bring near to you *Aharon*, your brother, and his sons with him, from the midst of the sons of *Yisra'eyl*, to adorn him for me, *Nadav* and *Aviyhu*, *Elazar* and *Iytamar*, the sons of *Aharon*, **2** and you will make garments of specialness for *Aharon*, your brother, for armament and for decoration, **3** and you, you will speak to all the skilled ones of heart, whom I filled with the wind[341] of skill, and they will make the garments of *Aharon* to set him apart, to adorn him for me, **4** and these are the garments which they will make, breastplate and ephod and cloak and tunic of woven material, turban and sash, and they will make garments of specialness for *Aharon*, your brother, and for his sons, to adorn him for me, **5** and they, they will take the gold and the blue and the purple and the kermes of the scarlet and the linen, **6** and they will make the ephod with gold, blue and purple, kermes of scarlet and twisted linen, a work of a thinking[342]. **7** He will have two shoulder pieces coupled together at the two of his extremities, and he will

[338] Meaning "west."
[339] This Hebrew word may refer to embroidery or an embroiderer.
[340] The word "go up" is referring to the rising flame of the lamp.
[341] The wind, or breath, of an individual is his character.
[342] This may be a work of thinking, in the sense of an intricate design, a work of a thinker, in the sense of a designer.

be coupled, **8** and the decorative band of his ephod, which is upon him, he will exist just like his work, gold, blue and purple and kermes of scarlet and twisted linen, **9** and you will take the two stones of the onyx, and you will engrave upon them the titles of the sons of *Yisra'eyl*. **10** Six from their titles upon the one stone and the six titles being left behind[343] upon the second stone, like their birthings[344]. **11** Like the work of a stone engraver, like the carvings of a seal, you will engrave the two stones according to the titles of the sons of *Yisra'eyl*, you will make them enclosed in plaits of gold, **12** and you will place the two stones upon the shoulder piece of the ephod, to be stones of remembrance for the sons of *Yisra'eyl*, and *Aharon* will lift up their titles to the face of ***YHWH***, upon his two shoulder pieces for a remembrance, **13** and you will make plaits of gold, **14** and two chains of clean gold are at the boundaries, you will make them a work of thick woven things, and you will place the chains of thick woven things upon the plaits, **15** and you will make a breastplate of decision, a work of thinking[345], like the work of the ephod you will make him, with gold, blue and purple and kermes of scarlet and twisted linen you will make him. **16** He will exist squared, doubled over, a finger span is his length, and a finger span is his width, **17** and you will set in him settings of stone, four rows of stone, a row of carnelian, olivine and emerald is the one row, **18** and the second row is turquoise, lapis lazuli and flint, **19** and the third row is opal, agate and amethyst, **20** and the fourth row is topaz and onyx and jasper, being woven with gold they will exist in their settings, **21** and the stones will exist according to the titles of the sons of *Yisra'eyl*, twelve according to their titles, carvings of the seal of each according to his title, they will exist for the twelve staffs[346], **22** and you will make upon the breastplate chains, the edging is a work of a thick woven thing of clean gold, **23** and you will make upon the breastplate two rings of gold, and you will place the two rings upon the two extremities of the breastplate, **24** and you will place the two thick woven things of gold upon the two rings at the extremities of the breastplate, **25** and the two extremities of the two thick woven cords you will place upon the two plaits, and you will place upon the shoulder pieces of the ephod to the forefront of his face, **26** and you will make two rings of gold, and you will place them upon the two extremities of the breastplate upon his lip, which is on the other side of the ephod, unto the inside, **27** and you will make two rings of gold, and you will place them upon the two shoulder pieces of the ephod, beneath the forefront of his face, alongside his joint, above the decorative band of the ephod, **28** and they will tie on the breastplate by his rings to the rings of the ephod with a cord of blue, to exist

---

[343] "Six titles being left behind" means "the other six titles."

[344] Or "according to their birthings."

[345] This may be a work of thinking, in the sense of an intricate design, a work of a thinker, in the sense of a designer.

[346] Or "tribes."

upon the decorative band of the ephod, and the breastplate will not be loosened from upon the ephod, **29** and *Aharon* lifted up the titles of the sons of *Yisra'eyl* in the breastplate of the decision upon his heart, in his coming to the special place garments of special place for a remembrance to the face of ***YHWH*** continually, **30** and you will place the *Uriym* and the *Tumiym* on the breastplate of the decision, and they will exist upon the heart of *Aharon* in his coming to the face of ***YHWH***, and *Aharon* will lift up the decision of the sons of *Yisra'eyl* upon his heart to the face of ***YHWH*** continually, **31** and you will make the cloak of the ephod entirely of blue, **32** and a mouth[347] for his head will exist in his midst, a lip[348] will exist for his mouth all around, a work of braiding[349], he will exist for him like the mouth of a collar, he will not be torn, **33** and you will make upon his hems pomegranates of blue and purple and kermes of scarlet, upon his hems all around, and bells of gold in their midst all around. **34** Bells of gold and pomegranates, bells of gold and pomegranates[350] are upon the hems of the cloak all around, **35** and he will exist upon *Aharon* to minister, and his voice[351] will be heard in his coming to the special place, to the face of ***YHWH***, and in his going out and he will not die, **36** and you will make a blossom of clean gold, and you will engrave upon him carvings of a seal, a special thing for ***YHWH***, **37** and you will place him upon a cord of blue, and he will exist upon the turban, to the forefront of the face of the turban he will exist, **38** and he will exist upon the forehead of *Aharon*, and *Aharon* will lift up the twistedness of the special things, which the sons of *Yisra'eyl* set apart for all the contributions of their special things, and he will exist upon his forehead continually, for the self-will for them[352] to the face of ***YHWH***, **39** and you will weave the tunic of linen, and you will make a turban of linen, and you will make a sash, a work of embroidering[353], **40** and for the sons of *Aharon* you will make tunics, and you will make for them sashes, and headdresses, you will make for them for armament and for decoration, **41** and you will clothe them, *Aharon* your brother and his sons with him, and you will smear them, and you will fill their hand[354], and you will set them apart, and they will be adorned for me, **42** and make for them

---

[347] That is an "opening."

[348] That is an "edge" or a "border."

[349] This may be the work of braiding or the work of a braider.

[350] The phrase "bells of gold and pomegranates" is written twice showing that they are to be placed on the garment in series.

[351] Meaning the "sound" of the bells.

[352] The phrase "for the self-will for them" means "that they will be accepted."

[353] This may refer to a work of embroidery or the work of an embroiderer.

[354] To "fill the hand" is an idiom of uncertain meaning, but the same phrase is used in Akkadian to mean the placing of a relevant tool or insignia (such as a scepter for a king) in the hand of one being installed in a high office.

undergarments of linen to cover over the flesh of nakedness from the waists, and unto the midsection they will exist, **43** and they will exist upon *Aharon* and upon his sons, in their coming to the appointed tent, or in their drawing near to the altar to minister in the special place, and they will not lift up twistedness or they will die, it is a ritual of a distant time for him and for his seed after him,

---

Chapter 29

1 and this is the matter which you will do for them to set them apart to be adorned for me, take one bull, a son of the cattle, and two whole bucks, **2** and unleavened bread and unleavened pierced bread mixed in the oil, and unleavened thin bread smeared in the oil, from the flour of wheat you will make them, **3** and you will place them upon one basket, and you will make them come near with the basket and the bull and the two bucks, **4** and you will make *Aharon* and his sons come near the opening of the appointed tent, and you will bathe them in the waters, **5** and you will take the garments, and you will clothe *Aharon* with the tunic and with the cloak of the ephod and with the ephod and with the breastplate, and you will gird him with the decorative band of the ephod, **6** and you will place the turban upon his head, and you will place the special thing of dedication[355] upon the turban, **7** and you will take the oil of ointment, and you will pour it down upon his head, and you will smear him, **8** and you will make his sons come near, and you will clothe them with tunics, **9** and you will gird up *Aharon* and his sons with the sash, and you will saddle them with the headdresses, and the administration will exist for them, a ritual of a distant time, and you will fill the hand[356] of *Aharon* and the hand of his sons, **10** and you will make the bull come near to the face of the appointed tent, and *Aharon*, and his sons, will support their hands upon the head of the bull, **11** and you will slay the bull to the face of ***YHWH*** at the opening of the appointed place, **12** and you will take from the blood of the bull and you will place it upon the horns of the altar with your finger, and you will pour out all the blood at the foundation of the altar, **13** and you will take all the fat covering, the insides, and the lobe upon the heavy one[357], and the two kidneys, and the fat which is upon them, and you will burn incense[358] unto the altar, **14** and you will cremate the flesh of the bull, and his skin, and his dung, in the fire outside

---

[355] That is a "crown."

[356] To "fill the hand" is an idiom of uncertain meaning, but the same phrase is used in Akkadian to mean the placing of a relevant tool or insignia (such as a scepter for a king) in the hand of one being installed in a high office.

[357] "The heavy one" is the "liver," the heaviest organ of the body.

[358] The phrase "and you will burn incense" may also be interpreted as "and you will burn them as incense."

the camp, he is a failure, **15** and you will take the one buck, and *Aharon* and his sons will support their hands upon the head of the buck, **16** and you will slay the buck, and you will take his blood and you will sprinkle it upon the altar all around, **17** and you will divide the buck into pieces according to his pieces[359], and you will bathe his insides and his legs, and you will place them upon his pieces and upon his head, **18** and you will burn as incense all of the buck unto the altar, he is an ascension offering for ***YHWH***, a sweet aroma, he is a fire offering for ***YHWH***, **19** and you will take the second buck, and *Aharon*, and his sons, will support their hands upon the head of the buck, **20** and you will slay the buck, and you will take from his blood and you will place it upon the tip of the ear of *Aharon* and upon the tip of the right ear of his sons, and upon the right thumb of their hands, and upon the right thumb of their feet, and you will sprinkle the blood upon the altar all around, **21** and you will take from the blood which is upon the altar, and from the oil of the ointment, and you will spatter it upon *Aharon* and upon his garments and upon his sons and upon the garments of his sons with him, and he will set him apart, and his garments, and his sons, and the garments of his sons with him, **22** and you will take from the buck the fat and the rump and the fat covering and the insides and the heavy lobe[360] and the two kidneys and the fat which is upon them and the right thigh, given that the buck, he is an installation, **23** and one round bread and one pierced bread of oil and one thin bread from the basket of the unleavened bread, which is to the face of ***YHWH***, **24** and you will place all of it upon the palms of *Aharon* and upon the palms of his sons, and you will wave them for a wave offering to the face of ***YHWH***, **25** and you will take them from their hand, and you will burn them as incense unto the altar, upon the ascension offering for a sweet aroma to the face of ***YHWH***, he is a fire offering for ***YHWH***, **26** and you will take the chest from the buck of the installation, which is for *Aharon*, and you will wave him for a wave offering to the face of ***YHWH***, and he will exist for you for a share, **27** and you will set apart the chest of the wave offering and the thigh of the offering, which was waved and which was raised from the buck of the installation, out of which is for *Aharon* and out of which is for his sons, **28** and he will exist for *Aharon* and for his sons for a custom of a distant time from the sons of *Yisra'eyl*, given that he is an offering, and the offering will exist from the sons of *Yisra'eyl*, from their offerings of restitution, their offerings to ***YHWH***, **29** and the garments of specialness, which belong to *Aharon*, will exist for his sons after him, to be smeared with them, and their hand to be filled[361] with them. **30** For seven days the administrator, from his

---

[359] "To his pieces" means that the animal would be divided (cut) at each section (piece, joint).

[360] "The heavy lobe" is the liver, the heaviest organ in the body.

[361] To "fill the hand" is an idiom of uncertain meaning, but the same phrase is used in Akkadian to mean the placing of a relevant tool or insignia (such as a scepter for a king) in the hand of one being installed in a high office.

sons, that is in place of him, will wear them when he will come to the appointed tent, to minister in the special place, **31** and you will take the buck of the installation, and you will boil his flesh in the unique area, **32** and *Aharon*, and his sons, will eat the flesh of the buck and the bread which is in the basket at the opening of the appointed tent, **33** and they will eat them, which was to make a covering with them to fill their hand[362] to set them apart, and a stranger will not eat it, given that they are a special thing, **34** and if anything is left behind from the flesh of the installation, and from the bread until the morning, then you will cremate what is being left behind in the fire, he will not be eaten, given that he is a special thing, **35** and you will do for *Aharon* and for his sons just like this, just like all that I directed you, for seven days you will fill their hand, **36** and you will do the bull of failure daily concerning the atonements, and you will bear the blame upon the altar with your making a covering upon him, and you will smear him for setting him apart. **37** For seven days you will make a covering upon the altar, you will set him apart and the altar will exist as a special of specials[363], all the ones touching the altar will be set apart, **38** and this is what you will do upon the altar, two sheep, a son[364] of a year, daily, continually. **39** You will do the one sheep in the morning, and you will do the second sheep between the evenings[365], **40** and one-tenth part of flour mixed in a quarter of the *hiyn* of crushed oil, and a pouring of a fourth of the *hiyn* of wine for the one sheep, **41** and you will do the second sheep between the evenings like the donation of the morning, and you will do her like her pouring, it is for a sweet aroma, a fire offering for ***YHWH***. **42** It is a continual ascension offering for your generations at the opening of the appointed tent to the face of ***YHWH***, where I will meet with you there, to speak to you there, **43** and I will meet with the sons of *Yisra'eyl* there, and he will be set apart with my armament, **44** and I will set apart the appointed tent and the altar and *Aharon* and his sons, I will set them apart, to be adorned for me, **45** and I will dwell in the midst of the sons of *Yisra'eyl*, and I will exist for them for *Elohiym*, **46** and they will know that I am ***YHWH*** their *Elohiym*, who made them go out from the land of *Mits'rayim*, for me to dwell in their midst, I am ***YHWH*** their *Elohiym*,

---

[362] To "fill the hand" is an idiom of uncertain meaning, but the same phrase is used in Akkadian to mean the placing of a relevant tool or insignia (such as a scepter for a king) in the hand of one being installed in a high office. (also in verse 34)

[363] The phrase "special of specials" means a "very special thing, one or place."

[364] "Son" is an idiom for years "old."

[365] The phrase "between the evenings" is of uncertain meaning but may be the time between sunset and dark. (also in verse 34)

Chapter 30

1 and you will make an altar, a place to burn incense smoke, you will make him of wood of acacia. **2** A *ammah* is his length and an *ammah* is his width, he will exist squared, and two *ammah*s is his height, from him are his horns, **3** and you will overlay him with clean gold, his roof and his walls, all around, and his horns, and you will make for him a molding of gold all around, **4** and you will make two rings of gold for him under his molding, upon his two ribs, you will make them upon his two sides, and he will exist for houses[366], for the strands to lift him up in them, **5** and you will make the strands of wood of acacia, and you will overlay them with gold, **6** and you will place him to the front of the tent curtain, which is upon the box of the evidence, to the face of the lid, which is upon the evidence, where I will meet with you there, **7** and *Aharon* will burn incense upon him, an incense of aromatic spices, morning by morning, in his making the lamps do well[367], he will make her burn incense, **8** and with *Aharon* making the lamp go up between the evenings[368], he will make her burn as incense, a continual incense to the face of ***YHWH*** for your generations. **9** You will not bring up upon him incense of a stranger[369], and you will not pour upon him an ascension offering, or a donation or a pouring, **10** and *Aharon* will make a covering upon his horns, one time in the year from the blood of failure of the atonement, one time in the year he will make a covering upon him for your generations, he is a special of specials[370] for ***YHWH***, **11** and ***YHWH*** spoke to *Mosheh* saying, **12** given that you will lift up the head[371] of the sons of *Yisra'eyl* for them to be registered, and each will give a covering of his soul to ***YHWH*** with their registering, and a striking[372] will not exist in them with their registering. **13** This is what all the ones crossing over upon the registered will give, one-half of the *sheqel*, with the *sheqel* of the special place, twenty *gerah*s is the *sheqel*, one-half of the *sheqel* is the offering for ***YHWH***. **14** All the ones crossing over upon the registered, from a son[373] of twenty years and upward, will give an offering of ***YHWH***. **15** The rich will not give an increase and the helpless will not give less from the one-half of the *sheqel*, it is for

---

366 Or "housings."

367 "Making the lamps do well" is probably referring to trimming the wicks so that they burn properly.

368 The phrase "between the evenings" is of uncertain meaning but may be the time between sunset and dark.

369 The phrase incense of a stranger" can also be translated as "strange incense."

370 The phrase "special of specials" means a "very special thing, one or place."

371 "Lift up the head" means to "count."

372 That is a pestilence, plague or other disaster.

373 "Son" is an idiom for years "old."

giving an offering of ***YHWH*** for making a covering upon your souls, **16** and you will take the silver of the atonement from the sons of *Yisra'eyl*, and you will give him upon the service of the appointed tent, and he will exist for the sons of *Yisra'eyl* for a remembrance to the face of ***YHWH*** for making a covering upon your souls, **17** and ***YHWH*** spoke to *Mosheh* saying, **18** and you will make a cauldron of copper, and his base of copper, it is for bathing, and you will place him between the appointed tent and the altar, and you will place unto there the waters, **19** and *Aharon* and his sons will bathe from him, their hands and their feet. **20** In their coming to the appointed tent, they will bathe with waters and they will not die, or in their drawing near to the altar to minister to burn incense, it is a fire offering for ***YHWH***, **21** and they will bathe their hands and their feet and they will not die, and she will exist for them as a custom of a distant time, for him and for his seed, for their generations, **22** and ***YHWH*** spoke to *Mosheh* saying, **23** and you, take for you the head[374] sweet spices, free flowing myrrh will be five hundred, and cinnamon of sweet spice will be one-half of him, that is fifty and two hundred, and a stalk of sweet spice will be fifty and two hundred, **24** and cassia will be five hundred, by the *sheqel* of the special place, and olive oil will be a *hiyn*, **25** and you will make him an oil of ointment of specialness, a spice mixture, an ointment mixture, a work of compounding[375], he will exist as an oil of ointment of specialness, **26** and you will smear with him the appointed tent, and the box of the evidence, **27** and the table and all his utensils, and the lampstand and her utensils, and the altar of the incense, **28** and the altar of the ascension offering and all his utensils, and the cauldron and his base, **29** and you will set them apart, and they will exist as a special of specials[376], all the ones touching them is set apart, **30** and you will smear *Aharon* and his sons, and you will set them apart to be adorned for me, **31** and to the sons of *Yisra'eyl* you will speak saying, this oil of ointment of specialness will exist for me for your generations. **32** Upon the flesh of the human he is not poured, and with the sum[377] you will not make it like that one, he is a special thing, a special thing will exist for you. **33** A man who will compound like that one, and which will give from him upon a stranger, then he will be cut from his peoples, **34** and ***YHWH*** said to *Mosheh*, take for you aromatic spices, *nataph* and onycha and galbanum, aromatic spices and refined frankincense, he will exist strand in strand[378], **35** and you will make

---

[374] Meaning "chief" or "principle."

[375] This may be a "work of compounding," in the sense of a "mixture," or made by a "compounder" in the sense of a "mixer."

[376] The phrase "special of specials" means a "very special thing, one or place."

[377] The "sum" is the proportions mentioned in the previous verses.

[378] "Strand in strand" means an equal portion of each.

her an incense, a spice mixture, a work of compounding[379], a clean
seasoning of specialness, **36** and you will pulverize some of her, beat to
make small, and you will place some of her to the face of the evidence in the
appointed tent, where I will meet with you there, she will exist for you as a
special of specials[380], **37** and the incense which you will make with her
sum[381], you will not make for you, it is a special thing, she will exist for you
for ***YHWH***. **38** A man who will make it like that one, to smell with her[382],
then he will be cut from his peoples,

Chapter 31

1 and ***YHWH*** spoke to *Mosheh* saying, **2** see, I called out by title *Betsaleyl*[383],
son of *Uriy*, son of *Hhur* belonging to the branch of *Yehudah*, **3** and I filled
him with the wind[384] of *Elohiym*, with skill and with intelligence and with
discernment and with all kinds of business. **4** To think of inventions, to make
things with the gold and with the silver and with the copper, **5** and with the
engraving of stone for filling, and with the engraving of trees[385] for making
things with all kinds of business, **6** and look, I gave him *Ahaliyav*, son of
Ahhiysamahh, belonging to the branch of *Dan*, and in the heart of all the
skilled ones of heart I gave skill, and they will make all that I directed you.
7 The appointed tent, and the box for the evidence, and the lid which is
upon him, and all the utensils of the tent, **8** and the table, and his utensils,
and the clean lampstand and all her utensils, and the altar of the incense,
9 and the altar of the ascension offering and all his utensils, and the
cauldron and his base, **10** and the garments of the braided work, and the
garments of specialness for *Aharon* the administrator, and the garments of
his sons, for them to be adorned, **11** and the oil of ointment, and the incense

---

379 This may be a "work of compounding," in the sense of a "mixture," or made by a "compounder" in the sense of a "mixer."

380 The phrase "special of specials" means a "very special thing, one or place."

381 The "sum" is the proportions mentioned in the previous verses.

382 Probably meaning "to smell the same as her," where the "her" is the incense smoke, a feminine noun.

383 The phrase "I called out by title *Betsaleyl*" can mean, "I called *Betsaleyl* by name," but can also be translated as "I met with the title (meaning character or person) of *Betsaleyl*," as the Hebrew verb קרא may mean to "call out" or to "meet."

384 The wind, or breath, of an individual is his character.

385 When the Hebrew word עֵץ is written in the singular, as it is here, it can mean tree or trees. When it is written in the plural form, it usually means "wood." If the original text read עֵצִים, the plural form, then this would be translated as "wood."

of aromatic spices for the special place, just like all that I directed you, they will do, **12** and ***YHWH*** said to *Mosheh* saying, **13** and you, speak to the sons of *Yisra'eyl* saying, surely you will safeguard my ceasings, given that she is a sign between me and you for your generations, to know that I am ***YHWH*** setting you apart, **14** and you will safeguard the ceasing, given that she is a special time for you, anyone defiling her will surely be killed, given that all the ones doing a business in her, that soul will be cut from inside her peoples. **15** Six days business will be done, and in the seventh day there will be a ceasing, a rest period, a special time for ***YHWH***, all the ones doing business in the day of the ceasing will surely be killed, **16** and the sons of *Yisra'eyl* will safeguard the ceasing, to do the ceasing to their generations, it is a covenant of a distant time. **17** Between me and the sons of *Yisra'eyl*, she is a sign for a distant time, given that in six days ***YHWH*** made the skies and the land, and in the seventh day he ceased and he breathed deeply[386], **18** and he gave to *Mosheh*, as he finished speaking with him in the hill of *Sinai*, the two slabs of the evidence, the slabs of stone written with the finger of *Elohiym*,

---

Chapter 32

1 and the people saw that *Mosheh* refrained to go down from the hill, and the people were rounded up upon *Aharon* and they said to him, rise, make for us *Elohiym*[387] which will walk to our faces, given that this *Mosheh*, the man which made us go up from the land of *Mits'rayim*, we do not know what came to pass to him, **2** and *Aharon* said to them, tear off the ornamental rings of gold which are in the ears of your women, your sons and your daughters and bring them to me, **3** and the people tore off the ornamental rings of gold which were in their ears and they brought them to *Aharon*, **4** and he took them from their hand, and he smacked him with the engraving tool, and he made him into a cast image of a bullock, and they said, *Yisra'eyl*, these are your *Elohiym*[388] which made you go up from the

---

386 "Breathe deeply" means "to take a break" or "to refresh ones' self."

387 When the word "*Elohiym*," a plural word, is used as the subject of a verb, the verb normally identifies the subject as a masculine singular. Therefore, the word "*Elohiym*" is being used in a singular sense. However, in this verse, the verb "walk" identifies the subject of the verb, "*Elohiym*," as a masculine plural noun. This may simply be an alternate grammatical verb and noun construct, or the word *Elohiym* is meant to be understood as a plural in this verse. (Compare with Exodus 32:4, 32:5 and 32:8.)

388 The word "*Elohiym*" is being used as a masculine plural noun in this verse, as it is modified with the masculine plural pronoun "these." However, the image representing the "*Elohiym*" is a single bullock. (Compare with Exodus 32:1, 32:5 and 32:8.)

land of *Mits'rayim*, **5** and *Aharon* saw it and he built an altar to his[389] face, and *Aharon* called out and he said, tomorrow is a feast to ***YHWH***, **6** and they departed early the next day, and they made ascension offerings go up, and they made offerings of restitution draw near, and the people settled to eat and gulp, and they rose to mock, **7** and ***YHWH*** spoke to *Mosheh*, walk, go down, given that your people, which you made go up from the land of *Mits'rayim*, are damaged. **8** They quickly turned aside from the road which I directed them, they made for themselves a cast image of a bullock, and they bent themselves down to him[390] and they sacrificed to him, and they said, *Yisra'eyl*, these are your *Elohiym*[391], which made you go up from the land of *Mits'rayim*, **9** and ***YHWH*** said to *Mosheh*, I saw this people and look, he is a hard necked people, **10** and now leave me, and my nose will flare up in them, and I will finish[392] them, and I will make you into a great nation, **11** and *Mosheh* twisted[393] the face of ***YHWH*** his *Elohiym*, and he said, ***YHWH***, why is your nose flared up with your people, which you made go out from the land of *Mits'rayim*, with great strength and with a forceful hand. **12** Why will *Mits'rayim* say, saying, in dysfunction he made them go out to kill them in the hills and to finish them from upon the face of the ground[394], turn back from the burning wrath of your nose, and repent concerning the dysfunction for your people. **13** Remember *Avraham*, *Yits'hhaq* and *Yisra'eyl* your servants, which you swore to them by yourself, and you spoke to them, I will make your seed increase like the stars of the skies, and all this land, which I said I will give to your seed and they will inherit it to a distant time, **14** and ***YHWH*** repented upon the dysfunction, which he spoke to do to his people, **15** and *Mosheh* turned, and he went down from the hill, and the two slabs of the evidence were in his hand, the slabs written on their two sides, on this side and on that side they were written, **16** and the slabs, they are the work of *Elohiym*, and the thing written was a thing written of *Elohiym*, he engraved upon the slabs, **17** and *Yehoshu'a* heard the voice of the people with a loud noise, and he said to *Mosheh*, it is the voice of battle in the camp, **18** and he said, it is not a voice in answer of bravery, and it is not a

---

389 In this verse the "*Elohiym*" is being identified with a masculine singular pronoun. (Compare with Exodus 32:1, 32:4 and 32:8.)

390 The pronoun "him," identifies the word "*Elohiym*" as a masculine singular noun. In addition, the image representing the "*Elohiym*" is a single bullock. (Compare with Exodus 32:1, 32:4 and 32:5 and the following Footnote.)

391 The word "*Elohiym*" is identified as a masculine plural noun, as it is modified with the masculine plural pronoun "these." (Compare with the previous Footnote and Exodus 32:1, 32:4 and 32:5.)

392 The context implies that the word "finish" means to "destroy."

393 The root of the Hebrew word ויחל may be חול (to twist), חלל (to pierce) or חלה (to be sick).

394 The phrase "to finish them from upon the face of the ground" means "to remove them from the land."

voice in answer of defeat, it is a voice in answer of wine[395] that I am hearing, **19** and it came to pass just as he came near to the camp, and he saw the bullock and the dances, and the nose of *Mosheh* flared up[396], and he threw out the slabs from his hand, and he cracked them under the hill[397], **20** and he took the bullock which they made and he cremated it in the fire, and he ground it until that is beaten small, and he dispersed it upon the face of the waters, and he made the sons of *Yisra'eyl* drink it, **21** and *Mosheh* said to *Aharon*, what did this people do to you, given that you brought upon him a great failure, **22** and *Aharon* said, do not let the nose of my lord flare up[398], you, you know the people, given that he is in dysfunction, **23** and they said to me, make for us *Elohiym*[399] which will walk to our faces, given that this *Mosheh*, the man which made us go up from the land of *Mits'rayim*, we do not know what came to pass to him, **24** and I said to them, whoever has gold, tear it off of yourself, and they gave it to me, and I sent him in the fire, and this bullock went out, **25** and *Mosheh* saw the people, given that he is loosened, given that *Aharon* loosened him for a derision in their risers[400], **26** and *Mosheh* stood in the gate of the camp, and he said, who is for ***YHWH***, come to me, and all the sons of *Lewi* gathered to him, **27** and he said to them, in this way, ***YHWH*** the *Elohiym* of *Yisra'eyl* said, each will place his sword upon his midsection[401], cross over and turn back from one gate to the other gate in the camp, and kill each his brother, and each his companion, and each his near one, **28** and the sons of *Lewi* did just like the word of *Mosheh*, and about three thousand men fell from the people in that day, **29** and *Mosheh* said, fill your hand[402] today for ***YHWH***, given that each is with his son and with his brother, and to give to you today a present, **30** and it came to pass the next day, and *Mosheh* said to the people, you, you failed a great failure, and now I will go up to ***YHWH***, possibly I will cover it on behalf of your failure, **31** and *Mosheh* turned back to ***YHWH*** and he said, please, this people failed a great failure, and they made for themselves *Elohiym* of gold, **32** and now, if you will lift up their failure, but if not, please wipe me away from your scroll which you wrote, **33** and ***YHWH*** said to *Mosheh*, who is it that failed me, I will wipe him away from my scroll, **34** and

---

395 The text appears to be missing a word after "answer," possibly "rejoicing," but the Septuagint has "wine."

396 The "flaring of the nose" is an idiom for a fierce anger.

397 "Under the hill" meaning "at the bottom of the hill."

398 The "flaring of the nose" is an idiom for a fierce anger.

399 See Exodus 32:1

400 Probably meaning "enemies," ones who "rise up" against them.

401 "Place his sword upon his midsection" means to "strap a sword onto the waist."

402 To "fill the hand" is an idiom of uncertain meaning, but the same phrase is used in Akkadian to mean the placing of a relevant tool or insignia (such as a scepter for a king) in the hand of one being installed in a high office.

now, walk, guide the people to where I spoke to you, look, my messenger will walk to your face, and in the day of my registering, then I will register upon them their failure, **35** and ***YHWH*** smote the people according to who made the bullock, which *Aharon* made,

---

Chapter 33

1 and ***YHWH*** spoke to *Mosheh*, walk, go up from this place, you and the people which you made go up from the land of *Mits'rayim*, which I swore to *Avraham* to *Yits'hhaq* and to *Ya'aqov* saying, I will give her to your seed,
2 and I will send a messenger to your face, and I will cast out the one of *Kena'an*, the one of *Emor* and the one of *Hhet* and the one of *Perez*, the one of *Hhiw* and the one of *Yevus*. **3** To a land issuing fat[403] and honey[404], given that I will not go up in *among* you, given that you are a hard necked people, otherwise, I will finish[405] you in the road, **4** and the people heard this dysfunctional word, and they mourned, and each did not set down[406] his trappings upon him, **5** and ***YHWH*** said to *Mosheh*, say to the sons of *Yisra'eyl*, you are a hard necked people, I will go up in among you one moment, and I will finish[407] you, and now, make your trappings go down from upon you[408], and I will know what I will do to you, **6** and the sons of *Yisra'eyl* delivered[409] their trappings by the hill of *Hhorev*, **7** and *Mosheh* will take the tent and he will extend[410] him outside of the camp, far from the camp, and he will call out to him at the appointed tent, and it will come to pass, the ones searching out ***YHWH*** will go out to the appointed tent, which is outside of the camp, **8** and it will come to pass, when *Mosheh* is about to go out to the tent, all the people will rise, and they will stand up, each at the opening of his tent, and they will stare after *Mosheh*, until his coming unto the tent, **9** and it will come to pass, when *Mosheh* is about to come unto the tent, the pillar of the cloud will go down, and he will stand at the opening of the tent, and he will speak with *Mosheh*, **10** and all the people saw the pillar of the cloud standing at the opening of the tent, and all the people rose, and they bent themselves down, each at the opening of his tent, **11** and ***YHWH*** spoke to *Mosheh* face to face, just as a man will speak to his companion, and

---

403 This Hebrew word can also mean "milk."
404 The Hebrew word דבש means a "sticky mass" and can also mean "dates" from the palm tree.
405 The context implies that the word "finish" means to "destroy."
406 "Set down" in this context means to "put on."
407 The context implies that the word "finish" means to "destroy."
408 "Make your trappings go down from upon you" in this context means to "take off your trappings.
409 The context implies that the word "delivered" means "removed."
410 That is to "stretch out" or to "set up."

he turned back to the camp, and his minister, *Yehoshu'a*, the son of *Nun*, a
young man, will not move away from the midst of the tent, **12** and *Mosheh*
said to ***YHWH***, see, you are saying to me, make this people go up, and you,
you did not make me know who you will send with me, and you, you said, I
know you by title[411], and also you found beauty[412] in my eyes, **13** and now,
please, if I find beauty in your eyes, please, make me know your road[413], and
I will know you, so that I will find beauty in your eyes and see that your
people are this nation, **14** and he said, my face will walk[414], and I will make a
rest for you[415], **15** and he said to him, if your face is not walking, do not
make us go up from this place, **16** and how will it be known then that I, and
your people, found beauty in your eyes, is it not with your walking with us,
then I and your people will be distinct out of all the people which are upon
the face of the ground, **17** and ***YHWH*** said to *Mosheh*, also this word which
you spoke, I will do, given that you found beauty in my eyes, and I know you
by title[416], **18** and he said, please make me see your armament, **19** and he
said, I will make all my function cross over upon your face, and I will call out
YHWH by title[417] to your face, and I will show beauty to who I will show
beauty, and I will have compassion to who I will have compassion, **20** and he
said, you will not be able to see my face, given that the human will not see
me and live, **21** and ***YHWH*** said, look, an area is by me, and you will be
standing up upon the boulder, **22** and it will come to pass with the crossing
over of my armament, and I will place you in the fissure of the boulder, and I
will fence my palm[418] around you until I cross over, **23** and I will make my
palm turn aside and you will see my backs[419], but my face will not appear,

---

[411] “I know you by title” is an idiom meaning “I know your character,” or “I know all about you.”

[412] “Find beauty” means to “be accepted.” (also in verses 13, 16 and 17)

[413] “Know your road” is an idiom meaning “teach me your ways.”

[414] “My face will walk” means “my presence will go.”

[415] “Make a rest for you” may be translated as “give you rest.”

[416] “I know you by title” is an idiom meaning “I know your character,” or “I know all about you.”

[417] The phrase “I will call out ***YHWH*** by title” can mean, “I will call ***YHWH*** by name,” but can also be translated as “and I will meet with the title (meaning character or person) of ***YHWH***,” as the Hebrew verb קרא may mean to “call out” or to “meet.”

[418] This may be the palm of a hand, a palm tree or anything that is palm-shaped. (also in verse 23)

[419] The phrase “my backs” may also be translated as “behind me.”

Chapter 34

1 and ***YHWH*** said to *Mosheh*, sculpt for yourself two slabs of stone like the
first ones, and I will write upon the slabs the words, which existed upon the
first slabs, which you cracked, **2** and be ready for the morning, and you will
go up in the morning to the hill of *Sinai*, and you will stand up to me there
upon the head of the hill, **3** and no man will go up with you, and also, do not
let a man appear in all the hill, also do not let the flocks and the cattle feed
on the forefront of that hill, **4** and he sculpted two slabs of stone like the
first ones, and *Mosheh* departed early in the morning, and he went up to the
hill of *Sinai*, just as ***YHWH*** directed him, and he took in his hand the two
slabs of stone, **5** and ***YHWH*** went down in the cloud, and he stationed
himself with him there, and he called out ***YHWH*** by title[420], **6** and ***YHWH***
crossed over upon his face, and he called out, ***YHWH***, ***YHWH***, the mighty
one[421], compassionate and gracious, slow of nostrils[422], and abundant in
kindness and truth. **7** Preserving kindness to the thousands, lifting up[423]
twistedness and offense and failure, but he will not completely acquit[424],
registering the twistedness of the fathers upon the sons and upon the sons
of the sons, upon the third generations and upon the fourth generation,
8 and *Mosheh* hurried and he bowed the head unto the land and he bent
himself down, **9** and he said, please, if I found beauty[425] in your eyes *Adonai*,
please, *Adonai* will walk inside us, given that he is a hard necked people, and
you will forgive our twistedness and our failure, and you will inherit us,
10 and he said, look, I am cutting a covenant before all your people, I will do
performances, which has not been shaped[426] in all the land and in all the
nations, and all the people, which you are inside, will see the work of ***YHWH***,
given that what I am doing with you, is to be feared. **11** Safeguard for you
what I am directing you today, look at me casting out from your face[427] the
one of *Emor* and the one of *Kena'an* and the one of *Hhet* and the one of

---

420 The phrase "he called out ***YHWH*** by title" can mean, "he called ***YHWH*** by name," but can also be translated as "and he met with the title (meaning character or person) of ***YHWH***," as the Hebrew verb קרא may mean to "call out" or to "meet."

421 The phrase וַיִּקְרָא יְהוָה יְהוָה אֵל may be translated as, "and he called out, ***YHWH***, ***YHWH***, the mighty one," "and ***YHWH*** called out, ***YHWH*** is a mighty one" or "and ***YHWH*** called out ***YHWH*** the mighty one."

422 "Slow of nostrils" is an idiom meaning "patient."

423 "Lifting up" means "forgiving."

424 The *Septuagint* reads "he will not acquit the guilty," where the word "guilty" is not found in the Hebrew text, but may have accidentally been dropped from the text.

425 "Find beauty" means to "be accepted."

426 "Not been shaped" means that it has not been done before.

427 "From your face" is an idiom meaning "from your presence."

Perez and the one of *Hhiw* and the one of *Yevus*. **12** Be safeguarded to yourself, otherwise you will cut a covenant for a settler of the land which you are coming upon, otherwise he will exist for a snare in among you, **13** given that their altars you must break down, and their monuments you must shatter, and his groves you must cut, **14** given that you will not bend yourself down to another mighty one, given that ***YHWH*** is zealous, his title is the mighty one, he is zealous. **15** Otherwise you will cut a covenant for a settler of the land, and they will be a whore after their *Elohiym*, and they will sacrifice to their *Elohiym*, and he will call out to you and you will eat of his altar, **16** and you will take from his daughters for your sons, and his daughters will be a whore after their *Elohiym*, and they will make your sons be a whore after their *Elohiym*. **17** You will not make for you an *Elohiym* of a cast image. **18** You will safeguard the feast of the unleavened bread, seven days you will eat the unleavened bread which I directed you for an appointed time in the month of the green grain, given that in the month of the green grain you went out from *Mits'rayim*. **19** All the bursting of the bowels[428] is for me, all your livestock, the males[429] bursting of the ox and ram, **20** and the burstings of the donkey you will ransom with a ram, and if you will not ransom it, then you will behead[430] him, all the firstborn of your sons you will ransom and they will not appear to my face empty[431]. **21** Six days you will serve and in the seventh day you will cease with the plowing, and with the harvesting you will cease, **22** and you will do the feast of weeks for you, first-fruits of the harvest of the wheat, and a feast of the gathering at the circuit[432] of the year. **23** Three times in the year all your men will appear at the face of the lord ***YHWH,*** the *Elohiym* of *Yisra'eyl*, **24** given that I will dispossess the nations from your face, and I will widen your borders, and a man will not crave your land with you going up to appear at the face ***YHWH*** your *Elohiym* three times in the year. **25** You will not slay the blood of my sacrifice upon the leavened bread, and the sacrifice of the feast of the *Pesahh* will not stay the night to the morning. **26** You will bring the summit of the first-fruits[433] of your ground to the house of ***YHWH*** your *Elohiym*, you will not boil a male kid in the fat[434] of his mother, **27** and ***YHWH*** said to *Mosheh*, write for yourself these words, given that by the mouth of these

---

[428] The "bursting of the bowels" is the childbirths.

[429] The Hebrew word תִּזָּכֵר means "you will be remembered," but the context implies that this word may have originally been written as הַזָּכָר meaning "the male."

[430] This Hebrew verb can mean to "behead" or "break the neck."

[431] The word פָּנָי appears to be missing the prefix ל (to). As it is written, the sentence could be translated as "and my face will not appear empty."

[432] Meaning "end."

[433] "The summit of the first-fruits" may mean the "first" or the "best" of the first-fruits.

[434] Or "milk.

words, I wrote you and *Yisra'eyl* a covenant, **28** and he existed there with **YHWH** forty days and forty nights, he did not eat bread and he did not gulp waters, and he wrote upon the slabs the words of the covenant, ten of the words[435], **29** and it came to pass with *Mosheh* going down from the hill of *Sinai*, and the two slabs of the evidence were in the hand of *Mosheh*, with his going down from the hill, and *Mosheh* had not known that the skin of his face had horns[436] with his speaking with him, **30** and *Aharon*, and all the sons of *Yisra'eyl*, saw *Mosheh*, and look, the skin of his face had horns, and they feared to draw near to him, **31** and *Mosheh* called out to them, and *Aharon* and all the captains in the company turned back to him, and *Mosheh* spoke to them, **32** and afterward all the sons of *Yisra'eyl* were drawn near, and he directed them with all which **YHWH** spoke with him in the hill of *Sinai*, **33** and *Mosheh* finished speaking with them, and he placed a hood upon his face, **34** and with *Mosheh* coming to the face of **YHWH** to speak with him, he turned aside the hood until his going out, and he went out and he spoke to the sons of *Yisra'eyl* with what he directed, **35** and the sons of *Yisra'eyl* saw the face of *Mosheh*, given that the skin of the face of *Mosheh* had horns, and *Mosheh* turned back the hood upon his face until his coming to speak with him,

---

Chapter 35

1 and *Mosheh* rounded up all the company of the sons of *Yisra'eyl*, and he said to them, these are the words which **YHWH** directed them[437] to do. **2** Six days business will be done, and in the seventh day a special time will exist for you, it is a ceasing, a rest period for **YHWH**, anyone doing business in him will be killed. **3** You will not ignite a fire in any of your settlings in the day of the ceasing, **4** and *Mosheh* said to all the company of the sons of *Yisra'eyl* saying, this is the word which **YHWH** directed saying, **5** take from you an offering for **YHWH**, all willing of his heart will bring the offering of **YHWH**, gold, and silver, and copper, **6** and blue, and purple, and kermes of scarlet, and linen, and she-goats[438], **7** and skins of bucks being red, and skins of deer, and acacia wood, **8** and oil for the luminary, and with sweet spices for the oil of ointment and for the incense of aromatic spices, **9** and stones of the onyx, and stones of the installations for the ephod and for the breastplate, **10** and all the skilled ones of heart with you will come, and they will make all which **YHWH** directed. **11** The dwelling, his tent, his roof covering, his hooks and

---

[435] This Hebrew word can also mean "matters."
[436] The Hebrew phrase קָרַן עוֹר פָּנָיו literally means "the skin of his face had horns," but many interpret this figuratively to mean that "rays of light" came from his face, an amazing sight in either case. (also in verses 30 and 35)
[437] Context implies that the pronoun "them" is in error and should be "you."
[438] Specifically, the hair of the goats.

his boards, his wood bars, his pillars and his footings. **12** The box and his strands, the lid, and the tent curtain of the screen. **13** The table and his strands and all his utensils, and the bread of the face, **14** and the lampstand of the luminary and all her utensils and her lamps, and the oil of the luminary, **15** and the altar of the incense and his strands, and the oil of ointment, and the incense of aromatic spices, and the screen of the opening for the opening of the dwelling. **16** The altar of the ascension offering, and the copper grate which is for him, his strands and all his utensils, the cauldron and his base. **17** The slings of the courtyard, his pillars and her footings, and the screen of the gate of the courtyard. **18** The tent pegs of the dwelling, and the tent pegs of the courtyard, and their strings. **19** The garments of the braided work to minister in the special place, the garments of specialness for *Aharon* the administrator, and the garments of his sons to be adorned, **20** and all the company of the sons of *Yisra'eyl* will go out from before the face of *Mosheh*, **21** and they will come, every man which lifted up his heart and all whose wind[439] willingly offered him, they brought the offering of ***YHWH*** for the business of the appointed tent, and for all his service, and for the garments of specialness, **22** and they will come, the men also the women, all willing of heart had brought nose rings and ornamental rings and rings and arm bands, all utensils of gold, and every man which waved a wave offering of gold to ***YHWH***, **23** and every man which was found with blue, and purple, and kermes of scarlet, and linen, and she-goats[440], and skins of bucks being red, and skins of deer, they brought it. **24** Any one raising an offering of silver and copper brought the offering of ***YHWH***, and anyone which was found with acacia wood for all the business of the service, they brought it, **25** and every woman skilled of heart spun with her hands, and they brought yarn, the blue, and the purple, kermes of scarlet, and the linen, **26** and all the women whose heart lifted them up in skill, they spun the she-goats, **27** and the captains brought the stones of the onyx and the stones of the installations[441] for the ephod and for the breastplate, **28** and the sweet spice, and the oil for the luminary and for the oil of ointment and for the incense of aromatic spices. **29** Every man and woman whose heart willingly offered them to bring things for all the business which ***YHWH*** directed to do by the hand of *Mosheh*, the sons of *Yisra'eyl* brought a freewill offering for ***YHWH***, **30** and *Mosheh* said to the sons of *Yisra'eyl*, see, ***YHWH*** called out by title *Betsaleyl*[442], son of *Uriy*, son of *Hhur*, belonging to

---

[439] The wind, or breath, of an individual is his character.

[440] Specifically, the hair of the goats. (also in verse 26)

[441] That is the "settings."

[442] The phrase "***YHWH*** called out by title *Betsaleyl*" can mean, "I called *Betsaleyl* by name," but can also be translated as "I met with the title (meaning character or person) of *Betsaleyl*," as the Hebrew verb קרא may mean to "call out" or to "meet."

the branch of *Yehudah*, **31** and he filled him with the wind[443] of *Elohiym*, with skill, with intelligence, and with discernment, and with all business, **32** and to think inventions to make things with the gold and with the silver and with the copper, **33** and with the engraving of stone to fill things, and with the engraving of trees[444] to make things with all the business of invention, **34** and he placed in his heart to teach, he and *Ahaliyav*, son of *Ahhiysamahh*, belonging to the branch of *Dan*. **35** He filled them with the skill of heart to do all the business of the engraver and thinking[445], and embroidering[446] with blue, and with purple, with kermes of the scarlet, and with the linen, and the braider, for doing all the business of thinking of inventions.

Chapter 36

1 and *Betsaleyl*, and *Ahaliyav*, and all the men skilled of heart, which ***YHWH*** gave skill and intelligence in them, to know how to make all the business of the service of the special place, to make things for all which ***YHWH*** directed, **2** and *Mosheh* called out to *Betsaleyl*, and *Ahaliyav*, and all the men skilled of heart, which ***YHWH*** gave skill in his heart, all whose heart lifted him up, to come near to the business to do her, **3** and they took from before the face of *Mosheh* all the offerings which the sons of *Yisra'eyl* brought for the business of the service of the special place, to do her, and they, they brought to him more freewill offerings, morning by morning, **4** and all the skilled ones, the ones doing all the business of the special place, came, each man from his business which they were doing, **5** and they said to *Mosheh* saying, the people are making an increase in number to bring more than is sufficient for the service for the business, which ***YHWH*** directed to do her, **6** and *Mosheh* directed, and they made the voice cross over in the camp saying, do not let a man or woman do more business for the offering of the special place, and the people were restricted from bringing, **7** and the business was sufficient for all the business to do her, and some was left behind, **8** and all the skilled ones of heart with doing the business with the dwelling made ten curtains of twisted linen with blue, and purple, and kermes of scarlet, keruvs of a work

---

[443] The wind, or breath, of an individual is his character.

[444] When the Hebrew word עֵץ is written in the singular, as it is here, it always means tree or trees. When it is written in the plural form, it usually means "wood." If the original text read עֵצִים, the plural form, then this would be translated as "wood."

[445] This may be a work of thinking, in the sense of an intricate design, a work of a thinker, in the sense of a designer.

[446] This may refer to a work of embroidery or the work of an embroiderer.

of thinking[447], he made them. **9** The length of the one curtain is eight and twenty by the *ammah*, and the width is four by the *ammah*, the one curtain measurement is one for all the curtains, **10** and he will couple five of the curtains unit to unit, and five curtains he will couple unit to unit, **11** and he made loops of blue upon the lip of the one curtain from the extremity in the joint, so he did with the lip of the outer curtain in the second joint. **12** He made fifty loops in the one curtain, and he made fifty loops in the extremity of the curtain which is in the second joint receiving the loops unit to unit, **13** and he made fifty hooks of gold, and he coupled the curtains unit to unit in the hooks, and he existed as one dwelling, **14** and he made the curtains of she-goats[448] for a tent upon the dwelling, he made eleven curtains. **15** The length of the one curtain is thirty by the *ammah*, and four *ammah*s is the width, the one curtain measurement is one for the eleven curtains, **16** and he coupled five of the curtains alone and six of the curtains alone, **17** and he made fifty loops upon the lip of the outer curtain in the joint, and fifty loops he made upon the lip of the curtain of the second coupling, **18** and he made fifty copper hooks for coupling the tent to exist as a unit, **19** and he made a roof covering for the tent from skins of bucks being red, and a roof covering from skins of deer on top, **20** and he made the boards for the dwelling of acacia wood, standing[449]. **21** Ten *ammah*s is the length of the board, and an *ammah* and a half of the *ammah* is the width of the one board. **22** Two hands[450] for the one board for being joined together unit to unit, so he made for all the boards of the dwelling, **23** and he made the boards for the dwelling, twenty boards to the edge, unto the south of the south, **24** and forty footings of silver he made under the twenty boards, two footings under the one board for his two hands and two footings under the other board for his two hands, **25** and for the second rib of the dwelling, at the north edge, he made twenty boards, **26** and their forty footings of silver, two footings under the one board and two footings under the other board, **27** and for the two flanks of the dwelling unto the sea[451] he made six boards, **28** and two boards he made for the corner posts of the dwelling in the two flanks, **29** and they existed being double below, and together they existed whole to his head for the one ring, so he did exist for the two of them, for two of the buttresses, **30** and eight boards and their footings of silver

[447] This may be a work of thinking, in the sense of an intricate design, a work of a thinker, in the sense of a designer.
[448] Specifically, the hair of the goats.
[449] The contextual meaning of this Hebrew word is uncertain. It may mean "standing acacia wood" or "acacia wood standing up."
[450] These "hands" are probably notched tenons which are cut into the board to join the boards together. (also in verse 24)
[451] Meaning "west."

existed, sixteen footings, two footings[452], two footings under the other board, **31** and he made wood bars of acacia wood, five for the boards of the one rib of the dwelling, **32** and five wood bars for the boards of the second rib of the dwelling, and five wood bars for the boards of the two flanks of the dwelling unto the sea[453], **33** and he made the middlemost wood bar to flee away[454] in the midst of the boards from the extremity to the other extremity, **34** and he overlaid the boards with gold, and he made their rings with gold, houses[455] for the wood bars, and he overlaid the wood bars with gold, **35** and he made the tent curtain with blue, and purple, and kermes of scarlet, and twisted linen, with keruvs of a work of thinking[456], he made her, **36** and he made for her four pillars of acacia, and he overlaid them with gold, their pegs with gold, and he poured down[457] for them four footings of silver, **37** and he made a screen for the opening of the tent of blue, and purple, and kermes of scarlet, and twisted linen, a work of embroidering[458], **38** and his five pillars and their pegs, and he overlaid their heads and their binders with gold, and their five footings with copper,

---

Chapter 37

1 and *Betsaleyl* made the box of acacia wood, two *ammah*s and a half is his length, and an *ammah* and a half is his width, and an *ammah* and a half is his height, **2** and he overlaid him with clean gold, from the inside and from the outside, and he made for him a molding of gold all around, **3** and he poured down[459] for him four rings of gold upon his four footsteps[460] and two rings upon his one rib, and two rings upon his second rib, **4** and he made strands of acacia wood, and he overlaid them with gold, **5** and he brought the strands in the rings upon the ribs of the box to lift up the box, **6** and he made a lid of clean gold, two *ammah*s and a half is her length, and an *ammah* and a half is her width, **7** and he made two keruvs of gold, a beaten work, he made them from the two extremities of the lid. **8** One *keruv* from

---

452 The Hebrew text appears to be missing the phrase "under the one board, and" after this word (compare with Exodus 36:26).

453 Meaning "west."

454 "Flee away" probably means "pass through."

455 Or "housings."

456 This may be a work of thinking, in the sense of an intricate design, a work of a thinker, in the sense of a designer.

457 In this context, to "pour down" means to "cast" an object from a molten metal.

458 This may refer to a work of embroidery or the work of an embroiderer.

459 In this context, to "pour down" means to "cast" an object from a molten metal.

460 Or "feet."

this extremity, and the other *keruv* from that extremity, from the lid he made the keruvs, from the two ends of his extremities, **9** and the keruvs were spreading out the wings above, fencing around with their wings upon the lid, and their faces each to his brother, the faces of the keruvs will exist toward the lid, **10** and he made the table of acacia wood, two *ammah*s is his length, and an *ammah* is his width, and an *ammah* and a half is his height, **11** and he overlaid him with clean gold, and he made for him a molding of gold all around, **12** and he made for him a rim, a hand span all around, and he made a molding of gold for him all around, **13** and he poured down[461] for him four rings of gold, and he placed the rings upon the four edges which is for his four feet. **14** The rings existed alongside the rim, houses[462] for the strands to lift up the table, **15** and he made the strands of acacia wood, and he overlaid them with gold to lift up the table, **16** and he made the utensils which are upon the table, his platters, and his palms[463] and his sacrificial bowls and his jugs, which will be for pouring with them, clean gold[464], **17** and he made the lampstand with clean gold, a beaten work, and he made the lampstand, her midsection, and her stalk, her bowls, her knobs and her buds existed out of her[465], **18** and six stalks are going out from her sides, three stalks of the lampstand out of her one side, and three stalks of the lampstand out of her second side. **19** Three bowls, being almond shaped in the stalk of the one with a knob and a bud, and three bowls, being almond shaped in the stalk of the other with a knob and a bud, so it is for the six stalks going out from the lampstand, **20** and in the lampstand are four bowls being almond shaped with her knobs and her buds, **21** and a knob under two of the stalks out of her, and a knob under two of the stalks out of her, and a knob under two of the stalks out of her, for the six stalks going out from her. **22** Their knobs and their stalks out of her, all of her will exist as one beaten work of clean gold, **23** and he made her seven lamps, and her tongs, and her fire pans, with clean gold. **24** A *kikar* of clean gold he made her and all her utensils, **25** and he made the altar of incense of acacia wood, an *ammah* is his length, and an *ammah* is his width, it is squared, and two *ammah*s is his height, out of him existed his horns, **26** and he overlaid him with clean gold, his roof, and his walls all around, and his horns, and he made for him a molding of gold all around, **27** and he made two rings of gold for him under

---

[461] In this context, to "pour down" means to "cast" an object from a molten metal.

[462] Or "housings."

[463] The Hebrew word for the "palms" can also mean "palm" shaped and here refers to "spoons" or "shovels."

[464] The phrase "and he made them with" appears to be missing before "clean gold" (compare with Exodus 25:29).

[465] "Out of her" means that each of these parts is beaten (molded) out of the one piece.

his molding upon his two ribs, upon his two sides, for houses[466] for the
strands to lift him up with them, **28** and he made the strands of acacia
wood, and he overlaid them with gold, **29** and he made the oil of ointment
of specialness, and the clean incense of the aromatic spices, the work of
compounding[467],

Chapter 38

1 and he made the altar of the ascension offering of acacia wood, five
*ammah*s is his length, and five *ammah*s is his width, it is square, and three
*ammah*s is his height, **2** and he made his horns upon his four corners, out of
him his horns will exist, and he overlaid him with copper, **3** and he made all
the utensils of the altar, the pots, and the shovels, and the sprinkling basins,
the forks, and the fire pans, he made all his utensils with copper, **4** and he
made for the altar a grate work of netting with copper under his outer rim,
from beneath unto his half, **5** and he poured down[468] four rings in four
extremities for the copper grate, houses[469] for the strands, **6** and he made
the strands of acacia wood, and he overlaid them with copper, **7** and he
brought the strands in the rings upon the ribs of the altar to lift him up with
them, he made him with hollowed out slabs, **8** and he made the cauldron
with copper, and his base with copper, with reflections of the musterers
who muster at the opening of the appointed tent, **9** and he made the
courtyard to the edge, unto the south of the south, slings of the courtyard
are of twisted linen, a hundred by the *ammah*. **10** Their twenty pillars and
their twenty footings of copper, the pegs of the pillars and their binders of
silver, **11** and to the north edge, a hundred by the *ammah*, their twenty
pillars and their twenty footings of copper, the pegs of the pillars and their
binders of silver, **12** and to the edge of the sea[470], fifty slings by the *ammah*,
their ten pillars and their ten footings, the pegs of the pillars and their silver
binders, **13** and to the edge unto the east, unto the sunrise, it is fifty
*ammah*s. **14** The slings are fifteen *ammah*s for the shoulder piece, their
three pillars and their three footings, **15** and for the second shoulder piece,
from this one and from that one, for the gate of the courtyard are slings,
fifteen *ammah*s, their three pillars and their three footings. **16** All the slings
of the courtyard all around are of twisted linen, **17** and the footings for the
pillars of copper, the pegs of the pillars and their binders of silver, and the

---

466 Or "housings."

467 This may be a "work of compounding," in the sense of a "mixture," or made by a "compounder" in the sense of a "mixer."

468 In this context, to "pour down" means to "cast" an object from a molten metal.

469 Or "housings."

470 Meaning "west."

metal plating of their heads of silver, and all the pillars of the courtyard are being attached with silver, **18** and the screen of the gate of the courtyard is a work of embroidering[471] with blue, and purple, and kermes of scarlet, and twisted linen, and twenty *ammah*s is the length, and the height with the width is five *ammah*s alongside the slings of the courtyard, **19** and their four pillars and their four footings of copper, their pegs of silver, and the metal plating of their heads and their binders of silver, **20** and all the tent pegs for the dwelling and for the courtyard all around are of copper. **21** These are registered of the dwelling, the dwelling of the evidence, which he registered by the mouth of *Mosheh*, the service of the ones of *Lewi*, by the hand of *Iytamar*, the son of *Aharon*, the administrator, **22** and *Betsaleyl*, the son of *Uriy*, the son of *Hhur*, belonging to the branch of *Yehudah*, had made all which ***YHWH*** directed *Mosheh*, **23** and with him is *Ahaliyav*, the son of *Ahhiysamahh*, belonging to the branch of *Dan*, an engraver, and a thinker, and an embroiderer with the blue, and with the purple, and with the kermes of the scarlet, and with the linen. **24** All the gold used for the business in all the business of the special place, the gold of the wave offering was nine and twenty kikars, and seven hundred and thirty *sheqel*s by the *sheqel* of the special place, **25** and the silver registered of the company, a hundred *kikar*, and a thousand and seven hundred and five and seventy *sheqel*s by the *sheqel* of the special place. **26** A *beqa* for the skull[472], one-half of the *sheqel* by the *sheqel* of the special place for all the ones crossing over upon the registered, from a son[473] of twenty years and upward, to the six hundred thousand and three thousand and five hundred and fifty, **27** and a hundred kikars of silver existed for pouring down[474] the footings of the special place, and the footings of the tent curtain, a hundred footings for the hundred kikars, a *kikar* for a footing, **28** and with the thousand and seven hundred and five and seventy[475] he made the pegs for the pillars, and he overlaid their heads[476] and he attached them, **29** and the copper of the wave offering was seventy kikars and two thousand and four hundred *sheqel*s, **30** and he made in her the footings of the opening of the appointed tent, and the copper altar, and the copper grate which belongs to him and all the utensils of the altar, **31** and the footings of the courtyard all around, and the footings of the gate of the courtyard, and all the tent pegs of the dwelling, and all the tent pegs of the courtyard all around,

---

[471] This may refer to a work of embroidery or the work of an embroiderer.
[472] Meaning "individual."
[473] "Son" is an idiom for years "old."
[474] In this context, to "pour down" means to "cast" an object from a molten metal.
[475] The text appears to be missing the word "*sheqel*s" after this Hebrew word.
[476] That is the "top."

Chapter 39

1 and from the blue, and the purple, and the kermes of the scarlet they made the garments of braided work, to minister in the special place, and they made the garments of specialness which are for *Aharon*, just as ***YHWH*** directed *Mosheh*, **2** and he made the ephod of gold, blue, and purple, and kermes of scarlet, and twisted linen, **3** and they hammered the wires of gold, and he severed the cords to use in the midst of the blue, and in the midst of the purple, and in the midst of the kermes of the scarlet, and in the midst of the linen, a work of thinking[477]. **4** They made the shoulder pieces for him, a coupling, upon his two extremities it is coupled, **5** and the decorative band of his ephod, which is upon him, he is just like his work, of gold, blue, and purple, and kermes of scarlet, and twisted linen, just as ***YHWH*** directed *Mosheh*, **6** and they made the stones of the onyx, enclosed in plaits of gold, being engraved as carvings of a seal according to the titles of the sons of *Yisra'eyl*, **7** and he placed them upon the shoulder pieces of the ephod, stones of remembrance for the sons of *Yisra'eyl*, just as ***YHWH*** directed *Mosheh*, **8** and he made the breastplate, a work of thinking[478], like the work of the ephod of gold, blue, and purple, and kermes of scarlet, and twisted linen. **9** He existed squared, doubled over they made the breastplate, a finger span is his length, and a finger span is his width, doubled over, **10** and they set in him four rows of stone, a row of carnelian, olivine and emerald was the one row, **11** and the second row, turquoise, lapiz-lazuli and flint, **12** and the third row, opal, agate and amethyst, **13** and the fourth row, topaz and onyx and jasper, being woven with gold they will exist in their settings, **14** and the stones were according to the titles of the sons of *Yisra'eyl*, twelve according to their titles, carvings of the seal of each according to his title, they will exist for the twelve staffs[479], **15** and they made upon the breastplate chains, the edging is a work of a thick woven thing of clean gold, **16** and they made two plaits of gold, and two rings of gold, and they placed the two rings upon the two extremities of the breastplate, **17** and they placed the two thick woven things of gold upon the two rings, upon the extremities of the breastplate, **18** and the two extremities of the two thick woven things, they placed upon the two plaits, and they placed upon the shoulder pieces of the ephod, to the forefront of his face, **19** and they made two rings of gold, and they placed them upon the two extremities of the breastplate upon his lip, which is on the other side of the ephod, unto the inside, **20** and they made two rings of gold, and they placed them upon the two shoulder pieces of the ephod, beneath the forefront of his face,

---

477 This may be a work of thinking, in the sense of an intricate design, a work of a thinker, in the sense of a designer.

478 This may be a work of thinking, in the sense of an intricate design, a work of a thinker, in the sense of a designer.

479 Or "tribes."

alongside his joint, above the decorative band of the ephod, **21** and they tied
on the breastplate by his rings to the rings of the ephod with a cord of blue,
to exist upon the decorative band of the ephod, and the breastplate will not
be loosened from upon the ephod, just as ***YHWH*** directed *Mosheh*, **22** and
he made the cloak of the ephod, a work of braiding[480], entirely with blue,
23 and the mouth[481] of the cloak in his midst, like the mouth of the collar, a
lip[482] for his mouth all around, he will not be torn, **24** and they made upon
the hems of the cloak pomegranates of blue, and purple, and kermes of
scarlet, and twisted[483], **25** and they made bells of clean gold and they placed
the bells in the midst of the pomegranates upon the hems of the cloak all
around in the midst of the pomegranates. **26** Bell and pomegranate, bell and
pomegranate[484] are upon the hems of the cloak all around to minister, just
as ***YHWH*** directed *Mosheh*, **27** and they made the tunics of linen, a work of
braiding[485] for *Aharon* and for his sons, **28** and the turban of linen and the
bonnets of the headdress of linen, and the undergarments of linen, twisted
linen, **29** and the sash of twisted linen, and blue, and purple, and kermes of
scarlet, a work of embroidering[486], just as ***YHWH*** directed *Mosheh*, **30** and
they made the blossom of the special thing of dedication[487] of clean gold,
and they wrote upon him a thing written, carvings of a seal, a special thing
for ***YHWH***, **31** and they placed upon him a cord of blue, to place upon the
top of the turban from above, just as ***YHWH*** directed *Mosheh*, **32** and all the
service of the dwelling of the appointed tent was finished, and the sons of
Yisra'eyl made it just like what ***YHWH*** directed *Mosheh*, so they made,
33 and they brought the dwelling to *Mosheh*, the tent and all his utensils, his
hooks, his boards, his wood bars, and his pillars, and his footings, **34** and the
roof covering of skins of the bucks being red, and the roof covering of skins
of the deer, and the tent curtain of the screen. **35** The box of the evidence
and his strands and the lid. **36** The table with all his utensils, and the bread
of the face. **37** The clean lampstand, with her lamps, the lamp of rank[488], and
all her utensils, and the oil of the luminary, **38** and the altar of gold, and the
oil of ointment, and the incense of aromatic spices, and the screen of the
opening of the tent. **39** The altar of copper, and the grate of copper which is
for him, his strands, and all his utensils, the cauldron and his base. **40** The
slings of the courtyard, her pillars and her footings, and the screen for the

---

[480] This may be the work of braiding or the work of a braider.
[481] Or "opening."
[482] Or "edge."
[483] The word "linen" appears to be missing after this Hebrew word.
[484] The phrase "bells and pomegranate" is written twice showing that they are to be placed on the garment in series.
[485] This may be the work of braiding or the work of a braider.
[486] This may refer to a work of embroidery or the work of an embroiderer.
[487] That is a "crown."
[488] "The lamp of rank" means "the row of lamps."

gate of the courtyard, his strings, and her tent pegs, and all the utensils of the service of the dwelling, for the appointed tent. **41** The garments of braided work to minister in the special place, the garments of specialness for *Aharon* the administrator, and the garments of his sons to adorn them. **42** Just like all that ***YHWH*** directed *Mosheh*, so the sons of *Yisra'eyl* made all the service, **43** and *Mosheh* saw all the business, and look, they made her just as ***YHWH*** directed, so they made it, and *Mosheh* exalted them,

---

Chapter 40

1 and ***YHWH*** spoke to *Mosheh* saying, **2** in the first new moon, on the first day of the new moon[489], you will make the dwelling of the appointed tent rise, **3** and you will place the box of the evidence there, and you will fence around the box with the tent curtain, **4** and you will bring the table, and you will arrange his arrangement, and you will bring the lampstand, and you will bring up her lamps, **5** and you will place the altar of gold for the incense for the face of the box of the evidence, and you will place the screen of the opening for the dwelling, **6** and you will place the altar of the ascension offering to the face of the opening of the dwelling of the appointed tent, **7** and you will place the cauldron between the appointed tent and the altar, and you will place waters in there, **8** and you will place the courtyard all around, and you will place the screen of the gate of the courtyard, **9** and you will take the oil of ointment, and you will smear the dwelling and all which is in him, and you will set him, and all his utensils, apart, and he will exist as a special thing, **10** and you will smear the altar of the ascension offering and all his utensils, and you will set the altar apart, and the altar, a special of specials[490], will exist, **11** and you will smear the cauldron and his base, and you will set him apart, **12** and you will bring near *Aharon* and his sons to the opening of the appointed tent, and you will bathe them in the waters, **13** and you will clothe *Aharon* with the garments of specialness, and you will smear him, and you will set him apart, and he will be adorned for me, **14** and you will bring near his sons, and you will clothe them with tunics, **15** and you will smear them just as you smeared their father, and they will be adorned for me, and their smearing will surely exist for them, for an administration of a distant time, for their generations, **16** and *Mosheh* did just like all that ***YHWH*** directed him, so he did, **17** and it came to pass, in the first new moon, in the second year, on the first day of the new moon, the dwelling was made

---

[489] The phrase בְּאֶחָד לַחֹדֶשׁ always means "the first day of the new moon" (compare with Exodus 40:17). Therefore, it appears that the phrase בְּיוֹם הַחֹדֶשׁ הָרִאשׁוֹן is written incorrectly and should be written as בְּחֹדֶשׁ הָרִאשׁוֹן (in the first new moon).

[490] The phrase "special of specials" means a "very special thing, one or place."

to rise, **18** and *Mosheh* made the dwelling rise, and he placed his footings, and he placed his boards, and he placed his wood bars, and he made his pillars rise, **19** and he spread out the tent upon the dwelling, and he placed the roof covering of the tent upon the top of him, just as ***YHWH*** directed *Mosheh*, **20** and he took, and he placed the evidence to[491] the box, and he placed the strands upon the box, and he placed the lid upon the top of the box, **21** and he brought the box to the dwelling, and he placed the tent curtain of the screen, and he fenced around upon the box of the evidence, just as ***YHWH*** directed *Mosheh*, **22** and he placed the table in the appointed tent, upon the midsection of the dwelling, unto the north, outside the tent curtain, **23** and he arranged upon him the bread for the face of ***YHWH***, just as ***YHWH*** directed *Mosheh*, **24** and he placed the lampstand in the appointed tent, in front of the table, upon the midsection of the dwelling, unto the south, **25** and he made the lamps go up[492] to the face of ***YHWH***, just as ***YHWH*** directed *Mosheh*, **26** and he placed the altar of gold in the appointed tent, to the face of the tent curtain, **27** and he burned incense upon him, an incense of aromatic spices, just as ***YHWH*** directed *Mosheh*, **28** and he placed the screen of the opening to the dwelling, **29** and the altar of the ascension offering he placed at the opening of the dwelling of the appointed place, and he made the ascension offering and the donation go up upon him, just as ***YHWH*** directed *Mosheh*, **30** and he placed the cauldron between the appointed tent and the altar, and he placed the waters to bathe unto there, **31** and they will bathe from him, *Mosheh* and *Aharon* and his sons, their hands and their feet. **32** In their coming to the appointed tent, and in their coming near to the altar, they will bathe, just as ***YHWH*** directed *Mosheh*, **33** and he made the courtyard all around rise to the dwelling, and to the altar he placed the screen of the gate of the courtyard, and *Mosheh* finished the business, **34** and the cloud covered over the appointed tent, and the armament of ***YHWH*** filled the dwelling, **35** and *Mosheh* was not able to come to the appointed tent, given that the cloud dwelled upon him, and the armament of ***YHWH*** had filled the dwelling, **36** and in the going up of the cloud from upon the dwelling, the sons of *Yisra'eyl* will journey in all their breaking camps, **37** and if the cloud will not go up, then they will not journey until the day of his going up, **38** given that the cloud of ***YHWH*** is upon the dwelling in the daytime, and fire will exist in him in the night to the eyes of all the house of *Yisra'eyl* in all their breaking camps,

---

[491] Probably meaning "inside."

[492] "Made the lamps go up" means to light the wicks.

Benner's Translation of the Torah

The Book of Leviticus

Chapter 1

1 and he called out to *Mosheh*, and ***YHWH*** spoke to him from the appointed tent saying, **2** speak to the sons of *Yisra'eyl*, and you will say to them, each that will bring from you a donation to ***YHWH***, from the beast, from the cattle, from the flocks, you will bring near your donation. **3** If his donation is an ascension offering from the cattle, it will be a whole male, he will bring him near to the opening of the appointed tent, he will bring him near for his self-will, to the face of ***YHWH***, **4** and he will support his hand upon the head of the ascension offering, and he will be acceptable to him[493], for making a covering upon him, **5** and he will slay the son of the cattle to the face of ***YHWH***, and the sons of *Aharon*, the administrators, will bring near the blood, and they will sprinkle the blood upon the altar all around where the opening of the appointed tent is, **6** and he will strip off the ascension offering, and he will divide her into pieces to her pieces, **7** and the sons of *Aharon*, the administrators, will give fire upon the altar, and they will arrange the wood upon the fire, **8** and the sons of *Aharon*, the administrators, will arrange the pieces, the head, the suet, upon the wood, which is upon the fire, which is upon the altar, **9** and he will bathe his insides and his legs in the waters, and the administrator will burn it all as incense upon the altar, an ascension offering of a fire offering, a sweet aroma to ***YHWH***, **10** and if the donation is from the flocks, from the sheep or from the she-goats, for an ascension offering, it will be a whole male, he will bring him near, **11** and he will slay him upon the midsection of the altar unto the north, to the face of ***YHWH***, and the sons of *Aharon*, the administrators, will sprinkle his blood upon the altar all around, **12** and he will divide him into pieces to his pieces, and his head and his suet, and the administrator will arrange them upon the wood, which is upon the fire, which is upon the altar, **13** and he will bathe the insides and the legs in the waters, and the administrator will bring near all, and he will burn it as incense upon the altar, an ascension offering, he is a fire offering, a sweet aroma to ***YHWH***, **14** and if the ascension offering is from the flyers, his donation to ***YHWH***, then he will bring near from the turtledoves or from the sons of the doves his donation, **15** and the administrator will bring him near to the altar, and he will snap off his head, and he will burn it as incense upon the altar, and his blood will be drained upon the wall of the altar, **16** and he will remove

---

493 If the "to" is referring to ***YHWH***, then this should be translated as "to him," but if the "to" is referring to the one bringing the sacrifice it should be translated as "for him."

his[494] crop with her plumage, and he will throw her out beside the altar unto the east, to the area of the fatness, **17** and he will split him in two by his wings, he will not separate, and the administrator will burn him as incense upon the altar, upon the wood, which is upon the fire, an ascension offering, he is a fire offering, a sweet aroma to ***YHWH***,

---

Chapter 2

1 and a soul that will bring near a donation of deposit for ***YHWH***, flour will exist as his donation, and he will pour down upon her oil, and he will give upon her frankincense, **2** and he will bring her to the sons of *Aharon*, the administrators, and he will grasp from there, filling his handful from her flour and from the oil upon all for her frankincense, and the administrator will burn her memorial as incense upon the altar, a fire offering, a sweet aroma to ***YHWH***, **3** and from the deposit being left behind, it belongs to *Aharon* and to his sons, it is a special of specials[495] from the fire offerings of ***YHWH***, **4** and, given that you will bring near a donation of deposit, oven baked, flour of unleavened pierced breads mixed with the oil and unleavened thin breads smeared with the oil, **5** and if your donation is a deposit upon the pan, flour mixed with the oil, she will be unleavened bread. **6** Crumble her fragments, and you will pour down upon her oil, she is a deposit, **7** and if your donation is a deposit of the boiling pot, the flour will be made with the oil, **8** and you will bring the deposit, which he will make from these, to ***YHWH***, and he will bring it near to the administrator, and he will draw her near to the altar, **9** and the administrator will raise her memorial up from the deposit, and he will burn incense upon the altar, a fire offering, a sweet aroma to ***YHWH***, **10** and from the deposit being left behind, it belongs to *Aharon* and to his sons, it is a special of specials from the fire offerings of ***YHWH***. **11** All the deposit, which you will bring near to ***YHWH***, you will not make leavened bread, given that you will not burn any leaven or any honey as incense from him, a fire offering for ***YHWH***. **12** The donation of the summit[496], you will bring them near to ***YHWH*** and to the altar, they will not go up[497] for a sweet aroma, **13** and all the donations of your deposit you will season with salt, and you will not cease the salt of the covenant of your *Elohiym* from upon your deposit, upon all your donations you will bring near with salt, **14** and if you will bring near a deposit of the

---

[494] The turtledove and dove are feminine words in Hebrew, therefore the pronoun "him" appears to be in error and should be "her" (compare with the next word-her plumage).

[495] The phrase "special of specials" means a "very special thing, one or place." (also in verse 10)

[496] The "summit" may be the "best" or the "first" of the produce.

[497] In the sense of not being burned on the fire.

first-fruits for ***YHWH***, it will be green grain dried by the fire, beaten grain of the plantation, you will bring near the deposit of your first-fruits, **15** and you will give upon her oil, and you will place upon her frankincense, she is a deposit, **16** and the administrator will make incense with her memorial, from her beaten grain and from the oil, with all of her frankincense, a fire offering for ***YHWH***,

---

Chapter 3

1 and if his donation is a sacrifice of offerings of restitution, if he is bringing near from the cattle, if a male or a female, a whole one, he will bring him near to the face of ***YHWH***, **2** and he will support his hand upon the head of his donation and he will slay him at the opening of the appointed tent, and the sons of *Aharon*, the administrators, will sprinkle the blood upon the altar all around, **3** and he will bring near, from the sacrifice of the offerings of restitution, a fire offering for ***YHWH***, the fat covering, the inside and all the fat which is upon the inside, **4** and the two kidneys and the fat, which is upon them, which is upon the hips, and the lobe upon the heavy one[498] with the kidneys he will remove, **5** and the sons of *Aharon* will burn him as incense upon the altar upon the ascension offering, which is upon the wood, which is upon the fire, a fire offering, a sweet aroma to ***YHWH***, **6** and if his donation is from the flocks for a sacrifice of offerings of restitution to ***YHWH***, it will be a whole male or female, he will bring him near. **7** If he is bringing near a sheep for his donation, he will bring him near to the face of ***YHWH***, **8** and he will support his hand upon the head of his donation, and he will slay him to the face of the appointed tent, and the sons of *Aharon* will sprinkle his blood upon the altar all around, **9** and he will bring near, from the sacrifice of the offerings of restitution, a fire offering for ***YHWH***, his fat, the rump, everything alongside the spine he will remove and the fat covering the inside and all the fat which is upon the inside, **10** and the two kidneys and the fat, which is upon them, which is upon the hips, and the lobe upon the heavy one with the kidneys he will remove, **11** and the administrator will burn him as incense upon the altar, it is a bread offering to ***YHWH***, **12** and if his donation is a she-goat, he will bring him near to the face of ***YHWH***, **13** and he will support his hand upon his head, and he will slay him to the face of the appointed tent, and the sons of *Aharon* will sprinkle his blood upon the altar all around, **14** and he will bring near from him his donation, a fire offering to ***YHWH***, the fat covering, the inside, and all the fat which is upon the inside, **15** and the two kidneys and the fat which is upon them, which is upon the hips, and the lobe upon the heavy one with the kidneys, he will remove, **16** and the administrator will burn them as

---

498 "The heavy one" is the "liver," the heaviest organ of the body. (also in verses 10 and 15)

incense upon the altar, it is a bread offering for a sweet aroma, all the fat is for ***YHWH***. **17** It is a distant custom for your generations in all your settlings, you will not eat any of the fat or any of the blood,

---

Chapter 4

1 and ***YHWH*** spoke to *Mosheh* saying, **2** speak to the sons of *Yisra'eyl* saying, a soul that will fail with an error from any of the directives of ***YHWH***, which were not done, and he will do from one of them. **3** If the smeared administrator will fail, it will be guiltiness of the people, and he will bring near, for his failure because he failed, a bull son, a whole cattle to ***YHWH*** for the failure, **4** and he will bring the bull to the opening of the appointed tent, to the face of ***YHWH***, and he will support his hand upon the head of the bull, and he will slay the bull to the face of ***YHWH***, **5** and the smeared administrator will take from the blood of the bull and he will bring him to the appointed tent, **6** and the administrator will dip his finger in the blood and he will spatter from the blood seven times to the face of ***YHWH***, at the face of the special tent curtain, **7** and the administrator will place from the blood upon the horns of the altar of incense smoke of the aromatic spices to the face of ***YHWH***, which is in the appointed tent, and he will pour out all the blood of the bull to the bottom base of the altar of the ascension offering, which is at the opening of the appointed tent, **8** and he will raise up all the fat of the bull of the failure, the fat of the covering upon the insides and all the fat which is upon the insides, **9** and the two kidneys and the fat, which is upon them, which is upon the hips, and the lobe upon the heavy one[499] with the kidneys he will remove. **10** Just as they were raised up from the ox of the sacrifice of the offerings of restitution, and the administrator will burn them as incense upon the altar of the ascension offering, **11** and the skin of the bull and all his flesh upon his head and upon his legs and his inside and his dung, **12** and he will bring out all of the bull to the outside of the camp, to the clean area for pouring out the fatness, and he will cremate him upon the wood with the fire, upon the pouring out of the fatness he will be cremated, **13** and if all the company of *Yisra'eyl* will go astray, and a word[500] was out of sight from the eyes of the assembly, and they did anyone of the directives of ***YHWH***, which was not to be done, then they will be guilty, **14** and the failure, which they failed, will be known upon her, and the assembly will bring near a son of a bull of the cattle for the failure, and they will bring him to the face of the appointed tent, **15** and the bearded ones will support the company with their hands upon the head of the bull to the face of ***YHWH***, and they will slay the bull to the face of ***YHWH***, **16** and the smeared administrator will bring the blood from the bull to the appointed

---

[499] The "liver," which is the heaviest organ in the body.
[500] This Hebrew word may also mean "matter."

tent, **17** and the administrator will dip his finger in the blood and he will spatter it seven times to the face of ***YHWH***, at the face of the tent curtain, **18** and from the blood, he will place it upon the horns of the altar, which is to the face of ***YHWH***, which is in the appointed tent, and he will pour out all the blood to the bottom base of the altar of the ascension offering, which is at the opening of the appointed tent, **19** and he will raise up all his fat from him, and he will burn it as incense upon the altar, **20** and he will do to the bull just as he did to the bull of the failure, so he will do to him, and the administrator will make a covering upon them and he will be forgiven for them, **21** and he will bring out the bull to the outside of the camp, and he will cremate him just as he cremated the first bull, he is the failure of the assembly. **22** When a captain fails, and he does one of any of the directives of ***YHWH*** his *Elohiym*, which was not to be done in error, then he is guilty. **23** Or if his failure, which he failed in her, is made known to him, then he will bring his donation, a hairy goat of the she-goats, a whole male, **24** and he will support his hand upon the head of the hairy goat, and he will slay him in the area which he slays the ascension offering, to the face of ***YHWH***, he is the failure, **25** and the administrator will take from the blood of the failure with his finger, and he will place it upon the horns of the altar of the ascension offering, and he will pour out his blood to the bottom base of the altar of the ascension offering, **26** and he will burn all his fat as incense upon the altar, like the fat of the sacrifice of the offerings of restitution, and the administrator will make a covering upon him because of his failure, and he will be forgiven for him, **27** and if one soul from the people of the land will fail with an error, by doing one of the directives of ***YHWH*** which was not to be done, then he will be guilty. **28** Or his failure is made known to him, which he failed, and he brings his donation, a hairy goat of the she-goats, a whole female for his failure which he failed, **29** and he will support his hand upon the head of the failure, and he will slay the failure in the area of the ascension offering, **30** and the administrator will take from her blood and he will place it upon the horns of the altar of the ascension offering, and he will pour out her blood to the bottom base of the altar, **31** and he will remove all her fat just as he removed the fat from upon the sacrifice of the offerings of restitution, and the administrator will burn it as incense upon the altar for a sweet aroma to ***YHWH***, and the administrator will make a covering upon him and he will be forgiven for him, **32** and if he will bring a sheep for his donation for the failure, a whole female he will bring, **33** and he will support his hand upon the head of the failure, and he will slay her for the failure in the area which the ascension offering is slain, **34** and the administrator will take from the blood of the failure with his finger, and he will place it upon the horns of the altar of the ascension offering, and he will pour out all her blood to the bottom base of the altar, **35** and he will remove all her fat just as he removed the fat of the sheep from the sacrifice of the offerings of restitution, and the administrator will burn them as incense upon the altar, fire offerings of ***YHWH***, and the administrator will make a covering upon him and his failure which he failed, and he will be forgiven for him,

---

Chapter 5

1 and a soul that will fail and will hear the voice of an oath and he[501] is a
witness, whether he saw or knew, if he will not tell, then he will lift up his
twistedness. **2** Or a soul which will touch any word[502] of dirtiness, or a
carcass of a dirty living one, or a carcass of a dirty living[503] one, or the
carcass of a dirty swarmer, and he was out of sight from him, then he is dirty
and he will be guilty. **3** Or if he will touch a dirty human, for all of his
dirtiness, which he is dirty for, and he will be out of sight from him, and he
knew, then he will be guilty. **4** Or a soul that will swear by uttering with lips
to make dysfunctional or make well, for all which the human will utter with
a swearing, and he be out of sight from him, and he knew, then he will be
guilty to one of these, **5** and it will come to pass when he is guilty to one of
these, and he will confess what he failed upon her, **6** and he will bring his
guilt to ***YHWH*** because of his failure, which he failed, a female from the
flocks of sheep or a hairy goat of the she-goats for the failure, and the
administrator will make a covering upon him because of his failure, **7** and if
his hand cannot sufficiently touch[504] a ram, then he will bring his guilt, which
he failed, two turtledoves or two sons of the dove to ***YHWH***, one for a
failure and one for an ascension offering, **8** and he will bring them to the
administrator, and he will bring near what is for the failure first, and he will
snap off his head from the forefront of his neck and he will not separate it,
9 and he will spatter from the blood of the failure upon the wall of the altar,
and the remaining blood will be drained to the bottom base of the altar, he
is the failure, **10** and he will do the second as an ascension offering,
according to the decision, and the administrator will make a covering upon
him because of his failure, which he failed, and he will be forgiven for him,
11 and if his hand is not able to overtake[505] two turtledoves or two sons of
the dove, then he will bring his donation, because he failed, a tenth of an
eyphah of flour for the failure, he will not place oil upon her, and he will not
give frankincense upon her, given that she is the failure, **12** and he will bring
her to the administrator, and the administrator will grasp from her a filling
of his handful, it is a memorial, and he will burn it as incense upon the altar
upon the fire offerings of ***YHWH***, she is the failure, **13** and the administrator
will make a covering upon him, upon his failure, because he failed, from one

---

501 The gender of the subject changes from feminine to masculine.

502 This Hebrew word can also mean a "thing."

503 A euphemism for a "creature."

504 To touch in the sense of being able to afford.

505 To overtake in the sense of acquiring.

of these, and he will be forgiven for him, and she will exist for the administrator as the deposit, **14** and ***YHWH*** spoke to *Mosheh* saying, **15** a soul that will transgress a transgression and is a failure in error from the special ones of ***YHWH***, then he will bring his guilt to ***YHWH***, a whole buck from the flocks, with your arrangement of silver *sheqel*s, with the special *sheqel* for the guilt, **16** and he will make restitution for when he failed by the special thing, and he will cause to add his fifth upon him, and he will give him to the administrator, and the administrator will make a covering upon him with the buck of the guilt, and he will be forgiven for him, **17** and if a soul that failed and did one of any of the directives of ***YHWH***, which was not to be done, and he did not know, then he will be guilty and he will lift up his twistedness, **18** and he will bring a whole buck from the flocks, with your arrangement for the guilt, to the administrator, and the administrator will make a covering upon him concerning his error, which her erred and he did not know, and he will be forgiven for him. **19** It is guilt, he is very guilty to ***YHWH***, **20 (6:1)** and ***YHWH*** spoke to *Mosheh* saying, **21 (6:2)** a soul that fails and transgresses a transgression with ***YHWH***, and he lies to his neighbor about a deposit or security deposit of the hand or with plucking or oppresses his neighbor. **22 (6:3)** Or he finds a lost thing and he lies about her, and he swears according to falsehood, anyone of the things which the human did, it is for failing in them, **23 (6:4)** and it will come to pass, given that he failed and he is guilty, and he returns the plucked thing which he plucked, or the oppression which he oppressed, or the deposited thing which he set over him, or the lost thing which he found. **24 (6:5)** Or from all which he will swear according to the falsehood, and he will make his restitution with his head[506], and he will cause his fifths to be added upon him, he will give him that which belongs to him in the day of his guiltiness, **25 (6:6)** and he will bring his guilt to ***YHWH***, a whole buck from the flocks with your arrangement for the guilt, to the administrator, **26 (6:7)** and the administrator will make a covering upon him to the face of ***YHWH***, and he will be forgiven for him upon anyone from which he does for guiltiness with her,

---

Chapter 6

1 (6:8) and ***YHWH*** spoke to *Mosheh* saying, **2 (6:9)** direct *Aharon* and his sons to say, this is the teaching of the ascension offering, she is the rising upon the smoldering fire upon the altar all the night until the morning, and the fire of the altar will be smoldering in her, **3 (6:10)** and the administrator will wear his long garment of strand, and he will wear undergarments of strand upon his flesh, and he will raise up the fatness which the fire will eat with the ascension offering upon the altar, and he will place him beside the

---

506 Meaning "with his principle."

altar, **4 (6:11)** and he will strip off his garments and he will wear other garments, and he will bring out the fatness to the outside of the camp to the clean area, **5 (6:12)** and the fire upon the altar will be made to smolder in him, she will not be quenched, and the administrator will burn upon her wood every morning, and he will arrange upon her the ascension offering and he will make the fats of the offerings of restitution burn as incense upon her. **6 (6:13)** The fire will be made to smolder continually upon the altar, she will not be quenched, **7 (6:14)** and this is the teaching of the deposit, the sons of *Aharon* will bring her near to the face of ***YHWH***, to the face of the altar, **8 (6:15)** and he will raise up from him with his handful from the flour of the deposit, and from the oil and all the frankincense which is upon the deposit, and he will burn it as incense upon the altar, a sweet aroma, her memorial to ***YHWH***, **9 (6:16)** and *Aharon* and his sons will eat the one being left behind from her, she will be eaten with unleavened breads in the unique area, in the courtyard of the appointed tent they will eat her. **10 (6:17)** Leavened bread will not be baked, I gave her for their distribution, from my fire offerings, she is a special of specials[507], like the failure and like the guilt. **11 (6:18)** Every male among the sons of *Aharon* will eat her, it is a custom of a distant time for your generations, it is from the fire offerings of ***YHWH***, all that touch them, he will set apart, **12 (6:19)** and ***YHWH*** spoke to *Mosheh* saying, **13 (6:20)** this is the donation of *Aharon* and his sons which they will bring near to ***YHWH*** in the day he is being smeared, a tenth of the *eyphah* of flour, a continual deposit, one half of her in the morning and one of her in the evening. **14 (6:21)** She will be made with the oil upon the pan, being fried you will bring her, you will bring near the cooked things of the deposit of fragments, it is a sweet aroma to ***YHWH***, **15 (6:22)** and the smeared administrator under him from his sons will make her, it is a custom of a distant time to ***YHWH***, she will be entirely burned as incense, **16 (6:23)** and every deposit of the administrator will entirely exist, she will not be eaten, **17 (6:24)** and ***YHWH*** spoke to *Mosheh* saying, **18 (6:25)** speak to *Aharon* and to his sons saying, this is the teaching of the failure in the area which you will slay the ascension offering, you will slay the failure to the face of ***YHWH***, she is a special of specials. **19 (6:26)** The administrator, the one bearing the blame with her, will eat her in the unique area, she will be eaten in the courtyard of the appointed tent. **20 (6:27)** Anything that touches her flesh will be set apart, and when he will spatter her blood upon the garment, when he will spatter upon her, you will wash it in the unique area, **21 (6:28)** and the utensil of clay which she is being boiled in will be cracked, or if she is being boiled in a utensil of copper, then he will be scoured and he will be flushed in the waters. **22 (6:29)** All the males among the administrators will eat her, she is a special of specials, **23 (6:30)** and every failure which he will bring from her blood to the appointed tent to

---

507 The phrase "special of specials" means a "very special thing, one or place." (also in verses 18 and 22)

make a covering in the special place will not be eaten in the fire, you will cremate it,

---

Chapter 7

1 and this is the teaching of the guilt, he is a special of specials[508]. **2** In the area where he will slay the ascension offering he will slay the guilt offering, he will sprinkle his blood upon the altar all around, **3** and he will bring all his fat near, the rump, the fat covering, the insides, **4** and the two kidneys and the fat which is upon them which is upon the hips, and the lobe upon the heavy one with the kidneys he will remove, **5** and the administrator will burn them as incense upon the altar, a fire offering to ***YHWH***, he is the guilt. **6** All the males with the administrators will eat him, he is a special of specials. **7** Like the failure, like the guilt, it is one teaching for them, the administrator, which will make a covering with him, it will exist for him, **8** and the administrator bringing near the ascension offering of a man, the skin of the ascension offering, which he brought near to the administrator, he will exist for him, **9** and all the deposits, which will be baked in the oven, and all that was made in the boiling pot and upon the pan, belongs to the administrator, the one bringing her, she will exist for him, **10** and all the deposits mixed in the oil and dried out, belong to all the sons of *Aharon*, she will exist each like his brother, **11** and this is the teaching of the sacrifice, the offerings of restitution, which he will bring near to ***YHWH***. **12** If it is for thanks, he will bring him near, and he will bring it near upon the sacrifice of the thanks, pierced unleavened breads mixed in the oil, and thin unleavened breads smeared with oil, and flour being fried, pierced breads mixed with the oil. **13** Upon the pierced breads is leavened bread, he will bring near his donation upon the sacrifice of thanks, it is his offerings of restitution, **14** and he will bring near from himself a unit from all the donation offerings to ***YHWH***, it will belong to the administrator, the one sprinkling the blood of the offerings of restitution, he will exist for him, **15** and the flesh of the sacrifice of thanks is his offerings of restitution, in the day his donation will be eaten, he will not leave any from him until morning, **16** but if the sacrifice of his donation is a vow or freewill offering, in the day his sacrifice is brought near, he will be eaten, and that being left behind from him on the morrow, he will be eaten, **17** and that being left behind from the flesh of the sacrifice in the third day, will be cremated in the fire, **18** and if the flesh of the sacrifice of his offerings of restitution will surely be eaten in the third day, the one bringing him near will not be accepted, he will not be considered, he will exist foul, and the soul eating from him will lift up her twistedness, **19** and the flesh which touches any dirty thing will not be eaten, he will be

---

[508] The phrase "special of specials" means a "very special thing, one or place." (also in verses 4 and 6)

cremated in the fire, and the flesh of all clean things, he will eat the flesh, **20** and the soul which will eat flesh from the sacrifice of the offerings of restitution which belongs to ***YHWH***, then his dirtiness is upon him, and that soul will be cut from her people, **21** and the soul that will touch any dirty thing, a dirty human or dirty beast or any filthy dirty thing, and ate from the flesh of the sacrifice of the offerings of restitution, which belong to ***YHWH***, then that soul will be cut from her people, **22** and ***YHWH*** spoke to *Mosheh* saying, **23** speak to the sons of *Yisra'eyl* saying, all the fat of the ox and sheep and she-goats you will not eat, **24** and the fat of a carcass and the fat of a torn thing will be done for any business, but you must not eat him, **25** given that all eating the fat from the beast, which is brought near from the fire offering to ***YHWH***, and the soul that is eating will be cut from her people, **26** and all the blood, belonging to the flyer or to the beast, you will not eat in all your settlings. **27** Any soul which will eat any blood, then that soul will be cut from her people, **28** and ***YHWH*** spoke to *Mosheh* saying, **29** speak to the sons of *Yisra'eyl* saying, the one bringing near a sacrifice of his offering of restitution to ***YHWH***, he will bring his donation to ***YHWH*** from the sacrifice of his offerings of restitution. **30** His hands will bring the fire offerings of ***YHWH***, the fat upon the chest he will bring with the chest, to make him wave, a waving to the face of ***YHWH***, **31** and the administrator will make the fat burn as incense upon the altar, and the chest will exist for *Aharon* and for his sons, **32** and the right thigh you will give as an offering to the administrator from the sacrifices of your offerings of restitution. **33** The one from the sons of *Aharon* bringing near the blood of the offerings of restitution, and the fat, the right thigh will exist for him for a share, **34** given that the chest of the waving and the thigh of the offering, I took from the sons of *Yisra'eyl* from the sacrifices of their offerings of restitution, and I will give them to *Aharon* the administrator and to his sons from the sons of *Yisra'eyl* for a distant custom. **35** This is the ointment of *Aharon* and the ointment of his sons from the fire offerings of ***YHWH***, in the day he brought them near to be adorned for ***YHWH***. **36** Which ***YHWH*** directed to give to them in the day of his smearing them from the sons of *Yisra'eyl*, a distant custom for their generations. **37** This is the teaching for the ascension offering, for the deposit and for the failure and for the guilt and for the settings and for the sacrifice of offerings of restitution. **38** Which ***YHWH*** directed *Mosheh* in the hill of *Sinai* in the day of his directing the sons of *Yisra'eyl* to bring near their donations to ***YHWH*** in the wilderness of *Sinai*,

---

Chapter 8

1 and ***YHWH*** spoke to *Mosheh* saying, **2** take *Aharon* and his sons with him and the garments and the oil of ointment and the bull of failure and two bucks and the wicker basket of unleavened breads, **3** and cause to assemble all the company to the opening of the appointed tent, **4** and *Mosheh* did just

as ***YHWH*** directed him, and the company assembled to the opening of the
appointed tent, **5** and *Mosheh* said to the company, this is the word which
YHWH directed to do, **6** and *Mosheh* brought near *Aharon* and his sons and
he bathed them in the waters, **7** and he placed upon him the tunic, and he
girded him up with a sash, and he caused him to wear the cloak, and he
placed upon him the *Ephod*, and he girded him up with the decorative band
of the *Ephod*, and he girded for him with him, **8** and he placed upon him the
breastplate, and he placed on the breastplate the *Uriym* and the *Tumiym*,
9 and he placed the turban upon his head, and he placed upon the turban,
to the forefront of his face, the gold blossom, the special thing of
dedication[509], just as ***YHWH*** directed *Mosheh*, **10** and *Mosheh* took the oil of
ointment and he smeared the dwelling and all which was in him, and he set
them apart, **11** and he spattered some of him upon the altar seven times,
and he smeared the altar and all his utensils and the cauldron and his base
to set them apart, **12** and he poured down some of the oil of ointment upon
the head of *Aharon*, and he smeared him to set him apart, **13** and *Mosheh*
brought near the sons of *Aharon*, and he caused them to wear tunics, and
he girded them up with a sash, and he saddled them with headdresses just
as ***YHWH*** directed *Mosheh*, **14** and he drew near the bull of failure and
Aharon and his sons supported their hands upon the head of the bull of
failure, **15** and he slew it, and *Mosheh* took the blood and placed it upon the
horns of the altar, all around, with his finger, and he purified the altar, and
he poured down the blood at the bottom base of the altar, and he set him
apart to make a covering over him, **16** and he took all the fat which was
upon the inside, and the heavy lobe[510], and the two kidneys, and their fat,
and *Mosheh* burned incense upon the altar,**17** and the bull and his skin and
his flesh and his dung he cremated in the fire outside the camp, just as
YHWH directed *Mosheh*, **18** and he brought near the buck of the ascension
offering, and *Aharon* and his sons supported their hands upon the head of
the buck, **19** and he slew it, and *Mosheh* sprinkled the blood upon the altar,
all around, **20** and he divided the buck into pieces, according to his pieces,
and *Mosheh* burned as incense the head and the pieces and the suet, **21** and
the inside and the legs, and he bathed in the waters and *Mosheh* burned as
incense all of the buck upon the altar, he was an ascension offering for a
sweet aroma, he was a fire offering to ***YHWH***, just as ***YHWH*** directed
Mosheh, **22** and he brought near the second buck, the buck of installation,
and *Aharon* and his sons supported their hands upon the head of the buck,
23 and he slew, and *Mosheh* took from his blood and he placed it upon the
tip of the right ear of *Aharon* and upon the thumb of his right hand and
upon the thumb of his right foot, **24** and he brought near the sons of *Aharon*
and *Mosheh* placed some of the blood upon their right ear and upon the
thumb of their right hand and upon the thumb of their right foot, and

[509] That is a "crown."

[510] "The heavy lobe" is the liver, the heaviest organ in the body.

Mosheh sprinkled the blood upon the altar, all around, **25** and he took the fat and the rump and all the fat which is upon the inside and the heavy lobe[511] and the two kidneys and their fat and the right thigh, **26** and from the wicker basket of the unleavened breads, which is to the face of ***YHWH***, he took one of the pierced unleavened bread, one of the pierced bread of oil, and one of the thin bread, and he placed upon the fats and upon the right thigh, **27** and he placed all of it upon the palms of *Aharon* and upon the palms of his sons, and he waved them, a waving to the face of ***YHWH***, **28** and *Mosheh* took them from upon their palms, and he burned it as incense upon the altar, upon the ascension offering of installation, they are for a sweet aroma, he is a fire offering to ***YHWH***, **29** and *Mosheh* took the chest, and he waved him, a waving to the face of ***YHWH***, from the buck of installation, belonging to *Mosheh*, he existed for a share, just as ***YHWH*** directed *Mosheh*, **30** and *Mosheh* took some of the oil of ointment and from the blood, which was upon the altar, and he spattered it upon *Aharon*, upon his garments and upon his sons and upon the garments of his sons with him, and he set apart *Aharon*, his garments and his sons and the garments of his sons with him, **31** and *Mosheh* said to *Aharon* and to his sons, boil the flesh at the opening of the appointed tent and there you will eat him and the bread which is in the wicker basket of installation, just as I directed, saying, *Aharon* and his sons will eat him, **32** and that being left behind of the flesh and of the bread, you will cremate in the fire, **33** and from the opening of the appointed tent you will not go out seven days, until the day of fillings, the days of your installation, given that seven days he will fill your hand[512].
34 Just as is done in this day, ***YHWH*** directed to do, to make a covering upon you, **35** and the opening of the appointed tent you will settle day and night seven days, and you will safeguard the charge of ***YHWH***, and you will not die, since I directed, **36** and *Aharon* did, and his sons, all the words that ***YHWH*** directed, by the hand of *Mosheh*,

---

Chapter 9

1 and it came to pass in the eighth day, *Mosheh* called out to *Aharon* and to his sons and to the bearded ones of *Yisra'eyl*, **2** and he said to *Aharon*, take for you a bullock, a son of the cattle, for the failure, and a buck for the ascension offering, whole ones, and bring near to the face of ***YHWH***, **3** and to the sons of *Yisra'eyl* you will speak saying, take a hairy goat of the she-goats for the failure, and a bullock and a sheep, sons of a year[513], whole

---

[511] "The heavy lobe" is the liver, the heaviest organ in the body.
[512] To "fill the hand" is an idiom of uncertain meaning, but the same phrase is used in Akkadian to mean the placing of a relevant tool or insignia (such as a scepter for a king) in the hand of one being installed in a high office.
[513] "Son of a year" is an idiom for "one year old."

ones, for the ascension offering, **4** and an ox and a buck for the offering of
restitution, for a sacrifice to the face of ***YHWH***, and a deposit mixed in the
oil, given that today ***YHWH*** appeared to you, **5** and they took what *Mosheh*
directed to the face of the appointed tent, and all the company came near,
and they stood to the face of ***YHWH***, **6** and *Mosheh* said, this is the word
that ***YHWH*** directed you to do, and the armament of ***YHWH*** appeared to
you, **7** and *Mosheh* said to *Aharon*, come near to the altar and do your
failure and your ascension offering and make a covering on behalf of
yourself and on behalf of the people, and do the donation of the people,
and make a covering on their behalf, just as ***YHWH*** directed, **8** and *Aharon*
came near to the altar, and he slew the bullock of the failure, which
belonged to him, **9** and the sons of *Aharon* brought near the blood to him,
and he dipped his finger in the blood, and he placed it upon the horns of the
altar, and he poured down the blood to the bottom base of the altar, **10** and
the fat and the kidneys and the heavy lobe[514] from the failure, he burned as
incense upon the altar, just as ***YHWH*** directed *Mosheh*, **11** and the flesh and
the skin he cremated in the fire outside the camp, **12** and he slew the
ascension offering, and the sons of *Aharon* revealed to him the blood, and
he sprinkled him upon the altar all around, **13** and they revealed the
ascension offering to him, to her pieces and the head, and he burned it as
incense upon the altar, **14** and he bathed the insides and the legs, and he
burned them as incense upon the ascension offering, unto the altar, **15** and
he brought near the donation of the people, and he took the hairy goat, the
failure, which belonged to the people, and slew him, and he bore the blame
with him like the first one, **16** and he brought near the ascension offering,
and he did her according to the decision, **17** and he brought near the
deposit, and he filled his palm from her, and he burned it as incense upon
the altar apart from the ascension offering of the morning, **18** and he slew
the ox and the buck of the sacrifice of the offerings of restitution, which
belonged to the people, and the sons of *Aharon* revealed the blood to him,
and he sprinkled him upon the altar, all around, **19** and the fats from the ox
and from the buck the rump, and what is covering over the kidneys and the
lobe of the heavy lobe, **20** and they placed the fats upon the chest, and he
made the fats burn as incense unto the altar, **21** and the chest and the right
thigh *Aharon* waved a waving to the face of ***YHWH***, just as *Mosheh* directed,
22 and *Aharon* lifted up his hand to the people, and he exalted them, and he
went down from doing the failure and the ascension offering and the
offerings of restitution, **23** and *Mosheh* came, and *Aharon*, to the appointed
tent, and they went out and they exalted the people, and the armament of
YHWH appeared to all the people, **24** and a fire came out from before the
face of ***YHWH***, and she ate the ascension offering and the fats upon the

---

514 "The heavy lobe" is the liver, the heaviest organ in the body. (also in verse 19)

altar, and all the people saw, and they shouted aloud and they fell upon their faces,

---

Chapter 10

1 and the sons of *Aharon*, *Nadav* and *Aviyhu*, each took his fire pan, and they placed fire in them, and they placed incense smoke upon her, and they brought strange fire near to the face of ***YHWH***, which he did not direct them, **2** and fire went out from before the face of ***YHWH*** and she at them and they died to the face of ***YHWH***, **3** and *Mosheh* said to *Aharon*, this is what ***YHWH*** spoke, saying, with ones near me I will be set apart, and upon the face of all the people I will be heavy, and *Aharon* was silent, **4** and *Mosheh* called out to *Miysha'eyl* and to *El'tsaphan*, the sons of *Uziy'eyl*, the uncle of *Aharon*, and said to them, come near, lift up your brothers from the face of the special place to the outside of the camp, **5** and they came near and they lifted them up with their tunics, to the outside of the camp, just as *Mosheh* spoke, **6** and *Mosheh* said to *Aharon*, and to *Elazar* and to *Iytamar*, his sons, you will not loose your heads, and you will not rip your garments, and you will not die, and he will snap upon all the company, and your brothers, all the house of *Yisra'eyl* will weep the cremating, which ***YHWH*** cremated, **7** and you will not go out from the opening of the appointed tent, otherwise you will die, given that the oil of ointment of ***YHWH*** is upon you, and they did according to the word of *Mosheh*, **8** and ***YHWH*** spoke to *Aharon* saying, **9** you will not gulp wine and liquor, you and your sons with you, when coming to the appointed tent, and you will not die, it is a distant custom for your generations, **10** and to make a separation between the special and the ordinary and between the dirty and the clean, **11** and to teach the sons of *Yisra'eyl* all the customs that ***YHWH*** spoke to them by the hand of *Mosheh*, **12** and *Mosheh* spoke to *Aharon*, and to *Elazar* and to *Iytamar* his sons, the ones being left behind, take the deposit, the one being left behind from the fire offerings of ***YHWH***, and eat the unleavened breads beside the altar, given that she is a special of specials[515], **13** and you will eat her in the unique area, given that she is your custom, and a custom of your sons, from the fire offerings of ***YHWH***, since I have been directed, **14** and the chest of the waving and the thigh of the offering you will eat in the clean area, you and your sons and your daughters with you, given that it is your custom and the custom of your sons, they were given from the sacrifices of the offerings of restitution of the sons of *Yisra'eyl*. **15** The thigh of the offering and the chest of the waving they will bring upon the fire offerings of the fat, to make a waving to the face of ***YHWH***, and he will exist for you and for your sons with you, it is for a distant custom just as ***YHWH*** directed,

---

[515] The phrase "special of specials" means a "very special thing, one or place."

16 and *Mosheh* diligently sought the hairy goat of the failure, and look, he was cremated, and he snapped upon *Elazar* and upon *Iytamar*, the sons of *Aharon*, the ones being left behind, saying, **17** why did you not eat the failure in the special area, given that she was a special of specials[516], and he gave her to you to lift up the twistedness of the company to cover over them to the face of ***YHWH***. **18** Though her blood was not brought to the special place within, you will surely eat her in the special place, just as I directed, **19** and *Aharon* spoke to *Mosheh*, though today they brought near their failure and their ascension offering to the face of ***YHWH***, and they[517] called me out like this, and I will eat the failure today, will it do well in the eyes of ***YHWH***, **20** and *Mosheh* heard and it did well in his eyes,

---

Chapter 11

1 and ***YHWH*** spoke to *Mosheh* and to *Aharon*, saying to them. **2** Speak to the sons of *Yisra'eyl*, saying, these are the living ones that you will eat from all the beasts which are upon the land. **3** All being cleaved of the hoof, and splitting hoofs split in two, and making the cud go up among the beasts, you will eat her. **4** Surely of these you will not eat, from ones making the cud go up or from ones cleaving of the hoof, the camel, given that he is making the cud go up, but his hoof is without a cleaving, he is dirty to you, **5** and the rabbit, given that he is making the cud go up, but the hoof is not cleaved, he is dirty to you, **6** and the hare, given that she is making the cud go up, but the hoof is not cleaved, she is dirty to you, **7** and the swine, given that he is cleaving the hoof and the split hoof is split in two, but he does not chew the cud, he is dirty to you. **8** You will not eat from their flesh and you will not touch their carcass, they are dirty to you. **9** Of these you will eat, from all which are in the waters, all which have to him a fin and scales, in the waters, in the seas, in the wadis, them you will eat, **10** and all which are without to him a fin and scales, in the seas and in the wadis, from all the swarmers of the waters and from all the living souls which are in the waters, they are filthy to you, **11** and they will exist as filthy to you, you will not eat from their flesh and you will detest their carcass. **12** All of them that are without fins and scales in the waters, he is filthy to you, **13** and these you will detest from the flyers, they will not be eaten, they are filthy, the eagle, and the bearded vulture, and the osprey, **14** and the vulture, and the hawk to her kind. **15** All raven to his kind, **16** and the daughter of the owl[518], and the

---

516 The phrase "special of specials" means a "very special thing, one or place."

517 As the "they" is the feminine plural pronoun, it is referring to the "failure" and the "ascension offering," not the sons of Aharon.

518 The meaning of "daughter of the owl" is uncertain; most translations ignore the word "daughter."

nighthawk, and the seagull, and the falcon to his kind, **17** and the little owl,
and the cormorant, and the eared owl, **18** and the ibis, and the pelican, and
the gier-eagle, **19** and the stork, the heron to her kind, and the grouse, and
the bat[519]. **20** All the swarmers of the flyers, the ones walking[520] upon four,
he is filthy to you. **21** Surely of these you will eat, from all the swarmers of
the flyers, the ones walking upon four, which have to him legs above his
feet, to leap with them upon the land. **22** Of these from them you will eat,
the swarming locust to his kind, and the locust to his kind, and the leaping
locust to his kind, and the grasshopper to his kind, **23** and all the swarmers
of the flyers which have to him four feet, he is filthy to you, **24** and to these
you will make yourself dirty, every touching with their carcass, he will be
dirty until the evening, **25** and all the ones lifting up their carcass, he will
wash his garments and he will be dirty until the evening. **26** To every beast
which she is cleaving of the hoof and is not splitting in two and is not
bringing up the cud, they are dirty for you, all the ones touching them will be
dirty, **27** and everyone walking upon his palms, among every living thing
walking upon four, they are dirty for you, everyone touching their carcass
will be dirty until the evening, **28** and the one lifting up their carcass will
wash his garments and he will be dirty until the evening, they are dirty to
you, **29** and this is dirty to you among the swarmers swarming upon the
land, the weasel and the mouse and the tortoise to his kind, **30** and the
ferret and the chameleon and the lizard and the snail and the ibis. **31** These
are the dirty ones to you among all the swarmers, everyone touching them
in their death will be dirty until evening, **32** and all of them in their death
which will fall upon him, he will be dirty, including any utensil of wood or
garment or skin or sack, every utensil which will be done for business he will
bring them in the waters, and he will be dirty until evening then he will be
clean, **33** and every utensil of clay which they will fall into his midst, all which
is in his midst will be dirty and you will crack him. **34** From all the foodstuff
which will be eaten, which waters will come upon will be dirty, and all drink
which can be gulped in every utensil will be dirty, **35** and all which will fall
from their carcass upon him will be dirty, oven and earthenware, he will be
broken down, they are dirty, and they will exist as dirty things to you.
36 Surely, from the eye[521] and cistern, a collection of waters, he will exist
clean, but touching with their carcass he will be dirty, **37** and if their carcass
will fall upon any seed sown which will be sown, he is clean, **38** and if he
placed waters upon the seed, and their carcass fell upon him, he is dirty,

---

[519] Because all English translations identify this list of creatures as "birds" (see verse 13), the addition of the "bat" has often been used to show ignorance of the author of the text. However, as the Hebrew word "oph" simply means "a creature that flies," the addition of the bat is justifiable.

[520] The word "walking" also means "going," and may apply to flyers as they "go" on two feet and with two wings.

[521] That is, a fountain.

39 and if the beast, which belongs to you for food, dies, the one touching
her carcass will be dirty until the evening, **40** and the one eating her carcass
will wash his garments and he will be dirty until the evening, and the one
lifting up her carcass will wash his garments and he will be dirty until the
evening, **41** and every swarming swarmer upon the land is filthy, he will not
be eaten. **42** All walking upon the belly and all walking upon four, as well as
all making an increase of feet[522], for all the swarming swarmers upon the
land, you will not eat them, given that they are filthy. **43** You will not detest
your souls with all the swarming swarmers, and you will not make yourself
be dirty with them, and you will be dirty with them, **44** given that I am
YHWH your *Elohiym* and you will set yourself apart and you will exist as
unique ones, given that I am unique, and you will not make your souls be
dirty with all the treading swarmers upon the land, **45** given that I am
YHWH, the one making you go up from the land of *Mits'rayim*, to exist for
you for *Elohiym*, and you will exist as unique ones, given that I am unique.
46 This is the teaching of the beast and the flyer and every living treading
soul in the waters, and for every swarming soul upon the land. **47** For
making a separation between the dirty and the clean and between the living
thing to be eaten and the living thing which will not be eaten,

---

Chapter 12

1 and ***YHWH*** spoke to *Mosheh*, saying, **2** speak to the sons of *Yisra'eyl*,
saying, a woman that will produce and bring forth a male, then she will be
dirty seven days, like the days of removal of her illness, she will be dirty,
3 and in the eighth day, the flesh of his foreskin will be snipped off, **4** and
thirty and three days she will settle in the bloodshed of the cleanliness, with
all special things she will not touch, and she will not come to the sanctuary
until the filling of the days of her cleanliness, **5** and if she will bring forth a
female, then she will be dirty two weeks, like her removal, and sixty and six
days she will settle upon the bloodshed of cleanliness, **6** and in the filling of
the days of her cleanliness for a son or for a daughter, she will bring a year
old sheep for an ascension offering, a son of a dove or a turtledove for the
failure, to the opening of the appointed tent, to the administrator, **7** and he
will bring him near to the face of ***YHWH***, and he will make a covering upon
her, and she will be clean from the fountain of her bloodshed, this is the
teaching of the bringing forth for the male or for the female, **8** and if she
does not find her hand sufficient with a ram, then she will take two
turtledoves or two sons of a dove, one for the ascension offering and one
for the failure, and the administrator will make a covering upon her and she
will be clean,

---

[522] The phrase "making an increase of feet" means "have many feet."

Chapter 13

1 and ***YHWH*** spoke to *Mosheh* and to *Aharon*, saying, **2** a human that has in the skin of his flesh a lifting up or a scab or a bright spot, and has in the skin of his flesh a plague of infection, then he will be brought to *Aharon* the administrator or to one of his sons the administrators, **3** and the administrator will see the plague in the skin of the flesh, and a hair in the plague turned white, and the appearance of the plague is sunken from the skin of his flesh, he is the plague of infection, and the administrator will see him and he will declare him dirty, **4** and if the bright spot is white, she is in the skin of his flesh and her appearance is not sunken from the skin and a hair is not turned white, then the administrator will shut the plague seven days, **5** and the administrator will see him in the seventh day and look, the plague stood in his eyes, the plague did not spread across the skin, then the administrator will cause him to be shut a second seven days, **6** and the administrator will see him in the second seventh day, and look, dimness of the plague and the plague did not spread across the skin, then the administrator will declare him clean, she is a scab, and he will wash his garments and he will be clean, **7** but if spreading across, the scab of the skin will seize hold, after he appears to the administrator for his cleanliness, he will appear a second time to the administrator, **8** and the administrator will see, and look, the scab spread across the skin, and the administrator will declare him dirty, she is an infection. **9** A plague of infection that exists in the human will be brought to the administrator, **10** and the administrator will see, and look, a lifting up of white on the skin, and the hair turned white, and a reviving[523] of the living flesh in the elevation[524]. **11** It is an infection, she is sleeping in the skin of his flesh, and the administrator will declare him dirty, he will not cause him shut, given that he is dirty, **12** and if the infection in the skin will completely burst out, and the infection will cover over all the skin of the plague, from his head to his feet to all the appearance of the eyes of the administrator[525], **13** and the administrator will see, and look, the infection covered over all his flesh, then the plague of all of him will be declared clean, he turned white, he is clean, **14** and in the day living[526] flesh appears in him, he will be dirty, **15** and the administrator will see the living flesh, and he will declare him dirty, the living flesh is dirty, he is an infection. **16** Or, given that the living flesh will turn back, and he was turned to white, and he will come to the administrator, **17** and the administrator will see him, and look, the plague was turned white, and the administrator will declare the plague clean, he is clean, **18** and the flesh that

---

523 Probably meaning "tender" or "raw."

524 Probably meaning "swelling."

525 The phrase "to all the appearance of the eyes of the administrator" means "as far as the administrator can see."

526 Probably meaning "tender" or "raw."

exists in him, in his skin are boils, and he will be healed, **19** and in the place
of the boils exists a lifting up of white, or a white reddish bright spot, then
he will appear to the administrator, **20** and the administrator will see, and
look, her appearance is low from the skin, and her hair turned white, then
the administrator will declare him dirty, she is a plague of infection, she will
burst out in the boils, **21** and if the administrator will see her, and look, no
white hair is in her, and she is not low from the skin, and she is dim, then the
administrator will cause him to shut seven days, **22** but if spreading across,
seizing hold in the skin, then the administrator will declare him dirty, she is a
plague, **23** and if the bright spot stands in her place, and does not spread
across, she is the searing boils, and the administrator will declare him clean.
24 Or the flesh that exists in his skin is a singe scar of fire, and the reviving of
the singe scar exists as a bright spot, white reddish or white, **25** then the
administrator will see her, and look, the hair turned white in the bright spot,
and her appearance is sunken from the skin, she is an infection, in the singe
scar she will burst out, and the administrator will declare him dirty, she is a
plague of infection, **26** and if the administrator will see her, and look, it is
without a white hair in the bright spot, and she is not low from the skin, and
she is dim, then the administrator will cause him to shut seven days, **27** and
the administrator will see him in the seventh day, if spreading across seizing
hold in the skin, then the administrator will declare him dirty, she is a plague
of infection, **28** and if the bright spot stands in her place, and does not
spread across in the skin and she is dim, she is a lifting up of the singe scar,
and the administrator will declare him clean, given that she is a searing of a
singe scar, **29** and a man or woman that exists in him a plague in the head or
in the beard, **30** and the administrator will see the plague, and look, his
appearance is sunken from the skin, and a scrawny yellow hair is in him, and
the administrator will declare him dirty, he is an eruption, he is an infection
of the head or beard, **31** and, given that the administrator will see the
plague of eruption, and look, his appearance is not sunken from the skin,
and the hair is not black as coal in him, and the administrator will cause to
shut the plague of eruption seven days, **32** and the administrator will see the
plague in the seventh day, and look, the eruption did not spread across, and
a yellow hair did not exist in him, and the appearance of the eruption was
not sunken from the skin, **33** and he will shave himself, but he will not shave
the eruption, and the administrator will cause shut the eruption a second
seven days, **34** and the administrator will see the eruption in the seventh
day, and look, the eruption did not spread across in the skin, and his
appearance is not sunken from the skin, and the administrator will declare
him clean, and he will wash his garments and he will be clean, **35** but if the
eruption completely spread across in the skin after his cleaning, **36** then the
administrator will see him, and look, the eruption spread across in the skin,
the administrator will not investigate for the yellow hair, he is dirty, **37** but if
in his eyes the eruption stands and a black as coal hair sprang up in him, the
eruption is healed, he is clean, and the administrator will declare him clean,

38 and a man or woman that exists in the skin of their flesh white bright
spots, **39** and the administrator will see, and look, in the skin of their flesh
are dim white bright spots, he is a rash burst out in the skin, he is clean,
40 and a man whose hair has fallen out of his head, he is bald, he is clean,
41 and if from the edge of his face the hair fell out of his head, he has a bald
forehead, he is clean, **42** and, given that a white reddish plague will exist
with the baldness or with the bald forehead, she is an infection bursting out
in his bald spot or in his bare spot, **43** and the administrator will see him,
and look, the white reddish plague is lifted up in his bald spot or in his bare
spot, like the appearance of an infection of the skin of the flesh. **44** He is an
infected man, he is dirty, the administrator will declare him completely dirty,
his plague is in his head, **45** and the infected one, which the plague is in him,
his garments will be ripped, and his head will be loosed[527], and upon the
upper lip he will enwrap, and he will be very dirty, he will call out dirty. **46** All
the days which the plague is in him he will be dirty, he is dirty, he will settle
alone, he will settle his settling outside of the camp, **47** and the garment
that the plague of infection exists in, in a garment of wool, or in a garment
of flax. **48** Or in the warp or in the mixture[528], to the flax and to the wool, or
in the skin or in any business of skin[529], **49** but if the greenish or reddish
plague exists in the garment or in the skin or in the warp or in the mixture or
any utensil of skin, he is a plague of infection, and he will be caused to
appear to the administrator, **50** and the administrator will see the plague,
and he will cause the plague to be shut seven days, **51** and he will see the
plague in the seventh day, given that the plague spread across in the
garment, or in the warp or in the mixture or in the skin, to anything that will
be done to the skin for business, the plague is an irritating infection, he is
dirty, **52** and he will cremate the garment or the warp or the mixture, in the
wool or in the flax, or any utensil of the skin that the plague exists in him,
given that she is an irritating infection, you will cremate it in the fire, **53** and
the administrator will see, and look, if the plague did not spread across in
the garment, or in the warp or in the mixture or in any utensil of skin, **54** and
the administrator will direct and they will wash the plague that is in him, and
he will cause him to be shut a second seven days, **55** and the administrator
will see after the plague is washed, and look, the plague did not overturn his
eye[530], and the plague did not spread across, he is dirty, you will cremate
him in the fire, she is a pit in his bald spot or in his bare spot, **56** and the
administrator will see, and look, if the plague is dim after washing him, then
he will tear him from the garment or from the skin or from the warp or from

---

[527] That is, "uncovered" or "bare."

[528] That is the "woof."

[529] "Business of skin" is a person working with leather.

[530] The phrase "did not overturn his eye" means "did not change color."

the mixture, **57** and if she[531] appears yet again in the garment or in the warp or in the mixture or in any utensil of skin, she is a bursting out, you will cremate what the plague is in the fire, **58** and the garment or the warp or the mixture or any utensil of skin, you will wash, and if the plague turns aside from them, then he will be washed a second time, and he will be clean. **59** This is the teaching of the plague of infection of a garment of wool or flax or the warp or the mixture or any utensil of skin, for his cleanliness or for his dirtiness,

---

Chapter 14

1 and ***YHWH*** will speak to *Mosheh* saying, **2** this will be the teaching of the one being infected in the day of his cleanliness, and he will be brought to the administrator, **3** and the administrator will go out to the outside of the camp, and the administrator will see, and look, the plague infection was healed from the infected one, **4** and the administrator will direct, and the one being clean will take two living clean birds and cedar wood and scarlet of kermes and hyssop, **5** and the administrator will direct, and he will slay the one bird to a utensil of clay[532] upon living waters[533]. **6** He will take the living bird and the cedar wood and the scarlet kermes and the hyssop and he will dip them and the living bird in blood of the slain bird upon the living waters, **7** and he will spatter upon the ones being made clean from the infection seven times, then he will declare him clean and he will send the living bird upon the face of the field, **8** and he will wash the garments of the one being made clean, and he will shave all his hair, and he will bathe in the waters and he will be clean, and after he will come to the camp and he will settle outside of his tent for seven days, **9** and it will come to pass in the seventh day, he will shave all his hair, his head and his beard and the arches of his eyes, and all his hair he will shave, and he will wash his garments, and he will bathe his flesh in the waters and he will be clean, **10** and in the eighth day he will take two whole sheep and one whole sheep, a daughter of a year, and three one-tenths of flour, it is a deposit, mixed in the oil of one log of oil, **11** and the administrator, the one making clean, will make the man to be made clean, stand with them, to the face of ***YHWH*** at the opening of the appointed tent, **12** and the administrator will take the one sheep and he will bring him near for guilt, and the log of oil, and he will wave them as a waving to the face of ***YHWH***, **13** and he will slay the sheep in the area which he slays the failure and the ascension offering in the special area, given that

---

531 The Hebrew word for "touch" (plague) is a masculine noun. In verse 56 the masculine pronoun "him" is used for this word, but here, this verb uses the feminine pronoun "she" and appears to be in error.

532 A "utensil of clay" is a clay vessel.

533 Meaning "running."

he is like the failure of the guilt for the administrator, he is the special of
specials[534], **14** and the administrator will take from the blood of the guilt and
the administrator will place it upon the tip of the right ear of the ones being
made clean, and upon the thumb of his right hand and upon the thumb of
his right foot, **15** and the administrator will take from the log of oil and he
will pour down upon the palm of the left hand of the administrator, **16** and
the administrator will dip his right finger in the oil which is upon the palm of
his left hand and he will spatter the oil on his finger seven times to the face
of ***YHWH***, **17** and from the remainder of the oil which is upon his palm, the
administrator will place upon the tip of the right ear of the one being made
clean, and upon the thumb of his right hand and upon the thumb of his right
foot, upon the blood of the guilt, **18** and the oil that is left behind which is
upon the palm, the administrator will place it upon the head of the one
being made clean, and the administrator will make a covering upon him to
the face of ***YHWH***, **19** and the administrator will do the failure and he will
make a covering upon the ones being made clean from his dirtiness, and
after, he will slay the ascension offering, **20** and the administrator will make
the ascension offering go up, and the deposit, unto the altar, and the
administrator will make restitution upon him and he will be clean, **21** but if
he is helpless and his hand is unable to reach[535], then he will take one sheep,
guilt for a waving to make a covering upon him, and one tenth of flour
mixed in the oil for a deposit and a log of oil, **22** and two turtledoves or two
sons of a dove, which his hand will reach[536], and one will exist for a failure
and the other one will be for an ascension offering, **23** and he will bring
them in the eighth day for his cleanliness to the administrator to the
opening of the appointed tent to the face of ***YHWH***, **24** and the
administrator will take the sheep of the guilt and the log of the oil and the
administrator will wave them, a waving to the face of ***YHWH***, **25** and he will
slay the sheep of the guilt and the administrator will take from the blood of
the guilt and he will place it upon the tip of the right ear to the one being
made clean and upon the thumb of his right hand and upon the thumb of his
right foot, **26** and from the oil, the administrator will pour down upon the
palm of the left hand of the administrator, **27** and the administrator will
spatter the oil, which is upon the palm of his left hand, on his right finger
seven times to the face of ***YHWH***, **28** and the administrator will place from
the oil which is upon his palm upon the right ear of the one being made
clean and upon the thumb of his right hand and upon the thumb of his right
toe, upon the area of the blood of guilt, **29** and the oil that is being left
behind, which is upon the palm of the administrator, he will place it upon
the head of the one being made clean to make a covering upon him to the

---

[534] The phrase "special of specials" means a "very special thing, one or place."

[535] Meaning to "acquire possessions."

[536] Meaning "acquire."

face of ***YHWH***, **30** and he will do the one from the turtledoves or from the sons of the dove, from which his hand will reach. **31** That which his hand has reached is for the one failure and for the one ascension offering upon the deposit, and the administrator will make a covering upon the one being made clean to the face of ***YHWH***. **32** This is the teaching in who has a plague of infection in him, who is not able to reach[537] his hand for his cleansing, **33** and ***YHWH*** spoke to *Mosheh* and to *Aharon* saying, **34** given that you will come to the land of *Kena'an* which I am giving to you for a holdings, and I will give a plague of infection in a house of the land of your holdings, **35** then the one who the house belongs to will come and he will tell it to the administrator saying, something like a plague was seen to me in the house, **36** and the administrator will direct and they will clear out the house before the administrator comes to see the plague, and all that is in the house will not be dirty, and after that the administrator will come to see the house, **37** and he will see the plague, and look, the plague is in the walls of the house, greenish or reddish spots, and their appearance is lower from the wall, **38** then the administrator will go out[538] from the house to the opening of the house, and he will shut the house for seven days, **39** and the administrator will return in the seventh day and he will see, and look, the plague spread across in the walls of the house, **40** then the administrator will direct, and they will extract the stones which have the plague in them, and they will throw them out to the outside of the city, to the dirty area, **41** and he will cause the house to be scraped off from the inside and all around, and they will pour out the dirt which they caused to be scraped off to the outside of the city, to the dirty area, **42** and they will take other stones, and they will bring them to be in place of the stones, and he will take other dirt and he will plaster the house, **43** and if the plague return and he bursts out in the house after he extracted the stones and after the scraping off the house and after being plastered, **44** and the administrator will come and he will see, and look, the plague spread across in the house, she[539] is an irritating infection, he[540] is dirty, **45** and he will break down the house, his stones, his wood, and all the dirt of the house, and he will bring it out to the outside of the city, to the dirty area, **46** and the one coming to the house all the days he caused him to be shut, he will be dirty until the evening, **47** and the one lying down in the house, he will wash his garments and the one eating in the house, he will wash his garments, **48** and if the administrator certainly comes and he will see, and look, the plague did not spread across

---

537 Meaning to "acquire" what is needed.

538 This verb is written in the perfect tense, "and he went out," but the context implies that this should be written in the imperfect tense, "and he will go out."

539 This pronoun is referring to "infection," the only feminine word in this verse.

540 This pronoun is referring to the word "house."

in the house after the house has been plastered, given that the plague was
healed, **49** and, for purifying the house, he will take two birds and a tree of
cedar and a scarlet kermes and hyssop, **50** and he will slay the one bird in a
utensil of clay upon living waters, **51** and he will take the tree of cedar and
the hyssop and the scarlet kermes and the living bird, and he will dip them in
the blood of the slain bird and the living waters, and he will spatter it on the
house seven times, **52** and he will purify the house with the blood of the bird
and with the living waters and with the living bird and with the cedar tree
and with the hyssop and with the scarlet kermes, **53** and he will send the
living bird to the outside of the city, to the face of the field, and he will make
a covering upon the house, and he will be clean. **54** This is the teaching for
every plague of infection and for the eruption, **55** and for an infection of a
garment and for the house, **56** and for the elevation and for the scab and for
the bright spot. **57** To teach in the day of dirtiness and in the day of
cleanliness, this is the teaching of the infection[541],

Chapter 15

1 and ***YHWH*** spoke to *Mosheh* and to *Aharon* saying, **2** speak to the sons of
Yisra'eyl and you will say to them, each man that exists with an issuing from
a discharge of his flesh, he is dirty, **3** and this will be his dirtiness with his
discharge, his flesh flowed out with his discharge or his flesh was sealed
from his discharge, she is his dirtiness. **4** Every lying place where he lies
down upon with the issuing, will be dirty, and every utensil which he settles
upon will be dirty, **5** and a man which touches his lying place will wash his
garments and he will bathe in the waters and he will be dirty until evening,
6 and the one settling upon the utensil, who settles upon him with an
issuing, he will wash his garments and he will bathe in the waters and he will
be dirty until the evening, **7** and the one touching the flesh with the issuing,
he will wash his garments and he will bathe in the waters and he will be
dirty until the evening, **8** and if the issuing spit on the clean one[542], then he
will wash his garments and he will bathe in the waters and he will be dirty
until the evening, **9** and every saddle which he rides upon with the issuing
will be dirty, **10** and everyone touching anything which will exist under him
will be dirty until the evening, and the one lifting them up will wash his
garments and he will bathe in the waters and he will be dirty until the
evening, **11** and everyone he touches with the issuing and did not flush his
hands in the waters, then he will wash his garments and he will bath in the
waters and he will be dirty until the evening, **12** and a utensil of clay which

---

[541] An alternate translation may be; "to teach when it is dirty and when it is clean, this is the teaching of the infection."

[542] An alternate translation may be "and if the one with the issuing spits on a clean person."

he touches with the issuing will be cracked and every utensil of wood will be flushed in the waters, **13** and if the one with the issuing will be clean from his discharge, then he will count to himself seven days for his cleanness, then he will wash his garments and he will bathe his flesh in living waters and he will be clean, **14** and in the eighth day he will take for himself two turtledoves or two sons of the dove, and he will come to the face of ***YHWH***, to the opening of the appointed tent, and he will give them to the administrator, **15** and the administrator will do them, one is the failure and the other one is the ascension offering, and the administrator will make a covering upon him, to the face of ***YHWH*** because of his discharge, **16** and a man that has a lying down of seed[543] go out from him, then he will bathe all his flesh in the waters and he will be dirty until the evening, **17** and every garment and every skin which exists the lying down of seed upon him will be washed in the waters and will be dirty until the evening, **18** and a woman that a man lies down with and has a laying down of seed, then they will bathe in the waters and they will be dirty until the evening, **19** and a woman that will have an issuing, the blood of her discharge is in her flesh, she will exist seven days in her removal, and anyone touching her will be dirty until evening, **20** and anything which she lays down upon in her removal will be dirty, and anything which she settles upon will be dirty, **21** and anyone touching her lying place, he will wash his garments and he will bathe in the waters and he will be dirty until the evening, **22** and anyone touching any utensil which she settled upon, he will wash his garments and he will bathe in the waters and he will be dirty until the evening, **23** and if he is upon the lying place or upon the utensil which she settled upon, with his touch, he will be dirty until the evening, **24** and if a man will surely lie down with her, and her removal existed upon him, then he will be dirty seven days, and every lying place which he lies down upon will be dirty, **25** and a woman that will issue a discharge of her blood an abundance of days, not in the appointed time of her removal, or that she will issue upon her removal, she will exist all the days of the discharge of her dirtiness like the days of her removal, she is dirty. **26** Every lying place which she lies down upon all the days of her discharge is like the lying place of her removal, and every utensil which she settles upon is dirty, he will be dirty like the dirtiness of her removal, **27** and everyone touching them will be dirty, and he will wash his garments in the waters and he will be dirty until the evening, **28** but if she was clean from her discharge and she counted seven days for herself, then after that she will be clean, **29** and in the eighth day she will take for herself two turtledoves or two sons of a dove and she will bring them to the administrator, to the opening of the appointed tent, **30** and the administrator will do the one for a failure and the other one for an ascension offering, and the administrator will make a covering upon her, to the face of ***YHWH*** because of the discharge of her dirtiness, **31** and you will

[543] The "lying down of seed" is the emission of seed during copulation.

dedicate the sons of *Yisra'eyl* from their dirtiness and they will not die from being dirty in my dwelling which is in the midst of them. **32** This is the teaching of the one issuing, and from his laying down of seed which will go out from him, for her dirtiness is in her, **33** and the illness in her removal, and the issuing of his discharge of the male or the female, and for a man which lies down with dirtiness,

---

Chapter 16

1 and ***YHWH*** spoke to *Mosheh* after the death of the two sons of *Aharon* in their coming near to the face of ***YHWH***, **2** and ***YHWH*** said to *Mosheh*, speak to *Aharon* your brother, and do not come in every appointed time to the special tent curtain of the house, to the face of the lid which is upon the box, and he will not die, given that I will be seen in the cloud upon the lid, **3** In this, *Aharon* will come to the special place with a bull, a son of cattle, for a failure, and a buck for an ascension offering. **4** He will wear a special tunic of strand and undergarments of strand will exist upon his flesh, and he will gird up with a sash of strand, and he will wind around with a turban of strand, they are special garments, and he will bathe his flesh in the waters, and he will wear them, **5** and he will take from the company of the sons of *Yisra'eyl* two hairy goats of the she-goats for a failure and one buck for an ascension offering, **6** and *Aharon* will bring near the bull of the failure which is for himself, and he will make a covering on his behalf and on behalf of his house, **7** and he will take the two hairy goats and he will make them stand to the face of ***YHWH***, at the opening of the appointed tent, **8** and *Aharon* will place upon the two hairy goats lots, one lot is for ***YHWH*** and one lot is for *Azazeyl*[544], **9** and *Aharon* will bring near the hairy goat, which went up[545] upon him the lot for ***YHWH***, and he will do him[546] as a failure, **10** and the hairy goat which went up[547] upon him the lot for *Azazeyl*, he will stand living to the face of ***YHWH*** to make a covering upon him, to send him for *Azazeyl* unto the wilderness, **11** and *Aharon* will bring near the bull of the failure which is for himself, and he will make a covering on behalf of himself and on behalf of his house, and he will slay the bull of the failure which is for himself, **12** and he will take the filling of the fire pan, the embers of the fire, from upon the altar from before the face of ***YHWH***, and a filling of his cupped hand, incense smoke of scrawny aromatic spices, and he will bring inside to the tent curtain, **13** and he will place the incense smoke upon the fire to the face of ***YHWH***, and the cloud of incense smoke will cover over the

---

[544] Most translations have "scapegoat," but the context implies that this is the name of a person or other entity.

[545] Meaning the one that was "selected."

[546] That is, "offer him."

[547] Meaning the one that was "selected."

lid which is upon the evidence, and he will not die, **14** and he will take from
the blood of the bull, and he will spatter with his finger upon the east face of
the lid, and to the face of the lid he will spatter seven times from the blood
with his finger, **15** and he will slay the hairy goat of the failure which is for
the people, and he will bring his blood to the inside, to the tent curtain, and
he will do with his blood, just as he did to the blood of the bull, and he will
spatter him upon the lid and to the face of the lid, **16** and he will make a
covering upon the special place because of the dirtiness of the sons of
Yisra'eyl, and because of their offenses for all their failures, and so he will do
this for the appointed tent dwelling with them in the midst of their dirtiness,
17 and there will not exist any human in the appointed tent when he comes
in to make a covering in the special place, until his going out, and he will
make a covering on his behalf and on the behalf of his house and on behalf
of all the assembly of *Yisra'eyl*, **18** and he will go out to the altar which is to
the face of ***YHWH***, and he will make a covering upon him, and he will take
from the blood of the bull and from the blood of the hairy goat, and he will
place them upon the horns of the altar all around, **19** and he will spatter
upon him from the blood with his finger seven times, and he will make him
clean, and he will set him apart from the dirty ones of *Yisra'eyl*, **20** and he
will finish making a covering for the special place and the appointed tent
and the altar, and he will bring near the living hairy goat, **21** and *Aharon* will
support his two hands upon the head of the living hairy goat, and he will
confess upon him all the twistedness of the sons of *Yisra'eyl* and all their
offenses for all their failures, and he will place them upon the head of the
hairy goat, and he will send it by the hand of a ready man unto the
wilderness, **22** and the hairy goat will lift up upon himself all their
twistedness to the uninhabited land, and he will send the hairy goat into the
wilderness, **23** and *Aharon* will come to the appointed tent and he will strip
off the garments of strand which he wore in his coming to the special place,
and he will make them rest there, **24** and he will bathe his flesh in the
waters in the unique area, and he will wear his garments, and he will go out
and he will do his ascension offering and the ascension offering of the
people, and he will make restitution on his behalf and on behalf of the
people, **25** and the fat of the failure he will burn as incense upon the altar,
26 and the one sending the hairy goat for *Azazeyl* will wash his garments and
he will bathe his flesh in the waters and after this he will come to the camp,
27 and the bull of the failure, and the hairy goat of the failure, whose blood
was brought to make a covering in the special place, he will bring it out to
the outside of the camp, and they will cremate their skin and their flesh and
their dung in the fire, **28** and the one cremating them will wash his flesh in
the waters, and after this he will come to the camp, **29** and she will exist for
you for a distant custom, in the seventh new moon in the tenth one to the
new moon[548] you will afflict your souls and you will not do any business, the

[548] That is the "tenth day of the new moon."

native and the immigrant immigrating in your midst, **30** given that in this day he will make restitution upon you to make you clean from all your failures, to the face of ***YHWH*** you will be clean. **31** She is a ceasing rest period for you, and you will afflict your souls, it is a distant custom, **32** and the administrator, who smeared himself and filled his hand[549] to be adorned in place of his father, will make restitution, and he will wear the garments of strand, the special garments, **33** and he will make a covering for the special sanctuary, and the appointed tent and the altar he will make a covering, and upon the administrators and upon the people of the assembly he will make a covering, **34** and this will exist for you for a distant custom to make a covering upon the sons of *Yisra'eyl* from all their failures once in the year, and he will do just as ***YHWH*** directed *Mosheh*,

---

Chapter 17

1 and ***YHWH*** spoke to *Mosheh* saying, **2** speak to *Aharon* and to his sons and to all the sons of *Yisra'eyl*, and you will say to them this word which ***YHWH*** directed, saying, **3** each man from the house of *Yisra'eyl* which will slay an ox or a sheep or a she-goat in the camp, or which he will slay outside the camp, **4** and did not bring it to the opening of the appointed tent to bring near a donation for ***YHWH***, to the face of the dwelling of ***YHWH***, blood is considered for the man, this is blood poured out, and this man will be cut from the inside of his people. **5** For that which the sons of *Yisra'eyl* will bring their sacrifices which they are sacrificing upon the face of the field, and they will bring them to ***YHWH***, to the opening of the appointed tent, to the administrator, and they will sacrifice them as the sacrifices of the offering of restitutions to ***YHWH***, **6** and the administrator will sprinkle the blood upon the altar of ***YHWH***, the opening of the appointed tent, and he will burn as incense the fat for a sweet aroma to ***YHWH***, **7** and they will not sacrifice ever again their sacrifices to the hairy goats, which they were harloting after, this will be a distant custom for them for their generations, **8** and to them you will say, each man from the house of *Yisra'eyl*, and from the immigrant which immigrated in their midst, which will bring up an ascension offering or sacrifice, **9** and he will not bring him to the opening of the appointed tent to do[550] him for ***YHWH***, this man will be cut from his peoples, **10** and each man from the house of *Yisra'eyl*, and from the immigrant immigrating in your midst, that eats any blood, then I will place my face in the soul of the one eating the blood, and I will cause her[551] to be cut from inside her people,

---

[549] To "fill the hand" is an idiom of uncertain meaning, but the same phrase is used in Akkadian to mean the placing of a relevant tool or insignia (such as a scepter for a king) in the hand of one being installed in a high office.
[550] That is to "sacrifice."
[551] Referring to the "soul," a feminine noun.

11 given that the soul of flesh, she is in the blood, and I, I will give him to you
upon the altar to make a covering upon your souls, given that the blood that
is in the soul will make restitution. **12** Therefore, I said to the sons of
Yisra'eyl, every soul among you will not eat blood, and the immigrant
immigrating in your midst will not eat blood, **13** and each man from the sons
of *Yisra'eyl*, and from the immigrant immigrating in their midst, who will
hunt living game or the flyer, will be eaten and he will pour out his blood,
and he will cover it over with the dirt[552], **14** given that the soul of all flesh is
his blood, he is in his soul, and I said to the sons of *Yisra'eyl*, you will not eat
the blood of all flesh, given that the soul of all flesh is blood, anyone eating
him will be cut, **15** and any soul who will eat a carcass and torn, by a native
or by the immigrant, he will wash his garments and he will bathe in the
waters, and he will be dirty until the evening and then he will be clean,
16 but if he will not wash and he will not bathe his flesh, then he will lift up
his twistedness,

Chapter 18

1 and ***YHWH*** spoke to *Mosheh* saying, **2** speak to the sons of *Yisra'eyl*, and
you will say to them, I am ***YHWH*** your *Elohiym*. **3** Like the work of the land of
Mits'rayim that you settled in, you will not do, and like the work of the land
of *Kena'an* that I am making you come unto, you will not do, and you will
not walk in their customs. **4** My decisions you will do, and my customs you
will safeguard, to walk in them, I am ***YHWH*** your *Elohiym*, **5** and you will
safeguard my customs and my decisions, the human that does them will
then live in them, I am ***YHWH***. **6** Each man belonging to all the kin of his
flesh, you will not come near to remove the cover of nakedness, I am ***YHWH***.
7 The nakedness of your father and the nakedness of your mother, you will
not remove the cover, she is your mother, you will not remove the cover of
her nakedness. **8** The nakedness of the woman of your father you will not
remove the cover, she is the nakedness of your father. **9** The nakedness of
your sister, the daughter of your father, or the daughter of your mother, the
kindred of the house or the kindred of outside, you will not remove the
cover of their nakedness. **10** The nakedness of the daughter of your son or
the daughter of your daughter, you will not remove the cover of their
nakedness, given that they are your nakedness. **11** The nakedness of the
daughter of the woman of your father, kindred of your father, she is your
sister, you will not remove the cover of her nakedness. **12** The nakedness of
the sister of your father, you will not remove the cover, she is the kin of your
father. **13** The nakedness of the sister of your mother, you will not remove
the cover, given that she is kin of your mother. **14** The nakedness of the
brother of your father, you will not remove the cover, you will not come

---

[552] That is the "dust" of the ground where the blood is poured.

near to his woman, she is your aunt. **15** The nakedness of your daughter-in-law, you will not remove the cover, she is the woman of your son, you will not remove the cover of her nakedness. **16** The nakedness of the woman of your brother, you will not remove the cover, she is the nakedness of your brother. **17** The nakedness of a woman and her daughter, you will not remove the cover, the daughter of her son and the daughter of her daughter, you will not take to remove the cover of her nakedness, they are kin, she is mischief, **18** and you will not take a woman to her sister to press in to remove the cover of her nakedness, upon her with her living,[553] **19** and you will not come near to a woman in the removal of her dirtiness, to remove the cover of her nakedness, **20** and you will not give copulation for seed to a woman of your neighbor, for her dirtiness is in her, **21** and you will not give your seed to be made to cross over to *Molekh*, and you will not defile the title of your *Elohiym*, I am ***YHWH***, **22** and with a male you will not lie down in the lying places of a woman, this is disgusting, **23** and you will not give your copulation in any beast, for her dirtiness is in her, and you will not stand a woman to the face of a beast for her to be squared[554], this is an unnatural mix, **24** and you will not make yourself dirty with all of these, given that with all these, the nations are dirty, which I am sending from your faces, **25** and the land was dirty, and I registered her twistedness upon her, and the land vomited her settlers, **26** and you, you will safeguard my customs and my decisions, and you will not do any of these disgusting things, the native and the immigrant immigrating in your midst, **27** given that all these disgusting things the men of the land, which are to your faces, did, and the land will be dirty, **28** and the land will not vomit you when you make her dirty, like when she vomited the nation which is to your faces, **29** given that anyone who will do all these disgusting things, then the souls doing this will be cut from inside their people, **30** and you will safeguard my charge by not doing these disgusting customs, which have been done to your faces, and you will not make yourself dirty in them, I am ***YHWH*** your *Elohiym*,

Chapter 19

1 and ***YHWH*** spoke to *Mosheh* saying, **2** speak to all the company of the sons of *Yisra'eyl* and you will say to them, you will exist as unique ones, given that I, ***YHWH*** your *Elohiym*, am unique. **3** Each of you will fear his mother and his father, you will safeguard my ceasings, I am ***YHWH*** your *Elohiym*. **4** You will not turn to the worthless ones and you will not make an *Elohiym* of a cast

---

[553] An alternate translation of this verse may be, "and you will not take a woman in addition to her sister to be her rival, to remove the cover of her nakedness, while her sister is still living,"

[554] Meaning to be "on all fours" for procreation.

image for yourself, I am ***YHWH*** your *Elohiym*, **5** and, given that you sacrifice him as a sacrifice of offering of restitutions to ***YHWH***, by the will of yourself you will sacrifice him. **6** In the day of your sacrifice he will be eaten, and on the morrow, and what is being left behind until the third day will be cremated in the fire, **7** and if he will surely be eaten in the third day, he is foul, he will not be accepted, **8** and the ones eating him will have his twistedness lifted up, given that he defiled the specialness of ***YHWH***, that soul will be cut from her peoples, **9** and with your severing[555] of the harvest in your land, you will not finish the edge of your field to sever it, and the gleanings of your harvest you will not pick up, **10** and your vineyard you will not glean, and the fallen grapes of your vineyard you will not pick up, you will leave them for the afflicted and for the immigrant, I am ***YHWH*** your *Elohiym*. **11** You will not steal and you will not deal falsely and you will not deal falsely a man with his neighbor, **12** and you will not swear with my title to falseness, and you will not defile my title *Elohiym*, I am ***YHWH***. **13** You will not oppress your companion and you will not pluck away[556], you will not stay the night[557] what is made[558] by your hireling until morning. **14** You will not belittle a silent one, and to the face of blind you will not place a stumbling block, and you will fear your *Elohiym*, I am ***YHWH***. **15** You will not do wickedness in the decision, you will not lift up the face of the helpless and you will not give honor to the face of the great one, with steadfastness you will decide your neighbor. **16** You will not walk as a talebearer with your people, you will not stand upon the blood of your companion, I am ***YHWH***. **17** You will not hate your brother in your heart, you will certainly make a rebuking of your neighbor, and you will not lift up upon him failure, **18** and you will not avenge and you will not keep[559] the sons of your people, and you will love your companion like one of you, I am ***YHWH***. **19** My customs you will safeguard, your beasts you will not cause to be squared[560] with diverse kinds, your fields you will not sow with diverse kinds, and garments of diverse kinds of linsey-woolsey you will not go up upon you[561], **20** and a man that lies down with a woman for the laying down of seed, and she is a maid, being a consort of a man and certainly not ransomed, freedom will

---

[555] That is the "reaping."

[556] That is to "steal."

[557] That is to "keep for the night."

[558] That is the wages "made" by the hireling.

[559] The Hebrew word meaning "keep" is defined as "to hold onto to preserve, protect or hold in reserve," but is problematic as it does not fit with the context. Many translations resolve this by adding the word "grudge," "keep a grudge," and it would appear that this Hebrew word, or a similar word, is missing from the text. The Greek *Septuagint* reads, "and you will not be angry," and may preserve a more correct Hebrew version.

[560] Meaning to be "on all fours" for procreation.

[561] To "go up upon you" means to "wear."

not be given her, there will be punishment, they will not be made to die, given that she was not free, **21** and he will bring his guilt to ***YHWH*** to the opening of the appointed tent, a buck of guilt, **22** and the administrator will make restitution upon him with the buck of guilt to the face of ***YHWH***, concerning his failure which he failed, and he will be forgiven for him from his failure which he failed, **23** and, given that you will come to the land, and you will plant every tree of nourishment, and you will consider uncircumcised his foreskin, his produce, three years he will exist to you as foreskin, he will not be eaten, **24** and in the fourth year all his produce will exist as special, shining things to ***YHWH***, **25** and in the fifth year you will eat his produce, his production will again be for you, I am ***YHWH*** your *Elohiym*. **26** You will not eat upon the blood, you will not predict, and you will not conjure. **27** You will not encircle the edge of your head, and you will not damage the edge of your beard, **28** and a slicing for the soul you will not give in your flesh, and a writing of a tattoo you not give in you, I am ***YHWH***. **29** You will not defile your daughter by making her be a harlot, and the land will not be a harlot, and the land will be filled with mischief. **30** My ceasings you will safeguard and my sanctuary you will fear, I am ***YHWH***. **31** You will not turn to the necromancers and you will not search out the knowers, for her dirtiness is in them, I am ***YHWH*** your *Elohiym*. **32** You will rise to the face of gray-headed ones, and you will give honor to the face of bearded ones, and you will fear your *Elohiym*, I am ***YHWH***, **33** and, given that an immigrant will immigrate with you in your land, you will not cause him suppression. **34** Like a native from you, he will exist with you, the immigrant immigrating with you, and you will love him like the ones of you, given that you existed as immigrants in the land of *Mits'rayim*, I am ***YHWH*** your *Elohiym*. **35** You will not do wickedness in the decision, in the measurement, in the weight and in the quantity. **36** Steadfast balances, steadfast stones[562], steadfast *eyphah* and a steadfast *hiyn*, he will exist for you, I am ***YHWH*** your *Elohiym* who caused you to go out from the land of *Mits'rayim*, **37** and you will safeguard all my customs and all my decisions, and you will do them, I am ***YHWH***,

---

Chapter 20

1 and ***YHWH*** spoke to *Mosheh* saying, **2** and to the sons of *Yisra'eyl* you will say, each man from the sons of *Yisra'eyl* and from the immigrant immigrating in *Yisra'eyl*, who give from his seed to *Molekh*, he will certainly be killed, the people of the land will kill him by stoning with the stone, **3** and I, I will give my face in that man, and I will cause him to be cut from inside his people, given that from his seed he gave to *Molekh*, because of that he dirtied my sanctuary, and defiled my special title, **4** and if the people of the

---

[562] Measured stones were used in the balances for weights.

land will surely cause their eyes to be out of sight from that man, in his giving from his seed to *Molekh*, to not kill him, **5** then I will place my face in that man and in his clan, and I will cause him and all the ones being a harlot after him, being a harlot after *Molekh*, to be cut from inside their people, **6** and the soul that will turn to the necromancers and to the knowers, to be a harlot after them, then I will give my face in that soul, and I will cause him to be cut from inside his people, **7** and you will set yourself apart, and you will exist as unique ones, given that I am ***YHWH*** your *Elohiym*, **8** and you will safeguard my customs, and you will do them, I am ***YHWH*** setting you apart, **9** given that each man which will belittle his father and his mother, he will certainly be killed, he belittled his father and his mother, his blood is on him, **10** and a man that will commit adultery with the woman of his companion, will certainly be killed, the one committing adultery and the one committing adultery[563], **11** and the man that will lie down with the woman of his father, he removed the cover of the nakedness of his father, the two of them will certainly be killed, their blood is on them, **12** and a man who will lie down with his daughter-in-law, the two of them will certainly be killed, they did an unnatural mix, their blood is on them, **13** and a man who will lie down with a male, lying places of a woman, the two of them did a disgusting thing, they will certainly be killed, their blood is on them, **14** and a man who will take a woman and her mother, this is mischief, they will cremate him and them in the fire, and mischief will not exist in your midst, **15** and a man who will give his copulation in a beast, he will certainly be killed, and they will kill the beast, **16** and a woman who will come near to any beast to be squared[564] with her, then you will kill the woman and the beast, they will certainly be killed, their blood is on them, **17** and a man who will take his sister, the daughter of his father or the daughter of his mother, and he will see her nakedness, and she will see his nakedness, this is kindness[565], and they will be cut to the eyes of the sons of their people, he removed the cover of the nakedness of his sister, he will lift up his twistedness, **18** and a man who will lay down with a woman of illness, and he will remove the cover of her nakedness, he caused the uncovering of her fountain, and she, she removed the cover of the fountain of her bloodshed, and the two of them will be cut from inside their people, **19** and the nakedness of the sister of your mother and the sister of your father, you will not remove the cover, given his kin he caused to be uncovered, they will lift up their twistedness, **20** and a man who will lay down with his aunt, he removed the cover of the nakedness of his uncle, they will lift up their failure, they will die barren, **21** and a man

563 The phrase "committing adultery" is written twice in the Hebrew text. One is referring to the "man" and the other is referring to the "woman."

564 Meaning to be "on all fours" for procreation.

565 The context implies that the Hebrew word for "kindness" (חסד / *hhesed*) is incorrect and may be a misspelling for another word, such as "diminish" (חסר / *hhaser*), which is spelled almost the same.

who will take the woman of his brother, this is a removal, he removed the cover of the nakedness of his brother, they will exist barren, **22** and you will safeguard all my customs and all my decisions, and you will do them, and the land that I brought you unto there to settle in will not vomit you, **23** and you will not walk in the customs of the nations which I am sending from your faces, given that all these they did, and I loathed them, **24** and I said to you, you, you will possess their ground and I will give her to you to possess her, a land issuing fat and honey, I am ***YHWH*** your *Elohiym* who caused you to be separated from the peoples, **25** and you will cause a separation between the clean beast to the dirty, and between the dirty flyer to the clean, and you will not make your souls detestable with the beast and with the flyer and with any that tread the ground which I separated for you for being dirty, **26** and you will exist for me as unique ones, given that I ***YHWH*** am unique, and I caused you to be separated from the people, to exist for me, **27** and a man or woman who will exist in them a necromancer or a knower, they will certainly be killed with the stone, they will kill them by stoning, their blood is on them,

---

Chapter 21

1 and ***YHWH*** said to *Mosheh*, say to the administrators, the sons of *Aharon*, and you will say to them, he will not be dirty for a soul in his people. **2** Instead, for his kin, the one near him, for his mother and for his father and for his son and for his daughter and for his brother, **3** and for his sister, the virgin, the one near to him, who does not have a man, for her he will be dirty. **4** A master in his people will not be dirty, to defile himself. **5** They will not make bald a bald spot on their head, and the edge of their beard they will not shave, and in their flesh they will not slice a slicing. **6** They will exist as unique ones to their *Elohiym*, and they will not defile the title of their *Elohiym*, given that the fire offerings of ***YHWH***, the bread of their *Elohiym*, they are bringing near, and they will be special. **7** A woman being a harlot and drilled they will not take, and a woman cast out from her man they will not take, given that he is unique to his *Elohiym*, **8** and you will set him apart, given that the bread of your *Elohiym* he is bringing near, he exists unique for you, given that unique am I, ***YHWH***, the one setting you apart, **9** and the daughter of each administrator that will be defiled by being a harlot, she is defiling her father, you will cremate in the fire, **10** and the great administrator from his brothers, which will have poured the oil of the ointment down upon his head, and he will fill his hand[566] to wear the garments, he will not loose his head, and his garments he will not rip, **11** and

---

[566] To "fill the hand" is an idiom of uncertain meaning, but the same phrase is used in Akkadian to mean the placing of a relevant tool or insignia (such as a scepter for a king) in the hand of one being installed in a high office.

he will not come upon any soul of the dying, for his father and for his mother he will not be dirty, **12** and from the sanctuary he will not go out, and he will not defile the sanctuary of his *Elohiym*, given that the dedication of oil of ointment of his *Elohiym* is upon him, I am ***YHWH***, **13** and he, he will take a woman in her virginity. **14** A widow and a casted out one and a drilled one, one being a harlot, he will not take these, but if there is a virgin from his people he will take a woman, **15** and he will not defile his seed in his people, given that I am ***YHWH*** setting him apart, **16** and ***YHWH*** spoke to *Mosheh* saying, **17** speak to *Aharon* saying, a man from your seed to their generations who will exist in him a blemish, he will not come near to bring near the bread of his *Elohiym*, **18** given that every man who in him is a blemish, he will not come near, a blind man or a lame one or a perforated[567] one or one being superfluous, **19** or a man who exists in him a shattering of the foot or a shattering of the hand, **20** or a hunchback or scrawny or a cataract in his eye or an irritation or a skin sore or crumbled testicles. **21** Every man, which is in him a blemish, from the seed of *Aharon* the administrator, will not draw near to bring near the fire offerings of ***YHWH***, a blemish is in him, he will not draw near to bring near the bread of his *Elohiym*. **22** The bread of his *Elohiym*, from the very special ones, and from the special ones, he will eat. **23** Surely, to the tent curtain he will not come and to the altar he will not draw near, given that a blemish is in him, and he will not defile my sanctuaries, given that I am ***YHWH***, setting them apart, **24** and *Mosheh* spoke to *Aharon* and to his sons and to all the sons of *Yisra'eyl*,

---

Chapter 22

1 and ***YHWH*** spoke to *Mosheh* saying, **2** speak to *Aharon* and to his sons, and they will be dedicated from the special things of the sons of *Yisra'eyl*, and they will not defile my special title, which they are setting apart for me, I am ***YHWH***. **3** Say to them, to your generations, every man from all your seed that will come near to the special things, which the sons of *Yisra'eyl* will set apart for ***YHWH***, and his dirtiness is upon him, and that soul will be cut from before my face, I am ***YHWH***. **4** Each man from the seed of *Aharon* and is infected or issuing, he will not eat the special things, until he is clean, and anyone touching a dirty soul or a man that had the lying down of seed going out from him, **5** or a man that touched any swarmer that is dirty to him, or with a human that is dirty to him to all his dirtiness. **6** A soul that touches in him, then she[568] will be dirty until the evening, and he will not eat from the special things, unless he bathed his flesh in the waters, **7** and the sun

---

[567] Of uncertain meaning.
[568] Referring to the "soul," a feminine noun.

came[569], and he will be clean, and afterward he will eat from the special things, given that he is his bread. **8** A carcass or a torn one he will not eat, for her dirtiness is in her, I am ***YHWH***, **9** and they will safeguard my charge and they will not lift up upon him failure, and they will die in him if he defiles her, I am ***YHWH*** setting them apart, **10** and anyone being a stranger will not eat the special thing, a settler of the administrator or a hireling will not eat the special thing, **11** and the administrator that will purchase a soul, he is the material of his purchase, he will eat with him, and the ones born of his house, they will eat his bread, **12** and the daughter of the administrator that will exist to a man being a stranger, she will not eat the special offering, **13** and the daughter of the administrator that will exist as a widow or is casted out or is without seed, and she is returned to the house of her father like in her young age, from the bread of her father she will eat, and anyone being a stranger will not eat with him, **14** and a man that will eat the special thing in error, then he will add his fifth part upon him and he will give to the administrator with the special thing, **15** and the sons of *Yisra'eyl* will not defile the special things that they raise up to ***YHWH***, **16** and they will lift them up, the twistedness of guilt, in their eating their special things, given that I am ***YHWH*** setting them apart, **17** and ***YHWH*** spoke to *Mosheh* saying, **18** speak to *Aharon* and to his sons, and to the sons of *Yisra'eyl*, and you will say to them, each man from the house of *Yisra'eyl* and from the immigrant in *Yisra'eyl*, which will bring near his donation for all their vows and for all their freewill offerings, which they bring near to ***YHWH*** for an ascension offering. **19** For yourself, a whole male of the cattle, of the sheep and[570] of the she-goats. **20** All that have in him a blemish you will not bring near, given that he will not exist for you for yourself, **21** and a man that will bring near a sacrifice of offerings of restitution to ***YHWH***, to perform a vow or for a freewill offering in the cattle or in the flocks, he will exist whole, to be accepted not any blemish will exist in him. **22** Blindness or cracked or cut sharply or an ulcer or an irritation or a skin sore, you will not bring these near to ***YHWH***, and a fire offering you will not give from them upon the altar to ***YHWH***, **23** and an ox or a ram, being superfluous or deformed, that you will make freewill offering of him, or for a vow, will not be accepted. **24** Or pressed firmly or smashed or drawn away or cut, you will not bring near to ***YHWH***, and in your land you will not do, **25** and from the hand of the son of a foreigner you will not bring near the bread of your *Elohiym* from any of these, given that their corruption is in them, a blemish is in them, they will not be accepted for you, **26** and ***YHWH*** spoke to *Mosheh* saying, **27** an ox or sheep or she-goat that will be brought forth, will exist seven days under his mother, and from the eighth day and further will be accepted for a donation of a fire offering for ***YHWH***, **28** and an ox or a ram, you will not slay him and his son in one day, **29** and when you will sacrifice him as a sacrifice of thanks

---

[569] This Hebrew word can also imply the "going down" of the sun.
[570] The prefix meaning "and" can also mean "or."

to ***YHWH***, you will sacrifice him by your own will. **30** In that day he will be eaten, you will not leave anything behind from him until morning, I am ***YHWH***, **31** and you will safeguard my directives, and you will do them, I am ***YHWH***, **32** and you will not defile my special title, and I will be set apart in the midst of the sons of *Yisra'eyl*, I am ***YHWH*** setting you apart. **33** The one causing you to go out from the land of *Mits'rayim*, to exist for you for *Elohiym*, I am ***YHWH***,

---

Chapter 23

1 and ***YHWH*** spoke to *Mosheh* saying, **2** speak to the sons of *Yisra'eyl*, and you will say to them, the appointed times of ***YHWH*** that you will call out, these are special meetings, they are appointed times. **3** Six days business will be done, and in the seventh day is a ceasing rest period, a special meeting, no business will be done, she is a ceasing for ***YHWH*** in all your settling places. **4** These are the appointed times of ***YHWH***, special meetings which you will call out in their appointed time. **5** In the first new moon, on the fourteenth[571] of the new moon, between the evenings[572], is the *Pesahh* for ***YHWH***, **6** and on the fifteenth day of this new moon is the feast of unleavened bread for ***YHWH***, seven days you will eat unleavened bread. **7** In the first day a special meeting will exist for you, you will not do any business of service, **8** and you will bring near a fire offering to ***YHWH*** seven days, in the seventh day is a special meeting, you will not do any business of service, **9** and ***YHWH*** spoke to *Mosheh* saying, **10** speak to the sons of *Yisra'eyl*, and you will say to them, when you will come to the land that I am giving to you, and you will sever her harvest, and you will bring a sheaf of the summit of your harvest to the administrator, **11** and he will wave the sheaf to the face of ***YHWH*** for your own will, on the morrow of the ceasing the administrator will make his waving, **12** and in the day you make your waving of the sheaf, a whole sheep, a son of his year, is for an ascension offering to ***YHWH***, **13** and his deposit is two tenths of flour mixed in the oil, a fire offering to ***YHWH***, a sweet aroma, and her[573] pouring of wine, a fourth of a *hiyn*, **14** and bread and roasted grain and plantation crops you will not eat, until the bone of the day[574] that you bring the donation of your *Elohiym*, a distant custom for your generations in all your settlings, **15** and you will count for you from the

---

571 The word "day" may be missing from the text (compare with Lev 23:6).
572 As the word for "evening" is written in the double plural. This is literally translated as "between the 'two' evenings," but is of uncertain meaning. It may be the time between sunset and dark or between sunrise (as the word ערב literally means the "mixing" of light) and sunset.
573 The "her" is probably referring to the "deposit," a feminine word.
574 "Bone of this day" is an idiom of uncertain meaning, but may mean "this very same day" or the "middle of this day." (also in verses 21, 28 and 29)

morrow of the ceasing from the day you bring the sheaf of the waving, seven whole ceasings exist. **16** Unto the morrow of the seventh ceasing, you will count fifty days, and you will bring near a new deposit for ***YHWH***. **17** From your settlings you will bring the bread of waving, two, two tenths of flour, they will exist as leavened bread, they will be baked, first-fruits for ***YHWH***, **18** and you will bring near upon the bread seven whole sheep, sons of a year, and one bull, son of cattle, and two bucks, they will exist as ascension offerings for ***YHWH***, and their deposit and their pourings are a fire offering, a sweet aroma to ***YHWH***, **19** and you will do one hairy goat of the she-goats for a failure and two sheep, sons of a year, for a sacrifice of offering of restitution, **20** and the administrator will wave them with the bread of the first-fruits, waving to the face of ***YHWH***, concerning the two sheep, they will exist special for ***YHWH*** and for the administrator, **21** and you will call out in the bone of that day, he will exist as a special meeting, you will not do any business of service, a distant custom in all your settlings to your generations, **22** and in your severing of the harvest of your land, you will not finish the edge of your field, in your severing and gleanings of your harvest you will not pick up, they are for the afflicted and for the immigrant, you will leave them, I am ***YHWH*** your *Elohiym*, **23** and ***YHWH*** spoke to *Mosheh* saying, **24** speak to the sons of *Yisra'eyl* saying, in the seventh new moon, on the first of the new moon is a rest period, it will exist for you as a remembrance of a signal, a special meeting. **25** You will not do any business of service and you will bring near a fire offering to ***YHWH***, **26** and ***YHWH*** spoke to *Mosheh* saying, **27** surely, on the tenth of this seventh new moon is a day of atonements, he will exist for you as a special meeting and you will afflict your souls, and you will bring near a fire offering to ***YHWH***, **28** and you will not do any business in the bone of this day, given that he is a day of atonements to make restitution upon you to the face of ***YHWH*** your *Elohiym*, **29** given that any soul that is not afflicted in the bone of this day will be cut from her people, **30** and any soul that does business in the bone of this day, then I will cause that soul to perish from inside her people. **31** You will not do any business, a distant custom for your generations in all your settlings. **32** He is a ceasing of rest period for you, and you will afflict your souls in the ninth of the new moon in the evening, from evening until evening[575] you will cease your ceasings, **33** and ***YHWH*** spoke to *Mosheh* saying, **34** speak to the sons of *Yisra'eyl* saying, in the fifteenth day of this seventh new moon, a feast of booths, seven days for ***YHWH***. **35** On the first day is a special meeting, you will not do any business of service. **36** Seven days you will bring near a fire offering to ***YHWH***, on the eighth day, a special meeting will exist for you, and you will bring near a fire offering to ***YHWH***, she is a conference, you will not do any business of service. **37** These are the appointed times of ***YHWH*** that you will call them out, special meetings to

[575] The phrase "from the evening until evenings" is of uncertain meaning, but may be the time between sunset and dark.

bring near a fire offering to ***YHWH***, an ascension offering and a deposit, a sacrifice and pourings, a thing of a day in his day. **38** Apart from the ceasings of ***YHWH***, and besides your contributions, and besides all your vows, and besides all your freewill offerings, which you will give to ***YHWH***. **39** Surely, on the fifteenth day of the seventh new moon, in the gathering of your production of the land, you will hold a feast, a feast of ***YHWH***, seven days, on the first day is a rest period, and on the eighth day is a rest period, **40** and you will take for you in the first day produce of an honorable tree, palms of the date palms and a bough of a thick woven tree, and willows of the wadi, and your rejoicing to the face of ***YHWH*** your *Elohiym*, seven days, **41** and you will hold his feast, a feast to ***YHWH***, seven days in the year, a distant custom for your generations, in the seventh new moon you will hold his feast. **42** You will settle in the booths seven days, every native in *Yisra'eyl* will settle in the booths. **43** So that your generations will know that in the booths I made the sons of *Yisra'eyl* turn back in my bringing them out from the land of *Mits'rayim*, I am ***YHWH*** your *Elohiym*, **44** and *Mosheh* spoke about the appointed times of ***YHWH*** to the sons of *Yisra'eyl*,

---

Chapter 24

1 and ***YHWH*** spoke to *Mosheh* saying, **2** direct the sons of *Yisra'eyl*, and they will take to you refined olive oil, smashed for the luminary[576], to make the lamp continually go up[577]. **3** From the outside of the tent curtain of the evidence, in the appointed tent, *Aharon* will arrange him, from the evening until morning, to the face of ***YHWH*** continually, a distant custom for your generations. **4** Upon the clean lampstand he will arrange the lamps to the face of ***YHWH*** continually, **5** and you will take flour and you will bake twelve pierced breads, two tenths will exist in one pierced bread, **6** and you will place them in two arrangements, six in a line upon the clean table to the face of ***YHWH***, **7** and you will place refined frankincense upon the line, and she will exist for the bread for a memorial, a fire offering to ***YHWH***. **8** In the ceasing day[578] he will arrange him to the face of ***YHWH*** continually, from the sons of *Yisra'eyl*, a distant covenant, **9** and she will exist for *Aharon* and for his sons, and they will eat him in the unique area, given that he is special of specials[579] for him, from the fire offerings of ***YHWH***, it is a distant custom, **10** and a son of a woman, one of *Yisra'eyl*, went out, and he is a son of a man, one of *Mits'rayim*, in the midst of the sons of *Yisra'eyl*, and they were

---

[576] Meaning the "lamps."

[577] Meaning to "burn."

[578] The phrase "in the ceasing day" is duplicated, either by accident or for the purpose of identifying "every ceasing day."

[579] The phrase "special of specials" means a "very special thing, one or place."

struggling in the camp, the son, one of *Yisra'eyl*, and the man, one of
Yisra'eyl, **11** and the son of the woman, the one of *Yisra'eyl*, pierced through
the title, and he belittled it, and they brought him to *Mosheh*, and the title
of his mother is *Sh'lomiyt*, daughter of *Divriy*, belonging to the branch of
Dan, **12** and they will make him rest in the custody, to spread out to them by
the mouth of ***YHWH***, **13** and ***YHWH*** spoke to *Mosheh* saying, **14** bring out
the belittling one to the outside of the camp, and all the ones hearing will
support their hands upon his head, and all the company will kill him by
stoning, **15** and to the sons of *Yisra'eyl* you will speak saying, each man that
will belittle his *Elohiym*, and he will lift up his failure, **16** and the one piercing
through the title of ***YHWH*** will surely be killed, all the company will surely
kill him by stoning, like the immigrant, like a native, in his piercing through
the title, he will be killed, **17** and a man that will attack any soul of a human
will certainly be killed, **18** and the one attacking a soul of a beast will make
restitution for her, a being in place of a beast, **19** and a man that will give a
blemish to his neighbor, just as he did so, will be done to him. **20** Shattering
in place of shattering, eye in place of eye, tooth in place of tooth, just as he
will place a blemish in the human, so will he be placed in him, **21** and the
one attacking a beast, he will make restitution for her, and the one hitting a
human will be killed. **22** One decision will exist for you, like the immigrant
like the native he will exist, given that I am ***YHWH*** your *Elohiym*, **23** and
Mosheh spoke to the sons of *Yisra'eyl*, and they brought out the belittling
one to the outside of the camp, and killed him by stoning with stones, and
the sons of *Yisra'eyl* did just as ***YHWH*** directed *Mosheh*,

---

Chapter 25

1 and ***YHWH*** spoke to *Mosheh* in the hill of *Sinai* saying, **2** speak to the sons
of *Yisra'eyl* and you will say to them, given that you will come to the land
which I am giving to you, and the land will cease a ceasing for ***YHWH***. **3** Six
years you will sow your field, and six years you will pluck your vineyard and
you will gather her production, **4** and in the seventh year a ceasing rest
period will exist for the land, a ceasing for ***YHWH***, you will not sow your
field, and you will not pluck your vineyard. **5** You will not sever the after
growth of your harvest, you will not fence in the grapes of your dedicated
place, a year of a rest period will exist for the land, **6** and a ceasing of the
land will exist for you for food, for you and for your servants and for your
bondwoman and for your hireling and for your settlers immigrating with
you, **7** and for your beast and for the living ones[580] which are in your land, all
of her production will exist for eating, **8** and you will count for yourself seven
ceasings of years, seven years seven times, and days of seven ceasings of
years will exist for you, nine and forty years, **9** and you will make the ram

---

[580] A euphemism for the wild animals.

horn a signal to cross over in the tenth one of the seventh new moon, on the
day of atonements you will make the ram horn cross over in all your land,
10 and you will set apart the year, the fiftieth year, and you will call out a
free flowing in the land to all her settlers, she, she will exist for you as a
jubilee, and you will turn back a man to his holdings, and a man to his clan
you will turn back. **11** She is a jubilee year, the fiftieth year will exist for you,
you will not sow, and you will not sever her after growth, and you will not
fence in her dedicated places, **12** given that she is a special jubilee, she will
exist for you, from the field you will eat her production. **13** In the year of this
jubilee you will turn a man to his holdings, **14** and, given that you will sell
merchandise to your neighbor, or purchase from the hand of your neighbor,
you will not make a man suppressed by his brother. **15** By the number of
years after the jubilee you will purchase from your neighbor, by the number
of years he will sell productions to you. **16** By the mouth[581] of an abundance
of years you will make his acquirings increase, and by the mouth of the
lesser years you will make his acquirings less, given that the number of
productions he is selling to you, **17** and you will not make a man suppressed
by his neighbor, and you will fear your *Elohiym*, given that I am ***YHWH*** your
Elohiym, **18** and you will do my customs, and my decisions you will
safeguard, and you will do them, and you will settle upon the land in safety,
19 and the land will give her produce, and you will eat to satisfaction, and
you will settle safely upon her, **20** and, given that you will say, what will we
eat in the seventh year, though we will not sow and we will not gather his
productions, **21** then I will direct my presents to you in the sixth year, and
she will do the production for the three years, **22** and you will sow the
eighth year, and you will eat from the stored production until the ninth year,
until her production comes, you will eat what is stored, **23** and the land will
not be sold permanently, given that the land belongs to me, given that you
are immigrants and settlers with me, **24** and in all the land of your holdings,
you will give redemption to the land, **25** given that your brother will be low,
and he will sell his holdings, and a near one to him will come redeeming him,
and he will redeem the merchandise of his brother, **26** and a man that will
not exist for him a redeemer, and his hand will reach, and he will find as
sufficient his redemption, **27** and he will plan the years of his merchandise,
and he will make the exceedings turn back to the man which he sold to him,
and he will turn back to his holdings, **28** and if his hand did not find
sufficiency to turn back to him, then his merchandise will exist in the hand of
the one purchasing him, until the year of the jubilee, and he will go out in
the jubilee, and he will turn back to his holdings, **29** and a man that will sell a
settling house of the city rampart, then his redemption will exist until the
year be whole for his merchandise, the days his redemption will exist,
30 and if he will not be able to redeem until his filling of a whole year, then
the house, which is in the city that belongs to him in the rampart, will rise to

---

581 Meaning "according to."

permanence to his purchaser to his generations, he will not go out in the jubilee, **31** and the courtyard houses that are without a rampart all around, he will be considered upon the field of the land, redemption will exist for him, and in the jubilee, he will go out, **32** and the cities of the ones of *Lewi*, houses of the cities of their holdings, redemption of distance will exist to the ones of *Lewi*, **33** and that which he will redeem from the ones of *Lewi*, and he will go out, the merchandise of the house and the city of his holdings, in the jubilee, given that the houses of the cities of the ones of *Lewi*, she is their holdings in the midst of the sons of *Yisra'eyl*, **34** and the fields of the open spaces of their cities will not be sold, given that he is a distant holdings for them, **35** and, given that your brother will be low, and his hand will totter with you, and you will seize him, immigrant and settler, and he will live with you. **36** You will not take from him usury and interest, and you will fear your *Elohiym*, and your brother is living with you. **37** You will not give your silver to him in usury, and you will not give your foodstuff in great number. **38** I am ***YHWH*** your *Elohiym*, who made you go out from the land of *Mits'rayim*, to give to you the land of *Kena'an*, to exist for you for *Elohiym*, **39** and, given that your brother will be low with you, and he will be sold to you, you will not serve with him, as service of a servant[582]. **40** Like a hireling, like a settler, he will exist with you until the year of the jubilee, he will serve with you, **41** and he will go out from with you, he and his sons with him, and he will turn back to his clan, and to the holdings of his fathers he will turn back, **42** given that they are my servants, which I made them go out from the land of *Mits'rayim*, they will not be sold as merchandise, a servant. **43** You will not rule in him with a whip, and you will fear your *Elohiym*, **44** and your servant and your bondwoman, which will exist for you from the nations that are all around you, from them you will purchase a servant and a bondwoman, **45** and also from the sons of the immigrating settlers with you, from them you will purchase, and their clan that is with you, which they brought forth in your land, and they will exist for you for holdings, **46** and you will inherit them for your sons after you, for the possessing of holdings, for a distant time with them you will serve, and with your brothers, the sons of *Yisra'eyl*, each with his brother, you will not rule in him with a whip, **47** and, given that the hand of an immigrant and the settler with you will reach, and your brother with him will be low, and he will be sold to an immigrant settling with you, or to an offshoot of the clan of an immigrant. **48** After he was sold, redemption will exist for him, one of his brothers will redeem him. **49** Or his uncle, or a son of his uncle, will redeem him, or from the remains of his flesh from his clan will redeem him, or his hand will reach and he will be redeemed, **50** and he will plan with his purchaser from the year of his being sold to him until the year of the jubilee, and the silver of his

[582] The Hebrew verb תעבד is written in the *qal* form, but may be in error and should have been written in the *hiphil* form. In which case this phrase would be translated as "you will not make him serve in the service of a servant."

merchandise will exist with the number of years like the days of a hireling that will exist with him. **51** If there is yet an abundance in years, by their mouth he will cause to turn back his redemption from the silver of his acquiring, **52** and if a small amount will remain in the years until the year of the jubilee, then he will plan with him, according to the mouth of his years, he will make his redemption turn back. **53** Like a hireling, year by year, he will exist with him, he will not rule him with a whip to your eyes, **54** and if he will not be redeemed by these, then he will go out in the year of the jubilee, he and his sons with him, **55** given that to me are the sons of *Yisra'eyl* are servants, they are my servants, which I made them go out from the land of *Mits'rayim*, I am ***YHWH*** your *Elohiym*.

Chapter 26

1 You will not make for you worthless ones, and sculpture and monument you will not make rise for you, and stone of imagery you will not place in your land to bow yourself down upon her, given that I am ***YHWH*** your *Elohiym*. **2** My ceasings you will safeguard, and my sanctuary you will fear, I am ***YHWH***. **3** If in my customs you will walk, and my directives you will safeguard, and you will do them, **4** then I will give your rain showers in their appointed time, and the land will give her produce, and the tree of the field will give his produce, **5** and the threshing will overtake the vintage for you, and the vintage will overtake the seed, and you will eat your bread to satisfaction, and you will settle safely in the land, **6** and I will give completeness in the land, and you will lay down, and without trembling, and I will make the dysfunctional living ones[583] cease from the land, and the sword will not cross over in your land, **7** and you will pursue your attackers, and they will fall to your faces by the sword, **8** and five from you will pursue a hundred, and a hundred from you will pursue a myriad, and your attackers will fall to your faces by the sword, **9** and I will turn to you, and I will make you reproduce, and I will make you increase, and I will make my covenant rise with you, **10** and you will eat the stores that are being stored, and you will make the storage go out from the face of the new ones, **11** and I will place my dwelling in your midst, and my soul will not cast you away, **12** and I will walk myself in your midst, and I will exist for you for *Elohiym*, and you, you will exist for me for a people. **13** I am ***YHWH*** your *Elohiym* who made you go out from the land of *Mits'rayim*, from existing for them as servants, and I will crack the poles of your yoke, and I will make you walk vertical, **14** but if you will not listen to me, and you will not do all these directives, **15** and if you will reject my customs, and if your soul will cast away my decisions, to not do all my directives to cause you to break my covenant. **16** Moreover, I will do this to you, and I will make register upon you dismay,

[583] A euphemism for wild beasts.

the consumption and the fever, a finishing of the eyes, and making the soul
sorrowful, and you will sow your seed to emptiness, and your attackers will
eat him, **17** and I will place my face with you, and you will be smitten at the
face of your attackers, and your haters will rule over you, and you will flee
without anyone pursuing you, **18** and if unto these you will not listen to me,
then I will add seven times upon your failures to correct you, **19** and I will
crack the majesty of your boldness, and I will make your skies like iron and
your land like brass, **20** and your strength will be whole in emptiness, and
your land will not give her produce, and the tree of the land will not give his
produce, **21** and if you will walk contrary with me, and you will not consent
to listen to me, then I will add a hitting upon you seven times according to
your failures, **22** and I will cause to send among you living ones of the
field[584], and she[585] will make you be childless, and she will make you be less,
and the roads will be desolate, **23** and if in these you will not be corrected
for me, and you will walk contrary with me, **24** then moreover I, I will walk
contrary with you, and I, also I, will attack you seven times over your
failures, **25** and I will bring upon you a sword, avenging vengeance of a
covenant, and you will be gathered to your cities, and I will send an
epidemic in your midst, and you will be given into the hand of the attackers.
26 In my cracking your branch of bread, and ten women will bake your bread
in one oven, and they will make your bread turn back by the weight, and you
will eat, but you will not be satisfied, **27** and if in this you will not listen to
me, and you will walk contrary with me, **28** then I will walk contrary with you
in a fury, and moreover I, I will correct you seven times over your failures,
29 and you will eat the flesh of your sons, and the flesh of your daughters
you will eat, **30** and I will cause your platforms to be destroyed, and I will
cause your sun idols to be cut, and I will place your corpses upon the corpses
of your idols, and my soul will cast you away, **31** and I will make your cities
dried out, and I will make your sanctuaries desolate, and I will not smell your
sweet aroma, **32** and I, I, will make the land desolate, and your attackers
settling in her will desolate her, **33** and I will disperse you in the nations, and
I will make the sword draw out after you, and your land will exist desolate,
and your cities will exist dried out. **34** At that time the land will accept her
ceasings all the days of her being desolate, and you will be in the land of
your attackers, at that time the land will cease, and she will accept her
ceasings. **35** All the days of her being made desolate, she will cease, because
she did not cease with your ceasings with you settling upon her, **36** and the
ones remaining in you, then I will bring faintness in their heart in the lands
of their attackers, and the voice of a leaf twirling will pursue them, and they
will flee, fleeing the sword, and they will fall and without a pursuer, **37** and
they will topple, each with his brother, as from the face of a sword, and
without a pursuer, and a high place will not exist for you to the face of your

---

[584] The "living ones of the field" is a euphemism for "wild animals."
[585] The "she" is referring to the word "living," a singular feminine noun.

attackers, **38** and you will perish in the nations, and the land of your attackers will eat you, **39** and the ones remaining in you, they will be rotted in their twistedness in the lands of your attackers, and moreover, in the twistedness of their fathers with them, they will be rotted, **40** and they will confess their twistedness and the twistedness of their fathers, in their transgression that they transgressed in me, and moreover that they walked contrary with me. **41** Moreover I, I will walk contrary with them, and I brought them in the land of their attackers, or at that time their uncircumcised heart will be lowered, and at that time they will accept their twistedness, **42** and I will remember my covenant with *Ya'aqov*, and moreover my covenant with *Yits'hhaq*, and moreover my covenant with *Avraham* I will remember, and I will remember the land, **43** and the land will be left from them, and she will accept her ceasings in being made desolate from them, and they will accept their twistedness, seeing as, and in seeing as in my directions they rejected, and my customs their soul casted away, **44** and moreover, also this, in their existing in the land of their attackers, I did not reject them, and I did not cast them away to finish them by breaking my covenant with them, given that I am ***YHWH*** their *Elohiym*, **45** and I remembered for them the covenant of the first ones that I brought out from the land of *Mits'rayim* to the eyes of the nations, to exist for them as *Elohiym*, I am ***YHWH***. **46** These are the customs and the decisions and the teachings that ***YHWH*** gave between him and between the sons of *Yisra'eyl* on the hill of *Sinai* by the hand of *Mosheh*,

Chapter 27

1 and ***YHWH*** spoke to *Mosheh* saying, **2** speak to the sons of *Yisra'eyl* and you will say to them, a man that will perform a vow, by your valuation souls belong to ***YHWH***, **3** and your valuation will exist, the male, from a son of twenty years and until a son of sixty years, and your valuation will exist, fifty *sheqel*s of silver, by the special *sheqel*, **4** and if she is a female, your valuation will exist of thirty *sheqel*s, **5** and if from a son of five years and until a son of twenty years, and your valuation will exist, the male, twenty *sheqel*s, and for the female, ten *sheqel*s, **6** and if from a son of a new moon and until a son of five years, then your valuation will exist, the male, five *sheqel*s of silver, and to the female your valuation is three *sheqel*s of silver, **7** and if from a son of sixty years and upward, if a male, then your valuation will exist, fifteen *sheqel*s, and for the female, ten *sheqel*s, **8** and if he be low from your valuation, then he will make him stand to the face of the administrator, and the administrator will value him by the mouth[586] of what the hand making a vow will overtake, the administrator will value him, **9** and if a beast that they will bring near, a donation for ***YHWH***, all that he will give

[586] The phrase "by the mouth" means "according to."

from him belong to ***YHWH***, he will exist special. **10** He will not pass him over, and he will not convert him, a functional for a dysfunctional or a dysfunction for a functional, and if he convert beast for a beast, and he will exist, he and his exchange will exist special, **11** and if any dirty beast, which they will not bring her near for a donation to ***YHWH***, then he will make the beast stand to the face of the administrators, **12** and the administrator will value her between the functional and the dysfunctional, like your valuation of the administrator, so he will exist, **13** but if he will surely redeem her, and he will add a fifth of him upon your valuation, **14** and a man that will make his house set apart as special for ***YHWH***, and the administrator will value him between the functional and dysfunctional, just as the administrator will value him, so he will rise, **15** and if the one making set apart will redeem his house, then he will add a fifth of silver of your valuation upon him, and he will exist for him, **16** and if from the field of his holdings a man will set it apart for ***YHWH***, then your valuation will exist by the mouth[587] of his seed, the seed of a *hhomer* of barleys with fifty *sheqel*s of silver. **17** If from the year of the jubilee, he will make his field set apart, like your valuation he will rise, **18** but if after the jubilee, he will make his field set apart, then the administrator will plan for him, the silver by the mouth[588] of the years being left behind until the year of the jubilee, then he will be taken away from your valuation, **19** and if he will surely redeem the field, the one making him set apart, then he will add a fifth of the silver of your valuation, and he will rise for him, **20** and if he will not redeem the field, or if he will sell the field to another man, he will not be redeemed again, **21** and the field will exist in his going out in the jubilee, special to ***YHWH***, like the assigned field, his holdings will exist for the administrator, **22** and if a field acquired of him, which is not from the field of his holdings, he will set it apart for ***YHWH***, **23** and the administrator will plan for him the worth of your arrangement until the year of the jubilee, and he will give your arrangement in that day, special for ***YHWH***. **24** In the year of the jubilee he will turn back the field to whom he purchased him from, to who belonged to him the holdings of the land, **25** and all your arrangements will exist by the special *sheqel*, twenty *gerah*s will be the *sheqel*. **26** Only the firstborn, which will be the firstborn for ***YHWH*** in the beasts, a man will not set him apart if of the ox, if of the ram, he belongs to ***YHWH***, **27** and if in the dirty beast, and he will ransom by your arrangement, then he will add five parts of him upon him, and if he will not be redeemed, he will be sold by your arrangement. **28** Only all the assigned, which a man assigned for ***YHWH***, from all that belongs to him, from the human and the beast and from the field of his holdings, he will not be sold, and he will not be redeemed, every assigned one is a special of

---

[587] Meaning "according to."

[588] The phrase "by the mouth" means "according to."

special[589], he belongs to ***YHWH***. **29** Every assigned one that will be assigned from the human, he will not be ransomed, he must surely be killed, **30** and all the tenth part of the land, from the seed of the land, from the produce of the tree, belong to ***YHWH***, he is special for ***YHWH***, **31** and if a man will surely redeem from his tenth part, he will add a fifth of him upon him, **32** and all the tenth part of the cattle and the flocks, all that will cross over under the staff[590], the tenth will exist special for ***YHWH***. **33** He will not investigate between the functional and the dysfunctional, and he will not convert him, but if he will surely convert him, then he and his exchange will exist as special, he will not be redeemed. **34** These are the directives that ***YHWH*** directed *Mosheh* to the sons of *Yisra'eyl* in the hill of *Sinai*,

---

589 The phrase "special of specials" means a "very special thing, one or place."

590 Livestock was counted when they passed under the staff of the shepherd as they entered the gate.

The Book of Numbers

Chapter 1

1 and ***YHWH*** spoke to *Mosheh* in the wilderness of *Sinai* in the appointed tent on the first of the second new moon of the second year of their going out from the land of *Mits'rayim* saying, **2** lift up the head of all the company of the sons of *Yisra'eyl*, to their clans, to the house of their fathers, number the titles of every male according to their skull. **3** From a son of twenty years and upward unto all the ones going out in the army of *Yisra'eyl*, you will register them by their armies, you and *Aharon*, **4** and with you, each man will exist for the branch, a man for the head of the house of his fathers is he, **5** and these are the titles of the men that will stand with you for *Re'uven*, *Elitsur* the son of *Shedeyur*. **6** For *Shimon*, *Shelumi'eyl* the son of *Tsurishaddai*. **7** For *Yehudah*, *Nahhshon* the son of *Amiynadav*. **8** For *Yis'sas'khar*, *Nataneyl* the son of *Tso'ar*. **9** For *Zevulun*, *Eli'av* the son of *Hheylon*. **10** For the sons of *Yoseph*, for *Ephrayim* the son of *Elishama* the son of *Amihud*, for *Menasheh*, *Gamli'eyl* the son of *Pedatsur*. **11** For *Binyamin*, *Avidan* the son of *Gidoni*. **12** For *Dan*, *Ahhi'ezer* the son of *Amishaddai*. **13** For *Asher*, *Pagi'eyl* the son of *Akhran*. **14** For *Gad*, *Elyasaph* the son of *De'u'eyl*. **15** For *Naphtali*, *Ahhira* the son of *Eynan*. **16** These are the selected ones of the company, captains of the branch of their fathers, they are heads of thousands of *Yisra'eyl*, **17** and *Mosheh* took, and *Aharon*, these men, which were pierced through by titles, **18** and they made all the company assemble on the first of the second new moon, and they brought forth upon their clans, to the house of their fathers, by the number of the titles, from a son of twenty years and upward, according to their skull. **19** Just as ***YHWH*** directed *Mosheh*, and he registered them in the wilderness of *Sinai*, **20** and the sons of *Re'uven*, the firstborn of *Yisra'eyl*, existed, their birthings according to their clans, according to the house of their fathers, by the number of titles, according to their skull, every male from a son of twenty years and upward, all going out for the army. **21** Their registered ones belonging to the branch of *Re'uven*, forty-six thousand and five hundred. **22** To the sons of *Shimon*, their birthings according to their clans, according to the house of their fathers, his registered ones by the number of titles, according to their skull, every male from a son of twenty years and upward, all going out for the army. **23** Their registered ones belonging to the branch of *Shimon* is fifty-nine thousand and three hundred. **24** To the sons of *Gad*, their birthings according to their clans, according to the house of their fathers, by the number of titles, from a son of twenty years and upward, all going out for the army. **25** Their registered ones belonging to the branch of *Gad* is forty-five thousand and six hundred and fifty. **26** To the

sons of *Yehudah*, their birthings according to their clans, according to the
house of their fathers, by the number of titles, from a son of twenty years
and upward, all going out for the army. **27** Their registered ones belonging
to the branch of *Yehudah* is seventy-four thousand and six hundred. **28** To
the sons of *Yis'sas'khar*, their birthings according to their clans, according to
the house of their fathers, by the number of titles, from a son of twenty
years and upward, going out for the army. **29** Their registered ones
belonging to the branch of *Yis'sas'khar* is fifty-four thousand and four
hundred. **30** To the sons of *Zevulun*, their birthings according to their clans,
according to the house of their fathers, by the number of titles, from a son
of twenty years and upward, all going out for the army. **31** Their registered
ones belonging to the branch of *Zevulun* is fifty-seven thousand and four
hundred. **32** To the sons of *Yoseph*, to the sons of *Ephrayim*, their birthings
according to their clans, according to the house of their fathers, by the
number of titles, from a son of twenty years and upward, all going out for
the army. **33** Their registered ones belonging to the branch of *Ephrayim* is
forty thousand and five hundred. **34** To the sons of *Menasheh*, their
birthings according to their clans, according to the house of their fathers, by
the number of titles, from a son of twenty years and upward, all going out
for the army. **35** Their registered ones belonging to the branch of *Menasheh*
is thirty-two thousand and two hundred. **36** To the sons of *Binyamin*, their
birthings according to their clans, according to the house of their fathers, by
the number of titles, from a son of twenty years and upward, all going out
for the army. **37** Their registered ones belonging to the branch of *Binyamin*
is thirty-five thousand and four hundred. **38** To the sons of *Dan*, their
birthings according to their clans, according to the house of their fathers, by
the number of titles, from a son of twenty years and upward, all going out
for the army. **39** Their registered ones belonging to the branch of *Dan* is
sixty-two thousand and seven hundred. **40** To the sons of *Asher*, their
birthings according to their clans, according to the house of their fathers, by
the number of titles, from a son of twenty years and upward, all going out
for the army. **41** Their registered ones belonging to the branch of *Asher* is
forty-one thousand and five hundred. **42** To the sons of *Naphtali*, their
birthings according to their clans, according to the house of their fathers, by
the number of titles, from a son of twenty years and upward, all going out
for the army. **43** Their registered ones belonging to the branch of *Naphtali* is
fifty-three thousand and four hundred. **44** These are the registered ones,
which *Mosheh* registered, and *Aharon* and the captains of *Yisra'eyl*, twelve
men, one man to the house of his fathers existed, **45** and all the registered
sons of *Yisra'eyl* existed, according to the house of their fathers, from a son
of twenty years and upward, all going out for the army in *Yisra'eyl*, **46** and all
the registered ones existed, six hundred thousand, and three thousand, and
five hundred and fifty, **47** and the ones of *Lewi*, according to the branch of
their fathers, they did not register themselves in their midst, **48** and ***YHWH***
spoke to *Mosheh* saying, **49** surely, the branch of *Lewi* will not register their

head, you will not lift up in the midst of the sons of *Yisra'eyl*, **50** and you will make the ones of *Lewi* register by the dwelling place of the evidence, and by all his utensils, and by all that belongs to him, they, they will lift up the dwelling and all his utensils, and they, they will administer him and they will camp all around the dwelling, **51** and in the journeying, the ones of *Lewi* will make the dwelling go down, and in the camping of the dwelling, the ones of *Lewi* will make the dwelling rise, and the stranger inside will be killed, **52** and the sons of *Yisra'eyl* will camp, each by his camp and each by his banner belonging to their armies, **53** and the ones of *Lewi* will camp all around the dwelling of the evidence, and a splinter will not exist upon the company of the sons of *Yisra'eyl*, and the ones of *Lewi* will safeguard the charge of the dwelling of the evidence, **54** and the sons of *Yisra'eyl* will do everything just as ***YHWH*** directed *Mosheh*, so they did,

---

Chapter 2

1 and ***YHWH*** spoke to *Mosheh* and to *Aharon* saying, **2** each by his banner, with the signs according to the house of their fathers, the sons of *Yisra'eyl* will camp, opposite all around the appointed tent they will camp, **3** and the ones camping to the east, toward the sunrise, is the banner of the camp of *Yehudah*, by their armies, and the captain for the sons of *Yehudah* is *Nahhshon* the son of *Amiynadav*, **4** and his army and their registered ones are seventy-four thousand and six hundred, **5** and the ones camping by him, the branch of *Yis'sas'khar*, and the captain for the sons of *Yis'sas'khar* is *Nataneyl* the son of *Tso'ar*, **6** and his army and his registered ones are fifty-four thousand and four hundred. **7** The branch of *Zevulun*, and the captain for the sons of *Zevulun* is *Eli'av* the son of *Hheylon*, **8** and his army and his registered ones are fifty-seven thousand and four hundred. **9** All the registered ones for the camp of *Yehudah* are a hundred thousand and eighty thousand and six thousand and four hundred for their armies, they will journey first. **10** The banner of the camp of *Re'uven* is unto the south for their armies, and the captain for the sons of *Re'uven* is *Elitsur* the son of *Shedeyur*, **11** and his army and his registered ones are forty-six thousand and five hundred, **12** and the ones camping by him is the branch of *Shimon*, and the captain for the sons of *Shimon* is *Shelumi'eyl* the son of *Tsurishaddai*, **13** and his army and their registered ones are fifty-nine thousand and three hundred, **14** and the branch of *Gad*, and the captain for the sons of *Gad* is *Elyasaph* the son of *Re'u'eyl*, **15** and his army, and their registered ones are forty-five thousand and six hundred and fifty. **16** All the registered ones belonging to the camp of *Re'uven* are a hundred thousand and fifty-one thousand and four hundred and fifty for their armies, they will journey second, **17** and the appointed tent, the camp of the ones of *Lewi*, journeyed in the midst of the camps, just as they will camp, so they will journey, each according to his hand[591] belonging to their banners. **18** The banner of the camp of *Ephrayim* is unto the west for their armies, and the captain for the sons of *Ephrayim* is *Elishama* the son of *Amihud*, **19** and his army, and their registered ones are forty thousand and five hundred, **20** and by him, the branch of *Menasheh*, and the captain of the sons of *Menasheh* is *Gamli'eyl* the son of *Pedatsur*, **21** and his army, and their registered ones are thirty-two thousand and two hundred, **22** and the branch of *Binyamin*, and the captain for the sons of *Binyamin* is *Avidan* the son of *Gidoni*, **23** and his army, and their registered ones if thirty-five thousand and four hundred. **24** All the registered ones belonging to the camp of *Ephrayim* are a hundred thousand and eight thousand and a hundred for their armies, they will journey third. **25** The banner of the camp of *Dan* is unto the north for their armies, and the captain for the sons of *Dan* is *Ahhi'ezer* the son of *Amishaddai*, **26** and his army and their registered ones are sixty-two thousand and seven hundred, **27** and the ones camping by him are the branch of *Asher*, and the captain for the sons of *Asher* is *Pagi'eyl* the son of *Akhran*, **28** and his army and their registered ones are forty-one thousand and five hundred, **29** and the branch of *Naphtali*, and the captain for the sons of *Naphtali* is *Ahhira* the son of *Eynan*, **30** and his army and their registered ones are fifty-three thousand and four hundred. **31** All the registered ones for the camp of *Dan* are a hundred thousand and fifty-seven thousand and six hundred, they will journey last according to their banners. **32** These are the registered ones of the sons of *Yisra'eyl*, according to the house of their fathers, all the registered ones, the camps for their armies, six hundred thousand and three thousand and five hundred and fifty, **33** and the ones of *Lewi*, they will not register themselves in the midst of the sons of *Yisra'eyl*, just as ***YHWH*** directed *Mosheh*, **34** and the sons of *Yisra'eyl* will do everything just as ***YHWH*** directed *Mosheh*, so they camped according to their banners, and so they journeyed, each according to his clan by the house of his fathers,

---

Chapter 3

1 and these are the birthings of *Aharon* and *Mosheh* in the day ***YHWH*** spoke with *Mosheh* on the hill of *Sinai*, **2** and these are the titles of the sons of *Aharon*, the firstborn is *Nadav*, and *Aviyhu*, *Elazar* and *Iytamar*. **3** These are the titles of the sons of *Aharon*, the smeared administrators, who filled his hand[592] to be adorned, **4** and *Nadav* died, and *Aviyhu*, to the face of ***YHWH*** in their bringing near strange fire to the face of ***YHWH*** in the wilderness of

---

[591] Meaning his place, position or station.

[592] To "fill the hand" is an idiom of uncertain meaning, but the same phrase is used in Akkadian to mean the placing of a relevant tool or insignia (such as a scepter for a king) in the hand of one being installed in a high office.

Sinai, and sons did not exist for them, so *Elazar* was adorned, and *Iytamar*, in place of *Aharon* their father, **5** and ***YHWH*** spoke to *Mosheh* saying, **6** bring near the branch of *Lewi*, and you will make him stand to the face of *Aharon* the administrator, and they will minister with him, **7** and they will safeguard his charge and the charge of all the company to the face of the appointed tent, to serve with the service of the dwelling, **8** and they will safeguard all the utensils of the appointed tent, and the charge of the sons of *Yisra'eyl*, to serve with the service of the dwelling, **9** and you will give the ones of *Lewi* to *Aharon* and to his sons, each of them are given to him from the sons of *Yisra'eyl*, **10** and *Aharon* and his sons you will register, and they will safeguard their administration, and the stranger inside will be killed, **11** and ***YHWH*** spoke to *Mosheh* saying, **12** and I, look, I took the ones of *Lewi* from the midst of the sons of *Yisra'eyl* in place of all the firstborn bursting the bowels from the sons of *Yisra'eyl*, and the ones of *Lewi* exist for me, **13** given that belonging to me are all the firstborn on the day I hit all the firstborn in the land of *Mits'rayim*, and I will set apart for me all the firstborn in *Yisra'eyl*, from the human until the beast, for me they will exist, I am ***YHWH***, **14** and ***YHWH*** spoke to *Mosheh* in the wilderness of *Sinai* saying, **15** register the sons of *Lewi* according to their house, according to their clans, every male from the son of a new moon and upward you will register them, **16** and *Mosheh* registered them by the mouth of ***YHWH*** just as he directed, **17** and these are the sons of *Lewi* by their titles, *Gershon* and *Qehat* and *Merari*, **18** and these are the titles of the sons of *Gershon* according to their clan, *Liyvniy* and *Shiymiy*, **19** and the sons of *Qehat* according to their clans, *Amram* and Yits'har, *Hhevron* and *Uziy'eyl*, **20** and the sons of *Merari* according to their clans, *Mahh'liy* and *Mushiy*, these are they, the clans of *Lewi* according to the house of their fathers. **21** To *Gershon*, the clan of *Liyvniy* and the clan of *Shiymiy*, these are they, the clans of *Gershon*. **22** Their numbered ones, in number, every male from a son of a new moon and upward, their registered ones are seven thousand and five hundred. **23** The clans of *Gershon*, behind the dwelling they will camp, unto the west, **24** and the captain of the house of the father belonging to *Gershon*, *Elyasaph* the son of *La'eyl*, **25** and the charge of the sons of *Gershon* in the appointed tent, the dwelling and the tent, his roof covering and the screen of the opening of the appointed tent, **26** and the slings of the courtyard, and the screen of the opening of the courtyard which is by the dwelling and by the altar all around, and his strings for all of his service, **27** and to *Qehat*, the clan of *Amram*, and the clan of Yits'har, and the clan of *Hhevron*, and the clan of *Uziy'eyl*, these are they, the clans of *Qehat*. **28** By number, every male, from a son of a new moon and upward, eight thousand and six hundred safeguarding the special charge. **29** The clans of the sons of *Qehat*, they will camp by the midsection of the dwelling, unto the south, **30** and the captain of the house of the father belonging to the clans of *Qehat* is *Elitsaphan* the son of *Uziy'eyl*, **31** and their charge is the box and the table and the lampstand and the altars, and the special utensils that they will

minister with, and the screen and his service, **32** and the captain of the
captains of the *Lewi* is *Elazar* the son of *Aharon* the administrator, oversight
of the safeguarding of the special charge. **33** To *Merari* is the clan of the
Mahh'liy and the clan of the *Mushiy*, these are they, the clans of *Merari*,
34 and they are registered by number, every male from a son of a new moon
and upward is six thousand and two hundred, **35** and the captain of the
house of the father belonging to the clans of *Merari* is *Tsuri'eyl* the son of
Avihha'il, by the midsection of the dwelling they will camp, unto the north,
36 and the oversight of the charge of the sons of *Merari* is the boards of the
dwelling and his wood bars and his pillars and his footings and all his utensils
and all his service, **37** and the pillars of the courtyard all around and their
footings and their tent pegs and their strings, **38** and the ones camping to
the face of the dwelling to the east, to the face of the appointed tent to the
sunrise, *Mosheh* and *Aharon* and his sons, safeguarding the charge of the
sanctuary, for the charge of the sons of *Yisra'eyl*, and the stranger inside will
be killed. **39** All the registered ones of the ones of *Lewi* that *Mosheh*
registered, by the mouth of ***YHWH***, to their clans, every male from a son of a
new moon and upward, twenty-two thousand, **40** and ***YHWH*** said to
Mosheh, register all the firstborn males belonging to the sons of *Yisra'eyl*,
from a son of a new moon and upward, and lift up the number of their titles,
41 and you will take the ones of *Lewi* belonging to me, I am ***YHWH***, in place
of all the firstborn among the sons of *Yisra'eyl*, and the beasts of the ones of
Lewi in place of all the firstborn among the beasts of the sons of *Yisra'eyl*,
42 and *Mosheh* registered, just as ***YHWH*** directed him, all the firstborn
among the sons of *Yisra'eyl*, **43** and all the firstborn males existed, by the
number of their titles, from a son of a new moon and upward, according to
their registered ones, twenty-two thousand, seventy-three and two
hundred, **44** and ***YHWH*** spoke to *Mosheh* saying, **45** take the ones of *Lewi* in
place of all the firstborn among the sons of *Yisra'eyl*, and the beasts of the
ones of *Lewi* in place of their beasts, the ones of *Lewi* will exist for me, I am
YHWH, **46** and the redeemed ones of the seventy-three and the two
hundred, the ones exceeding over the ones of the *Lewi*, from the firstborn of
the sons of *Yisra'eyl*, **47** and you will take five, five *sheqel*s for the skull, with
the special *sheqel* you will take, twenty *gerah*s is the *sheqel*, **48** and you will
give the silver to *Aharon* and to his sons, the redeemed ones exceeding
them, **49** and *Mosheh* took the silver, the ransom price, from the exceeding
ones over the redeemed ones of the *Lewi*. **50** From the firstborn sons of
Yisra'eyl he took the silver, sixty-five and three hundred and a thousand, in
the special *sheqel*, **51** and *Mosheh* gave the silver of the redeemed ones to
Aharon, and to his sons, by the mouth of ***YHWH***, just as ***YHWH*** directed
Mosheh,

Chapter 4

1 and ***YHWH*** spoke to *Mosheh* and to *Aharon* saying, **2** lift up the head[593] of the sons of *Qehat* from the midst of the sons of *Lewi*, according their clans, according to the house of their fathers. **3** From a son of thirty years and upward, and until a son of fifty years, each came for the army to do the business of the appointed tent. **4** This is the service of the sons of *Qehat* in the appointed tent, the special of specials[594], **5** and *Aharon* will come, and his sons, in the journeying of the camp, and they will bring down the tent curtain of the screen, and they will cover over the box of the evidence with her, **6** and they will place upon him the outer covering of skin of the deer, and they will spread out the garment, entirely of blue, above, and they will place his strands, **7** and upon the table of the face they will spread out the garment of blue, and they will place upon him the platters and the palms and the sacrificial bowl and the pouring jug and the continual bread will exist upon him, **8** and they will spread out upon them a garment of scarlet kermes, and they will cover him over with a roof covering of skin of deer, and they will place his strands, **9** and they will take the garment of blue and they will cover over the lampstand of the luminary, and her lamps and her tongs and her fire pan, and all the utensils of her oil that they will minister to her with them, **10** and they will place her and all her utensils on the roof covering of a skin of deer, and they will place it upon the bar, **11** and upon the gold altar they will spread out a garment of blue, and they will cover him over with the roof covering of a skin of deer, and they will place his strands, **12** and they will take all the utensils of ministry that they will minister with in the special place, and they will place on the garment of blue, and they will cover them over with the roof covering of a skin of deer, and they will place it upon the bar, **13** and they will remove the fat of the altar and they will spread out upon him a garment of purple, **14** and they will place upon him all his utensils that they will minister upon him with them, the fire pans and the shovels and the sprinkling basins and all the utensils of the altar, and they will spread out upon him an outer covering of a skin of deer, and they will place his strands, **15** and *Aharon* finished, and his sons, to cover over the special things and all the special utensils, with the journeying of the camp, and after this the sons of *Qehat* will come to lift it up, but they will not touch the special things or they will die, these are the loads of the sons of *Qehat* in the appointed tent, **16** and the oversight of *Elazar* the son of *Aharon* the administrator, is the oil of the luminary and the aromatic spices of the incense smoke, and the continual deposit, and the ointment oil, the oversight of all that is in him, in the special place, and in his utensils, **17** and

---

593 "Lift up the head" is an idiom for "counting heads."

594 The phrase "special of specials" means a "very special thing, one or place."

YHWH spoke to *Mosheh* and to *Aharon* saying, **18** do not cut the staff[595] of the clans of the ones of *Qehat* from the midst of the ones of the *Lewi*, **19** and this, do to them and live, and they will not die in their drawing near to the special of specials[596], *Aharon* and his sons will come and they will place them, each man according to his service and his load, **20** and they will not come to see, like the swallowing[597] of the special place, or they will die, **21** and ***YHWH*** spoke to *Mosheh* saying, **22** lift up the head[598] of the sons of *Gershon*, them also, according to the house of their fathers, according to their clans. **23** From a son of thirty years and upward, until a son of fifty years, you will register them, all the ones coming to muster the army, to serve the service in the appointed tent. **24** This is the service of the clans of *Gershon* to serve and to load, **25** and they will lift up the curtains of the dwelling and the appointed tent, his roof covering and the roof covering of deer which is upon him on top, and the screen of the opening of the appointed tent, **26** and the slings of the courtyard and the screen of the opening of the gate of the courtyard that is upon the dwelling and upon the altar all around, and their strings, and all the utensils of their service, and all that he will make for them, and they will serve. **27** By the mouth of *Aharon* and his sons, all the service of the sons of *Gershon* will exist for all their loads, and for all of their service, and you will register upon them with the charge of all their loads. **28** This is the service of the clans of the sons of *Gershon* in the appointed tent, and their charge is in the hand of *Iytamar* the son of *Aharon* the administrator. **29** The sons of *Merari* according to their clans, according to the house of their fathers, you will register them. **30** From a son of thirty years and upward, and until a son of fifty years, you will register them, all the ones coming to the army, to serve the service of the appointed tent, **31** and this is the charge of their load for all their service in the appointed tent, the boards of the dwelling and his wood bars, and his pillars, and his footings, **32** and the pillars of the courtyard all around and their footings and their tent pegs and their strings, for all their utensils, and for all their service, and by the titles you will register the utensils of the charge of their load. **33** This is the service of the clans of the sons of *Merari*, for all their service in the appointed tent, by the hand of *Iytamar* the son of *Aharon* the administrator, **34** and *Mosheh* will register, and *Aharon* and the captains of the company, the sons of *Qehat* according to their clans and according to the house of their fathers. **35** From a son of thirty years and upward, and until a son of fifty years, all the ones coming to the army for the service in the appointed tent, **36** and their registered ones will exist according to their clans, two thousand seven hundred and fifty. **37** These are

---

[595] That is the "tribe."

[596] The phrase "special of specials" means a "very special thing, one or place."

[597] Probably means "even for a moment."

[598] "Lift up the head" is an idiom for "counting heads."

the registered ones of the clans of *Qehat*, all the ones serving in the appointed tent which *Mosheh* registered, and *Aharon*, by the mouth of ***YHWH***, by the hand of *Mosheh*, **38** and the registered of the sons of *Gershon*, according to their clans and according to the house of their fathers. **39** From a son of thirty years and upward, and until a son of fifty years, all the ones coming to the army for the service in the appointed tent, **40** and their registered ones will exist according to their clans, according to the house of their fathers, two thousand and six hundred and thirty. **41** These are the registered ones of the clans of the sons of *Gershon*, all the ones serving in the appointed tent which *Mosheh* registered, and *Aharon*, by the mouth of ***YHWH***, **42** and the registered of the clans of the sons of *Merari*, according to their clans, according to the house of their fathers. **43** From a son of thirty years and upward, and until a son of fifty years, all the ones coming to the army for the service in the appointed tent, **44** and their registered ones will exist, according to their clans, three thousand and two hundred. **45** These are the registered ones of the clans of the sons of *Merari* which *Mosheh* registered, and *Aharon*, by the mouth of ***YHWH***, by the hand of *Mosheh*. **46** All the registered which *Mosheh* registered, and *Aharon*, and the captains of *Yisra'eyl*, the ones of *Lewi*, according to their clans and according to the house of their fathers. **47** From a son of thirty years and upward, and until a son of fifty years, all the ones coming to serve the service of the service[599] and service the load in the appointed tent, **48** and their registered ones existed, eight thousand and five hundred and eighty. **49** By the mouth of ***YHWH*** he registered them, by the hand of *Mosheh*, each man upon his service and his load upon him, and registered him, which ***YHWH*** directed *Mosheh*,

---

Chapter 5

1 and ***YHWH*** spoke to *Mosheh* saying, **2** direct the sons of *Yisra'eyl*, and they will send from the camp all the infected, all the ones issuing, and every dirty one to the soul[600]. **3** From the male until the female you will send, to the outside of the camp you will send them, and they will not dirty their camps, which I am dwelling in the midst of them, **4** and the sons of *Yisra'eyl* will do so, and they sent them to the outside of the camp, just as ***YHWH*** spoke to *Mosheh*, so the sons of *Yisra'eyl* did do, **5** and ***YHWH*** spoke to *Mosheh* saying, **6** speak to the sons of *Yisra'eyl*, a man or a woman that will do from any of the failures of the human to transgress a transgression in ***YHWH***, then that soul will be guilty, **7** and they will confess their failures that they did,

---

[599] It is possible that the Hebrew word for "service" was accidentally written twice by the scribe, or one of these words should have been the word "army." (see verses 30, 35, 39 and 43)

[600] The meaning of the phrase "to the soul" is uncertain.

and they will turn back his guilt in his head, and a fifth of him he will add upon him, and he will give it to him he did the guilt, **8** and if the man is without a redeemer to turn back the guilt to him, the guilt to be turned back belongs to ***YHWH***, belongs to the administrator, apart from the buck of the atonement that will make a covering for him upon him, **9** and every offerings for all the special things of the sons of *Yisra'eyl*, which they will bring near to the administrator will exist for him, **10** and a man, his special things will exist for him, a man which will give to the administrator will exist for him, **11** and ***YHWH*** spoke to *Mosheh* saying, **12** speak to the sons of *Yisra'eyl*, and you will say to them, each man whose woman will go aside and she will transgress with him a transgression, **13** and a man will lay her down a lying down of seed, and he will be out of sight from the eyes of her man, and she was hidden, and she, she was dirty and without a witness for her, and she, she was not seized, **14** and a wind of zealousness crossed over upon him, and he was zealous with his woman, and she, she was dirty or a wind of zealousness crossed over upon him, and he was zealous with his woman, and she, she was not dirty, **15** then the man will bring his woman to the administrator, and he brought her donation upon her, a tenth *eyphah* of grain flour of barley, he will not pour down upon him the oil, and he will not place upon him frankincense, given that it is a deposit of zealousness, a deposit of remembrance, making a remembrance of twistedness, **16** and he will bring her near the administrator, and he will make her stand to the face of ***YHWH***, **17** and the administrator will take unique waters in a utensil of clay, and from the dirt that exists in the bottom of the dwelling, the administrator will take and he will give to the waters, **18** and the administrator will make the woman stand to the face of ***YHWH***, and he will loose[601] the head of the woman, and he will place upon her palms the deposit of remembrance, she is a deposit of zealousness, and in the hand of the administrator will exist the bitter waters that causes the spitting upon[602], **19** and the administrator will make her swear, and he will say to the woman, if a man did not lay down with you, and if you did not go aside to dirtiness in place of your man, you will be acquitted from this bitter waters causing the spitting upon, **20** and you, if you did go aside in place of your man, and if you were dirty and the man placed in you his copulation, apart from your man, **21** then the administrator will make the woman swear with the swearing of the oath, and the administrator will say to the woman, ***YHWH*** will give you for an oath and for a swearing in the midst of your people, in ***YHWH*** giving your midsection a falling, and your womb a swelling, **22** and this waters causing the spitting upon will come in your abdomen to make the womb swell, and to make the midsection fall, and the woman will say, so be it, so be it, **23** and the administrator will write these oaths in the scroll, and he will wipe them away with the bitter waters, **24** and he will

---

[601] This may refer to the loosening of the hair or the removing of a covering.
[602] A "spitting upon" is a curse. (also in verse 19)

make the woman drink the bitter waters causing the spitting upon, and the bitter water causing the spitting upon will come in her for bitterness, **25** and the administrator will take from the hand of the woman the deposit of zealousness, and he will wave the deposit to the face of ***YHWH***, and he will bring her near to the altar, **26** and the administrator will grasp from the deposit of her memorial, and he will burn it as incense on the altar, and after, he will make the woman drink the waters, **27** and he will make her drink the waters, and it will come to pass, if she be dirty and she transgressed a transgression with her man, and the waters causing the spitting upon comes in her for bitterness, and her womb swells and her midsection falls, and the woman will exist for an oath in the inside of her people, **28** and if the woman was not being dirty, then she is clean, and she will be acquitted, then she will be sown with seed. **29** This is the teaching of the zealousness, when the woman will go aside in place of her man, then she will be dirty. **30** Or a man that the wind of zealousness will cross over upon him, and he will be zealous of his woman, then he will make the woman stand to the face of ***YHWH***, and the administrator will do to her all this teaching, **31** and the man will be acquitted from twistedness and that woman will lift up her twistedness,

---

Chapter 6

1 and ***YHWH*** spoke to *Mosheh* saying, **2** speak to the sons of *Yisra'eyl*, and you will say to them, a man or woman that will perform to make a vow, a vow of dedication, to be dedicated to ***YHWH***. **3** From wine and liquor he will dedicate, vinegar of wine and vinegar of liquor he will not gulp, and any juice of grapes he will not gulp, and moist or dry grapes he will not eat. **4** All the days of his dedication, from all that will be made from the grapevine, the wine, the kernels and even the grape skin he will not eat. **5** All the days of the vow of his dedication, a razor will not cross over upon his head, until the filling of the days that he dedicated to ***YHWH***, he will exist unique, magnified is the long hair of his head. **6** All the days of his dedication to ***YHWH***, he will not come upon a dying soul. **7** For his father and for his mother, for his brother and for his sister, he will not be dirty for them in their death, given that the dedication of his *Elohiym* is upon his head. **8** All the days of his dedication he will be unique for ***YHWH***, **9** and if the dying dies upon him suddenly in an instant, and he dirtied the head of his dedication, then he will shave his head on the day of his cleanness, on the seventh day he will shave him, **10** and on the eighth day he will bring two turtledoves or two sons of a dove, to the administrator, to the opening of the appointed tent, **11** and the administrator will do one for the failure and one for an ascension offering, and he will make a covering upon him, from that he failed upon the soul, and he will set his head apart in that day, **12** and he will dedicate to ***YHWH*** the days of his dedication, and he will bring a sheep, a son of his year for

guilt, and the first days will fail, given that his dedication was dirtied, **13** and
this is the teaching of the dedicated, in the day of the fullness of the days of
his dedication, he will bring him to the opening of the appointed tent,
14 and he will bring near his donation for ***YHWH***, a sheep of a son of his
year, a whole one for an ascension offering, and one sheep, a daughter of
her year, a whole one for a failure, and one whole buck for offerings of
restitution, **15** and a wicker basket of unleavened breads, flour of pierced
breads mixed with the oil, and thin bread of unleavened bread smeared with
the oil, and their deposit, and their pourings, **16** and the administrator will
bring near to the face of ***YHWH***, and he will do his failure and his ascension
offering, **17** and he will do the buck for a sacrifice of offerings of restitution
for ***YHWH*** upon the wicker basket of the unleavened breads, and the
administrator will do his deposit and his pourings, **18** and the dedicated will
shave the head of his dedication at the opening of the appointed tent, and
he will take the hair of the head of his dedication and he will place it upon
the fire which is under the sacrifice of the offerings of restitution, **19** and the
administrator will take the boiled arm from the buck and one pierced bread
of unleavened bread from the wicker basket, and the thin bread of one
unleavened bread, and he will place them upon the palms of the dedicated
after he shaved his dedication, **20** and the administrator will wave them, a
waving to the face of ***YHWH***, he is special for the administrator, with the
chest of waving and with the thigh of offering, and afterward the dedicated
will gulp the wine. **21** This is the teaching of the dedicated, who will make a
vow of his donation to ***YHWH*** concerning his dedication, besides what his
hand will overtake, according to the mouth of his vow, which he will make
so he will do concerning the teaching of his dedication, **22** and ***YHWH*** spoke
to *Mosheh* saying, **23** speak to *Aharon* and to his sons saying, in this way you
will exalt the sons of *Yisra'eyl* saying to them. **24** ***YHWH*** will exalt you and he
will safeguard you. **25** ***YHWH*** will make his face shine toward you and he will
provide you with protection. **26** ***YHWH*** will lift up his face toward you and he
will place completeness to you, **27** and they will place my title upon the sons
of *Yisra'eyl*, and I, I will exalt them,

Chapter 7

1 and it came to pass, in the day *Mosheh* finished making the dwelling rise,
and he smeared him, and he set him apart and all his utensils, and the altar
and all his utensils, and he smeared them, and set them apart, **2** and the
captains of *Yisra'eyl* brought near[603] the heads of the house of their fathers,

---

[603] The construction of this passage implies that the captains brought near the "heads of the house of their fathers," but as the "heads" are the captains, we can assume that the captains "brought near" an offering, which is what we find in the next verse.

they are the captains of the branches, they are the ones standing over the registered ones, **3** and they brought their donation to the face of ***YHWH***, six covered carts and twelve cattle, a cart upon two of the captains and one ox[604], and they will bring them near to the face of the dwelling, **4** and ***YHWH*** said to *Mosheh* saying, **5** take from them, and they will exist to serve at the service of the appointed tent, and you will give them to the ones of the *Lewi*, each according to the mouth of his service, **6** and *Mosheh* will take the carts and the cattle and he will give them to the ones of the *Lewi*. **7** Two carts and four of the cattle he gave to the sons of *Gershon*, according to the mouth of their service, **8** and four carts and eight of the cattle he gave to the sons of *Merari*, according to the mouth of their service, by the hand of *Iytamar* the son of *Aharon* the administrator, **9** and to the sons of *Qehat* he did not give, given that the special service is upon them, they will lift with the shoulder, **10** and the captains will bring near a devotion of the altar in the day of his being smeared, and the captains will bring near their donation to the face of the altar, **11** and ***YHWH*** said to *Mosheh*, each captain for each day, they will bring their donation near to the devotion of the altar, **12** and it came to pass, the one bringing near his donation on the first day was *Nahhshon* the son of *Amiynadav*, belonging to the branch of *Yehudah*, **13** and his donation was one silver platter weighting a hundred and thirty, one silver sprinkling basin of seventy *sheqel*s by the special *sheqel*, both of them full of flour mixed with the oil of the deposit. **14** One gold spoon of ten, full of incense. **15** One bull, a son of the cattle, one buck, one sheep, a son of his year, for an ascension offering. **16** One hairy goat of the she-goats for a failure, **17** and for the sacrifice of the offerings of restitution, two cattle, five bucks, five male goats, five sheep, sons of a year, this is the donation of *Nahhshon* the son of *Amiynadav*. **18** On the second day *Nataneyl* the son of *Tso'ar*, the captain of *Yis'sas'khar*, brought near, **19** and he brought near his donation, one silver platter weighing a hundred and thirty, one silver sprinkling basin of seventy *sheqel*s by the special *sheqel*, both of them full of flour mixed with the oil of the deposit. **20** One gold spoon of ten, full of incense. **21** One bull, a son of the cattle, one buck, one sheep, a son of his year, for an ascension offering. **22** One hairy goat of the she-goats for a failure, **23** and for the sacrifice of the offerings of restitution, two cattle, five bucks, five male goats, five sheep, sons of a year, this is the donation of *Nataneyl* the son of *Tso'ar*. **24** On the third day the captain for the sons of *Zevulun*, *Eli'av* the son of *Hheylon*. **25** His donation, one silver platter weighing a hundred and thirty, one silver sprinkling basin of seventy *sheqel*s by the special *sheqel*, both of them full of flour mixed with the oil of the deposit. **26** One gold spoon of ten, full of incense. **27** One bull, a son of the cattle, one buck, one sheep, a son of his year, for an ascension offering. **28** One hairy goat of the she-goats for a failure, **29** and for the sacrifice of the offerings of restitution, two cattle, five bucks, five male goats, five

---

[604] That is, "one cart and one ox for each of the two captains."

sheep, sons of a year, this is the donation of *Eli'av* the son of *Hheylon*. **30** On
the fourth day the captain for the sons of *Re'uven*, *Elitsur* the son of
Shedeyur. **31** His donation, one silver platter weighing a hundred and thirty,
one silver sprinkling basin of seventy *sheqel*s by the special *sheqel*, both of
them full of flour mixed with the oil of the deposit. **32** One gold spoon of
ten, full of incense. **33** One bull, a son of the cattle, one buck, one sheep, a
son of his year, for an ascension offering. **34** One hairy goat of the she-goats
for a failure, **35** and for the sacrifice of the offerings of restitution, two
cattle, five bucks, five male goats, five sheep, sons of a year, this is the
donation of *Elitsur* the son of *Shedeyur*. **36** On the fifth day the captain for
the sons of *Shimon*, *Shelumi'eyl* the son of *Tsurishaddai*. **37** His donation,
one silver platter weighing a hundred and thirty, one silver sprinkling basin
of seventy *sheqel*s by the special *sheqel*, both of them full of flour mixed
with the oil of the deposit. **38** One gold spoon of ten, full of incense. **39** One
bull, a son of the cattle, one buck, one sheep, a son of his year, for an
ascension offering. **40** One hairy goat of the she-goats for a failure, **41** and
for the sacrifice of the offerings of restitution, two cattle, five bucks, five
male goats, five sheep, sons of a year, this is the donation of *Shelumi'eyl* the
son of *Tsurishaddai*. **42** On the sixth day the captain for the sons of *Gad*,
Elyasaph the son of *De'u'eyl*. **43** His donation, one silver platter weighing a
hundred and thirty, one silver sprinkling basin of seventy *sheqel*s by the
special *sheqel*, both of them full of flour mixed with the oil of the deposit.
44 One gold spoon of ten, full of incense. **45** One bull, a son of the cattle,
one buck, one sheep, a son of his year, for an ascension offering. **46** One
hairy goat of the she-goats for a failure, **47** and for the sacrifice of the
offerings of restitution, two cattle, five bucks, five male goats, five sheep,
sons of a year, this is the donation of *Elyasaph* the son of *De'u'eyl*. **48** On the
seventh day the captain for the sons of *Ephrayim*, *Elishama* the son of
Amihud. **49** His donation, one silver platter weighing a hundred and thirty,
one silver sprinkling basin of seventy *sheqel*s by the special *sheqel*, both of
them full of flour mixed with the oil of the deposit. **50** One gold spoon of
ten, full of incense. **51** One bull, a son of the cattle, one buck, one sheep, a
son of his year, for an ascension offering. **52** One hairy goat of the she-goats
for a failure, **53** and for the sacrifice of the offerings of restitution, two
cattle, five bucks, five male goats, five sheep, sons of a year, this is the
donation of *Elishama* the son of *Amihud*. **54** On the eighth day the captain
for the sons of *Menasheh*, *Gamli'eyl* the son of *Pedatsur*. **55** His donation,
one silver platter weighing a hundred and thirty, one silver sprinkling basin
of seventy *sheqel*s by the special *sheqel*, both of them full of flour mixed
with the oil of the deposit. **56** One gold spoon of ten, full of incense. **57** One
bull, a son of the cattle, one buck, one sheep, a son of his year, for an
ascension offering. **58** One hairy goat of the she-goats for a failure, **59** and
for the sacrifice of the offerings of restitution, two cattle, five bucks, five
male goats, five sheep, sons of a year, this is the donation of *Gamli'eyl* the
son of *Pedatsur*. **60** On the ninth day the captain for the sons of *Binyamin*,

Avidan the son of *Gidoni*. **61** His donation, one silver platter weighing a hundred and thirty, one silver sprinkling basin of seventy *sheqel*s by the special *sheqel*, both of them full of flour mixed with the oil of the deposit. **62** One gold spoon of ten, full of incense. **63** One bull, a son of the cattle, one buck, one sheep, a son of his year, for an ascension offering. **64** One hairy goat of the she-goats for a failure, **65** and for the sacrifice of the offerings of restitution, two cattle, five bucks, five male goats, five sheep, sons of a year, this is the donation of *Avidan* the son of *Gidoni*. **66** On the tenth day the captain for the sons of *Dan*, *Ahhi'ezer* the son of *Amishaddai*. **67** His donation, one silver platter weighing a hundred and thirty, one silver sprinkling basin of seventy *sheqel*s by the special *sheqel*, both of them full of flour mixed with the oil of the deposit. **68** One gold spoon of ten, full of incense. **69** One bull, a son of the cattle, one buck, one sheep, a son of his year, for an ascension offering. **70** One hairy goat of the she-goats for a failure, **71** and for the sacrifice of the offerings of restitution, two cattle, five bucks, five male goats, five sheep, sons of a year, this is the donation of *Ahhi'ezer* the son of *Amishaddai*. **72** On the eleventh day the captain for the sons of *Asher*, *Pagi'eyl* the son of *Akhran*. **73** His donation, one silver platter weighing a hundred and thirty, one silver sprinkling basin of seventy *sheqel*s by the special *sheqel*, both of them full of flour mixed with the oil of the deposit. **74** One gold spoon of ten, full of incense. **75** One bull, a son of the cattle, one buck, one sheep, a son of his year, for an ascension offering. **76** One hairy goat of the she-goats for a failure, **77** and for the sacrifice of the offerings of restitution, two cattle, five bucks, five male goats, five sheep, sons of a year, this is the donation of *Pagi'eyl* the son of *Akhran*. **78** On the twelfth day the captain for the sons of *Naphtali*, *Ahhira* the son of *Eynan*. **79** His donation, one silver platter weighing a hundred and thirty, one silver sprinkling basin of seventy *sheqel*s by the special *sheqel*, both of them full of flour mixed with the oil of the deposit. **80** One gold spoon of ten, full of incense. **81** One bull, a son of the cattle, one buck, one sheep, a son of his year, for an ascension offering. **82** One hairy goat of the she-goats for a failure, **83** and for the sacrifice of the offerings of restitution, two cattle, five bucks, five male goats, five sheep, sons of a year, this is the donation of *Ahhira* the son of *Eynan*. **84** This is the devotion of the altar in the day of him being smeared, from the captains of *Yisra'eyl*, twelve silver platters, twelve silver sprinkling basins, twelve gold spoons. **85** A hundred and thirty for the one silver platter, and seventy for the one sprinkling basin, all the silver utensils, two thousand and four hundred by the special *sheqel*. **86** Twelve spoons of gold full of incense, each spoon ten by the special *sheqel*, a hundred and twenty for all the gold spoons. **87** All the cattle for the ascension offering are twelve bulls, twelve bucks, twelve sheep, sons of a year, and their deposit, and twelve hairy goats of the she-goats for the failure, **88** and all the cattle for the sacrifice of offerings of restitution, twenty and four bulls, sixty bucks, sixty male goats, sixty sheep, sons of a year, this is the devotion of the altar after him being smeared, **89** and with

Mosheh coming to the appointed tent to speak with him, he heard the voice
speaking to him from upon the lid, which is upon the box of evidence, from
between the two keruvs, and he spoke to him,

Chapter 8

1 and ***YHWH*** spoke to *Mosheh* saying, **2** speak to *Aharon*, and you will say to
him, in your making the lamps go up[605], to the forefront of the face of the
lampstand, the seven lamps will make light, **3** and *Aharon* will do so to the
forefront of the face of the lampstand, and he will make her light go up, just
as ***YHWH*** directed *Mosheh*, **4** and this is the work of the lampstand, a beaten
work of gold, unto her midsection, unto her bud, she is a beaten work, like
the appearance that ***YHWH*** made *Mosheh* see, so he did do with the
lampstand, **5** and ***YHWH*** spoke to *Mosheh* saying, **6** take the ones of *Lewi*
from the midst of the sons of *Yisra'eyl*, and you will declare them clean,
7 and in this way you will do for them, to declare them clean, spatter the
waters of failure upon them, and they will make a razor cross over upon all
their flesh, and they will wash their garments, and they will be declared
clean, **8** and they will take a bull, a son of the cattle, and his deposit of flour
mixed in the oil, and a second bull, a son of the cattle, you will take for a
failure, **9** and you will bring the ones of *Lewi* near to the face of the
appointed tent, and you will assemble all the company of the sons of
Yisra'eyl, **10** and you will bring the ones of *Lewi* near to the face of ***YHWH***,
and the sons of *Yisra'eyl* will support their hands upon the ones of *Lewi*,
11 and *Aharon* will wave the ones of *Lewi*, a waving to the face of ***YHWH***,
from the sons of *Yisra'eyl*, and they will exist to serve the service of ***YHWH***,
12 and the ones of *Lewi* will support their hands upon the head of the bulls,
and do the one of failure, and the one of an ascension offering, to ***YHWH*** to
make a covering upon the ones of *Lewi*, **13** and you will make the ones of
Lewi stand to the face of *Aharon* and to the faces of his sons, and you will
wave them, a waving to ***YHWH***, **14** and you will make the ones of *Lewi*
separate from the midst of the sons of *Yisra'eyl*, and the ones of *Lewi* will
exist for me, **15** and after this, the ones of *Lewi* will come to serve the
appointed tent, and you will declare them clean, and you will make them
wave a waving, **16** given that each of them were certainly given to me from
the midst of the sons of *Yisra'eyl*, in place of the bursting of all the bowels[606]
of the firstborn from all the sons of *Yisra'eyl*, I will take them for me,
17 given that all the firstborn in the sons of *Yisra'eyl* belong to me, among
the human and among the beast, in the day I hit the firstborn in the land of
Mits'rayim, I set them apart for me, **18** and I took the ones of *Lewi* in place
of all the firstborn in the sons of *Yisra'eyl*, **19** and I gave the ones of *Lewi*,

---

[605] Meaning "to light the lamps." (also in verse 3)

[606] The phrase "bursting bowels" means "give birth."

given to *Aharon* and to his sons from the midst of the sons of *Yisra'eyl*, to serve the service of the sons of *Yisra'eyl* in the appointed tent, and to make a covering upon the sons of *Yisra'eyl*, and a striking[607] will not exist in the sons of *Yisra'eyl* with the sons of *Yisra'eyl* drawing near to the special place, **20** and *Mosheh*, and *Aharon* and all the company of the sons of *Yisra'eyl*, did to the ones of *Lewi* everything that ***YHWH*** directed *Mosheh* concerning the ones of *Lewi*, so the sons of *Yisra'eyl* did to them, **21** and the ones of *Lewi* purified themselves, and they washed their garments, and *Aharon* made a waving of them, waving to the face of ***YHWH***, and *Aharon* made a covering upon them to make them clean, **22** and after this, the ones of *Lewi* came to serve their service in the appointed tent, to the face of *Aharon* and to the faces of his sons, just as ***YHWH*** directed *Mosheh* upon the ones of *Lewi*, so they did to them, **23** and ***YHWH*** spoke to *Mosheh* saying, **24** this is what belongs to the ones of *Lewi*, from a son of five and twenty years and upward, he will come to muster the army in the service of the appointed tent, **25** and from a son of fifty years, he will turn back from the army of the service and he will not serve again, **26** and he will minister to his brothers in the appointed tent to safeguard the charge, and he will not serve a service, like this way you will do to the ones of *Lewi* concerning their custodies,

---

Chapter 9

1 and ***YHWH*** spoke to *Mosheh* in the wilderness of *Sinai*, in the second year of them going out from the land of *Mits'rayim*, in the first new moon, saying, **2** and the sons of *Yisra'eyl* will do the *Pesahh* in his appointed time. **3** On the fourteenth day, on this new moon, between the evenings[608], you will do him in his appointed time, like all his customs and like all his decisions, you will do him, **4** and *Mosheh* spoke to the sons of *Yisra'eyl* to do the *Pesahh*, **5** and they did do the *Pesahh* on the first, on the fourteenth day to the new moon, between the evenings, in the wilderness of *Sinai*, according to all that ***YHWH*** directed *Mosheh*, so the sons of *Yisra'eyl* did do, **6** and it came to pass, men which existed dirty by the soul of a human[609], and they were not able to do the *Pesahh* in that day, and they came near to the face of *Mosheh* and to the face of *Aharon* in that day, **7** and those men said to him, we are dirty by a soul of a human, why will we be taken away by not bringing near a donation of ***YHWH*** in his appointed time, in the midst of

---

607 That is a "plague."

608 As the word for "evening" is written in the double plural. This is literally translated as "between the 'two' evenings," but is of uncertain meaning. It may be the time between sunset and dark or between sunrise (as the word ערב literally means the "mixing" of light) and sunset. (also in verse 5)

609 This is referring to a person who becomes dirty due to being in contact with another person, probably a dead body.

the sons of *Yisra'eyl*, **8** and *Mosheh* said to them, stand, and I will hear what ***YHWH*** will direct for you, **9** and ***YHWH*** spoke to *Mosheh* saying, **10** speak to the sons of *Yisra'eyl* saying, any man that is dirty by the soul[610], or on a distant road, for you or for your generations, and he will make a *Pesahh* to ***YHWH***. **11** In the second new moon, on the fourteenth day, between the evenings[611], they will do him[612], with unleavened breads and bitter herbs they will eat him. **12** They will not leave anything from him until morning, and they will not crack a bone in him, according to all the customs of the *Pesahh* they will do him, **13** and the man who is clean and did not exist on a road, and he terminated to do the *Pesahh*, then that soul will be cut from her peoples, given that he did not bring near a donation of ***YHWH*** in his appointed time, that man will lift up his failure, **14** and, given that an immigrant will immigrate with you, and he will do a *Pesahh* to ***YHWH***, according to the custom of the *Pesahh*, and according to his decision, so he will do, one custom will exist for you and for an immigrant and for a native of the land, **15** and in the day the dwelling is made to rise, the cloud covered over the dwelling, to the tent of evidence, and in the evening what looks like the appearance of fire will exist upon the dwelling until morning. **16** So he will exist continually, the cloud will cover him over, and the appearance of fire by night, **17** and according to the cloud going up from upon the tent, after so, the sons of *Yisra'eyl* will journey, and in the area the cloud will dwell there, there the sons of *Yisra'eyl* will camp. **18** By the mouth of ***YHWH*** the sons of *Yisra'eyl* will journey, and by the mouth of ***YHWH*** they will camp, all the days that the cloud will dwell upon the dwelling they will camp, **19** and in the cloud prolonging upon the dwelling an abundance of days, then the sons of *Yisra'eyl* will safeguard the charge of ***YHWH***, and they will not journey, **20** and there it is, when the cloud will exist a number of days over the dwelling, according to the mouth of ***YHWH*** they will camp, and according to the mouth of ***YHWH*** they will journey, **21** and there it is, when the cloud will exist from evening until morning, and the cloud will be going up in the morning and they will journey, whether daytime or night, and the cloud will be going up and they will journey. **22** Whether two days or a new moon or days, in the prolonging of the cloud upon the dwelling, to dwell upon him, the sons of *Yisra'eyl* will camp, they will not journey, and in his going up they will journey. **23** According to the mouth of ***YHWH*** they will camp, and according to the mouth of ***YHWH*** they will journey, they will safeguard the charge of ***YHWH***, according to the mouth of ***YHWH*** by the hand of *Mosheh*,

---

[610] Probably meaning a "dead body."

[611] As the word for "evening" is written in the double plural, this is literally translated as "between the 'two' evenings," but is of uncertain meaning. It may be the time between sunset and dark or between sunrise (as the word ערב literally means the "mixing" of light) and sunset.

[612] The "him" is "*Pesahh*."

Chapter 10

1 and ***YHWH*** spoke to *Mosheh* saying, **2** make for you two silver straight
trumpets, beaten work you will make them, and they will exist for you for
the meeting of the company, and for the journeying with the camps, **3** and
they will blow in them, and all the company will meet with you at the
opening of the appointed tent, **4** and if with one[613] they will blow, and they
will meet with you, the captains, the heads of thousands of *Yisra'eyl*, **5** and
you will blow a signal, and the camps camping to the east will journey, **6** and
you will blow a second signal, and the camps camping to the south will
journey, a signal they will blow for their journeys, **7** and make the assembly
assemble, you will blow and you will not make a signal, **8** and the sons of
Aharon, the administrators, will blow in the straight trumpet, and they will
exist for you to a distant custom to your generations, **9** and, given that you
will come to battle in your land, against the enemy, the one pressing in on
you, and you will make a signal with the straight trumpet, and you will be
remembered to the face of ***YHWH*** your *Elohiym*, and you will be rescued
from your attackers, **10** and in the day of your rejoicing, and in your
appointed times, and in the heads of your new moons, then you will blow
with the straight trumpet over your ascension offerings and over your
sacrifices of offerings of restitution, and they will exist for you for a
remembrance to the face of your *Elohiym*, I am ***YHWH*** your *Elohiym*, **11** and
it will come to pass in the second year, in the second new moon, on the
twentieth of the new moon, the cloud went up from upon the dwelling of
the evidence, **12** and the sons of *Yisra'eyl* will journey in their journeys from
the wilderness of *Sinai*, and the cloud dwelt in the wilderness of *Paran*,
13 and they journeyed at the first according to the mouth of ***YHWH*** by the
hand of *Mosheh*, **14** and the banner of the camp of the sons of *Yehudah*
journeyed at the first, by their armies, and over his army is *Nahhshon* the
son of *Amiynadav*, **15** and over the army of the branch of the sons of
Yis'sas'khar is *Nataneyl* the son of *Tso'ar*, **16** and over the army of the
branch of the sons of *Zevulun* is *Eli'av* the son of *Hheylon*, **17** and the
dwelling will be brought down, and the sons of *Gershon* and the sons of
Merari will journey, lifting up the dwelling, **18** and the banner of the camp of
Re'uven will journey according to their armies, and over his army is *Elitsur*
the son of *Shedeyur*, **19** and over the army of the branch of the sons of
Shimon is *Shelumi'eyl* the son of *Tsurishaddai*, **20** and over the army of the
branch of the sons of *Gad* is *Elyasaph* the son of *De'u'eyl*, **21** and the ones of
Qehat will journey, lifting up the sanctuary, and they will make the dwelling
rise until their coming, **22** and the banner of the camp of the sons of
Ephrayim will journey according to their armies, and over his army is
Elishama the son of *Amihud*, **23** and over the army of the branch of the sons
of *Menasheh* is *Gamli'eyl* the son of *Pedatsur*, **24** and over the army of the

[613] That is one of the trumpets.

branch of the sons of *Binyamin* is *Avidan* the son of *Gidoni*, **25** and the
banner of the camp of the sons of *Dan* will journey, gathering[614] for all the
camps, according to their armies, and over his army is *Ahhi'ezer* the son of
Amishaddai, **26** and over the army of the branch of the sons of *Asher* is
Pagi'eyl the son of *Akhran*, **27** and over the army of the branch of the sons
of *Naphtali* is *Ahhira* the son of *Eynan*. **28** These are the journeys of the sons
of *Yisra'eyl* according to their armies, and they journeyed, **29** and *Mosheh*
said to *Hhovav* the son of *Re'u'eyl*, the one of *Mid'yan*, an in-law of *Mosheh*,
we are journeying to the area which ***YHWH*** said, I will give him to you, walk
with us and we will make it go well for you, given that ***YHWH*** had spoken
function over *Yisra'eyl*, **30** and he said to him, I will not walk, instead I will
walk to my land and to my kindred, **31** and he said, please do not leave us,
since you know our camping in the wilderness, and you will exist for us for
eyes, **32** and it will come to pass that you will walk with us, and it will come
to pass that function, which ***YHWH*** will make go well with us, and we will
make it go well with you, **33** and they journeyed from the hill of ***YHWH***, a
road of three days, and the box of the covenant of ***YHWH*** was journeying to
their face, a road of three days to scout for them an oasis, **34** and the cloud
of ***YHWH*** was upon them by day in their journeying from the camp, **35** and it
came to pass with the journeying of the box, and *Mosheh* said, ***YHWH*** will
rise and your attackers will scatter abroad, and your haters will flee from
your face, **36** and in her resting he will say, ***YHWH*** will return, a myriad of
thousands of *Yisra'eyl*,

Chapter 11

1 and the people were complaining of their dysfunction in the ears of
YHWH, and ***YHWH*** heard, and his nose flared up and the fire of ***YHWH***
burned in them and ate at the extremity of the camp, **2** and the people cried
out to *Mosheh*, and *Mosheh* pleaded to ***YHWH*** and the fire was drowned,
3 and he called the title of that area *Taveyrah*, given that the fire of ***YHWH***
burned in them, **4** and the mixed multitude that is in among him, they will
yearn a yearning, and they will turn back and they will weep, also the sons of
Yisra'eyl, and they said, who will make us eat flesh. **5** We remembered the
fish, which we freely ate in *Mits'rayim*, the cucumbers and the melons and
the herbage and the onions and the garlics, **6** and now our souls are dry,
without anything except for the *Mahn* before our eyes, **7** and the *Mahn*, he
is like coriander seed, and his eye[615] is like the eye of amber. **8** The people
went, and they picked it up, and they ground it in the millstones, or they
ground it to pieces with the mortar and pestle, and they boiled it in the
skillet, and they made him into baked breads, and his flavor is like the flavor

---

614 Possibly meaning they are the "rearguard" of the camp.
615 The word "eye"may mean "appearance" in this context.

of the fresh oil, **9** and with the coming down of the dew upon the camp at night, the *Mahn* will come down upon him, **10** and *Mosheh* heard the people weeping to his clans, each to the opening of his tent, and the nose of ***YHWH*** flared up greatly, and in the eyes of *Mosheh* it is dysfunctional, **11** and *Mosheh* said to ***YHWH***, why did you make dysfunction for your servant, and why did I not find beauty in your eyes, to place the load of all these people upon me. **12** Did I, I conceive all these people if I brought him forth, given that you said to me, lift him up in your bosom just as the securing one will lift up the suckling upon the ground that you swore to his fathers. **13** From where is there for me flesh to give to all these people, given that they weep upon me saying, give us flesh and we will eat. **14** I will not be able, I am alone, to lift up all this people, given that it is heavy for me, **15** and if you are doing it just like this to me, please kill me, kill if I found beauty in your eyes, and I will not see my dysfunction, **16** and ***YHWH*** said to *Mosheh*, gather for me seventy men from the bearded ones of *Yisra'eyl* that you know, given that they are bearded ones of the people, and his officers, and you will take them to the appointed tent and you will station themselves there with you, **17** and I will come down and I will speak with you there, and I will set aside from the wind that is upon you and I will place it upon them, and they will lift up with you the load of the people, and you will not lift it up yourself alone, **18** and to the people you will say, they will set themselves apart for tomorrow, and you will eat flesh, given that you wept in the ears of ***YHWH*** saying, who will make us eat flesh, given that it was functional for us in *Mits'rayim*, and ***YHWH*** will give to you flesh and you will eat. **19** You must not eat one day, and not two days, and not five days, and not ten days, and not twenty days. **20** Until a new moon of days, until which will come out from your nose, and he will exist for you for vomit, seeing as that you rejected ***YHWH***, who is among you, and you will weep to his face saying, why is this that we went out from *Mits'rayim*, **21** and *Mosheh* said, six hundred thousand on foot are the people, which I am among, and you, you said I will give flesh to them, and they will eat a new moon of days. **22** Will flocks and cattle be slain for them, then will he find for them, if all the fish of the sea will be gathered for them, then will he find for them, **23** and ***YHWH*** said to *Mosheh*, is the hand of ***YHWH*** severed, now you will see if my word will meet you or not, **24** and *Mosheh* went out and he spoke to the people the words of ***YHWH***, and he gathered the seventy men from the bearded ones of the people, and he made them stand all around the tent, **25** and ***YHWH*** went down in a cloud, and he spoke to him, and he caused the wind that was upon him to be set aside, and he gave it upon the seventy bearded men, and it came to pass it was like the wind rested upon them, and they announced, and they did not add, **26** and two men remained in the camp, the title of the one is *Eldad*, and the title of the second is *Meydad*, and the wind rested upon them, and they are in the writings, and they did not go out unto the tent, and they announced in the camp, **27** and the young man ran, and he told to *Mosheh*, and he said, *Eldad* and *Meydad* are announcing in the camp, **28** and *Yehoshu'a* the son of *Nun*, the minister of *Mosheh*, one from the youth, answered and he said, my lord *Mosheh*, restrict them, **29** and *Mosheh* said to him, are you being zealous for me, and who will give all the people of ***YHWH*** announcers, given that ***YHWH*** gave his wind upon them, **30** and *Mosheh* was gathered to the camp, he and the bearded ones of *Yisra'eyl*, **31** and the wind journeyed from ***YHWH***, and he swept quail from the sea, and he left them alone upon the camp, like the road of a day in this way all around the camp[616], and like two *ammahs*[617] upon the face of the land, **32** and the people rose all that day and all the night and all the day of the morrow, and they gathered the quail, and the one making the least gathered ten hhomers, and they spread for them, spreading all around the camp. **33** The flesh is still between their teeth before he will be cut, and the nose of ***YHWH*** flared up, and ***YHWH*** will attack within the people, a great abundant hitting, **34** and he called out the title of that area *Qivrot-Hata'awah*, given that there they buried the yearning people. **35** From *Qivrot-Hata'awah* the people journeyed to *Hhatsarot*, and they existed in *Hhatsarot*,

---

Chapter 12

1 and *Mir'yam* spoke, and *Aharon*, with *Mosheh*, on account of the woman of *Kush* which he took, given that he took a woman of *Kush*, **2** and they said, is it only with *Mosheh* ***YHWH*** will speak, is it also not with us ***YHWH*** will speak and hear, **3** and the man *Mosheh*, a very gentle one, more than all the humans which are upon the face of the ground, **4** and ***YHWH*** said suddenly to *Mosheh*, and to *Aharon*, and to *Mir'yam*, the three of you go out to the appointed tent, and the three of them went out, **5** and ***YHWH*** went down in a pillar of cloud, and he stood at the opening of the tent, and he called out *Aharon* and *Mir'yam*, and the two of them went out, **6** and he said, please hear my words, if your announcer of ***YHWH*** will exist, I will make myself known to him in an appearance, in the dream I will speak with him. **7** Not so my servant *Mosheh*, in all my house he is being secure. **8** Mouth to mouth I will speak with him, and by appearance, and not in riddles, and the resemblance of ***YHWH*** will make him stare, and why are you not afraid to speak with my servant, with *Mosheh*, **9** and the nose of ***YHWH*** flared up with them and he walked, **10** and the cloud turned aside from upon the tent, and look, *Mir'yam* is being infected like the snow, and *Aharon* turned to

---

616 "Like the road of a day in this way all around the camp" means "a day's journey" in every direction from the camp.
617 That is, "like a depth of two *ammahs*."

Mir'yam, and look, she is being infected, **11** and *Aharon* said to *Mosheh*, excuse me my lord, please do not set down upon us a failure, because we have been foolish, and because we failed. **12** Please do not let her exist like the dying, when in his going out from the bowels of his mother, and his flesh will be half eaten, **13** and *Mosheh* cried out to ***YHWH*** saying, mighty one, please heal, please for her, **14** and ***YHWH*** said to *Mosheh*, and her father surely spat in her face, will she not be shamed seven days, she will be shut seven days outside of the camp, and after she will be gathered, **15** and *Mir'yam* was shut outside of the camp seven days, and the people did not journey until *Mir'yam* will be gathered, **16** and after, the people journeyed from *Hhatsarot*, and they camped in the wilderness of *Paran*,

---

Chapter 13

1 and ***YHWH*** spoke to *Mosheh* saying, **2** send for you men, and they will scout the land of *Kena'an* which I am giving to the sons of *Yisra'eyl*, one of each man belonging to the branch of his fathers you will send, everyone a captain among them, **3** and *Mosheh* sent them from the wilderness of *Paran*, according to the mouth of ***YHWH***, all of them are men, heads of the sons of *Yisra'eyl* are they, **4** and these are their titles, belonging to the branch of *Re'uven*, *Shamu'a* the son of *Zakur*. **5** Belonging to the branch of *Shimon* is *Shaphat* the son of the one of *Hhoriy*. **6** Belonging to the branch of *Yehudah* is *Kaleyv* the son of *Yephunah*. **7** Belonging to the branch of *Yis'sas'khar* is *Yigal* the son of *Yoseph*. **8** Belonging to the branch of *Ephrayim* is *Hosheya* the son of *Nun*. **9** Belonging to the branch of *Binyamin* is *Palti* the son of *Raphu*. **10** Belonging to the branch of *Zevulun* is *Gad'di'eyl* the son of *Sodi*. **11** Belonging to the branch of *Yoseph*, belonging to the branch of *Menasheh* is *Gad'diy* the son of *Susiy*. **12** Belonging to the branch of *Dan* is *Ami'eyl* the son of *Gemali*. **13** Belonging to the branch of *Asher* is *Setur* the son of *Mika'eyl*. **14** Belonging to the branch of *Naphtali* is *Nahhbi* the son of *Waphsi*. **15** Belonging to the branch of *Gad* is *Ge'u'eyl* the son of *Makhi*. **16** These are the titles of the men which *Mosheh* sent to scout the land, and *Mosheh* called out to *Hosheya* the son *Nun*, *Yehoshu'a*, **17** and *Mosheh* sent them to scout the land of *Kena'an*, and he said to them, go up there in the south, and you will go up the hill, **18** and you will see the land, what she is, and the people settling upon her, is he forceful or frail, is he small amount or if abundant, **19** and what the land is, which he is settling in, is she functional or if dysfunctional, and what are the cities which he is settling in, in camps or if in fortifications[618], **20** and what the land is, is she

---

[618] Probably meaning "walls" as in "walled cities" in contrast to just camps.

fat or if lean, are there trees in her or if without, and strengthen yourself,
and you will take from the produce of the land, and the days are the days of
the first-fruits of the grapes, **21** and they went up and they scouted the land
from the wilderness of *Tsin* as far as *Rehhov*, to the coming of *Hhamat*,
22 and they went up in the south, and they came as far as *Hhevron*, and
there is *Ahhiman*, *Sheyshai* and *Talmai* of the *Anaq*, and *Hhevron* was built
seven years before *Tso'an* of *Mits'rayim*, **23** and they came as far as the wadi
of *Eshkol*, and they cut from there a vine and one cluster of grapes, and they
lifted him up on a branch by two, and including pomegranates and figs.
24 For that area was called wadi of *Eshkol*, on account of the cluster which
the sons of *Yisra'eyl* cut from there, **25** and they turned back from scouting
the land at the conclusion of forty days, **26** and they walked and they came
to *Mosheh* and to *Aharon* and to all the company of the sons of *Yisra'eyl*, to
the wilderness of *Paran*, unto *Qadesh*, and they returned to them word, and
they showed all the company the produce of the land, **27** and they
recounted to him, and they said, we came to the land that you sent us, and
also she is issuing fat and honey, and this is her produce. **28** In the end, given
that the people, the settlers, are strong in the land, and a great many of the
cities are fenced in, and also the boys of the *Anaq* we saw there. **29** *Amaleq*
is settling in the land of the south, and the ones of *Hhet*, and the ones of
Yevus, and the ones of *Emor* are settlers on the hill, and the ones of *Kena'an*
are settlers upon the sea and upon the hand[619] of the *Yarden*, **30** and *Kaleyv*
silenced the people for *Mosheh*, and he said, we will surely go up and we
will possess her, given that we are surely able for her, **31** and the men which
went up with him said, we are not able to go up to the people, given that he
is more forceful than us, **32** and they made a slander go out concerning the
land that they scouted for the sons of *Yisra'eyl* saying, the land that we
crossed over in to scout is a land that is eating her settlers, and all the
people that we saw in her midst were men of measurements, **33** and there
we saw the ones of *Nephilim*, the sons of *Anaq*, the ones of *Nephilim*, and
we existed in our eyes like grasshoppers, and so we existed in their eyes,

---

Chapter 14

1 and all the company lifted up, and they gave their voice, and the people
wept in that night, **2** and all the sons of *Yisra'eyl* murmured upon *Mosheh*
and upon *Aharon*, and all the company said to them, would that we died in
the land of *Mits'rayim* or in that wilderness would that we died, **3** and why is
YHWH making us come to this land to fall on the sword, our women and our
babies will exist for plunder, is it not functional for us to turn back unto
Mits'rayim, **4** and they said, each to his brother, we will make a head[620], and

---

619 Probably meaning on the "banks."
620 That is, a "leader."

we will turn back unto *Mits'rayim*, **5** and *Mosheh* fell, and *Aharon*, upon
their faces, to the face of all the assembly of the company of the sons of
Yisra'eyl, **6** and *Yehoshu'a* the son of *Nun*, and *Kaleyv* the son of *Yephunah*,
from the scouts of the land, tore their garments, **7** and they said to all the
company of the sons of *Yisra'eyl* saying, the land that we crossed over in to
scout is a very great functional land. **8** If ***YHWH*** is delighted in us, and he will
bring us to this land, then he will give to us the land that is issuing fat and
honey. **9** Surely you will not rebel with ***YHWH***, and you, you will not fear the
people of the land, given that our bread is them, their shadow[621] turned
aside from upon them, and ***YHWH*** is with us, you will not fear them, **10** and
all the company said to kill them by stoning with stones, and the armament
of ***YHWH*** appeared in the appointed tent to all the sons of *Yisra'eyl*, **11** and
YHWH said to *Mosheh*, how long will this people provoke me, and how long
will they not be secure in me with all the signs that I did inside him. **12** I will
hit him with an epidemic, and I will dispossess him, and I will make you for a
great nation and more numerous than him, **13** and *Mosheh* said to ***YHWH***,
then *Mits'rayim* will hear that you brought up in your strength this people
from inside them, **14** and they will say to the settlers of this land, they heard
that you, ***YHWH***, are inside this people, that eye to eye you, ***YHWH***, are
seen, and your cloud is standing upon them, and in the pillar of the cloud
you are walking before them in the daytime, and in a pillar fire at night,
15 and you will kill this people, like one man, and they will say, the nations
that heard your report are saying, **16** because ***YHWH*** is not able to bring this
people to the land that he swore to them, and he will slay them in the
wilderness, **17** and now, please, the strength of *Adonai* will magnify, just as
you spoke saying, **18** ***YHWH***, slow of nostrils[622] and abundant of kindness,
lifting up twistedness and offense, and he will not completely acquit,
registering the twistedness of the fathers upon the sons, upon the third
generation, and upon the fourth generation. **19** Please forgive the
twistedness of this people, according to the magnificence of your kindness,
and just as you lifted up this people from *Mits'rayim* and until this point,
20 and ***YHWH*** said, I forgave according to your word, **21** and yet I am living,
and the armament of ***YHWH*** will be filled in all the land, **22** given that all the
men seeing my armament, and my signs, which I did in *Mits'rayim* and in the
wilderness, and they will test me these ten times, and they did not hear my
voice. **23** If[623] they will see the land that I swore to their fathers, and all the
ones provoking me will not see her, **24** but my servant *Kaleyv*, consequently
another wind existed with him, and he filled[624] after me, then I will bring
him to the land that he came unto, and his seed will dispossess her, **25** and

---

621 That is, "protection," in the sense of being in the shade of a covering,

622 "Slow of nostrils" is an idiom meaning "patient."

623 The *Septuagint* has the word "not" and if this is the original reading, the first phrase of this sentence would read, "they will not see the land."

624 Probably meaning "follow."

the ones of *Amaleq*, and the ones of *Kena'an* are settling in the valley,
tomorrow turn and journey for yourself the wilderness, by the road of the
sea of reeds[625], **26** and ***YHWH*** spoke to *Mosheh* and to *Aharon*, saying, **27** for
how long for this dysfunctional company, which they are murmuring upon
me, the murmuring of the sons of *Yisra'eyl*, which they are murmuring upon
me, I heard. **28** Saying to them, a living one am I, declared ***YHWH***, therefore
just as you speak in my ears, so I will do to you. **29** In this wilderness your
corpses will fall, and all your registered ones, for all your numbered from a
son of twenty years and upward, which murmured upon me. **30** If[626] you,
you will come to the land that I lifted up by my hand for you to dwell in,
except *Kaleyv* the son of *Yephunah* and *Yehoshu'a* the son of *Nun*, **31** and
your babies, which you said will exist for plunder, and I will bring them, and
they will know the land that you rejected, **32** and your corpses, they will fall
in this wilderness, **33** and your sons will exist as feeders in the wilderness
forty years, and they will lift up your whoredom until the whole of your
corpses are in the wilderness. **34** By the number of days which you scouted
the land, forty days, a day for the year you will lift your twistedness of forty
years, and you will know my defiance. **35** I ***YHWH*** will speak, if I do not do
this to all of this dysfunctional company meeting with me in this wilderness,
they will be whole, and there they will die, **36** and the men that *Mosheh* sent
to scout the land, and they will turn back and all the company will be
murmuring upon him by bringing out a slander concerning the land, **37** and
the men bringing out the slander of the dysfunctional land will die in
pestilence to the face of ***YHWH***, **38** and *Yehoshu'a* the son of *Nun*, and
Kaleyv the son of *Yephunah*, will live from those men walking to scout the
land, **39** and *Mosheh* spoke these words to all the sons of *Yisra'eyl*, and the
people mourned greatly, **40** and they departed early in the morning, and
they went up to the head of the hill saying, look at us, and we went up to
the area which ***YHWH*** said, given that we failed, **41** and *Mosheh* said, why is
this, you are crossing over[627] the mouth[628] of ***YHWH***, and she, she[629] will not
prosper. **42** You will not go up, given that you are without ***YHWH*** inside you,
and you will not be smitten to the face of your attackers, **43** given that the

---

625 "Sea of reeds," or "*Yam Suph*," is usually mistranslated as "red sea."

626 The context implies that this Hebrew word should be "NOT," in which case, this phrase would read, "you, you will not come."

627 Meaning "violate" or "transgress."

628 Meaning "words."

629 What the "she" is referring to is uncertain as this would be referring to a feminine noun, which is not found in the text. However, the context implies it is the "crossing over the mouth of ***YHWH***," in which case one would expect the word "he," rather than "she." the Greek *Septuagint* reads "you will not prosper." the Hebrew word תִּצְלָח can mean "you will prosper," and if this is the correct reading then the preceding phrase "and she" would have to have originally been "and you."

ones of *Amaleq* and the ones of *Kena'an* are there to your faces, and you will fall by the sword, given that you turned back from after ***YHWH***, and ***YHWH*** will not exist with you, **44** and they presumed to go up to the head of the hill, and the box of the covenant of ***YHWH*** and *Mosheh* did not move away from the inside of the camp, **45** and the ones of *Amaleq* went down, and the ones of *Kena'an* settled in that hill, and they hit them, and they smashed them as far as the *Hharmah*,

Chapter 15

1 and ***YHWH*** spoke to *Mosheh* saying, **2** speak to the sons of *Yisra'eyl*, and you will say to them, given that you will come to the land of your settlings, which I am giving to you, **3** and you will do a fire offering to ***YHWH***, an ascension offering or a sacrifice to perform a vow, or with a freewill offering, or with your appointed things to make a sweet aroma to ***YHWH***, from the cattle or from the flocks, **4** and he will bring near the bringing near of his donation to ***YHWH***, a deposit of flour, one-tenth mixed in a fourth of the *hiyn* of oil, **5** and wine for the pouring, a fourth of the *hiyn*, you will place upon the ascension offering, or to the sacrifice for the one sheep. **6** Or for the buck you will do a deposit of flour, two-tenths mixed with the oil, a third of the *hiyn*, **7** and wine for the pouring, a third of the *hiyn*, you will bring near a sweet aroma to ***YHWH***, **8** and when you will do a son of the cattle, an ascension offering or a sacrifice, to perform a vow, or offerings of restitution for ***YHWH***, **9** and he will bring near with the son of the cattle, a deposit of three-tenths of flour mixed with a half *hiyn* of oil, **10** and you will bring near wine for the pouring, a half *hiyn*, a fire offering, a sweet aroma to ***YHWH***. **11** In this same way he will do to the one ox, or to the one buck, or to the ram among the sheep or the she-goats. **12** According to the number which you will do, in this same way you will do to another according to their number. **13** Every native will do these in the same way, to bring near a fire offering, a sweet aroma to ***YHWH***, **14** and, given that an immigrant will immigrate with you, or which is in your midst to your generations, and he will do a fire offering, a sweet aroma to ***YHWH***, just as you will do, so he will do. **15** The assembly, one custom for you and for the immigrating immigrant, a distant custom to your generations, like you, like the immigrant, he will exist to the face of ***YHWH***. **16** One teaching and one decision will exist for you and for the immigrating immigrant with you, **17** and ***YHWH*** spoke to *Mosheh* saying, **18** speak to the sons of *Yisra'eyl*, and you will say to them, in your coming to the land which I am bringing you unto there, **19** and it will come to pass in your eating from the bread of the land, you will make an offering rise up to ***YHWH***. **20** The summit of your bread meal of pierced bread you will make rise up as an offering, like the offering of the floor[630], so

[630] Probably the "threshing floor."

you will make her rise up. **21** From the summit of your bread meals you will give to ***YHWH***, an offering for your generations, **22** and, given that you will go astray and you will not do all these directives which ***YHWH*** spoke to *Mosheh*. **23** All which ***YHWH*** directed to you by the hand of *Mosheh*, from the day when ***YHWH*** directed and further to your generations, **24** and it will come to pass, if from the eyes of the company she has been done for an error, then all the company will do one bull, a son of the cattle for an ascension offering, for a sweet aroma to ***YHWH***, and his deposit and his pouring will be according to the decision, and one hairy goat of the she-goats for a failure, **25** and the administrator will make a covering upon all the company of the sons of *Yisra'eyl*, and he will be forgiven for them, given that that is an error, and they, they will bring their donation of a fire offering to ***YHWH***, and their failure to the face of ***YHWH*** concerning their error, **26** and he will be forgiven for all the company of the sons of *Yisra'eyl*, and for the immigrating immigrant in their midst, given that all the people are in error, **27** and if one soul will fail in error, then she will bring near a she-goat, a daughter of her year for a failure, **28** and the administrator will make a covering upon the erring soul, with the failing in the error to the face of ***YHWH***, to make a covering upon him, and he will be forgiven for him. **29** The native among the sons of *Yisra'eyl* and for the immigrating immigrant in their midst is one teaching, he[631] will exist to you, to the one doing an error, **30** and the soul that will do with a raised hand, from the native and from the immigrant, he[632] is taunting ***YHWH***, and that soul will be cut from inside her people, **31** given that he disdained the word of ***YHWH*** and he broke his directive, that soul will surely be cut, her twistedness is in her, **32** and the sons of *Yisra'eyl* existed in the wilderness, and they found a man collecting wood on the day of ceasing, **33** and the ones finding him collecting wood brought him near to *Mosheh* and to *Aharon* and to all the company, **34** and they made him rest in custody, given that it was not understood what will be done to him, **35** and ***YHWH*** said to *Mosheh*, he will certainly be killed, all the company will kill him by stoning with stones outside the camp, **36** and all the company made him go out outside of the camp, and they killed him with stones and he died, just as ***YHWH*** directed *Mosheh*, **37** and ***YHWH*** said to *Mosheh* saying, **38** speak to the sons of *Yisra'eyl*, and you will say to them, and they will make for themselves fringes upon the wings of their garments, and they will place upon the fringe of the wing a cord of blue, **39** and he will

---

[631] The context implies that the "he" is the "one teaching," but as the word "teaching" is a feminine noun, either the gender of this verb is incorrect and should be "she will exist" (in which case this would be translated as "one teaching will exist for you"), or it is referring to another unidentified masculine noun.

[632] This masculine pronoun is referring to the native and immigrant (masculine nouns). The feminine pronouns in this and the next verse are referring to the "soul" (feminine noun).

exist to you for fringe, and you will see him and you will remember all the
directives of ***YHWH***, and you will do them, and you will not scout after your
heart and after your eyes, which you are being a harlot after them. **40** So
that you will remember and you will do all my directives, and you will exist
as unique ones to your *Elohiym*. **41** I am ***YHWH*** your *Elohiym*, who brought
you out from the land of *Mits'rayim*, to exist for you for *Elohiym*, I am ***YHWH***
your *Elohiym*,

Chapter 16

1 and *Qorahh* the son of *Qehat* the son of *Lewi* took, and *Datan* and *Aviram*
the sons of *Eli'av*, and On the son of *Pelet*, the sons of *Re'uven*, **2** and they
rose to the face of *Mosheh* and the men of the sons of *Yisra'eyl*, two
hundred and fifty, captains of the witness, selected ones of the appointed,
men of the title, **3** and they were assembled over *Mosheh* and over *Aharon*,
and they said to them, it is abundant for you[633], given that all the company,
all of them, are unique ones, and in their midst is ***YHWH***, so why do you lift
yourself up over the assembly of ***YHWH***, **4** and *Mosheh* heard, and he fell
upon his face, **5** and he spoke to *Qorahh* and to all his company saying,
morning, and ***YHWH*** will make known who is for him and who is unique, and
he will bring him near and who he will choose with him, he will bring near to
him. **6** Do this, take for yourself firepans, *Qorahh* and all his company, **7** and
place in them fire, and they will place upon them incense smoke to the face
of ***YHWH*** tomorrow, and the man that ***YHWH*** will choose will exist, he is the
unique one, it is abundant for you sons of *Lewi*, **8** and *Mosheh* said to
Qorahh, sons of *Lewi* please hear. **9** Is it a small thing for you, given that
Elohiym caused you to be separated from the company of *Yisra'eyl*, to bring
you near to him to serve in the service of the dwelling of ***YHWH***, and to
stand to the face of the company to minister them, **10** and he brought you
near and all your brothers, the sons of *Lewi* with you, and you are searching
out also the administration. **11** Because of this, you and all your company,
the ones meeting against ***YHWH***, and *Aharon*, what of him, given that you
will be murmuring against him, **12** and *Mosheh* sent to call out to *Datan* and
to *Aviram*, the sons of *Eli'av*, and they said, we will not go up. **13** Is it a small
thing, given that you will bring us up from the land issuing fat and honey to
kill us in the wilderness, given that you are surely making yourself ruler over
us also. **14** Moreover, you did not bring us to a land issuing fat and honey, or
given to us an inheritance of the field and vineyard, will you pick out the
eyes of those men, we will not go up, **15** and for *Mosheh*, he greatly flared
up, and he said to ***YHWH***, do not turn to their deposit, I did not lift up one
donkey from them, and I will not make one from them be dysfunctional,

---

[633] This phrase has been interpreted to mean, "You have gone too far" or "Enough of you." (also in verse 7)

16 and *Mosheh* said to *Qorahh*, you and all your company, exist to the face of ***YHWH***, you and they and *Aharon* tomorrow, **17** and each will take his fire pan, and you will place upon them incense smoke, and you will bring it near to the face of ***YHWH*** each his fire pan, two hundred and fifty, and you and *Aharon*, each his fire pan, **18** and each will take his fire pan, and they will place upon them fire, and they will place upon them incense smoke, and they will stand at the opening of the appointed tent, and *Mosheh* and *Aharon*, **19** and *Qorahh* will assemble upon them all the company to the opening of the appointed tent, and the armament of ***YHWH*** appeared to all the company, **20** and ***YHWH*** spoke to *Mosheh* and to *Aharon* saying, **21** be separated from the midst of this company and I will finish them in just a moment, **22** and they fell upon their faces and they said, mighty one, *Elohiym* of the winds belonging to all flesh, the one man will fail, but you will snap upon all the company, **23** and ***YHWH*** spoke to *Mosheh* saying, **24** speak to the company saying, be brought up from all around to the dwelling of *Qorahh*, *Datan* and *Aviram*, **25** and *Mosheh* rose and he walked to *Datan* and *Aviram*, and the bearded ones of *Yisra'eyl* walked after him, **26** and he spoke to the company saying, turn aside please, from upon the tents of these lost men, and you will not touch anything that belongs to them, otherwise you will add to all their failure, **27** and they were brought up from upon the dwelling of *Qorahh*, *Datan* and *Aviram*, from all around, and *Datan* and *Aviram* went out standing up at the opening of their tents, and their women and their sons and their babies, **28** and *Mosheh* said, in this you will certainly know that ***YHWH*** sent me to do all these works, given that it is not from my heart. **29** If these will die like a death of all the humans, or the oversight of all the humans will be registered upon them, ***YHWH*** did not send me, **30** but if ***YHWH*** will shape a shape[634], and the ground will part her mouth, and she will swallow them and all that belongs to them, and the living ones will go down unto the underworld, then you will know that these men provoked ***YHWH***, **31** and it came to pass, as he finished to speak all these words, and the ground that was under them was cleaved open, **32** and the land opened her mouth and she swallowed them and their houses and all the humans that belonged to *Qorahh* and all the goods, **33** and they went down, and all the living ones that belonged to them, unto the underworld, and the land covered over upon them, and they perished from the midst of the assembly, **34** and all *Yisra'eyl* that was all around them, fled to their voice, given that they said, otherwise the land will swallow us, **35** and fire went out from ***YHWH*** and she[635] ate two hundred and fifty men bringing near the incense smoke,

---

[634] "Shape a shape" probably means "to bring about something great."

[635] Referring to the fire, a feminine word in Hebrew.

Chapter 17

1 (16:36) and ***YHWH*** spoke to *Mosheh* saying, **2 (16:37)** say to *Elazar* the son
of *Aharon* the administrator, and he raised up the fire pans from between
the cremating, and the fire dispersed further, given that they were set apart.
3 (16:38) With the fire pans of these ones of failure in their souls, and they
will make with them flat wires, metal plating for the altar, given that they
brought them near to the face of ***YHWH***, and they are set apart, and they
will exist for a sign for the sons of *Yisra'eyl*, **4 (16:39)** and *Elazar* the
administrator will take the copper fire pans, which were brought near the
cremating, and they will hammer them, metal plating for the altar. **5
(16:40)** A remembrance for the sons of *Yisra'eyl*, so that when a stranger
man, who is not from the seed of *Aharon*, will come near, to cause incense
smoke to burn to the face of ***YHWH***, and he will not exist like *Qorahh* and
like his company, just as ***YHWH*** spoke to him by the hand of *Mosheh*, **6
(16:41)** and all the company of the sons of *Yisra'eyl* were murmuring, on the
morrow, upon *Mosheh* and upon *Aharon* saying, you, you will kill the people
of ***YHWH***, **7 (16:42)** and it came to pass in the assembling of the company
upon *Mosheh* and upon *Aharon*, they turned to the appointed tent, and
look, the cloud covered him over, and the armament of ***YHWH*** appeared, **8
(16:43)** and *Mosheh* came, and *Aharon*, to the face of the appointed tent, **9
(16:44)** and ***YHWH*** spoke to *Mosheh* saying, **10 (16:45)** be lifted from the
midst of this company, and I will finish them in like a moment, and they fell
upon their faces, **11 (16:46)** and *Mosheh* said to *Aharon*, take the fire pan
and place upon her fire from the altar, and place incense smoke, and quickly
walk to the company and make restitution upon them, given that the
splinter[636] went out from before the face of ***YHWH***, the striking began, **12
(16:47)** and *Aharon* took, just as *Mosheh* spoke, and he ran to the midst of
the assembly, and look, the striking began in the people, and he placed the
incense smoke, and he made a covering upon the people, **13 (16:48)** and he
will stand between the dying and the living, and the pestilence was stopped,
14 (16:49) and the ones dying in the pestilence were fourteen thousand and
seven hundred, apart from the ones dying because of the word[637] of
Qorahh, **15 (16:50)** and *Aharon* turned back to *Mosheh*, to the opening of
the appointed tent, and the pestilence had been stopped, **16 (17:1)** and
YHWH spoke to *Mosheh* saying, **17 (17:2)** speak to the sons of *Yisra'eyl*, and
take from them every branch for the house of the father, from all their
captains belonging to their fathers, twelve branches, you will write each of
his titles upon his branch, **18 (17:3)** and the title of *Aharon* you will write
upon the branch of *Lewi*, given that one branch for the head of the house of
their fathers, **19 (17:4)** and you will make them rest in the appointed tent, to

[636] That is a "fierce anger" in the sense of smashing a piece of wood resulting in flying splinters of wood.

[637] This Hebrew word can also mean "matter."

the face of the evidence, where I will meet with you there, **20 (17:5)** and it will come to pass, the man which I will choose, his branch will burst out[638], and I will make the murmuring of the sons of *Yisra'eyl* subside from upon me, which they were murmuring upon you, **21 (17:6)** and *Mosheh* spoke to the sons of *Yisra'eyl*, and all their captains gave to him a branch for each captain belonging to the house of their fathers, twelve branches, and the branch of *Aharon* is in the midst of their branches, **22 (17:7)** and *Mosheh* made the branches rest to the face of ***YHWH*** in the tent of evidence, **23 (17:8)** and it came to pass on the morrow, and *Mosheh* came to the tent of evidence, and look, the branch of *Aharon* belonging to the house of *Lewi* burst out, and a bud went out, and the blossom bloomed, and he yielded an almond, **24 (17:9)** and *Mosheh* brought out all the branches from before the face of ***YHWH***, to all the sons of *Yisra'eyl*, and they saw and each took his branch, **25 (17:10)** and ***YHWH*** said to *Mosheh*, turn back the branch of *Aharon* to the face of the evidence for a charge, for a sign to the sons of rebelliousness, and you will bring an end to their murmurings from upon me and they will not die, **26 (17:11)** and *Mosheh* did just as ***YHWH*** directed him, so he did, **27 (17:12)** and the sons of *Yisra'eyl* said to *Mosheh* saying, though we expired, all of us perished, we perished. **28 (17:13)** All the ones inside, the ones inside the dwelling of ***YHWH*** will die, is it that the whole of us are to expire,

---

Chapter 18

1 and ***YHWH*** said to *Aharon*, you, and your sons and the house of your father with you, will lift up the twistedness of the sanctuary, and you, and your sons with you, will lift up the twistedness of your administration, **2** and also your brothers, the branch of *Lewi*, the staff of your father, bring near with you, and they will be joined upon you, and they will minister with you, and you and your sons with you, to the face of the tent of evidence, **3** and they will safeguard your charge and the charge of all the tent, only to the special utensils and to the altar they will not come near, and they will not die, also they, also you, **4** and they will be joined upon you, and they will safeguard the charge of the appointed tent, for all the service of the tent, and a stranger will not come near to you, **5** and you will safeguard the charge of the special place, and the charge of the altar, and he will not again splinter upon the sons of *Yisra'eyl*, **6** and I, look, I took your brothers, the ones of *Lewi*, from the midst of the sons of *Yisra'eyl*, for you, a contribution given to ***YHWH*** to serve the service of the appointed tent, **7** and you, and your sons with you, will safeguard your administration, for all the things of the altar and inside the tent curtain, and you will serve, a service of a contribution I will give your administration, and the stranger, the one inside,

---

[638] That is, "to bring forth buds."

will be killed, **8** and ***YHWH*** spoke to *Aharon*, and I, look, I gave to you a charge of my offerings, for all the special things of the sons of *Yisra'eyl*, to you I gave them to smear, and to your sons for a distant custom. **9** This will exist for you from the special of specials[639] from the fire, for all their donations, for all their deposits, and for all their failures, and for all their guilt, which they will return to me, that is the special of specials for you and for your sons. **10** In the special of specials you will eat him, every male will eat him, he will exist special for you, **11** and this is for you, the offering of their gift, for all the wavings of the sons of *Yisra'eyl*, for you I gave them, and to your sons and to your daughters with you, for a distant custom, every clean one in your house will eat him. **12** All the fat[640] of the fresh oil and all the fat of the fresh wine and cereal, their summit[641], which they will give to ***YHWH***, I gave them to you. **13** The first-fruits of all that is in their land, that they will bring to ***YHWH***, will exist for you, every clean one in your house will eat them. **14** Every assigned thing in *Yisra'eyl* will exist for you. **15 everyone** bursting the bowels among all the flesh, that they will bring near to ***YHWH***, among the humans and among the beasts, will exist for you, but you will surely ransom the firstborn of the human, and the firstborn of the dirty beast you will ransom, **16** and his ransomed one, from a son of a new moon, you will ransom with your arrangement, silver of five *sheqel*s with the special *sheqel*s, he is twenty *gerah*s. **17** Surely the firstborn of the ox or the firstborn of the sheep or the firstborn of the she-goat you will not ransom, they are special, you will sprinkle their blood upon the altar, you will burn their fat as incense, a fire offering for a sweet aroma to ***YHWH***, **18** and their flesh will exist for you, like the chest of the waving and like the right thigh, he will exist for you. **19** All the special offerings that the sons of *Yisra'eyl* will make rise up to ***YHWH***, I gave to you and to your sons and to your daughters with you for a distant custom, a covenant of salt, she is distant to the face of ***YHWH***, for you and for your seed with you. **20** and ***YHWH*** said to *Aharon*, you will not inherit in their land, and a distribution will not exist for you in their midst, I am your distribution and your inheritance in the midst of the sons of *Yisra'eyl*, **21** and to the sons of *Lewi*, look, I gave every tenth part in *Yisra'eyl* for an inheritance, for their service that they are serving the service of the appointed tent, **22** and the sons of *Yisra'eyl* will not come near again to the appointed tent to lift up a failure to die, **23** and that one of *Lewi* will serve the service of the appointed tent, and they, they will lift up their twistedness, a distant custom to your generations, and in the midst of the sons of *Yisra'eyl* they will not inherit an inheritance, **24** given that the tenth part of the sons of *Yisra'eyl*, an offering that they will make raise up to ***YHWH***, I gave to the ones of *Lewi* for an inheritance, therefore I said to

---

639 The phrase "special of specials" means a "very special thing, one or place." (also in verse 10)
640 Meaning the "best."
641 Meaning the "first."

them, in the midst of the sons of *Yisra'eyl* they will not inherit an inheritance, **25** and ***YHWH*** spoke to *Mosheh* saying, **26** and to the ones of *Lewi* you will speak and you will say to them, when you take from the sons of *Yisra'eyl* the tenth part, which I gave to you from them, for your inheritance, and you will raise up from him an offering of ***YHWH***, a tenth part from the tenth part, **27** and your offering will be considered to you like cereal from the floor[642], and like the fullness from the wine trough. **28** So you will raise up, also you, an offering of ***YHWH*** from all your tenth parts which you will take from the sons of *Yisra'eyl*, and you will give from him the offering of ***YHWH*** to *Aharon* the administrator. **29** From all your contributions, you will raise up every offering of ***YHWH*** from all his fat, from his sanctuary, **30** and you will say to them, in your raising up his fat from him, and he will be considered to the ones of *Lewi* like the production of the floor, and like the production of the wine trough, **31** and you will eat him in every place, you and your house, given that he is your wage for you for your service in the appointed tent, **32** and you will not lift up upon him a failure, in your raising up his fat from him, and the special things of the sons of *Yisra'eyl* you will not defile and you will not die,

---

Chapter 19

1 and ***YHWH*** spoke to *Mosheh* and to *Aharon* saying, **2** this is the custom of the teaching which ***YHWH*** directed saying, speak to the sons of *Yisra'eyl* and they will take for you a whole red cow which is without a blemish in her, which a yoke did not go up upon her, **3** and you will give her to *Elazar* the administrator, and he will bring her out to the outside of the camp, and he will slay her to his face, **4** and *Elazar* the administrator will take from her blood with his finger, and he will spatter from her blood seven times in front of the face of the appointed tent, **5** and he will cremate the cow to his eyes, her skin and her flesh and her blood with her dung he will cremate, **6** and the administrator will take a tree of cedar and hyssop and a scarlet kermes, and he will throw them into the midst of the cremating of the cow, **7** and the administrator will wash his garments, and he will bathe his flesh in the waters, and after he will come to the camp, and the administrator will be dirty until the evening, **8** and the one cremating her will wash his garments in the waters, and he will bathe his flesh in the waters, and he will be dirty until the evening, **9** and a clean man will gather the ash of the cow, and he will make it rest outside the camp in the clean area, and she will exist for the company of the sons of *Yisra'eyl* for a charge for the waters of removal, she is a failure, **10** and the one gathering the ash of the cow will wash his garments, and he will be dirty until the evening, and she will exist for the sons of *Yisra'eyl* and for the immigrant immigrating in their midst for a

---

[642] That is the "threshing floor." (also in verse 30)

distant custom. **11** The one touching with the dying of any human soul, then he will be dirty seven days. **12** He, he will purify himself with him in the third day, and in the seventh day he will be clean, but if he will not purify himself in the third day, then in the seventh day he will not be clean. **13** Anyone touching with the dying of a human soul which will die, and he did not purify himself, he dirtied the dwelling of ***YHWH***, and that soul will be cut from *Yisra'eyl*, given that the waters of removal were not sprinkled upon him, he will exist dirty yet again, his dirtiness is in him. **14** This is the teaching of a human that will die in a tent, anyone coming to the tent, and anyone that is in the tent, he will be dirty seven days, **15** and any utensil opened, which is without a bracelet of cord[643] upon him, he is dirty, **16** and all that will touch upon the face of the field with the one drilled of the sword, or with the dying, or with a human bone, or in the grave, he will be dirty seven days, **17** and for the dirty one, they will take from the dirt of the cremating of the failure, and he will place upon him the living waters into a vessel, **18** and a clean man will take hyssop and he will dip it in the waters, and he will spatter it upon the tent and upon all the utensils, and upon the souls which exist there, and upon the one touching the bone or one drilled or one dying or a grave, **19** and the clean one will spatter upon the dirty one on the third day, and on the seventh day, and he will purify him on the seventh day, and he will wash his garments, and he will bathe in the waters, and he will be clean in the evening, **20** and the man that will be dirty and does not purify himself, then that soul will be cut from the midst of the assembly, given that he made the sanctuary of ***YHWH*** dirty, the waters of removal was not sprinkled upon him, he is dirty, **21** and she will exist for them for a distant custom, and the one spattering the waters of removal will wash his garments and the one touching the waters of removal will be dirty until the evening, **22** and all which the dirty one will touch will be dirty, and the soul touching will be dirty until the evening,

---

Chapter 20

1 and the sons of *Yisra'eyl*, all the company, came to the wilderness of *Tsin*, in the first new moon, and the people settled in *Qadesh*, and there *Mir'yam* died, and she was buried there, **2** and waters did not exist for the company and they assembled upon *Mosheh* and upon *Aharon*, **3** and the people disputed with *Mosheh* and they said, saying, and would that we expired with the expiring of our brothers to the face of ***YHWH***, **4** and why did you bring the assembly of ***YHWH*** to this wilderness, to die there, we, and our cattle, **5** and why did you bring us up from *Mits'rayim*, to bring us to this area of dysfunction, not an area of seed and fig and grapevine and pomegranate and without waters to gulp, **6** and *Mosheh* came, and *Aharon*, from the face

---

[643] The "bracelet of cord" is some type of covering or lid for the container.

of the assembly to the opening of the appointed tent, and they fell upon their faces, and the armament of ***YHWH*** appeared to them, **7** and ***YHWH*** spoke to *Mosheh* saying, **8** take the branch and assemble the company, you and *Aharon* your brother, and you will speak to the cliff before their eyes, and he will give his waters, and you will bring to them the waters from the cliff, and you will make the company and their cattle drink, **9** and *Mosheh* took the branch from before the face of ***YHWH***, just as he directed him, **10** and *Mosheh* and *Aharon* made the assembly assemble to the face of the cliff, and he said to them, the ones disobeying, please hear, will we bring out to you waters from this cliff, **11** and *Mosheh* raised up his hand and he hit the cliff with his branch two times, and abundant waters came out, and the company and the cattle gulped, **12** and ***YHWH*** said to *Mosheh* and to *Aharon*, seeing as you did not support me, to make me set apart to the eyes of the sons of *Yisra'eyl*, because of this you will not bring this assembly to the land which I gave to them. **13** This is the waters of *Meriyvah*, because the sons of *Yisra'eyl* disputed with ***YHWH***, and he was set apart in them, **14** and *Mosheh* sent messengers from *Qadesh* to the king of *Edom*, in this way your brother *Yisra'eyl* said, you, you know all the trouble which has found us, **15** and our fathers went down unto *Mits'rayim*, and we settled in *Mits'rayim* an abundance of days, and *Mits'rayim* did dysfunction to us and to our fathers, **16** and we cried out to ***YHWH*** and he heard our voice, and he sent a messenger, and he brought us out from *Mits'rayim*, and look, we are in *Qadesh*, a city at the extremity of your border. **17** We will cross over please in your land, we will not cross over in the field or in the vineyard, and we will not gulp waters of a well, the road of the king we will walk, we will not extend the right hand, or the left hand[644], until when we cross over your border, **18** and *Edom* said to him, you will not cross over in me, otherwise, with the sword I will go out to meet you, **19** and the sons of *Yisra'eyl* said to him, in the highway we will go up, and if we gulp your waters, I, and my livestock, then I will give their value, only without a word, with my feet I will cross over[645], **20** and he said, you will not cross over, and *Edom* went out to meet him with many people and with a forceful hand, **21** and *Edom* refused to allow *Yisra'eyl* to cross over in his border, and *Yisra'eyl* extended from upon him[646], **22** and the sons of *Yisra'eyl*, all the company, journeyed from *Qadesh*, and they came to the hill of *Hor*, **23** and ***YHWH*** said to *Mosheh* and to *Aharon* in *Hor* the hill, upon the border of the land of *Edom*, saying, **24** *aharon* will be gathered to his people, given that he will not come to the land which I gave to the sons of *Yisra'eyl*, because you disobeyed my mouth toward the waters of *Meriyvah*. **25** Take *Aharon* and *Elazar* his son, and

---

644 The phrase "extend the right hand or left hand" means that they will not "go to the left or the right" of the road.

645 An alternate translation of this phrase may be, "I will cross over with nothing but my feet."

646 An alternate translation is "and *Yisra'eyl* turned away from him."

bring them up to *Hor* the hill, **26** and make *Aharon* strip off his garments, and you will make *Elazar* his son wear them, and *Aharon* will be gathered and he will die there, **27** and *Mosheh* did just as ***YHWH*** directed, and they went up to *Hor*, the hill, to the eyes of all the company, **28** and *Mosheh* made *Aharon* strip off his garments, and he made *Elazar* his son wear them, and *Aharon* died there on the head of the hill, and *Mosheh* went down, and *Elazar*, from the hill, **29** and all the company saw that *Aharon* expired, and all the house of *Yisra'eyl* wept for *Aharon* three days,

---

Chapter 21

1 and the one of *Kena'an*, the king of *Arad*, the one settling the south, heard that *Yisra'eyl* came by the road of the *Atariym*, and he fought with *Yisra'eyl*, and he captured from him captives, **2** and *Yisra'eyl* made a vow, a vow to ***YHWH***, and he said, if you will surely give this people in my hand, then I will assign their cities, **3** and ***YHWH*** heard the voice of *Yisra'eyl*, and he gave the one of *Kena'an*, and he made them assign their cities, and he called out the title of the area *Hharmah*, **4** and they journeyed from *Hor*, the hill, by the road of the sea of reeds[647], to go around the land of *Edom*, and the soul of the people was severed in the road, **5** and the people spoke with *Elohiym* and with *Mosheh*, why did you bring us up from *Mits'rayim* to die in the wilderness, given that there is no bread and no waters, and our soul loathed the lightweight bread, **6** and ***YHWH*** sent with the people the venomous serpents and they bit the people, and an abundance of people from *Yisra'eyl* died, **7** and the people came to *Mosheh* and they said, we failed, given that we spoke with ***YHWH*** and with you, intercede to ***YHWH*** and he will make the serpent turn aside from upon us, and *Mosheh* interceded on behalf of the people, **8** and ***YHWH*** said to *Mosheh*, make for you a venomous one and place him upon a standard, and it will come to pass, all the ones bitten and will see him and will live, **9** and *Mosheh* made a copper serpent, and he placed him upon the standard, and it came to pass, if the serpent bit a man, and he will stare toward the copper serpent, and he will live, **10** and the sons of *Yisra'eyl* journeyed, and they camped in *Ovot*, **11** and they journeyed from *Ovot*, and they camped in *Iyey-Ha'a'variym*, in the wilderness, which is upon the face of *Mo'av* from the sunrise of the sun. **12** From there they journeyed, and they camped in the wadi of *Zered*. **13** From there they journeyed, and they camped on the other side of *Arnon*, which is in the wilderness, the going out from the border of the ones of *Emor*, given that *Arnon* is the border of *Mo'av*, between *Mo'av* and the ones of *Emor*. **14** Therefore he will be said in the scroll of the battles of ***YHWH***, and *Waheyv* in *Suphah* and the wadis of *Arnon*, **15** and the banks of the wadis, which extend to the settling of *Ar*, and he will be leaning to the border of

---

647 "Sea of reeds," or "*Yam Suph*," is usually mistranslated as "red sea."

Mo'av, **16** and from there, unto *B'er,* that is the well which ***YHWH*** said to
Mosheh, gather the people and I will give to them waters. **17** At that time,
Yisra'eyl sang this song, go up well, answer her. **18** A well, nobles dug her
out, the willing ones of the people dug her, with the inscribers with their
staves, and from the wilderness, *Matanah,* **19** and from *Matanah,*
Nahhali'eyl, and from *Nahhali'eyl, Bamot,* **20** and from *Bamot,* the steep
valley, which is in the field of *Mo'av,* the head of the *Pisgah,* and she looks
down upon the face of the desolate wilderness, **21** and *Yisra'eyl* sent
messengers to *Sihhon,* king of the ones of *Emor,* saying, **22** I will cross over in
your land, we will not extend in the field or in the vineyard, we will not gulp
waters of the well, in the road of the king we will walk until when we cross
over your border, **23** and *Sihhon* did not give *Yisra'eyl* to cross over in his
border, and *Sihhon* gathered all his people, and he went out to meet
Yisra'eyl unto the wilderness, and he came unto *Yahats,* and he fought with
Yisra'eyl, **24** and *Yisra'eyl* attacked by the mouth of the sword, and he
possessed his land from *Arnon* as far as *Yaboq,* unto the sons of *Amon,* given
that the border of the sons of *Amon* was strong, **25** and *Yisra'eyl* took all
these cities, and *Yisra'eyl* settled in all the cities of the ones of *Emor* in
Hheshbon, and in all her daughters[648], **26** given that *Hheshbon,* she is the city
of *Sihhon,* the king of the ones of *Emor,* and he, he waged war with the first
king of *Mo'av,* and he took all his land from his hand as far as *Arnon.*
27 Therefore, the regulators will say, come *Hheshbon,* the city of *Sihhon* will
be built and will prepare itself, **28** given that fire went out from *Hheshbon,* a
glimmering from the metropolis of *Sihhon,* eating *Ar* of *Mo'av,* masters of
the platforms of *Arnon.* **29** Oh to you *Mo'av,* you perished, the people of
Kemosh, he gave his sons, the escaped ones, and his daughters, into
captivity to *Sihhon,* the king of the ones of *Emor,* **30** and we threw them,
Hheshbon perished as far as *Dibon,* and we made desolate as far as
Nophahh, which is as far as *Meydva,* **31** and *Yisra'eyl* settled in the land of
the ones of *Emor,* **32** and *Mosheh* sent to tread about *Yazeyr,* and they
trapped her daughters, and he possessed the ones of *Emor* which were
there, **33** and they turned and they went down the road of *Bashan,* and *Og*
the king of the *Bashan* went out to meet them, he and all his people, for the
battle of *Ed're'i,* **34** and ***YHWH*** said to *Mosheh,* you will not fear him, given
that in your hand I gave him and all his people and his land, and you will do
to him just as you did to *Sihhon* the king of the ones of *Emor,* which were
settling in *Hheshbon,* **35** and they attacked him and his sons and all his
people, until not one survivor of him remained, and they possessed his land,

---

[648] Hamlets of the larger cities were called "daughters" of the city. (also in verse 32)

Chapter 22

1 and the sons of *Yisra'eyl* journeyed, and they camped in the deserts of
Mo'av, from the other side to the *Yarden* of *Ye'rey'hho*, **2** and *Balaq* the son
of *Tsipor* saw all which *Yisra'eyl* did to the ones of *Emor*, **3** and *Mo'av*
immigrated from the face of the many people, given that he was abundant,
and *Mo'av* was loathed from the face of the sons of *Yisra'eyl*, **4** and *Mo'av*
said to the bearded ones of *Mid'yan*, now the assembly will lick all around
us, like the licking of the ox at the green field, and *Balaq* the son of *Tsipor*
was king to *Mo'av* in that appointed time, **5** and he sent messengers to
Bilam the son of *Be'or*, unto *Petor*, which is upon the river of the land of the
sons of his people, to call out to him saying, look, a people went out from
Mits'rayim, look, he covered over the eye of that land, settling in front of
me, **6** and now, please walk, spit upon for me this people, given that he is
more numerous than me, possibly I will be able, we will attack him, and I will
cast him out from the land, given that I know what you will exalt will be
exalted, and what you spit upon will be spit upon, **7** and the bearded ones of
Mo'av and the bearded ones of *Mid'yan* walked, and divinations were in
their hand, and they came to *Bilam*, and they spoke to him the words of
Balaq, **8** and he said to them, stay here the night, and I will bring you back
word, just as ***YHWH*** spoke to me, and the nobles of *Mo'av* settled with
Bilam, **9** and *Elohiym* came to *Bilam*, and he said, who are these men with
you, **10** and *Bilam* said to the *Elohiym*, *Balaq* the son of *Tsipor*, king of
Mo'av, he sent to me saying[649], **11** Look, the people are going out from
Mits'rayim, and he covered over the eye of that land, now walk, hollow him
out for me, possibly I will be able to fight him, and I will cast him out, **12** and
Elohiym said to *Bilam*, you will not walk with them, you will not spit upon
the people, given that he is exalted, **13** and *Bilam* rose in the morning, and
he said to the nobles of *Balaq*, walk to your land, given that ***YHWH*** refused
to give me to walk with you, **14** and the nobles of *Mo'av* rose, and they
came to *Balaq*, and they said, *Bilam* refused to walk with us, **15** and again
Balaq sent nobles, abundant ones and being heavier[650] than these, **16** and
they came to *Bilam*, and they said to him, in this way *Balaq* the son of *Tsipor*
said, please, you will not be withheld from walking to me, **17** given that I will
certainly honor you greatly, and everything that you will say to me, I will do,
and please walk, hollow out for me this people, **18** and *Bilam* answered, and
he said to the servants of *Balaq*, if *Balaq* will give to me the fillings of his
house, silver and gold, I will not be able to cross over the mouth of ***YHWH***
my *Elohiym* to do small or great, **19** and now, please, you settle in this[651] also
the night, and I will know what more ***YHWH*** is speaking with me, **20** and

---

[649] In the *Septuagint* this verse ends with the word "saying" and is probably missing from the Masoretic Hebrew text.

[650] Heavy in the sense of being honored and respected.

[651] This Hebrew word may mean "here."

Elohiym came to *Bilam* at night, and he said to him, if the men come to call out to you, rise, walk to them, but only the word which I will speak to you, him you will do, **21** and *Bilam* rose in the morning, and he saddled his she-donkey, and he walked with the nobles of *Mo'av*, **22** and the nose of *Elohiym* flared up, given that he is walking, and a messenger of ***YHWH*** stationed himself in the road as an opponent to him, and he is riding upon his she-donkey, and two of his young men with him, **23** and the she-donkey saw the messenger of ***YHWH*** standing up in the road, and his sword was pulled out in his hand, and the she-donkey extended from the road, and she walked in the field, and *Bilam* attacked the she-donkey to make her extend to the road, **24** and the messenger of ***YHWH*** stood in a narrow way of the vineyard, from this fence and from this fence, **25** and the she-donkey saw the messenger of ***YHWH***, and she squeezed to the wall, and she squeezed the foot of *Bilam* to the wall, and he again attacked her, **26** and the messenger of ***YHWH*** again crossed over, and he stood in the narrow area, which was without a road to extend to the right hand or left hand, **27** and the she-donkey saw the messenger of ***YHWH***, and she stretched out under *Bilam*, and *Bilam* flared up his nose, and he attacked the she-donkey with the rod, **28** and ***YHWH*** opened the mouth of the she-donkey, and she said to *Bilam*, what did I do to you, given that you attacked me these three times, **29** and *Bilam* said to the she-donkey, given that you abused me, would that there is a sword in my hand, for now I would kill you, **30** and the she-donkey said to *Bilam*, am I not your she-donkey which you ride upon your whole life until this day, am I in the habit to do to you in this way, and he said, no, **31** and ***YHWH*** removed the cover of the eyes of *Bilam* and he saw the messenger of ***YHWH*** standing up in the road and his sword pulled out in his hand, and he bowed the head and he bent himself down to his nostrils, **32** and the messenger of ***YHWH*** said to him, why did you attack this she-donkey three times, look, I, I went out to the opponent, given that the road was handed over to be face to face with me, **33** and the she-donkey saw me, and she extended to my face these three times, possibly she extended from my face, given that now I also killed you, and her sign caused me to live, **34** and *Bilam* said to the messenger of ***YHWH***, I failed, given that I did not know you were standing to meet me in the road, and now, if it is dysfunctional in your eyes, I will turn back to me, **35** and the messenger of ***YHWH*** said to *Bilam*, walk with the men, but in the end, the word which I will speak to you, you will speak, and *Bilam* walked with the nobles of *Balaq*, **36** and *Balaq* heard that *Bilam* came, and he went out to meet him at the city of *Mo'av*, which is upon the border of *Arnon*, which is in the extremity of the border, **37** and *Balaq* said to *Bilam*, did I surely not send to you to call you out, why did you not walk to me, will I indeed not be able to honor you, **38** and *Bilam* said to *Balaq*, look, I came to you, now, will I surely be able to speak anything, the word which *Elohiym* placed in my mouth, I will speak, **39** and *Bilam* walked with *Balaq*, and they came to the metropolis of *Hhutsot*, **40** and *Balaq* sacrificed cattle and flocks, and he sent to *Bilam*, and to the nobles which were with him, **41** and it came to pass in the morning, and *Balaq* took *Bilam*, and he made him go up to the platforms of *Ba'al*, and he saw from there the extremity of the people,

---

Chapter 23

1 and *Bilam* said to *Balaq*, build for me here seven altars, and prepare for me here seven bulls and seven bucks, **2** and *Balaq* did just as *Bilam* spoke, and *Balaq* brought up[652], and *Bilam*, a bull and a buck on the altar, **3** and *Bilam* said to *Balaq*, stand up upon your ascension offering, and I will walk, possibly ***YHWH*** will come to meet me, and the word that he will cause me to see, and I will tell it to you, and he walked to a bare place, **4** and *Elohiym* met *Bilam*, and he said to him, seven of the altars I arranged, and I brought up a bull and a buck on the altar, **5** and ***YHWH*** placed a word in the mouth of *Bilam*, and he said, turn back to *Balaq*, and in this way you will speak, **6** and he turned back to him, and look, he is standing upon his ascension offering and all the nobles of *Mo'av*, **7** and he lifted up his parable, and he said, from *Aram Balaq* the king of *Mo'av* guided me from the hills of the east, walking, spitting upon *Ya'aqov* for me, and walk, enrage *Yisra'eyl*. **8** What will I hollow out, the mighty one did not hollow her out, and what will I enrage, ***YHWH*** did not enrage, **9** given that from the head of the boulders I will see him, and from the knolls I will look upon him, though the people will dwell alone, and in the nations he will not think of himself. **10** Who reckoned the dirt of *Ya'aqov*, or number a fourth part of *Yisra'eyl*, my soul will die a death of the straight ones, and my end will exist like him, **11** and *Balaq* said to *Bilam*, what did you do to me, I took you to hollow out my attackers, and look, you certainly exalted, **12** and he answered, and he said, will I not safeguard to speak what ***YHWH*** placed in my mouth. **13** Please, walk with me to another area where you will see from there the far end, his extremity you will see, but all of him you will not see, then hollow him out for me from there, **14** and they took him to the field of *Tsophim*, to the head of the *Pisgah*, and he built seven altars, and he brought up a bull and a buck on the altar, **15** and he said to *Balaq*, stand yourself up in this way upon your ascension offering, and I, I will be met in this way, **16** and ***YHWH*** met with *Bilam*, and he placed a word in his mouth, and he said, turn back to *Balaq* and in this way you will speak, **17** and he came to him, and looked at him standing up upon his ascension offerings, and the nobles of *Mo'av* with him, and *Balaq* said to him, what did ***YHWH*** speak, **18** and he lifted up his parable, and he said, rise *Balaq* and hear, pay attention unto me, son of *Tsipor*. **19** The mighty one is not a man that he will lie, or a son of a human that he will comfort himself, did he say, and will he not do, and did he speak, and will he not make her rise. **20** Look, I took exalt, and he exalted, and I will

---

[652] That is, "offer up" as a sacrifice.

not make her turn back. **21** He did not stare at the barrenness in *Ya'aqov*,
and he did not see the labor in *Yisra'eyl*, ***YHWH*** his *Elohiym* is with him, and
the signal of the king is in him. **22** The mighty one brought them from
Mits'rayim, he is like the bulk of the rhinoceros, **23** given that there is no
prediction in *Ya'aqov* and there is no divination in *Yisra'eyl*, according to the
appointed time it will be said to *Ya'aqov* and to *Yisra'eyl*, what did the
mighty one do. **24** Though the people will rise like a lioness, he will lift
himself up like a lion, he will not lay down until he eats the prey, and the
blood of the drilled ones he will gulp, **25** and *Balaq* said to *Bilam*, you will
also certainly not hollow him out, you will also certainly not exalt him,
26 and *Bilam* answered and he said to *Balaq*, did I not speak to you saying,
all that ***YHWH*** spoke with him I will do, **27** and *Balaq* said to *Bilam*, please
walk, I will take you to the other area, possibly it will be straight in the eyes
of the *Elohiym*, and you will hollow him out for me from there, **28** and *Balaq*
took *Bilam*, the head[653] of *Pe'or*, the place looking down upon the face of
the desolate wilderness, **29** and *Bilam* said to *Balaq*, build for me in this
place seven altars, and prepare for me in this place seven bulls and seven
bucks, **30** and *Balaq* did just as *Bilam* said, and he brought up a bull and a
buck on the altar[654],

Chapter 24

1 and *Bilam* saw that it was functional in the eyes of ***YHWH*** to exalt *Yisra'eyl*,
and he did not walk as in times past to meet predictions, and he set his face
down to the wilderness, **2** and *Bilam* lifted up his eyes and he saw *Yisra'eyl*
dwelling to his staffs[655], and the wind of *Elohiym* existed upon him, **3** and he
lifted up his parable, and he said, *Bilam* the son of *Be'or* declared, and the
warrior of the wide open eye declared. **4** The one hearing the statements of
the mighty one declared, who had a vision of *Shaddai* perceived, falling, and
removed the cover of the eyes. **5** How functional is your tent *Ya'aqov*, your
dwellings *Yisra'eyl*. **6** Like the wadis they were extended, like the gardens
upon the river, like aloes ***YHWH*** planted, like cedars upon the waters. **7** He
will flow waters from his buckets, and his seed in abundant waters, and he
will raise up from *Agag* his king, and his empire will lift itself up. **8** The
mighty one brought him out from *Mits'rayim*, like the bulk of the rhinoceros
is to him, he will eat the nations of his narrow ones[656], and he will gnaw
their bones, and arrows will strike through. **9** He stooped, he laid down like a
lion, and like a lioness, who will raise him, the ones exalting you are exalted,

---

653 Meaning the top of mount *Pe'or*.
654 Probably meaning "on each altar."
655 Meaning that he saw them dwelling in their camps according to their standards.
656 That is, "his enemies."

and the ones spitting upon you are spat upon, **10** and *Balaq* flared up the nose to *Bilam*, and he clasped his palms, and *Balaq* said to *Bilam*, I called you out to hollow out my attackers, and look, you certainly exalted these three times, **11** and now, flee away for you to your area, I said, I will certainly honor you, and look, ***YHWH*** withheld you from the armament, **12** and *Bilam* said to *Balaq*, did I not also speak to your messengers which you sent to me saying, **13** if *Balaq* will give to me the filling of his house of silver and gold, I will not be able to cross over the mouth of ***YHWH*** to do function or dysfunction from my heart, what ***YHWH*** will speak, that I will speak, **14** and now, look at me walking to my people, walk, I will give you advice of what this people will do to your people in the end of days, **15** and he lifted up his parable, and he said, *Bilam* the son of *Be'or* declared, and the warrior of the wide open eye declared. **16** The one hearing the statements of the mighty one declared, and the one knowing the discernment of *Elyon*, the vision of *Shaddai* he will perceive, falling, and removed the cover of the eyes. **17** I will see him, but not now, I will look upon him, but not near, a star will take steps from *Ya'aqov*, and a staff will rise from *Yisra'eyl*, and he will strike through the edges of *Mo'av*, and he will toss out all the sons of *Shet*, **18** and *Edom* will exist as property, and *Se'iyr* will exist as the property of his attackers, and *Yisra'eyl* is doing a force, **19** and he went down from *Ya'aqov*, and he made the survivor[657] from the city perish, **20** and he saw *Amaleq*, and he lifted up his parable, and he said, the summit[658] of the nations is *Amaleq*, and his end is until the perishing[659], **21** and he saw the one of *Qayin*, and he lifted up his parable, and said, consistency is your settling, and placed in the cliff is your nest. **22** Instead *Qayin* will exist for burning, until when *Ashur* will capture you, **23** and he lifted up his parable, and he said, oh, who will live, the mighty one is placing him, **24** and nomads from the hand of the ones of *Kit*, and they afflicted *Ashur*, and they afflicted *Ever*, and also he until perishing, **25** and *Bilam* rose, and he walked, and he turned back to his area, and also *Balaq* walked to his road,

---

Chapter 25

1 and *Yisra'eyl* settled in the *Shitiym*, and the people began to be a harlot to the daughters of *Mo'av*, **2** and they called out to the people for sacrifices of their *Elohiym*, and the people ate, and they bent themselves down to their *Elohiym*, **3** and *Yisra'eyl* was fastened to *Ba'al-Pe'or* and ***YHWH*** flared up his nose with *Yisra'eyl*, **4** and ***YHWH*** said to *Mosheh*, take all the heads of the people and hang them before ***YHWH*** opposite the sun, and the flaming

---

657 While the Hebrew word is singular, context implies that it is plural.
658 Meaning the "beginning," "first," "best" or "most important."
659 The *Septuagint* has "his seed will perish."

wrath of the nose of ***YHWH*** was turned back from *Yisra'eyl*, **5** and *Mosheh* said to the deciding ones of *Yisra'eyl*, kill each of his men, the ones being fastened to *Ba'al-Pe'or*, **6** and look, a man from the sons of *Yisra'eyl* came, and he brought near to his brothers the one of *Mid'yan*[660] to the eyes of *Mosheh*, and to the eyes of all the company of the sons of *Yisra'eyl*, and they were weeping at the opening of the appointed tent, **7** and *Piynhhas* the son of *Elazar*, the son of *Aharon* the administrator, saw, and he rose from the midst of the company, and he took a spear in his hand, **8** and he came after the man of *Yisra'eyl* to the hut, and he pierced the two of them, the man of *Yisra'eyl*, and the woman through her stomach, and the pestilence was stopped from upon the sons of *Yisra'eyl*, **9** and the ones dying in the pestilence were twenty-four thousand, **10** and ***YHWH*** spoke to *Mosheh* saying, **11** piynhhas the son of *Elazar*, the son of *Aharon* the administrator, had turned back my fury from upon the sons of *Yisra'eyl*, with his being zealous of my zealousness in their midst, and I did not finish the sons of *Yisra'eyl* with my zealousness. **12** Because of this say, look at me, giving to him my covenant of completeness, **13** and she existed for him, and to his seed after him, a covenant of a distant administration, because he was being zealous for his *Elohiym*, and he covered over the sons of *Yisra'eyl*, **14** and the title of the man of *Yisra'eyl*, the one being attacked, who was attacked with the one of *Mid'yan*, was *Zimri* the son of *Salu*, the captain of the house of the father belonging to the one of *Shimon*, **15** and the title of the woman, the one being attacked, the one of *Mid'yan* was *Kazbi*, the daughter of *Tsur*, the head of the tribes of the father in *Mid'yan* is he, **16** and ***YHWH*** spoke to *Mosheh* saying, **17** press in to the ones of *Mid'yan*, and you will attack them, **18** given that they are pressing in on you with their craftiness, because they were crafty toward you in the matter of *Pe'or*, and in the matter of *Kazbi* the daughter of the captain of *Mid'yan*, their sister, the one being attacked in the day of the pestilence, in the matter of *Pe'or*, **19** and it came to pass after the pestilence,[661]

Chapter 26

1 and ***YHWH*** said to *Mosheh*, and to *Elazar* the son of *Aharon* the administrator, saying, **2** lift up the head of every company of the sons of *Yisra'eyl*, from a son of twenty years and upward, belonging to the house of their fathers, all are going out into the army of *Yisra'eyl*, **3** and *Mosheh* spoke, and *Elazar* the administrator, to them in the deserts of *Mo'av*, upon

---

660 The possessive suffix is feminine identifying this as a woman from *Mid'yan*. (also in verse 14)

661 In both the Aleppo and Leningrad Codices, this verse follows verse 18 and 26:1 begins a new paragraph. However, context implies that this verse should be part of 26:1, just as it is in the *Septuagint*.

the *Yarden* of *Ye'rey'hho*, saying, **4** from a son of twenty years and upward, just as ***YHWH*** directed *Mosheh* and the sons of *Yisra'eyl*, the ones going out from the land of *Mits'rayim*. **5** *Re'uven* the firstborn of *Yisra'eyl*, sons of *Re'uven*, *Hhanokh* is the clan of the ones of *Hhanokh*, belonging to *Palu* is the clan of the ones of *Palu*. **6** Belonging to *Hhetsron* is the clan of the ones of *Hhetsron*, belonging to *Karmi* is the clan of the *Karmi*. **7** These are the clans of the ones of *Re'uven*, and their registered ones existed forty-three thousand and seven hundred and thirty, **8** and the sons of *Palu*, *Eli'av*, **9** and the sons of *Eli'av*, *Nemu'eyl* and *Datan* and *Aviram*, this is *Datan* and *Aviram*, the ones called out of the company, who struggled with *Mosheh* and with *Aharon* in the company of *Qorahh*, in their struggling with ***YHWH***, **10** and the land opened her mouth and she swallowed them and *Qorahh*, in the death of the company, in the eating of the fire of the two hundred and fifty men, and they existed for a standard[662], **11** and the sons of *Qorahh* did not die. **12** The sons of *Shimon* to their clans, to *Nemu'eyl* is the clan of the ones of *Nemu'eyl*, to *Yamin* is the clan of the ones of *Yamin*, to *Yakhin* is the clan of the ones of *Yakhin*. **13** To *Zerahh* is the clan of the ones of *Zerahh*, to *Sha'ul* is the clan of the ones of *Sha'ul*. **14** These are the clans of the ones of *Shimon*, twenty-two thousand and two hundred. **15** The sons of *Gad* to their clans, to *Tsaphon* is the clan of the ones of *Tsaphon*, to *Hhagi* is the clan of the ones of *Hhagi*, to *Shuni* is the clan of the *Shuni*. **16** To *Azni* is the clan of the ones of *Azni*, to *Eyriy* is the clan of the ones of *Eyriy*. **17** To *Arwad* is the clan of the ones of *Arwad*, to *Areliy* is the clan of the ones of *Areliy*. **18** These are the clans of the sons of *Gad* to their registered ones, forty thousand and five hundred. **19** The sons of *Yehudah*, *Eyr* and *Onan*, and *Eyr* died, and *Onan* is in the land of *Kena'an*, **20** and the sons of *Yehudah* existed to their clans, to *Sheylah* is the clan of the ones of *Sheylah*, to *Perets* is the clan of the ones of *Perets*, to *Zerahh* is the clan of the ones of *Zerahh*, **21** and the sons of *Perets* existed, to *Hhetsron* is the clan of the ones of *Hhetsron*, to *Hhamul* is the clan of the ones of *Hhamul*. **22** These are the clans of *Yehudah* to their registered ones, seventy-six thousand and five hundred. **23** The sons of *Yis'sas'khar* to their clans, *Tola* is the clan of the ones of *Tola*, to *Pu'a* is the clan of the ones of *Pun*. **24** To *Yashuv* is the clan of the ones of *Yashuv*, to *Shimron* is the clan of the ones of *Shimron*. **25** These are the clans of *Yis'sas'khar* to their registered ones, sixty-four thousand and three hundred. **26** The sons of *Zevulun* to their clans, to *Sered* is the clan of the ones of *Sered*, to *Elyon* is the clan of the ones of *Elyon*, to *Yahh'le'el* is the clan of the ones of *Yahh'le'el*. **27** These are the clans of the ones of *Zevulun* to their registered ones, sixty thousand and five hundred. **28** The sons of *Yoseph* to their clans, *Menasheh* and *Ephrayim*. **29** The sons of *Menasheh*, to *Makhir* is the clan of the ones of *Makhir*, and *Makhir* brought forth *Gil'ad*, to *Gil'ad* is the clan of the ones of *Gil'ad*. **30** These are the sons of *Gil'ad*, *I'ezer* is the clan of the ones of *I'ezer*, to *Hheleq* is the clan of the ones of *Hheleq*, **31** and

---

[662] This may also be translated as, "for a sign."

Asri'eyl is the clan of the ones of the *Asri'eyl*, and *Shekhem* is the clan of the ones of *Shekhem*, **32** and *Shemida* is the clan of the ones of *Shemida*, and *Hheypher* is the clan of the ones of *Hheypher*, **33** and *Tselaph'hhad* is the son of *Hheypher*, sons did not exist to him, instead daughters, and the title of his daughters were *Tselaph'hhad*, *Mahhlah* and *No'ah*, *Hhaglah*, *Milkah* and *Tirtsah*. **34** These are the clans of *Menasheh* and their registered ones, fifty-two thousand and seven hundred. **35** These are the sons of *Ephrayim* to their clans, to *Shutelahh* is the clan of the ones of *Shutelahh*, to *Bekher* is the clan of the ones of *Bekher*, to *Tahhan* is the clan of the ones of *Tahhan*, **36** and these are the sons of *Shutelahh*, to *Eyran* is the clan of the ones of *Eyran*. **37** These are the clans of the sons of *Ephrayim* to their registered ones, thirty-two thousand and five hundred, these are the sons of *Yoseph* to their clans. **38** The sons of *Binyamin* to their clans, to *Bela* is the clan of the ones of *Bela*, to *Ashbeyl* is the clan of the ones of *Ashbeyl*, to *Ahhiram* is the clan of the ones of *Ahhiram*. **39** To *Sheshupham* is the clan of the ones of *Sheshupham*, to *Hhupham* is the clan of the ones of *Hhupham*, **40** and the sons of *Bela* were *Ard* and *Na'aman*, to *Ard*[663] is the clan of the ones of *Ard*, to *Na'aman* is the clan of the ones of *Na'amah*. **41** These are the sons of *Binyamin* to their clans and their registered ones, forty-five thousand and six hundred. **42** These are the sons of *Dan* to their clans, to *Shuhham* is the clan of the ones of the *Shuhham*, these are the clans of *Dan* to their clans. **43** All the clans of the ones of *Shuhham* to their registered ones, sixty-four thousand and four hundred. **44** The sons of *Asher* to their clans, to *Yimnah* is the clan of the *Yimnah*, to *Yishwiy* is the clan of the *Yishwiy*, to *Beri'ah* is the clan of the ones of *Beri'ah*. **45** To the sons of *Beri'ah*, to *Hhever* is the clan of the ones of *Hhever*, to *Malki'el* is the clan of the ones of *Malki'el*, **46** and the title of the daughter of *Asher* is *Serahh*. **47** These are the clans of the sons of *Asher* to their registered ones, fifty-three thousand and four hundred. **48** The sons of *Naphtali* to their clans, to *Yahhtse'el* is the clan of the ones of *Yahhtse'el*, to *Guni* is the clans of the ones of *Guni*. **49** To *Yetser* is the clan of the ones of *Yetser*, to *Shalem* is the clan of the ones of *Shalem*. **50** These are the clans of *Naphtali* to their clans, to their registered ones, forty-five thousand and four hundred. **51** These are the registered ones of the sons *Yisra'eyl*, six hundred thousand and a thousand, seven hundred and thirty, **52** and ***YHWH*** spoke to *Mosheh* saying, **53** to these the land will be distributed by inheritance, by the number of titles. **54** To the abundant[664] you will make his inheritance increase, and to the small amount[665] you will make his inheritance be less, each according to his being registered he is given his inheritance. **55** Only by a lot will the land be distributed, to the titles of the branch of their fathers they will inherit. **56** According to the lot

---

663 The phrase "to *Ard*" is accidentally omitted from the text, but is found in the *Septuagint*.

664 That is, "the many."

665 That is, "the few."

his inheritance will be distributed between the abundant and the small
amount[666], **57** and these are the registered ones of the ones of *Lewi* to their
clans, to *Gershon* is the clan of the ones of *Gershon*, to *Qehat* is the clan of
the ones of *Qehat*, to *Merari* is the clan of the ones of *Merari*. **58** These are
the clans of *Lewi*, the clan of the ones of *Liyvniy*, the clan of the ones of
Hhevron, the clan of the ones of *Mahh'liy*, the clan of the *Mushiy*, the clan of
the ones of the *Qorahh*, and *Qehat* had brought forth *Amram*, **59** and the
title of the woman of *Amram* is *Yokheved* the daughter of *Lewi*, the one who
was brought forth to *Lewi* in *Mits'rayim*, and she brought forth to *Amram*,
Aharon and *Mosheh* and *Mir'yam* their sister, **60** and *Nadav* and *Aviyhu*,
Elazar and *Iytamar* were brought forth to *Aharon*, **61** and *Nadav* died, and
Aviyhu, in their bringing near strange fire to the face of ***YHWH***, **62** and their
registered ones were twenty-three thousand, every male from a son of the
new moon and upward, given that did not register themselves in the midst
of the sons of *Yisra'eyl*, given that an inheritance was not given to them in
the midst of the sons of *Yisra'eyl*. **63** These are the registered ones of
Mosheh and *Elazar* the administrator, who registered the sons of *Yisra'eyl* in
the deserts of *Mo'av*, by the *Yarden* of *Ye'rey'hho*, **64** and in these a man did
not exist from the registered ones of *Mosheh* and *Aharon* the administrator,
which they registered the sons of *Yisra'eyl* in the wilderness of *Sinai*,
65 given that ***YHWH*** said to them they will surely die in the wilderness, and a
man was not left behind from them, except *Kaleyv* the son of *Yephunah* and
Yehoshu'a the son of *Nun*,

Chapter 27

1 and the daughters of *Tselaph'hhad*, the son of *Hheypher* the son of *Gil'ad*
the son of *Makhir* the son of *Menasheh*, belonging to the clan of *Menasheh*
the son of *Yoseph*, came near, and these are the titles of his daughters,
Mahhlah, *No'ah* and *Hhaglah* and *Milkah* and *Tirtsah*, **2** and they stood to
the face of *Mosheh* and to the face of *Elazar* the administrator, and to the
faces of the captains and all the company at the opening of the appointed
tent saying, **3** our father died in the wilderness, and he, he did not exist in
the midst of the company of the ones meeting upon ***YHWH*** in the company
of *Qorahh*, given that in his failure he died and sons did not exist for him.
4 Why will the title of our father be taken away from the midst of his clan,
given that he is without a son, give to us holdings in the midst of the
brothers of our father, **5** and *Mosheh* brought near their decision to the face
of ***YHWH***, **6** and ***YHWH*** said to *Mosheh* saying, **7** so the daughters of
Tselaph'hhad are speaking, you will surely give to them holdings of an
inheritance in the midst of the brothers of their father, and you will make
the inheritance of their father cross over to them, **8** and to the sons of

---

[666] That is, "between the many and the few."

Yisra'eyl, you will speak saying, a man that dies and he is without a son, then you will make his inheritance cross over to his daughter, **9** and if he is without a daughter, then you will give his inheritance to his brothers, **10** and if he is without brothers, then you will give his inheritance to the brothers of his father, **11** and if his father is without brothers, then you will give his inheritance to his kin, the one near to him from his clan, and he will possess her, and she will exist for the sons of *Yisra'eyl* for a custom of decision, just as ***YHWH*** directed *Mosheh*, **12** and ***YHWH*** said to *Mosheh*, go up to this hill of the ones of *Ever*[667], and see the land which I gave to the sons of *Yisra'eyl*, **13** and you will see her, and you will be gathered to your people, also you, just as *Aharon* your brother was gathered. **14** Just as you disobeyed my mouth in the wilderness of *Tsin*, in the contention of the company, to set me apart in the waters before their eyes, they are the waters of *Meriyvah* of *Qadesh*, the wilderness of *Tsin*, **15** and *Mosheh* spoke to ***YHWH*** saying, **16** ***YHWH*** the *Elohiym* of the winds to all the flesh will register a man over the company. **17** Who will go out to their faces, and who will come to their faces, and who will bring them out, and who will bring them, and the company of ***YHWH*** will not exist like the flocks which are without a feeding one[668], **18** and ***YHWH*** said to *Mosheh*, take for you *Yehoshu'a* the son of *Nun*, a man which has the wind in him, and you will support your hand upon him, **19** and you will make him stand to the face of *Elazar* the administrator, and to the faces of all the company, and you will direct him to their eyes, **20** and you will give from your splendor upon him so that all the company of the sons of *Yisra'eyl* will hear, **21** and to the face of *Elazar* the administrator he will stand, and he will inquire for him in the decision of the *Uriym* to the face of ***YHWH*** by his mouth they will go out, and by his mouth they will come, he and all the sons of *Yisra'eyl* with him, and all the company, **22** and *Mosheh* did just as ***YHWH*** directed him, and he took *Yehoshu'a* and he made him stand to the face of *Elazar* the administrator and to the face of all the company, **23** and he supported his hands upon him, and he directed him just as ***YHWH*** spoke by the hand of *Mosheh*,

---

Chapter 28

1 and ***YHWH*** spoke to *Mosheh* saying, **2** direct the sons of *Yisra'eyl*, and you will say to them, my donation, my bread, for my fire offerings, my sweet aroma, you will safeguard to bring near to me in his appointed time, **3** and you will say to them, this is the fire offering which you will bring near to ***YHWH***, two sheep, sons of a year, whole ones, daily, an ascension offering continually. **4** One of the sheep you will do in the morning and the second

---

[667] This could also be translated as "hill of Ivrim" (hill of the Hebrews).
[668] That is, a "shepherd."

sheep you will do between the evenings[669], **5** and a tenth of the *eyphah* of flour for a deposit, mixed in smashed oil of a fourth of the *hiyn*. **6** A continual ascension offering, the one done in the hill of *Sinai*, for a sweet aroma, a fire offering to ***YHWH***, **7** and his pouring of the fourth of the *hiyn* for the one sheep in the special place, make the pouring of liquor pour to ***YHWH***, **8** and the second sheep you will do between the evenings, like the morning deposit, and like his pouring you will do the fire offering, a sweet aroma to ***YHWH***, **9** and in the day of ceasing, two sheep, sons of a year, whole ones, and two-tenths of flour, a deposit of mixed in the oil and his pouring. **10** an ascension offering of ceasing in his ceasing, in addition to the continual ascension offering and her pouring, **11** and in the heads of your new moons you will bring near an ascension offering to ***YHWH***, two bulls, sons of the cattle, and one buck, seven sheep, sons of a year, whole ones, **12** and three-tenths of flour of the deposit mixed in the oil for the one bull, and two-tenths of flour of the deposit mixed in the oil for the one buck, **13** and one-tenth of flour of a deposit mixed in the oil for the one sheep, an ascension offering, a sweet aroma, a fire offering to ***YHWH***, **14** and their pourings is half the *hiyn* of wine, he will exist for the bull, and a third of the *hiyn* for the buck, and a fourth of the *hiyn* for the sheep, this is the ascension offering of the new moon in his new moon, for the new moons of the year, **15** and one hairy goat of the she-goats for failure to ***YHWH***, besides the continual ascension offering that will be done and his pouring, **16** and in the first new moon on the fourteenth day of the new moon is the *Pesahh* for ***YHWH***, **17** and on the fifteenth day of this new moon is a feast of seven days, unleavened breads will be eaten. **18** On the first day is a special meeting, you will not do any business of service, **19** and you will bring near a fire offering, an ascension offering, to ***YHWH***, two bulls of the sons of cattle, and one buck, and seven sheep, sons of a year, whole ones, they will exist for you, **20** and their deposit of flour mixed in the oil, three-tenths for the bull and two-tenths for the buck you will do. **21** One-tenth you will do for each sheep of the seven sheep, **22** and one hairy goat, a failure to cover over you. **23** Apart from the ascension offering of the morning, which is for the continual ascension offering, you will do these. **24** Like these you will do daily, seven days, the bread of the fire offering is a sweet aroma to ***YHWH***, besides the continual ascension offering that will be done, and his pouring, **25** and in the seventh day a special meeting will exist for you, you will not do any business of service, **26** and the day of the first-fruits, in your bringing near a new deposit for ***YHWH***, in your weeks, a special meeting will exist for you, you will not do any business of service, **27** and you will bring near an ascension offering for a sweet aroma to ***YHWH***, two bulls, sons of the cattle, one buck, seven sheep, sons of a year, **28** and their deposit of flour mixed in the oil, three-tenths for one bull and two-tenths for one buck. **29** One-tenth

---

[669] The phrase "between the evenings" is of uncertain meaning but may be the time between sunset and dark.

for each sheep of the seven sheep. **30** One hairy goat of the she-goats to
cover over you. **31** Apart from the continual ascension offering, and his
deposit you will do, whole ones will exist for you and their pourings,

---

Chapter 29

1 and in the seventh new moon, in the first of the new moon, a special
meeting will exist for you, you will not do any business of service, he will
exist as a day of a signal for you, **2** and you will do an ascension offering for a
sweet aroma to ***YHWH***, one bull, son of the cattle, one buck, seven sheep,
sons of a year, whole ones, **3** and their deposit of flour mixed in the oil,
three-tenths for the bull, two-tenths for the buck, **4** and one-tenth for each
sheep of the seven sheep, **5** and one hairy goat of the she-goats is the failure
to cover over you. **6** Apart from the ascension offering of the new moon and
her deposit, and the continual ascension offering and her deposit, and their
pourings like their decision, for a sweet aroma, a fire offering to ***YHWH***,
7 and on the tenth of this seventh new moon a special meeting will exist for
you, and you will afflict your souls, you will not do any business, **8** and you
will bring near an ascension offering to ***YHWH***, a sweet aroma, one bull, son
of the cattle, one buck, seven sheep, sons of a year, whole ones, they will
exist for you, **9** and their deposit of flour mixed in the oil, three-tenths for
the bull, two-tenths for the one buck. **10** One-tenth for each sheep of the
seven sheep. **11** One hairy goat of the she-goats is the failure, apart from the
failure of the atonements and continual ascension offerings, and her deposit
and their pourings, **12** and on the fifteenth day to the seventh new moon a
special meeting will exist for you, you will not do any business of service,
and you will hold a feast to ***YHWH*** seven days, **13** and you will bring near an
ascension offering, a fire offering, a sweet aroma to ***YHWH***, thirteen bulls,
sons of the cattle, two bucks, fourteen sheep, sons of a year, they will exist
as whole ones, **14** and their deposit of flour mixed in the oil, three-tenths for
each bull of the thirteen bulls, two-tenths to each buck of the two bucks,
15 and one-tenth for each sheep of the fourteen sheep, **16** and one hairy
goat of the she-goats is the failure apart from the continual ascension
offering, her deposit and her pouring, **17** and on the second day, twelve
bulls, sons of the cattle, two bucks, fourteen sheep, sons of a year, whole
ones, **18** and their deposit and their pouring for the bulls, for the bucks and
for the sheep, by their number, according to the decision, **19** and one hairy
goat of the she-goats for the failure apart from the continual ascension
offering and her deposit and their pourings, **20** and on the third day eleven
bulls, two bucks, fourteen sheep, sons of a year, whole ones, **21** and their
deposit and their pourings for the bulls, for the bucks and for the sheep, by
their number, according to the decision, **22** and one hairy goat is the failure,
apart from the continual ascension offering and her deposit and her
pouring, **23** and on the fourth day, ten bulls, two bucks, fourteen sheep,

sons of a year, whole ones. **24** Their deposit and their pourings for the bulls, for the bucks and for the sheep, by their number, according to the decision, **25** and one hairy goat of the she-goats is the failure apart from the continual ascension offering, her deposit and her pouring, **26** and on the fifth day, nine bulls, two bucks, fourteen sheep, sons of a year, whole ones. **27** Their deposit and their pourings for the bulls, for the bucks and for the sheep, by their number, according to the decision, **28** and one hairy goat is the failure apart from the continual ascension offering, her deposit and her pouring, **29** and on the sixth day, eight bulls, two bucks, fourteen sheep, sons of a year, whole ones. **30** Their deposit and their pourings for the bulls, for the bucks and for the sheep, by their number, according to the decision, **31** and one hairy goat is the failure apart from the continual ascension offering, her deposit and her pouring, **32** and on the seventh day, seven bulls, two bucks, fourteen sheep, sons of a year, whole ones. **33** Their deposit and their pourings for the bulls, for the bucks and for the sheep, by their number, according to the decision, **34** and one hairy goat is the failure apart from the continual ascension offering, her deposit and her pouring, **35** and on the eighth day a conference will exist for you, you will not do any business of service, **36** and you will bring near an ascension offering, a fire offering, a sweet aroma to ***YHWH***, one bull, one buck, seven sheep, sons of a year, whole ones. **37** Their deposit and their pourings for the bull, for the buck and for the sheep, by their number, according to the decision, **38** and one hairy goat is the failure, apart from the continual ascension offering, her deposit and her pouring, **39** and you will do these for ***YHWH*** in your appointed times, apart from your vows and your freewill offerings, for your ascension offerings, and for your deposits, and for your pourings, and for your offerings of restitution,

---

Chapter 30

1 (29:40) and *Mosheh* said to the sons of *Yisra'eyl*, according to all which ***YHWH*** directed *Mosheh*, **2 (30:1)** and *Mosheh* spoke to the heads of the branches of the sons of *Yisra'eyl* saying, this is the word which ***YHWH*** directed. **3 (30:2)** A man that will make a vow to ***YHWH***, or swear a swearing, to tie up a bond upon his soul, he will not defile his word, according to all the goings out from his mouth he will do, **4 (30:3)** and a woman that will make a vow to ***YHWH***, and she will tie up a bond in the house of her father in her young age, **5 (30:4)** and her father will hear her vow and her bond, which she tied up upon her soul, and her father will make her keep silent, and all her vows will rise, and every bond which she tied up upon her soul will rise, **6 (30:5)** and if her father forbid her in the day of his hearing, all her vows and her bonds which she tied up upon her soul will not rise, and ***YHWH*** will forgive her, given that her father forbid her, **7 (30:6)** and if she will exist for a man, and her vows upon her or the utterance of her lips which she tied up upon her soul, **8 (30:7)** and her man heard in the day of his hearing, and he will make her keep silent, then her vows will rise, and her bond which she tied up upon her soul will rise, **9 (30:8)** and if in the day her man hears, he will forbid her sign[670], and he will break her vow which was upon her, and the utterance of her lips which she tied up upon her soul, then ***YHWH*** will forgive her, **10 (30:9)** and the vow of a widow and the casted out ones, all which she tied up upon her soul will rise upon her, **11 (30:10)** and if in the house of her man, she made a vow, or she tied up a bond upon her soul in swearing, **12 (30:11)** and her man heard, and he kept silent at her, he did not forbid her, and all her vows will rise, and every bond which she tied up upon her soul will rise, **13 (30:12)** and if her man will certainly make them broken in the day of his hearing, everything going out of her lips concerning her vow and to the bond of her soul will not rise, and her man made them broken, and ***YHWH*** will forgive her. **14 (30:13)** Every vow and every swearing of a bond to afflict the soul, her man will make him rise or her man will make him broken, **15 (30:14)** but if her man will certainly keep silent at her, from day to day, then he will make all of her vows rise, or all of her bonds which are upon her, he will make them rise, given that he kept silent at her in the day of his hearing, **16 (30:15)** but if he will make them broken after his hearing, then he will lift up her twistedness. **17 (30:16)** These are the customs which ***YHWH*** directed *Mosheh* between a man to his woman, between a father to his daughter in her young age, in the house of her father,

---

Chapter 31

1 and ***YHWH*** spoke to *Mosheh* saying, **2** sons of *Yisra'eyl*, avenge a vengeance on the ones of *Mid'yan*, afterward you will be gathered to your people, **3** and *Mosheh* spoke to the people saying, arm from among you men for the army, and they will exist upon *Mid'yan* to give vengeance of ***YHWH*** in *Mid'yan*. **4** A thousand to the branch, a thousand to the branch, to every branch in *Yisra'eyl* you will send to the army, **5** and a thousand to the branch will be committed from the thousands of *Yisra'eyl*, twelve thousand armed ones of the army, **6** and *Mosheh* sent them, a thousand to the branch for the army, them and *Piynhhas* the son of *Elazar* the administrator, to the army, and special utensils and the straight trumpets of the signal in his hand, **7** and they mustered upon *Mid'yan*, just as ***YHWH*** directed *Mosheh*, and they killed every male, **8** and they killed the kings of *Mid'yan* in addition to their drilled ones, *Ewi* and *Reqem* and *Tsur* and *Hhur* and *Reva*, five kings of *Mid'yan*, and *Bilam* the son of *Be'or* they killed with the sword, **9** and the

---

[670] The meaning of "forbid her sign" is unknown. The Hebrew word אות (*ot*) means a "sign," but all other translations treat this as the word את (*et*) and translated this phrase simply as "forbid her."

sons of *Yisra'eyl* captured the women of *Mid'yan*, and their babies and all their beasts and all their livestock, and all their force they plundered, **10** and all of their cities with their settlers, and all their rows of tents, they cremated in the fire, **11** and they took all the spoils and all the booty of the humans and of the beasts, **12** and they brought to *Mosheh* and to *Elazar* the administrator, and to the company of the sons of *Yisra'eyl*, the captives and the booty and the spoils to the camp, to the deserts of *Mo'av*, which is by the *Yarden* of *Ye'rey'hho*, **13** and *Mosheh* and *Elazar* the administrator went out, and all the captains of the company, to meet them outside of the camp, **14** and *Mosheh* snapped upon the registered ones of the force, the nobles of thousands and nobles of hundreds, the ones coming from the army of the battle, **15** and *Mosheh* said to them, did you keep all the females alive. **16** Though they existed for the sons of *Yisra'eyl* by the word[671] of *Bilam* to commit transgression in ***YHWH*** concerning the word of *Pe'or*, and the pestilence existed in the company of ***YHWH***, **17** and now, kill all the males in the babies, and kill all the women knowing a man at the lying place of a male, **18** and all the babies with the women who did not know the lying place of a male, keep them alive for you, **19** and you, camp outside the camp seven days, all the ones killing a soul, all the ones touching a drilled one, you will purify yourself on the third day, and on the seventh day, you and your captives[672], **20** and every garment and every utensil of skin, and every work of she-goats[673], and every utensil of wood, you will purify, **21** and *Elazar* the administrator said to the men of the army, the ones coming to battle, this is the custom of the teaching that ***YHWH*** directed *Mosheh*. **22** Surely the gold and the silver, the copper, the iron, the tin and the lead. **23** Everything that will come in the fire, you will make cross over in the fire, and he will surely be clean, with the waters of removal he will be purified, and all that will not come in the fire you will make cross over in the waters, **24** and you will wash your garments on the seventh day and clean them, and after you will come to the camp, **25** and ***YHWH*** said to *Mosheh* saying, **26** lift up the head[674] of the booty of the captives among the human and the beast, you and *Elazar* the administrator and the heads of the fathers of the company, **27** and you will divide the booty between the ones seizing hold the battle, the ones going out to the army, and between all the company, **28** and you will raise up a tribute to ***YHWH*** from the men of the battle, the ones going out to the army, one soul from the five hundred, from the humans and from the cattle and from the donkeys and from the flocks. **29** From one half of them you will take, and you will give it to *Elazar* the administrator, an offering of ***YHWH***, **30** and from the one half of the sons of *Yisra'eyl* you will take one of the

---

671 This Hebrew word can also mean "matter."

672 This Hebrew noun is in the singular, but the context implies that it should be a plural.

673 "Work of goats" means "made of goat skins" or possible "goat hair."

674 "Lifting up the head" means "to count."

taken hold from the fifty, from the humans, from the cattle, from the donkeys and from the flocks, from every beast, and you will give them to the ones of *Lewi*, the ones safeguarding the charge of the dwelling of ***YHWH***,
31 and *Mosheh* did, and *Elazar* the administrator, just as ***YHWH*** directed *Mosheh*, **32** and the booty existed, the remainder of the plunder that the people of the army plundered, six hundred and seventy-five thousand flocks,
33 and seventy-two thousand cattle, **34** and sixty-one thousand donkeys,
35 and human souls from the women that did not know the lying place of a male, every soul is thirty-two thousand, **36** and half the spoils existed as a distribution of the ones going out in the army, the number of the flocks is three hundred thousand and thirty-seven thousand and five hundred,
37 and the tribute existed for ***YHWH***, from the flocks is six hundred and seventy-five, **38** and the cattle is thirty-six thousand, and their tribute to ***YHWH*** is seventy-two, **39** and the donkeys is thirty thousand and five hundred, and their tribute to ***YHWH*** is sixty-one, **40** and human souls is sixteen thousand, and their tribute to ***YHWH*** is thirty-two souls, **41** and *Mosheh* gave the tribute of offering of ***YHWH*** to *Elazar* the administrator, just as ***YHWH*** directed *Mosheh*, **42** and from one half of the sons of *Yisra'eyl* that *Mosheh* divided from the men of the ones mustering, **43** and half the spoils of the company existed from the flocks, three hundred thousand and thirty-seven thousand and five hundred, **44** and the cattle is thirty-six thousand, **45** and donkeys is thirty thousand and five hundred, **46** and human souls is sixteen thousand, **47** and *Mosheh* took from one half of the sons of *Yisra'eyl*, taking hold one from the fifty, from the humans and from the beasts, and he gave them to the ones of *Lewi*, safeguarding the charge of the dwelling of ***YHWH***, just as ***YHWH*** directed *Mosheh*, **48** and the registered ones that belonged to the thousands of the army, the nobles of the thousands and the nobles of the hundreds, came near to *Mosheh*,
49 and they said to *Mosheh*, your servants had lifted up the head[675] of men of the battle that are in our hand, and a man was not registered from us,
50 and we brought near a donation of ***YHWH***, each that found a utensil of gold, armlet and bracelet, ring, earing and arm band, to cover over our souls to the face of ***YHWH***, **51** and *Mosheh*, and *Elazar* the administrator, took the gold from them, every utensil of work, **52** and all the gold of the offering that they raised up to ***YHWH*** was sixteen thousand, seven hundred and fifty *sheqel*s, from the nobles of the thousands and from the nobles of the hundreds. **53** The men of the army had plundered each for himself, **54** and *Mosheh*, and *Elazar* the administrator, took the gold from the nobles of the thousands and the hundreds, and they brought him[676] to the appointed tent, a remembrance to the sons to the face of ***YHWH***,

---

[675] Meaning "counted."

[676] Referring to the "gold," a masculine singular noun.

Chapter 32

1 and abundant livestock existed to the sons of *Re'uven*, and to the sons of
Gad a numerous many, and they saw the land of *Yazeyr*, the land of *Gil'ad*,
and look, the area is an area of livestock, **2** and the sons of *Gad* and the sons
of *Re'uven* came, and they said to *Mosheh* and to *Elazar* the administrator
and to the captains of the company, saying, **3** atarot and *Dibon* and *Yazeyr*
and *Nimrah* and *Hheshbon* and *Elaley* and *Sevam* and *Nevo* and *Be'on*, **4** the
land that ***YHWH*** attacked to the face of the company of *Yisra'eyl*, she is a
land of livestock, and belonging to your servants is livestock, **5** and they said,
if we find beauty in your eyes, give this land to your servants for holdings, do
not make us cross over the *Yarden*, **6** and *Mosheh* said to the sons of *Gad*
and to the sons of *Re'uven*, will your brother come to the battle, and you,
you will settle here, **7** and why must you forbid the heart of the sons of
Yisra'eyl from crossing over to the land that ***YHWH*** gave to them. **8** In this
way your fathers did in sending me them from *Qadesh Barneya* to see the
land, **9** and they went up unto the wadi of *Eshkol*, and they saw the land,
and they forbid the heart of the sons of *Yisra'eyl* by not coming to the land
that ***YHWH*** gave to them, **10** and the nose of ***YHWH*** flared up in that day,
and he was swearing, saying, **11** if the men will see, the ones going up from
Mits'rayim, from a son of twenty years and upward, the ground which I
swore to *Avraham*, to *Yits'hhaq* and to *Ya'aqov*, given that they were not
filled after me.**12** Except *Kaleyv* the son of *Yephunah*, the one of *Qenaz*, and
Yehoshu'a the son of *Nun*, given that they were filled after ***YHWH***, **13** and
the nose of ***YHWH*** flared up in *Yisra'eyl*, and he made them stagger in the
wilderness forty years, until all the generation, the one doing the
dysfunction in the eyes of ***YHWH***, be whole, **14** and look, you rose in place of
your fathers, a great amount of men, failures, to consume again upon the
flaming wrath of the nose of ***YHWH*** to *Yisra'eyl*. **15** When you must turn
back from following after him, then he will continue to make him rest in the
wilderness, and you will certainly damage all this people,**16** and they drew
near to him, and they said, fences of flocks we will build for our livestock
here, and the cities for our babies, **17** and we, we will be armed, making
haste to the face of the sons of *Yisra'eyl*, until we bring them to their area,
and our babies settle in the cities of fortification, from the face of the
settlers of the land. **18** We will not turn back to our houses until the sons of
Yisra'eyl inherit each his inheritance, **19** given that we will not inherit with
them on the other side of the *Yarden* and further, given that our inheritance
came to us from the other side of the *Yarden* unto the sunrise, **20** and
Mosheh said to them, if you must do this word, if you will be armed to the
face of ***YHWH*** for the battle, **21** and all your armed ones will cross over the
Yarden, to the face of ***YHWH***, until he makes his attackers be dispossessed
from his face, **22** and the land was subdued to the face of ***YHWH***, and after
you will turn back, and you will exist as innocent ones from ***YHWH*** and from
Yisra'eyl, and this land will exist for you for holdings to the face of ***YHWH***,

23 and if you will not do so, look, you failed to ***YHWH***, and know that your failure will find you. **24** Build for you cities for your babies, and fences for your flocks, and what is going out from your mouth you will do, **25** and the sons of *Gad* and the sons of *Re'uven* said to *Mosheh* saying, your servants will do just as my lord directed. **26** Our babies, our women, our livestock, and all our beasts will exist there in the cities of the *Gil'ad*, **27** and your servants will cross over, all the armed ones of the army to the face of ***YHWH*** for the battle, just as my lord is speaking, **28** and *Mosheh* directed *Elazar* the administrator and *Yehoshu'a* the son of *Nun* and the heads of the fathers of the branches to the sons of *Yisra'eyl*, **29** and *Mosheh* said to them, if the sons of *Gad* and the sons of *Re'uven* will cross over with you at the *Yarden*, all the armed ones for the battle to the face of ***YHWH***, and the land will be subdued to your faces, and you will give to them the land of *Gil'ad* for holdings, **30** and if the armed ones will not cross over with you, then they will take hold[677] in your midst in the land of *Kena'an*, **31** and the sons of *Gad* and the sons of *Re'uven* answered saying, what ***YHWH*** spoke to your servants, so we will do. **32** We, we will cross over, armed ones to the face of ***YHWH***, to the land of *Kena'an*, and with us are the holdings of our inheritance on the other side of the *Yarden*, **33** and *Mosheh* gave to them, to the sons of *Gad*, and to the sons of *Re'uven*, and to the half staff[678] of *Menasheh* the son of *Yoseph*, the kingdom of *Sihhon*, the king of the ones of *Emor*, and the kingdom of *Og*, the king of the *Bashan*, the land belongs to her cities, in the borders, the cities of the land all around, **34** and the sons of *Gad* built *Dibon* and *Atarot* and *Aro'eyr*, **35** and *At'rot-Shophan* and *Yazeyr* and *Yagbahah*, **36** and *Beyt-Nimrah* and *Beyt-Haran*, the cities of fortification and the fences of the flocks, **37** and the sons of *Re'uven* built *Hheshbon* and *Elaley* and *Qiryatayim*, **38** and *Nevo* and *Ba'al-Me'on*, going around the title[679], and *Sevam*, and they called out by titles the titles of the cities which they built, **39** and the sons of *Makhir*, the son of *Menasheh*, walked unto *Gil'ad*, and they trapped her, and possessing the ones of *Emor* who were in her, **40** and *Mosheh* gave the *Gil'ad* to *Makhir*, the son of *Menasheh*, and he settled in her, **41** and *Ya'ir*, the son of *Menasheh*, walked, and he trapped their towns, and he called them *Hhawot*[680] *Ya'ir*, **42** and *Novahh* walked, and he trapped *Qenat* and her daughters[681], and he called her *Novahh* with his title.

---

677 Meaning that they will take possession of a land.

678 That is, "tribe."

679 Meaning that the title of these places has been "changed."

680 This Hebrew word could also be a noun meaning "towns of..."

681 The villages outside of the city are called the "daughters" of the city.

Chapter 33

1 These are the journeys of the sons of *Yisra'eyl* who went out from the land of *Mits'rayim*, by their armies, by the hand of *Mosheh* and *Aharon*, **2** and *Mosheh* wrote about their goings out, by their journeys, according to the mouth of ***YHWH***, and these are their journeys by their goings out, **3** and they journeyed from *Ra'meses* in the first new moon, on the fifteenth day of the first new moon, from the morrow of the *Pesahh* the sons of *Yisra'eyl* went out, by the hand raising, to the eyes of all *Mits'rayim*, **4** and *Mits'rayim* is burying those among them who were attacked by ***YHWH***, all the firstborn, and ***YHWH*** did judgments on their *Elohiym*, **5** and the sons of *Yisra'eyl* journeyed from *Ra'meses*, and they camped in *Suk'kot*, **6** and they journeyed from *Suk'kot*, and they camped in *Eytam*, which is in the extremity of the wilderness, **7** and they journeyed from *Eytam*, and they turned back upon *Piy-Hahhiyrot*, which is upon the face of *Ba'al-Tsephon*, and they camped to the face of *Migdol*, **8** and they journeyed from the face of *Hhirot*, and they crossed over in the midst of the sea, unto the wilderness, and they walked a road three days in the wilderness of *Eytam*, and they camped in *Marah*, **9** and they journeyed from *Marah*, and they came unto *Eyliym*, and in *Eyliym* were twelve eyes[682] of waters and seventy date palms, and they camped there, **10** and they journeyed from *Eyliym*, and they camped upon the sea of reeds[683], **11** and they journeyed from the sea of reeds, and they camped in the wilderness of *Sin*, **12** and they journeyed from the wilderness of *Sin*, and they camped in *Daphqah*, **13** and they journeyed from *Daphqah*, and they camped in *Alush*, **14** and they journeyed from *Alush*, and they camped in *Rephiydiym*, and waters did not exist there for the people to gulp, **15** and they journeyed from *Rephiydiym*, and they camped in the wilderness of *Sinai*, **16** and they journeyed from the wilderness of *Sinai*, and they camped in *Qivrot-Hata'awah*, **17** and they journeyed from *Qivrot-Hata'awah*, and they camped in *Hhatsarot*, **18** and they journeyed from *Hhatsarot*, and they camped in *Ritmah*, **19** and they journeyed from *Ritmah*, and they camped in *Rimon-Perets*, **20** and they journeyed from *Rimon-Perets*, and they camped in *Lavan*, **21** and they journeyed from *Livnah*, and they camped in *Risah*, **22** and they journeyed from *Risah*, and they camped in *Qe'hey'latah*, **23** and they journeyed from *Qe'hey'latah*, and they camped in the hill of *Shapher*, **24** and they journeyed from the hill of *Shapher*, and they camped in *Hharadah*, **25** and they journeyed from *Hharadah*, and they camped in *Maqheylot*, **26** and they journeyed from *Maqheylot*, and they camped in *Tahhat*, **27** and they journeyed from *Tahhat*, and they camped in *Terahh*, **28** and they journeyed from *Terahh*, and they camped in *Mitqah*, **29** and they journeyed from *Mitqah*, and they camped in *Hhashmonah*, **30** and they

---

[682] That is a "spring."

[683] "Sea of reeds," or "*Yam Suph*," is usually mistranslated as "red sea." (also in verse 11)

journeyed from *Hhashmonah*, and they camped in *Moseyrot*, **31** and they
journeyed from *Moseyrot*, and they camped in *B'ney-Ya'aqan*, **32** and they
journeyed from *B'ney-Ya'aqan*, and they camped in *Hhor-Hagidgad*, **33** and
they journeyed from *Hhor-Hagidgad*, and they camped in *Yatvatah*, **34** and
they journeyed from *Yatvatah*, and they camped in *Evronah*, **35** and they
journeyed from *Evronah*, and they camped in *Etsi'on-Gaver*, **36** and they
journeyed from *Etsi'on-Gaver*, and they camped in the wilderness of *Tsin*,
she is *Qadesh*, **37** and they journeyed from *Qadesh*, and they camped on *Hor*
the hill, in the extremity of the land of *Edom*, **38** and *Aharon* the
administrator went up to *Hor* the hill, by the mouth of ***YHWH***, and he died
there, in the fortieth year of the sons of *Yisra'eyl* going out from the land of
Mits'rayim, in the fifth new moon, on the first of the new moon, **39** and
Aharon was a son of twenty-three and a hundred years in his death on *Hor*
the hill, **40** and king *Arad* the *Kena'an* and the one settling in the south, in
the land of *Kena'an*, heard about the coming of the sons of *Yisra'eyl*, **41** and
they journeyed from *Hor* the hill, and they camped in *Tsalmonah*, **42** and
they journeyed from *Tsalmonah*, and they camped in *Punon*, **43** and they
journeyed from *Punon*, and they camped in *Ovot*, **44** and they journeyed
from *Ovot*, and they camped in *Iyey-Ha'a'variym*, in the border of *Mo'av*,
45 and they journeyed from *Iy'yim*, and they camped in *Dibon-Gad*, **46** and
they journeyed from *Dibon-Gad*, and they camped in *Almon-Divlatayim*,
47 and they journeyed from *Almon-Divlatayim* and they camped in the hills
of the ones of *Ever*[684], to the face of *Nevo*, **48** and they journeyed from the
hills of the ones of *Ever*, and they camped in the deserts of *Mo'av*, upon the
Yarden of *Ye'rey'hho*, **49** and they camped upon the *Yarden* from *Beyt-Hayishmot*, unto *Aveyl-Hashit'tim*, in the deserts of *Mo'av*, **50** and ***YHWH***
spoke to *Mosheh* in the deserts of *Mo'av*, upon the *Yarden* of *Ye'rey'hho*,
saying, **51** speak to the sons of *Yisra'eyl*, and you will say to them, given that
you are crossing over the *Yarden* to the land of *Kena'an*, **52** and you will
dispossess all the ones settling the land from your faces, and you will cause
to perish all their imagery, and all their cast images you will cause to perish,
and all their platforms you will destroy, **53** and you will dispossess the land,
and you will settle in her, given that to you I gave the land for possessing
her, **54** and you will inherit the land by lot for your clans, for an abundance
you will make his inheritance increase, and for the few you will make his
inheritance less, according to what the lot will go out to him unto there, he
will exist for him, according to the branch of your fathers you will inherit,
55 and if you will not dispossess the settlers in the land from your faces, and
it will come to pass that you will leave some behind, they will be
stickerbushes in your eyes, and prickly thorns in your sides, and they will

[684] Or, "the hills of the Ivrim" (the hills of the Hebrews). Also in verse 48.

press in on you upon the land which you are settling in, **56** and it will come to pass, just as I resembled[685] to do to them, I will do to you,

---

Chapter 34

1 and ***YHWH*** spoke to *Mosheh* saying, **2** direct the sons of *Yisra'eyl*, and you will say to them, given that you are coming to the land of *Kena'an*, this is the land that will fall on you as an inheritance, the land of *Kena'an* to her borders, **3** then the south edge will exist for you from the wilderness of *Tsin* upon the hands of *Edom*, and the south border from the extremity of the salt sea unto the east will exist for you, **4** and the border will go around to you from the south to the ascent of Aqrabiym[686], and he will cross over unto *Tsin*, and his goings will exist from the south to *Qadesh Barneya*, and he will go out to *Hhatsar-Adar*, and he will cross over unto *Atsmon*, **5** and the border will go around from *Atsmon* unto the wadi of *Mits'rayim*[687], and his goings will exist unto the sea, **6** and the border of the sea[688], the great sea, will exist for you, and this border will exist for you as the border of the sea, **7** and this will exist for you as the northern border, from the great sea you will point for you *Hor* the hill. **8** From *Hor* the hill you will point to the coming of *Hhamat*, and the goings of the border will exist unto *Tsedad*, **9** and the border went out unto Ziphron, and his goings will exist at *Hhatsar-Eynan*, this will exist for you as the northern border, **10** and you point out for yourself unto the eastern border, from *Hhatsar-Eynan* unto *Shepham*, **11** and the border will go down from *Shepham* to *Rivlah*, from the east to *Ayin*, and the border will go down, and he will wipe away[689] upon the shoulder of the sea of *Kineret* unto the east, **12** and the border will go down unto the *Yarden*, and his goings will exist at the sea of salt, this is the land that will exist for you by her borders all around, **13** and *Mosheh* directed the sons of *Yisra'eyl* saying, this is the land that you will inherit by lot, which ***YHWH*** directed to give to the nine branches and the half branch, **14** given that the branch of the sons of the ones of *Re'uven* belonging to the house of

---

685 This Hebrew word can mean to "compare" and in this context means to "do the same to one as the other."

686 The Hebrew phrase למעלה עקרבים can be translated as "to the ascent of Aqrabiym" or "to Ma'aleh Aqrabiym" (compare the Young's Literal Translation and the King James Version of this verse and Joshua 15:3).

687 The phrase נחלה מצרים could also be translated as "unto the inheritance of *Mits'rayim*" as the word נחלה can mean "unto the wadi" or "inheritance" (compare with verse 2).

688 This phrase can also be translated as "the western border" (also at the end of the verse), which is the (Mediterranean) Sea.

689 This Hebrew word may be written in error for another word that means "extends to" or "reaches."

their fathers will take, and the branch of the sons of the ones of *Gad* belonging to the house of their fathers and the half branch of *Menasheh* will take their inheritance. **15** Two of the branches and the half branch will take their inheritance from the other side of the *Yarden* of *Ye'rey'hho*, unto the east, unto the sunrise, **16** and ***YHWH*** spoke to *Mosheh* saying, **17** these are the titles of the men that will inherit the land for you, *Elazar* the administrator, and *Yehoshu'a* the son of *Nun*, **18** and one captain, one captain from a branch you will take to inherit the land, **19** and these are the titles of the men for the branch of *Yehudah*, *Kaleyv* the son of *Yephunah*, **20** and to the branch of the sons of *Shimon*, *Shemu'eyl* the son of *Amihud*. **21** To the branch of *Binyamin*, *Elidad* the son of *Kislon*, **22** and to the branch of the sons of *Dan*, captain *Buqi* the son of *Yagli*. **23** To the sons of *Yoseph*, to the branch of the sons of *Menasheh*, captain *Hhani'eyl* the son of *Ephod*, **24** and to the branch of the sons of *Ephrayim*, captain *Qemu'el* the son of *Shaphtan*, **25** and to the branch of the sons of *Zevulun*, captain *Elitsaphan* the son of Parnakh, **26** and to the branch of the sons of *Yis'sas'khar*, captain *Palti'eyl* the son of *Azan*, **27** and to the branch of the sons of *Asher*, captain *Ahhihud* the son of *Shelomiy*, **28** and to the branch of the sons of *Naphtali*, captain *Pedah'eyl* the son of *Amihud*. **29** These are who ***YHWH*** directed for an inheritance with the sons of *Yisra'eyl* in the land of *Kena'an*,

Chapter 35

1 and ***YHWH*** spoke to *Mosheh* in the deserts of *Mo'av*, upon the *Yarden* of *Ye'rey'hho*, saying, **2** direct the sons of *Yisra'eyl*, and they will give to the ones of *Lewi* from the inheritance of their holdings cities to settle, and open spaces for the cities all around them you will give to the ones of *Lewi*, **3** and the cities will exist for them to settle, and their open spaces will exist for their beasts and for their goods and for all their living ones, **4** and the open spaces of the cities that you will give to the ones of *Lewi* are from the wall of the city and unto the outside a thousand *ammah* all around, **5** and you will measure from the outside of the city unto the east edge two thousand *ammah*, and the south edge two thousand *ammah*, and the west edge two thousand *ammah*, and the north edge two thousand *ammah*, and the city in the midst of this, open spaces of the city will exist for them, **6** and the cities that you will give to the ones of *Lewi* are the six cities of asylum that you will give the murderers fleeing unto there, and beside them you will give forty-two cities. **7** All the cities that you will give to the ones of *Lewi* is forty-eight cities, them and their open spaces, **8** and the cities that you will give from the holdings of the sons of *Yisra'eyl*, from the abundant you will increase, and from the small you will give less, each according to his inheritance that they will inherit, he will give from his cities to the ones of *Lewi*, **9** and ***YHWH*** spoke to *Mosheh* saying, **10** speak to the sons of *Yisra'eyl*, and you will say to them, given that you are crossing over the *Yarden* unto the land of *Kena'an*,

11 and you will bring near[690] for you cities, cities of asylum will exist for you,
and a murderer attacking a soul in error will flee unto there, **12** and the
cities will exist for you for an asylum from the redeeming one, and the
murderer will not die until his standing to the face of the company for a
decision, **13** and the cities which you will give are six cities, they will exist for
you as an asylum. **14** You will give the three cities on the other side of the
Yarden, and three cities you will give in the land of *Kena'an*, they will exist as
cities of asylum. **15** For the sons of *Yisra'eyl* and for an immigrant and for the
settlers in their midst, these six cities will exist for an asylum for ones fleeing
unto there, all the attackers of a soul in error, **16** and if he will attack him
with a utensil of iron, and he dies, he is a murderer, the murderer will
certainly die, **17** and if with a stone of the hand that he will die by her, he
attacked him, and he died, he is a murderer, the murderer will certainly be
put to death. **18** Or with a utensil of wood of the hand that he will die by
him, he attacked him, and he died, he is a murderer, the murderer will
certainly be put to death. **19** He is the redeemer of blood, he will kill the
murderer in his reaching him, he will kill him, **20** and if in hate he pushes him
away[691], or he threw upon him in ambush and he died. **21** Or in hostility he
attacks him by his hand and he certainly dies, the attacker will be killed, he is
a murderer, the redeemer of blood will kill the murderer in his reaching him,
22 and if in an instant, without hostility, he pushed him away, or he threw
upon him any utensil without ambush. **23** Or with any stone that he will die
by her without seeing, and he caused to fall upon him and he died, and he is
not his attacker, and not searching out his dysfunction, **24** and the company
will decide between the attacker and the redeemer of blood according to
these decisions, **25** and the company will deliver the murderer from the
hand of the redeemer of blood, and the company will turn him back to the
city of his asylum where he fled unto there, and he will settle in her until the
death of the great administrator who was smeared with the special oil,
26 and if the murderer will ever go out the border of the city of his asylum
where he fled unto there, **27** and the redeemer of blood will find him
outside the border of the city of his asylum, and the redeemer of blood will
murder the murderer, he is without blood, **28** given that in the city of his
asylum he settled until the death of the great administrator, and after the
death of the great administrator the murderer will turn back to the land of
his holdings, **29** and these will exist for you for a custom of decision to your
generations in all your settlings. **30** Anyone attacking a soul by the mouth of
witnesses, he will murder the murderer, and one witness will not answer
over a soul to die, **31** and you will not take a covering for a soul of a
murderer that is lost to die[692], given that he will surely be killed, **32** and you

690 That is to "appoint."

691 This verb means to push, throw or cast, but in this context appears to mean to "stab." (also in verse 22)

692 "Lost to die" means "condemned to death."

will not take a covering[693] to flee to the city of his asylum, to turn back to settle in the land until the death of the administrator, **33** and you will not make the land filthy which you are in, given that the blood, he will make the land filthy, and to the land, he will be covered for the blood that is poured out in her, except by the blood of the one pouring him out, **34** and you will not make the land dirty which you are settling in, which I am dwelling in her midst, given that I am ***YHWH*** dwelling in the midst of the sons of *Yisra'eyl*,

Chapter 36

1 and the heads of the fathers to the clans of *Gil'ad*, the son of *Makhir*, the son of *Menasheh*, from the clans of the sons of *Yoseph*, will come near, and they will speak to the face of *Mosheh*, and to the face of the captains of the heads of the fathers to the sons of *Yisra'eyl*, **2** and they said, ***YHWH*** directed my lord to give the land by inheritance by lot to the sons of *Yisra'eyl*, and my lord was directed by ***YHWH*** to give the inheritance of *Tselaph'hhad* our brother to his daughters, **3** and they will exist for one from the sons of the staffs[694] of the sons of *Yisra'eyl* for women, and the inheritance will be taken away from the inheritance of our fathers, and he will add upon the inheritance of the branch which will exist for them, and from the lot of our inheritance will be taken away, **4** and if the jubilee will exist for the sons of *Yisra'eyl*, and the inheritance will be added upon the inheritance of the branch that will exist for them, and from the inheritance of the branch of our fathers, the inheritance will be taken away, **5** and *Mosheh* will direct the sons of *Yisra'eyl* according to the mouth of ***YHWH*** saying, so is the branch of the sons of *Yoseph* is speaking. **6** This is the word which ***YHWH*** directed to the daughters of *Tselaph'hhad* saying, for the function in their eyes they will exist for women, surely for the clan of the branch of their fathers they will exist for women, **7** and the inheritance will not go around to the sons of *Yisra'eyl* from branch to branch, given that each in the inheritance of the branch of his fathers the sons of *Yisra'eyl* will adhere, **8** and any daughter possessing an inheritance from the branches of the sons of *Yisra'eyl*, she will exist for a woman to one from the clan of her father so that the sons of *Yisra'eyl* will possess each the inheritance of his fathers, **9** and inheritance will not go around from a branch to another branch, given that each branch of the sons of *Yisra'eyl* will adhere to his inheritance. **10** Just as ***YHWH*** directed *Mosheh*, so the daughters of *Tselaph'hhad* did do, **11** and *Mahhlah*, *Tirtsah* and *Hhaglah* and *Milkah* and *No'ah*, the daughters of *Tselaph'hhad*, existed for the sons of their uncles for women. **12** From the clans of the sons of *Menasheh*, the son of *Yoseph*, existed for women, and the inheritance existed upon the branch of the clan of their father. **13** These are the

693 A "ransom."

694 That is a "branch" or "tribe."

directives and the decisions which ***YHWH*** directed by the hand of *Mosheh,* to the sons of *Yisra'eyl,* in the deserts of *Mo'av,* upon the *Yarden* of *Ye'rey'hho*.

The Book of Deuteronomy

Chapter 1

1 These are the words which *Mosheh* spoke to all of *Yisra'eyl* on the other side of the *Yarden*, in the wilderness, in the desert, in front of the reeds[695], between *Paran* and *Tophel*, and *Lavan* and *Hhatsarot* and *Di-Zahav*. **2** Eleven days from *Hhorev*, the road of the hill of *Se'iyr*, unto *Qadesh Barneya*, **3** and it came to pass in the fortieth year, in the eleventh new moon, on the first of the new moon, *Mosheh* spoke to the sons of *Yisra'eyl* all that ***YHWH*** directed him concerning them. **4** After his attacking *Sihhon* the king of the ones of *Emor*, which were settling in *Hheshbon*, and *Og* the king the *Bashan*, which were settling in *Ashterot* in *Ed're'i*. **5** On the other side of the *Yarden*, in the land of *Mo'av*, *Mosheh* agreed, he explained this teaching saying, **6** ***YHWH*** our *Elohiym* spoke to us in *Hhorev* saying, abundant for you settling on this hill[696]. **7** turn and journey for you, and come to the hill of the ones of *Emor*, and to all his dwellers, in the desert, on the hill, and in the lowland, and in the south, and in the shore of the sea, the land of the ones of *Kena'an* and the *Levanon*, unto the great river, the river of *Perat*. **8** See, I will give to your faces the land, come and possess the land which ***YHWH*** swore to your fathers, to *Avraham*, to *Yits'hhaq*, and to *Ya'aqov*, to give to them and to their seed after them, **9** and I will say to you in that appointed time saying, I will not be able to lift you up myself. **10** ***YHWH*** your *Elohiym* increased you, and look, today you are like the stars of the skies for an abundance. **11** ***YHWH*** *Elohiym* of your fathers will add upon you a thousand times like you, and he will exalt you just as he spoke to you. **12** How will I lift up by myself your heavy burden and your load and your dispute. **13** Provide for you skilled men, and understanding and knowing to your staffs[697], and I will place them as your heads, **14** and you answered me, and you said, the word which you spoke to do is functional, **15** and I took the heads of your staffs, skilled and knowing men, and I made them heads upon you, nobles of thousands, nobles of hundreds, and nobles of fifties[698], and nobles of tens[699], and officers for your staffs, **16** and I directed your deciders in that appointed time saying, hear between your brothers, and you decide

---

695 Probably referring to ים סוף (*Yam Suph*), the sea of reeds, but is usually mistranslated as "the Red Sea."

696 Meaning, "you have settled long enough on this hill."

697 That is, "tribes." (also in verse 15)

698 This Hebrew word means "fifty," but in context this word may be translated as "fifties."

699 This Hebrew word means "twenty," but in context this word may be translated as "tens."

steadfastly between a man and his brother and his immigrant. **17** You will not pay attention to faces in the decision, like the small, like the great, you must hear, you will not be afraid of the face of man, given that the decision belongs to *Elohiym*, and the word which will be hard for you, you must come near to me and I will hear him, **18** and I directed you in that appointed time all the words which you must do, **19** and we journeyed from *Hhorev*, and we walked all that great and fearful wilderness which you saw, the road of the hill of the ones *Emor*, just as ***YHWH*** our *Elohiym* directed us, and we came unto *Qadesh Barneya*, **20** and I said to you, you came unto the hill of the ones of *Emor*, which ***YHWH*** our *Elohiym* is giving to us. **21** See, ***YHWH*** your *Elohiym* placed to your face the land, go up, possess, just as ***YHWH*** *Elohiym* of your fathers spoke to you, you will not fear and you will not be shattered, **22** and you must come near to me, all of you, and you will say, let us send men to our face, and they will dig out for us the land, and they will turn back to us a word about the road which we will go up in, and the cities which we will come to, **23** and the word will do well in my eyes, and I will take from you twelve men, one man to a staff, **24** and they turned, and they went up unto the hill, and they came unto the wadi of *Eshkol*, and they treaded about her, **25** and they took in their hand from the produce of the land, and they brought down to us, and they turned back to us a word, and they said, functional is the land which ***YHWH*** our *Elohiym* is giving to us, **26** and you did not consent to go up, and you disobeyed the mouth of ***YHWH*** your *Elohiym*, **27** and you whispered in your tents, and you said, with hate ***YHWH*** brought us out from the land of *Mits'rayim* to give us into the hand of the ones of *Emor* to destroy us. **28** Wherever are we going up, our brothers melted away our heart saying, a great people and taller than us, great cities and fenced in to the skies, and also the sons of the ones of *Anaq* we saw there, **29** and I said to you, you must not be terrified, and you must not fear them. **30** ***YHWH*** your *Elohiym*, the one walking to your faces, he will fight for you, just as he did for you in *Mits'rayim* to your eyes, **31** and in the wilderness, which you saw, when ***YHWH*** your *Elohiym* lifted you up, just as a man lifts up his son, in all the roads which you walk until your coming unto this area, **32** and in this word you are not secure in ***YHWH*** your *Elohiym*. **33** The one walking to your faces in the road to scout for you the area for you to camp, in the fire of the night, to show you in the road which you will walk in, and in the cloud of daytime, **34** and ***YHWH*** heard the voice of your words, and he snapped and he swore, saying, **35** not[700] a man, with these men of this dysfunctional generation, see the functional land, which I swore to give to your fathers. **36** With the exception of *Kaleyv* the son of *Yephunah*, he, he will see her, and to him I will give the land which he took steps in, and to his sons, seeing that he was fully after ***YHWH***. **37** Also with

[700] While this Hebrew word means "if," context requires that it be translated as "not."

me ***YHWH*** snorted[701] on account of you, saying, you also will not come there. **38** *Yehoshu'a* the son of nun, the one standing to your face, he, he will come unto there, strengthen him, given that he, he will cause *Yisra'eyl* to inherit her, **39** and your babies, which you said is for plunder, will exist, and your sons, which do not know today function or dysfunction, they, they will come unto there, and to them I will give her, and they will possess her, **40** and you, turn for yourselves, and journey unto the wilderness, the road of the sea of reeds[702], **41** and you answered, and you said to me, we failed ***YHWH***, we, we will go up and we will be fighting, as all which ***YHWH*** our *Elohiym* directed us, and you girded up each his utensils of battle, and you readied to go up unto the hill, **42** and ***YHWH*** said to me, saying to them, you will not go up, and you will not fight, given that I am not inside you, and you will not be smitten to the face of your attackers, **43** and I spoke to you, and you did not hear, and you disobeyed the mouth of ***YHWH***, and you simmered, and you went up unto the hill, **44** and the ones of *Emor*, the settlers on that hill, went out to meet them, and they pursued you just as the bees will do, and they smashed you in *Se'iyr* unto *Hharmah*, **45** and you turned back, and you wept to the face of ***YHWH***, and ***YHWH*** did not hear your voice, and he did not pay attention to you, **46** and you settled in *Qadesh*, an abundance of days, according to the days which you settled,

Chapter 2

1 and we turned, and we journeyed unto the wilderness, the road of the sea of reeds, just as ***YHWH*** spoke to me, and we went around the hill of *Se'iyr*, an abundance of days, **2** and ***YHWH*** said to me, saying, **3** abundant[703] for you going around this hill, you turn unto the north, **4** and direct the people to say, you are crossing over into the border of your brothers, the sons of *Esaw*, the settlers in *Se'iyr*, and they feared you, and you were very safeguarded. **5** You will not meddle with them, given that I will not give to you from their land even a stepping of the palm of the foot, given that to *Esaw* I gave the hill of *Se'iyr* as a heritage. **6** You will exchange foodstuff from them with silver, and you will eat, and you will also dig waters from them with silver, and you will gulp, **7** given that ***YHWH*** your *Elohiym* will exalt you in all the work of your hand, he knows your walking in this great wilderness these forty years, ***YHWH*** your *Elohiym* is with you, you were not diminished a thing, **8** and we will cross over from our brothers, the sons of *Esaw*, the ones settling in *Se'iyr* from the road of the desert from *Eylot* and from *Etsi'on-Gaver*, and we will turn, and we will cross over the road of the

[701] Meaning that he was "angry."
[702] "Sea of reeds," or "*Yam Suph*," is usually mistranslated as "red sea." (also in verse 2:1)
[703] Meaning "it is sufficient."

wilderness of *Mo'av*, **9** and ***YHWH*** said to me, do not smack *Mo'av*, and do not meddle in their battles, given that I will not give to you from his land as a heritage, given that to the sons of *Lot* I have given *Ar* as a heritage. **10** The ones of *Eym* settled to the face of her, a great people, and abundant, and tall like the ones of *Anaq*. **11** The ones of *Rapha* will be considered, moreover they are like the ones of *Anaq*, and the ones of *Mo'av* call them the ones of *Eym*, **12** and the ones of *Hhor* settled in *Se'iyr* before, the sons of *Esaw* will possess them, and they will destroy them from their face, and they settled in their place, just as *Yisra'eyl* did to the land of their heritage which ***YHWH*** gave to them. **13** Now rise, and cross over for yourself the wadi of *Zered*, and we crossed over wadi of *Zered*, **14** and the days which we walked from *Qadesh Barneya*, until when we crossed over wadi of *Zered*, is thirty and eight years, until all the generation of the men of battle are whole from inside the camp, just as ***YHWH*** swore to them, **15** and also the hand of ***YHWH*** existed in them to confuse them from inside the camp until they be whole, **16** and it came to pass, just as all the men of battle were whole, dying in the inside of the people, **17** and ***YHWH*** spoke to me saying, **18** you are crossing over today, the border of *Mo'av*, *Ar*, **19** and you will come near the forefront of the sons of *Amon*, you will not smack them down, and you will not meddle in them, given that I will not give from the land of the sons of *Amon* to you as a heritage, given that to the sons of *Lot* I gave her as a heritage. **20** The land of the ones of *Rapha* is considered, moreover is she, the ones of *Rapha* settled in her before, and the ones of *Amon* called them the ones of *Zamzum*. **21** A great people, and abundant, and tall like the ones of *Anaq*, and ***YHWH*** will destroy them from their face, and they possessed them, and they settled in their place. **22** Just as he did to the sons of *Esaw*, the settlers in *Se'iyr*, when he destroyed the ones of *Hhor* from their face, and they possessed them, and they settled in their place until this day, **23** and the ones of *Awi*, the ones settling in *Hhatsariym* until *Ghaza*, the ones of *Kaphtor*, the ones going out from *Kaphtor*, and they destroyed them and they settled in their place. **24** Rise, journey, and cross over the wadi of *Arnon*, see, I gave in your hand *Sihhon*, the king of *Hheshbon*, the ones of *Emor*, and his land, begin, possess, and meddle yourself with him in battle. **25** This day I will begin to place the awe of you and the fearfulness of you upon the face of the people under all the skies when they hear a report of you, and they will shake and they will twist from your face, **26** and I sent messengers from the wilderness of *Qedeymot* to *Sihhon* the king of *Hheshbon*, words of completeness, saying, **27** I will cross over in your land, only on the road will I walk, I will not turn aside from the right hand or the left hand. **28** You will exchange for me foodstuff for silver, and I will eat, and waters for silver you will give me, and I will gulp, only I will cross over with my feet. **29** Just as the sons of *Esaw*, the ones settling in *Se'iyr*, and the ones of *Mo'av*, the ones settling in *Ar*, did to me, until when I will cross over the *Yarden*, to the land which ***YHWH*** our *Elohiym* is giving to us, **30** and *Sihhon*, the king of *Hheshbon* did not consent to let us to cross over in him, given that ***YHWH*** made his wind be hard, and he made his heart be strong, so as to give him in your hand like this day, **31** and ***YHWH*** said to me, see, I began to give to your face *Sihhon* and his land, begin, possess for the possessing of his land, **32** and *Sihhon* went out to meet us, he and all his people, for the battle unto *Yahats*, **33** and ***YHWH*** our *Elohiym* gave him to our face, and we attacked him and his sons and all his people, **34** and we trapped all his cities in that appointed time, and we perforated every city, the mortal men and the women and the babies, we did not let a survivor remain. **35** Only the beasts we plundered for us, and the spoils of the cities which we trapped. **36** From *Aro'eyr*, which is upon the lip of the wadi of *Arnon*, and the city which is by the wadi, and as far as *Gil'ad*, a metropolis did not exist which was lifted high from us, ***YHWH*** our *Elohiym* gave to our face the whole thing. **37** Only to the land of the sons of *Amon* you did not come near any hand[704] of the wadi of *Yaboq*, and the hill cities which ***YHWH*** our *Elohiym* directed,

---

Chapter 3

1 and we turned, and we went up the road of *Bashan*, and *Og* the king of *Bashan* went out to meet us, he and all his people for the battle at *Ed're'i*, **2** and ***YHWH*** said to me, you will not fear him, given that in your hands I gave him and all his people and his land, and you will do to him just as you did to *Sihhon* the king of the ones of *Emor*, which settled in *Hheshbon*, **3** and ***YHWH*** our *Elohiym* gave in our hands also *Og* the king of *Bashan* and all his people, and we attacked him until none of his survivors remained, **4** and we trapped all his cities in that appointed time, a metropolis did not exist which we did not take from them, sixty cities of all the region of *Argov*, the kingdom of *Og* in *Bashan*. **5** All these cities were fenced in with high ramparts, doors and wood bars, apart from the great many city villages, **6** and we perforated them just as we did to *Sihhon* the king of *Hheshbon*, perforating every city, mortal men, the women and the babies, **7** and every beast and spoil of the cities we plundered for us, **8** and we will take in that appointed time the land from the hand of the two kings of the ones of *Emor*, which is on the other side of the *Yarden* from the wadi of *Arnon*, unto the hill of *Hhermon*. **9** The ones of *Tsidon* called *Hhermon Siryon* and the ones of *Emor* called him *Senir*. **10** All the cities of the plain, and all *Gil'ad* and all *Bashan*, unto *Salkah* and *Ed're'i*, the cities of the kingdom of *Og* in *Bashan*, **11** given that only *Og* the king of *Bashan* remained from the remainder of the ones of *Rapha*, look, his mattress is a mattress of iron, is she not in *Ravah* of the sons of *Amon*, nine *ammah*s is her length and four *ammah*s is her width, with the *ammah* of man. **12** and this land we will possess in that appointed time, from *Aro'eyr* which is upon the wadi of *Arnon*, and half the hill of *Gil'ad* and his cities I gave to the ones of *Re'uven* and to the ones of

---

704 That is the "banks" of the wadi.

Gad, **13** and the remainder of *Gil'ad* and all *Bashan*, the kingdom of *Og*, I
gave to the half staff of *Menasheh* all the region of *Argov* to all that *Bashan*,
he will be called the land of the ones of *Rapha*. **14** *Ya'ir* the son of *Menasheh*
took all the region of *Argov* unto the border of the ones *Geshur* and the
ones of *Ma'akhah*, and he called them by his title, *Bashan Hhawot Ya'ir* until
this day, **15** and to *Makhir* I gave *Gil'ad*, **16** and to the ones of *Re'uven* and to
the ones of *Gad* I gave from *Gil'ad* and until the wadi of *Arnon*, the midst of
the wadi and the border and until *Yaboq* the wadi, the border of the sons of
Amon, **17** and the desert and the *Yarden* and the border from *Kineret*, and
unto the sea of the desert, the salt sea, under the ravines of *Pisgah* unto the
sunrise, **18** and I directed you in that appointed time saying, ***YHWH*** your
Elohiym gave to you this land to possess her, armed you will cross over to
the face of your brothers, the sons of *Yisra'eyl*, all the sons of the force.
19 Only your women and your babies and your livestock, I know that
livestock is abundant for you, they will settle in your cities which I gave to
you. **20** Until ***YHWH*** will give rest to your brothers, like you, and they will
also possess the land which ***YHWH*** your *Elohiym* is giving to them on the
other side of the *Yarden*, and each of you will turn back to his heritage which
I gave to you, **21** and *Yehoshu'a* I directed in that appointed time, saying,
your eyes are seeing all which ***YHWH*** your *Elohiym* did to these two kings, so
YHWH will do to all the kingdoms which you are crossing over unto there.
22 You will not fear them, given that ***YHWH*** your *Elohiym*, he is fighting for
you, **23** and I beseeched ***YHWH*** in that appointed time, saying, **24** *adonai*
YHWH, you, you began to show your servant your magnificence, and your
forceful hand, for who is a mighty one in the skies and in the land, who will
do like your works and like your bravery. **25** Please, I will cross over and I will
see the functional land that is on the other side of the *Yarden*, this
functional hill, and the *Levanon*, **26** and ***YHWH*** crossed himself over with me
on account of you, and he did not listen to me, and ***YHWH*** said to me,
abundant are you, you will not again speak to me again with this word.
27 Go up to the head of the *Pisgah* and lift up your eyes unto the sea, and
unto the north, and unto the south, and unto the sunrise, and see with your
eyes, given that you will not cross over this *Yarden*, **28** and direct *Yehoshu'a*,
and strengthen him and make him strong, given that he will cross over to
the face of this people, and he will make them inherit the land which you
will see, **29** and we will settle in the steep valley, in front of *Beyt-Pe'or*,

---

Chapter 4

1 and now *Yisra'eyl* listen to the customs and to the decisions which I am
teaching you to do so that you will live, and you will come and you will
possess the land which ***YHWH***, the *Elohiym* of your fathers, is giving to you.
2 You will not add upon the word, which I am directing you, and you will not
take away from him, safeguard the directives of ***YHWH*** your *Elohiym*, which

I am directing you. **3** Your eyes are seeing what ***YHWH*** did in *Ba'al Pe'or*, given that every man that walked after *Ba'al Pe'or* ***YHWH*** your *Elohiym* destroyed from inside you, **4** and you, the fasteners with ***YHWH*** your *Elohiym*, all of you are living today. **5** See, I taught you customs and decisions, just as ***YHWH*** my *Elohiym* did, so it is inside the land when you come unto there to possess her, **6** and you will safeguard, and you will do, given that she is your skill and your understanding to the eyes of the peoples, who must hear all these customs, and they will say, only a people skilled and with understanding is this great nation, **7** given that who is a great nation that belongs to him, an *Elohiym* near to him like our *Elohiym* ***YHWH***, in all we called out to him, **8** and who is a great nation, which belongs to him steadfast customs and decisions according to all this teaching, which I am giving to your faces today. **9** Be safeguarded for yourself and safeguard your soul much, otherwise you will forget the things which your eyes saw, and otherwise they will turn aside from your heart all the days of your life, and you will make them known to your sons and to the sons of your sons. **10** The day when you stood to the face of ***YHWH*** your *Elohiym* in *Hhorev*, with ***YHWH*** saying to me, assemble for me the people, and I will make them hear my words, because they must learn to fear me all the days which they are living upon the ground, and their sons they must teach, **11** and you must come near, and you must stand under the hill, and the hill is burning with fire unto the heart of the skies, a dark cloud and thick darkness, **12** and ***YHWH*** spoke to you from the midst of the fire, a voice of words you are hearing, and a resemblance you are not seeing, with the exception of the voice, **13** and he told you his covenant which he directed you to do, the ten words, and he wrote them upon two slabs of stone, **14** and ***YHWH*** directed me in that appointed time to teach you customs and decisions, for you to do them in the land which you are crossing over unto there to possess her, **15** and you will carefully safeguard your souls, given that you did not see any resemblance in the day ***YHWH*** spoke to you in *Hhorev* from the midst of the fire. **16** Otherwise, you will cause damage, and you will make for yourselves a sculpture of resemblance of every figure, a pattern of male or female. **17** A pattern of every beast which is in the land, a pattern of every bird of the wing which will fly in the skies. **18** A pattern of every treader in the ground, a pattern of every fish which is in the waters under the land, **19** and otherwise, you will lift up your eyes and you will see the sun and the moon and the stars and all the army of the skies, and you will be driven out[705], and you will bend yourselves down to them, and you will serve them, which ***YHWH*** your *Elohiym* distributed them to all the people under all the skies, **20** and ***YHWH*** took you, and he made you go out from the iron crucible, from *Mits'rayim*, to exist for him for a people an inheritance like this day, **21** and ***YHWH*** had snorted at me because of your

[705] Not in the sense of "away," but "toward."

words[706], and he swore to not let me cross over the *Yarden*, and to not let me come to the functional land which ***YHWH*** your *Elohiym* is giving to you for an inheritance, **22** given that I am dying in this land, without me crossing over the *Yarden*, but you are crossing over, and you will possess this functional land. **23** Safeguard yourselves, otherwise you will forget the covenant of ***YHWH*** your *Elohiym* which he cut with you, and you will do for yourselves a sculpture, a resemblance of anything, which ***YHWH*** your *Elohiym* directed you, **24** given that ***YHWH*** your *Elohiym* is an eating fire, he is a zealous mighty one, **25** given that you will cause to bring forth sons and sons of sons, and you will sleep in the land, and you will cause damage, and you will do a sculpture, a resemblance of anything, and you will do dysfunction in the eyes of ***YHWH*** your *Elohiym* to make him angry. **26** I warned the skies and the land about you today, given that you will most certainly perish quickly from upon the land which you are crossing over the *Yarden* unto there to possess her, you shall not prolong the days upon her, given that you will most certainly be destroyed, **27** and ***YHWH*** will scatter you abroad in the peoples, and you will remain mortal men of number in the nations which ***YHWH*** will drive you unto there, **28** and there you will serve *Elohiym*[707], works of human hands of tree and stone, which cannot see and cannot hear and cannot eat and cannot smell, **29** and you will search out from there ***YHWH*** your *Elohiym*, and you will find, given that you will seek him with all your heart and with all your soul. **30** In the narrows of you[708], and all these words[709] find you in the end days, and you turn back unto ***YHWH*** your *Elohiym*, and you hear his voice, **31** given that ***YHWH*** your *Elohiym* is a compassionate mighty one, he will not make you sink down, and he will not damage you, and he will not forget the covenant of your fathers which he swore to them, **32** given that, please inquire to the first days, which existed to your face from the day which *Elohiym* shaped the human upon the land, and to the extremity of the skies and unto the extremity of the skies[710], had anything existed like this great word or anything heard like him. **33** Did the people hear the voice of *Elohiym* speaking from the midst of the fire, just as you heard, and did he live. **34** Or did *Elohiym* test to come to take for him a nation from inside a nation, with trials, with signs, and with wonders and with battle and with a forceful hand, and with an extended arm, and with great fearings, like all that ***YHWH*** did to you in *Mits'rayim* to your eyes. **35** You, you were shown, to know that ***YHWH***, he is the *Elohiym*, without another besides him. **36** From the skies he

---

[706] This Hebrew word can also mean "things."

[707] In context, this Hebrew word is plural and is referring to other *Elohiym* made of wood and stone.

[708] The phrase "in the narrows for you" may be interpreted as, "when you are in distress."

[709] Or "things."

[710] Meaning "from one end of the skies to the other."

made you hear his voice to correct you, and upon the land he showed you his great fire, and his words you heard from the midst of the fire, **37** and now, given that he loved your fathers, and he chose in his seed after him, and he brought you out, with his face, with his great strength, from *Mits'rayim*. **38** To dispossess great nations and more numerous than you from your face, to bring you, to give to you their land as an inheritance like this day, **39** and you will know today, and you will turn back to your heart, given that ***YHWH***, he is the *Elohiym* in the skies above and upon the land below, without another, **40** and you will safeguard his customs and his directives, which I am directing you today, that he will do well for you and for your sons after you, and so that you will prolong the days upon the ground which ***YHWH*** your *Elohiym* is giving to you all the days. **41** At that time *Mosheh* will separate three cities on the other side of the *Yarden*, unto the sunrise of the sun[711]. **42** A murderer that unknowingly murdered his companion will flee unto there, and he was not hating him previously, and he will flee to one of these cities, and he will live. **43** *Betser* in the wilderness, in the land of the plain, to the ones of *Re'uven*, and *Ramot* in *Gil'ad*, to the ones of *Gad*, and *Golan* in *Bashan*, to the ones of *Menasheh*, **44** and this is the teaching which *Mosheh* placed to the face of the sons of *Yisra'eyl*. **45** These are the witnesses, and the customs, and the decisions, which *Mosheh* spoke to the sons of *Yisra'eyl* in their going out from *Mits'rayim*. **46** On the other side of the *Yarden*, in the steep valley, in front of the *Beyt-Pe'or*, in the land of *Sihhon*, the king of the ones of *Emor*, who are settling in *Hheshbon*, who *Mosheh* and the sons of *Yisra'eyl* attacked in their going out from *Mits'rayim*, **47** and they possessed his land and the land of *Og*, king of the *Bashan*, two kings of the ones of *Emor*, which are on the other side of the *Yarden*, the sunrise of the sun. **48** From *Aro'eyr*, which is upon the lip[712] of the wadi of *Arnon*, and unto the hill of *Si'on*, he is *Hhermon*, **49** and all the desert, the other side of the *Yarden*, unto the sunrise, and unto the sea, the desert under the ravines of the *Pisgah*,

---

Chapter 5

1 and *Mosheh* called out to all of *Yisra'eyl*, and he said to them, hear *Yisra'eyl* the customs and the decisions which I am speaking in your ears today, and you will learn them, and you will safeguard to do them. **2** ***YHWH*** is our *Elohiym*, he cut with us a covenant in *Hhorev*. **3** ***YHWH*** did not cut this covenant with our fathers but with us, we these here today, all us living ones. **4** Face to face ***YHWH*** spoke with you on the hill from the midst of the fire. **5** I am standing between ***YHWH*** and you in that appointed time, to tell you the word of ***YHWH***, given that you feared from the face of the fire, and

---

711 That is the "east." (also in verse 47)

712 The "edge" or "bank."

you did not go up on the hill, saying, **6** I am ***YHWH*** your *Elohiym*, which I
brought you out from the land of *Mits'rayim*, from the house of servants.
7 Other *Elohiym* will not exist for you upon my face. **8** You will not do for
yourselves a sculpture, any resemblance which is in the skies above and
which is on the land below and which is in the waters below the land. **9** You
will not bend yourself down to them, and you will not serve them, given that
I am ***YHWH*** your *Elohiym*, a zealous mighty one, registering twistedness of
the fathers upon the sons and upon the third generation, and upon the
fourth generation to the ones hating me, **10** and do kindness to the
thousands to the ones loving me and safeguarding my directives. **11** You will
not lift up the title of ***YHWH*** your *Elohiym* for falseness, given that ***YHWH***
will not acquit one who will lift up his title to falseness. **12** Safeguard the day
of ceasing, to set him apart just as ***YHWH*** your *Elohiym* directed you. **13** Six
days you will serve and you will do your business, **14** and the seventh day is
a ceasing for ***YHWH*** your *Elohiym*, you will not do business, you and your
sons and your daughters and your servants and your bondwomen and your
ox and your donkey and all your beasts and your immigrants that are in your
gates, so that your servant will rest, and your bondwomen, like you, **15** and
you will remember that you existed as a servant in the land of *Mits'rayim*,
and ***YHWH*** your *Elohiym* brought you out from there with a forceful hand
and with an extended arm, therefore ***YHWH*** your *Elohiym* directed you to
do the day of ceasing. **16** Honor your father and your mother just as ***YHWH***
your *Elohiym* directed you, so that your days will certainly be prolonged, and
so that he will go well for you upon the ground which ***YHWH*** your *Elohiym* is
giving to you. **17** You will not murder, **18** and you will not commit adultery,
19 and you will not steal, **20** and you will not afflict a witness of falseness on
your companion, **21** and you will not crave the woman of your companion,
and you will not yearn for the house of your companion, his field and his
servant and his bondwoman, his ox and his donkey and all that belongs to
your companion. **22** These words ***YHWH*** spoke to all of your assembly, on
the hill, from the midst of the fire, the cloud and the thick darkness, a great
voice, and he did not add, and he wrote them upon two slabs of stone, and
he gave them to me, **23** and it came to pass, when you hear the voice from
the midst of the darkness, and the hill burning with fire, and you came near
to me, all the heads of your staffs[713], and your bearded ones, **24** and you
said, though ***YHWH*** our *Elohiym* showed us his armament and his
magnificence and his voice, we heard from the midst of the fire this day, and
we saw that *Elohiym* will speak with the human and he lived, **25** and now,
why will we die, given that this great fire will eat us if we again hear the
voice of ***YHWH*** our *Elohiym* again, and we will die, **26** given that, who of all
flesh, who heard the voice of the living *Elohiym* speaking from the midst of
the fire, like one of us and lived. **27** Come near, you, and hear all that ***YHWH***
our *Elohiym* will say, and you, you will speak to us all that ***YHWH*** our

[713] "Staff" is a euphemism for a "tribe."

Elohiym spoke to you, and we will hear and we will do, **28** and ***YHWH*** heard the voice of your words in your speaking to me, and ***YHWH*** said to me, I heard the voice of the words of this people which they spoke to you, they did well, all which they spoke. **29** Who will give, and their heart will exist, this belongs to them, to fear me and to safeguard all my directives all the days, so that he will do well to them and to their sons to a distant time.
30 Walk, say to them, turn back for yourselves to your tents, **31** and you, here, stand by me, and I will speak to you all the directives and the customs and the decisions, that you will teach them, and they will do in the land which I am giving to them to possess her, **32** and you will safeguard to do just as ***YHWH*** your *Elohiym* directed you, you will not turn aside the right hand or the left hand. **33** In all the road which ***YHWH*** your *Elohiym* directed you, you will walk, so that you will certainly live, and he will go well for you, and you will make the days prolonged in the land, which you will possess,

---

Chapter 6

1 and this is the directive, the customs, and the decisions, which ***YHWH*** your *Elohiym* directed, to teach you to do in the land, which you are crossing over unto there to possess her. **2** So that you will fear ***YHWH*** your *Elohiym*, to safeguard all his customs and his directives, which I am directing you, you and your son and the son of your son, all the days of your life, and so that you will make your days prolonged, **3** and you will hear, *Yisra'eyl*, and you will safeguard to do, that it will go well for you, and that you will certainly greatly increase, just as ***YHWH*** the *Elohiym* of your fathers spoke to you, a land issuing fat and honey. **4** Hear *Yisra'eyl*, ***YHWH*** our *Elohiym*, ***YHWH*** a unit,[714] **5** and you will love ***YHWH*** your *Elohiym* with all your heart and with all your soul and with all your everything, **6** and these words, which I am directing you today, will exist upon your heart, **7** and you will whet them for your sons, and you will speak with them in your settlings, in your house and in your walking in the road, and your lying down, and in your rising, **8** and you will tie them for a sign upon your hand, and they will exist for markers between your eyes, **9** and you will write them upon the doorposts of your house and on your gates, **10** and it came to pass, given that ***YHWH*** your *Elohiym* will bring you to the land which he swore to your fathers, to *Avraham*, to *Yits'hhaq*, and to *Ya'aqov*, to give to you great and functional cities, which you did not build, **11** and houses full of every functional thing which you did not fill, and hewn cisterns which you did not hew, vineyards and olives which you did not plant, and you will eat and you will be satisfied.
12 Safeguard yourselves, otherwise you will forget ***YHWH*** who brought you out from the land of *Mits'rayim*, from the house of servants. **13** ***YHWH*** your

---

[714] This verse could also be translated as "hear *Yisra'eyl*, ***YHWH*** is our *Elohiym*, ***YHWH*** is one,

Elohiym you will fear, and him you will serve, and in his title you will swear. **14** You must not walk after other *Elohiym* from the *Elohiym* of the people which are all around you, **15** given that ***YHWH*** your *Elohiym* is a zealous mighty one in among you, otherwise, ***YHWH*** your *Elohiym* will flare up the nose with you, and he will destroy you from upon the face of the ground. **16** You will not test ***YHWH*** your *Elohiym*, just as you tested in *Mas'sah*[715]. **17** You must certainly safeguard the directives of ***YHWH*** your *Elohiym*, and his witnesses and his customs, which he directed you, **18** and you did the straight and functional thing in the eyes of ***YHWH***, so that he will do well for you, and you will come and you will possess the functional land, which ***YHWH*** sworn to your fathers, **19** to push away everyone attacking you from your face, just as ***YHWH*** spoke, **20** given that your son will inquire of you tomorrow saying, what are the witnesses, and the customs, and the decisions, which ***YHWH*** our *Elohiym* directed you, **21** and you will say to your son, we existed as servants to *Paroh* in *Mits'rayim*, and ***YHWH*** brought us out from *Mits'rayim* with a forceful hand, **22** and ***YHWH*** gave signs and great and dysfunctional wonders in *Mits'rayim*, in *Paroh*, and in all his house, to our eyes, **23** and he brought us out from there, to bring us, to give us, the land which he swore to our fathers, **24** and ***YHWH*** directed us to do all these customs, to fear ***YHWH*** our *Elohiym*, for function for us all the days, to keep us alive like this day, **25** and steadfastness will exist for us, given that we will safeguard to do all these directives to the face of ***YHWH*** our *Elohiym*, just as he directed us,

Chapter 7

1 given that ***YHWH*** your *Elohiym* brought you to the land, which you came unto there to possess, and he cast off the abundant nations from your face, the ones of *Hhet*, and the ones of *Girgash*, and the ones of *Emor*, and the ones of *Kena'an*, and the ones of *Perez*, and the ones of *Hhiw*, and the ones of *Yevus*, seven nations more abundant and numerous nations than you, **2** and ***YHWH*** your *Elohiym* will give them to your face, and you will attack them, you will completely perforate them, you will not cut them a covenant, and you will not provide them protection, **3** and you will not make yourselves be in-laws with them, you will not give your daughters to his sons, and his daughters you will not take for your sons, **4** given that he will make your son turn aside from after me, and they will serve other *Elohiym*, and the nose of ***YHWH*** will flare up with you, and he will quickly destroy you. **5** Instead, in this way, you will do to them, their altars you will break down, and their monuments you will crack, and their groves you must cut down, and their sculptures you must cremate in the fire, **6** given that you are

---

[715] The *Septuagint* assumes this Hebrew word is a noun and not a proper name and would then be translated as "with a trial" or "with temptation."

a unique people for ***YHWH*** your *Elohiym*, with you ***YHWH*** your *Elohiym* chose to exist, to be for himself for a people, a jewel from all the peoples, which are upon the face of the ground. **7** Not because you are great in number, more than all the peoples, ***YHWH*** attached with you, and he chose you, given that you are the fewest from all the peoples, **8** given that from the affection of ***YHWH*** for you, and his safeguarding the swearing that he swore to your fathers, ***YHWH*** brought you out with a forceful hand, and he ransomed you from the house of servants, from the hand of *Paroh*, the king of *Mits'rayim*, **9** and you knew that ***YHWH*** your *Elohiym*, he is the mighty *Elohiym*, the one being secure, safeguarding the covenant, and kindness to the ones loving him and safeguarding his directives to a thousand generations, **10** and making restitution[716] to the ones hating him to his face, to make him perish, he will not delay to the one hating him to his face, he will make restitution for him, **11** and you will safeguard the directives and the customs and the decisions, which I am directing you today to do them, **12** and consequently, it will come to pass, you must hear these decisions, and you will safeguard, and you will do them, then ***YHWH*** your *Elohiym* will safeguard you, the covenant and the kindness, which he swore to your fathers, **13** and he loved you, and he exalted you, and he made you increase, and he exalted the produce of your womb, and the produce of your ground, your cereal and your fresh wine and your fresh oil, the birth of your bovine, and the young sheep of your flocks upon the ground, which he swore to your fathers to give you. **14** Exalted you will be, more than all the peoples, sterility will not exist in you or in your beast, **15** and ***YHWH*** turned aside from you all infirmity and all diseases of *Mits'rayim*, the dysfunctional things which you knew, he will not place them in you, and he will give them to all the ones hating you, **16** and you will eat[717] all the people which ***YHWH*** your *Elohiym* is giving to you, you will not spare your eye upon them, and you will not serve their *Elohiym*, given that he is a snare for you, **17** given that you will say in your heart, abundant are these nations more than me, how will I be able to dispossess them. **18** You will not fear them, you will certainly remember what ***YHWH*** your *Elohiym* did to *Paroh* and to all *Mits'rayim*. **19** The great trials which your eyes saw, and the signs, and the wonders, and the forceful hand, and the extended arm which ***YHWH*** your *Elohiym* brought you out, so will ***YHWH*** your *Elohiym* do to all the peoples which you are fearing from their face, **20** and also the hornet ***YHWH*** your *Elohiym* will send in them, until the ones remaining and the ones hiding from your face perish. **21** You will not be terrified from their face, given that ***YHWH*** your *Elohiym* is in among you, the great mighty one and fearful one, **22** and ***YHWH*** your *Elohiym* cast off these nations from your face little by little, you will not be

---

[716] While this verb is usually used in the context of repaying another that one has wronged, it can also be used in the context of repaying another that has caused wrong,

[717] Meaning to "destroy," in the same sense that fire "eats" the wood.

able to finish them quickly, otherwise living ones of the field[718] will increase upon you, **23** and ***YHWH*** your *Elohiym* gave them to your face, and he will roar at them, a great tumult until they are destroyed, **24** and he will give their kings in your hand, and you will cause their title to perish from under the skies, a man will not station himself in your face until you destroy them. **25** The sculptures of their *Elohiym* you must cremate in the fire, you will not crave the silver and gold upon them or take it for yourself, otherwise you will be snared by him, given that this is disgusting to ***YHWH*** your *Elohiym*, **26** and you will not bring a disgusting thing to your house, or you will be assigned like him, you shall detest him, and you shall abhor him, given that he is assigned.

Chapter 8

1 All the directives, which I am directing you today you must safeguard to do, so that you must live, and you will increase, and you will come, and you will possess the land which ***YHWH*** swore to your fathers, **2** and you will remember every road which ***YHWH*** your *Elohiym* made you walk these forty years in the wilderness, in order to afflict you, to test you to know what is in your heart, will you safeguard his directives or not, **3** and he afflicted you, and he made you be hungry, and he made you eat the *Mahn*, which you did not know, and your fathers certainly could not know, in order for you to know that not by bread alone the human will live, given that by all the goings out of the mouth of ***YHWH*** will the human live. **4** Your apparel did not wear out from upon you, and your foot did not swell up these forty years, **5** and you will know with your heart, that just as a man will correct his son, ***YHWH*** your *Elohiym* is correcting you, **6** and you will safeguard the directives of ***YHWH*** your *Elohiym*, to walk in his road, and to fear him, **7** given that ***YHWH*** your *Elohiym* brought you to a functional land, a land of wadis of waters, eyes[719], and deep water going out[720] in the level valley and in the hill. **8** Land of wheat and barley and grapevine and fig and pomegranate, land of olive oil and honey. **9** A land which is not in poverty, you will eat her bread, you will not diminish anything in her, a land which her stones are iron, and from her hills you will hew copper, **10** and you will eat, and you will be satisfied, and you will exalt ***YHWH*** your *Elohiym* because of the functional land, which he gave to you. **11** Safeguard yourself, otherwise you will forget ***YHWH*** your *Elohiym* by not safeguarding his directives and his decisions and his customs, which I am directing you today. **12** Otherwise, you will eat and you will be satisfied, and you will build functional houses, and you will settle, **13** and your cattle and your flocks, they shall increase, and silver and gold

---

[718] "Living ones of the field" are "wild beasts."

[719] That is, "fountains."

[720] That is, "springs."

will increase for you, all that belongs to you will increase, **14** and your heart will rise up, and you will forget ***YHWH*** your *Elohiym*, the one bringing you out from the land of *Mits'rayim*, from the house of servants. **15** Who is the one making you walk in the great wilderness, and who is the one being fearful[721] of the venomous serpents and scorpions and a thirsty land that is without waters, who is the one bringing for you waters from the quartz boulder. **16** Who is the one making you eat *Mahn* in the wilderness, which your fathers could not know, in order to afflict you, and in order to test you, **17** and you will say in your heart, my strength and the brawn of my hand did for me this force, **18** and you will remember ***YHWH*** your *Elohiym*, given that he is the one giving to you strength to do force, so that his covenant will rise, which he swore to your fathers like this day, **19** and it will come to pass, if you completely forget ***YHWH*** your *Elohiym*, and you walk after other *Elohiym*, and you serve them, and you bend yourself down to them, I warn you today that you will certainly perish. **20** Like the nations, which ***YHWH*** is making perish from your faces, so you must perish, consequently, you will not listen to the voice of ***YHWH*** your *Elohiym*.

Chapter 9

1 Hear *Yisra'eyl*, you are crossing over today the *Yarden* to come to possess nations greater and more numerous than you, cities great and fenced to the skies. **2** People great and tall, sons of the ones of *Anaq*, which you knew, and you heard, who will station himself to face the sons of the ones of *Anaq*, **3** and you will know today that ***YHWH*** your *Elohiym*, he is the one crossing over to your face, he is an eating fire, he will destroy them, and he will lower them to your face, and you will dispossess them, and you will make them perish quickly, just as ***YHWH*** spoke to you. **4** You will not say in your heart, with ***YHWH*** your *Elohiym* is pushing them away from your face, saying, with my steadfastness ***YHWH*** brought me to possess this land, and in the waywardness of these nations ***YHWH*** is dispossessing them from your face. **5** Not with your steadfastness or with the straightness of your heart, you will come to possess their land, given that with the waywardness of these nations, ***YHWH*** your *Elohiym* dispossessed them from your face, so that the word which ***YHWH*** swore to your fathers, to *Avraham*, to *Yits'hhaq* and to *Ya'aqov* will rise, **6** and you will know that not with your steadfastness ***YHWH*** your *Elohiym* is giving to you this functional land to possess her, given that you are a hard neck people. **7** Remember, you will not forget that you made ***YHWH*** your *Elohiym* snap in the wilderness, from the day when you

---

721 If the letter ה (the Hebrew letter *hey*) prefixed to this Hebrew verb is the definite article (the) instead of an interrogative participle, an alternate translation would be, "the great and fearful wilderness" (see Deuteronomy 1:19).

went out from the land of *Mits'rayim*, until your coming to this area, you
existed as ones disobeying with ***YHWH***, **8** and in *Hhorev* you caused ***YHWH***
to snap, and ***YHWH*** snorted concerning you to destroy you. **9** In my going up
unto the hill to take the slabs of stone, the slabs of the covenant which
YHWH cut with you, and I settled on the hill forty days and forty nights,
bread I did not eat and waters I did not gulp, **10** and ***YHWH*** gave to me the
two slabs of stone, written with the finger of *Elohiym*, and upon them,
according to all the words which ***YHWH*** spoke with you on the hill from the
midst of the fire in the day of the assembly, **11** and it came to pass, at the
conclusion of the forty days and forty nights, ***YHWH*** gave to me the two
slabs of stone, the slabs of the covenant, **12** and ***YHWH*** said to me, rise,
quickly go down from this, given that your people, which you brought out
from *Mits'rayim*, did damage, they quickly turned aside from the road which
I directed them, they made for themselves a cast image, **13** and ***YHWH*** said
to me saying, I saw this people, and look the people, they have a hard neck.
14 Sink down from me, and I will destroy them, and I will wipe their title
away from under the skies, and I will make you for a numerous and
abundant nation, more than them, **15** and I turned, and I came down from
the hill, and the hill was burning with the fire, and the two slabs of the
covenant upon my two hands, **16** and I saw, and look, you failed ***YHWH*** your
Elohiym, you made for you a bullock of a cast image, you turned aside
quickly from the road which ***YHWH*** directed you, **17** and I seized hold of the
two slabs, and I threw them from upon my two hands, and I cracked them to
your eyes, **18** and I threw myself to the face of ***YHWH*** like the first forty days
and forty nights, bread I did not eat and waters I did not gulp, on account of
all your failures which you failed, to do dysfunction in the eyes of ***YHWH*** to
make him angry, **19** given that I was afraid from the face of the nose, and
the fury which ***YHWH*** snapped upon you, to destroy you, and ***YHWH*** heard
me also in that time, **20** and in *Aharon* ***YHWH*** snorted much to destroy him,
and I interceded also concerning *Aharon* in that appointed time, **21** and your
failure which you did, the bullock I took and I cremated him in the fire, and I
smashed him, grinding well until he was beat small to dirt, and I threw his
dirt to the wadi, the one going down from the hill, **22** and in *Taveyrah*, and
in the *Mas'sah*, and in *Qivrot-Hata'awah*, you were making ***YHWH*** snap,
23 and ***YHWH*** sent you from *Qadesh Barneya* saying, go up and possess the
land which I gave to you, and you disobeyed the mouth of ***YHWH*** your
Elohiym, and you did not make yourselves secure in him, and you did not
hear his voice. **24** You were disobeying ***YHWH*** from the day I knew you,
25 and I threw myself to the face of ***YHWH***, forty days and forty nights which
I threw myself, given that ***YHWH*** said to destroy you, **26** and I interceded to
YHWH, and I said, *Adonai* ***YHWH***, you will not damage your people and your
inheritance, which you ransomed in your greatness, which you brought out
from *Mits'rayim* with a forceful hand. **27** Remember your servants *Avraham*,
Yits'hhaq and *Ya'aqov*, you will not turn toward the stubbornness of this
people, and his being lost and his failure. **28** Otherwise the land which you

made us go out from there will say, ***YHWH*** was not able to bring them to the land which he spoke to them, and from his hate of them he brought them to the wilderness to kill them, **29** and they, your people, and your inheritance, which you brought out with your great strength and your extended arm.

Chapter 10

1 In that appointed time ***YHWH*** said to me, sculpt for yourself two slabs of stone like the first ones, and go up to me unto the hill, and you will make for yourself a box of wood, **2** and I will write upon the slabs the words which existed upon the first slabs, which you cracked, and you will place them in the box, **3** and I made a box of wood of acacia, and I sculpted two slabs of stone like the first ones, and I brought up unto the hill the two slabs in my hand, **4** and he wrote upon the slabs like the first things written, the ten words which ***YHWH*** spoke to you on the hill from the midst of the fire in the day of assembly, and ***YHWH*** gave them to me, **5** and I turned, and I went down from the hill, and I placed the slabs in the box which I made, and they existed there just as ***YHWH*** directed me, **6** and the sons of *Yisra'eyl* journeyed from the wells of *B'ney-Ya'aqan* to *Moseyrah*, there *Aharon* died, and he was buried there, and *Elazar* his son was adorned in place of him. **7** From there they journeyed to the *Gudgodah*, and from the *Gudgodah* to *Yatvatah*, a land of wadis of waters. **8** In that appointed time ***YHWH*** separated the staff of *Lewi*, to lift up the box of the covenant of ***YHWH***, to stand to the face of ***YHWH***, to minister to him, and to respect his title until this day. **9** Therefore, a distribution and inheritance with his brothers does not exist for *Lewi*, ***YHWH***, he is his inheritance, just as ***YHWH*** your *Elohiym* spoke to him, **10** and I, I stood on the hill like the first days, forty days and forty nights, and ***YHWH*** heard me, also in that time ***YHWH*** did not consent to damage you, **11** and ***YHWH*** said to me, rise, walk to journey to the face of the people, and they will come and they will possess the land, which I swore to their fathers to give to them, **12** and now *Yisra'eyl*, what is ***YHWH*** your *Elohiym* enquiring from you, except to fear ***YHWH*** your *Elohiym*, to walk in all his roads, and to love him, and to serve ***YHWH*** your *Elohiym* with all your heart and with all your soul. **13** To safeguard the directives of ***YHWH*** and his customs, which I am directing you today to be functional[722] for you[723]. **14** Though, belonging to ***YHWH*** your *Elohiym* is the skies, the skies of the skies, the land, and all which is in her. **15** Only with your fathers was ***YHWH*** attached to love them, and he chose on their seed after them, on you, from all the peoples like this day, **16** and you will snip off the foreskin of your

---

[722] The word טוֹב (*tov*) is a noun meaning "functional," but if this was the verb טוּב (*tuv*), then this would be a verb meaning "do good."

[723] If the previous word is a verb, then the alternate translation would be, "to do good for you."

heart, and your neck you will not be made hard again, **17** given that ***YHWH*** your *Elohiym*, he is *Elohiym* of the *Elohiym*, lords of the lords[724], the mighty one, the great one, the courageous one, and the one being feared, who will not lift up face and will not take a bribe. **18** Making a decision of orphan and widow, and loving the immigrant to give him bread and apparel, **19** and you will love the immigrant, given that you existed as immigrants in the land of *Mits'rayim*. **20** ***YHWH*** your *Elohiym*, you will fear him, him you will serve, and in him you will adhere, and in his title you will be sworn. **21** He is your adoration, and he is your *Elohiym* who did for you these great and the fearful things which your eyes saw. **22** With seventy souls your fathers went down unto *Mits'rayim*, and now ***YHWH*** your *Elohiym* placed you like the stars of the skies for an abundance,

---

Chapter 11

1 and you will love ***YHWH*** your *Elohiym*, and you will safeguard his charge, and his decisions, and his directives all the days, **2** and you will know today, given that it is not with your sons who did not know and did not see the discipline of ***YHWH*** your *Elohiym*, his magnificence, his forceful hand and his extended arm, **3** and his signs, and his works, which he did in the midst of *Mits'rayim* to *Paroh* the king of *Mits'rayim* and to all his land, **4** and what he did to the forces of *Mits'rayim*, to his horses and to his vehicles, when he made the waters of the sea of reeds[725] float upon their faces in their pursuing after you, and ***YHWH*** caused them to perish until this day, **5** and what he did to you in the wilderness until your coming unto this area, **6** and what he did to *Datan* and to *Aviram*, the sons of *Eli'av* the son of *Re'uven*, when the land parted her mouth and she swallowed them, and with their houses and their tents, and all the substance which was at their feet, in the inside of all *Yisra'eyl*, **7** given that your eyes are seeing all the great work of ***YHWH*** which he did, **8** and you will safeguard all the directives which I am directing you today, so that you will seize, and you will come, and you will possess the land which you are crossing over unto to possess her, **9** and so that you will prolong the days upon the ground, which ***YHWH*** swore to your fathers to give them and to their seed, a land issuing fat and honey, **10** given that the land which you came unto there to possess her, she is not like the land of *Mits'rayim* which you went out from there, where you sowed your seed and you made drink with your foot, like the green garden, **11** and the land which you are crossing over unto there to possess her, a land of hills and level valleys, by the precipitation of the skies you will gulp waters. **12** A

---

[724] While this phrase, "lords of the lords," is correct, it should be noted that most Hebrew names (titles) for ***YHWH*** are in the plural, so this could be translated as "lord of the lords."

[725] "Sea of reeds," or "*Yam Suph*," is usually mistranslated as "red sea."

land which ***YHWH*** your *Elohiym* is seeking her, continually the eyes of ***YHWH*** your *Elohiym* are on her, from the summit of the year and until the end of the year, **13** and it will come to pass, if you will certainly listen to my directives which I directed you today, to love ***YHWH*** your *Elohiym* and to serve him with all your heart and with all your soul, **14** and I will give your land precipitation in his appointed time, the first rain and the late rain, and you will gather your cereal, and your fresh wine and your fresh oil, **15** and I will give herbs in your field for your beast, and you will eat and you will be satisfied. **16** Safeguard yourselves, otherwise your heart will spread wide, and you will turn aside, and you will serve other *Elohiym*, and you will bend yourselves down to them, **17** and the nose of ***YHWH*** flared up with you, and he will stop the skies and precipitation will not exist, and the ground will not give her produce, and you will perish quickly from upon the functional land which ***YHWH*** is giving to you, **18** and you will place my words upon your heart and upon your soul, and you will tie them for a sign upon your hand, and they will exist for markers between your eyes, **19** and you will learn them with your sons, to speak about them in your settling in your house, and in your walk in the road, and in your lying down, and in your rising, **20** and you will write them upon the doorposts of your house and on your gates. **21** So that your days will increase, and the days of your sons, upon the ground, which ***YHWH*** swore to your fathers to give to them, like the days of the skies upon the land, **22** given that if you will certainly safeguard all these directives which I am directing you to do, to love ***YHWH***, to walk in all his roads and to adhere with him, **23** and ***YHWH*** will dispossess all these nations from before your faces, and you will possess great nations more numerous than you. **24** All the area which you will take steps with the palm of your foot will exist for you, from the wilderness, and the *Levanon*, from the river, the river *Perat*, and until the last[726] sea will exist as your border. **25** A man will not station himself in your faces[727], your awe and your fearing ***YHWH*** will give upon the face of all the land which you will take steps in, just as he spoke to you. **26** See, I am giving to your faces today a present and an annoyance. **27** A present when you will listen to the directives of ***YHWH*** your *Elohiym*, which I am directing you today, **28** and an annoyance if you will not listen to the directives of ***YHWH*** your *Elohiym*, and you will turn aside from the road which I directed you today, to walk after other *Elohiym* which you did not know, **29** and it will come to pass that ***YHWH*** your *Elohiym* will bring you to the land which you came unto to possess her, and you will place the present upon the hill of *Gerizim*, and the annoyance upon the hill of *Eyval*. **30** Are they not on the other side of the *Yarden*, after the road of the entrance of the sun, in the land of the ones of *Kena'an*, the ones settling in

---

726 Probably meaning "the farthest sea."

727 An alternate translation would be "no man will station himself in front of you."

the desert the forefront of *Gilgal*, beside the great trees of *Moreh*[728],
31 given that you are crossing over the *Yarden* to come to possess the land which ***YHWH*** your *Elohiym* is giving to you, and you will possess her, and you will settle in her, **32** and you will safeguard to do all the customs and the decisions which I am giving to your faces today.

Chapter 12

1 These are the customs and the decisions which you must safeguard to do in the land which ***YHWH***, the *Elohiym* of your fathers, gave to you to possess her all the days which you are living upon the ground. **2** You must
completely destroy all the areas where the nations, which you are possessing, served their *Elohiym*, upon the raised up hills and upon the knolls and under all the flourishing trees, **3** and you will break down their
altars, and you will crack their monuments, and their groves you must cremate in the fire, and the sculptures of their *Elohiym* you must cut down, and you will destroy their title from this area. **4** You must not do so to ***YHWH***
your *Elohiym*. **5** Except to the area where ***YHWH*** your *Elohiym* will choose from all your staffs[729] to place his title there for his dwelling, you will seek and you will come unto there, **6** and you will bring unto there your ascension
offerings, and your sacrifices, and from your tenth parts, and the offering of your hand, and your vows, and your freewill offerings, and the firstborn of your cattle and your flocks, **7** and you will eat there to the face of ***YHWH***
your *Elohiym*, and your rejoicing with all the sending of your hand[730], you and your house, because ***YHWH*** your *Elohiym* respected you. **8** You must not
do like everything we are doing here today, every man the straight thing in his eyes, **9** given that you did not come until now to the oasis[731], and to the
inheritance, which ***YHWH*** your *Elohiym* is giving to you, **10** and you will cross
over the *Yarden*, and you will settle in the land which ***YHWH*** your *Elohiym* is making you inherit, and he will make you rest from all your attackers from all around, and you will settle safely, **11** and it will come to pass, the area
which ***YHWH*** your *Elohiym* will choose for himself to make his title dwell there, unto there you will bring all which I am directing you, your ascension offerings and your sacrifices from your tenth parts, and the offering of your hand, and all your chosen vows which you will vow to ***YHWH***, **12** and your
rejoicing to the face of ***YHWH*** your *Elohiym*, you and your sons and your daughters and your servants, and your bondwomen, and the *Lewi* which are

---

728 This name can be the name of a place, the noun מורה (*moreh*), from the root ירה (*Y.R.H*) meaning "teacher," or the participle form of the verb מרה (*M.R.H*) meaning "disobeying."

729 That is, "tribes."

730 Meaning "everything that your hands do."

731 A euphemism for a "place of rest or" in a "state of rest."

in your gates, given that he is without a distribution or inheritance with you. **13** Safeguard yourselves, otherwise you will bring up your ascension offerings in every area which you will see. **14** Except in the area which ***YHWH*** will choose in one of your staffs[732], there you will bring up your ascension offerings, and there you will do all which I am directing you. **15** Only with all the desire of your soul will you sacrifice, and you will eat flesh like a present of ***YHWH*** your *Elohiym*, which he gave to you, in all your gates the dirty and the clean will eat him, like the gazelle and like the buck. **16** Only the blood you will not eat upon the land, you will pour him out like waters. **17** You will not be able to eat in your gates the tenth part of your cereal, and your fresh wine, and your fresh oil, and the firstborn of your cattle and your flocks, and all your vows which you make a vow, and your freewill offering, and your hand offering. **18** Except to the face of ***YHWH*** your *Elohiym* will you eat him in the area which ***YHWH*** your *Elohiym* chose, you, and your son, and your daughter, and your servant, and your bondwoman, and the *Lewi* which is in your gates, and you will rejoice to the face of ***YHWH*** your *Elohiym* in all your hand is sending[733]. **19** Safeguard yourself, otherwise you will leave[734] the *Lewi* all your days upon your ground, **20** given that ***YHWH*** your *Elohiym* will make wide your border, just as he spoke to you, and you will say, I will eat flesh, given that your soul will yearn to eat flesh, with all the desire of your soul you will eat flesh, **21** given that the area which ***YHWH*** your *Elohiym* chose to place his title there will be far from you, and you will sacrifice from your cattle and from your flocks which ***YHWH*** gave to you, just as I directed you, and you will eat in your gates with all the desire of your soul. **22** Surely, just as the gazelle will be eaten, and the buck, so will the dirty and the clean eat him, together they will eat him. **23** Only seize by not eating the blood[735], given that the blood, he is the soul, and you will not eat the soul with the flesh. **24** You will not eat him, upon the land you will pour him like waters. **25** You will not eat him so that he will do well for you and for your sons after you, given that you will do the straight thing in the eyes of ***YHWH***. **26** Only your special things which exist for you, and your vows you will lift up, and you will come to the area which ***YHWH*** will choose, **27** and you will do your ascension offerings, the flesh and the blood upon the altar of ***YHWH*** your *Elohiym*, and the blood of your sacrifices will be poured out upon the altar of ***YHWH*** your *Elohiym*, and the flesh you will eat. **28** Safeguard yourself, and you will hear all these words which I am directing you, so that he will do well for you and for your sons after you until a distant time, given that you will do the functional and the straight thing in the eyes of ***YHWH*** your *Elohiym*, **29** given that ***YHWH*** your *Elohiym* will cut the nations which you came unto there to possess

---

[732] That is, "tribes."

[733] That is, "doing."

[734] Meaning to "forsake."

[735] An alternate translation is "but refrain from eating the blood."

them from your face, and you will possess them, and you will settle in their land. **30** Be safeguarded for yourself[736], otherwise you will be ensnared after them, after their being destroyed from your face, and otherwise you will seek their *Elohiym* to say, how do these nations serve their *Elohiym*, and I will do so also. **31** You will not do so for ***YHWH*** your *Elohiym*, given that all the disgusting things which they did to their *Elohiym*, ***YHWH*** hated, given that even their sons and their daughters they will cremate in the fire to their *Elohiym*.

Chapter 13

1 (12:32) All the words which I am directing you, him you will safeguard to do, you will not add upon him and you will not take away from him. **2**
(13:1) When an announcer or a dreamer of dreams will rise from in among you, and he will give to you a sign or a wonder, **3 (13:2)** and the sign or the wonder will come, which he spoke to you, saying, we will walk after other *Elohiym* which you did not know and we will serve them. **4 (13:3)** You will not listen to the words of that announcer or to that dreamer of dreams, given that ***YHWH*** your *Elohiym* is testing you to know if you are loving ***YHWH*** your *Elohiym* with all your heart and with all your soul. **5 (13:4)** You will walk after ***YHWH*** your *Elohiym*, and him you will fear, and his directives you will safeguard, and in his voice you will hear, and him you will serve, and in him you must adhere, **6 (13:5)** and that announcer or that dreamer of dreams, will be killed, given that he spoke of turning aside from ***YHWH*** your *Elohiym*, the one bringing you out from the land of *Mits'rayim*, and the one ransoming you from the house of servants, to drive you out from the road which ***YHWH*** your *Elohiym* directed you to walk in her, and you will burn the dysfunctional one from inside you, **7 (13:6)** given that your brother, the son of your mother, or your son, or your daughter, or the woman of your bosom, or your companion which is like your soul, will persuade you in hiding[737] saying, we will walk and we will serve other *Elohiym*, which you did not know, you and your fathers. **8 (13:7)** From the *Elohiym* of the people, which are all around you, the ones near to you, or the ones distant from you, from the extremity of the land and until the extremity of the land. **9**
(13:8) You will not consent to him, and you will not listen to him, and your eye will not spare him, and you will not show pity, and you will not cover him over[738], **10 (13:9)** given that you will surely kill him, your hand will exist in him first to kill him, and the hand of all the people last, **11 (13:10)** and you will stone him with stones, and he will die, given that he searched out to drive you out from upon ***YHWH*** your *Elohiym*, the one bringing you out from

---

[736] This could also be translated as "be on your guard."
[737] Or "in secret."
[738] Meaning "hide."

the land of *Mits'rayim*, from the house of servants, **12 (13:11)** and all *Yisra'eyl* will hear, and they must fear, and they will not again do like this dysfunctional word in among you, **13 (13:12)** given that you heard in one of your cities which ***YHWH*** your *Elohiym* is giving to you to settle there, saying, **14 (13:13)** the men, the sons of *Beli'ya'al*, went out from inside you, and they drove the settlers of their city out saying, we will walk and we will serve other *Elohiym* which you did not know, **15 (13:14)** and you will seek, and you will examine, and you will inquire thoroughly, and look, truth, the thing is being prepared, this disgusting thing is being done in among you. **16 (13:15)** You will certainly attack the settlers of that city by the mouth[739] of the sword, perforate her and all which are in her, and her beast by the mouth of the sword, **17 (13:16)** and all her spoils you will gather together unto the midst of the street, and you will entirely cremate in the fire the city and all her spoils to ***YHWH*** your *Elohiym*, and she will exist a distant ruin, she will not be built again, **18 (13:17)** and nothing will adhere in your hand from the perforated things, so that ***YHWH*** will turn back from the flaming wrath of his anger, and he will give to you tenderness, and he will have compassion, and he will make you increase, just as he swore to your fathers, **19 (13:18)** given that you will hear the voice of ***YHWH*** your *Elohiym* to safeguard all his directives which I am directing you today, to do the straight thing in the eyes of ***YHWH*** your *Elohiym*.

Chapter 14

1 You are sons belonging to ***YHWH*** your *Elohiym*, you will not band yourselves together, and you will not place a bald spot between your eyes for the dying, **2** given that you are a unique people belonging to ***YHWH*** your *Elohiym*, and ***YHWH*** chose you to exist for him for a people, a jewel from all the people which are upon the face of the ground. **3** You will not eat anything disgusting. **4** These are the beasts which you will eat, ox, ram of sheep and ram of she-goats. **5** Buck and gazelle and roebuck and wild goat and antelope and oryx and mountain sheep, **6** and every beast cleaving the hoof and splitting the hoof in two, with the beast bringing up the cud, her you will eat. **7** Surely this you will not eat, from the ones bringing up the cud, or from the ones cleaving the hoof in two, the camel and the hare and the rabbit, given that they are bringing up the cud, but the hoof is not cleaved, they are dirty for you, **8** and the swine, given that he has a cleaving hoof, but not a cud, he is dirty for you, from their flesh you will not eat and their carcass you will not touch. **9** This you will eat from all that is in the waters, all that have a fin and scales you will eat, **10** and all that are without a fin and scales you will not eat, he is dirty for you. **11** Every clean bird you will eat, **12** and these, which you will not eat from them, the eagle and the

---

[739] Meaning the "edge."

bearded vulture and the osprey, **13** and the kite and the hawk and the vulture to her kind, **14** and every raven to his kind, **15** and the daughter of the owl[740] and the nighthawk and the seagull and the falcon to his kind. **16** The little owl and the eared owl and the ibis, **17** and the pelican and the gier-eagle and the cormorant, **18** and the stork and the heron to her kind, and the grouse and the bat, **19** and all the flying swarmers, he is dirty for you, they will not be eaten, **20** and the clean flyers you will eat. **21** You will not eat any carcass, you will give her to the immigrant who is in your gates, and he will eat her, or sell it to a foreigner, given that you are a unique people for ***YHWH*** your *Elohiym*, you will not boil a male kid in the fat of his mother. **22** You will certainly give a tenth of all the production of your seed, the ones going out of the field year by year, **23** and you will eat to the face of ***YHWH*** your *Elohiym*, in the area which he will choose to make his title dwell there, a tenth part of your cereal, your fresh wine and your fresh oil, and the firstborn of your cattle and of your flocks, so that you will learn to fear ***YHWH*** your *Elohiym* all the days, **24** and when the road will increase[741] from you, given that you will not be able to lift him up, given that the area will be far from you, which ***YHWH*** your *Elohiym* will choose to place his title there, given that ***YHWH*** your *Elohiym* will respect you, **25** and you will replace it into silver, and you will smack the silver in your hand, and you will walk to the area which ***YHWH*** your *Elohiym* chose for himself, **26** and you will replace the silver with anything that your soul will yearn, with the cattle and with the flocks and with the wine and with the liquor and with anything that your soul will inquire, and you will eat there to the face of ***YHWH*** your *Elohiym*, and you will rejoice, you and your house, **27** and *Lewi* which is in your gates, you will not leave[742] him, given that he is without a distribution and inheritance with you. **28** At the extremity[743] of three years, you will bring out all the tenth part of your production in that year, and you will make it rest in your gates, **29** and *Lewi* will come, given that he is without a distribution and inheritance with you, and the immigrant, and the orphan, and the widow that is in your gates, and they will eat and they will be satisfied, so that ***YHWH*** your *Elohiym* will respect you, in all the work of your hand which you will do.

---

[740] The meaning of "daughter of the owl" is uncertain; most translations ignore the word "daughter." the *Septuagint* has just στρουθὸν (*strouthon*) meaning "sparrow."

[741] Meaning "the road is too long for you."

[742] Or "forget."

[743] Meaning "at the end."

Chapter 15

1 At the conclusion of seven years, you will release, **2** and this is the word of
the release to release, every master of a loan, his hand which he will lend
with his companion, he will not push his companion and his brother, given
that he called out a release to ***YHWH***. **3** The foreigner you will push, and
what will belong to you with your brother, you will make your hand release.
4 In the end there will not exist within you a needy one, given that ***YHWH***
will respect you in the land which ***YHWH*** your *Elohiym* is giving to you as an
inheritance to possess her, **5** Only if you will certainly hear the voice of
YHWH your *Elohiym*, to safeguard to do all these directives, which I am
directing you today, **6** given that ***YHWH*** your *Elohiym* respected you, just as
he spoke to you, and you will cause an abundance of nations to make a
pledge, but you will not make a pledge, and you will regulate with the
abundance of nations, but in you they will not regulate. **7** When the needy
will exist within you from one of your brothers, in one of your gates, in your
land which ***YHWH*** your *Elohiym* is giving to you, you will not make your
heart be strong, and you will not close your hand from your brother, **8** given
that your hand will surely be open to him, and you will surely cause him to
make a pledge, sufficient for his lacking, which will diminish for him.
9 Safeguard yourself, otherwise a word will exist with your heart, the
unaware will gain saying, the seventh year, the year of the release came
near, and your eye will be dysfunctional with your needy brother, and you
will not give to him, and he will call out concerning you to ***YHWH***, and failure
will exist in you. **10** You will surely give to him, and your heart will not be
dysfunctional in your giving to him, given that on account of this word,
YHWH your *Elohiym* will respect you in all your work and in all the sending
of your hand, **11** given that the needy will not terminate from inside the
land, therefore I am directing you to say, your hand will surely open to your
brother, for your afflicted and for your needy in your land. **12** When your
brother, the one of *Ever*[744] or the one of *Ever*[745], will be sold to you, and he
will serve you six years, and in the seventh year you will send him free from
with you, **13** and when you will send him free from with you, you will not
send him empty. **14** You will surely cause him to be encompassed from your
flocks, and from your floor and from your wine trough, what ***YHWH*** your
Elohiym respected you, you will give him, **15** and you will remember that you
existed as a servant in the land of *Mits'rayim*, and ***YHWH*** your *Elohiym* will
ransom you, therefore I am directing you this word today, **16** and it will
come to pass that he will say to you, I will not go out from among you, given
that he loved you and your house, given that it is functional for him with
you, **17** and you will take the awl, and you will give it in his ear, and in the
door, and he will exist for you a distant servant, and moreover for your

---

[744] This Hebrew word is in the masculine and means a "Hebrew."
[745] This Hebrew word is in the feminine and means "Hebrewess."

bondwoman you will do so. **18** He will not be hard in your eyes in sending him free from among you, given that a double of the wage of a hireling he served you six years, and ***YHWH*** your *Elohiym* will respect you in all that you will do. **19** Every firstborn which will be brought forth in your cattle and in your flocks, the male you will set apart for ***YHWH*** your *Elohiym*, you will not serve[746] with the firstborn of your oxen, and you will not shear the firstborn of your flocks. **20** To the face of ***YHWH*** your *Elohiym* you will eat him, year by year, in the area which ***YHWH*** will choose, you and your house, **21** and if in him will exist a blemish, lame or blind, any dysfunctional blemish, you will not sacrifice him to ***YHWH*** your *Elohiym*. **22** You will eat him in your gates, the dirty and the clean together, like the gazelle and like the buck. **23** Only his blood you will not eat, you will pour him out upon the land like waters.

Chapter 16

1 Safeguard the new moon of the green grain, and you will do *Pesahh* for ***YHWH*** your *Elohiym*, given that in the new moon of the green grain ***YHWH*** your *Elohiym* brought you out from *Mits'rayim* by night, **2** and you will sacrifice the *Pesahh* to ***YHWH*** your *Elohiym*, flocks and cattle, in the area where ***YHWH*** will choose to place his title there. **3** You will not eat with him leavened breads seven days, you will eat with him unleavened breads, bread of affliction, given that in haste you went out from the land of *Mits'rayim*, so that you will remember the day of going out from the land of *Mits'rayim* all the days of your life, **4** and leaven will not be seen for you in all your borders seven days, and nothing will stay the night from the flesh which you will sacrifice in the evening on the first day to the morning. **5** You will not be able to sacrifice the *Pesahh* in one of your gates which ***YHWH*** your *Elohiym* is giving to you. **6** Except to the area which ***YHWH*** your *Elohiym* will choose to place his title there, you will sacrifice the *Pesahh* in the evening, at the coming of the sun, the appointed time of your going out from *Mits'rayim*, **7** and you will boil, and you will eat, in the area which ***YHWH*** your *Elohiym* will choose in him, and you will turn in the morning, and you will walk to your tents. **8** Six days you will eat unleavened breads, and on the seventh day is a conference to ***YHWH*** your *Elohiym*, you will not do business. **9** Seven weeks you will count for you, from the beginning of the sickle with the grain stalk you will begin to count seven weeks, **10** and you will do the feast of weeks to ***YHWH*** your *Elohiym*, a proportion of the freewill offering of your hand, which you will give, just as ***YHWH*** your *Elohiym* respected you, **11** and you will rejoice to the face of ***YHWH*** your *Elohiym*, you and your sons and your daughters and your servant and your bondwoman and the *Lewi* which are in your gates, and the immigrant and the orphan and the widow which are in among you, in the area which ***YHWH*** will choose to place his title

---

[746] Or "work."

there, **12** and you will remember that you existed as a servant in *Mits'rayim*, and you will safeguard, and you will do these customs. **13** You will do the feast of booths for you seven days, in your gathering from your floor and from your wine trough, **14** and you will rejoice in your feasts, you and your son and your daughter and your servant and your bondwoman and the *Lewi* and the immigrant and the orphan and the widow which are in your gates. **15** Seven days you will hold a feast for ***YHWH*** your *Elohiym* in the area which ***YHWH*** will choose, given that ***YHWH*** your *Elohiym* will respect all your production and all the work of your hands, and you will surely exist rejoicing. **16** Three times in the year all your men will appear at the face of ***YHWH*** your *Elohiym* in the area which he will choose, in the feast of unleavened breads and in the feast of weeks and in the feast of booths, but will not appear at the face of ***YHWH*** empty. **17** Each according to the contribution of his hand, according to the present of ***YHWH*** your *Elohiym* which he gave to you. **18** Deciders and officers you will make for you in all your gates, which ***YHWH*** your *Elohiym* is giving to you for your staffs[747], and they will decide for the people, a decision of steadfastness. **19** You will not turn away from a decision, you will not pay attention to faces, and you will not take a bribe, given that the bribe will blind the eyes of the skilled ones, and will twist the words of steadfastness backwards. **20** You will pursue complete steadfastness so that you will live, and you will possess the land which ***YHWH*** your *Elohiym* is giving to you. **21** You will not plant for yourself a grove of any tree beside the altar of ***YHWH*** your *Elohiym* which you will make for yourself, **22** and you will not raise for yourself a monument which ***YHWH*** your *Elohiym* hated.

Chapter 17

1 You will not sacrifice to ***YHWH*** your *Elohiym* an ox or a ram, which will exist in him a blemish, anything dysfunctional, given that he is disgusting to ***YHWH*** your *Elohiym*. **2** If a man or woman will be found in among you, in one of your gates which ***YHWH*** your *Elohiym* is giving to you, which will do dysfunction in the eyes of ***YHWH*** your *Elohiym*, to cross over[748] his covenant, **3** and he will walk and he will serve other *Elohiym*, and he will bend himself down to them, and to the sun or to the moon or to any army of the skies which I did not direct, **4** and he will be told to you, and you will hear and you will thoroughly seek, and look, truth, the thing is being prepared, this disgusting thing was done in *Yisra'eyl*, **5** and you will bring out that man or that woman which did this dysfunctional thing, to your gates, the man or the woman, and you will stone them with stones and they will die. **6** By the mouth of two witnesses or three witnesses, the dying will be

---

[747] Meaning "tribes."

[748] Meaning to ignore or violate.

killed, he will not be killed by the mouth of one witness. **7** The hand of the witnesses will exist on him first to kill him, and the hand of all the people after, and you will burn the dysfunction from inside you. **8** When a word is too difficult for you for a decision, between blood and blood, between plea to plea, and between touch and touch, disputed words in your gates, then you will rise and you will go up to the area which ***YHWH*** your *Elohiym* will choose for himself, **9** and you will come to the administrators, the ones of *Lewi*, and to the deciders which will exist in those days, and you will seek, and they will tell to you the word of the decision, **10** and you will do according to the word which they will tell to you from that area which ***YHWH*** will choose, and you will safeguard to do according to all which they will throw you. **11** According to the teaching which they will throw you, and according to the decision which they will say to you, you will do, you will not turn aside the right hand or the left hand from the word which they will tell to you, **12** and the man which will do arrogance, by not hearing the administrator, the one standing to minister ***YHWH*** your *Elohiym* there, or to the decider, and that man will die, and you will burn the dysfunction from *Yisra'eyl*, **13** and all the people will hear and they will fear, and he will not simmer again, **14** given that you will come to the land which ***YHWH*** your *Elohiym* is giving to you, and you will possess her, and you will settle in her, and you will say, I will place upon me a king like all the nations which are all around me. **15** You will surely place upon you a king which ***YHWH*** your *Elohiym* will choose in him, from among your brothers you will place upon you a king, you will not be able to give upon you a foreign man who is not of your brothers, **16** but he will not make an increase for himself of horses, and he will not turn the people back unto *Mits'rayim* in order to increase horses, and ***YHWH*** said to you, you will not again turn back in this road again, **17** and he will not make an increase for himself of women, and he will not turn aside his heart, and much silver and gold he will not make an increase for himself, **18** and it will come to pass, as he settles upon the seat of his kingdom, and he will write for himself a double[749] of this teaching upon a scroll from the faces of the administrators, the ones of *Lewi*, **19** and she will exist with him, and he will call out[750] in him all the days of his life, so that he will learn to fear ***YHWH*** his *Elohiym*, to safeguard all the words of this teaching and these customs, to do them. **20** By not raising up his heart from his brothers, and by not turning aside from the directive, the right hand or the left hand, so that he will prolong the days upon his kingdom, he and his sons in among *Yisra'eyl*.

---

[749] That is a "copy."

[750] Meaning "read."

Chapter 18

1 A distribution and an inheritance with *Yisra'eyl* will not exist for the administrators, the ones of *Lewi*, any staff[751] of *Lewi*, fire offerings of ***YHWH*** and his inheritance he must eat, **2** and an inheritance will not exist for him in among his brothers, ***YHWH***, he is his inheritance just as he spoke to him, **3** and this will be the decision of the administrators from the people, from ones sacrificing the sacrifice, if an ox, if a ram, and he will give it to the administrator the arm and the jaws and the stomach. **4** The summit[752] of your cereal, your fresh wine, and the summit of the fleece of your flocks, you will give to him, **5** given that in him ***YHWH*** your *Elohiym* chose from all your staffs[753], to stand, to minister in the title of ***YHWH***, he and his sons, all the days, **6** and when the *Lewi* will come from one of your gates from all *Yisra'eyl*, where he immigrated there, and he will come with all the desire of his soul to the area which ***YHWH*** chose, **7** and he will minister in the title of ***YHWH*** his *Elohiym*, like all his brothers, the ones of *Lewi*, the ones standing there to the face of ***YHWH***. **8** Distribution like distribution they will eat, apart from his merchandise with the fathers, **9** given that you came to the land which ***YHWH*** your *Elohiym* is giving to you, you will not learn to do the disgusting things of those nations. **10** One will not be found among you making his son or his daughter to cross over in the fire, a divining one of divinations, conjurer or a predictor or a sorcerer. **11** Or a coupler of coupling or inquirer, necromancer or knower or seeker to the dying[754], **12** given that all of these doings are the disgusting things of ***YHWH***, and on account of these disgusting things ***YHWH*** your *Elohiym* is dispossessing them from your face. **13** You will exist whole with ***YHWH*** your *Elohiym*, **14** given that these nations, which you are possessing, they listened to the conjurer and to the diviner, and you, not so did ***YHWH*** your *Elohiym* give to you. **15** An announcer from among you, from your brothers, like one of me, ***YHWH*** your *Elohiym* will make rise, to him you must listen. **16** Just as all you inquired from ***YHWH*** your *Elohiym* in *Hhorev*, in the day of assembly, saying, not again to hear the voice of ***YHWH*** my *Elohiym*, and this great fire I will not see again, and I will not die, **17** and ***YHWH*** said to me, they did well which they spoke. **18** An announcer I will make rise for them from among their brothers, like one of you, and I will give my words in his mouth, and he will speak to them all which I will direct him, **19** and it will come to pass, the man which will not listen to my words which he will speak in my title, I, I will seek it from him, **20** but the announcer which will simmer to speak a word in my title, which I did not direct him to speak, or which he will speak in the title of another *Elohiym*, then that announcer will die, **21** and, given that you will

[751] A "tribe."

[752] This may be the "best" or the "first."

[753] Meaning "tribes."

[754] Or "the dead."

say in your heart, how will we know the word which ***YHWH*** did not speak to him. **22** When the announcer will speak in the title of ***YHWH***, and the word will not exist, and will not come, which is the word which ***YHWH*** did not speak to him, the announcer spoke him in arrogance, you will not be afraid of him,

---

Chapter 19

1 given that ***YHWH*** your *Elohiym* will cut the nations, their land which ***YHWH*** your *Elohiym* is giving to you, and you will possess them, and you will settle in their cities and in their houses. **2** Three cities you will separate for you in the midst of your land which ***YHWH*** your *Elohiym* is giving to you to possess. **3** You will prepare for you the road, and you will make the border of your land which ***YHWH*** your *Elohiym* will make you inherit threefold[755], and he will exist for fleeing unto there every murderer, **4** and this is the word of the murderer which will flee unto there that he will live, one who will attack his companion with unaware discernment[756], and he is not hating him previously, **5** and when he will come with his companion in the forest to carve trees, and his hand will be driven out with the ax to cut the tree, and the iron is cast off from the tree[757], and he will find[758] his companion, and he died, he will flee to one of these cities and he will live. **6** Otherwise the redeemer of blood will pursue after the murderer, given that his heart is heated, and he will overtake him, given that the road is long, and he will attack him, the soul, and to him is without a decision of death, given that he was not hating him previously. **7** Therefore I am directing you to say, three cities you will separate for you, **8** and if ***YHWH*** your *Elohiym* will widen your border just as he swore to your fathers, and to give to you all the land which he spoke to give to your fathers, **9** given that you will safeguard all these directives to do her, which I am directing you today, to love ***YHWH*** your *Elohiym*, and to walk in his road all the days, and you will add to you again three cities upon these three, **10** and the blood of innocent will not be poured out inside your land which ***YHWH*** your *Elohiym* is giving to you, an inheritance, and bloodshed will exist upon you, **11** and, given that a man will exist hating his companion, and he will ambush him, and he will rise upon him, and he will attack him, a soul, and he will die, then he will flee to one of these cities, **12** and the bearded ones of his city will send, and they will take him from there, and they will give him in the hand of the redeemer of blood, and he will die. **13** Your eye will not spare him, and you will burn the blood of the innocent from *Yisra'eyl*, and he will go well for you. **14** You will not

---

[755] That is, "three parts."

[756] "Unaware discernment" means "unknowingly."

[757] Meaning the ax head flew off the handle.

[758] "He will find" means that the iron of the ax head will "strike."

overtake the border of your companion which they bound first in your
inheritance, which you will inherit in the land which ***YHWH*** your *Elohiym* is
giving to you to possess. **15** A witness of one will not rise with a man for
every twistedness and for every failure which he failed, according to the
mouth of two witnesses or according to the mouth of three witnesses a
word will rise. **16** If a witness of violence will rise with a man to answer in
him a turning aside, **17** and the two men, which belong to them a dispute,
will stand to the faces of the administrators and the deciders which exist in
their days, **18** and the deciders will seek to do well, and look, a false witness,
the false witness afflicted his brother, **19** and you will do to him just as he
plotted to do to his brother, and you will burn the dysfunction from inside
you, **20** and the remaining ones will hear, and they will fear, and they will
not again do again like the word of this dysfunction in among you, **21** and
your eye will not spare, soul with soul, eye with eye, tooth with tooth, hand
with hand, foot with foot,

Chapter 20

1 given that you will go out to battle, upon your attackers, and you will see
the horse and vehicle, a people more abundant than you, you will not fear
them, given that ***YHWH*** your *Elohiym* is with you, bringing you up from the
land of *Mits'rayim*, **2** and it will come to pass, as you come near to battle,
and the administrator will be drawn near, and he will speak to the people,
3 and he will say to them, listen *Yisra'eyl*, you are near the day to battle
upon your attackers, your heart will not be soft, you will not fear, and you
will not hasten, and you will not be terrified from their faces, **4** given that
YHWH your *Elohiym* is the one walking with you to fight for you with your
attackers to rescue you, **5** and the officers will speak to the people saying,
who is the man which built a new house and did not devote himself, he will
walk and he will turn back to his house, otherwise he will die in battle, and
the other man will devote himself, **6** and who is the man which planted a
vineyard and has not begun him, he will walk and he will turn back to his
house, otherwise he will die in battle and the other man will begin him,
7 and who is the man which will betroth a woman and he will not take her,
he will walk and he will turn back to his house, otherwise he will die in
battle, and the other man will take her, **8** and the officers will add to speak
to the people, and they will say, who is the man fearing and the tender heart
will walk and he will turn back to his house, and the heart of his brothers will
not be melted away like his heart, **9** and it will come to pass, as the officers
finish speaking to the people, and they will register the nobles of the armies
by the head of the people, **10** given that you will come near to the city to
fight upon her, and you will call out to her for completeness, **11** and it will
come to pass, if completeness, she will afflict you, and she will open to you,
and it will come to pass, all the people being found in her, they will exist for

you for task work, and they will serve you, **12** and if not, she will make restitution with you, and she will make battle with you, and you will smack upon her, **13** and ***YHWH*** your *Elohiym* will give her in your hand, and you will attack all her men by the mouth[759] of the sword. **14** Only the women and the babies and the beast and all which will exist in the city, all her spoils you will plunder for yourself, and you will eat the spoils of your attackers which ***YHWH*** your *Elohiym* gave to you. **15** So you will do to all the very distant cities from you, because they are not from the cities of these nations. **16** Only from the cities of these peoples, which ***YHWH*** your *Elohiym* is giving to you as an inheritance, you will not keep alive any breath, **17** given that you will completely perforate them, the ones of *Hhet* and the ones of *Emor*, the ones of *Kena'an* and the ones of *Perez*, the ones of *Hhiw* and the ones of *Yevus*, just as ***YHWH*** your *Elohiym* directed you. **18** So that when they will not teach you to do all their disgusting things which they do to their *Elohiym*, and you will fail to ***YHWH*** your *Elohiym*. **19** When you fence in[760] a city an abundance of days, to be fought upon her, to seize hold of her, you will not damage her trees, to drive out upon him the ax, given that from him you will eat, and him you will not cut, given that for the human is the tree of the field[761], to come from your face with the smacking. **20** Only the trees which you will know, given that he is not a tree of nourishment, him you will damage, and you will cut, and you will build a smacking[762] upon the city that is doing battle with you until her going down.

Chapter 21

1 If one will be found drilled in the ground, which ***YHWH*** your *Elohiym* is giving to you to possess her, falling in the field, it is not known who attacked him, **2** then the bearded ones will go out, and your deciders, and they will measure to the cities which are all around the drilled one, **3** and it will come to pass, the nearest city to the drilled one, and the bearded ones of that city will take a heifer of the cattle which has not served, which did not draw in a yoke, **4** and the bearded ones of that city will bring down the heifer to a consistent wadi, which was not served and which was not sown, and they will behead there the heifer in the wadi, **5** and the administrators, the sons of *Lewi*, will be drawn near, given that in them ***YHWH*** your *Elohiym* chose to minister to him, and to respect in the title of ***YHWH***, and upon their mouth every dispute and every touch will exist, **6** and all the bearded ones of that city, the ones near to the drilled one, they will bathe their hands upon the heifer, the one beheaded in the wadi, **7** and they will answer, and they will

[759] That is, the "edge."
[760] Meaning to "siege."
[761] Or "in the sieging."
[762] That is, "siege works."

say, our hands did not pour out this blood, and our eyes did not see. **8** A covering to your people of *Yisra'eyl*, who you, ***YHWH***, ransomed, and you will not give innocent blood in among your people of *Yisra'eyl*, and the blood will cover for them, **9** and you, you will burn the innocent blood from inside you, given that you will do the straight thing in the eyes of ***YHWH***, **10** given that you will go out to the battle upon your attackers, and ***YHWH*** your *Elohiym* will give him in your hands, and you will capture his captives, **11** and you will see in the captives a woman of beauty of form, and you will attach with her, and you will take for you for a woman, **12** and you will bring her to the midst of your house, and she will shave her head, and she will do her points[763], **13** and she will turn aside the apparel of her captivity from upon her, and she will settle in your house, and she will weep for her father and her mother a moon of days, and afterward you will come to her, and you will marry her, and she will exist for you for a woman, **14** and it will come to pass, if you did not delight in her, and you will send her to her soul, and you will surely not sell her with silver, you will not bundle her under, because you afflicted her. **15** If two women will exist for a man, one is loved and one is hated, and they will bring forth for him sons, the loved one and the hated one, and the firstborn son will exist to the hated one, **16** and it will come to pass in the day of making his sons, which will exist for him, to inherit him, he will not be able to make the son of the loved one be the firstborn over the face of the son of the hated one, the firstborn, **17** but he will recognize the firstborn son of the hated one, to give to him a mouth of two[764] in all which will be found for him, given that he is the summit of his vigor, for him is the decision of the birthright. **18** When a son will exist for a man, being stubborn and disobeying, he is not hearing the voice of his father or the voice of his mother, and they correct him and he will not listen to them, **19** then his father and his mother will seize hold of him, and bring him out to the bearded ones of his city and to the gate of his area, **20** and they will say to the bearded ones of his city, this is our son, being stubborn and disobeying, he is not hearing our voice, gluttoning and imbibing, **21** and all the men of his city will kill him by stoning with stones, and he will die, and you will burn the dysfunction from among you, and all *Yisra'eyl* will hear and they will fear, **22** and when a failure will exist in a man, a decision of death, and he will be killed, and you will hang him upon a tree. **23** You will not let his carcass stay the night upon the tree, given that you will surely bury him in that day, given that a hanged one is an annoyance of *Elohiym*, and you will not dirty your ground which ***YHWH*** your *Elohiym* is giving to you as an inheritance.

---

[763] That is, "finger-nails."

[764] A "mouth of two" is a double portion of the inheritance.

Chapter 22

1 You will not see an ox of your brother, or his ram, be driven out, and you will be out of sight from them, you will surely turn them back to your brother, **2** and if your brother is not near to you, and you do not know him, then you will gather him to the midst of your house, and he will exist with you until your brother seeks him, and you will turn him back to him, **3** and so you will do to his donkey, and so you will to his apparel, and so you will do to any lost thing of your brother, which will perish[765] from him, and you will find, you will not be able to be out of sight. **4** You will not see the donkey of your brother, or his ox, falling in the road, and you will be out of sight from them, you will surely make them rise with him. **5** A utensil of a warrior will not exist upon a woman, and a warrior will not wear the apparel of a woman, given that all these doings are disgusting of ***YHWH*** your *Elohiym*. **6** When a nest of a bird will meet to your face in the road, in any tree or upon the land, chicks or eggs, and the mother is stretching out upon the chicks or upon the eggs, you will not take the mother with the sons. **7** You will surely send the mother, and the sons you will take for you, so that it will go well for you, and you will make your days prolonged. **8** When you will build a new house, then you will make a parapet for your roof, and you will not place blood on your house when the one falling falls from him. **9** You will not sow your vineyard of diverse kinds, otherwise the ripe fruit of the seed which you will sow, and the production of the vineyard will be set apart. **10** You will not scratch[766] with an ox and with the donkey together. **11** You will not wear linsey-woolsey wool and flax things together. **12** You will make tassels for you upon the four wings of your raiment, which you will cover over with her. **13** When a man will take a woman, and he will come to her and he will hate her, **14** and he placed on her workings of words, and he will bring out upon her a title of dysfunction, and he will say, this woman I took, and I came near to her, and I did not find virginity for her, **15** and the father of the young woman, and her mother, will take and bring out the signs of virginity of the young woman to the bearded ones of the city unto the gate, **16** and the father of the young woman will say to the bearded ones, my daughter I gave to this man for a woman, and he hated her, **17** and look, he, he placed workings of the words saying, I did not find virginity for your daughter, and these are the signs of the virginity of my daughter, and they will spread out the apparel to the face of the bearded ones of the city, **18** and the bearded ones of that city took the man, and they corrected him, **19** and they fined him a hundred silver, and they will give it to the father of the young woman, given that he brought out a title of dysfunction upon the virgin of *Yisra'eyl*, and she will exist to him for a woman, he will not be able to send her all his days, **20** and if this word is truth, the sign of virginity will

---

[765] Or "be lost."

[766] That is, "plow."

not be found for the young woman, **21** then bring out the young woman to the opening of the house of her father, and the men of her city will stone her with stones, and she will die, given that she did folly in *Yisra'eyl*, to be a harlot of the house of her father, and you will burn the dysfunction from inside you, **22** given that the man lying down with a woman, married of a master, and they will die, also the two of them, the man lying down with the woman and the woman, and you will burn the dysfunction from *Yisra'eyl*.
23 If there will exist a young woman, a virgin, betrothed to a man, and a man will find her in the city, and he will lay down with her, **24** then you will bring the two of them out to the gate of that city, and you will stone them with stones, and they will die, the young woman because of the word[767] that she did not cry out in the city, and the man because of the matter that he afflicted the woman of his companion, and you will burn the dysfunction from inside you, **25** but if in the field the man will find the young woman, the one betrothed, and the man will seize her, and he will lay down with her, then the man which laid down with her will die alone, **26** but to the young woman you will not do a thing, for the young woman is without a failure of death, given that just as a man will rise upon his companion and murder him, a soul, so is this word, **27** given that in the field he found her, the young woman, the one betrothed, cried out, and without a rescuer for her. **28** If a man will find a young woman, a virgin which is not betrothed, and he seized hold of her, and lay down with her, and they will be found, **29** then the man, the one lying down with her, will give to the father of the young woman fifty silver, and she will exist to him for a woman, because he afflicted her, he will not be able to send her all his days.

Chapter 23

1 (22:30) A man will not take the woman of his father, he will not remove the cover of the wing of his father. **2 (23:1)** One who is wounded, broken or a cut penis, will not come in the assembly of ***YHWH***. **3 (23:2)** A bastard will not come in the assembly of ***YHWH***, also the tenth generation of him will not come in the assembly of ***YHWH***. **4 (23:3)** Not one of *Amon* or one of *Mo'av* will come,, in the assembly of ***YHWH***, also the tenth generation of them will not come in the assembly of ***YHWH***, until a distant time. **5 (23:4)** Because of the word that they did not face toward you with the bread and with the waters in the road, in your going out from *Mits'rayim*, and because he hired upon you *Bilam* the son of *Be'or* from *Petor Aram-Nahara'im* to belittle you, **6 (23:5)** and ***YHWH*** your *Elohiym* did not consent to listen to *Bilam*, and ***YHWH*** your *Elohiym* overturned for you the annoyance for a present, given that ***YHWH*** your *Elohiym* loved you. **7 (23:6)** You will not seek their completeness and their function all your days

[767] This Hebrew word can also mean "matter." (also in verse 23:5)

to a distant time. **8 (23:7)** You will not abhor one of *Edom*, given that he is your brother, you will not abhor one of *Mits'rayim*, given that you existed as an immigrant in his land. **9 (23:8)** Sons, which will be brought forth to them, the third generation will come to them in the assembly of ***YHWH***, **10 (23:9)** given that the camp will go out upon your attackers, and you will be safeguarded from all words of dysfunction. **11 (23:10)** When a man that is not clean from an event of the night, will exist in you, and he will go out to the outside of the camp, he will not come to the midst of the camp, **12 (23:11)** and it will come to pass in the turning of the evening, he will bathe in the waters, and as the sun comes, he will come to the midst of the camp, **13 (23:12)** and a hand will exist for you outside the camp, and you will go out unto there, outside, **14 (23:13)** and a tent peg will exist for you with your tools, and it will come to pass in your settling outside, and you will dig out in her, and you will turn back, and you will cover over your going out[768], **15 (23:14)** given that ***YHWH*** your *Elohiym* is walking inside your camp to deliver you, and to give your attackers to your face, and it will come to pass, your camps are unique, and he will not see in you a naked thing and he will turn back from after you. **16 (23:15)** You will not deliver a servant to his lords that was delivered to you from his lords. **17 (23:16)** With you, he will settle in among you, in the area which he will choose, in one of your gates, in the functional one for him, you will not suppress him. **18 (23:17)** A prostitute will not exist from the daughters of *Yisra'eyl*, and a male prostitute will not exist from the sons of *Yisra'eyl*. **19 (23:18)** You will not bring the wage of a harlot, or the price of a dog, into the house of ***YHWH*** your *Elohiym*, for any vow, also both of them are disgusting to ***YHWH*** your *Elohiym*. **20 (23:19)** You will not cause your brother to bite a usury of silver, a usury of foodstuff, a usury of anything which he will bite. **21 (23:20)** To the foreigner you will cause to bite, but to your brother you will not cause to bite, so that ***YHWH*** your *Elohiym* will respect you in all that your hand is sending upon the land where you are going unto there to possess her, **22 (23:21)** given that you will make a vow to ***YHWH*** your *Elohiym*, you will not delay to make his restitution, given that ***YHWH*** your *Elohiym* will surely seek him with you, and failure will exist in you, **23 (23:22)** and when you will terminate to make a vow, a failure will not exist in you. **24 (23:23)** The going out of your lips you will safeguard and you will do, just as you made a vow of a freewill offering to ***YHWH*** your *Elohiym*, you will speak with your mouth. **25 (23:24)** When you will come in the vineyard of your companion, and you will eat grapes, as many as your soul wants, but you will not place any in your utensil. **26 (23:25)** When you will come in the grain stalks of your companion, and you will crop off a head of wheat with your hand, but you will not wave a sickle upon the grain stalk of your companion.

---

[768] That is, "excrement."

Chapter 24

1 When a man will take a woman, and he will marry her, and it will come to pass, if she will not find beauty in his eyes, given that he found a nakedness of a thing in her, then he will write a scroll of divorce, and he will give it in her hand, and he will send her from his house, **2** and she will go out from his house, and she will walk, and she will exist for another man, **3** and the last man will hate her, and he will write for her a scroll of divorce, and he will give it in her hand, and he will send her from his house, or when the last man which took her for him for a woman will die. **4** Her first master, who sent her turning back, will not be able to take her to exist for him for a woman, after that she will be made dirty, given that she is disgusting to the face of ***YHWH***, and you will not fail the land which ***YHWH*** your *Elohiym* is giving to you as an inheritance. **5** When a man will take a new woman, he will not go out in the army, and he will not cross over upon him for anything, he will exist innocent to his house one year, and he will rejoice with his woman which he took. **6** He will not take millstones or vehicle as a pledge, given that he is taking a soul as a pledge. **7** If a man is found stealing a soul from his brothers, from the sons of *Yisra'eyl*, and he bundled himself in him, and he will sell him, then that thief will die, and you will burn the dysfunction from inside you. **8** Be safeguarded in the touch of the infection, to greatly safeguard, and to do just as the administrators, the ones of *Lewi*, will throw at you, just as I directed them, you will safeguard to do. **9** Remember what ***YHWH*** your *Elohiym* did to *Mir'yam* in the road, in your going out from *Mits'rayim*, **10** given that you will lend to your companion a loan of anything, you will not come to his house to take his pledge. **11** You will stand in the outside, and the man that you are lending to him, he will bring out to you the pledge, to the outside, **12** and if he is a man of affliction, you will not lay down with his pledge. **13** You will certainly make the pledge turn back to him with the coming[769] of the sun, and he will lay down with his outer garment, and he will respect you, and steadfastness will exist to you to the face of ***YHWH*** your *Elohiym*. **14** You will not oppress a hireling, one afflicted and needy, from your brothers or from your immigrants, which are in your land, in your gates. **15** In his day you will give his wage, and the sun will not come[770] upon him, given that he is afflicted, and he belongs to him for a lifting up of his soul, and he will not call out upon you to ***YHWH***, and failure will exist in you. **16** Your fathers will not be killed because of the sons, and the sons will not be killed because of the fathers, each will be killed with his failure. **17** You will not cause to extend[771] a decision of an immigrant or orphan, and you will not take a garment of widow as a pledge, **18** and you will remember that you existed as a servant in *Mits'rayim*, and ***YHWH*** your

---

[769] Or "going."

[770] Or "go."

[771] Probably meaning "to pervert."

Elohiym ransomed you from there, therefore I am directing you to do this word. **19** When you sever your harvest in your field, and you forget the sheaf in the field, you will not turn back to take him, he will exist for the immigrant, for the orphan and for the widow, so that ***YHWH*** your *Elohiym* will respect you in all the work of your hands. **20** When you knock your olives, you will not decorate[772] after you, he will exist for the immigrant, for the orphan and for the widow. **21** When you fence in your vineyard, you will not roll after you, he will exist for the immigrant, for the orphan and for the widow, **22** and you will remember that you existed as a servant in *Mits'rayim*, therefore I am directing you to do this word.

Chapter 25

1 When a dispute will exist between men, and they will be drawn near to the decision, and they will decide them, and they will make the steadfast one be steadfast, and they will make the lost depart, **2** and it will come to pass, if a son attacks the lost, and the decider will make him fall, and he will attack him to his face, according to the sufficiency of his waywardness, by the number. **3** He will attack him forty times, he will not add, otherwise he will add to his attack many more of the hittings, and your brother will be dry to your eyes. **4** You will not muzzle the ox with the threshing. **5** When brothers will settle together, and one of them will die, and is without a son to him, the woman of the dead one will not exist unto the one outside, to a strange man, her brother-in-law will come upon her, and he will take her for him for a woman, and he will do the marriage duty with her, **6** and it will come to pass, the firstborn, which she will bring forth, will rise upon the title of his dead brother, and he will not wipe his title from *Yisra'eyl*, **7** and if the man will not delight to take his sister-in-law, and his sister-in-law will go up unto the gate, to the bearded ones, and she will say, he refused to do the marriage duty for me, to make his brother raise a title in *Yisra'eyl*, he did not consent to do the marriage duty for me, **8** and the bearded ones of his city called out to him, and they spoke to him, he stood, and he said, I did not delight to take her, **9** and his sister-in-law will be drawn near to him, to the eyes of the bearded ones, and she will extract his sandal from upon his foot, and she will spit in his face, and she will answer, and she will say, as in this way it will be done to the man which will not build the house of his brother, **10** and his title will be called out in *Yisra'eyl*, the house of the extracted one of the sandal. **11** When men will struggle together, a man and his brother, and the woman of the one will come near to deliver her man from the hand of his attacker, and she will send her hand, and she will seize his genitals, **12** then you will slice off her palm, your eye will not spare. **13** A stone and

[772] The meaning of this Hebrew verb in the context of the passage is not certain.

stone, great and small[773], will not exist for you in your bag. **14** An *eyphah* and *eyphah*, great and small[774], will not exist for you in your house. **15** A complete and steadfast stone will exist for you, a complete and steadfast *eyphah* will exist for you, so that your days upon the ground, which ***YHWH*** your *Elohiym* is giving to you, will be prolonged, **16** given that anyone doing these, anyone doing wicked, is disgusting to ***YHWH*** your *Elohiym*. **17** Remember what *Amaleq* did to you in the road in your going out from *Mits'rayim*. **18** When he met you in the road, and he attacked your rear, all the ones being shattered behind you, and you were tired and weary, and he did not fear *Elohiym*, **19** and it will come to pass, with ***YHWH*** your *Elohiym* making rest for you from all your attackers, from all around in the land, which ***YHWH*** your *Elohiym* is giving to you as an inheritance to possess her, you will wipe away the memory of *Amaleq* from under the skies, you will not forget,

Chapter 26

1 and it will come to pass, when you come to the land, which ***YHWH*** your *Elohiym* is giving to you as an inheritance, and you will possess her, and you will settle in her, **2** and you will take from the summit of all the produce of the ground, which you will bring from your land, which ***YHWH*** your *Elohiym* is giving to you, and you will place in the reed basket, and you will walk to the area which ***YHWH*** your *Elohiym* will choose for his title to dwell there, **3** and you will come to the administrator, which will exist in those days, and you will say to him, I will tell today to ***YHWH*** your *Elohiym*, given that I came to the land, which ***YHWH*** swore to our fathers to give to us, **4** and the administrator will take the reed basket from your hand, and he will make him rest to the face of the altar of ***YHWH*** your *Elohiym*, **5** and you will answer, and you will say to the face of ***YHWH*** your *Elohiym*, a perishing one of *Aram* is my father, and he will go down unto *Mits'rayim*, and he will immigrate there with a few mortal men, and he will exist there for a great, numerous and abundant nation, **6** and the ones of *Mits'rayim* will make us dysfunctional, and they will afflict us, and they will place upon us a hard service, **7** and we cried out to ***YHWH*** the *Elohiym* of our fathers, and ***YHWH*** heard our voice, and he saw our affliction and our labor and our squeezing, **8** and ***YHWH*** brought us out from *Mits'rayim* with a forceful hand, and with an extended arm, and with a great fearing, and with signs, and with wonders, **9** and he brought us to this area, and he gave to us this land issuing fat and honey, **10** and now look, I brought the summit of the produce of the

[773] This may also be translated as "a great stone and a small stone," or "a heavy stone and a light stone."
[774] This may also be translated as "a great *eyphah* and a small *eyphah*," or "a heavy *eyphah* and a light *eyphah*."

ground, which you ***YHWH*** gave to me, and you will make him rest to the face of ***YHWH*** your *Elohiym*, and you will bend yourself down to the face of ***YHWH*** your *Elohiym*, **11** and you will rejoice in all the functional things which ***YHWH*** your *Elohiym* gave to you, and to your house, you and the one of *Lewi*, and the immigrant which is in among you. **12** When you will finish giving a tenth of all the tenth part of your production in the third year, the year of the tenth part, and you will give to *Lewi*, to the immigrant, to the orphan, and to the widow, and they will eat in your gates, and they will be satisfied, **13** and you will say to the face of ***YHWH*** your *Elohiym*, I burned the special thing from the house, and also I gave him to *Lewi* and to the immigrant, to the orphan and to the widow, like all your directives which you directed me, I did not cross over from your directives, and I did not forget. **14** I did not eat in my barrenness from him, and I did not burn from him in dirtiness, and I did not give from him to the dying, I heard the voice of ***YHWH*** my *Elohiym*, I did as all which you directed me. **15** Look down from your special habitation from the skies, and respect your people *Yisra'eyl*, and the ground which you gave to us, just as you swore to our fathers, a land issuing fat and honey. **16** This day ***YHWH*** your *Elohiym* is directing you to do these customs and decisions, and you will safeguard and you will do them with all your heart and with all your soul. **17** You made ***YHWH*** say today[775], to exist for you for *Elohiym*, and to walk in his road, and to safeguard his customs, and his directives, and his decisions, and to hear his voice, **18** and ***YHWH*** made you say today, to exist for him for a jeweled people, just as he spoke to you, and to safeguard all his directives, **19** and to make you above all the nations which he did, for adoration, and for a name, and for a decoration, and to make you a unique people for ***YHWH*** your *Elohiym*, just as he spoke,

---

Chapter 27

1 and *Mosheh*, and the bearded one of *Yisra'eyl*, directed the people saying, safeguard all the directives which I am directing you today, **2** and it will come to pass, in the day when you will cross over the *Yarden*, to the land which ***YHWH*** your *Elohiym* is giving to you, and you will make great stones rise up for you, and you will plaster them with lime, **3** and you will write upon them all the words of this teaching, in your crossing over, so that when you will come to the land which ***YHWH*** your *Elohiym* is giving to you, a land issuing fat and honey, just as ***YHWH*** the *Elohiym* of your fathers spoke to you, **4** and it will come to pass, in your crossing over the *Yarden*, you will make these stones rise, which I am directing you today, in the hill of *Eyval*, and you will

---

[775] While this phrase literally reads, "You made ***YHWH*** say today," the *Septuagint* reads, "You have chosen ***YHWH*** (theos *Bera* God) today." This may preserve the original Hebrew wording for this phrase.

plaster them with lime, **5** and you will build there an altar to ***YHWH*** your *Elohiym*, an altar of stones, you will not wave upon them iron[776]. **6** You will build the altar of ***YHWH*** your *Elohiym* with complete stones, and you will bring upon him an ascension offering for ***YHWH*** your *Elohiym*, **7** and you will sacrifice an offering of restitution, and you will eat there, and you will rejoice to the face of ***YHWH*** your *Elohiym*, **8** and you will write upon the stones all the words of this teaching, well explained, **9** and *Mosheh*, and the administrators, the ones of *Lewi*, spoke to all *Yisra'eyl* saying, *Yisra'eyl*, take heed and hear this day, you will exist for a people for ***YHWH*** your *Elohiym*, **10** and you will hear the voice of ***YHWH*** your *Elohiym*, and you will do his directives and his customs, which I am directing you today, **11** and *Mosheh* directed the people in that day saying, **12** these will stand to respect the people upon the hill of *Gerizim*, in your crossing over the *Yarden*, *Shimon* and *Lewi* and *Yehudah* and *Yis'sas'khar* and *Yoseph* and *Binyamin*, **13** and these will stand upon the annoyance in the hill *Eyval*, *Re'uven*, *Gad* and *Asher* and *Zevulun*, *Dan* and *Naphtali*, **14** and the ones of *Lewi* will answer, and they will say to all the men of *Yisra'eyl*, a voice rising up. **15** Spat upon is the man who will make a sculpture and a cast image, disgusting of ***YHWH***, the work of the hands of the engraver, and he will place it in hiding, and all the people will answer and they will say, so be it. **16** Spat upon is the one making his father and his mother dry, and all the people said, so be it. **17** Spat upon is the one making the border of his companion be overtaken, and all the people said, so be it. **18** Spat upon is the one making the blind go astray in the road, and all the people said, so be it. **19** Spat upon is the one making the decision of the immigrant, orphan and widow extended, and all the people said, so be it. **20** Spat upon is the one lying down with the woman of his father, given that he removed the cover of the wing of his father, and all the people said, so be it. **21** Spat upon is the one lying down with any beast, and all the people said, so be it. **22** Spat upon is the one lying down with his sister, the daughter of his father or the daughter of his mother, and all the people said, so be it. **23** Spat upon is the one lying down with his in-law, and all the people said, so be it. **24** Spat upon is the one attacking his companion in hiding, and all the people said, so be it. **25** Spat upon is the one taking a bribe to attack a soul of innocent blood, and all the people said, so be it. **26** Spat upon is one who will not make the words of this teaching rise, to do them, and all the people said, so be it,

Chapter 28

1 and it will come to pass, if you will diligently hear the voice of ***YHWH*** your *Elohiym*, to safeguard to do all his directives, which I am directing you today, then ***YHWH*** your *Elohiym* will make you above all the nations of the land,

[776] Meaning "you will not hew them with an iron tool."

2 and these presents will come upon you, given that you will hear the voice
of ***YHWH*** your *Elohiym*. **3** Respected are you in the city and respected are
you in the field. **4** Respected are the produce of your womb, and the
produce of your ground, and the produce of your beast, the birth of your
bovine and the young sheep of your flocks. **5** Respected are your reed basket
and your kneading bowl. **6** Respected are you in your coming, and respected
are you in your going out. **7** ***YHWH*** will make your attackers, the ones rising
upon you, be smitten to your face, in one road, they will go out to you and
they will flee your face on seven roads. **8** ***YHWH*** will direct with you the
present in your barns and in all your hand sends, and he will respect you in
the land, which ***YHWH*** your *Elohiym* is giving to you. **9** ***YHWH*** will make you
rise for him for a unique people, just as he swore to you, given that you will
safeguard the directives of ***YHWH*** your *Elohiym*, and you will walk in his
roads, **10** and the people of the land will see that the title of ***YHWH*** will
come to meet with you, and they will fear you, **11** and ***YHWH*** will leave
behind you the functional produce of your womb, and the produce of your
beast, and the produce of your ground, upon the ground which ***YHWH***
swore to your fathers to give to you. **12** ***YHWH*** will open for you his
functional supply house, the skies will give the precipitation of your land in
his appointed time, and to respect all the work of your hand, and you will
make many nations join, but you will not join, **13** and ***YHWH*** will give to the
head and not to the tail, and you will only exist on top, and you will not exist
at the bottom, given that you heard the directives of ***YHWH*** your *Elohiym*,
which I am directing you today to safeguard and to do, **14** and you will not
turn aside from any of the words which I am directing you today, the right
hand and the left hand, to walk after other *Elohiym* to serve them, **15** and it
will come to pass, if you will not hear the voice of ***YHWH*** your *Elohiym*, to
safeguard to do all his directives and his customs, which I am directing you
today, then all these annoyances will come upon you, and they will overtake
you. **16** Spat upon are you in the city, and spat upon are you in the field.
17 Spat upon are your reed basket and your kneading bowl. **18** Spat upon
are the produce of your womb, and the produce of your ground, the birth of
your bovine and the young sheep of your flocks. **19** Spat upon are you in
your coming, and spat upon you in your going out, **20** and ***YHWH*** will send in
you the spitting and the tumult and the reproof, in all the sending of your
hand which you will do, until you are destroyed and until you perish quickly
from the face of the dysfunction of your works, because you left me.
21 ***YHWH*** will make the epidemic adhere in you until his finishing with you
from upon the ground, which you came unto there to possess her. **22** ***YHWH***
will attack you with consumption, and with fever, and with inflammation,
and with a burning flame, and with the sword, and with the blasting, and
with the mildew, and they will pursue you until you perish, **23** and your skies
which are over your head will exist as copper, and the land which is under
you as iron. **24** ***YHWH*** will make dust and dirt precipitate on your land, from
the skies it will go down until you are destroyed. **25** ***YHWH*** will make you be

smitten to the face of your attackers, in one road you will go out to him, but in seven roads you will flee from his face, and you will exist for an agitation to all the kingdoms of the land, **26** and your carcass will exist for nourishment to all the flyers of the skies, and to the beast of the land, and no one to make them tremble. **27** ***YHWH*** will attack you with boils of *Mits'rayim*, and with tumors, and with the irritation, and with the itch, which you will not be able to heal. **28** ***YHWH*** will attack you with madness, and with blindness, and with an astonishment of the heart, **29** and you will be groping in the noontime, just as the blind grope in the thick gloominess, and you will not prosper with your roads, and you will surely be oppressed and plucked away all the days, and there is no rescuer. **30** You will betroth a woman, but another man will copulate her, you will build a house, but you will not settle in him, you will plant a vineyard, but you will not drill him. **31** Your ox is butchered to your eyes, and you will not eat from him, your donkey is plucked away from before your face, and you will not turn him back to you, your flocks are given to your attackers, and there is no rescuer for you. **32** Your sons and your daughters are given to other people, and your eyes are seeing and consuming for them all the day, and there is no might of your hand. **33** The produce of your ground and all your toil, people which you do not know will eat, and you will only be oppressed and crushed all the days, **34** and you will be raving from the appearance of your eyes which you will see. **35** ***YHWH*** will attack you with boils, dysfunction upon the knees and upon the thighs, which you will not be able to heal, from the palm of your foot and unto the top of your head. **36** ***YHWH*** will make you walk, and your king, which you will make rise over you, to a nation, which you did not know, you and your father, and there you will serve other *Elohiym*, tree and stone, **37** and you will exist for a desolation, for a parable, and for a piercing in all the people which ***YHWH*** will drive you unto there. **38** You will bring many seeds out to the field, but you will gather a small amount, given that the swarming locust will devour him. **39** You will plant vineyards, and you will serve, but you will not gulp wine, and you will not gather food, given that the kermes will eat him. **40** Olives will exist for you in all your borders, but you will not pour down oil, given that your olive will cast off. **41** You will bring forth sons and daughters, but they will not exist for you, given that they will walk in captivity. **42** All your trees and produce of your ground, the whirring locust will possess. **43** The immigrant who is in among you will go up upon you very high, but you, you will go down very low. **44** He, he will make you join, but you, you will not make him join, he, he will exist for a head, and you, you will exist for a tail, **45** and all these annoyances will come upon you, and they will pursue you, and they will overtake you until you are destroyed, given that you did not hear the voice of ***YHWH*** your *Elohiym*, to safeguard his directives, and his customs, which he directed you, **46** and they will exist in you for a sign and for a wonder, and in your seed until a distant time. **47** Because you did not serve ***YHWH*** your *Elohiym* with rejoicing and with a functional heart, from all the abundance, **48** and you will

serve your attackers which ***YHWH*** will send him in you, with hunger, and
with thirst, and with nakedness, and with wanting of all, and he will give you
a yoke of iron upon the back of your neck, until he will make him destroy
you, **49** and ***YHWH*** will lift up upon you a distant nation, from the extremity
of the land, just as the eagle will dive, the tongue of a nation which you will
not hear. **50** A nation, strong of face, which will not lift up the face of the
bearded one, and the young man he will not provide protection, **51** and he
will eat the produce of your beast, and the produce of your ground, until
you are destroyed, because he will not let remain the cereal, fresh wine and
fresh oil, the birth of your bovine and the young sheep of your flock, until his
making you perish, **52** and he will make you pressed in in all your gates until
the going down of your high and fenced in ramparts, which you are clinging
on them in all your land, and he will make you pressed in in all your gates, in
all your land, which ***YHWH*** your *Elohiym* gave to you, **53** and you will eat the
produce of your womb, the flesh of your sons and your daughters, which
YHWH your *Elohiym* gave to you, with a smacking and with stress, which
your attacker will harass you. **54** The tender man in you, and the very soft,
his eye will be dysfunctional with his brother and with the woman of his
bosom, and with the remainder of his sons which he will leave behind.
55 Giving to one of them from the flesh of his sons, which he will eat,
because nothing remains for him, with the smacking and with stress, which
your attacker in all your gates will harass you. **56** The tender one in you, and
the soft one, which did not test the palm of her foot, leaving it in place upon
the land, from the softness and from the tenderness, her eye will be
dysfunctional with the man of her bosom and with her son and with her
daughter. **57** and with her infant, the one going out from between her feet,
and with her sons which she will bring forth, given that you will eat them, in
wanting all things in hiding, in the smacked and in the stress, which your
attacker in your gates will harass you. **58** If you will not safeguard to do all
the words of this teaching written in this scroll, to fear this heavy and fearful
title of ***YHWH*** your *Elohiym*, **59** and ***YHWH*** will make your hittings perform,
and the hittings of your seed, great hittings, and being secure, and
dysfunctional infirmities, and being secure, **60** and he will return in you all
the diseases of *Mits'rayim*, which you were afraid from their face, and they
will adhere in you. **61** Also, every infirmity and every hitting, which is not
written in the scroll of this teaching, ***YHWH*** will bring them up upon you
until you be destroyed, **62** and you will be left with a few mortal men,
because you existed like the stars of the skies, for an abundance, given that
you did not hear the voice of ***YHWH*** your *Elohiym*, **63** and it will come to
pass, just as ***YHWH*** skipped with joy over you, to make you do well, and to
make you increase, so will ***YHWH*** skip with joy over you, to make you perish,
and to destroy you, and you will be torn away from upon the ground which
you came unto there to possess her, **64** and ***YHWH*** will scatter you abroad in
all the peoples from the extremity of the land, and unto the extremity of the
land, and you will serve there other *Elohiym* which you did not know, you

and your fathers, tree and stone, **65** and in these nations you will not repose, and an oasis will not exist for the palm of your foot, and ***YHWH*** will give to you there a shaking heart, and a failing of the eyes, and a brooding soul, **66** and your life will hang for you from the opposite, and you will shake in awe night and day, and you will not be secure in your life. **67** In the morning you will say, who will make it evening, and in the evening you will say, who will make it morning, from the awe of your heart, when you will shake in awe, and from the appearance of your eyes, which you will see, **68** and ***YHWH*** will make you turn back to *Mits'rayim* in ships, by the road when I will say to you, you will not continue to see her, and you will sell yourself there to your attackers, for servants and for maids, but without a purchaser. **69 (29:1)** These are the words of the covenant which ***YHWH*** directed *Mosheh*, to cut with the sons of *Yisra'eyl* in the land of *Mo'av*, besides the covenant which he cut with them in *Hhorev*,

Chapter 29

1 (29:2) and *Mosheh* called out to all *Yisra'eyl*, and he said to them, you saw all which ***YHWH*** did to your eyes in the land of *Mits'rayim* to *Paroh*, and to all his servants, and to all his land. **2 (29:3)** The great trials which your eyes saw, the signs and those great wonders, **3 (29:4)** and ***YHWH*** did not give to you a heart to know, and eyes to see, and ears to hear, until this day, **4 (29:5)** and I made you walk forty years in the wilderness, your outer garments did not wear out, and your sandals did not wear out from upon your feet. **5 (29:6)** Bread you did not eat, and wine and liquor you did not gulp, so that you will know that I am ***YHWH*** your *Elohiym*, **6 (29:7)** and you came to this area, and *Sihhon* the king of *Hheshbon*, and *Og* the king of the *Bashan*, met us for battle, and we attacked, **7 (29:8)** and we took their land, and gave it for an inheritance to the ones of *Re'uven*, and to the ones of *Gad*, and to the half staff[777] of the ones of *Menasheh*, **8 (29:9)** and you will safeguard the words of this covenant, and you will do them, so that you will calculate all which you must do. **9 (29:10)** You are standing up today, all of you, to the face of ***YHWH*** your *Elohiym*, your heads, your staffs, your bearded ones, and your officers, all the men of *Yisra'eyl*. **10 (29:11)** Your babies, your women and your immigrant which are in among your camp, from the carver of your trees, until the drawer of your waters. **11 (29:12)** For your crossing over in the covenant of ***YHWH*** your *Elohiym*, and with his oath, which ***YHWH*** your *Elohiym* is cutting with you today. **12 (29:13)** So that you will rise today for him for a people, and he, he will exist for you for an *Elohiym*, just as he spoke to you, and just as he swore to your fathers, to *Avraham*, to *Yits'hhaq*, and to *Ya'aqov*, **13 (29:14)** and not with you alone am I cutting this covenant and this oath, **14 (29:15)** but with who is here

[777] Meaning "tribe."

with us, standing today to the face of ***YHWH*** our *Elohiym*, and with who is not here with us today, **15 (29:16)** given that you, you knew that we settled in the land of *Mits'rayim*, and how we crossed over in among the nations which you crossed over, **16 (29:17)** and you saw their filthiness, and their idols of tree and stone, silver and gold, which are with them. **17 (29:18)** Otherwise, there is in you a man, or woman, or clan, or staff[778], which is turning his heart today from ***YHWH*** our *Elohiym*, to walk, to serve the *Elohiym* of these nations, otherwise there is in you a root reproducing venom and hemlock, **18 (29:19)** and it will come to pass, in his hearing the words of this oath, and he exalted himself in his heart saying, completeness will exist in me, given that in the imagination of my heart, I will walk, so that the watered will consume the thirst. **19 (29:20)** ***YHWH*** will not consent to forgive him, given that at that time the nose of ***YHWH*** smoked, and his zealousness with that man, and all of the oath written on this scroll will stretch out with him, and ***YHWH*** will wipe his title away from under the skies, **20 (29:21)** and ***YHWH*** will separate him for dysfunction, from all the staffs of *Yisra'eyl*, in accordance with all the oaths of the covenant written on the scroll of this teaching, **21 (29:22)** and he said, the last generation of your sons, which will rise after you, and the foreigner which will come from a distant land, and they will see the hitting of that land and her sick ones, which ***YHWH*** made sick in her. **22 (29:23)** Brimstone and salt are cremating all her land, she will not be sown, and you will not spring up, and not any herb will go up in her, like the overthrowing of *Sedom* and *Ghamorah*, *Admah* and *Tseviim*, which ***YHWH*** overturned with his nose and with his fury, **23 (29:24)** and all the nations will say, why did ***YHWH*** do like in this way to this land, what is this great flaming nose, **24 (29:25)** and they will say, because they left the covenant of ***YHWH***, the *Elohiym* of their fathers, which he cut with them, with his bringing them out from the land of *Mits'rayim*, **25 (29:26)** and they will walk, and they will serve other *Elohiym*, and they will bend themselves down to them, *Elohiym* which they did not know, and he did not distribute for them, **26 (29:27)** and the nose of ***YHWH*** flared up in that land, to bring upon her all the annoyances written in this scroll, **27 (29:28)** and ***YHWH*** will root them out from upon their ground with a nose, and with fury and with great splinters, and he will make them thrown out to another land, like this day. **28 (29:29)** The hidden things belong to ***YHWH*** our *Elohiym*, and the uncovered things belong to us and to our sons until a distant time, to do all the words of this teaching,

---

[778] Meaning "tribe."

Chapter 30

1 and it will come to pass, when all these words[779] will come upon you, the
present and the annoyance, which I gave to your face, and you will turn back
to your heart in all the nations, where ***YHWH*** your *Elohiym* drove you out
unto there, **2** and you will turn back unto ***YHWH*** your *Elohiym*, and you will
hear his voice, according to what I am directing you today, you and your
sons, with all your heart and with all your soul, **3** and ***YHWH*** your *Elohiym*
will return your captives, and he will have compassion on you, and he will
return and he will gather you together from all the people where ***YHWH***
your *Elohiym* scattered you abroad. **4** If your driven out ones will exist in the
extremity of the skies, from there ***YHWH*** your *Elohiym* will gather you
together, and from there he will take you, **5** and ***YHWH*** your *Elohiym* will
bring you to the land which your fathers possessed, and you will possess
her, and he will make it go well for you, and he will increase you more than
your fathers, **6** and ***YHWH*** your *Elohiym* will snip off your heart, and the
heart of your seed, to love ***YHWH*** your *Elohiym* with all your heart, and with
all your soul, so that you live, **7** and ***YHWH*** your *Elohiym* gave all these oaths
upon your attackers, and upon your haters which pursue you, **8** and you, you
will turn back, and you will hear the voice of ***YHWH***, and you will do all his
directives which I am directing you today, **9** and ***YHWH*** your *Elohiym* will
leave you behind with all the work of your hand, and with the produce of
your womb, and with the produce of your beast, and with the produce of
your ground, for function, given that ***YHWH*** will return the skipping with joy
over you, for function, just as he skipped with joy over your fathers, **10** given
that you will hear the voice of ***YHWH*** your *Elohiym*, to safeguard his
directives and his customs written on the scroll of this teaching, given that
you will return to ***YHWH*** your *Elohiym* with all your heart and with all your
soul, **11** given that this directive, which I am directing you today, she is not
too difficult for you, and she is not distant. **12** She is not in the skies saying,
who will go up for us unto the skies, and take her for us, and make us hear
her, and do her, **13** and she is not on the other side of the sea saying, who
will cross over for us to the other side of the sea, and take her for us, and
make us hear her, and do her, **14** given that the word is very near to us, it is
in your mouth and in your heart to do him. **15** See, I gave to your face today,
life and function and death and dysfunction, **16** given that I am directing you
today to love ***YHWH*** your *Elohiym*, to walk in his roads, and to safeguard his
directives, and his customs, and his decisions, and you will live, and you will
increase, and ***YHWH*** your *Elohiym* will respect you in the land which you are
coming unto there to possess her, **17** but if your heart will turn, and you will
not hear, then you will be driven out, and you will bend yourself down to
other *Elohiym*, and you will serve them. **18** I will tell to you today, given that
you must certainly perish, you must not prolong the days upon the ground

[779] Or "things."

which you are crossing over the *Yarden* to come unto there to possess her. **19** I will warn the skies and the land about you today, I will place to your face life and death, the present and the annoyance, and you will choose life so that you will live, you and your seed. **20** To love ***YHWH*** your *Elohiym*, to hear his voice, and to adhere to him, given that he is your life, and the length of your days to settle upon the ground, which ***YHWH*** swore to your fathers, to *Avraham*, to *Yits'hhaq* and to *Ya'aqov*, to give to them,

---

Chapter 31

1 and *Mosheh* walked, and he spoke these words to all *Yisra'eyl*, **2** and he said to them, a son of one hundred and twenty years am I today, I will not again be able to go out and to come, and ***YHWH*** said to me, you will not cross over this *Yarden*. **3** ***YHWH*** your *Elohiym*, he is crossing over to your face, he will destroy these nations from before you, and you will possess them, *Yehoshu'a*, he is crossing over to your face, just as ***YHWH*** spoke, **4** and ***YHWH*** will do to them just as he did to *Sihhon*, and to *Og*, kings of the ones of *Emor*, and to their land, which he will destroy them, **5** and ***YHWH*** gave them to your faces, and you will do to them according to all the directives which I am directing you. **6** Seize and be strong, you will not fear, and you will not be terrified from their faces, given that ***YHWH*** your *Elohiym*, he is the one walking with you, he will not let you sink down, and he will not leave you, **7** and *Mosheh* called out to *Yehoshu'a*, and he said to him to the eyes of all *Yisra'eyl*, seize and be strong, given that you, you will come with this people to the land that ***YHWH*** swore to their fathers to give to them, and you, you will make them inherit her, **8** and ***YHWH***, he is the one walking to your face, he will exist with you, he will not let you sink down, and he will not leave you, you will not fear, and you will not be shattered, **9** and *Mosheh* wrote this teaching, and he gave her to the administrators, the sons of *Lewi*, the ones lifting up the box of the covenant of ***YHWH***, and to all the bearded ones of *Yisra'eyl*, **10** and *Mosheh* directed them saying, at the conclusion of seven years, in the appointed year of the release, in the feast of booths. **11** All *Yisra'eyl* will come to appear at the face of ***YHWH*** your *Elohiym*, in the area which he will choose, this teaching will be called out[780] before all *Yisra'eyl* in their ears. **12** Make the people assemble, the men and the women and the babies and your immigrant which is in your gates, so that they will hear, and so that they will learn, and they will fear ***YHWH*** your *Elohiym*, and they will safeguard to do all the words of this teaching, **13** and their sons which they did not know, they will hear, and they will learn to fear ***YHWH*** your *Elohiym* all the days which you live upon the ground, which you are crossing over the *Yarden* unto there to possess her, **14** and ***YHWH*** said to *Mosheh*, though your days came near to die, meet with *Yehoshu'a*, and

---

[780] That is, "read."

station yourselves in the appointed tent, and I will direct him, and *Mosheh* walked, and *Yehoshu'a*, and they were made to stand up in the appointed tent, **15** and ***YHWH*** appeared in the tent, in the pillar of cloud, and the pillar of the cloud stood over the opening of the tent, **16** and ***YHWH*** said to *Mosheh*, look, you are lying down with your fathers, and this people will rise, and he will be a harlot following the *Elohiym* of the foreigner of the land where he came unto there in among him, and he will leave me, and he will break my covenant, which I cut with him, **17** and my nose will flare up with him in that day, and I will leave him, and I will make my face hidden from them, and he will exist for eating, and an abundance of dysfunction and persecution will find him, and he will say in that day, is it not so because I am without *Elohiym* in among me, these dysfunctions will find me, **18** and I will certainly make my face hidden in that day, concerning all the dysfunction which he will do, given that he will turn to other *Elohiym*, **19** and now, write for you this song, and teach her to the sons of *Yisra'eyl*, place her in their mouth, so that this song will exist for me for a witness in the sons of *Yisra'eyl*, **20** given that I will bring him to the ground which I swore to his fathers, issuing fat and honey, and he will eat, and he will be satisfied, and he will make fat, and he will turn to other *Elohiym*, and they will serve them, and they will provoke me, and they will break my covenant, **21** and it will come to pass, given that an abundance of dysfunction and persecution will find him, and this song will answer to his face for a witness, given that she will not be forgotten from the mouth of his seed, given that I knew his thoughts, which he is doing, before the day I bring him to the land which I swore, **22** and *Mosheh* wrote this song in that day, and he taught her to the sons of *Yisra'eyl*, **23** and he directed *Yehoshu'a* the son of *Nun*, and he said, seize and be strong, given that you, you will bring the sons of *Yisra'eyl* to the land which I swore to them, and I, I will exist with you, **24** and it came to pass, as *Mosheh* finished to write the words of this teaching upon the scroll until they be whole, **25** and *Mosheh* directed the ones of *Lewi*, the ones lifting up the box of the covenant of ***YHWH***, saying, **26** take the scroll of this teaching, and you will place him beside the box of the covenant of ***YHWH*** your *Elohiym*, and he will exist there with you for a witness, **27** given that I, I knew your rebellion, and your hard neck, with me still living with you today, you will be disobeying with ***YHWH***, and moreover, even after my death. **28** Assemble for me all the bearded ones of your staffs[781], and your officers, and I will speak in their ears these words, and I will make the skies and the land witness with them, **29** given that I know, after my death, that you will certainly damage, and you will turn aside from the road which I am directing you, and the dysfunction will call you out in the end of days, given that you will do the dysfunction in the eyes of ***YHWH*** to make him angry by the work

---

[781] Or "tribes."

of your hands, **30** and *Mosheh* spoke in the ears of all the assembly of *Yisra'eyl* with the words of this song until their being whole[782].

Chapter 32

1 Pay attention skies, and I will speak, and the land will hear the statements
of my mouth. **2** My learning will drop like precipitation, my speech will flow
like dew, like raindrops upon the grass, and like showers upon herbs, **3** given
that I will call out the title of ***YHWH***, provide magnificence to our *Elohiym*.
4 The boulder, his deeds are whole, given that all his roads are a decision, a
mighty one secure and without wickedness, steadfast and straight is he.
5 He did damage to him, their blemish is not his sons, a crooked and twisted
generation. **6** Will you yield to ***YHWH*** this foolish and unskilled people, is he
not your father that purchased you, he, he made you, and he will prepare
you. **7** Remember the distant days, understand the years of generation and
generation, inquire your father, and he will tell you, your bearded ones, and
they will say to you. **8** With *Elyon* making an inheritance of the nations, with
his dividing apart the sons of human, he will make the borders of the
peoples stand up to the number of the sons of *Yisra'eyl*[783], **9** given that the
distribution of ***YHWH*** is his people, *Ya'aqov* is the region of his inheritance.
10 He will find him in the land of wilderness, and in the confusion of a
howling desolate wilderness he will make him go around, he will make him
understand, he will preserve him like the deep blackness[784] of his eye.
11 Like an eagle he will stir up his nest, his young pigeons he will flutter, he
will spread out his wings, he will take him, he will lift him up upon his
feathers. **12** ***YHWH*** alone will guide him, and with him is no mighty one of a
foreigner. **13** They will ride upon the platforms of the land, and he will eat
the bounties of the field, and they will suckle honey from the cliff, and oil
from the quartz of a boulder. **14** Cheese of cattle, and fat of the flocks, with
fat of the depressions, and bucks of the sons of *Bashan*, and male goats,
with the fat of the kidneys of wheat, and blood of the grape you will gulp the
slime, **15** and *Yeshurun* will grow fat, and he will kick, you will grow fat, you
will cover over, and he left alone the powerful one that made him, and he
made the boulder of his relief fade. **16** They will make him zealous with
strange things, with disgusting things he will make him angry. **17** They will
sacrifice to the beasts, not the powerful one, *Elohiym* they did not know,
new things from nearby came, your fathers did not storm[785] them. **18** A
boulder brought you forth, you will be unmindful, and you will forget the

[782] That is; until the end (of the words).

[783] The *Septuagint* here has the word θεοῦ (*theou*) and the Dead Sea Scrolls have אל (*el*), both meaning "mighty one."

[784] The "pupil" of the eye.

[785] In context, this word means "to fear," as you would fear a violent storm.

mighty one twisting you, **19** and ***YHWH*** saw, and he was provoked from the
anger of his sons and his daughters, **20** and he will say, I will hide my face
from them, I will see what is their end, given that they are an upside down
generation, sons with no secureness in them. **21** They, they made me be
zealous with no mighty one, they will make me angry in their vanity, and I, I
will make them be zealous with no people, with a foolish nation I will make
them angry, **22** given that a fire is kindled in my nose, and she[786] will
smolder unto the underworld of the lower part, and she will eat the land
and her product, and she will make the foundations of the hills blaze. **23** I
will make dysfunction consume upon him, my arrow I will finish in them.
24 Exhausted of hunger, and fought of a spark, and a harsh destruction, and
I will send the tooth of beasts in them, with the fury of a crawler of the dirt.
25 In the outside the sword will be childless, and in the chambers is terror,
also the chosen one, also the virgin, suckling with a gray-headed man. **26** I
said I will make them blown away, I will cease from man their memory.
27 Unless the anger of an attacker I will fear, otherwise their narrow ones[787]
will recognize, otherwise they will say our hands are rising, and ***YHWH*** had
not made all this, **28** given that they are a nation perishing of counsel, and
no intelligence is in them. **29** Would that they be skilled, they will calculate
this, they must understand to their end. **30** How will one pursue a thousand,
and two make a myriad flee, if not, given that their boulder sold them, and
YHWH shut them in, **31** given that their boulder is not like our boulder, and
our attacking are judges, **32** given that from the grapevine of *Sedom* is their
grapevine, and from the cropland of *Ghamorah* is his grapes, grapes of
venom, clusters of gall for them. **33** The fury of the crocodiles[788] is their
wine, and the venom of asps is cruel. **34** Is he not stored by me in my supply
house. **35** To me is vengeance, and recompense to the appointed time, their
foot will totter, given that it is near the day of their calamity, and he will
make haste the prepared things for them, **36** given that ***YHWH*** will
moderate his people, and upon his servants he will repent, given that he will
see that a hand wavered, and in the end stopped and left, **37** and he will say,
where is his *Elohiym*, they will take refuge in a boulder. **38** Because the fat of
their sacrifices they will eat, they will gulp the wine of your pouring out, they
will rise, and they will help you, he will exist upon you a hiding[789]. **39** See
now, given that I, I am he, and there is no *Elohiym* by me, I, I will kill and
keep alive, I struck through, and I, I will heal, and none can deliver from my

---

786 The "she" is referring to the "fire," a feminine noun.

787 Or "their adversaries."

788 This Hebrew word is translated in various ways, including; whale, sea-monster, dragon, serpent, asp and jackal (see Exodus 7:9, Deuteronomy 32:33, Nehemiah 2:13, Job 7:12). According to these texts, this is a very large creature that lives on the land and in the water, which is characteristic of the crocodile.

789 This phrase probably means "he will exist for you as a hiding-place."

hand, **40** given that I will lift my hand up to the skies, and I will say, I am living for a distant time. **41** If I whet my flashing sword, and my hand will take hold on a decision, I will make vengeance turn back to my narrow ones[790], and to my haters I will make restitution. **42** I will make my arrow drunk from blood, and my sword will eat flesh, from the blood of the drilled[791] and the captive, from the head of the long hair of the attacker. **43** Shout aloud nations, his people, given that the blood of his servants will rise, and vengeance will return to his narrow ones, and he will cover his ground, his people, **44** and *Mosheh* came, and he spoke all the words of this song in the ears of the people, he and *Hosheya* the son of *Nun*, **45** and *Mosheh* finished to speak all these words to all *Yisra'eyl*, **46** and he said to them, place your heart to all the words which I am warning with you today, which you will direct your sons to safeguard, to do all the words of this teaching, **47** given that he is not an empty word from you, given that he is your life, and in this word, you will prolong the days upon the ground which you are crossing over the *Yarden*, unto there, to possess her, **48** and ***YHWH*** spoke to *Mosheh* in the bone of this day[792] saying, **49** go up to this hill of the ones of *Ever*, the hill of *Nevo*, which is in the land of *Mo'av*, which is to the face of *Ye'rey'hho*, and see the land of *Kena'an*, which I am giving to the sons of *Yisra'eyl* for holdings, **50** and die in the hill, which you are going up unto there, and be gathered to your people, just as *Aharon* your brother died in *Hor* the hill, and he was gathered to his people. **51** Because you transgressed with me in the midst of the sons of *Yisra'eyl* in the waters of *Meriyvah Qadesh* of the wilderness of *Tsin*, because you did not set my sign apart in the midst of the sons of *Yisra'eyl*, **52** given that from the opposite side you will see the land, and unto there you will not come to the land which I am giving to the sons of *Yisra'eyl*,

---

Chapter 33

1 and this is the present which *Mosheh*, the man of *Elohiym*, respected the sons of *Yisra'eyl* to the face of his death, **2** and he said, ***YHWH*** came from *Sinai*, and he came up[793] from *Se'iyr* to them, he shone from the hill of *Paran*, and he arrived from the myriads of special ones, from his right hand, *Eyshdat* is for them. **3** Moreover, cherishing the peoples, all his unique ones are in your hand, and they, they are sitting down at your foot, he will lift up your words. **4** *Mosheh* directed a teaching to us, a possession of the

---

[790] That is, "adversaries."

[791] Meaning "slain."

[792] "Bone of this day" is an idiom of uncertain meaning, but may mean "this very same day" or the "middle of this day."

[793] This could also be translated as, "and ***YHWH*** said from *Sinai*, he came up."

assembly of *Ya'aqov*, **5** and he was king in *Yeshurun*, in the heads of the people gathered together, the staffs[794] of *Yisra'eyl*. **6** *Re'uven* will live, and he will not die, and his mortal men will be a number, **7** and this is for *Yehudah*, and he will say, hear ***YHWH*** the voice of *Yehudah*, and to his people you will bring him, his hands are abundant for him, and help from his narrow ones[795], you will exist, **8** and to *Lewi* he said, your *Tumiym* and your *Uriym* are for each of your kind ones, whom you tested in *Mas'sah*, you will dispute him upon the waters of *Meriyvah*. **9** The one saying to his father and to his mother, I did not see him, and his brother he did not recognize, and his son he did not know, given that they safeguarded your speech, and your covenant they preserved. **10** They will throw[796] your decisions to *Ya'aqov*, and your teachings to *Yisra'eyl*, they will place incense smoke in your nose, and entirely upon your altar. **11** Respect ***YHWH***, his force, and the deed of his hands you will accept, strike through the waists of his rising ones, and the ones hating him, they must not rise. **12** To *Binyamin* he said, the cherished of ***YHWH*** will dwell with safety upon him, blanketing upon him all the day, and between his shoulder pieces he dwelled, **13** and to *Yoseph* he said, being respected of ***YHWH*** is his land, from the precious skies, from the dew, and from the deep water stretching out below, **14** and from the precious productions of the sun, and from the precious things brought out of the moons, **15** and from the head of the hills of the east, and from the precious distant knolls, **16** and from the precious land and her filling, and the self-will of my dwelling is a thorn bush, she will come to the head of *Yoseph*, and to the top of the head of the dedicated one of his brothers. **17** The firstborn of his ox is honor for him, and the horns of the rhinoceros are his horns, with them he will gore the people together to the far end of the land, and they are the myriads of *Ephrayim*, and they are the thousands of *Menasheh*, **18** and to *Zevulun* he said, rejoice *Zevulun* in your going out, and *Yis'sas'khar* in your tents. **19** The people of the hill they will call out, there they will sacrifice steadfast sacrifices, given that the abounding seas they will suckle, and boarding up the submerged sand, **20** and to *Gad* he said, respected is the one making *Gad* wide, like a lioness he dwelled, and he will tear into pieces the arm, moreover the top of the head, **21** and he saw the summit for himself, given that there the parcel of the inscriber is boarded up, and he arrived with the heads of the people, he did the steadfastness of ***YHWH***, and his decisions with *Yisra'eyl*, **22** and to *Dan* he said, *Dan* is a whelp of a lion, he will jump from *Bashan*, **23** and to *Naphtali* he said, *Naphtali*, plenty of self-will and full of the presents of ***YHWH***, possess the sea and the southern, **24** and to *Asher* he said, respected from the sons of *Asher*, he will exist, accepted of his brothers, and dipping his foot in the oil. **25** Iron and copper are your sandals, and like your days is your toughness.

[794] Or "tribes."

[795] That is, "his adversaries."

[796] That is, "teach" or "point out."

26 There is none like the mighty one of *Yeshurun*, riding the skies with your
help, and with his pride is a dust cloud. **27** The habitation of *Elohiym* of the
east, and below is the distant[797] arms, and he cast out the attacker from
your face, and he said, destroy, **28** and *Yisra'eyl* will dwell safely alone, the
eye[798] of *Ya'aqov* is a land of cereal and fresh wine, moreover his skies will
drop dew. **29** Happy are you, *Yisra'eyl*, who is like one of you, a people
rescued by ***YHWH***, the shield of your help, and what is the sword of your
pride, and your attackers will be denied to you, and you, upon their
platforms you will take steps,

Chapter 34

1 and *Mosheh* went up from the deserts of *Mo'av* to the hill of *Nevo*, the
head of *Pisgah*, which is upon the face of *Ye'rey'hho*, and ***YHWH*** showed
him all the land, the *Gil'ad* until *Dan*, **2** and all of *Naphtali*, and the land of
Ephrayim and *Menasheh*, and all the land of *Yehudah*, as far as the last sea,
3 and the south, and the roundness of the level valley of *Ye'rey'hho*, the city
of date palms as far as *Tso'ar*, **4** and ***YHWH*** said to him, this is the land which
I swore to *Avraham*, to *Yits'hhaq* and to *Ya'aqov*, saying, to your seed I will
give her, I will show you with your eyes, and unto there you will not cross
over, **5** and *Mosheh*, the servant of ***YHWH***, died there in the land of *Mo'av*,
according to the mouth of ***YHWH***, **6** and he buried him in the steep valley, in
the land of *Mo'av*, at the forefront of *Beyt-Pe'or*, and no man knows his
burying place unto this day, **7** and *Mosheh* was a son of a hundred and
twenty years in his death, his eyes did not dim, and his moistness did not
flee, **8** and the sons of *Yisra'eyl* wept for *Mosheh* in the deserts of *Mo'av*
thirty days, and the days of weeping and mourning of *Mosheh* were whole,
9 and *Yehoshu'a* the son of *Nun* was filled with the wind of skill, given that
Mosheh supported his hands upon him, and the sons of *Yisra'eyl* listened to
him, and they did just as ***YHWH*** directed *Mosheh*, **10** and an announcer did
not rise again in *Yisra'eyl* like *Mosheh*, who knew ***YHWH*** face to face. **11** To
all the signs and wonders, which ***YHWH*** sent him to do in the land of
Mits'rayim to *Paroh*, and to all his servants, and to all his land, **12** and for
every forceful hand, and for every great fearing, which *Mosheh* did to the
eyes of *Yisra'eyl*.

---

797 "Distant" in time, as in "ancient."

798 This Hebrew word also means a "spring" or "fountain."

Glossary

Abdomen: #4578
Abhor: #8581
Abide: #5115
Able: #3201
Abode: #5116
Abounding: #8228
About, tread: #7270, #8637
About: #5921
Above: #4605, #5921, #5945
Abroad, scatter: #6327
Abundance: #7230
Abundant: #6105, #7227, #7228
Abused: #5953
Acacia: #7848
Accept: #7521
Accepted: #7522
According to: #5921, #6310
Account, on: #182, #1558, #5668, #5674
Accumulate: #7408
Acquired: #4736
Acquiring: #4901
Acquisition: #4943
Acquit: #5352
Across, spread: #6581
Act as midwife: #3205
Add: #3254
Adder: #8207
Addition, in: #5921
Adhere: #1692
Administer: #8334
Administration: #3550
Administrator: #3548
Adoration: #8416
Adorn: #3547
Adultery, commit: #5003
Advance: #6275
Advice, give: #3289
Afar: #7368
Affection: #160
Afflict: #6031
Affliction: #6040, #6041
Afraid: #3016, #3025
After growth: #5599
After: #310, #314, #7093
Afterward: #310
Again, yet: #5750
Again: #1157, #5703, #5704, #3254, #5750
Against: #5921
Agate: #7618
Age, extreme old: #2208
Age, full: #3624
Age, old: #2209
Age, young: #5271
Age: #2207
Agitation: #2113, #2189
Ago, three days: #8032
Agony: #2427
Agree: #225, #2974
Alarm: #8643
Alive, keep: #2421, #2425
All around: #5439
All, at: #7535
All: #3605
Allow: #5414
Almond shaped: #8246
Almond: #8247
Aloe: #174
Alone, leave: #5203
Alone, that: #905, #906
Alone: #905, #906, #910
Alongside: #5980

Aloud, shout: #7442, #7444
Also: #1157, #5703, #5704, #1571, #5750, #5921
Altar: #4196
Amazed: #2302
Amber: #916
Ambush: #693, #6660
Amethyst: #306
Ammah: #520
Among: #3605, #5868, #5973, #7130, #7131
Amount, great: #8635
Amount, measured: #8506
Amount, small: #4592
Amplify: #1711
Anger: #3708
Angry: #3707
Announce: #5012
Announcer: #5030, #5031
Annoyance: #7045
Another: #259, #312, #5750
Answer: #6030
Antelope: #1788
Anything: #3972
Apart from: #1107
Apart, divide: #6504
Apart, set: #6942
Apart: #905, #906
Apparel: #8071
Appear: #7200, #7202, #7207, #7212
Appearance: #4758
Appoint: #3259
Appointed time: #6256
Appointed: #4150, #4151
Appointment: #4150, #4151
Approach: #579
Arch: #1354, #1610
Area: #4725
Arm band: #3558
Arm for battle: #2571
Arm: #2220, #2502
Armament: #3519
Armlet: #685
Army: #6635
Aroma: #7381
Aromatic spice: #5561
Around, all: #5439
Around, dancing: #1524
Around, fence: #5526
Around, go: #5437
Around, wind: #6801
Around, wrap: #5749
Arrange: #6186
Arrangement: #6187
Arrive: #857
Arrogance: #2087
Arrow: #2671
As far as: #1157, #5703, #5704
As well as: #1157, #5703, #5704
Ascension offering: #1473, #5930
Ascent: #4608
Ash: #665, #666
Ashamed: #954
Aside, go: #7847
Aside, set: #680
Aside, turn: #5493, #7787, #8323
Aside, turning: #5627
Aside: #905, #906
Asp: #6620
Ass, wild: #6501
Assemble: #6950, #7035
Assembly: #6951, #3862, #6952
Assign: #2763
Assigned: #2764
Astonishment: #8541
Astray, go: #7686
Asylum: #4733

Bat: #5847
Bathe: #7364
Battering ram: #4239
Battle, arm for: #2571
Battle: #4421
Be a harlot: #2181
Be put to death: #4191
Be white: #3835
Bear the blame: #2398
Beard: #2205, #2206
Bearded vulture: #6538
Beast: #929, #930
Beat out: #1849
Beat small: #1854
Beat: #5221, #6470
Beaten grain: #1643
Beaten work: #4749
Beautiful: #3303, #3304
Beauty: #2580
Because of what: #834
Because: #834, #3588, #5921, #5921, #8478
Bed: #4296
Bee: #1682
Begin: #2490
Beginning: #7218, #7389
Behalf: #1157, #5703, #5704
Behead: #6202
Behind, leave: #3498
Behind: #310
Belittle: #7043
Bell: #6472
Belly: #1512
Belonging to: #413
Beloved: #1730
Below: #8478
Bend down: #7812
Bend the knee: #86
Beneath: #4295
Benefit: #5532, #5533
Beqa: #1235
Beseech: #2589, #2603
Beside: #681
Besides: #905, #906
Best: #4315, #7218, #7389
Betray: #7411
Betroth: #781
Between: #996, #1143
Beyond: #1157, #5703, #5704, #1973
Bind up: #481
Bind: #6123
Binder: #2838
Bird of prey: #5861
Bird: #6833
Birth: #7698
Birthed: #3209
Birthing: #8435
Birthright: #1062
Bite: #5391
Bitter herbs: #4472
Bitter: #4751, #4752, #4843
Black as coal: #7838, #7815
Black, burn: #3648
Black, deep: #380
Black: #2345
Blame, bear the: #2398
Blanket: #2653
Blast: #7710
Blasting: #7711
Blaze: #3857
Blazing: #3858
Blemish: #3971
Blind: #5786, #5787
Blindness: #5788
Block, stumbling: #4383
Blood: #1818
Bloodshed: #1818
Bloom: #6692
Blossom: #6731, #6733

Bring up: #5927
Bring, quickly: #7323
Broken: #1793
Brooding: #1671
Brother: #251, #1889
Brother-in-law: #2993
Brought near: #7126
Brought out: #1645
Bruise, striped: #2250
Buck: #352, #353, #354
Bucket: #1805
Bud: #6525
Budding: #1392
Build up: #5549
Build: #1129
Bulk: #8443
Bull: #6499
Bullock: #5695
Bulrush: #1573
Bunch: #92
Bundle: #6014
Burden, heavy: #2960
Burden: #5450
Burial place: #6900
Burn black: #3648
Burn incense: #6999, #7000
Burn, place to: #4729
Burn: #1197
Burning flame: #2746
Burning: #1200
Burst out: #6524
Bursting: #6363
Bury: #6912
Bush, thorn: #5572
Business: #4399
Butcher: #2873
Buttocks: #8357
Buttress: #4740
Cake: #1690
Calamity: #343
Calculate: #7919
Call out: #7121
Camel, young: #1070
Camel: #1581
Camp: #2583, #4264
Campsite: #8466
Cannot: #3808
Captain: #5387
Captive: #7628, #7633
Captivity: #7622
Capture: #7617
Caravan: #736
Carcass: #5038
Carnelian: #124
Carry: #5445
Cart: #5699
Cartilage: #1634
Carve: #2404
Cassia: #6916
Cast away: #1602
Cast down: #2040
Cast image: #4541
Cast off: #5394
Cast out: #1644
Cataract: #8400
Cattle: #1165, #1241
Cauldron: #3595
Cave: #4380, #4631
Cease: #7673
Ceasing: #7674, #7676
Cedar: #730
Center: #2676
Cereal: #1715
Chain: #8331, #8333
Chamber: #2315
Chameleon: #3581
Change: #2498, #8132, #8138
Charge: #4931
Chariot: #4818
Cheese: #2529

Confuse: #2000
Confusion: #8414
Conjure: #6049
Consent: #14
Consequence: #6118
Consequently: #6118
Consider: #2803
Considered uncircumcised: #6188
Consistency: #386
Consort: #2778
Consume: #5595
Consuming: #3616
Consumption: #7829
Contention: #4808
Continually: #8548
Continue: #5750
Contrary: #7147
Contribution: #4979
Convert: #4171
Convict: #7561
Cooked: #8601
Copper: #5178
Copulate: #7693
Copulation: #7903
Coral: #7215
Cord: #6616
Coriander: #1407
Cormorant: #7994
Corner post: #4742
Corner: #6438
Corpse: #6297
Correct: #3256
Corruption: #4893
Couch: #3326
Counsel: #6098
Count: #5608
Couple: #2266, #2267, #2270, #2271
Coupling: #2279
Courageous: #1368
Courtyard: #2691
Covenant: #1285
Cover over: #3680, #3780
Cover, remove the: #1540
Cover: #3722
Covered: #6632
Covering, outer: #3681
Covering, roof: #4372
Covering: #3723, #3724
Cow: #6510
Crack: #7665
Craftiness: #5231
Craftsman: #2794
Crafty: #5230
Crash: #7582, #7583
Crave: #2530
Craving: #3700
Crawl: #2119
Creature: #2416
Creek: #3105
Cremate: #5635, #8313
Cremating: #8316
Crimson: #8438
Crocodile: #8565, #8577
Crooked: #6141
Crop off: #6998
Crop: #4760
Cropland: #7709, #8309
Cross over: #5668, #5674
Crossing: #4569
Crown: #5145
Crucible: #3564
Cruel: #393
Crumble: #6626
Crumbled: #4790
Crush: #7465, #7533, #7567
Cry out: #6817
Cry: #6818
Cucumber: #7180

Cud: #1625
Cup: #3563
Cupped hand: #2651
Curdle: #7087
Curtain, tent: #6532
Curtain: #3407
Custody: #4929
Custom: #2706, #2708
Cut down: #1438
Cut in two: #1334
Cut off: #5243
Cut piece: #1335
Cut sharply: #2742, #2782
Cut: #3772
Daily: #3117
Damage: #7843
Damaging: #4889
Dance: #4246
Dancing around: #1524
Dark: #2824, #2825
Darken: #2821
Darkness, thick: #6205
Darkness: #2822
Dash to pieces: #7492
Date palm: #8558
Daub: #7874
Daughter: #1323
Daughter-in-law: #3618
Dawn: #7837
Day, next: #4283
Day: #3117
Daytime: #3119
Dead: #7496
Deal deceitfully: #2048
Deal falsely: #8266
Death, be put to: #4191
Death: #4192, #4194
Deceit: #4820
Deceitfully, deal: #2048
Deceive: #5377, #5378, #5383
Decide: #8199
Decision: #4941
Declare clean: #2891
Declare: #5001, #5002
Decorate: #6286
Decoration: #8597
Decorative band: #2805
Dedicate: #5144
Dedicated: #5139
Dedication: #5145
Deed: #6467
Deep black: #380
Deep water: #8415
Deeply, breathe: #5314
Deer: #8476
Defeat: #2476
Defiance: #8569
Defile: #2490
Deform: #7038
Delay: #309
Delicacy: #4303
Delight: #2654
Delightful: #5276
Deliver up: #4042
Deliver: #5337, #5462, #5534
Delivers: #579
Deny: #3584
Depart early: #7925
Depart: #7561
Deposit, security: #8667
Deposit: #3240, #4503
Deposited: #6487
Depression: #3733
Depth: #4688
Derision: #8103
Desert: #6160
Desire: #185
Desolate wilderness: #3452
Desolate: #8047, #8077, #8074
Despise: #936

Despised: #937
Destroy: #6, #8, #7843, #8045
Destruction: #6986
Detest: #8262
Devote: #2596
Devotion: #2598
Devour: #2628
Dew: #2919
Die: #4191
Difficult, too: #6381
Dig out: #2658, #2659
Dig: #3738, #3739
Dim: #3543
Diminish: #2637
Dimness: #3544
Dip: #2881
Direct: #6680
Directive: #4687
Dirt: #6083
Dirty: #2930, #2933, #2931, #2932
Discernment: #1847
Discharge: #2101
Discipline: #4561, #4148
Discord: #4090
Disdain: #959
Disease: #4064
Disgrace: #2781
Disgusting: #8441
Dislocate: #3363
Dismay: #928
Disobey: #4784
Disperse: #2219
Dispossess: #3423
Dispute: #7378, #7379
Dissolve: #4127
Distance: #7350
Distant: #5769
Distinct: #6395
Distress: #3334, #3335, #6087
Distressing pain: #6089, #6091, #6092
Distribute: #2505
Distribution: #2506
Disturb: #5916
Dive: #1675
Diverse kind: #3610
Divide apart: #6504
Divide into pieces: #5408
Divide: #2673
Divided part: #1506
Divination: #7081
Divine: #7080
Divorce: #3748
Do not: #408
Do sorcery: #3784
Do well: #3190
Doe: #355
Dog: #3611
Donation: #7133
Donkey: #2543, #2565
Door: #1817
Doorpost: #4201
Double over: #3717
Double: #4932, #8382
Dough: #1217
Dove: #3123
Down, bend: #7812
Down, break: #5422
Down, bring: #3381
Down, cast: #2040
Down, come: #3381
Down, cut: #1438
Down, drop: #5413
Down, go: #3381
Down, lie: #7901
Down, look: #8259
Down, lying: #7902
Down, pour: #3251, #3332

End, far: #657
End, in the: #657
End: #319, #8622
Endorse: #1984
Endow: #2064
Enemy: #6145, #6862
Engrave: #2801, #6603, #6605
Engraver: #2791, #2796
Engraving tool: #2747
Engraving: #2799
Enrage: #2194
Ensnare: #5367
Entangled: #943
Entirely: #3632
Entrance: #3996
Entwine: #6617
Envelop: #5848
Envious: #7065
Enwrap: #5844
Ephod: #642, #646
Epidemic: #1698
Equate: #7737, #7738
Err: #7683
Error: #7684
Eruption: #5424
Escaped: #6412, #6413
Escaping: #6405
Establish: #3559
Estimate: #3699
Eunuch: #5631
Even though: #834, #3588
Evening: #6153
Event: #7137
Ever: #1157, #5703, #5704, #5750
Every: #3605, #3966
Everyone: #5315
Evidence: #5715
Ewe: #7353
Exalt: #1288
Examine: #2713
Exceed: #5736
Except: #1115, #3588
Exception, with the: #2108
Exchange: #7666, #8545
Exhale: #5301
Exhausted: #4198
Exist: #1961
Experienced: #2593
Expire: #1478
Explain: #874
Expose: #4286
Extend: #5186
Extract: #2502
Extreme old age: #2208
Extremity: #7097, #7098
Eye: #5869
Eyphah: #374
Face to face: #5046
Face toward: #6923
Face, in the: #5048
Face: #3942, #6440
Fade: #5034
Fail: #2398
Failing: #3631
Failure: #2399, #2400, #2401, #2403
Faint: #3856, #4816
Falcon: #5322
Fall upon: #7779
Fall: #5307
Fallen grape: #6528
False: #8267
Falsely, deal: #8266
Falseness: #7723
Family idol: #8655
Famine: #7459
Far be it: #2486
Far end: #657
Far: #7368

Flee away: #1272
Flee: #5127
Fleece: #1488
Fleeing: #4499
Flesh: #1154, #1320
Flint: #3095
Float: #6687
Flocks: #6629, #6792
Flood: #3999
Floor: #1637
Flour, grain: #7058
Flour: #5560
Flourishing: #7488
Flow out: #7325
Flow: #5140
Flowing, free: #1865
Flush: #7857
Flutter: #7363
Fly: #5774
Flyer: #5775
Follow: #310
Following: #8669
Folly: #5039
Food, gather: #103
Food, provide: #3938
Food, tasty: #4574
Food: #402
Foodstuff: #400
Fool: #5036
Foolish: #2973
Foot, on: #7273
Foot: #6471, #7272
Footing: #134
Footstep: #6471
Forbid: #5106
Force: #2428
Forceful: #2389, #2390, #2391
Forefront: #4136
Forehead: #4696
Foreign: #5237
Foreigner: #5235, #5236
Foreskin: #6190
Forest: #3264, #3293
Forget: #7911
Forgive: #5545
Fork: #4207
Form: #8389
Forth, bring: #3205
Fortification: #4013
Fortune: #1409
Forty: #702, #705
Foul: #6292
Foundation: #4143, #4144, #4145, #4146
Founded: #3245
Fountain: #4726
Four: #702, #705
Fourth generation: #7256
Fourth part: #7255
Fourth: #7243
Fragment: #6595
Frail: #7504
Frankincense: #3828
Free flowing: #1865
Free: #2666, #2670
Freedom: #2668
Freely: #2600
Freewill offering: #5071
Fresh oil: #3323
Fresh wine: #8492
Fresh: #3955
Friend: #7468
Fringe: #6734
Frog: #6854
From, apart: #1107
Front, in: #5227
Fruit press: #1831
Fruit, choice: #2173
Fruit, ripe: #4395
Fruitful: #6500

Grain, green: #24
Grain, roasted: #7039
Grain: #1250
Grant: #7592
Grape skin: #2085
Grape, fallen: #6528
Grape: #6025
Grapevine: #1612
Grapple: #79
Grasp: #2392, #7061
Grass, marsh: #260
Grass: #1877
Grasshopper: #2284
Grate: #4345
Grave: #6913
Gray-headed: #7872
Great amount: #8635
Great number: #4768
Great tree: #436, #437
Greatly: #3966
Green grain: #24
Green: #3418, #3419
Greenish: #3422
Grief: #4786
Grind: #2912
Groaning: #5009
Grope: #4184, #4959
Ground to pieces: #1743
Ground, dry: #3004
Ground: #127
Grouse: #1744
Grove: #842
Grow fat: #8080
Growth, after: #5599
Grudge, hold a: #7852
Guardian: #8104, #8109
Guide: #5148
Guilt: #817, #818
Guiltiness: #819
Guilty: #816
Gulp: #8354
Gust: #5380
Guzzle: #1572
Habit, in the: #5532, #5533
Habitation: #4583, #4585
Hailstones: #1259
Hair, long: #6545
Hair: #8163, #8181, #8185
Hairy goat: #8163, #8166
Half the spoils: #4275
Half, one: #4276
Half: #2677
Halter: #7448
Hammer: #7554
Hand over: #3399
Hand span: #2947
Hand, cupped: #2651
Hand, left: #8040, #8041, #8042
Hand, right: #3225
Hand, throw: #1911, #3034
Hand: #3027, #3197
Handful: #7062
Hang: #3363, #8511, #8518
Happiness: #837
Happy: #833, #835
Harass: #6693
Hard, press: #6484
Hard: #7185, #7186
Hardship: #6093
Hare: #768
Harlot, be a: #2181
Harm: #611
Harness: #5630, #8302
Harp: #3658
Harsh: #4815
Harvest: #7105
Haste, make: #2363, #5789
Haste: #2649
Hasten: #2648
Hate: #8130, #8135

Horse: #5483
Horseman: #6571
Hostility: #342
Hot: #2525, #2527
House, supply: #214
House: #1004
How long: #575, #4970, #8478
How many: #4100
How: #349, #834, #4100
However: #389, #403
Howl: #2980
Howling: #3214
Human: #120
Hunchback: #1384
Hundred: #3967
Hunger: #7457, #7458
Hungry: #7456
Hunt: #6679
Hunter: #6719
Hurl: #2909
Hurry: #4116, #4117
Hut: #6898
Hyssop: #231
Ibis: #8580
Ice: #7140
Idol, family: #8655
Idol, sun: #2553
Idol: #1544
If: #518, #3588
Ignite: #1197
Ill: #1738
Illness: #1739
Illuminate: #2094
Image, cast: #4541
Image: #6754
Imagery: #4906
Imagination: #8307
Imbibe: #5433
Imitate: #8591
Immigrant: #1616
Immigrate: #1481
Immigration: #4033
Impatient: #3811
In addition: #5921
In front: #5227
In law: #2860
In line: #4635
In misery: #3510
In order: #4616, #5668, #5674
In place: #4136, #8478
In the end: #657
In the face: #5048
In the habit: #5532, #5533
In the sense of drawing weapons: #2502
In this way: #3541, #3602
In, fence: #1219
In, press: #6887
Incense smoke: #6988, #7004
Incense, burn: #6999, #7000
Increase in number: #7231, #7232
Increase: #7235
Indeed: #552
Individual: #1538
Infant: #7988
Infect: #6879
Infection: #6883
Infirmity: #2483
Inflame: #1814
Inflammation: #1816
Inherit: #5157
Inheritance: #5159
In-law, be an: #2859
Innocence: #5356
Innocent: #5355
Inquire: #7592
Inscribe: #2710
Inside: #1004, #7130, #7131
Installation: #4394

Instant: #6621
Instead: #3588
Intelligence: #8394
Intercede: #6279, #6419
Interest: #8636
Interpret: #3887, #6622
Interpretation: #6623
Invade: #1464
Invention: #4284
Investigate: #1239
Iron: #1270
Irritate: #3992
Irritation: #1618
Is, there: #786, #3426
Island: #336, #339
Issue: #2100
Itch: #2775
Jar: #3537
Jasper: #3471
Jaw: #3895
Jewel: #5459
Join: #3867
Joined together: #7947
Joint: #4225
Journey: #4550, #4551, #5265
Joy, skip with: #7797
Jubilee: #3104
Judge: #6414
Judgment: #8201
Jug: #7184
Juice: #4952
Jump: #2187
Juniper: #7574
Just as: #834
Just like this: #3541, #3602
Keep alive: #2421, #2425
Keep back: #2820
Keep secret: #3582
Keep silent: #2790
Keep watch: #6822
Keep: #5201
Kermes: #8438
Kernel: #2785
Keruv: #3742
Kick: #1163
Kid, male: #1423
Kidney: #3629
Kikar: #3603
Kill by stoning: #7275
Kill: #2026, #4191
Kin: #7608
Kind one: #2623
Kind, diverse: #3610
Kind: #4327
Kindle: #6919
Kindness: #2617
Kindred: #4138
King: #4428
Kingdom: #4467
Kiss: #5401
Kite: #7201
Knead: #3888
Kneading bowl: #4863
Knee, bend the: #86
Knee: #1290
Kneel: #1288
Knife: #3979
Knob: #3730
Knock: #2251
Knoll: #1389
Know: #3045
Knower: #3049
Labor: #5999, #6001
Lace: #8288
Lack of: #1097
Lacking: #4270
Ladder: #5551
Lame: #6455
Lament: #5594
Lamenting: #4553

Lamp: #5216
Lampstand: #4501
Land, dry: #3006
Land, high: #780
Land, thirsty: #6774
Land: #776
Lapis lazuli: #5601
Last night: #570
Last: #314
Late rain: #4456
Late: #648
Laudanum: #3910
Laugh: #6711
Laughter: #6712
Lavish: #2107
Law, in: #2860
Law: #1881
Lay in wait: #6658
Lay waste: #1110
Lazy: #7503
Lead: #5095, #5777
Leader: #678
Leaf: #5929
Lean: #7330, #8172
Leap: #5425
Leaping locust: #2728
Learn: #3925
Learning: #3948
Leave alone: #5203
Leave behind: #3498
Leave in place: #3322
Leave: #5117, #5800, #5805, #7604
Leaven: #2556, #7603
Leavened bread: #2557
Left hand: #8040, #8041, #8042
Leg, upper: #7640
Leg: #3767
Lend: #5377, #5378, #5383, #5670
Length: #753
Lentil: #5742
Leopard: #5246
Less: #4591
Level valley: #1237
Lick: #3897, #3952
Lid: #3727
Lie down: #7901
Lie: #3576, #3577, #3584
Lieutenant: #7991
Life, whole: #5750
Life: #2416
Lift high: #7682
Lift up: #4984, #5375
Lift: #7426, #7318
Light: #215, #216, #217
Lightweight: #7052
Like, lion: #746
Likeness: #1823
Lime: #7875
Limp: #6760
Line, in: #4635
Linen: #905, #906, #7893, #8336
Linger: #4102
Linsey-woolsey: #8162
Lintel: #4947
Lion like: #746
Lion: #738
Lioness: #3833
Lip, upper: #8222
Lip: #8193
Liquor: #7941
Listen: #8085
Little one: #2191, #6810
Little owl: #3563
Little: #4592
Live: #2421, #2425
Lively: #2422
Liver: #3515, #3516

Marriage duty, do the: #2992
Marry: #1166
Marsh grass: #260
Marvel: #8539
Master: #1167
Material, woven: #8665
Material: #7075
Matter: #562, #1697, #1703
Mattress: #6210
Mature: #8535
Meal, bread: #6182
Measure: #4058
Measured amount: #8506
Measurement: #4060
Meat: #4202
Meddle: #1624
Meditate: #7742
Meet, come to: #7122, #7125, #7136
Meet: #7122, #7125, #7136
Meeting: #4744
Melon: #20
Melt away: #4549
Memorial: #234
Memory: #2143
Men: #2138
Mention: #2142
Merchandise: #4465, #4466
Messenger: #4397
Metal plating: #6826
Metal, precious: #1220, #1222
Metropolis: #7151
Middle: #2677, #8432
Middlemost: #8484
Midsection: #3409
Midst: #8432
Midwife, act as: #3205
Might have: #4592
Mighty one: #410
Mildew: #3420
Milk, give: #5763
Milk: #2459, #2461
Millstone: #7347
Mimic: #3887
Minister: #8334
Ministry: #8335
Mire: #3121
Miscarry: #7921
Mischief: #2154
Misery, in: #3510
Misery: #4341
Mist: #108
Mistake: #4870
Mix, unnatural: #8397
Mix: #1101
Mixed multitude: #628
Mixture, ointment: #4842
Mixture, spice: #7545
Mixture: #6154
Mock: #6711
Moderate: #1777
Moist: #3892, #3893
Mold: #3334, #3335
Molding: #2213
Moment: #7281, #7282
Month: #2320
Monument: #4676
Moon, new: #2320
Moon: #3391, #3394
More: #3254, #3966, #5750
Moreover: #637
Morning: #1242
Morrow: #4283
Mortal man: #4962
Mortar and pestle: #4085
Mortar: #2563
Mother: #517
Mound: #1530
Mount: #2042
Mountain-sheep: #2169

Number: #4557
Numerous: #6099
Nurse: #3243
Oak: #424, #427
Oasis: #4494, #4496
Oath: #423
Obedience: #3349
Occount, on: #4616
Off, cast: #5394
Off, crop: #6998
Off, cut: #5243
Off, flake: #2636
Off, scrape: #7096
Off, send: #7964, #7971
Off, shake: #5286, #5287
Off, slice: #7082, #7112
Off, snap: #4454
Off, snip: #4135
Off, strip: #6584
Off, tear: #6561
Offense: #6588
Offer willingly: #5068
Offering of restitution: #8002
Offering, ascension: #1473, #5930
Offering, fire: #801
Offering, freewill: #5071
Offering: #8641
Officer: #7860
Offshoot: #6133
Oh: #188
Oil, fresh: #3323
Oil, press out: #6671
Oil: #8081, #8082
Ointment mixture: #4842
Ointment: #4888
Old age: #2209
Old: #2204
Olive: #2132
Olivine: #6357
Om, turn away: #5186
Omer: #6016
On account: #182, #1558, #5668, #5674
On foot: #7273
On occount: #4616
On, tie: #7405
One half: #4276
One tenth: #6241
One, kind: #2623
One, little: #2191, #6810
One, mighty: #410
One, single: #8478
One, skilled: #2450
One, steadfast: #6662
One, tenth: #6218
One, that: #1119, #3644, #3926
One, this: #1976
Onion: #1211
Only: #389, #403, #905, #906, #7535
Onycha: #7827
Onyx: #7718
Opal: #3958
Open space: #4054
Open up: #6491
Open, cleave: #1234
Open, wide: #8365
Open: #6603, #6605
Opening: #6310, #6607, #6608
Opinion: #1843
Opponent: #7854
Opposite: #5048
Opposition: #7855
Oppress: #6231
Oppression: #6233
Or: #176, #518
Order, in: #4616, #5668, #5674
Ordinary: #2455
Ornament: #4030

Pack: #2943
Pain, distressing: #6089, #6091, #6092
Pale: #2353, #2715
Paleness: #2355, #2751
Palm, date: #8558
Palm: #3709, #3710
Pan, fire: #4289
Pan: #4227
Parable: #4912
Parapet: #4624
Parcel: #2513
Parching heat: #2721
Part, divided: #1506
Part, fifth: #2569, #2570
Part, fourth: #7255
Part, lower: #8482
Part, tenth: #4643
Part: #905, #906, #6475
Partner: #4828
Pass over: #2498
Pass, come to: #1961
Past time: #6927
Paste: #2560
Pasture: #4721
Path: #734
Pattern: #8403
Pay attention: #238, #239, #5234
Payment: #4909
Peasant: #6518
Pedestal: #4350
Peel: #6478
Peg, tent: #3489
Peg: #2053
Pelican: #6893
Penis: #8212
People: #5971
Perceive: #1957, #2372
Perforate: #2763
Perforated: #2764
Perform: #6381
Performance: #6382
Period, rest: #7677
Perish: #6, #8
Permanent: #6783
Persecution: #6869
Persuade: #5496, #6601
Pestilence: #4046
Pick out: #5365
Pick up: #3950
Piece, cut: #1335
Piece, shoulder: #3802
Piece: #5409
Pieces, dash to: #7492
Pieces, divide into: #5408
Pieces, ground to: #1743
Pieces, tear into: #2963
Pierce through: #5344
Pierce: #1856
Pierced bread: #2471
Piercing: #8148
Pigeon, young: #1469
Pile of ruins: #5856
Pile up: #6651
Pile: #6192
Pillar base: #7507
Pillar: #5982
Pipe, reed: #5748
Pistachio: #992
Pit: #6354, #6356
Pitch tent: #166, #167
Pitch: #2203
Pity, show: #2550
Pity: #2551
Place of lodging: #4411
Place to burn: #4729
Place, bare: #8205
Place, burial: #6900
Place, feeding: #4829

Place, high: #8617
Place, in: #4136, #8478
Place, leave in: #3322
Place, lying: #4904
Place: #3455, #7760, #5414, #7931
Plague: #5061
Plain: #4334
Plait: #4865
Plan: #2803
Plant: #5193
Plantation: #3759
Plaster: #2902
Platform: #1116
Plating, metal: #6826
Platter: #7086
Plea: #1779, #1781
Plead: #6419
Pleasant: #2532
Pleasantness: #5282
Please: #577, #4994
Pleasure: #5730
Pledge, make a: #5670
Pledge, take as a: #2254
Pledge: #5667
Plenty: #7647, #7649
Plot: #2161
Plowing: #2758
Plowshare: #855
Pluck away: #1497
Pluck out: #4871
Pluck up: #6131
Pluck: #2167, #2168
Plucked: #1500
Plucking: #1498, #1499
Plumage: #5339
Plunder: #957, #962
Point out: #184
Point, at this: #1988
Point, to this: #2008
Point: #3384, #6856, #8376
Pole: #4133
Pomegranate: #7416
Pool: #98, #99, #1293, #1295
Poplar: #3839
Possess: #3423
Possession: #4180, #4181
Possibly: #194
Post, corner: #4742
Post: #5333
Posterity: #5220
Pot, boiling: #4802
Pot: #5518
Pouch: #6872
Pour down: #3251, #3332
Pour out: #8210
Pour: #5258, #5259
Poured out: #5257
Pouring: #5262
Poverty: #4544
Power: #430, #433
Precious metal: #1220, #1222
Precious: #4022
Precipitate: #4305
Precipitation: #4306
Predict: #5172
Prediction: #5173
Pregnancy: #2032
Pregnant: #2030
Prepare: #3559
Prepared: #6264
Present: #1293, #1295, #3322
Preserve: #5341
Press firmly: #4600
Press hard: #6484
Press in: #6887
Press out oil: #6671
Press, fruit: #1831
Press: #7818

Pressing in, in the sense of: #2490
Presume: #6075
Previously: #8543
Prey, bird of: #5861
Prey: #2964, #2965
Price, bride: #4119
Price, ransom: #6306
Price: #4242
Prickly thorn: #6796
Pride: #1346
Prison: #5470
Prisoner: #615, #616
Produce a seed: #2232
Produce: #6529
Product: #2981
Production: #8393
Profit: #1215
Projectile: #7973
Prolong: #748
Property: #3424
Proportion: #4530
Prosper: #6743
Prostitute: #6945, #6948
Prostitution: #2183
Protection, provide: #2589, #2603
Protective: #2587
Provender: #4554
Provide food: #3938
Provide protection: #2589, #2603
Provide: #3051
Provisions: #6720
Provoke: #4843, #5006
Pruify: #2398
Pull out: #8025
Pulverize: #7833
Punishment: #1244
Purchase: #7069
Pure gold: #6337
Purge: #2398
Purple: #713
Pursue: #7291
Push away: #1920
Push: #5065
Pustule: #76
Qeshiytah: #7192
Quail: #7958
Quantity: #4884
Quarrel: #4079
Quarter: #7252, #7253
Quartz: #2496
Queen: #4436
Quench: #3518
Quickly bring: #7323
Quickly: #4118, #4120
Quietness: #5183
Quiver: #8522
Rabbit: #8227
Rafter: #6982
Raiment: #3682
Rain shower: #1653, #1730
Rain, first: #3138
Rain, late: #4456
Raindrop: #8164
Raise up: #7311
Ram horn: #7782
Ram, battering: #4239
Ram: #2089, #7716
Rampart: #2346
Rank: #4634
Ransom price: #6306
Ransom: #6299, #6304
Rash: #933
Rave: #7696
Raven: #6158
Ravine: #794
Raw: #4995
Razor: #8593

Reviving: #4241
Rhinoceros: #7214
Rib: #6763
Rich: #6223, #6238
Riches: #6239
Riddle: #2420
Ride: #7392
Right hand: #3225
Right, go: #541, #3231
Right: #3233
Rim, outer: #3749
Rim: #4526
Ring, nose: #2397
Ring, ornamental: #5141
Ring: #2885
Rip: #6533
Ripe fruit: #4395
Ripen: #1310, #2590
Rise up: #1342
Rise: #6965
Rising sun: #2225
River: #5104
Road: #1870
Roam: #7300
Roar: #1949
Roast: #6748
Roasted grain: #7039
Robe: #155
Robust: #7194
Rock wall: #7790, #7791
Rod: #4731
Roebuck: #3180
Roll: #1556
Rolling thing: #1534, #1536
Roof covering: #4372
Roof: #1406
Root out: #5428
Root: #8328
Rot: #4743
Roundness: #3603
Row of tents: #2918
Row: #2905
Ruddy: #132
Ruin: #8510
Ruins, pile of: #5856
Rule: #7287
Ruler, make self: #5493, #7787, #8323
Ruler: #5057
Rump: #451
Run: #7323
Sack, grain: #572
Sack: #8242
Sacrifice: #2076, #2077
Sacrificial bowl: #4518
Sad: #2196
Saddle: #2280, #4817
Saddlebag: #4942
Safeguard: #8104, #8109
Safeguarding: #8107
Safely: #983
Safety: #983
Salt: #4417, #4419
Sanctuary: #4720
Sand: #2344
Sandal: #5275
Sash: #73
Satisfaction: #7648
Satisfied: #7646
Saw: #2009
Say: #559
Scab: #4556, #5597
Scales: #7193
Scar, singe: #4348
Scarlet: #8144
Scatter abroad: #6327
Scatter: #5310
Scorpion: #6137
Scour: #4838
Scout: #7788, #8446

Shatter: #2826, #7665
Shattered: #2865, #7665
Shattering: #7667
Shave: #1548
Sheaf, bound: #485
Sheaf: #6016
Shear: #1494
She-donkey: #860
Sheep, young: #6251
Sheep: #3532, #3535, #3775
Sheet: #7549
She-goat: #5795
Sheqel: #8255
Shield: #4043
Shine: #215, #1984, #4110
Shining: #1974
Ship: #591
Shone: #3313
Shoot: #5322
Shore: #2348
Short: #3530
Shortness: #7115
Should: #1571, #3651
Shoulder piece: #3802
Shoulder: #7926
Shout aloud: #7442, #7444
Shouting out: #7769, #7771, #7773
Shovel: #3257
Show pity: #2550
Show: #7200, #7202, #7207, #7212
Shower, rain: #1653, #1730
Showers: #7241
Shrub: #7880
Shut up: #5640
Shut: #5462, #5534
Sick: #2470, #8463
Sickle: #2770
Sickness: #4245
Side, other: #5676
Side: #6654
Sigh: #584
Sight, out of: #5956
Sightlessness: #5575
Sign: #226
Signal: #7321, #8643
Silence: #2013
Silenced: #1745, #1822
Silent, keep: #2790
Silent: #1826, #2795
Silver: #3701
Simmer: #2102
Since: #1571, #2004, #2005, #3588
Sinew: #1517
Sing: #7891
Singe scar: #4348
Singeing: #3555
Single one: #8478
Sink down: #7503
Sink: #2883
Sister: #269
Sister-in-law: #2994
Sit down: #8497
Six: #8337, #8346
Sixth: #8345
Sixty: #8337, #8346
Skill: #2451
Skilled one: #2450
Skilled: #2449
Skillet: #6517
Skin bag: #2573
Skin sore: #3217
Skin, grape: #2085
Skin: #5785
Skip with joy: #7797
Skull: #1538
Sky: #8064
Slab: #3871

Spitting: #3994
Splendor: #1935
Splinter: #7110
Split in two: #8156
Split: #6385
Splitting: #8157
Spoil: #7998
Spoils, half the: #4275
Spoon: #3709, #3710
Spot, bald: #7144, #7146
Spot, bare: #1371, #1372
Spot, bright: #934
Spot: #2921, #8258
Spotted: #1261
Spread across: #6581
Spread out: #6566, #6567
Spread wide: #6601
Spread: #7849
Spring up: #6779
Spring: #4599
Sprinkle: #2236
Sprinkling basin: #4219
Sprout: #1876
Spy: #7270, #8637
Square: #7250, #7251
Squeeze: #3905
Squeezing: #3906
Stack: #1430
Staff: #7626
Stagger: #5128
Stair step: #4609
Stalk, grain: #7054
Stalk: #7070
Stand up: #5324
Stand: #5975, #5976
Standard: #5251
Star: #3556
Stare: #5027
Statement: #561
Station: #3320
Stave: #4938
Stay the night: #3885
Stay: #3176, #3186
Steadfast one: #6662
Steadfast: #6663, #6664
Steadfastness: #6666
Steal: #1589
Steel away: #1589
Steep valley: #1516
Step, stair: #4609
Step: #4096
Steps, take: #1869
Sterile: #6135
Stew: #5138
Stickerbush: #5519, #7899, #7900
Still: #1157, #5703, #5704, #5750
Stink: #887
Stir up: #5782, #5783
Stir: #926
Stomach: #6896
Stone stool: #70
Stone, hewn: #1496
Stone, sharp: #6864
Stone: #68, #5619
Stoning, kill by: #7275
Stool, stone: #70
Stool: #3676
Stoop: #3766
Stop: #6113
Storage: #3463, #3465
Store up: #686
Store: #3462, #3647
Storehouse: #4543
Stork: #2624
Storm: #5590, #8175
Straight trumpet: #2689
Straight: #3474, #3477
Straightness: #3476

Take refuge: #2620
Take steps: #1869
Take upon: #2974
Take: #1980, #3212, #3947
Talebearer: #7400
Talk: #4448
Tall: #7311
Tamarisk: #815
Tambourine: #8596
Task work: #4522, #4523
Tassel: #1434
Taste sweet: #4985, #4988
Tasty food: #4574
Tattoo: #7085
Taunt: #1442
Teach: #3384, #3925
Teaching: #8451
Tear away: #5255
Tear into pieces: #2963
Tear off: #6561
Tear: #7167
Teat: #1717
Tell: #5046
Ten: #6235, #6240, #6242
Tender: #7390
Tenderness: #7356, #7358, #7391
Tent curtain: #6532
Tent peg: #3489
Tent, pitch: #166, #167
Tent: #168
Tenth one: #6218
Tenth part: #4643
Tenth, give a: #6237
Tenth, one: #6241
Tenth: #6224
Tents, row of: #2918
Terminate: #2308
Terrified: #6206
Terror: #367
Test: #5254
Testicles: #810
Thank: #1911, #3034
Thanks: #8426
That alone: #905, #906
That one: #1119, #3644, #3926
That way: #3541, #3602
That, given: #3588
That, would: #3863
Theft: #1591
Then: #645
There is: #786, #3426
There: #3588, #8033
Therefore: #518, #3808, #5921
These: #411, #428, #1992
Thick darkness: #6205
Thick gloominess: #653
Thick woven: #5687, #5688
Thick: #5645, #5666
Thief: #1590
Thigh muscle: #5384
Thigh: #7784, #7785
Thin bread: #7550
Thin: #7534
Thing written: #4385
Thing, lost: #9
Thing, rolling: #1534, #1536
Thing, small: #4592
Think: #2803
Third generation: #8029
Third: #7992
Thirst: #6770, #6771, #6772, #6773
Thirsty land: #6774
Thirty: #7969, #7970
This one: #1976
This time: #6471
Thistle: #1863
Thorn bush: #5572
Thorn, bramble: #329

Tranquility: #7886
Transgress: #4603
Transgression: #4604
Trap: #3920
Trappings: #5716
Tread about: #7270, #8637
Tread: #7429, #7430
Treader: #7431
Treasure: #4301
Tree, great: #436, #437
Tree: #6086, #6097
Tremble: #2729
Trembling in fear: #2844
Trembling: #2730, #2731
Trial: #4530
Tribe: #523
Tributary: #6388
Tribute: #4371
Trouble: #8513
Trough, watering: #8268
Trough, wine: #3342
Trough: #7298
Trumpet, straight: #2689
Truth: #571
Tumor: #6076
Tumult: #4103
Tunic: #3801
Turban: #4701
Turn aside: #5493, #7787, #8323
Turn away: #8280
Turn back: #7725
Turn: #6437
Turning aside: #5627
Turquoise: #5306
Turtledove: #8449
Twenty: #6235, #6240, #6242
Twig: #8299
Twilight: #5939
Twin: #8380
Twirl: #5086
Twist backwards: #5557
Twist together: #7806
Twist: #2342, #5754
Twisted: #6618, #7806
Twistedness: #5771
Two, cut in: #1334
Two, split in: #8156
Two: #8147
Ty, do the marriage: #2992
Ulcer: #2990
Unable: #369, #370, #371
Unaware: #1097
Uncircumcised, considered: #6188
Uncircumcised: #6189
Uncle: #1730
Uncover: #1540, #6168
Under: #8478
Undergarment: #4370
Underneath: #8478
Understand: #995
Understanding: #998
Understood: #6566, #6567
Underworld: #7585
Unfilled: #922
Uninhabited: #1509
Unique: #6918
Unit: #259
Unite: #3161
Unknowingly: #1097, #1847
Unleavened bread: #4682
Unless: #3588, #3884
Unmindful: #7876
Unnatural mix: #8397
Unprotected: #6176
Unrecognizable, make self: #5234
Unseasoned: #8602
Up, boarded: #5603, #8226

Wanting: #2640
War, wage: #3898
Warm: #2552
Warn: #2094, #5749
Warp: #8358, #8359
Warrior: #1397, #1399
Wash: #3526
Waste, lay: #1110
Watch over: #974
Watch, keep: #6822
Watch, night: #821
Watch: #7200, #7202, #7207, #7212
Watchtower: #4707
Water, deep: #8415
Water, draw: #7579
Water: #4325
Watercourse: #2988
Watered: #7302
Watering trough: #8268
Wave: #5130
Waver: #235
Waving: #8573
Way, in this: #3541, #3602
Way, narrow: #4934
Way, that: #3541, #3602
Waywardness: #7564
Weaken: #2522
Wealthy: #2831
Weapons, in the sense of drawing: #2502
Wear out: #1086, #1089
Wear: #3847
Weary: #3022, #3023
Weasel: #2467
Weave: #7660
Week: #7620
Weep: #1058
Weeping, time of: #1068
Weeping: #1065
Weigh out: #238, #239
Weigh: #8254
Weight: #4948
Well, do: #3190
Well, go: #3190
Well: #875
West: #3220
What is needed: #1961
What is the reason: #4100
What, because of: #834
What: #834, #4100
Wheat, head of: #4425
Wheat: #2406
Wheel: #212
Whelp: #1482, #1484
When: #834, #3588
Where: #335, #346, #351, #375, #369, #370, #371, #834
Whereas: #834
Wherein: #2098
Wherever: #575
Whet: #8150
Whether: #176
Which: #834
While: #5750
Whip: #6531
Whirlwind: #5492
Whirring locust: #6767
Whisper: #7279
White, be: #3835
White: #3836
Who: #834, #4310
Whoever: #834
Whole life: #5750
Whole: #8549, #8552
Whom: #834
Whoredom: #2184
Whose: #834
Why: #335, #346, #351, #375, #4069, #4100, #5921

Wicked: #5766, #5767
Wickedness: #5932
Wicker basket: #5536
Wide open: #8365
Wide, spread: #6601
Wide: #7338, #7342
Widen: #7337
Widow: #490
Widowhood: #491
Width: #7341
Wild ass: #6501
Wild goat: #689
Wilderness, desolate: #3452
Wilderness: #4057
Willing: #5081
Willingly, offer: #5068
Willow: #6155
Wind around: #6801
Wind, east: #6921
Wind: #7305, #7307
Window: #2474
Wine trough: #3342
Wine, fresh: #8492
Wine: #3196
Wing: #3671
Winged, long: #83
Winter: #2779
Wipe away: #4229
Wire: #6341
With the exception: #2108
Withdraw: #2244
Wither: #6798
Withhold: #4513
Within: #3942, #6440
Without: #369, #370, #371, #3808, #3808
Witness: #5707, #5713
Wolf: #2061
Woman, young: #5291
Woman: #802
Womb: #990
Wonder: #4159
Wood bar: #1280, #1281
Wood: #6086, #6097
Wool: #6785
Word: #1697, #1703
Work over: #5953
Work, beaten: #4749
Work, braided: #8278, #8279
Work, task: #4522, #4523
Work: #4639
Workings: #5949
Works: #4611
Worth: #4373
Worthless: #457
Would that: #3863
Wound: #6481, #6482
Woven basket: #6803
Woven material: #8665
Woven, thick: #5687, #5688
Wrap around: #5749
Wrap, loin: #2290
Wrap: #5968
Wrapped, tightly: #3875
Wrath, flaming: #2740
Wrath: #5678, #5679
Wreath: #5850
Wrestling: #5319
Wrist: #6446
Write: #3789
Writing: #3793
Written, thing: #4385
Yarn: #4299
Year: #8141
Yearn: #183
Yearning: #8378
Yell out: #2199
Yell: #2201
Yellow: #6669
Yemim: #3222

Yesterday: #8543
Yet again: #5750
Yet, not: #2962
Yet: #5750
Yield: #1580
Yoke: #5923
Young age: #5271
Young camel: #1070
Young maiden: #5959
Young man: #5288, #5289
Young pigeon: #1469
Young sheep: #6251
Young woman: #5291
Youth: #979
Youthfulness: #6812
Zealous: #7065, #7067
Zealousness: #7068

Dictionary of Hebrew Names

Adah: Adornment. Strong's: #5711
Adbe'el: Mist in the mighty one. Strong's: #110
Admah: Ground. Strong's: #126, #128
Adonai: My lords. Strong's: #136
Adulam: Witness and a shepherd staff. Strong's: #5725, #5726
Agag: I will be overtop. Strong's: #90
Ahalivamah: Tent of the platform. Strong's: #173
Ahaliyav: Tent of father. Strong's: #171
Aharon: Light bringer (Uncertain meaning, but related to the word for light). Strong's: #175
Ahhi'ezer: My brother is help. Strong's: #295
Ahhihud: My brother is splendor. Strong's: #282
Ahhiman: My brother shares. Strong's: #289
Ahhira: My brother is dysfunctional. Strong's: #299
Ahhiram: My brother is raised. Strong's: #297, #298
Ahhiysamahh: My brother supports (May also mean "My brother of support."). Strong's: #294
Ahhuzat: Holdings. Strong's: #276
Akad: Delicate (Can also mean 'spark'). Strong's: #390
Akhbor: Mouse. Strong's: #5907
Akhran: Disturbed one. Strong's: #5918
Almodad: Mighty one of measuring (The origins of "modad" is uncertain). Strong's: #486
Almon-Divlatayim: Out of sight of two cakes (or "Out of sight of Divlatayim"). Strong's: #5963
Alon-Bakhut: Great tree of weeping. Strong's: #439
Alush: I will knead. Strong's: #442
Alwah: Wickedness. Strong's: #5933
Alwan: Loft. Strong's: #5935
Amaleq: People gathered up. Strong's: #6002, #6003
Ami'eyl: People of the mighty one. Strong's: #5988
Amihud: People of splendor. Strong's: #5989
Amishaddai: People of my breasts. Strong's: #5996
Amiynadav: My people offered willingly. Strong's: #5992
Ammah: A linear standard of measure equal to the length of the forearm; a cubit. Strong's: #520
Amon: Tribal. Strong's: #5983, #5984, #5985

Amram: People raised. Strong's: #6019

Amraphel: Sayer of the fall (Can also mean "One that speaks of secrets", "Sayer of darkness" or "Fall of the sayer."). Strong's: #569

Anah: Answered. Strong's: #6034

Anam: Affliction of waters. Strong's: #6047

Anaq: Neck band. Strong's: #6061, #6062

Aner: Young boy (Meaning and origin are uncertain). Strong's: #6063

Aqabariym: Sharp sighted. Strong's: #4610

Aqan: Sharp sighted. Strong's: #6130

Ar: Enemy (May also mean "city."). Strong's: #6144

Arad: Wild donkey. Strong's: #6166

Aram: Palace (From a root meaning "a high place," such as used for building palaces and forts). Strong's: #758

Aram-Nahara'im: Palace of two rivers. Strong's: #763

Aran: I will shout aloud. Strong's: #765

Araq: Gnawed. Strong's: #6208

Ararat: High land (Meaning uncertain. Possibly of foreign origin). Strong's: #780

Ard: I will go down. Strong's: #714

Areliy: Lion of my mighty one. Strong's: #692

Argov: I will clod. Strong's: #709

Arnon: I will shout aloud. Strong's: #769

Arodiy: My roaming. Strong's: #722

Aro'eyr: Unprotected. Strong's: #6177

Arpakhshad: I declined the breast. Strong's: #775

Arwad: Roaming. Strong's: #719, #721

Aryokh: Lion like. Strong's: #746

Ashbeyl: I will exchange (Can also mean "Fire of Bel"). Strong's: #788

Asher: Happy. Strong's: #836

Ashkanaz: Fire sprinkled. Strong's: #813

Ashterot: young sheep. Strong's: #6252

Ashterot-Qar'nayim: Horns of young sheep. Strong's: #6255

Ashur: Happy. Strong's: #804

Asiyr: Prisoner. Strong's: #617

Asnat: Belonging to Nat (Of Egyptian origin). Strong's: #621

Asri'eyl: My happiness is the mighty one. Strong's: #844, #845

Atariym: Sites. Strong's: #871

Atarot: Wreaths. Strong's: #5852

Atsmon: Abundant one. Strong's: #6111
At'rot-Shophan: Wreaths of Rabbit. Strong's: #5855
Aveyl-Hashit'tim: Mourning of the acacias (or "Mourning of Hashit'tim") Strong's: #63
Aveyl-Mitsrayim: Mourning of two straits (or "Mourning of Mitsrayim"). Strong's: #67
Avida: My father knows. Strong's: #28
Avidan: My father is a moderator (May also mean "father of a moderator," "father of Dan" or "My father is Dan."). Strong's: #27
Avihha'il: My father is a force. Strong's: #32
Aviram: My father is raised. Strong's: #48
Aviyasaph: My father gathers. Strong's: #23
Aviyhu: He is my father. Strong's: #30
Aviyma'el: My father is from the mighty one. Strong's: #39
Aviymelekh: My father is king (Can also mean "Father of the king."). Strong's: #40
Avraham: Father lifted. Strong's: #85
Avram: Father raised. Strong's: #87
Awi: Twist. Strong's: #5757, #5761
Awit: Ruined heaps. Strong's: #5762
Ay: Ruined heap. Strong's: #5857
Ayah: Hawk. Strong's: #345
Ayin: Eye. Strong's: #5871
Azan: Strong one. Strong's: #5821
Azazeyl: Strong waver. Strong's: #5799
Azni: My ear. Strong's: #241, #244
Ba'al: Master. Strong's: #1168
Ba'al-Hhanan: Master of beauty (Can also mean "Ba'al is Beauty"). Strong's: #1177
Ba'al-Me'on: Master of the habitation. Strong's: #1186
Ba'al-Pe'or: Master of the wide open. Strong's: #1187
Ba'al-Tsephon: Master of the north. Strong's: #1189
Balaq: He laid waste. Strong's: #1111
Bamot: Platforms. Strong's: #1120
Barneya: Grain rattles. Strong's: #6947
Bashan: Shame. Strong's: #1316
Basmat: Fragrance. Strong's: #1315
Bavel: Mixed up. Strong's: #894
Bedad: Alone. Strong's: #911

Be'eri: My well. Strong's: #882
Be'er-Lahhiy-Ro'iy: I see a well for life. Strong's: #883
Bekher: Young camel. Strong's: #1071
Bela: Swallowed. Strong's: #1106
Beli'ya'al: The unaware will gain. Strong's: #1100
Ben-Amiy: Son of my people. Strong's: #1151
Ben-Oni: Son of my vigor. Strong's: #1126
Be'on: In cohabitation. Strong's: #1194
Be'or: Igniting. Strong's: #1160
B'er: Well. Strong's: #876
Bera: In dysfunction (Can also mean "With shouting", "Son of evil", "A well" or "Declaring."). Strong's: #1298
Beqa: A dry weight measure equal to one-half *shekel* weight. Strong's: #1235
Bered: Hailstones. Strong's: #1260
Beri'ah: With a companion. Strong's: #1283
B'er-Sheva: Seven wells. Strong's: #884
Betsaleyl: In the shadow of the mighty one. Strong's: #1212
Betser: Precious metal. Strong's: #1221
Betu'el: Their house is the mighty one. Strong's: #1328
Beyt-El: House of the mighty one. Strong's: #1008
Beyt-Haran: House of the Hill country. Strong's: #1028
Beyt-Hayishmot: House of there is death (or "House of Hayishmot") Strong's: #1020
Beyt-Lehhem: House of bread. Strong's: #1035
Beyt-Nimrah: House of the leopard. Strong's: #1039
Beyt-Pe'or: House of the opened wide one (or "House of Pe'or"). Strong's: #1047
Bilam: None of the people. Strong's: #1109
Bilhah: Dismay. Strong's: #1090
Bilhan: Their dismay. Strong's: #1092
Binyamin: Son of the right hand. Strong's: #1144
Birsha: With the lost. Strong's: #1306
B'ney-Ya'aqan: Sons of he will be sharp sighted (or "sons of Ya'aqatan") Strong's: #1142
Botsrah: Sheep pen. Strong's: #1224
Buqi: Vacant. Strong's: #1231
Buz: Despised. Strong's: #938
Dameseq: Blood sack. Strong's: #1834
Dan: Moderator. Strong's: #1835

Daphqah: She beat out. Strong's: #1850

Datan: Lawful. Strong's: #1885

Dedan: Low country (Can also mean breasts or judge). Strong's: #1719

De'u'eyl: They knew the mighty one. Strong's: #1845

Devorah: Bee. Strong's: #1683

Dibon: Brooding. Strong's: #1769

Dibon-Gad: Plea offering. Strong's: #1769

Dinah: Plea. Strong's: #1783

Dinhavah: Plea offering. Strong's: #1838

Diqlah: Palm grove (Meaning and origin are uncertain). Strong's: #1853

Dishan: Thresher. Strong's: #1789

Dishon: Antelope. Strong's: #1787

Divriy: My word. Strong's: #1704

Di-Zahav: Sufficient gold. Strong's: #1774

Dodan: Low country (Can also mean friendship, breast or judge). Strong's: #1721

Dotan: Lawful. Strong's: #1886

Dumah: Silenced. Strong's: #1746

Eden: Pleasure. Strong's: #5731

Edom: Red. Strong's: #123, #130

Ed're'i: My energy. Strong's: #154

Ehyeh: I exist (Used only once, Exodus 3:14, where it is used as a proper name). Strong's: #1961

Elaley: The mighty one goes up. Strong's: #500

Elam: Ancient. Strong's: #5867

Elasar: Mighty one of the noble (Can also mean "Mighty one is a chastiser" or "Revolting from the mighty one."). Strong's: #495

Elazar: The mighty one helps. Strong's: #499

El-Beyt-El: Mighty one of the house of the mighty one (or "mighty one of Beyt El"). Strong's: #416

Elda'ah: The mighty one knows. Strong's: #420

Eldad: The mighty one is a teat. Strong's: #419

El-Elohey-Yisra'eyl: Mighty one of powers will turn aside the mighty one (or "mighty one of Elohiym of Yisra'el"). Strong's: #415

Eli'av: The mighty one is father. Strong's: #446

Elidad: My mighty one is a teat. Strong's: #449

Eli'ezer: My mighty one helps (Can also mean "Mighty one of help."). Strong's: #461

Eliphaz: My mighty one is pure gold. Strong's: #464
Elishah: My mighty one equates (or "My mighty one resembles." The meaning of the word "shah" is uncertain). Strong's: #473
Elishama: My mighty one heard. Strong's: #476
Elitsaphan: My mighty one concealed. Strong's: #469
Elitsur: My mighty one is a boulder. Strong's: #468
Eliysheva: My mighty one swears. Strong's: #472
Elohiym: Powers. Strong's: #430
Elqanah: The mighty one purchased. Strong's: #511
El-Ra'iy: The mighty one sees me. Strong's: #410 & #7200
El'tsaphan: The mighty one conceals. Strong's: #469
Elyasaph: The mighty one added. Strong's: #460
Elyon: Upper. Strong's: #5945
Emor: Sayer. Strong's: #567
Enosh: Man. Strong's: #583
Epher: Dirt. Strong's: #6081
Ephod: Ephod. Strong's: #641
Ephrat: I will interpret. Strong's: #672
Ephrayim: Ashes (Can also mean "fruitful" or "double fruit."). Strong's: #669
Ephron: Powdery. Strong's: #6085
Erekh: Slow. Strong's: #751
Esaw: Doing. Strong's: #6215
Eseq: Strife. Strong's: #6230
Eshban: I will grow. Strong's: #790
Eshkol: Cluster. Strong's: #812
Etsbon: Working. Strong's: #675
Etsi'on-Gaver: Abundant one. Strong's: #6100
Ever: Other side. Strong's: #5677, #5680, #5681, #5682
Evronah: Crossing one. Strong's: #5684
Ewi: My yearning. Strong's: #189
Eyhhiy: My brother. Strong's: #278
Eylah: Oak. Strong's: #425
Eyliym: Bucks. Strong's: #362
Eylon: Great tree. Strong's: #356
Eylot: Does. Strong's: #359
Eyl-Paran: Decorated Buck (The word Eyl can also mean ram, hart, tree, lintel, oak, mighty or strength). Strong's: #364
Eym: Terror. Strong's: #368
Eynan: Having an eye. Strong's: #5851

Eynayim: Eyes (or more literally, "Two eyes"). Strong's: #5879
Eyn-Mishpat: Eye of decision (Can also mean "Spring of judgement."). Strong's: #5880
Eyphah: A dry standard of measure equal to 3 *se'ah*s or 10 omers. The same as the liquid measure bath which is about 9 imperial gallons or 40 liters. Strong's: #374
Eyphah: Murkiness. Strong's: #5891
Eyr: Enemy (May also mean "city."). Strong's: #6147
Eyran: Bare one (May also mean "enemy" or "city."). Strong's: #6197
Eyriy: My bare skin. Strong's: #6179, #6180
Eyshdat: Fire Law. Strong's: #799+#1881
Eytam: Their plowshare. Strong's: #864
Eytser: He stored up. Strong's: #687
Eyval: Round stone. Strong's: #5858
Gad: Fortune. Strong's: #1410
Gad'di'eyl: My fortune is the mighty one. Strong's: #1427
Gad'diy: My fortune. Strong's: #1426
Gahham: Burnt. Strong's: #1514
Galeyd: Mound of the witness. Strong's: #1567
Gamli'eyl: My camel is the mighty one. Strong's: #1583
Gatam: Burnt Valley. Strong's: #1609
Gemali: My camel. Strong's: #1582
Gera: Seed of grain. Strong's: #1617
Gerar: Chewed. Strong's: #1642
Gerizim: Cuttings. Strong's: #1630
Gershom: Evicted. Strong's: #1647
Gershon: Evicted. Strong's: #1648
Geshur: Clinging. Strong's: #1650, #1651
Getar: Agitated. Strong's: #1666
Gerah: A dry weight measure equal to a 20th part of a shekel. Strong's: #1626
Ge'u'eyl: The mighty one will rise up. Strong's: #1345
Ghamorah: Submersion. Strong's: #6017
Ghaza: She-goat. Strong's: #5804
Gidoni: My hewn one. Strong's: #1441
Gil'ad: Dancing around the witness. Strong's: #1568
Gilgal: Rolling thing. Strong's: #1537
Girgash: Immigrant of clayey soil (Can also mean "dwelling on clayey soil."). Strong's: #1622
Giyhhon: Bursting forth. Strong's: #1521

Golan: Their burnt offerings. Strong's: #1474
Gomer: Concluded. Strong's: #1586
Goren-Ha'atad: Floor of the bramble thorn. Strong's: #329, #1637
Goshen: Drawing near. Strong's: #1657
Goyim: Nations. Strong's: #1471
Gudgodah: Fortunes. Strong's: #1412
Guni: My defender. Strong's: #1476
Hadad: The teat. Strong's: #1908
Hadar: Honor. Strong's: #1924
Hadoram: Their honor. Strong's: #1913
Hagar: The immigrant. Strong's: #1904
Ham: Roaring (From a root meaning "the roar of the sea"). Strong's: #1990
Haran: Hill country. Strong's: #2039
Hevel: Vanity. Strong's: #1893
Heymam: Confused. Strong's: #1967
Hhadad: He was sharp. Strong's: #2316
Hhagi: My feast. Strong's: #2291
Hhaglah: Partridge. Strong's: #2295
Hham: Father-in-law. Strong's: #2526
Hhamat: Skin bag (Can also mean heat, anger or wall). Strong's: #2574, #2575, #2577
Hhamor: Donkey. Strong's: #2544
Hhamul: Pitied. Strong's: #2538, #2539
Hhani'eyl: Beauty of the mighty one. Strong's: #2592
Hhanokh: Devoted. Strong's: #2585
Hharadah: Trembling. Strong's: #2732
Hharan: Flaming wrath. Strong's: #2771
Hharmah: Assigned. Strong's: #2767
Hhashmonah: Wealthy. Strong's: #2832
Hhatsar-Adar: Courtyard of he was eminent (or "Courtyard of Adar"). Strong's: #2692
Hhatsar-Eynan: Courtyard of Having an eye (or "Courtyard of Eynan"). Strong's: #2704
Hhatsariym: Courtyards. Strong's: #2699
Hhatsarmawet: Courtyard of death. Strong's: #2700
Hhatsarot: Courtyards. Strong's: #2698
Hhats'tson-Tamar: Dividing the date palm. Strong's: #2688
Hhawah: Town. Strong's: #2332

Hhawilah: Twist around (May have the meaning of "suffers pain" from the idea of twisting). Strong's: #2341
Hhawot: Towns. Strong's: #2334
Hhazo: His looking into. Strong's: #2375
Hheleq: Distribution. Strong's: #2507, #2516
Hhemdan: Desired. Strong's: #2533
Hhermon: Perforated one. Strong's: #2768
Hheshbon: Reason. Strong's: #2809
Hhet: Trembling in fear. Strong's: #2845, #2850
Hhetsron: Surrounded by a wall. Strong's: #2696
Hhever: Couple. Strong's: #2268
Hhevron: Association. Strong's: #2275, #2276
Hheylon: Window. Strong's: #2497
Hheypher: Dug out well. Strong's: #2660
Hhideqel: Rapid. Strong's: #2313
Hhirot: Cisterns. Strong's: #6367
Hhiw: Town. Strong's: #2340
Hhiyrah: Nobility. Strong's: #2437
Hhomer: A dry standard of measurement equal to 65 Imperial gallons. Strong's: #2563
Hhor: Pale. Strong's: #2752
Hhorev: Parching heat. Strong's: #2722
Hhor-Hagidgad: Parching heat. Strong's: #2735
Hhoriy: Paleness. Strong's: #2753
Hhovah: Withdrawing Strong's: #2327
Hhovav: Cherishing. Strong's: #2246
Hhul: Sand. Strong's: #2343
Hhupham: Their shore. Strong's: #2349
Hhupim: Shores. Strong's: #2650
Hhur: Pale. Strong's: #2354
Hhush: Hasty. Strong's: #2366
Hhusham: Hastily. Strong's: #2367
Hhutsot: Outsides. Strong's: #7155
Hiyn: A liquid measure equal to about 5 quarts (6 liters). Strong's: #1969
Hor: Hill. Strong's: #2023
Hosheya: Rescue. Strong's: #1954
I'ezer: An Island is help (or "Island of help"). Strong's: #372, #373
Irad: Fleet. Strong's: #5897

Iyey-Ha'a'variym: Pile of ruins of the ones of the other side (or "Pile of ruins of the ones of Eber"). Strong's: #5863

Iyram: Their city. Strong's: #5902

Iytamar: Island of the date palm. Strong's: #385

Iy'yim: Pile of ruins. Strong's: #5864

Kalahh: Full age. Strong's: #3625

Kaleyv: Dog. Strong's: #3612

Kalneh: Fortress of Anu. Strong's: #3641

Kaphtor: Knob. Strong's: #3731, #3732

Karmi: My vineyard. Strong's: #3756

Kasluhh: Fortified (Can also mean "hopes of life."). Strong's: #3695

Kazbi: My lie. Strong's: #3579

Kedarla'omer: Fighting for the sheaf. Strong's: #3540

Kemosh: Subduer. Strong's: #3645

Kena'an: Lowered. Strong's: #3667, #3669

Keran: Lyre. Strong's: #3763

Kesed: Increasing (Can also mean "Like a level field"). Strong's: #3777, #3778

Keruv: A supernatural creature (written as cherub in most translations), identified in other Semitic cultures as a winged lion, a Griffin. Strong's: #3742

Keziv: Lie. Strong's: #3580

Kikar: A dry standard of measure. Usually rendered as "talent" in most translations. However. the word “talent” is a transliteration of the Greek word talanton (a Greek coin), which is used in the Greek Septuagint for the Hebrew word "kikar." Strong's: #3603

Kineret: Harp. Strong's: #3672

Kislon: Confident one. Strong's: #3692

Kit: Bruiser (Can also mean breaking or bruising). Strong's: #3794

Kush: Blackish. Strong's: #3568, #3569, #3571

La'eyl: Belonging to the mighty one. Strong's: #3815

Lamekh: Despairing (Can also mean "suffering."). Strong's: #3929

Lavan: White. Strong's: #3837

Le'ah: Impatient. Strong's: #3812

Lehav: Glimmer. Strong's: #3853

Lesha: Crack open. Strong's: #3962

Letush: Sharpened. Strong's: #3912

Le'um: Community. Strong's: #3817

Levanon: White one. Strong's: #3844

Lewi: My joining. Strong's: #3878, #3881

Livnah: Brick (May also mean "White" or "Moon."). Strong's: #3841

Liyvniy: To my son (May also mean "for my son," or "my white). Strong's: #3845

Lot: Tightly wrapped. Strong's: #3876

Lotan: Wrapper. Strong's: #3877

Lud: Nativity (Can also mean "generation"). Strong's: #3865, #3866

Luz: Hazel. Strong's: #3870

Ma'akhah: Firmly pressed. Strong's: #4601

Madai: My long garments (Can also mean measure, judging, habit or covering). Strong's: #4074

Magdi'eyl: Precious is the mighty one. Strong's: #4025

Magog: Roofing. Strong's: #4031

Mahalalel: Shining of the mighty one. Strong's: #4111

Mahhalat: Sickened. Strong's: #4257, #4258

Mahhanayim: Two camps Strong's: #4266

Mahhlah: Sickness. Strong's: #4244

Mahh'liy: My Sickness. Strong's: #4249

Mahn: Share (The bread-like substance provided to the Israelites while in the wilderness. The actual meaning of this word is uncertain, but can mean "stringed instrument," "from," or "portion." In the Greek Septuagint, this word is written as "mahn" in the book of Exodus and "manna" in Numbers and Deuteronomy.). Strong's: #4478

Makhi: Being low. Strong's: #4352

Makhir: Price. Strong's: #4353

Makhpelah: Doubled. Strong's: #4375

Malki'el: My king is the mighty one. Strong's: #4439

Malkiy-Tsedeq: My king is steadfast (Can also mean "My king is Tsedeq" or "My king is righteousness."). Strong's: #4442

Mamre: Flapping wing (From a root meaning "bitter." Can also mean "rebellious"). Strong's: #4471

Manahhat: Oasis. Strong's: #4506

Maqheylot: Grasslands. Strong's: #4722

Marah: Bitter. Strong's: #4785

Masa: Load. Strong's: #4854

Mash: Drawn out. Strong's: #4851

Masreyqah: Choice vineyard. Strong's: #4957

Mas'sah: Trial. Strong's: #4532

Matanah: Contribution. Strong's: #4980

Matreyd: Continuous. Strong's: #4308
Medan: Discord. Strong's: #4091
Meheytaveyl: Favored of the mighty one. Strong's: #4105
Mehhuya'el: The mighty one is a battering ram. Strong's: #4232
Menasheh: Causing to overlook. Strong's: #4519
Merari: My bitterness. Strong's: #4847
Meriyvah: Contention. Strong's: #4809
Mesha: Tumultuous. Strong's: #4852
Meshek: Acquiring. Strong's: #4902
Metusha'el: His death he enquired (Can also mean "Their death asks."). Strong's: #4967
Metushelahh: His death sends (Can also be "Their death sends."). Strong's: #4968
Meydad: Throwing. Strong's: #4312
Meydva: Water of toughness. Strong's: #4311
Mey-Zahav: Waters of Gold. Strong's: #4314
Mid'yan: Quarrel. Strong's: #4080
Migdal-Eyder: Tower of the drove. Strong's: #4029
Migdol: Tower. Strong's: #4024
Mika'eyl: Who is like the mighty one. Strong's: #4317
Milkah: Queen. Strong's: #4435
Mir'yam: Bitter sea (Can also mean "rebellion."). Strong's: #4813
Mishma: Hearing. Strong's: #4927
Mitqah: Sweetness. Strong's: #4989
Mitspah: Watchtower. Strong's: #4708, #4709
Mits'rayim: Two straits (A double plural name). Strong's: #4713, #4714
Mivsam: Spice place. Strong's: #4017
Mivtsar: Fortification. Strong's: #4014
Miysha'eyl: Who enquired. Strong's: #4332
Miz'zah: Exhausted (Or may mean "fear"). Strong's: #4199
Mo'av: That one is father. Strong's: #4124
Molekh: Reigning. Strong's: #4432
Moreh: Teacher (Can also mean rain). Strong's: #4176
Moriyah: Yah is my teacher (Can also mean "seen of Yah," "chosen of Yah," "seeing Yah"). Strong's: #4179
Moseyrah: Straps. Strong's: #4149
Moseyrot: Straps. Strong's: #4149
Mosheh: Plucked out. Strong's: #4872
Mupim: Snakes. Strong's: #4649

Mushiy: My moving. Strong's: #4187
Na'amah: Delightful. Strong's: #5279
Na'aman: Pleasantness. Strong's: #5283
Nadav: He offered willingly. Strong's: #5070
Nahhali'eyl: Wadi of the mighty one. Strong's: #5160
Nahhat: Quietness. Strong's: #5184
Nahhbi: Withdrawn. Strong's: #5147
Nahhor: Snorting. Strong's: #5152
Nahhshon: Predictor. Strong's: #5177
Naphish: Deep breath. Strong's: #5305
Naphtali: My wrestling. Strong's: #5321
Naphtuhh: Doorway. Strong's: #5320
Nataneyl: The mighty one gave. Strong's: #5417
Nataph: An unknown spice. Strong's: #5198
Nemu'eyl: Sea of the mighty one. Strong's: #5241
Nepheg: Sprout up. Strong's: #5298
Nephilim: Making fall. Strong's: #5303
Nevayot: Flourishings. Strong's: #5032
Nevo: His flourishing. Strong's: #5015
Nimrah: Leopard. Strong's: #5247
Nimrod: Rebelling. Strong's: #5248
Ninweh: Abode of Ninus (Can also mean "handsome"). Strong's: #5210
No'ah: Staggering. Strong's: #5270
No'ahh: Rest. Strong's: #5146
Nod: Nodding. Strong's: #5113
Nophahh: Exhaling. Strong's: #5302
Novahh: Barking. Strong's: #5025
Nun: Continue. Strong's: #5126
Og: Baked bread (The meaning of the feminine Hebrew noun). Strong's: #5747
Ohad: United Strong's: #161
Omar: Matter. Strong's: #201
On: Vigor. Strong's: #204
Onam: Complainer. Strong's: #208
Onan: Complainer. Strong's: #209
Ophir: Reduced to ashes. Strong's: #211
Ovot: Necromancers. Strong's: #88
Padan: Suet. Strong's: #6307
Padan-Aram: Suet of the palace. Strong's: #6307

Pagi'eyl: Encounter of the mighty one. Strong's: #6295
Palti: My escaping. Strong's: #6406
Palti'eyl: My escaping of the mighty one. Strong's: #6409
Palu: Performing. Strong's: #6396
Paran: Decorated. Strong's: #6290
Parnakh: Fragile. Strong's: #6535
Paroh: Great house. Strong's: #6547
Patros: Southern region (Can also mean "persuasion of ruin."). Strong's: #6624, #6625
Pa'u: Screaming. Strong's: #6464
Pedah'eyl: The mighty one ransomed. Strong's: #6300
Pedatsur: Ransomed of the boulder. Strong's: #6301
Peleg: Tributary. Strong's: #6389
Peleshet: wallower. Strong's: #6429, #6430
Pelet: Swiftness. Strong's: #6431
Peni'el: Face of the mighty one. Strong's: #6439
Pe'or: Opened wide. Strong's: #1187, #6465
Perat: Fruitfulness. Strong's: #6578
Perets: Breach. Strong's: #6557
Perez: Peasant (Meaning "one who dwells in a village"). Strong's: #6522
Pesahh: Hopping (The day of deliverance from Egypt. Also, the feast remembering this day, and the lamb that is sacrificed for this feast). Strong's: #6453
Petor: Interpreting. Strong's: #6604
Pikhol: Mouth of all. Strong's: #6369
Pildash: Flame of fire. Strong's: #6394
Pinon: Around the corner. Strong's: #6373
Pisgah: Cleft. Strong's: #6449
Pishon: Scattered. Strong's: #6376
Pitom: City of justice (Of Egyptian origin). Strong's: #6619
Piy-Hahhiyrot: Mouth of the cisterns. Strong's: #6367
Piynhhas: Mouth of the serpent. Strong's: #6372
Potee-Phera: Belonging of long hair (or "Belonging of Phera," of Egyptian origin). Strong's: #6319
Potiphar: Belonging of a Bull (or "Belonging of Phar"). Strong's: #6318
Pu'a: Blown. Strong's: #6312
Pu'ah: Splendid. Strong's: #6326
Pun: Distracted. Strong's: #6325

Punon: Distracted one. Strong's: #6325
Put: Belonging (Meaning and origin are uncertain). Strong's: #6316
Putiy'eyl: Belonging of the might one. Strong's: #6317
Qadesh: prostitute. Strong's: #6946
Qadmon: Eastern (Can also mean "Easterner."). Strong's: #6935
Qayin: Spearhead. Strong's: #7014, #7017, #8423
Qedar: Gray. Strong's: #6938
Qedeymot: Past times. Strong's: #6932
Qedmah: Past time. Strong's: #6929
Qehat: Allied. Strong's: #6955
Qe'hey'latah: Her assembly. Strong's: #6954
Qemu'el: Rise mighty one. Strong's: #7055
Qenat: Purchased. Strong's: #7079
Qenaz: Stalker. Strong's: #7073, #7074
Qeshiytah: A unit of value, money. Strong's: #7192
Qeturah: Burnt incense. Strong's: #6989
Qeynan: Nesting. Strong's: #7018
Qiryat-Arba: Four walls. Strong's: #7153
Qiryatayim: Two metropolises. Strong's: #7156
Qivrot-Hata'awah: Graves of the yearning. Strong's: #6914
Qorahh: Balding. Strong's: #7141
Rahhel: Ewe. Strong's: #7354
Ramah: Mane of a horse. Strong's: #7484
Ra'meses: Child of the sun (Of Egyptian origin). Strong's: #7486
Ramot: Corals. Strong's: #7216
Rapha: Dead. Strong's: #7497
Raphu: Healed. Strong's: #7505
Ravah: Abundant. Strong's: #7237
Rehhov: Street. Strong's: #7340
Rehhovot: Streets. Strong's: #7344
Rehhovot-Ghir: Streets of the city. Strong's: #7344, #5892
Rephiydiym: Pillar base. Strong's: #7508
Reqem: Embroidery. Strong's: #7552
Resen: Halter. Strong's: #7449
Re'u: Companion. Strong's: #7466
Re'u'eyl: Companion of the mighty one. Strong's: #7467
Re'umah: Elevated. Strong's: #7208
Re'uven: See a son. Strong's: #7205
Reva: Quarter. Strong's: #7254
Rimon-Perets: Overthrown. Strong's: #7428

Riphat: Spoken (Can also mean remedy, medicine, release or pardon). Strong's: #7384
Risah: Overthrown. Strong's: #7446
Ritmah: Juniper. Strong's: #7575
Rivlah: Fruitful. Strong's: #7247
Rivqah: Fattening. Strong's: #7259
Rosh: Head. Strong's: #7220
Salkah: Migration. Strong's: #5548
Salu: Compared. Strong's: #5543
Samlah: Apparel. Strong's: #8072
Sarah: Noblewoman. Strong's: #8297
Sarai: my rulers. Strong's: #8283
Savtah: Go about. Strong's: #5454
Savtekha: Beating. Strong's: #5455
Se'ah: A dry standard of measure equal to 1/3 *ephah*. Strong's: #5429
Sedom: Scorching (Can also mean "burning" or "cement."). Strong's: #5467
Se'iyr: Hairy Goat. Strong's: #8165
Senir: Snow mountain. Strong's: #8149
Sephar: Scroll. Strong's: #5611
Serahh: Overhang. Strong's: #8294
Sered: Braided work. Strong's: #5624
Serug: Twig (From a root meaning "to be intertwined"). Strong's: #8286
Setur: Hid. Strong's: #5639
Seva: Drunkard. Strong's: #5434
Sevam: Balsam. Strong's: #7643
Sha'ah: A standard of measure. Strong's: #8180
Shaddai: My breasts. Strong's: #7706
Shalem: Offering of restitution. Strong's: #8004
Sham'mah: Desolate. Strong's: #8048
Shamu'a: Heard. Strong's: #8051
Shaphat: He decided. Strong's: #8202
Shapher: Bright. Strong's: #8234
Shaphtan: Judicial. Strong's: #8204
Sha'ul: Enquired. Strong's: #7586
Shaweh: Equal. Strong's: #7740
Shaweh-Qiryatayim: Equal walls. Strong's: #7741
Shedeyur: Breasts of light. Strong's: #7707

Shekhem: Shoulder. Strong's: #7927, #7928
Shelahh: Projectile. Strong's: #7974
Sheleph: Pulled out. Strong's: #8026
Shelomiy: My completeness. Strong's: #8015
Shelumi'eyl: Completeness of the mighty one. Strong's: #8017
Shem: Title. Strong's: #8035
Shemever: Title of the long winged (Can also mean "lofty flight."). Strong's: #8038
Shemida: My title is an opinion. Strong's: #8061, #8062
Shemu'eyl: His title is the mighty one. Strong's: #8050
Shepham: Scraped bare. Strong's: #8221
Shepho: Bare place. Strong's: #8195
Sheqel: A chief Hebrew weight standard of measurement. Strong's: #8255
Sheshupham: Adder. Strong's: #7781, #8197
Shet: Buttocks. Strong's: #8352
Sheva: Seven. Strong's: #7614
Sheylah: Request. Strong's: #7956
Sheyshai: My linens. Strong's: #8344
Shilem: Recompense. Strong's: #8006
Shimon: Hearer. Strong's: #8095
Shimron: Guard. Strong's: #8110
Shinar: Country of two rivers (Can also mean "sleeps"). Strong's: #8152
Shinav: Tooth of father (Can also mean "Changing father" or "Splendor of father."). Strong's: #8134
Shiphrah: Brightness. Strong's: #8236
Shitiym: Acacias. Strong's: #7851
Shivah: Sevenfold. Strong's: #7656
Shiymiy: My report. Strong's: #8096
Sh'lomiyt: One of Shalem. Strong's: #8019
Shoval: Upper leg. Strong's: #7732
Shu'a: Shouting out. Strong's: #7770
Shu'ahh: Sinking. Strong's: #7744
Shuhham: Pit digger. Strong's: #7748, #7749
Shuni: Fortunate one (May also mean "One of Shun" or "my sleep."). Strong's: #7764
Shur: Rock wall. Strong's: #7793
Shutelahh: Moistness sat down. Strong's: #7803, #8364
Sidim: Fields. Strong's: #7708

Sihhon: Meditating one. Strong's: #5511
Sin: Sharp thorn. Strong's: #5513
Sinai: My sharp thorns. Strong's: #5514
Si'on: High one. Strong's: #7865
Siryon: Harness. Strong's: #8303
Sitnah: Opposition. Strong's: #7856
Sitriy: My protection. Strong's: #5644
Sodi: My confidence. Strong's: #5476
Suk'kot: Booths. Strong's: #5523
Suphah: Whirlwind. Strong's: #5492
Susiy: horses. Strong's: #5485
Tahhan: Campsite. Strong's: #8465, #8470
Tahhash: Deer. Strong's: #8477
Tahhat: Under. Strong's: #8480
Talmai: My furrows. Strong's: #8526
Tamar: Date palm. Strong's: #8559
Tarshish: Topaz. Strong's: #8659
Taveyrah: Kindled. Strong's: #8404
Terahh: Stationed. Strong's: #8646
Tevahh: Slaughtering. Strong's: #2875
Teyma: Desert region. Strong's: #8485
Teyman: Southward. Strong's: #8487, #8489
Tidal: Yoke breaker (Meaning and origin are uncertain). Strong's: #8413
Timna: Withholding. Strong's: #8555
Timnat: Southward. Strong's: #8553
Tiras: Desirable (Meaning and origin are uncertain). Strong's: #8494
Tirtsah: You will accept. Strong's: #8656
Togarmah: You will gnaw her. Strong's: #8425
Tola: Kermes. Strong's: #8439
Tophel: Unseasoned. Strong's: #8603
Tsalmonah: Imaging. Strong's: #6758
Tsaphnat-Paneyahh: Treasury of the glorious rest. Strong's: #6847
Tsaphon: North. Strong's: #6827
Tsedad: Mountain side. Strong's: #6657
Tselaph'hhad: Shadow of awe. Strong's: #6765
Tsemar: Wool. Strong's: #6786
Tsepho: His watchman. Strong's: #6825
Tseviim: Gazelles. Strong's: #6636
Tsidon: Hunting. Strong's: #6721

Tsilah: Shadow. Strong's: #6741
Tsin: Flocks. Strong's: #6790
Tsiphyon: Watcher. Strong's: #6837
Tsipor: Bird. Strong's: #6834
Tsiporah: Bird. Strong's: #6855
Tsiv'on: Splashed. Strong's: #6649
Tso'an: Removed. Strong's: #6814
Tso'ar: Tiny (Meaning "insignificant."). Strong's: #6820, #6686
Tsohhar: Reddish gray. Strong's: #6714
Tsophim: Kept watch. Strong's: #6839
Tsur: Boulder. Strong's: #6701
Tsuri'eyl: My boulder is the mighty one. Strong's: #6700
Tsurishaddai: My boulder is my breasts (This name may also be written as "Tsur of Shaddai"). Strong's: #6701
Tumiym: Full strengths. Strong's: #8550
Tuval: You will bring. Strong's: #8422
Tuval-Qayin: You will bring the spearhead. Strong's: #8423
Ur: Light. Strong's: #218
Uriy: My light. Strong's: #221
Uriym: Lights. Strong's: #224
Uts: Plan. Strong's: #5780
Uval: Rounded. Strong's: #5745
Uzal: I will be lavished. Strong's: #187
Uziy'eyl: My boldness is the mighty one. Strong's: #5816
Waheyv: And a gift offering. Strong's: #2052
Waphsi: And my wrist. Strong's: #2058
Ya'aqov: He restrains. Strong's: #3290
Yaboq: He will empty out. Strong's: #2999
Yagbahah: He will be her highness. Strong's: #3011
Yagli: He will remove the cover. Strong's: #3020
Yah: Existing (The actual pronunciation of this name is not certain but probably "Yah."). Strong's: #3050
Yahats: Stamped down. Strong's: #3096
Yahh'le'el: The mighty one will stay. Strong's: #3177, #3178
Yahhtse'el: The mighty one will divide. Strong's: #3183
Ya'ir: He will make light. Strong's: #2971
Yakhin: He will prepare. Strong's: #3199
Yalam: He will be out of sight. Strong's: #3281
Yamin: Right hand. Strong's: #3226
Yaphet: Wonder. Strong's: #3315

Yaq'shan: Snarer. Strong's: #3370
Yaqtan: He will be small. Strong's: #3355
Yarden: Descender. Strong's: #3383
Yared: He will go down. Strong's: #3382
Yashuv: He will turn back. Strong's: #3437
Yatvatah: Her wellness. Strong's: #3193
Yaval: Watercourse. Strong's: #2989
Yawan: Mire (Closely related to the Hebrew word yayin meaning "wine"). Strong's: #3120
Yazeyr: He will help. Strong's: #3270
Yegar-Sa'haduta: Afraid of the record. Strong's: #3026
Yehoshu'a: Yah will rescue. Strong's: #3091
Yehudah: Thanksgiving. Strong's: #3063
Yehudit: Thanksgiving. Strong's: #3067
Ye'ish: He will hasten. Strong's: #3274
Yemim: The meaning of this word is uncertain and it is not known if this is a noun or a name. The Greek Septuagint transliterates this word as Ιαμιν (*iamin*). Strong's: #3222
Yemu'el: Day of the mighty one. Strong's: #3223
Yephunah: He will be turned. Strong's: #3312
Yerahh: Moon. Strong's: #3392
Ye'rey'hho: His moon. Strong's: #3405
Yeshurun: Straight one. Strong's: #3484
Yeter: Remainder. Strong's: #3500
Yetet: Nail. Strong's: #3509
Yetser: Thought. Strong's: #3337
Yetur: He will row. Strong's: #3195
Yevus: He will trample down. Strong's: #2982, #2983
YHWH: He will be (or YHWH. The actual pronunciation of this name is not certain). Strong's: #3068
YHWH-Nisiy: YHWH is my standard. Strong's: #3071
YHWH-Yireh: YHWH will see. Strong's: #3070
Yidlap: He will drip. Strong's: #3044
Yigal: He will redeem. Strong's: #3008
Yimnah: He will reckon. Strong's: #3232
Yish'baq: He will be let alone. Strong's: #3435
Yishma'el: The mighty one will hear. Strong's: #3458
Yishwah: He will equate (or "He will resemble"). Strong's: #3438
Yishwiy: He will equate me (or "He will resemble me"). Strong's: #3440, #3441

Yiskah: He will look forth. Strong's: #3252
Yisra'eyl: He turns the mighty one aside. Strong's: #3478
Yis'sas'khar: There is a wage. Strong's: #3485
Yitran: Reserver. Strong's: #3506
Yitro: His remainder. Strong's: #3503
Yits'har: He presses out oil. Strong's: #3324
Yits'hhaq: He laughs. Strong's: #3327
Yokheved: Yah is heavy. Strong's: #3115
Yoseph: Adding. Strong's: #3130
Yov: Howling. Strong's: #3102
Yovav: Howling. Strong's: #3103
Yuval: Creek. Strong's: #3106
Za'awan: Troubled. Strong's: #2190
Zakur: Remembered. Strong's: #2139
Zamzum: Mischievous. Strong's: #2157
Zerahh: Rising sun. Strong's: #2226, #2227
Zered: Exuberant. Strong's: #2218
Zevulun: Resident. Strong's: #2074
Zikh'riy: My memorial. Strong's: #2147
Zilpah: Trickling. Strong's: #2153
Zimran: Musician. Strong's: #2175
Zimri: My singer. Strong's: #2174
Ziphron: Fragrant one. Strong's: #2202
Zuz: Entryway. Strong's: #2104

Benner's Translation of the Torah

Benner's Translation of the Torah

Benner's Translation of the Torah